Entrepreneurial Finance

3E

J. CHRIS LEACH

UNIVERSITY OF COLORADO AT BOULDER

RONALD W. MELICHER

UNIVERSITY OF COLORADO AT BOULDER

SOUTH-WESTERN
CENGAGE Learning™

Australia · Brazil · Canada · Mexico · Singapore · Spain · United Kingdom · United States

Entrepreneurial Finance, **Third Edition**

J. Chris Leach, Ronald W. Melicher

VP/Editorial Director: Jack W. Calhoun

Editor-in-Chief: Alex von Rosenberg

Executive Editor: Mike Reynolds

Developmental Editor: Adele Scholtz

Marketing Manager: Jason Krall

Senior Marketing Communications Manager:
Jim Overly

Content Project Manager: Emily Nesheim

Senior Technology Project Manager: Matt McKinney

Production Technology Analyst: Adam Grafa

Manufacturing Coordinator: Kevin Kluck

Production Service: Newgen–Austin

Art Director: Bethany Casey

Internal Designer: Mike Stratton/Stratton Design

Production Artist: Patti Hudepohl

Cover Designer: Bethany Casey

Cover Image: Jon Berkeley/Getty Images, Inc.

For product information and technology assistance, contact us at
Cengage Learning Academic Resource Center, 1-800-423-0563

For permission to use material from this text or product,
submit all requests online at **www.cengage.com/permissions**
Further permissions questions can be emailed to
permissionrequest@cengage.com

Library of Congress Control Number: 2007943971
Student Edition ISBN 13: 978-0-324-56125-8
Student Edition ISBN 10: 0-324-56125-3

South-Western Cengage Learning
5191 Natorp Boulevard
Mason, OH 45040
USA

Cengage Learning products are represented in Canada by
Nelson Education, Ltd.

For your course and learning solutions, visit **academic.cengage.com**

Purchase any of our products at your local college store or at our
preferred online store **www.ichapters.com**

Printed in the United States of America
1 2 3 4 5 6 7 11 10 09 08

*To my wife Martha, our great joys Laura and John,
and the Life we share*

J. CHRIS LEACH

*To my parents, William and Lorraine, and to my wife,
Sharon, and our children, Michelle, Sean, and Thor*

RONALD W. MELICHER

Brief Contents

Contents

Preface

The life of an entrepreneur is exciting and dynamic. The challenge of envisioning a new product or service, infecting others with entrepreneurial zeal, and bringing a product to market can be one of the great learning experiences in life. All ventures require financing—taking investors' money today and expecting to return a significantly larger amount in the future. Typically, the return comes from the venture's public offering, sale, or merger. In the interim, the venture must manage its financial resources, communicate effectively with investors and partners, and create the harvest value expected by investors.

TEXTBOOK MOTIVATION

The purpose of the textbook is to introduce financial thinking, tools, and techniques adapted to the realm of entrepreneurship. We believe that, while much of traditional financial analysis may not be ideally suited to the venture context, there is great value in applying venture adaptations.

This entrepreneurial finance text introduces the theories, knowledge, and financial tools an entrepreneur needs to start, build, and harvest a successful venture. Sound financial management practices are essential to a venture's operation. The successful entrepreneur must know how and where to obtain the financing necessary to launch and develop the venture. Eventually, that same successful entrepreneur must know how and when to interact with financial institutions and regulatory agencies to take the venture to its potential and provide a return and liquidity for the venture's investors.

THE LIFE CYCLE APPROACH

We incorporate a life cycle approach to the material in this text. Successful ventures typically begin with an initial **development stage** where the entrepreneurial team generates ideas and assesses the associated business opportunities. Most entrepreneurs realize that a business plan can greatly improve the chance that an idea will become a commercially viable product or service. **Startup-stage** ventures focus on the formulation of a business model and plan. As marketing and selling products and services begins, **survival-stage** ventures often refocus or restructure. **Rapid-growth-stage** ventures increase their momentum, and begin to demonstrate value creation. **Maturity-stage** ventures typically look for ways to harvest the value created and provide a return to their investors.

Each stage in the life cycle requires a specific understanding of the financial management tools and techniques, potential investors and their mindset, and the financial institutions supporting that venture stage. During the early stages of a venture's life, cash management tools and survival planning are the dominant forms of financial analysis. Cash burn rates are very high and additional sources of financing are usually limited, making it critical for the successful venture to project and accommodate necessary operating costs. The need to measure and adjust investment in working capital and property, plant, and equipment is evident. The process of anticipating and accommodating costs and asset investments begins with the analysis of historical financial experience and then projects future financial positions using projected financial statements or their proxies. Successful ventures emerging from their survival stages can concentrate more on value creation and calibration. Consequently, our financial management emphases for this stage are valuation tools and techniques.

Equally important as sound financial management practices is the need for the entrepreneur to understand the types and sources of financial capital and the related investment processes. During the development stage, seed financing usually comes from the entrepreneur's personal assets and possibly from family and friends. Business angels and venture capitalists are important financing sources during the startup stage. First-round financing from business operations, venture capitalists, suppliers, customers, and commercial banks may be initiated during the survival stage. The rapid-growth stage involves second-round, mezzanine, and liquidity-stage financing from business operations, suppliers, customers, commercial banks, and investment bankers. Once a venture enters its maturity stage, seasoned financing replaces venture financing. Seasoned financing takes the form of cash flow from business operations, bank loans, and stocks and bonds issued with the assistance of investment bankers or others. Our approach is to introduce the types and sources of financial capital that become available as we progress through a successful venture's life cycle.

The successful entrepreneur must understand the legal environment regulating financial relationships among the venture, investors, and financial institutions, including venture capital funds and investment banks. We cover the basic securities laws and regulatory agencies, particularly the Securities and Exchange Commission (SEC), relevant to the entrepreneur when considering how to obtain financial capital at each stage.

To summarize, we take a comprehensive three-pronged stage-sensitive approach to entrepreneurial finance. Our coverage of entrepreneurship-adapted financial analysis and relevant institutional details provides a relevant financial analysis base for the entrepreneur in each of the various stages as he or she develops the idea, brings it to market, grows the venture's value, and ultimately provides an exit for venture investors. We identify and explain the types and sources of financing available during the various stages and introduce the relevant legal and regulatory environment the entrepreneur must consider when seeking financing throughout the venture's life cycle.

DISTINCTIVE FEATURES

This text considers a successful firm as it progresses through various maturity stages. Specific examples of stage-relevant skills and techniques we introduce include:

- **Brainstorming and Screening:** Chapter 2, From the Idea to the Business Plan, introduces qualitative and quantitative venture screening devices. Chapter 3, Organizing and Financing a New Venture, with its treatment of intellectual property, demonstrates important issues and concepts for the earliest-stage ventures.

- **Raising External Funds:** Chapter 8, Securities Law Considerations When Obtaining Venture Financing, introduces readers to the restrictions and warnings for the growing venture seeking external financing.

- **Venture Diagnostics and Valuation:** Chapter 9, Valuing Early-Stage Ventures, presents our versions of traditional valuation techniques important to internal and external perceptions of a venture's financial health. While the material is traditional, our treatment provides a unifying approach to projecting financial statements, extracting pseudo dividends, and assessing a venture's value.

- **Venture Capital Valuation Methods:** Chapter 10, Venture Capital Valuation Methods, introduces representative multistage venture capital valuation methods and interprets them relative to more traditional procedures. It provides a unified example of traditional pre-money and post-money valuations and the shortcuts employed by many venture capitalists.

- **Professional VCs:** Chapter 11, Professional Venture Capital, explores the historical development of venture capital and describes the professional venture investing cycle from determining the next fund objectives and policies to distributing cash and securities proceeds to investors.

- **Harvest:** Chapter 14, Harvesting the Business Venture Investment, considers a wide range of venture harvest strategies, including private sales (to outsiders, insiders, and family), transfers of assets, buyouts, and initial public offerings.

- **Turnaround Opportunities:** Chapter 15, Financially Troubled Ventures: Turnaround Opportunities? introduces important aspects of financial distress and alternative restructuring approaches (operations, asset, and financial) to rescue a struggling venture.

INTENDED AUDIENCE AND USE

The material contained in this text has been used successfully at the upper-division (junior/senior) undergraduate, MBA, and executive MBA levels. For MBAs, the course can easily be conducted in two ways. In the first, what we term the life cycle approach, we recommend the addition of illustrative cases, each at different life cycle stages. Recently, entrepreneurial finance cases have been available individually from the usual providers and in collected form in entrepreneurial case books. The second, or what we term the venture capital approach, emphasizes the money management aspects of financing entrepreneurial ventures. For this approach, we recommend supplementing the text treatments with venture capital cases (available individually or in collected case books) and journal articles covering private equity (venture capital) and initial public offerings (investment banking). For an abbreviated mini-semester course or compressed executive MBA, we recommend concentrating on the text and using our capstone cases as focal points for integrating the venture financing perspective.

We have also used this text for semester-long upper-division (junior/senior) undergraduate courses involving finance and nonfinance business majors. Most academic business programs require students to take basic background courses in both accounting and finance prior to upper-division courses such as entrepreneurial finance. Chapters 9, 10, and 13 present a rigorous and conceptually advanced approach to financial valuation. Our experience is that these chapters provide the greatest intellectual challenge and require relatively sophisticated spreadsheet skills. The third edition of this textbook has been written to support two different approaches to the undergraduate entrepreneurial finance course. A more rigorous approach challenges undergraduate students by covering all fifteen chapters (including all of the valuation material) and adopts a decision-making focus. An alternative, more descriptive entrepreneurial finance course would omit most, or all, of Part 4 (Chapters 9 and 10) and Chapter 13 from Part 5. For application, while the included capstone cases synthesize a great deal of the text's material, some instructors find it useful to have students prepare short cases in lieu of, or prior to, these capstones.

Regarding the accounting and basic finance background material in Chapters 4 and 5, we provide it for student and instructor convenience when the material has not been covered in prerequisite courses or in instances when a review of the materials is warranted. The remainder of the text can be used without explicit coverage of this review material. Additionally, for some adopters, it may be advantageous to alter the sequencing and coverage of the securities law and investment banking material, depending on student backgrounds and other course offerings.

ADDITIONS AND CHANGES IN THE THIRD EDITION

Overall changes to content and organization include:

- All chapters present new and updated materials, and several chapters have been reorganized to offer more flexibility and usability by moving selected technical materials to appendixes and end-of-chapter learning extensions.
- Chapter 2, From the Idea to the Business Plan, provides a more general treatment of how to screen venture opportunities with the venture opportunity screening (VOS) indicator's being moved to a learning extension while still being available to users who want to emphasize a formal screening application.
- Chapter 8, Securities Law Considerations When Obtaining Venture Financing, was substantially rewritten to stress important securities law concepts that an entrepreneur needs to know when raising venture financing with more technical

securities law information placed in end-of-chapter appendixes for users who want to place greater emphasis on securities laws in the entrepreneurial finance course.

- Chapter 9, Valuing Early-Stage Ventures, was rewritten employing more clearly described and less complex financial statement projections to determine a venture's discounted cash flow (DCF) equity value.

- Chapter 10, Venture Capital Valuation Methods, provides explanatory materials on the application of venture capital valuations and provides more clearly written materials on pre- and post-money valuations and venture capital shortcuts for estimating a venture's equity value.

- Chapter 13, Security Structures and Determining Enterprise Values, was moved from Part 4 in the previous edition to the last chapter in Part 5 of this edition to better reflect how more mature ventures with complex financial structures are valued for harvesting purposes. More complex valuation considerations involving options in the form of warrants are provided in an end-of-chapter learning extension.

- Chapter 15, Financially Troubled Ventures: Turnaround Opportunities? was rewritten to stress the importance of evaluating troubled ventures as possible turnaround opportunities with liquidation as a last consideration.

- New end-of-chapter questions and problems are provided to enhance the presentation of key concepts and applications, as well as to improve the learning process.

SUPPLEMENTS

Instructor's Manual with Test Bank

Written by the text authors, the Instructor's Manual includes short answers to end-of-chapter questions and answers to end-of-chapter problems. The Test Bank includes true/false and multiple-choice questions, as well as short test problems. Both the Instructor's Manual and the Test Bank are available on the text Web site for instructors only.

PowerPoint Lecture Slides

Created by the text authors, the PowerPoint slides present a point-by-point lecture outline, including graphics and equations, for instructors to use in the classroom. They are available on the text Web site for instructors only.

Excel Solutions

Excel Solutions to end-of-chapter problems requiring Excel are provided for instructors on the text Web site.

Text Web Site

The text Web site at academic.cengage.com/finance/leach provides access to supplements and to finance resources, including updated links to Web site activities provided in the text.

ACKNOWLEDGMENTS

During the several years we spent developing and delivering this material, we benefited from interactions with colleagues, students, entrepreneurs, and venture capitalists. We thank the numerous sections of students who became the sounding board for our presentation of this material. We also thank the members of the Venture Capital Association of Colorado who opened their professional lives and venture capital conferences to our students. Additionally, we have benefited from detailed valuable comments and input by Craig Wright and Michael Meresman. Clinton Talmo and Robert Donchez contributed to the preparation of the Instructor's Manual.

We recognize the moral support of the Deming Center for Entrepreneurship (Bob Deming, Dale Meyer, Denis Nock, Kathy Simon, and Paul Jerde) and the Coleman Foundation, who supported the research involved in our capstone cases.

We recognize the valuable contributions of our editorial staff at Cengage Learning, including Michael Mercier, our original acquisitions editor, who believed in our book enough to publish it; Mike Reynolds, our current Cengage Learning executive editor; and Adele Scholtz, our developmental editor. Also, we'd like to thank our production managers, Tamborah Moore and Emily Nesheim; and our marketing manager, Jason Krall. We also thank Martha Leach, who read and corrected a complete version of this third edition; and Andre Gygax, who provided several important corrections to a previous edition.

For their patience and insights offered during the process, we thank our colleagues who reviewed materials for this third edition or earlier editions of the text:

Brian Adams, University of Portland

M. J. Alhabeeb, University of Massachusetts

Olufunmilayo Arewa, Northwestern University

David Choi, Loyola Marymount University

Susan Coleman, University of Hartford

David Culpepper, Millsaps College

William C. Hudson, St. Cloud State University

Jeffrey June, Miami University

Miranda Lam, Salem State College

Michael S. Long, Rutgers University

Michael Owens, University of Tennessee at Chattanooga

Charles B. Ruscher, University of Arizona

Steven R. Scheff, Florida Gulf Coast University

Michael Williams, University of Denver

Finally, to our families, who kept asking if we were finished yet, we offer thanks for their sacrifice and support.

J. Chris Leach

Ronald W. Melicher

About the Authors

J. Chris Leach is Professor of Finance and the Robert H. and Beverly A. Deming Professor in Entrepreneurship at the Leeds School of Business, University of Colorado at Boulder. He received a Ph.D. in finance from Cornell University, began his teaching career at the Wharton School, and has been a visiting professor at Carnegie Mellon, the Indian School of Business, and the Stockholm Institute for Financial Research. His teaching experience includes courses for undergraduates, MBAs, executives, and Ph.D. students. He has been recognized as Graduate Professor of the Year and has received an award for MBA Teaching Excellence. His research on a variety of topics has been published in *The Review of Financial Studies*, *Journal of Business*, and *Journal of Financial and Quantitative Analysis*, among others.

Chris's business background includes various startups dating back to his late junior high days in the 1970s. More recently, he was the chairman of a New Mexico startup and, as an investor and adviser, participated in a late 1990s Silicon Valley startup that subsequently merged into a public company. His consulting activities include business plan advising, valuation, and deal structure for early-stage and small businesses.

Ronald W. Melicher is Professor of Finance and Chair of the Finance Division at the Leeds School of Business at the University of Colorado at Boulder. He earned his undergraduate, MBA, and doctoral degrees from Washington University in St. Louis, Missouri. While at the University of Colorado, he has received several distinguished teaching awards and was designated as a university-wide President's Teaching Scholar. He also has held the William H. Baugh Distinguished Scholar faculty position, served two previous terms as Chair of the Finance Division, served as the Faculty Director of the Boulder Campus MBA Program, and was the Academic Chair of the three-campus executive MBA program.

Ron has taught entrepreneurial finance at both the MBA and undergraduate levels. He also teaches corporate finance and financial strategy in the MBA and executive MBA programs and investment banking to undergraduate students. While on sabbatical leave from the University of Colorado, Ron has taught at the INSEAD Graduate School of Business in Fontainebleau, France, and at the University of Zurich in Zurich, Switzerland. He has delivered numerous university-offered executive education short courses and has taught in-house finance education materials for IBM and other firms. He has presented expert witness testimony on the cost of capital in regulatory proceedings and has provided consulting expertise in the areas of financial management and firm valuation.

Ron's research interests focus on mergers and acquisitions, corporate restructurings, and the financing of valuation of early-stage firms. His previous research has been published in major finance journals, including the *Journal of Finance, Journal of Financial and Quantitative Analysis, and Financial Management.* He is the co-author of *Introduction to Finance: Markets, Investments, and Financial Management,* Thirteenth Edition (John Wiley & Sons, 2008).

Part 1

BACKGROUND AND ENVIRONMENT

INTRODUCTION AND OVERVIEW

FIRST THOUGHTS

Only those individuals who have actually been entrepreneurs can say, "Been there, done that!" With aspiring entrepreneurs in mind, we start at the beginning and consider how entrepreneurial finance relates to the other aspects and challenges of launching a new venture. Our goal, as you progress through this text, is to equip you with the terms, tools, and techniques that help turn a business idea into a successful venture.

LOOKING AHEAD

Chapter 2 focuses on the transformation of an idea into a business opportunity, and the more formal representation of that opportunity as a business plan. Most successful ideas are grounded in sound business models. We present qualitative and quantitative screening exercises that can help determine an idea's commercial viability. We provide a brief discussion of a business plan's key elements.

CHAPTER LEARNING OBJECTIVES

This chapter presents an overview of entrepreneurial finance. We hope to convey the potential benefit of embracing entrepreneurial finance methods and techniques. We consider an entrepreneur's operating and financial decisions at each stage, as the venture progresses from idea to harvest. After completing this chapter, you will be able to:

1. Explain the economic importance of small and emerging businesses

2. Describe entrepreneurship and some characteristics of entrepreneurs

3. Indicate three megatrends providing waves of entrepreneurial opportunities

4. List and describe the seven principles of entrepreneurial finance

5. Discuss entrepreneurial finance and the role of the financial manager

6. Describe the various stages of a successful venture's life cycle

7. Identify by life cycle stage the relevant types of financing and investors

8. Understand the life cycle approach used in this book

It is estimated that more than one million new businesses are started in the United States each year. The Office of Advocacy of the U.S. Small Business Administration (SBA) documents that "employer firm births" have exceeded 600,000 annually in recent years.[1] Reasonable estimates place nonemployer (e.g., single person or small family) businesses started each year at a similar number. In addition to these formally organized startups, millions of commercial ideas are entertained and abandoned without the benefit of a formal organization. The incredible magnitude of potential entrepreneurial opportunities is a clear reflection of the commercial energy fostered by a market economy. We believe that the time you spend on this book's treatment of financial tools and techniques may be one of the most important investments you make.

1.1   ENTREPRENEURSHIP FUNDAMENTALS

Successful entrepreneurs recognize and develop a viable business opportunity, have confidence in the market potential for their new products and services, and are committed to "running the race." They keep success in sight even when others may have difficulty focusing.

WHO IS AN ENTREPRENEUR?

After working for a large corporation for nearly five years, you are considering launching a Web-based business. Product development and testing require financing that exceeds your limited personal resources. How much external financing do you need to make a credible attempt with the new venture? How much of the venture's ownership will you have to surrender to attract this initial financing?

A friend of yours, upon graduating from college three years ago, started a new business with the conviction that pumpkin stencils and special carving knives could foster an unprecedented commercial exploration of the market for Halloween crafts. Her firm has experienced phenomenal growth and is seeking financing for this season's inventory stockpiling. Do her options differ from yours? Do the possible investors for your startup and her later-stage venture differ?

Your neighbor is the chief executive officer (CEO) of a large firm founded twenty years ago. He has accumulated enormous paper wealth and, before retirement, wishes to diversify his investments. How do your neighbor's investment goals and your financial needs relate to one another? Is your neighbor a reasonable prospect for startup funding? Is he more likely to spend the money he has allocated for earlier-stage investing on his own idea for a new product? Does he see himself as an entrepreneur or as one who wants to enable and profit from other entrepreneurs?

---

[1] The Office of Advocacy of the SBA was created in 1976 by Congress to be an independent voice for small business within the federal government. Small business statistics are available at http://www.sba.gov/advo/.

Who will succeed? Who will fail? Who is an entrepreneur? Your pumpkin-carving friend? Your CEO neighbor? You? All of you or none of you? We offer no infallible formula or process for entrepreneurial success. None exists. We cannot tell you if you should drop a Fortune 500 career track and take up drinking from the entrepreneurial fire hose. We have no blueprint for the ideal entrepreneur and no genetic screening device to test you for the entrepreneurial gene. Even if we had such a test, rest assured that for many who test positive, the news might not be welcome, particularly to friends and family. The ups and downs of the entrepreneurial lifestyle are difficult for those supporting the entrepreneur financially and emotionally. Nonetheless, we believe that the tools and techniques we introduce can help entrepreneurs and others anticipate venture challenges, navigate through shortfalls, and achieve important milestones. Importantly for the entrepreneur, employees, backers, and their families, these tools and techniques can help smooth out an inevitably bumpy ride.

BASIC DEFINITIONS

While the academic definition of "entrepreneurship" has evolved, it is useful to formalize our context for the term. Jeffry Timmons and Stephen Spinelli suggest: "Entrepreneurship is a way of thinking, reasoning, and acting that is opportunity obsessed, holistic in approach, and leadership balanced."[2] We adopt a somewhat shorter definition: **Entrepreneurship** is the process of changing ideas into commercial opportunities and creating value. An **entrepreneur** is an individual who thinks, reasons, and acts to convert ideas into commercial opportunities and to create value. Whether entrepreneurial efforts succeed or fail, an entrepreneur's mission is to find economic opportunities, convert them into valuable products and services, and have their worth recognized in the marketplace.

entrepreneurship
process of changing ideas into commercial opportunities and creating value

entrepreneur
individual who thinks, reasons, and acts to convert ideas into commercial opportunities and to create value

CONCEPT CHECK

- What is the meaning of entrepreneurship?
- Who is an entrepreneur?

ENTREPRENEURIAL TRAITS OR CHARACTERISTICS

While we want to avoid most generalizations about entrepreneurial traits or characteristics, there are three we consider important. First, successful entrepreneurs recognize and seize commercial opportunities, frequently before others even have an inkling. Mark Twain once said, "I was seldom able to see an opportunity, until it ceased to be one." Second, successful entrepreneurs tend to be doggedly optimistic. The glass is never "half empty" and usually not even "half full." It is "full," and they are ready to call for more glasses. Third, successful entrepreneurs are

---

[2] Jeffry A. Timmons and Stephen Spinelli, *New Venture Creation*, 7th ed. (New York: McGraw-Hill/Irwin, 2007), p. 79.

not consumed entirely with the present. Their optimism is conditional. They know that certain events need to take place for this optimism to be justified. They do not treat venture planning as the enemy. Seeing a (conditionally) bright future, successful entrepreneurs plan a way to get there and begin to construct paths to obtain the required physical, financial, and human resources.

While there are caricatures, there is no prototypical entrepreneur. Many authors have tried to identify specific characteristics of successful entrepreneurs, but accurate generalizations have eluded them. There are numerous myths about entrepreneurs.[3] One hears that "entrepreneurs are born, not made." Yet many successful entrepreneurs have been, or will be, failing entrepreneurs if observed at different times in their lives. While identifying the fear of failure as a personal motivation propelling them forward, successful entrepreneurs are not paralyzed by this fear. If you see venture bumps as opportunities rather than obstacles, perhaps the entrepreneurial lifestyle is right for you.

CONCEPT CHECK

- What are some general traits or characteristics of entrepreneurs?

OPPORTUNITIES EXIST BUT NOT WITHOUT RISKS

If you feel the entrepreneurship bug biting, you are not alone. Remember, the annual number of new U.S. business formations runs in the millions. Small and growing enterprises are critical to the U.S. economy; small firms provide 60 to 80 percent of net new jobs.[4]

Firms with fewer than 500 employees represent over 99 percent of all employers and employ over half of the private workforce. They are responsible for about half of the private gross domestic product. During the past century, entrepreneurial firms' innovations included personal computers, heart pacemakers, optical scanners, soft contact lenses, and double-knit fabric. Entrepreneurial firms have long been major players in high-technology industries, where small businesses account for over one-fourth of all jobs and over one-half of U.S. innovations and new technologies. Small high-technology firms are responsible for twice as many product innovations per employee, and obtain more patents per sales dollar, than large high-technology firms. One government study suggests that some of the fastest-growing opportunities for small businesses are in the restaurant industry, medical and dental laboratories, residential care industries (housing for the elderly, group homes, etc.), credit reporting, child day care services, and equipment leasing.[5]

---

[3] Timmons and Spinelli address seventeen myths and realities about entrepreneurs, as well as summarize prior efforts to identify characteristics of successful entrepreneurs. Ibid., pp. 18–20.

[4] *Small Business Economic Indicators* (Washington, DC: U.S. Small Business Administration, Office of Advocacy, 2004). An electronic version of the study including tables is available at http://sba.gov/advo/press/04-26.html.

[5] "Small Business Answer Card" and "The Facts About Small Business" (Washington, DC: U.S. Small Business Administration, Office of Advocacy, 2000).

As much as we would like to encourage your entrepreneurial inclinations, it would be irresponsible for us to imply that starting and successfully operating a business is easy. As a basic financial principle, risk and return go together—the expectation of higher returns is accompanied by higher risks. According to the Small Business Association's Office of Advocacy, annual employer firm births averaged 581,000 for the 2000–2003 period. For the same period, employer firm terminations averaged 555,000 annually. In 2005, the estimated number of small business starts was 671,800 while the estimated number of closures was 544,800. The result was an estimated record of 5.99 million employer firms. Nonemployer firms also reached a new high at 19.86 million. There were 39,201 business bankruptcies in 2005, suggesting that some employer firm terminations reflect successful exit strategies for founding entrepreneurs.[6]

B. Phillips and B. A. Kirchhoff, using Dun & Bradstreet data, found that 76 percent of new firms were still in existence after two years of operation. Forty-seven percent of new firms survived four years, and 38 percent were still operating after six years.[7] In a more recent study of the U.S. Census Bureau's Business Information Tracking Series (BITS), Brian Headd found similar results. Sixty-six percent of new employers survived two years, 50 percent were still in existence after four years, and 40 percent survived at least six years. Headd also studied the U.S. Census Bureau's Characteristics of Business Owners (CBO) database that surveyed owners of closed firms on whether the owners felt their firms were successful or unsuccessful at the time of closure. The evidence suggests that about one-third of closed businesses were successful at closure. Thus, instead of closing due to bankruptcy, many owners may have exited their businesses by retiring or selling.[8]

Nearly half of business failures are due to economic factors such as inadequate sales, insufficient profits, and industry weakness. Of the remainder, almost 40 percent cite financial causes, such as excessive debt and insufficient financial capital. Other reasons include insufficient managerial experience, business conflicts, family problems, fraud, and disasters.[9]

Although the risks associated with starting a new entrepreneurial venture are large, there is always room for one more success. Successful entrepreneurs are able to anticipate and overcome the business risks that cause others to fail. While hard work and a little luck will help, an entrepreneur must be able to finance and manage the venture. Commercial vision, an unrelenting drive to succeed, the ability to build and engage a management team, a grasp of the risks

[6] *Small Business Economic Indicators and The Small Business Economy* (Washington, DC: U.S. Government Printing Office, 2006), Executive Summary and Chapter 1. For electronic access, see http://sba.gov/advo/research/sb_econ2006.pdf.

[7] B. Phillips and B. A. Kirchhoff, "Formation, Growth and Survival: Small Firm Dynamics in the U.S. Economy," *Small Business Economics* 1 (1989): pp. 65–74.

[8] Brian Headd, "Redefining Business Success: Distinguishing Between Closure and Failure," *Small Business Economics* 21 (2003): pp. 51–61.

[9] "Small Business Answer Card" and "The Facts About Small Business."

involved, and a willingness to plan for the future are some of the ingredients for success.

1.2 SOURCES OF ENTREPRENEURIAL OPPORTUNITIES

entrepreneurial opportunities
ideas with potential to create value through different or new, repackaged, or repositioned products, markets, processes, or services

Entrepreneurs are the primary engine of commercial change in the global economy. **Entrepreneurial opportunities** are ideas that have the potential to create value through new, repackaged, or repositioned products, markets, processes, or services. One study of *Inc.* magazine's 500 high-growth firms suggests that about 12 percent of founders feel their firms' successes are due to extraordinary ideas, while the remaining 88 percent feel their firms' successes are due to exceptional execution of ordinary ideas.[10] In a separate survey, Amar Bhide found that *Inc.* 500 founders often make use of existing ideas originating in their prior work experiences. Only 6 percent of his responding founders indicate that "no substitutes were available" for their products or services. In contrast, 58 percent say they succeeded even though competitors offer "identical or close substitutes."[11]

Megatrends are large societal, demographic, or technological trends or changes that are slow in forming but once in place continue for many years. In contrast, *fads* are not predictable, have short lives, and do not involve macro changes. Of course, there are many degrees between fads and megatrends that provide entrepreneurs with business opportunities. However, while entrepreneurial opportunities can come from an almost unlimited number of sources, we give special focus to the following three megatrend categories:

• Societal trends or changes
• Demographic trends or changes
• Technological trends or changes

SOCIETAL CHANGES

Many entrepreneurial endeavors are commercial reflections of broader societal changes. In 1982, John Naisbitt identified several major or megatrends shaping U.S.

---

[10] J. Case, "The Origins of Entrepreneurship," *Inc.*, June 1989, p. 51.

[11] Amar V. Bhide, *The Origin and Evolution of New Businesses* (New York: Oxford University Press, 2000).

society and the world.[12] Naisbitt recognized that the U.S. economy, by the early 1980s, centered on the creation and distribution of information. He argued that successful new technologies would center on the human response to information. Many of the commercial opportunities in the past two decades have capitalized on information creation and organization and its central role in human decision support.

Naisbitt also recognized that the United States was increasingly affected by a global economy and that Americans were rekindling the entrepreneurial spirit. It is now clear that almost all businesses face international competition and that the pace of entrepreneurial innovation is increasing throughout the world. To succeed in such an environment requires an understanding of current megatrends and the anticipation of new ones. While many possible trends are candidates for spawning entrepreneurial innovation, two that will undoubtedly influence future commercial opportunities are the demographic shifts associated with the baby boom generation and our increasingly information-oriented society.

Social, economic, and legal changes may occur within pervasive trends. Social changes are reflected in important changes in preferences about clothing styles, food (e.g., low-carb diets), travel and leisure, housing, and so forth. An anticipation of social change is the genesis of many entrepreneurial opportunities as innovators position themselves to satisfy the demand for the related new products and services. Economic shifts—the rise of two-career families, higher disposable incomes, changing savings patterns—also suggest entrepreneurial opportunities. Changes in our legal environment can introduce important economic opportunities by eliminating existing barriers to entry. For example, deregulation in the banking, transportation, and telecommunications industries has allowed entrepreneurs to provide cost-efficient, demand-driven alternatives.

CONCEPT CHECK

- What are megatrends, and how do they introduce new commercial opportunities?

DEMOGRAPHIC CHANGES

One major demographic trend continuing to shape the U.S. economy is the aging of the so-called baby boom generation. In 1993, Harry Dent documented major generation waves in the United States during the twentieth century.[13] By far, the

[12] John Naisbitt, *Megatrends* (New York: Warner Books, 1982). Although only two are presented here, Naisbitt identified six additional megatrends. For a follow-up look at the megatrends shaping our society, see John Naisbitt and Patricia Aburdene, *Megatrends 2000* (New York: Morrow, 1990). In a 2007 article in *Entrepreneur* magazine, five forces that shaped the face of entrepreneurship over the past three decades were identified as technology (the computer), the Internet (a network to link computers), globalization (everyone can sell worldwide), baby boomers (question-authority attitudes), and individualism (corporate restructurings forced individuals to look out for themselves). See Carol Tice, "Change Agents," *Entrepreneur* (May 2007), pp. 65–67.

[13] Harry S. Dent, Jr., *The Great Boom Ahead* (New York: Hyperion, 1993). Also see Harry S. Dent, Jr., *The Roaring 2000s* (New York: Simon & Schuster, 1998).

most important generation wave is the baby boom. After World War II, an unprecedented number of babies, approximately 79 million, were born in the United States from 1946 to 1964. As this generation has aged, it has repeatedly stressed the U.S. infrastructure. In the 1950s and 1960s, it pressured public school systems serving kindergarten through high school. By the 1970s and early 1980s, a period sometimes referred to as their innovation wave, boomers were heavily involved in developing, innovating, and adopting new technologies.

Dent estimates that the boomers' spending wave started in the early 1990s and peaked in the late 1990s and the first part of the twenty-first century. The tremendous expansion in the stock and bond markets during the 1980s and 1990s was, in part, due to the boomers' innovation and spending waves. Dent projects that the organization, or power, wave, where boomers dominate top managerial positions and possess the accumulated wealth to influence corporate America, will peak sometime in the 2020s.

For the entrepreneurially inclined, the good news is that the boomers continue to spend at record levels; "consumer confidence" is a key ingredient to America's continued prosperity and expansion. Financing continues to be available for solid business opportunities. Venture investing, although initially reeling after the decline at the turn of this century, is recovering. The aging boomers, with their earning and consumption power, continue to provide endless business opportunities. Many of the successful ones will provide goods and services tailored to this aging, and wealthy, generation. There will undoubtedly be other business opportunities relating to as yet unlabeled subsets of consumers. Entrepreneurs with the ability to understand demographic shifts and see the resulting new business opportunities will write their own success stories.

CONCEPT CHECK

• What is meant by the term "baby boom generation"?

TECHNOLOGICAL CHANGES

Technological change may be the most important source of entrepreneurial opportunities.[14] While the accurate dating of the arrival of major technological innovations is difficult, it is reasonable to say that the seeds of our information society were planted in the last half of the 1950s and early 1960s. Transatlantic cable telephone service began. The Soviet Union launched *Sputnik*, suggesting the possibility of global satellite communications. Transistors replaced vacuum

---

[14] For example, see Scott Shane, "Explaining Variation in Rates of Entrepreneurship in the United States: 1899–1988," *Journal of Management* 22 (1996): pp. 747–781; and Scott Shane, "Technology Opportunities and New Firm Creation," *Management Science* 47 (2001): pp. 205–220.

tubes in computers. Compilers opened the door to higher-level programming languages and the development of the computer "chip" was under way.

Perhaps the most important invention shuttling us from an industrial society to an information society is the computer chip.[15] Such chips are the backbone of all modern computing and enable the telecommunications applications and information systems that have changed the way almost everyone lives. The worldwide distribution of computer chips (and the software systems running on them) has paved the way for what may be the most significant innovation in global commerce since the merchant ship: the Internet. The Internet is an incredibly diffuse collection of computers networked together. It is hard to think of anything else in history that parallels the level of international coordination (individuals and entities) that the Internet has almost painlessly achieved—and all in a remarkably short time.[16] When the Internet's ability to provide nearly instant worldwide communication was combined with rapid transfer of graphic images, the Internet became the infrastructure for the "World Wide Web," a user-friendly and commercially attractive foundation for many new ways of doing business, including retail and wholesale operations through electronic commerce. In addition to the Web's commercial applications, the Internet has dramatically changed the way almost everyone goes about daily business. Internet functionality affects modern life in almost uncountable ways, including such common things as electronic mail, remote access, large file transfer (including pictures, music, and videos), instant messaging, and, more recently, cell phone–Web cross-functionality.

CONCEPT CHECK

- What innovations drove our move from an industrial society to an information society? Why?

---

[15] The U.S. Patent Office appears to recognize Jack Kilby and Robert Noyce as the computer chip's co-inventors. Kilby conducted research at Texas Instruments during the 1950s and filed for the first "computer chip" patent. Noyce filed after Kilby, but supposedly had a more useful design. Noyce later cofounded the Intel Corporation. See Lee Gomes, "Paternity Suits Some Better Than Others in the Invention Biz," *Wall Street Journal*, June 18, 1999, pp. A1, A10.

[16] The Internet had its beginning in late 1969 when researchers at UCLA, including Professor Leonard Kleinrock and graduate students Stephen Crocker and Vinton Cerf, linked two computers for purposes of exchanging data. This initial network project, supported by the Department of the Defense (DOD), was given the name Arpanet for Advanced Research Projects Agency Network. Other milestones include the inventing of network e-mail in 1971 and the use of the @ symbol in 1972. Cerf and Robert Kan invented the TCP protocol used in transporting data via the Internet in 1974. In 1982, the "Internet" was defined as a series of TCP/IP networks that were connected. In 1990, Tim Berners-Lee invented the World Wide Web and Arpanet ceased to exist. The commercial explosion really began after the creation of modern server software, hypertext markup language (HTML), and browsers (such as Mosaic, Netscape, and Internet Explorer). See Anick Jesdanun, "Happy Birthday to the Internet," *Daily Camera*, August 30, 2004, pp. 1B, 5B. The appendix in this chapter provides further information on the Internet's structure and the various constituent industries that provide goods and services to support the Internet.

1.3   THE INTERNET ECONOMY AND E-COMMERCE

e-commerce
the use of electronic means to conduct business online

Electronic commerce, or **e-commerce**, involves the use of electronic means to conduct business online. The Internet economy and e-commerce are here to stay. Simply put, we will never do business the same way we did before the Internet and the Web. It has become too easy to compare various suppliers' prices or check on the latest offer from our competitors to return to conducting business in the "darkness" tolerated only a few years ago. A simple example is online package tracking. Now, instead of using the phone to say a package is "in the mail," the sender is expected to provide a tracking number to be used on the Web so that the sender and the receiver can ascertain the veracity of this claim *and* follow the package along its route.

Attention is shifting from the age-old strategy of owning and controlling natural resources (tangibles), to a strategy of owning and controlling information (intangibles). Even Internet entrepreneurs who started their ventures intending to sell products and services have sometimes found themselves giving their products and services away in order to monitor their "users" and sell user demographic information. Information is an important, if not central, product in the modern global economy.

While new technologies suggest business opportunities, profitable commercial application of the new technologies often occurs after trial and error. Many attempts to exploit the Internet commercially were proposed, tried, and funded. Eventually, there was a wave of potentially appealing applications—and the vision was contagious. We are still trying to determine the winners. That is, we know the Internet provides significant efficiency improvements for commercial interaction; we're just not sure whether the winners are buyers, sellers, or both. As highlighted in a popular commercial, the Web lets suppliers compete for consumers' business, putting the consumer in an advantageous position. It is not clear whether this benefits suppliers in the long run.

It is fair to say that many e-commerce business plans were funded with the belief that part of the benefit could be captured by sellers, that is, producers and retailers. We now know that the Web so effectively facilitates price competition that it is hard for suppliers and retailers to protect margins. Much of the efficiency gains go to the buyers (in what economists call consumer surplus), making for a less-than-attractive seller business model. Although such a plan might have received funding a few years ago, building an e-commerce site to sell nondifferentiated goods at lower prices than are currently available is now a nonstarter. An important characteristic of the Internet is that physical barriers to entry are very low. That is, it is easy and relatively low cost to launch a competing Web e-commerce site. If your business model doesn't have a sustainable purchasing cost advantage, the Internet may help defeat your business model, as it allows scores of other retailers to quickly monitor and replicate whatever you're doing and drive everyone toward aggressive price competition and diminishing margins.

E-commerce may not deliver the margins once conjectured, but the Internet is still one of the most radical innovations in our lifetime. Expect it to provide profitable new venture opportunities for many years to come—consumers are probably hooked forever.

1.4 PRINCIPLES OF ENTREPRENEURIAL FINANCE

Entrepreneurial finance draws its basic principles from both entrepreneurship and finance. The seven principles we emphasize are:

- Real, human, and financial capital must be rented from owners
- Risk and expected reward go hand in hand
- While accounting is the language of business, cash is the currency
- New venture financing involves search, negotiation, and privacy
- A venture's financial objective is to increase value
- It is dangerous to assume that people act against their own self-interests
- Venture character and reputation can be assets or liabilities

REAL, HUMAN, AND FINANCIAL CAPITAL MUST BE RENTED FROM OWNERS

While it is true that commercial innovation exists outside the capitalist market context pervading the global economy, we will confine our remarks to that market context. When you obtain permission to use someone's land and building (real capital), you have to compensate the owner for the loss of its use otherwise. If there are many suppliers of buildings and many possible tenants, competition among them facilitates the allocation of the building to a commercially worthy purpose. While this may be obvious regarding buildings, it is equally true for financial capital (money). The *time value of money* is an important component of the rent one pays for using someone else's financial capital. When you rent the money, it cannot be rented to others, and you must expect to compensate the money's owner for that loss.

Entrepreneurs usually understand that quitting their day job and starting a new venture entails the loss of a regular paycheck. They will, in some fashion, expect the venture experience to compensate them for this loss. We recommend that they insert a line item for a fair wage for their services in their financial projections, but we realize that there are other nonpecuniary compensations at work. What may not be well understood is that a founder's own financial capital invested in the firm deserves a fair compensation. The seed money used to start the venture could have been put elsewhere to earn interest. The venture should expect to compensate *all* investors for using their financial capital. This is conceptually separate from any compensation for services rendered if the investors are also employees (human capital).

RISK AND EXPECTED REWARD GO HAND IN HAND

The time value of money is not the only cost involved in renting someone's financial (or other) capital. The total cost is typically significantly higher due to the possibility that the venture won't be able to pay. The rent is risky. One way humans express their dislike of this risk is to expect more when the rent is riskier. If the U.S. government promises $.05 for borrowing my dollar for a year, you can bet it will be virtually impossible to get someone to rent it to a risky new venture for that same $.05 per year. The expected compensation for the risk involved in renting money to a new venture swamps the time value of money. For example, a new venture investor might expect to get $.25 or even more per year for using her money at the same time the government is promising $.05. While this expectation may annoy you, it is set by competitive markets, and you don't have a lot of room to argue—if you want the money to build your new venture.

WHILE ACCOUNTING IS THE LANGUAGE OF BUSINESS, CASH IS THE CURRENCY

If you were going to be a missionary to a foreign country where some language other than English was the official language, you would probably take the time and effort to learn the language. Whether you like it or not—and many finance professors don't like it—accounting is the official language of business. It has a long and honorable history, and most of its practitioners believe in the basic principle that using accounting techniques, standards, and practices communicates a firm's financial position more accurately than if those customs are ignored. Accounting for entrepreneurial firms has two purposes. The first is the same as for any other business: to provide for checks, balances, integrity, and accountability in tracking a firm's conduct. We leave that aspect of entrepreneurial accounting to others. The second purpose, and our emphasis for the entrepreneurial finance context, is quantifying the future in a recognizable dialect of the official language. We will not shy away from the reality that entrepreneurs need to be able to quantify certain aspects of their venture's future and translate them into appropriate financial statements.

Although we recommend bending the knee to accounting when communicating a venture's vision to the financial community, we recognize that the day-to-day financial crises usually are about only one account: cash.[17] For example, while the income statement might look great when we book an additional $50,000 sale, the real concern will be how much, if any, was paid in cash. To be more specific, if the sale was on account, it will help at some time in the future when collected, but it can't be used to make payroll tomorrow. Rather than as a criticism of accounting, however, we lay this down as a challenge to entrepreneurs: Get enough accounting to see through the accruals to the cash account.

---

[17] It is often said that "cash is king!" It is certainly true that an entrepreneur who has enough cash to make it through the day can feel like the kingdom has survived another day. Cash here usually refers to bank balances and other highly liquid assets quickly converted into cash.

Accounting is not your enemy. It may take some investment for it to become your friend; you may be surprised how attached you become.

Entrepreneurs often underestimate the cash needed to get their ventures up and running. Consequently, we supplement traditional accounting measures—such as profit and return on investment—with measures that focus on what is happening to cash. *Cash burn* measures the gap between the cash being spent and that being collected from sales; it's typical for new ventures to experience a large cash burn, which is why they must seek additional investment from outsiders. Ultimately, to create value, a venture must produce more cash than it consumes. *Cash build* measures the excess of cash receipts over cash disbursements, including payments for additional investment.

NEW VENTURE FINANCING INVOLVES SEARCH, NEGOTIATION, AND PRIVACY

Much of corporate finance deals with the financial decisions of public companies raising money in public markets where a large number of investors and intermediaries compete. Corporate finance can concentrate much of its attention on **public financial markets** where standardized contracts or securities are traded on organized securities exchanges. In such markets, publicly traded prices may be considered good indicators of true values; investors who disagree are free to buy and sell the securities to express their sentiments to the contrary. We say that these public markets exhibit efficiency (prices that reflect information) and liquidity (investors who disagree with prevailing prices can buy and sell the security to object).

> **public financial markets**
> where standardized contracts or securities are traded on organized securities exchanges

Corporate finance tends to downplay, or even ignore, significant frictions in the markets for new venture financial capital. New ventures seldom have standby financing waiting to fill any gaps. Most are actively engaged in searching for financing. When they do find potential investors, competition is weak, and this leads to bargaining between the venture and its investors. Even after a deal is struck, the venture and its investors typically are locked into the funding arrangement, because the securities are privately placed (sold) and cannot easily be resold or repurchased to express satisfaction or discontent with the venture's progress. New ventures usually arrange financing in **private financial markets**. We often characterize such markets as relatively inefficient (prices may not reflect significant information known to the venture or its investors) and illiquid (investors who disagree cannot easily sell or buy to express discontent or approval). New venture financing tends to require serious search, intricate and invasive negotiation, and indefinitely long investing horizons for those buying the resulting privately held securities.

> **private financial markets**
> where customized contracts or securities are negotiated, created, and held with restrictions on how they can be transferred

A VENTURE'S FINANCIAL OBJECTIVE IS TO INCREASE VALUE

Entrepreneurs can start new ventures for a host of personal reasons. They may have either economic or altruistic motives. Many serial entrepreneurs may see the challenge as the biggest reason to start their next venture. It is only realistic to acknowledge that there can be many nonfinancial objectives for a new venture.

Nonetheless, whatever the myriad personal motivations for founders, investors, and employees, there is really only one overarching *financial* objective for the venture's owners: to increase value. While all the owners might not agree on social objectives (e.g., improving local employment or wages vs. international outsourcing), environmental objectives (e.g., providing an alternative delivery system using only recyclables vs. providing cheaper products), or other perfectly valid new venture considerations, if there were a way to increase the venture's value by $1 without interfering with these other nonfinancial objectives, all of the owners would want to take the $1.

There are other candidates for a venture's financial objective, including maximizing sales, profit, or return on investment. It is easy to understand why these measures don't quite summarize how venture owners feel about the venture's financial performance. Increasing sales seems to be good, but not at the cost of greatly diminished margins. Profit is a better candidate than sales, but it still doesn't provide an adequate summary. If a venture is profitable, but has to reinvest in assets so much that no return is available to pay the owners for the use of their money, profits don't thrill the owners as much as you might think. At some point, profit has to give rise to *free cash* to be returned to investors *in a timely manner*. Profits alone are not a good indicator of owner sentiment. The problem with having return on investment as the venture's financial objective is similar. When the profit is divided by the book value of equity, one gets a return on equity. If a venture started on a shoestring, currently has very little operating history, but has created incredibly valuable intellectual property, you would never want to use the venture's return on equity as serious input in deciding how much to ask from an interested potential acquirer. Return on equity will be low because profits are nonexistent and there is some book value of equity. Return on equity, particularly in new ventures, can be a very poor proxy for what owners care about: value.[18]

free cash
cash exceeding that which is needed to operate, pay creditors, and invest in assets

free cash flow
change in free cash over time

We said that profits must eventually turn into free cash in order to be available to provide a return to a venture's owners. More formally, **free cash** (or "surplus cash") is the cash exceeding that which is needed to operate, pay creditors, and invest in the assets. **Free cash flow** is the change in free cash over time.[19] We deal mostly with financial projections; accordingly, we will use *free cash flow* instead of the more accurate *projected free cash flow*. When we line up free cash flows and adjust them for risk and the time value of money, we get value, the best proxy for owner sentiment regarding a venture's prospects.

---

[18] Chapter 9 and Learning Supplement 9A provide a more rigorous exposition of how financial markets can resolve arguments between a venture's owners and create a consensus on how the venture should develop and invest. The interesting point in this resolution is that in the presence of tradable financial assets, all of the firm's owners can agree on maximizing firm value as the venture's *financial* objective.

[19] When we use the term "free cash flow" in this text, we are referring to free cash flow to the owners or equity investors in the venture unless specified otherwise. We discuss in great detail the process of valuing a venture using free cash flow to equity investors in Chapter 9. An alternative definition of free cash flow focuses on free cash flow available to interest-bearing debtholders and equity investors. This approach values the entire venture or enterprise and is discussed in Chapter 13.

- What is meant by free cash and free cash flow?
- How does risk affect an entrepreneurial venture's value?

IT IS DANGEROUS TO ASSUME THAT PEOPLE ACT AGAINST THEIR OWN SELF-INTERESTS

Economics is often regarded as a heartless discipline in which the view of human nature is that people are motivated primarily by greed and self-interest. We do not propose to debate such a claim here. However, having just said that increasing value is the owners' primary financial objective, perhaps we should explain how we see self-interest's entering into our principles of entrepreneurial finance. Rather than take a position on the ethical, religious, or philosophical underpinnings of the economic view of human behavior, we prefer to introduce the subject as a warning. When incentives are aligned, the presence of self-interest, even of moral or religious interest, is not at odds with economic incentives. When it's good for me to do a good job for you, we can debate the morality of my motives, but the likely result is that I will do a good job for you.

In contrast, when doing a good job for you involves wrecking my family, living in poverty, and seeking counseling, you should expect me to renegotiate, increase my risk taking, cut corners, and possibly even out-and-out default. We are not condoning or condemning such behavior; we are simply pointing out that incentives need to be aligned because ignoring self-interest is not a good idea. To put this in a financial context, there will be many times when financial and operational arrangements have to be renegotiated. This should be expected. It is unwise to assume that arrangements are durable in the new venture context. Owners will need to constantly monitor incentive alignments for everyone associated with the venture and be ready to renegotiate to improve failing alignments.

Of particular concern is when the need for external capital dictates that the entrepreneur will lose control at an early stage. To keep incentives aligned, it is common to provide contingent increases in the entrepreneur's ownership, through options grants, to improve the tie between her self-interest and the majority owners'. Watching out for managers' and other employees' self-interest usually dictates providing them with contingent options grants as the venture reaches milestones. Venture teams typically sacrifice lifestyle and leisure during the early stages. It is wise to allow them to visualize a future reward for their sacrifice. These future rewards are almost uniformly structured to help solve **owner-manager (agency) conflicts** in the new venture context.

Although not as common in the earliest-stage ventures, different types of investors can have dramatically different incentives depending on how their investments are structured. Perhaps the easiest way to see the potential for significant conflict and renegotiation is to consider a venture that has borrowed money to help fund itself (from friends, personal loans, or even credit cards). The **owner-debtholder conflict** is the divergence of the owners' self-interest from that of the

owner-manager (agency) conflicts
differences between manager's self-interest and that of the owners who hired him

owner-debtholder conflict
divergence of the owners' and lenders' self-interests as the firm gets close to bankruptcy

lenders as the firm gets close to bankruptcy. Although it's an extreme example, if the venture is indebted and doesn't have the cash to pay rent and payroll the following morning, it may be tempted to take whatever money it has and buy lottery tickets in the hopes of making rent and payroll. If the venture doesn't make rent and payroll, it will fold and the owners won't get anything. If they do nothing, they won't make payroll. If they take what little cash is left and buy lottery tickets, it costs them nothing and provides some chance that there will be value to their ownership tomorrow.

We are not advocating the purchase of lottery tickets; we're only suggesting that it would be prudent to expect this type of behavior in certain circumstances. We chose the extreme example to make a point: Everyone should keep an eye on others' self-interests and, when feasible, take steps to align incentives. If incentives aren't aligned, it is unwise to assume that temptation to cater to self-interest will be overcome. It would be best to anticipate the incentive conflicts and renegotiate to minimize value-destroying behavior.

CONCEPT CHECK

- What is the owner-manager (agency) conflict?
- What is the owner-debtholder conflict?

VENTURE CHARACTER AND REPUTATION CAN BE ASSETS OR LIABILITIES

While it is customary to talk about individual character, we think it is useful to point out that most of us characterize businesses as well. These characterizations, and the associated reputation, can grow and evolve as others accumulate evidence on how the individuals and the entity behave. Simple things, such as honest voice mail, on-time delivery and payment, courteous internal and external discourse, and appropriate e-mail etiquette, can be the building blocks for favorable venture character and reputation.

Of course, we all know that character goes both ways. A venture's negative character will be difficult or impossible to hide; customers, employers, and others can be expected to engage in substantially different behavior when doing business (if at all) with ventures having weak or negative characters. One doesn't have to look further than eBay auctions to see that buyers and sellers will treat you differently if you haven't substantiated your character in prior commercial interactions or, worse yet, you have exhibited bad or negative character.

One survey of successful entrepreneurs indicated that a majority felt that having high ethical standards was the most important factor in the long-term success of their ventures.[20] Taking the time and money to invest in the venture's

---

[20] Jeffry A. Timmons and Howard H. Stevenson, "Entrepreneurship Education in the 1980s," *75th Anniversary Entrepreneurship Symposium Proceedings* (Boston: Harvard Business School, 1983), pp. 115–134. For further discussion, see Timmons and Spinelli, *New Venture Creation*, chap. 9.

character will help ensure that it is an asset rather than a liability. Of course, it will be easier to build positive venture character if the founders possess that quality as individuals. In the earliest stages, the venture's character and the founders' character tend to coincide.

Is the financial objective of increasing value necessarily inconsistent with developing positive character and reputation? Certainly not! The typical situation is quite the opposite. It will be very difficult to increase value—an amount reflecting *all* of the venture's future economic interactions—if a venture does not pay sufficient attention to issues of character. Following laws, regulations, and responsible marketing and selling practices builds confidence and support for the entrepreneur and the venture. Having a good reputation can eliminate much of the hedging and frictions that result when a venture has unproven or negative character.

On a related issue, increasing a venture's value need not conflict with the venture's improving the society in which it operates. Entrepreneurial firms provide meaningful work and many of the new ideas, products, and services that improve our lives. Success in the marketplace not only provides prima facie evidence that someone (the customer) benefited from the venture's goods and services; it also creates wealth that can be used to continue the process or fund noncommercial endeavors. It is no secret that successful entrepreneurs are prime targets for charitable fundraising. Some firms, including Newman's Own and Pura Vida, were organized to sell goods and services in a competitive marketplace while designating charities as the recipients of the financial returns to ownership. Although the charities don't own the firms, they receive the financial benefit of ownership.[21] Increasing these ventures' values is the same as increasing the value of the stream of cash support promised to the charities. It need not be the case that ventures' financial objectives conflict with their nonfinancial objectives. Most ventures will not be organized with the explicit objective of benefiting charities. Nevertheless, new ventures can and do provide dramatic benefits to society, not just to their customers.

CONCEPT
CHECK

- Why is venture character important?

1.5 ROLE OF ENTREPRENEURIAL FINANCE

Entrepreneurial finance is the application and adaptation of financial tools and techniques to the planning, funding, operations, and valuation of an entrepreneurial venture. Entrepreneurial finance focuses on the financial management of

entrepreneurial finance
application and adaptation of financial tools and techniques to the planning, funding, operations, and valuation of an entrepreneurial venture

---

[21] Variants of the venture philanthropy model also have been created. For example, Ben Cohen, a cofounder of Ben & Jerry's Ice Cream, recently formed an investment fund that would buy firms operating in low-income areas with the intent of raising wages and employee benefits. Profits will be used to buy and operate other firms in the same way. See Jim Hopkins, "Ben & Jerry's Co-Founder to Try Venture Philanthropy," *USA Today*, August 7, 2001, p. B1.

a venture as it moves through its life cycle, beginning with its development stage and continuing through to when the entrepreneur exits or harvests the venture. Nearly every entrepreneurial firm will face major operating and financial problems during its early years, making entrepreneurial finance and the practice of sound financial management critical to the survival and success of the venture.

financial distress
when cash flow is insufficient to meet current debt obligations

Most entrepreneurial firms will need to regroup and restructure one or more times in order to succeed. **Financial distress** occurs when cash flow is insufficient to meet current liability obligations. Alleviating financial distress usually requires restructuring operations and assets or restructuring loan interest and scheduled principal payments. Anticipating and avoiding financial distress is one of the main reasons to study and apply entrepreneurial finance.

Generating cash flows is the responsibility of all areas of the venture—marketing, production/engineering, research and development, distribution, human resources, and finance/accounting. However, the entrepreneur and financial manager must help other members of the entrepreneurial team relate their actions to the growth of cash flow and value.[22] The financial manager is normally responsible for keeping the venture's financial records, preparing its financial statements, and planning its financial future.[23] Short-run planning typically involves projecting monthly financial statements forward for one to two years. The venture needs adequate cash to survive the short run. Financial plans indicate whether the venture is expecting a cash shortage. If so, the entrepreneur should seek additional financing to avert the shortage. Long-term financial planning typically involves projecting annual statements five years forward. While the reliability of longer-term projections may be lower, it is still important to anticipate large financial needs as soon as possible. Meeting those needs may dictate several rounds of financing in the first few years of operations.

The financial manager is responsible for monitoring the firm's operating efficiency and financial performance over time. Every successful venture must eventually produce operating profits and free cash flows. While it is common for a new venture to operate at a loss and deplete its cash reserves, it cannot continue indefinitely in that state. Venture investors, particularly in our post-dot-com age, expect ventures to have business models generating positive free cash flows in relatively short order. As the venture progresses through its early stages, it must control expenses and investments to the extent possible without undermining projected revenues.

In summary, financial management in an entrepreneurial venture involves record keeping, financial planning, monitoring the venture's use of assets, and arranging for any necessary financing. Of course, the bottom line of all these efforts is increasing the venture's value.

---

[22] Although the entrepreneur typically serves as the venture's "chief operating officer," the entrepreneur may also assume management responsibility over one of the functional areas, including serving as the venture's financial manager.

[23] For ventures in the development or startup stage, one individual typically is responsible for both basic accounting and financial management functions. However, as ventures succeed and grow, the accounting and finance functions often are separated, in part because of the sheer amount of record keeping that is required, particularly if a venture becomes a public corporation.

- What is entrepreneurial finance?
- What are the financial management responsibilities of the financial manager?

1.6 THE SUCCESSFUL VENTURE LIFE CYCLE

Successful ventures frequently follow a maturation process known as a life cycle. The **venture life cycle** begins in the development stage, has various growth stages, and "ends" in a maturity stage. While a venture's maturity can be expressed in terms of profits and/or cash flows, it is common practice to use revenues.[24] The five life cycle maturities are:

- Development stage
- Startup stage
- Survival stage
- Rapid-growth stage
- Maturity stage

venture life cycle
stages of a successful venture's life from development through various stages of revenue growth

As noted previously, **early-stage ventures** are new or very young firms with little operating histories. They are in their development, startup, or survival life cycle stages. **Seasoned firms** have produced successful operating histories and are in their rapid-growth or maturity life cycle stages.

Figure 1.1 depicts the five basic stages in a successful business venture's life cycle over an illustrated time period ranging from one and one-half years before startup up to about six years after startup. Some "ideas" may take less or more time to develop, and the various operating life cycle stages for a particular venture may be shorter or longer depending on the product or service being sold. As this text progresses, we address stage-specific aspects of a venture's organizational, operational, and financial needs from the viewpoint of what entrepreneurial finance has to offer.

early-stage ventures
new or very young firms with little operating history

seasoned firms
firms with successful operating histories and operating in their rapid-growth or maturity life cycle stages

DEVELOPMENT STAGE

During the **development stage**, the venture progresses from an idea to a promising business opportunity. Most new ventures begin with an idea for a potential product, service, or process. The feasibility of an idea is first put on trial during the development stage. Comments and initial reactions from friends and family

development stage
period involving the progression from an idea to a promising business opportunity

---

[24] For the typical venture, operating losses usually occur during the startup and survival stages with profits beginning and growing during the rapid-growth stage. Free cash flows generally lag operating profits because of the heavy investment in assets usually required during the first part of the rapid-growth stage. Most ventures burn more cash than they build during the early stages of their life cycles and don't start producing positive free cash flows until the latter part of their rapid-growth stages and during their maturity stages.

members (and entrepreneurship professors) form an initial test of whether the idea seems worth pursuing further. The reaction and interest level of trusted business professionals provides additional feedback. If early conversations evoke sufficient excitement (and, sometimes, even if they don't), the entrepreneur takes the next step: producing a prototype, delivering a trial service, or implementing a trial process.

In Figure 1.1, the development stage is depicted as occurring during the period of −1.5 to −.5 years (or about one year at most, on average) prior to market entry. Of course, the time to market is often a critical factor in whether a new idea is converted to a successful opportunity. For example, a new electronic commerce idea might move from inception to startup in several weeks or months. For other business models, the venture may spend considerably more time in the development stage.

STARTUP STAGE

startup stage

period when the venture is organized and developed and an initial revenue model is put in place

The second stage of a successful venture's life cycle is the **startup stage**, when the venture is organized, developed, and an initial revenue model is put in place. Figure 1.1 depicts the startup stage as typically occurring between years −.5 and +.5. In some instances, the process of acquiring necessary resources can take less than one year. For example, a business venture requiring little physical and intellectual capital and having simple production and delivery processes might progress from the initial idea to actual startup in one year or less. Revenue generation typically begins at what we have designated "time zero" as the venture begins operating and selling its first products and services.

FIGURE 1.1   Life Cycle Stages of the Successful Venture

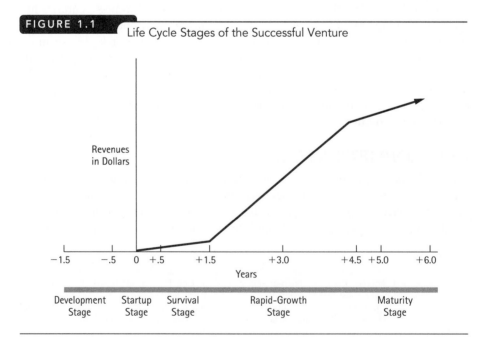

SURVIVAL STAGE

Figure 1.1 places the survival stage from about +.5 to +1.5 years, although different ventures will experience different timing. During the **survival stage**, revenues start to grow and help pay some, but typically not all, of the expenses. The gap is covered by borrowing or by allowing others to own a part of the venture. However, lenders and investors will provide financing only if they expect the venture's cash flows from operations to be large enough to repay their investments and provide for additional returns. Consequently, ventures in the survival stage begin to have serious concerns about the financial impression they leave on outsiders. Formal financial statements and planning begin to have useful external purposes.

survival stage
period when revenues start to grow and help pay some, but typically not all, of the expenses

RAPID-GROWTH STAGE

The fourth stage of a successful venture's life cycle is the **rapid-growth stage** when revenues and cash inflows grow very rapidly. Cash flows from operations grow much more quickly than do cash outflows, resulting in a large appreciation in the venture's value. This rapid growth often coincides with years +1.5 through +4.5. Ventures that successfully pass through the survival stage are often the recipients of substantial market share gains taken from less successful firms struggling in their own survival stage. Continued industry revenue growth and increased market share combine to propel the venture toward its lucrative financial future. During this period in a successful venture's life, value increases rapidly as revenues rise more quickly than expenses. The successful venture reaps the benefits of economies of scale in production and distribution.

rapid-growth stage
period of very rapid revenue and cash flow

MATURITY STAGE

The fifth stage in a successful venture's life cycle is the **maturity stage** when the growth of revenue and cash flow continues, but at much slower rates than in the rapid-growth stage. Although value continues to increase modestly, most venture value has already been created and recognized during the rapid-growth stage. Figure 1.1 depicts the maturity stage as occurring around years +4 and +5. The maturity stage often coincides with decisions by the entrepreneur and other investors to exit the venture through a sale or merger. We have truncated the venture at the end of six years in Figure 1.1 for illustrative purposes only. The successful venture may provide value to the entrepreneur, or to others if the entrepreneur has sold out, for many years to come. Our focus, however, is the period from the successful venture's development stage through its maturity stage, when the founders and venture investors decide whether to exit the venture or to remain at the helm.

maturity stage
period when the growth of revenue and cash flow continues but at a much slower rate than in the rapid-growth stage

A caveat is in order. Figure 1.1 represents a hypothetical length of time it takes for successful ventures to progress through development into maturity. The rapid pace of technological change shortens the life span of most products. The development time from the idea to viable business is often less than one year. For rapidly deployed ventures, the toughest part of the survival stage may be the first few months of operation. Within the first year, rapid growth can be experienced; mature-firm financing issues can arise before they would have traditionally been expected. Such rapid maturity, in addition to being a challenge in itself, represents a tremendous challenge for entrepreneurial team members. They must deploy a variety of financial skills within the first year.

CONCEPT CHECK

• What are the five stages of a successful venture's life cycle?

1.7   FINANCING THROUGH THE VENTURE LIFE CYCLE

Early-stage ventures often are undercapitalized from the beginning. This condition makes it essential that the entrepreneur understand, and attempt to tap, the various sources of financial capital as the venture progresses from development to startup and on through its survival stage. Once a venture is able to achieve a successful operating history, it becomes a seasoned firm; new sources (and larger amounts) of financial capital become attainable.

Figure 1.2 depicts the likely types of financing sources as well as the major players or providers of financial funds at each life cycle stage. Major types of financing include:

• Seed financing
• Startup financing
• First-round financing
• Second-round, mezzanine, and liquidity-stage financing
• Seasoned financing

SEED FINANCING

seed financing
funds needed to determine whether an idea can be converted into a viable business opportunity

During the development stage of a venture's life cycle, the primary source of funds is in the form of **seed financing** to determine whether the idea can be converted into a viable business opportunity. The primary source of funds at the development stage is the entrepreneur's own assets. As a supplement to this limited source, most new ventures will also resort to *financial bootstrapping*, that is, creative methods, including barter, to minimize the cash needed to fund the venture. Money from personal bank accounts and proceeds from selling other investments are likely sources of seed financing. It is quite common for founders to sell personal assets (e.g., an automobile or a home) or secure a loan by pledging these assets as collateral. The willingness to reduce one's standard of living by cutting expenditures helps alleviate the need for formal financing in the development-stage venture. Although it can be risky, entrepreneurs often use personal credit cards to help finance their businesses. Family members and friends also provide an

FIGURE 1.2   Types and Sources of Financing by Life Cycle Stage

1. VENTURE FINANCING

LIFE CYCLE STAGE	TYPES OF FINANCING	MAJOR SOURCES/PLAYERS
Development stage	Seed financing	Entrepreneur's assets Family and friends
Startup stage	Startup financing	Entrepreneur's assets Family and friends Business angels Venture capitalists
Survival stage	First-round financing	Business operations Venture capitalists Suppliers and customers Government assistance programs Commercial banks
Rapid-growth stage	Second-round financing Mezzanine financing Liquidity-stage financing	Business operations Suppliers and customers Commercial banks Investment bankers

2. SEASONED FINANCING

LIFE CYCLE STAGE	TYPES OF FINANCING	MAJOR SOURCES/PLAYERS
Maturity stage	Obtaining bank loans Issuing bonds Issuing stock	Business operations Commercial banks Investment bankers

important secondary source of seed financing; they may make loans to the entrepreneur or purchase an equity position in the business. (It is often said that family and friends invest in the entrepreneur rather than in a product or service.) Such financing is usually relatively inexpensive, at least compared with more formal venture investing. While there are a few professional and business angel investors (see below) that engage in seed-stage investing, they are not a typical source of financing at this stage.

STARTUP FINANCING

Startup financing coincides with the startup stage of the venture's life cycle; this is financing that takes the venture from having established a viable business opportunity to the point of initial production and sales. Startup financing is usually targeted at firms that have assembled a solid management team, developed a business model and plan, and are beginning to generate revenues. Depending on the demands placed on the entrepreneur's personal capital during the seed stage, the entrepreneur's remaining assets, if any, may serve as a source of startup financing. Family and friends may continue to provide financing during startup.

startup financing
funds needed to take a venture from having established a viable business opportunity to initial production and sales

However, the startup venture should begin to think about the advantages of approaching other, more formal, venture investors.

Although sales or revenues begin during the startup stage, the use of financial capital is generally much larger than the inflow of cash. Thus, most startup-stage ventures need external equity financing. This source of equity capital is referred to as **venture capital**, which is early-stage financial capital often involving substantial risk of total loss.[25] The flip side of this risk of total loss is the potential for extraordinarily high returns when an entrepreneurial venture is extremely successful. Venture capital investors will require the venture, if it has not yet done so, to organize formally in order to limit the risk assumed by venture investors to the amount invested.[26]

Two primary sources of formal external venture capital for startup-stage ventures, as indicated in Figure 1.2, are business angels and venture capitalists. **Business angels** are wealthy individuals, operating as informal or private investors, who provide venture financing for small businesses. They may invest individually or in joint efforts with others.[27] While business angels may be considered informal investors, they are not uninformed investors. Many business angels are self-made entrepreneur multimillionaires, generally well educated, who have substantial business and financial experience. Business angels typically invest in technologies, products, and services in which they have a personal interest and previous experience.

Venture capitalists (VCs) are individuals who join in formal, organized **venture capital firms** to raise and distribute venture capital to new and fast-growing ventures. Venture capital firms typically invest the capital they raise in several different ventures, in an effort to reduce the risk of total loss of their invested capital.[28]

FIRST-ROUND FINANCING

The survival stage in a venture's life cycle is critical to whether the venture will succeed and create value or be closed and liquidated. **First-round financing** is external equity financing typically provided by venture investors during the venture's survival stage to cover the cash shortfalls when expenses and investments exceed revenues. While some revenues begin during the startup stage, the race for market share generally results in a cash deficit. Financing is needed to cover

venture capital
early-stage financial capital often involving substantial risk of total loss

business angels
wealthy individuals operating as informal or private investors who provide venture financing for small businesses

venture capitalists (VCs)
individuals who join in formal, organized firms to raise and distribute venture capital to new and fast-growing ventures

venture capital firms
firms formed to raise and distribute venture capital to new and fast-growing ventures

first-round financing
equity funds provided during the survival stage to cover the cash shortfall when expenses and investments exceed revenues

---

[25] Venture capital sometimes has a debt component. That is, debt convertible into common stock, or straight debt accompanied by an equity kicker such as warrants, is sometimes purchased by venture investors. We will discuss hybrid financing instruments in Chapter 13.

[26] The legal forms for organizing small businesses are discussed in Chapter 3.

[27] For descriptive information on the angels market, see William Wetzel, "The Informal Venture Capital Markets: Aspects of Scale and Market Efficiency," *Journal of Business Venturing* 2 (Fall 1987): pp. 299–313. An interesting study of how earliest-stage technology ventures are financed is presented in William Wetzel and John Freear, "Who Bankrolls High-Tech Entrepreneurs?" *Journal of Business Venturing* 5 (March 1980): pp. 77–89.

[28] It has become common practice to use the terms "venture capitalists" (or VCs) and "venture capital firms" interchangeably. Chapter 11 provides a detailed discussion of the characteristics, methods, and procedures involved in raising professional venture capital.

the marketing expenditures and organizational investments required to bring the firm to full operation in the venture's commercial market. Depending on the nature of the business, the need for first-round financing may actually occur near the end of the startup stage.

As Figure 1.2 suggests, survival-stage ventures seek financing from a variety of external sources. For example, both suppliers and customers become important potential sources of financing. Ventures usually find it advantageous, and possibly necessary, to ask their suppliers for **trade credit**, allowing the venture to pay for purchases on a delayed basis. Having more time to pay supplier bills reduces the need for other sources of financial capital. Upstream users of the firm's goods and services also may be willing to provide formal capital or advances against future revenues. Of course, delayed payments to creditors and accelerated receipts from customers, while good for current cash flow, do impose a need for more careful financial planning.

Federal and some state and local governments provide some financing to small ventures during their survival stages. For example, the **Small Business Administration (SBA)** was established in 1953 by the federal government to provide financial assistance to small businesses. Many state and local governments have developed special **government assistance programs** designed to improve local economic conditions and to create jobs. These programs typically offer low-interest-rate loans and guarantee loans and may also involve tax incentives. Chapter 12 discusses such programs in greater detail.

Commercial banks, usually just called banks, are financial intermediaries that take deposits and make business and personal loans. Because commercial bankers prefer lending to established firms with two years of financial statements, it can be difficult for survival-stage ventures to secure bank financing.[29] Thus, while we show commercial banks as a possible source of financing during the survival stage, successful ventures will typically find it much easier to obtain bank loans during their rapid-growth and maturity stages.

SECOND-ROUND FINANCING

Figure 1.2 indicates that the major sources of financing during the rapid-growth stage come from business operations, suppliers and customers, commercial banks, and financing intermediated by investment bankers. Most ventures, upon reaching the rapid revenue growth stage, find that operating flows, while helpful, remain inadequate to finance the desired rate of growth. Rapid growth in revenues typically involves a prerequisite rapid growth in inventories and accounts receivable, which requires significant external funding. Because inventory expenses are usually paid prior to collecting on the sales related to those inventories, most firms commit sizable resources to investing in "working capital." With potentially large and fluctuating investments in receivables and inventories, it is more important than ever that the venture formally project its

trade credit
financing provided by suppliers in the form of delayed payments due on purchases made by the venture

Small Business Administration (SBA)
established by the federal government to provide financial assistance to small businesses

government assistance programs
financial support, such as low-interest-rate loans and tax incentives, provided by state and local governments to help small businesses

commercial banks
financial intermediaries that take deposits and make business and personal loans

---

[29] Survival- and even startup-stage ventures that might not be able to obtain direct loans from banks often can get indirect loans in the form of cash advances on credit cards issued by banks.

second-round financing
financing for ventures in their rapid-growth stage to support investments in working capital

cash needs. **Second-round financing** typically takes the form of venture capital needed to back working capital expansion.[30]

MEZZANINE FINANCING

One study suggests that, on average, it takes two and one-half years to achieve operating breakeven (i.e., where revenues from operating the business become large enough to equal the operating costs), and a little more than six years to recover an initial equity investment.[31] Thus, the typical successful venture is usually well into its rapid-growth stage before it breaks even. As the venture continues to grow after breaking even, it may need another infusion of financial capital from venture investors. During a venture's rapid-growth stage, **mezzanine financing** provides funds for plant expansion, marketing expenditures, working capital, and product or service improvements. Mezzanine financing is usually obtained through debt that often includes an equity "kicker" or "sweetener" in the form of **warrants**— rights or options to purchase the venture's stock at a specific price within a set time period. At the end of the mezzanine stage, the successful firm will be close to leaving the traditional domain of venture investing and will be prepared to attract funding from the public and large private markets.

mezzanine financing
funds for plant expansion, marketing expenditures, working capital, and product or service improvements

warrants
rights or options to purchase a venture's stock at a specific price within a specified time period

LIQUIDITY-STAGE FINANCING

The rapid-growth stage of a successful venture's life cycle typically provides venture investors with an opportunity to cash in on the return associated with their risk; it also provides access to the public or private capital necessary to continue the firm's mission. A venture, if organized as a corporation, may desire to provide venture investor liquidity by establishing a public market for its equity. Temporary or **bridge financing** may be used to permit a restructuring of current ownership and to fill the gap leading to the firm's first public offer of its equity in its **initial public offering (IPO)**. Typically, part of the proceeds of the public offering will be used to repay the bridge loan needed to keep the venture afloat until the offering. After (and sometimes during) an initial public offering, firms may directly sell founder and venture investor shares to the public market in a **secondary stock offering** of previously owned shares.

Firms not seeking a public market for their equity may attempt to slow to a growth rate that can be supported by internal funding, bank debt, and private equity. For such firms, investor liquidity may be achieved by the repurchase of investor shares, the payment of large dividends, or the sale of the venture to an acquirer. Existing and potential investors usually have strong preferences regarding the planned liquidity event. An investor's perception of the firm's willingness to provide venture investor liquidity affects the terms and conditions in all venture-financing rounds.

bridge financing
temporary financing needed to keep the venture afloat until the next offering

initial public offering (IPO)
a corporation's first sale of common stock to the investing public

secondary stock offering
founder and venture investor shares sold to the public

---

[30] Depending on the size of financial capital needs, ventures may go through several rounds of financing (e.g., first, second, third, fourth, etc.). Sometimes the various rounds of financing are referred to as "series," such as Series A, Series B, Series C, Series D, and so on.

[31] Cited in Timmons and Spinelli, *New Venture Creation*, pp. 390–391.

Investment banking firms advise and assist corporations regarding the structure, timing, and costs of issuing new securities. **Investment banker** is a broad term usually referring to an individual who advises and assists corporations in their security financing decisions. Investment bankers are particularly adroit at helping the successful venture firm undertake an initial public offering. Although it is more common for a firm to have an IPO during a time of rapid and profitable growth, it has become increasingly acceptable for firms with access to new ideas or technologies to go public with little or no operating history and before profitability has been established. Investment bankers also facilitate the sale of firms, through their mergers and acquisitions divisions.

Venture law firms specialize in providing legal services to young, fast-growing entrepreneurial firms. They can craft a firm's legal structure, its tax and licensing obligations, its intellectual property strategy, its employment agreements and incentive compensation, as well as the actual wording and structure of the securities it sells to others. An early and solid relationship with a law firm that specializes in the legal issues of new ventures can be a considerable asset as the firm grows and continues to seek financing.

SEASONED FINANCING

Seasoned financing takes place during the venture's maturity stage. As previously noted, venture investors typically complete their involvement with a successful venture before the venture's move into the maturity stage of its life cycle. Retained earnings from business operations are a major source of financing for the mature venture. If additional funds are needed, seasoned financing can be obtained in the form of loans from commercial banks or through new issues of bonds and stocks, usually with the aid of investment bankers. A mature firm with previously issued publicly traded securities can obtain debt and equity capital by selling additional securities through **seasoned securities offerings** to the public.

As a mature firm's growth rate declines to the growth rate for the whole economy, the firm's need for new external capital is not the matter of survival that it was in earlier stages. Mature firms frequently approach financing as a way to cut taxes, fine-tune investor returns, and provide capital for mergers, acquisitions, and extraordinary expansion. If they have created brand equity in their securities, they may choose to fund mergers and acquisitions by directly issuing securities to their targets. Mature private companies can sell seasoned versions of their securities directly to a restricted number and class of investors, but not to the general public. The time needed for an entrepreneurial firm to reach its maturity stage depends on its operating characteristics, the rate of technological change in the industry, and the drive, vision, talent, and depth of resources in its management team and venture investors.

---

investment banking firms
firms that advise and assist corporations regarding the type, timing, and costs of issuing new securities

investment banker
individual working for an investment banking firm who advises and assists corporations in their security financing decisions and regarding mergers and acquisitions

venture law firms
law firms specializing in providing legal services to young, fast-growing entrepreneurial firms

seasoned securities offering
the offering of securities by a firm that has previously offered the same or substantially similar securities

---

CONCEPT CHECK

- What types of venture financing are typically available at each stage of a successful venture's life cycle?
- What is seasoned financing?

1.8   LIFE CYCLE APPROACH FOR TEACHING ENTREPRENEURIAL FINANCE

We use a life cycle approach throughout this text to teach entrepreneurial finance. Figure 1.3 provides an overview of major operating and financial decisions faced by entrepreneurs as they manage their ventures during the five life cycle stages. The fact that the entrepreneur is continually creating useful information on the venture's viability and opportunities means that this approach, and the diagram depicted in Figure 1.3, should be viewed as being dynamic and ongoing. At each stage, and sometimes more than once during a stage, the entrepreneur needs to make critical decisions about the future of the venture. Should we abandon the idea or liquidate the venture? Should we rethink the idea, redesign a product or service, change manufacturing, selling, or distributing practices, or restructure the venture? Ultimately, the question becomes "Should we continue?"[32]

This text is divided into six parts. Part 1, "Background and Environment," consists of the first two chapters and focuses primarily on development-stage financial considerations faced by entrepreneurs. During the development stage, the entrepreneur screens or examines an idea from the perspective of whether it is likely to become a viable business opportunity, prepares a business plan for the idea that successfully passes the "opportunity screen," and obtains the seed financing necessary to carry out the venture's development stage. Earlier in this chapter, we provided a brief discussion of the sources of, and players involved in, seed financing. Sources of financing during the other life cycle stages also were presented. In Chapter 2, we introduce the ingredients of a sound business model that are necessary to convert an idea into a viable business opportunity. We also provide examples of qualitative and quantitative assessment exercises that can be used to help assess the business viability of an idea. The last part of the chapter discusses the key elements of a business plan.

Part 2, "Organizing and Operating the Venture," consists of Chapters 3, 4, and 5 and focuses on entrepreneurial finance topics relating primarily to the startup and survival life cycle stages as depicted in Figure 1.3. The preparation of a business plan serves as the link between the development stage and the startup stage. In order to start operating the business, the entrepreneur must first decide on the organizational form for the business, prepare pro forma or projected financial statements for the first several years of operation, and identify the amount and timing of startup financing that will be needed. Many entrepreneurs find that it is relatively easy to start a new venture; the hard part is surviving the first year or two of operation. In order to progress successfully through the survival stage, the entrepreneur must closely monitor the venture's

---

[32] While the entrepreneur may have the most at stake when making these decisions, investors (i.e., friends, family, and/or venture investors) and other constituencies (creditors, the management team, and other employees, etc.) will be affected by what the entrepreneur decides. Thus, we choose to use "we" instead of "I" when formulating these questions.

FIGURE 1.3 Life Cycle Approach: Venture Operating and Financial Decisions

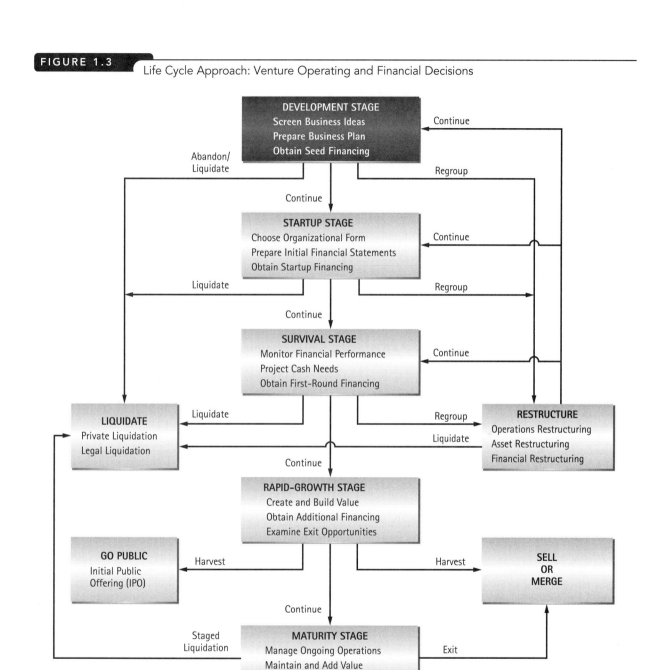

financial performance, understand and project cash needs, and obtain first-round financing.

In Chapter 3, we discuss the various forms of business organizations available to the entrepreneur, provide a discussion of the importance of developing intellectual property and ways to protect intellectual property, and discuss sources of early-stage financing needed during the startup and survival stages. In Chapter 4, we review the financial statements used to measure a venture's financial performance. Chapter 5 covers the evaluation of financial performance. It is worth noting that users of this text who have adequate finance/accounting backgrounds can bypass Chapters 4 and 5 without loss of continuity, as long as they have a fundamental understanding of cash flow concepts, including how ventures build and burn cash.

Part 3, "Planning for the Future," consists of Chapters 6, 7, and 8; it provides a transition from a venture's survival to its ability to experience rapid sales growth and the creation and growth of value. Again, we turn to the venture life cycle illustration in Figure 1.3. As a venture starts operating, both short-term and long-term plans must be prepared, monitored, and revised to adjust to actual performance and competitive pressures. Long-term financial planning requires the projection of annual financial statements covering the next few years, reflecting a venture's survival stage as well as what is expected for the venture as it succeeds and begins to grow rapidly. Of course, only those ventures that are able to survive by regrouping and restructuring will succeed in reaching their rapid-growth stages. Survival depends on generating sufficient cash flow to meet obligations as they come due in the short run, which makes it necessary for the venture to prepare monthly financial projections for the next year. Chapter 6 covers short-term and long-term financial planning topics.

Being able to move successfully from survival to rapid growth usually requires finding ways to generate several types and rounds of financing. Chapter 7 discusses the types and costs of financial capital available to the entrepreneur. Since the cost of financial capital also can be viewed as the rate of return required on a specific risk class of investment, the materials in this chapter are important to understanding how ventures are valued. Chapter 8 provides an introduction to securities law basics. Before the entrepreneur starts raising financial capital, it is important that she understand which actions are legal and which actions are illegal. Ignorance of the law is not an acceptable defense when issuing or selling securities.

Part 4, "Creating and Recognizing Venture Value," consists of Chapters 9 and 10. As previously noted, the financial goal of the entrepreneurial venture is to maximize the value of the venture to the owners. Most of a venture's value is achieved in the form of free cash flows generated during the latter part of the venture's rapid-growth stage and during the maturity stage. (See Figure 1.3.) In order to increase revenues rapidly, investments in inventories and fixed assets are necessary. Generally, these assets require additional financing. Once the assets are in place, however, the successful venture begins generating large and growing amounts of free cash flows. Chapter 9 discusses the fundamentals of financial valuation and covers the equity perspective of valuation. We present two methods for valuing a venture's equity: the maximum dividend method and the pseudo dividend method. Chapter 10 examines common venture investor short-cut methods for valuing the venture and relates them to the more detailed valuation methods introduced in Chapter 9.

Part 5, "Structuring Financing for the Growing Venture," consists of Chapters 11, 12, and 13. As entrepreneurial ventures move successfully through succeeding stages of their life cycles, financing sources often become more varied and, in some cases, more complex. Most entrepreneurial ventures will seek financial capital from venture investors during their progress from startup, through survival, and into the rapid-growth stage of their lifetime. Chapter 11 discusses the history of, and current practices used by, professional venture capitalists. Other intermediated financing is the topic of Chapter 12. In Chapter 13, we discuss security design, including issuing various classes of stock, debt that is convertible into common stock, and warrants. We also illustrate how ventures are valued from an enterprise perspective, which is the value of the venture to both debtholders and equity investors.

Part 6, "Exit and Turnaround Strategies," consists of Chapters 14 and 15. As depicted in Figure 1.3, it is during a venture's rapid-growth stage that entrepreneurs and outside venture investors examine possible exit opportunities to "harvest" the value they built. Chapter 14 examines alternative exit opportunities that include going public through an IPO, selling the venture to management or outside investors, and merging the venture with another firm.

Chapter 15 recognizes that, at one or more times during a venture's life cycle, financial distress may develop whereby a venture is unable to meet its debt obligations when they are due. Such a situation creates a need to regroup, reorganize, and even restructure in order to move the venture forward toward success. Restructuring may take the form of operations restructuring, asset restructuring, and/or financial restructuring. Sometimes it is necessary to seek legal protection while financial restructuring takes place. At the extreme, unsuccessful restructuring efforts may result in liquidation.

Now that we have introduced you to the world of entrepreneurial finance, we hope you apply yourself to learn the concepts, theory, and practice of finance as they relate to the entrepreneur. We remind you that mastering the materials in this book, while satisfying in itself, is really for the purpose of creating financial competence that increases the likelihood your entrepreneurial firm will survive, attract financial backing, and create value over time.

CONCEPT CHECK

- Why do many entrepreneurial ventures have to regroup and restructure?
- How can the entrepreneur exit or harvest the venture?

SUMMARY

This chapter provided an introduction to the world of entrepreneurial finance. We began by defining entrepreneurship and discussed the importance of small and growing ventures to the U.S. economy. We recognized that starting and successfully operating an entrepreneurial venture is not easy. At the same time, there is always room for one more successful entrepreneur.

We discussed the importance of understanding societal, demographic, and technological trends shaping our society and providing many lucrative entrepreneurial opportunities. Our attention then shifted to identifying and discussing the seven principles of entrepreneurial finance: (1) Real, human, and financial capital must be rented from owners. (2) Risk and expected reward go hand in hand.

(3) While accounting is the language of business, cash is the currency. (4) New venture financing involves search, negotiation, and privacy. (5) A venture's financial objective is to increase value. (6) It is dangerous to assume that people act against their own self-interests. (7) Venture character and reputation can be assets or liabilities. The financial objective is to increase the venture's value. Behaving fairly and honestly with the venture's constituencies builds confidence and support for the entrepreneur and the venture, which contributes to increasing the venture's value. Increasing value can be consistent with social responsibility, and many wealthy entrepreneurs have engaged in personal and venture philanthropy.

Conflicts may arise when incentives diverge as the new venture matures. While entrepreneurial ventures often can avoid or minimize the owner-manager agency problem, the owner-debtholder conflict will arise every time the venture faces financial distress. After discussing the principles of entrepreneurial finance, we turned our attention to defining entrepreneurial finance and described the responsibilities of a venture's financial manager.

We then identified and presented a five-stage life cycle that successful ventures typically endure. These stages are the development stage, the startup stage, the survival stage, the rapid-growth stage, and the maturity stage. Next, we discussed types of financing, and the sources and players involved at the various life cycle stages. Types of venture financing include seed financing, startup financing, first-round financing, second-round financing, and mezzanine financing. Liquidity-stage financing is important in allowing venture investors to achieve a tangible return through the sale of the venture or its securities. For ventures achieving their maturity stages, seasoned financing in the form of bank loans, bonds, and stocks is available to meet possible external financing needs.

We concluded the chapter with the presentation of our life cycle approach. We connected each chapter to the life cycle stage and topics it addresses from initial idea screening in Chapter 2 through the execution of exit strategies in Chapter 14. Chapter 15 provides guidance to the many entrepreneurial ventures that will suffer some form of financial distress. If these ventures are to survive and build value, they will need to successfully regroup, reorganize, and restructure.

KEY TERMS

bridge financing	government assistance programs	secondary stock offering
business angels	initial public offering (IPO)	seed financing
commercial banks	investment banker	Small Business Administration
development stage	investment banking firms	(SBA)
e-commerce	maturity stage	startup financing
early-stage ventures	mezzanine financing	startup stage
entrepreneur	owner-debtholder conflict	survival stage
entrepreneurial finance	owner-manager (agency) conflicts	trade credit
entrepreneurial opportunities	private financial markets	venture capital
entrepreneurship	public financial markets	venture capital firms
financial distress	rapid-growth stage	venture capitalists (VCs)
first-round financing	seasoned firms	venture law firms
free cash	seasoned securities offerings	venture life cycle
free cash flow	second-round financing	warrants

DISCUSSION QUESTIONS

1. What is entrepreneurship? What are some basic characteristics of entrepreneurs?

2. Why do businesses close or cease operating? What are the primary reasons why businesses fail?

3. What are three megatrend sources or categories for finding entrepreneurial opportunities?

4. What is e-commerce? Why are the Internet economy and e-commerce here to stay?

5. Identify the seven principles of entrepreneurial finance.

6. Explain the statement: "The time value of money is not the only cost involved in renting someone's financial capital."

7. How do public and private financial markets differ?

8. What is the financial goal of the entrepreneurial venture? What are the major components for estimating value?

9. From an agency relationship standpoint, describe the possible types of problems or conflicts of interest that could inhibit maximizing a venture's value.

10. Briefly discuss the likely importance of an entrepreneur's character and reputation on the success of a venture. What role does social responsibility play in the operation of an entrepreneurial venture?

11. What is entrepreneurial finance, and what are the responsibilities of the financial manager of an entrepreneurial venture?

12. What are the five stages in the life cycle of a successful venture?

13. New ventures are subject to periodic introspection on whether they should continue or liquidate. Explain the types of information you would expect to gather and how it would be used in each stage to aid an entrepreneur's approach to the venture's future.

14. Identify the types of financing that typically coincide with each stage of a successful venture's life cycle.

15. Identify the major sources, as well as the players, associated with each type of financing for each life cycle stage.

16. Describe the life cycle approach for teaching entrepreneurial finance.

INTERNET ACTIVITIES

1. Web-surfing exercise: Develop your own list of the five most important societal or economic trends currently shaping our society and providing major business opportunities. Use the World Wide Web to generate potential venture ideas related to the trends and to gather commentary and statistics on them.

2. Determine several "resources" available from the Small Business Administration for entrepreneurs that might be useful in starting, financing, and managing an entrepreneurial venture. The SBA Web site is http://www.sba.gov. Also, search the SBA's Office of Advocacy Web site at http://www.sba.gov/advo/ for information relating to recent annual numbers of employer firm births and the importance of small businesses to the U.S. economy.

EXERCISES/PROBLEMS

1. The following ventures are at different stages in their life cycles. Identify the likely stage for each venture and describe the type of financing each venture is likely to be seeking and identify potential sources for that financing.

   A. Phil Young, founder of Pedal Pushers, has an idea for a pedal replacement for children's bicycles. The Pedal Pusher will replace existing bicycle pedals with an easy-release stirrup to help smaller children hold their feet on the pedals. The Pedal Pusher will also glow in the dark and will provide a musical sound as the bicycle is pedaled. Phil is seeking some financial help in developing working prototypes.

   B. Petal Providers is a firm that is trying to model the U.S. floral industry after its European counterparts. European flower markets tend to have larger selections at lower prices. Revenues started at $1 million last year when the first "mega" Petal Providers floral outlet was opened. Revenues are expected to be $3 million this year and $15 million next year after two additional stores are opened.

2. The following ventures have supplied information on how they are being financed. Link the type and sources of financing to where each venture is likely to be in its life cycle.

   A. Voice River provides media-on-demand services via the Internet. Voice River raised $500,000 of founder's capital in April 2008 and "seed" financing of $1 million in September 2008 from the Sentinak Fund. The firm is currently seeking $6 million for a growth round of financing.

   B. Electronic Publishing raised $200,000 from three private investors and another $200,000 from SOFTLEND Holdings. The financial capital is to be used to complete software development of e-mail delivery and subscription management services.

3. Identify a successful entrepreneurial venture that has been in business at least three years.

   A. Use historical revenue information to examine how this particular venture moved through its life cycle stages. Determine the length of the development stage, the startup stage, and so forth.

   B. Determine the financing sources used during the various stages of the venture's life cycle.

   C. Identify the venture's equity owners and how shares have been distributed among the owners. What portion of ownership has been allocated to management team members? What, if any, agency conflicts can you identify?

4. Explain how you would choose between the following situations. Develop your answers from the perspective of the principles of entrepreneurial finance presented earlier in the chapter. You may develop your answers with or without making actual calculations.

   A. You have $1,000 to invest for one year (this would be a luxury for most entrepreneurs). You can set a 4 percent interest rate for one year at the Third First Bank or a 5 percent interest rate at the First Fourth Bank. Which savings account investment would you choose and why?

   B. A "friend" of yours will lend you $10,000 for one year if you agree to repay him $1,000 interest plus returning the $10,000 investment. A second "friend" has only $5,000 to lend to you but wants total funds of $5,400 in repayment at the end of one year. Which loan would you choose and why?

   C. You have the opportunity to invest $3,000 in one of two investments. The first investment would pay you either $2,700 or $3,300 at the end of one year depending on the success of the venture. The second investment would pay you either $2,000 or $4,000 at the end of one year depending on the success of the venture. Which investment would you choose and why? Would your answer change if your investment were only $1?

   D. An outside venture investor is considering investing $100,000 in either your new venture or another venture, or investing $50,000 in each venture. At the end of one year, the value of your venture might be either $0 or $1 million. The other venture is expected to be worth either $50,000 or $500,000 at the end of one year. Which investment choice (yours, the other venture, or half-and-half) do you think the venture investor would choose to invest in? Why?

5. Assume that you have been working on a first-generation "prototype" for a new product. An angel investor is "waiting in the wings," wanting to invest in a second-generation model or prototype. Unfortunately, you have run out of money and aren't able to finish the initial prototype. The business angel has previously said that she would "walk" if you cannot produce a working first-generation prototype.

A. What would you attempt to do to save your entrepreneurial venture?

B. Now let's assume that the angel investor will advance you the financing needed for the second-generation prototype based on your "word" that the first-generation prototype has been completed and is working? What would you do?

6. Following are some pairs of famous entrepreneurs. Associate the entrepreneurs with the companies they founded.

1. Steve Jobs and Steven Wozniak   A. Google

2. Bill Gates and Paul Allen   B. Ben & Jerry's

3. Larry Page and Sergey Brin   C. Microsoft

4. Ben Cohen and Jerry Greenfield   D. Apple, Inc.

SUPPLEMENTAL EXERCISES/PROBLEMS

[Note: These activities are for readers who have an understanding of financial statements.]

7. Phil Young, founder of Pedal Pushers, expects to spend the next six months developing and testing prototypes for a pedal replacement for children's bicycles. (See Part A of Problem 1 for a description of the proposed product.) Phil anticipates paying monthly rent of $700 for space in a local warehouse where the Pedal Pusher product will be designed, developed, and tested. Utility expenses for electricity and heat are estimated at $150 per month. Phil plans to pay himself a salary of $1,000 per month. Materials needed to build and test an initial prototype product are expected to cost $9,500. Each redesign and new prototype will require an additional $4,500 investment. Phil anticipates that before the final Pedal Pusher is ready for market at the end of six months, three prototypes will have been built and tested. Costs associated with test marketing the Pedal Pusher are estimated at $7,000.

A. Determine the amount of financial capital that Phil Young will need during the six months it will take to develop and test-market the Pedal Pusher.

B. What type of financial capital is needed? What are the likely sources of that capital for Phil Young?

C. What would be your estimate of the amount of financial capital needed if the product development period lasted nine months?

D. What compensation arrangements would you recommend as he hires additional members of the management team?

8. Let's assume that Phil Young does develop and successfully market the Pedal Pusher product discussed in Problems 1 and 7. Phil's venture will purchase materials for making the product from others, assemble the products at the Pedal Pusher venture's facilities, and hire product sales representatives to sell the Pedal Pusher through local retail and discount stores that sell children's bicycles. The costs of plastic pedals and extensions; bolts, washers, and nuts; reflective material; and a microchip to provide the music when the bicycle is pedaled are expected to be $2.33 per pair of Pedal Pushers. Assembly costs are projected at $1.50 per pair. Shipping and delivery costs are estimated at $.20 per pair, and Phil Young will have to pay commissions of $.30 per pair of pedals sold by the sales representatives.

A. What will it cost to produce and sell a pair of Pedal Pushers?

B. What price will Phil Young have to charge for a pair of Pedal Pushers if he wants a "markup" of 50 percent on each sale? At what price would retailers have to sell a pair of Pedal Pushers if they, in turn, desired a "markup" before their expenses of 40 percent?

C. Now that Pedal Pushers is up and operating, Phil Young feels he should be paid a salary of $5,000 per month. Other administrative expenses will be $2,500 per month. How many units (pairs) of Pedal Pushers will the venture have to sell to cover all operating and administrative costs during the first year of operation?

M I N I   C A S E

Interact Systems, Inc.

Interact Systems, Inc., has developed software tools that help hotel chains solve application integration problems. Interact's application integration server (AIS) provides a two-way interface between central reservations systems (CRSs) and property management systems (PMSs). At least two important trends in the hotel industry are relevant. First, hotels are shifting from manual to electronic booking of room reservations; electronic bookings will continue to increase as more reservations are made over the Internet. Second, competitive pressures are forcing hotels to implement yield management programs and to increase customer service. By integrating the CRS and PMS through Interact's AIS, inventories can be better managed, yields improved, and customer service enhanced.

All reservation traffic is routed from the CRS to individual hotel properties. This allows Interact Systems to create a database that can be used to track customers and to facilitate marketing programs, such as frequent-stay or VIP programs, as a way of increasing customer satisfaction. Interact forecasts application integration expenditures in the hospitality industry exceeding $1 billion by 2010.

Greg Thomas founded Interact Systems in 2004 and developed the firm's middleware software and hospitality applications. He has twelve years of systems applications experience and currently is Interact's chief technology officer. Eric Westskow joined Interact in early 2007 as president and CEO. He had worked in sales and marketing in the software industry for more than twenty years.

Interact Systems' AIS software development, which began in 2004, went through several design changes in 2005. The first product was sold and installed in 2006. Sales were only $500,000 in 2007. However, now that the firm has dependable market-tested AIS products ready to be shipped, revenues are expected to reach $20.8 million in 2010.

Greg Thomas founded Interact Systems with $50,000 of his own savings plus $50,000 from friends. Two private investors provided an additional $200,000 in 2005. In addition, $1 million was obtained from a venture capital firm, Katile Capital Partners, in early 2007 in exchange for an equity position in Interact. The firm currently is seeking an additional $5 million to finance sales growth.

A. Verify the two important trends that are developing in the hotel industry.

B. Describe how Interact Systems' AIS software products will benefit the hotel industry from a profitability standpoint.

C. Describe how Interact Systems' AIS software will help hotels improve customer satisfaction.

D. Describe the life cycle stages that Interact Systems has progressed through to date.

E. What types of venture financing have been obtained, or are being sought, by Interact?

F. Relate major sources or players with the venture financing described in Part E.

G. What types of agency problems or conflicts should the founding entrepreneur have anticipated?

Interact Systems, Inc. (continued)

H. What, if anything, should the founding entrepreneur have done in anticipation of agency conflicts?

I. Assuming the venture succeeds, what are the potential advantages to other stakeholders (customers, employees, and society more broadly)?

J. If internal sales growth projections are revised downward after the current financing round, what, if any, disclosure to stakeholders (investors, employees, customers, etc.) should occur? Why?

Appendix

INTERNET CONCEPTS AND DEVELOPMENTS

INTERNET INDUSTRY STRUCTURE

To develop a conceptual understanding of how the Internet works, we start with broadcast networks. Much of historical communication (including computer communications) employed "one-to-many" networking. In this broadcast setup, there is a centralized sender and decentralized receivers. When a new connection is added, the network's size increases by one sender-receiver pair. In such a network, adapting it to allow messages from the "receivers" to the "sender" and possibly other "receivers" involves communicating through the centralized "sender." This introduces significant scaling challenges owing to the constrained capacity of the centralized sender. In contrast, "many-to-many" networks such as the Internet allow every member to be a sender and a receiver, diminishing the tendency to bottleneck. Adding one new connection to an existing network of size N means adding N new sender-receiver pairs. Growth can be exponential.

Many-to-many networks require a physical infrastructure. Infrastructure firms build the physical network that connects individuals, businesses, and devices. Telecommunications firms and producers of end-user networking equipment are essential components of the Internet infrastructure. *Internet service providers (ISPs)* provide the links whereby individuals and businesses can communicate with each other and exchange information via the Internet. *Enabling technology firms* create the software and devices that process and organize the data that flow back and forth on the Internet. *Infomediary firms* offer Web sites that help consumers find and purchase products and services, as well as search for all kinds of information. *E-commerce firms*, including manufacturers, re-tailers, and their intermediaries, use Internet and Web technology to sell, or facil-itate the sale of, goods and services.

Traditional firms are often called brick-and-mortar firms. *Brick-and-mortar firms* have physical facilities in place for manufacturing, marketing, selling, and distributing their products and services. Many of these firms also have established brand loyalty for their products and services and are here to stay. However, many brick-and-mortar firms are moving toward becoming "click-and-mortar" firms. *Click-and-mortar firms* have established Web sites, and sometimes separate subsidiaries, to use the Internet to leverage their existing physical assets and their intangible assets such as brand loyalties and distribution systems. A click-and-mortar firm may be a manufacturer that sells its products directly to customers via the firm's Web site. The manufacturer produces, packs, and ships the ordered products.

Dot-com firms create and reinvent business opportunities based on existing and evolving technologies associated with the Internet. They sell products, ser-vices, and information; attempt to generate revenues from advertising on their Web sites; provide auction markets; and bring together businesses with existing supplier-customer relationships. While dot-com firms may be involved in all as-pects of the Internet network, much of the recent focus has been on their role as e-tailers (i.e., firms conducting retailing activities online).

During the late 1990s, the mere mention of a new dot-com idea might have brought forth multiple offers of venture capital funding. These funds oc-casionally were made available with little scrutiny or due diligence regarding the viability of the proposed business idea and model. As the new century be-gan, closer investigation showed that many dot-com ideas had virtually no chance of producing cash flow for their investors. This led venture investors to react strongly in the opposite direction, dramatically contracting the supply of venture capital. Many dot-coms ceased operations. A good illustration of adap-tation to this rather violent reversal is the experience of Omnicell, Inc., a firm that creates and sells software that facilitates the purchase and management of drugs and supplies for hospitals and other health care facilities. The firm was known as Omnicell.com in April 2000 when it filed for an IPO. However, owing to rapid deterioration in the valuation of dot-coms, the offering was withdrawn. In mid-2001, a decision was made to drop the dot-com from the end of the firm's name, and a second attempt at an IPO in August 2001 was successful.[33]

By 2003, much of the negative impact of the dot-com bust had worn off, and e-commerce was flourishing. The initial success of Google as a search engine

---

[33] See Raymond Hennessey, "Omnicell IPO Is Priced Low, but Rises 36%," *Wall Street Journal*, August 8, 2001, p. C14.

and the continued growth of online display advertising are examples that the Internet economy and e-commerce are here to stay.[34]

COMPONENTS OF THE INTERNET ECONOMY

The University of Texas Center for Research in Electronic Commerce has identified four segments of commercial activity within the Internet economy:[35]

- Infrastructure layer
- Applications infrastructure layer
- Intermediary layer
- Commerce layer

The Internet *infrastructure layer* provides the physical assets necessary to allow the many-to-many Internet network to actually work. This layer includes telecommunications firms, Internet service providers, companies that provide end-user access, and manufacturers of end-use networking equipment. Major players include Cisco, Corning, Hewlett-Packard, Sun, and IBM. The Internet *applications infrastructure layer* provides the fundamental basis for e-commerce to take place and also makes the Internet functional or operational. Included in this layer are providers of software products and platforms, consultants, and Web site designers, builders, and service providers. Examples of major players in this layer include Microsoft, Oracle, Adobe, and SAP. These are considered enabling technology firms.

The Internet *intermediary layer* involves firms that generate revenues not from direct transactions but from advertising, membership and subscription fees, and commissions. They are Web content providers, online advertisers, content aggregators, online brokerages, and market makers or intermediaries. Examples include Yahoo!, DoubleClick, Charles Schwab, and eBay. These are, primarily, infomediary firms. The Internet *commerce layer* consists of firms that conduct Web-based commerce transactions; it includes manufacturers selling online, airlines selling tickets online, the e-commerce click-and-mortar retailers, and even business-to-business e-commerce transactions. Examples are Amazon.com, Dell.com, Southwest.com, and the dot-com activities of Target and many other traditional retailers.

E-COMMERCE AND YOUR VENTURE

If your new venture will involve e-commerce—and it's harder every day to think of businesses that won't—some warnings may prove helpful. Internet etiquette

---

[34] For example, see Timothy J. Mullaney, "The E-Biz Surprise," *Business Week*, May 12, 2003, pp. 60–68. Also see Paul R. La Monica, "Online Ad Spending Surges," http://money.cnn.com/2007/06/06/news/companies/onlineads/index.htm.

[35] The source of information for this section was the Web site for the Center for Research in Electronic Commerce, McCombs School of Business, University of Texas at Austin (http://cism.bus.utexas.edu/) and http://www.InternetIndicators.com.

should not be ignored. For example, joining a lot of mailing lists and sending out general advertising messages ("spam") to list subscribers is not a good idea. While your hard work is only a delete key away, even that one short keystroke can anger recipients. If recipients become sufficiently annoyed, you may receive an exceedingly large amount of unpleasant replies (even if only from one recipient) in an act known as flaming. Also, the expectations of e-commerce customers can be quite high. In addition to great prices and immediate order placement, many e-customers expect instantaneous shipping confirmation and tracking information. It is worth your time to investigate the cultural aspects of Internet interaction.

A number of Internet-spawned terms have been invented to gauge and measure e-commerce activities. One measure of Web site popularity is the number of "hits," or visits, prospective customers make during a specified period, such as a day or a month. The use of the word "hits" has been replaced in some e-commerce vocabularies by "unique visitors," which is the number of unduplicated computer users who visited a Web site in a given time period. Computer users who visit the same site numerous times within a specified time period are known as "eyeballs." "Reach" is the percentage of total Web users in the United States who visited a Web site in a given time period. Additional e-commerce metrics in use are average minutes per visitor per time period and pages viewed in a specified time period. There is also an increasing focus on "cost per addition," which reflects how cost effective a venture is in finding new customers, and "churn rates," which measure how successful a venture is in keeping its customers.[36] E-commerce, after a period of obsession with revenue growth, is increasing its attention to gross margins and profits.

E-COMMERCE RESOURCES

While we recognize that some future entrepreneurial activities may not involve the Internet and e-commerce, we believe it will become increasingly difficult to identify business opportunities divorced from Internet concerns and competition. To help businesses make use of electronic commerce, the U.S. Congress created the CALS Shared Resource Center (CSRC) program in 1991. The program was renamed the Electronic Commerce Resource Center (ECRC) in 1994, and, by 1998, it had grown to encompass several regional centers.

Each ECRC provides outreach activities, training courses, and technical support to help businesses use electronic commerce effectively. Training courses are provided at little or no cost and cover such topics as "getting started with electronic commerce" and the "Internet series," which shows how to use the Web to reach new customers and serve existing customers better. Technical support includes demonstrations of electronic commerce technologies, guidance in selecting software providers, and even on-site support. Potential benefits of ECRC e-commerce training and technical support include reduced time to market,

---

[36]   See George Donnelly, "New @ttitude," *CFO* (June 1999): pp. 43–54.

improved operating efficiencies, and better payment processes.[37] As anyone who has recently watched television commercials can tell you, there are also many private fee-for-service firms ready, willing, and apparently able to help your venture explore e-commerce.

APPENDIX DISCUSSION QUESTIONS

1. Briefly describe the structure of the Internet industry.
2. Identify the four layers or segments of firms within the Internet economy.

---

[37] For more detailed information, contact the Electronic Commerce Resource Center Web site at http://www.ornl.gov/cals/ctc/ecrcpage.html. For examples of specific firm benefits from using an ECRC, see Jennifer Sehu, "Electronic Commerce Resources Centers Help Entrepreneurs Get Online," *CNNfn Small Business* (June 8, 1999).

Chapter 2

FROM THE IDEA TO THE BUSINESS PLAN

PREVIOUSLY COVERED

In Chapter 1, we presented an overview of entrepreneurial finance and, we hope, kindled your interest in learning more about the financial management tools and methods that can help entrepreneurs succeed. We aligned the types of financing, sources, and investors with a successful venture's stages of revenue growth. We explained how the progression through this book follows the venture life cycle.

LOOKING AHEAD

Part 2 focuses on starting a new venture and surviving the first year or two of operations. Chapter 3 covers the pros and cons of alternative business organizations, including tax and liability considerations the entrepreneur should consider when making choices regarding a new venture's formal organization. We discuss important intellectual property rights issues that can factor heavily in whether the venture survives and prospers. We consider potential seed and startup financing sources.

CHAPTER LEARNING OBJECTIVES

In this chapter, we examine how one can move from an idea to an assessment of the related business opportunity's feasibility. We introduce both qualitative and quantitative tools to facilitate this assessment. We conclude the chapter with an overview of the more formal document that incorporates, extends, and reinforces the initial feasibility assessment's analysis: the business plan. After completing this chapter, you will be able to:

1. Describe the process of moving from an idea to a business plan

2. Understand the components of a sound business model

3. Identify some of the best practices for high-growth, high-performance firms

4. Understand the importance of timing in venture success

5. Describe the use of a SWOT analysis as an initial "litmus test"

6. Identify the types of questions that a reasonable feasibility assessment addresses

7. Identify quantitative criteria that assist in assessing a new venture's feasibility and its ability to attract external financing

8. Describe the primary components of a typical business plan

Every new venture begins with an idea. Transforming this picture in one's mind into a product or service that satisfies, or creates and then satisfies, a consumer need is the first step in the entrepreneurial process. Only a small number of new business ideas become viable business opportunities with funded business plans. We know that venture capitalists invest in only 1 to 3 percent of business plans presented to them. To survive the massive winnowing, particularly when seeking professional venture capital, successful entrepreneurs overcome substantially long odds.

How do we know whether an idea has the potential to become a viable business opportunity? The answer is that we don't know with absolute certainty. There are many examples of good ideas that have flopped as business ventures. Likewise, there are many examples of ideas that were turned down by venture investors (and professors) before ultimately making the persistent entrepreneur a wealthy individual. While there is no infallible screening process, there are tools and techniques that can help you and prospective investors examine similarities between your potential venture and other successful ventures.

2.1 PROCESS FOR IDENTIFYING BUSINESS OPPORTUNITIES

In Chapter 1, we defined an *entrepreneur* as an individual who thinks, reasons, and acts to convert ideas into commercial opportunities and to create value. An entrepreneur may start a number of different types of businesses, including salary-replacement firms, lifestyle firms, and entrepreneurial firms or ventures. **Salary-replacement firms** provide their owners with income levels comparable to what they would have earned working for much larger firms. Examples include single-store retailers, restaurant owners, and financial and tax services providers. **Lifestyle firms** allow their owners to pursue specific lifestyles while being paid for doing what they like to do. Examples include owning and operating a ski instruction or whitewater rafting business.

Entrepreneurial ventures strive for high growth rates for revenue, profit, and cash flow. Typically, entrepreneurial ventures will not be able to grow at the targeted rate without attracting external investment above and beyond that provided by the entrepreneur and retained profits. Salary-replacement and lifestyle firms experience some of the trauma and rewards of the entrepreneurial lifestyle, but remain centered on a small-scale format with limited growth and employment opportunities. U.S. small businesses are predominately salary-replacement or lifestyle firms; many provide their owners with perceived business enjoyment

salary-replacement firms
firms that provide their owners with income levels comparable to what they could have earned working for much larger firms

lifestyle firms
firms that allow owners to pursue specific lifestyles while being paid for doing what they like to do

entrepreneurial ventures
entrepreneurial firms that are flows and performance oriented as reflected in rapid value creation over time

and a reasonable amount of wealth.[1] For such firms, rapid growth and (inter)national market domination are of secondary, if any, interest to the owners. While we don't want to diminish the contribution of this very large and economically critical class of entrepreneurial firms, we do want to make it clear that our focus is on the subset of entrepreneurial firms seeking growth and market domination. Such firms experience traumatic growth pains and are the primary targets for professional venture investing. To emphasize the particular challenges faced by such firms, we will refer to our growth-driven subset as *entrepreneurial ventures*.

In Chapter 1, we defined *entrepreneurial opportunities* as ideas that have the potential to create value through new, repackaged, or repositioned products, markets, processes, or services. Figure 2.1 depicts a graphic representation of moving from the idea or entrepreneurial opportunity stage through the feasibility analysis stage and into the business planning stage. Many introductory entrepreneurship textbooks spend considerable time on identifying ideas, conducting feasibility analyses, and preparing business plans.[2] Rather than repeating that material here, our objective is to provide insights into the process while maintaining an entrepreneurial finance perspective.

Once conceptualized, a new idea should be examined for its business feasibility. The second element in Figure 2.1 is an initial feasibility review. This review focuses on whether it is possible to convert the idea into a product or service meeting a lucrative unfilled need. Much insight can be gained from this initial feasibility "litmus test." Entrepreneurs pursuing a salary-replacement or lifestyle business requiring little outside financing may move rapidly from such a basic qualitative screen to preparing a business plan. However, for entrepreneurial ventures requiring external financing, a more rigorous feasibility analysis with qualitative and quantitative components offers important additional insights.

Later in this chapter, we will return to a simple initial approach and more detailed in-depth approaches to feasibility analysis. First, however, we want to discuss the basic ingredients of a sound business model. Knowing the best practices of successful startup businesses can help an entrepreneur make better judgments and distinctions when conducting a feasibility analysis or writing a business plan.

CONCEPT CHECK

- What are three types of startup firms?

---

[1]   For example, see Thomas J. Stanley and William D. Danko, *The Millionaire Next Door* (New York: Longstreet Press, 1996).

[2]   See Jeffry A. Timmons and Stephen Spinelli, *New Venture Creation*, 7th ed. (New York: McGraw-Hill/Irwin, 2007), chaps. 4, 5, and 6. Also see Bruce R. Barringer and R. Duane Ireland, *Entrepreneurship: Successfully Launching New Ventures*, 2nd ed. (Upper Saddle River, NJ: Pearson/Prentice Hall, 2008), chaps. 2, 3, and 4.

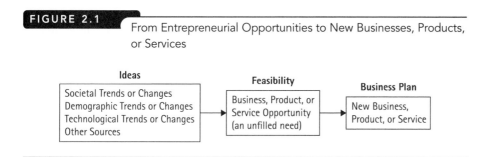

FIGURE 2.1 From Entrepreneurial Opportunities to New Businesses, Products, or Services

2.2 TO BE SUCCESSFUL, YOU MUST HAVE A SOUND BUSINESS MODEL

A good idea is not enough. If an entrepreneur hopes to turn an idea into a business opportunity, a viable business model should be in place. A **sound business model** provides a framework for the venture to:

- Generate revenues
- Make profits
- Produce free cash flows

sound business model
a plan to generate revenues, make profits, and produce free cash flows

Each of these components needs to be achieved within a reasonable time. Having a sound business model helps the entrepreneur attract financing and increase the likelihood that the venture will survive and build value over time.

COMPONENT 1: THE PLAN MUST GENERATE REVENUES

First, the venture must generate sales or revenues.[3] An important component of a venture's perceived present and future value is its current level of revenues (which may be zero, if the venture is in its development stage or at the beginning of its startup stage) and the expected growth of those revenues. A successful business model provides a product or service that customers will purchase. Sound marketing plans and selling efforts are almost always necessary to generate initial sales, and growth in sales over time.

In addition to marketing existing products and services, a venture's management team must develop and market new products and services to increase sales revenue. Branding the venture's products and services—to facilitate new product introduction and inhibit competitive inroads—is an important part of most ventures' marketing strategies. It would be easy if the venture could somehow keep selling its existing products and services at prevailing or higher prices. More

---

[3] We use the words "sales" and "revenues" interchangeably throughout this book since both connote a dollar amount. However, there are times when it is useful to refer to unit sales and the growth in units sold. Technically, revenues can grow by raising prices of the products or services being sold, by selling more units, or by a combination of both.

typically, however, innovation and competition drive down prices and erode the market share held by a venture's existing products and services. In extremely competitive industries, it can be difficult to increase existing product prices at all, even just to keep up with inflation. Anyone who has bought electronic goods in the last thirty years understands this.

It is common for ventures that get to market first, or that generate defensible intellectual property, to price new products or services at high markups. The realization of high margins, however, is the bait that lures new competitors into mimicking the first mover and into investing in research, development, and legal advice to chip away at protections offered by intellectual property rights. In a competitive market economy with restricted intellectual property rights (e.g., finite patent lives), no venture can expect to sustain abnormally high margins forever. The ravages of competition may be delayed; they cannot be avoided.

COMPONENT 2: THE PLAN MUST MAKE PROFITS

The second component of a sound business model is after-tax operating profits. A successful venture cannot target sales growth alone. It must target growth in total venture profitability even when prices decrease as sales grow. A venture's revenues must be large enough to exceed its costs of production and services, as well as pay the venture's management team, other employees, liabilities owed to its creditors, and tax obligations. A venture's management team must be capable of managing the firm's operations efficiently, and of finding and retaining the human resources necessary to carry out production and service functions. Seeking a sustainable competitive advantage on any or all of these fronts is an important component of long-term venture viability. In most cases, a successful venture that survives its rapid-growth stage understands that durable future revenues and profits require ongoing innovation, marketing, and attention to the industry's cost structure and competitive landscape.

Profitability, however, is still not enough. When a venture consumes resources, it diverts them from other potential uses. A basic principle of market economics and capitalism is that capital providers must be compensated for the venture's use of that capital. Capital can be loaned out to others or otherwise employed; consequently, the venture's plan must incorporate a return to capital providers over and above simple profitability. To understand this, suppose a venture requires a warehouse to store intermediate products before finishing them for sales. If the venture doesn't own that warehouse, it must be rented. This type of cost is easy to see because the rent typically appears directly on a statement of profits and losses (an income statement). No one overlooks the cost of this capital when there is a highly visible market for the use of that capital, and accounting conventions allow the venture to "expense" the rent payment.

Some forms of capital, however, are not so easy to see, and accounting conventions may not emphasize their immediacy and accumulation. For example, if a founder allows a sibling to invest $200,000 in a new venture, even the most charitable of siblings will likely expect to get the $200,000 back, with appreciation, at some future date. This is simply because that money could have been invested elsewhere. The expected appreciation is the cost of using the $200,000, even if it only went to purchase inventory (which appears as an asset on the venture's balance sheet rather than as a "rent" on the statement of profit and loss). Capital costs are real; while the associated payments may be deferred, no venture can ignore them in the long run. It is not prudent to ignore them even in the short run.

COMPONENT 3: THE PLAN MUST PRODUCE FREE CASH FLOWS

The third component of a sound business model is a future ability to pay accumulated equity capital costs by what many term "free cash flow to equity"—what remains of profits after all investment costs have been subtracted. A sound business model anticipates the cash flow associated with expansions in the venture's asset investments. In particular, growing firms typically need to expand their investments in inventories, facilities, and equipment.[4] Not all of the profit generated by selling a product (or providing a service) is "free" to be paid back to the investors when the venture must increase its asset investments.

Frequently, students (and entrepreneurs unfamiliar with accounting) will inquire where retained earnings are kept—as though they are stored inside a vault somewhere in venture headquarters. When the venture generates a profit that is not paid out to the owners, the account that grows is usually labeled "retained earnings." As this account increases over time (indicating profitability), it is natural to look for this great store of earnings and, presumably, value. However, in many—if not most—cases, these retained earnings are long gone, as the associated liquid asset (e.g., cash) was spent on increasing the assets so production and sales could rise. Only when the venture's profit rises above these reinvestment flows does it offer a free cash flow that can be used to repay the venture's capital providers.[5]

The venture's value to its owners is determined by the size and timing of its future free cash flows (to equity). However, having to wait to receive those future free cash flows imposes the opportunity cost of not having them now. That is, everyone would prefer to have the cash now rather than in the future. The opportunity cost of this delay is referred to as the time value of money and is due to the investor's foregone return on current use of the cash. In addition to the time value of money, investors expect to be compensated for risk—that is, the risk that the venture will be less successful than anticipated, or even a failure.

---

[4] We will occasionally refer to expenditures for plant and equipment as "capital expenditures," or CAPEX for short.

[5] While it is important to establish a sound business model where revenues will convert to profits and cash flows, it is growth or scalability of the model that creates value for the owners. The importance of growth is noted annually in various business publications. For example, see "Hot Growth Companies," *Business Week*, June 4, 2007, pp. 70–74; and "The Fastest-Growing Technology Companies," *Business 2.0*, June 2007, pp. 58–66.

CONCEPT CHECK

• What are the components of a sound business model?

2.3   LEARN FROM THE BEST PRACTICES OF SUCCESSFUL ENTREPRENEURIAL VENTURES

It is important to realize that one can learn critical lessons from the experiences of other entrepreneurs. Knowing some of the characteristics and practices of existing successful high-growth, high-performance entrepreneurial ventures can help an aspiring entrepreneur understand and deliver the necessary ingredients for success. Figure 2.2 lists some of the leading practices that Donald Sexton and Forrest Seale identified in a study of successful fast-growth (high-growth, high-performance) companies for the Kauffman Center for Entrepreneurial Leadership.[6] We group these leading or "best" practices into three categories: marketing, financial, and management.

BEST MARKETING PRACTICES

Successful high-growth, high-performance firms typically sell high-quality products and provide high-quality services. These firms generally develop and introduce new products or services considered to be the best in their industries. That is, they are product and service innovation leaders. Their products typically command higher prices and profit margins. Providing high-quality products or services, being product or service innovation leaders, and being able to sell products or provide services that command high profit margins are characteristics of successful entrepreneurial ventures. Successful ventures tend to offer high-quality products and services while demonstrating innovative leadership and market (pricing) power.

BEST FINANCIAL PRACTICES

Many successful entrepreneurs understand the financial challenges facing rapid-growth ventures. Not surprisingly, the financial planning function becomes critical to venture success and cannot be neglected even when the entrepreneur feels her talents are best suited to other areas such as product development, marketing, or operations. Financial plans incorporating multiple contingencies are important for dealing with the financial fragility of early-stage ventures. Slight delays, less-than-expected consumer acceptance, and key employee departure all have financial ramifications that can cripple a new venture and send it spiraling downward.

Even unexpected success can present significant financial challenges that may not be immediately obvious without a detailed financial plan. Anticipating the

---

[6]   Donald L. Sexton and Forrest I. Seale, *Leading Practices of Fast Growth Entrepreneurs: Pathways to High Performance* (Kansas City, MO: Kauffman Center for Entrepreneurial Leadership, 1997).

FIGURE 2.2   Best Practices of High-Growth, High-Performance Firms

Marketing Practices

- Deliver high-quality products or services
- Develop new products or services that are considered to be the best
- Offer products or services that command higher prices and margins
- Develop efficient distribution channels and superior service support facilities

Financial Practices

- Prepare detailed monthly financial plans for the next year and annual financial plans for the next five years
- Anticipate and obtain multiple rounds of financing as the venture grows
- Efficiently and effectively manage the firm's assets and financial resources and its operating performance
- Plan an exit strategy consistent with the entrepreneur's objectives and the firm's business plan

Management Practices

- Assemble a management team that is balanced in both functional area coverage and industry/market knowledge
- Employ a decision-making style that is viewed as being collaborative
- Identify and develop functional area managers who support entrepreneurial endeavors
- Assemble a board of directors that is balanced in terms of internal and external members

---

consequences of ramping up to meet a favorable demand shock due to unexpected success is an important prerequisite to being able to enjoy that unexpected success. Some examples of the financial tools that assist in anticipating challenges in a venture's potential future include at least one year of monthly cash-oriented projections and projected annual financial statements for the next three to five years. Rapid growth typically requires multiple rounds of financing. Successful ventures anticipate financing needs and search for the financing before the funds are actually required. Since most entrepreneurs want to retain control of the venture, their search for financing involves some important stated and unstated constraints that can significantly increase the time spent obtaining financing.

Successful high-growth firms understand the resources required to manage the firm's assets, financial resources, and operating performance, while putting out any current "fires" and monitoring and positioning the venture for future expansion. They also develop preliminary harvest or exit strategies and, at times, consider the ramifications of current financing, investment, and operating decisions on a potential future liquidity event. They may even reflect these contemplations in a formal business plan. Keep the following in mind as you look for the business opportunities in your ideas:

> *Everything started as a dream. You gotta have insight, know what you want. You gotta have a plan. Like I tell anybody, if you fail to plan, you're planning to fail.*
>
> —Lawrence Tureau (Mr. T), actor, 1993
> (interview with *The Onion*)

BEST MANAGEMENT PRACTICES

Successful entrepreneurial ventures assemble well-balanced and experienced management teams. Members of the teams have expertise across the functional areas of marketing, finance, and operations. They typically have prior success in the venture's industry and markets. While successful entrepreneurs exhibit many different managerial styles, they usually view decision making as a collaborative effort. It is critical that functional area managers share in the founder's entrepreneurial drive. Successful entrepreneurial ventures make use of the expertise provided by their boards of directors (or advisers). Summarizing, the effective entrepreneurial management team should (1) provide expertise in the functional areas of marketing, finance, and operations; (2) have successful experience in the venture's industry and markets; (3) work collaboratively; and (4) share the entrepreneurial spirit. A venture's management profile is extremely important. Some potential investors view a detailing of the management team as the most important section of a business plan.

BEST PRODUCTION OR OPERATIONS PRACTICES ARE ALSO IMPORTANT

Although Figure 2.2 does not include specific operations or production practices, we want to make sure that the importance of this functional area is not overlooked. Recall that the first item under marketing practices was to deliver high-quality products or services. It is the venture's production or operations area that carries this responsibility. Furthermore, products and services must be delivered on time. Businesses operate in real time. Customers want their products or services now or, at least, when they are promised. Otherwise, customers are likely to turn to a competitor who delivers on time. Remember that, as you move from the idea to a viable business opportunity and then to actual startup, many aspects of your products and services (like quality and timing) are critical.

• What is an entrepreneurial venture?

2.4   TIME TO MARKET AND OTHER TIMING IMPLICATIONS

Business opportunities exist in real time, and most ideas have a relatively narrow window of opportunity to be transformed into successful business ventures. Sometimes ideas are *ahead of their time*—at least, they are too early to become viable business opportunities for the inventor or innovator.[7] For example, although the

---

[7] Of course, patents and copyrights may provide some protection until an idea can become a viable business opportunity. We discuss intellectual property in Chapter 3.

Wright brothers were pioneers in flight, their prototype was not commercially viable. Military and early commercial uses exploiting related technologies marked the beginning of that viable business opportunity. Not long ago, neither the World Wide Web nor e-commerce existed. Selling groceries "online instead of in line" and writing electronic mortgage loans were not viable business opportunities until recently. Many innovations that are now technologically feasible (including online groceries) are still struggling to become the foundations of successful commercial ventures. Often, the first attempts to deploy a new technology only partially clear the necessary education and adoption hurdles and end up merely providing data for the next generation of ventures seeking to commercially exploit the new technology.

Ideas can also be *past their time*. That is, the window of opportunity may close when someone beats you to market or when the idea focuses on a technology that is abandoned shortly after the venture is launched. If you are thinking about starting an online auction business, it is certainly technologically feasible. However, it is probably a bit late, unless you exploit a lucrative niche that for some reason has remained undiscovered by the scores of other entrepreneurs who have considered launching online auctions in recent years. Similarly, an idea to construct an infrastructure of wires and cables, to provide voice and other services to customers in developing countries, may not be a viable business idea when wireless broadband technology offers a more cost-effective means of providing high-speed, high-capacity data and voice services.

Time to market, particularly when one is *first to market*, is often important in determining whether an idea becomes a viable business. Time is particularly critical when ideas involve information technology because the difference of a few months may determine success or failure. eBay, Inc., an online auction house, is an interesting example of a firm's moving quickly and successfully to dominate a type of Internet business (person-to-person). Pierre Omidyar launched eBay in September 1995 after a casual dinner conversation with his fiancée, an avid collector of Pez™ candy dispensers. Omidyar had his initial contact with Internet shopping in 1993 with a firm called eShop, which was subsequently purchased by Microsoft. He then developed Web applications at General Magic. With a vision of the potential demand for consumer trading via the Internet, Omidyar designed eBay as an initial experiment to assess consumer demand. When expectations were quickly exceeded, eBay became Omidyar's full-time job. eBay currently hosts well over two million auctions each day. Movement from the idea to the business opportunity and actual startup was very quick, even by Internet standards. As a result of being first and quick to market, eBay has not been seriously threatened by competition.

Of course, being *first to market* does not necessarily ensure success. Adam Osborne is generally given credit for having been first to market with a portable computer. Several of our faculty colleagues purchased "Osbornes" when they were introduced to the marketplace. Although we recall that the computer worked reasonably well, Adam Osborne had no sustainable competitive advantage. Other computer manufacturers that were more soundly financed and had larger support staffs quickly brought out their own versions of the portable computer; the rest is history. Dan Bricklin was first to market with spreadsheet software: VisiCalc, a name unfamiliar to most of our younger readers. VisiCalc was quickly buried by the introduction of Lotus 1-2-3, and, as we all know, the dominant product in the category was soon revealed to be Microsoft's Excel®.

CONCEPT CHECK

- What is meant by time to market?

2.5 INITIAL "LITMUS TEST" FOR EVALUATING THE BUSINESS FEASIBILITY OF AN IDEA

Good business ideas often result from creative thinking and hard work. They may reflect new insights into particular existing products, services, or processes. They can result from more widespread product and service trends related to the evolution of our societies (so-called "megatrends"). Of course, new business ideas can also be a response to confusion and chaos. Nottingham-Spirk, a successful industrial-design firm, sends employees to retail establishments such as Wal-Mart to generate product improvement ideas. They then have a "diverging" or brainstorming session involving several product designers. This initial meeting is followed by a second round of "converging" meetings where the ideas are judged.[8]

viable venture opportunity

an opportunity that creates or meets a customer need, provides an initial competitive advantage, is timely in terms of time to market, and offers the expectation of added value to investors

The key ingredient is that an idea provide an opportunity to create economic value for the entrepreneur (and others). In other words, a **viable venture opportunity** must meet (or create and meet) a customer need, provide at least an initial competitive advantage, have an attractive time-to-market profile, and offer the expectation of attractive investment returns.[9] We know that, during the development stage, it is normal for ideas to be abandoned along the way as the entrepreneur and venture investors evaluate whether an idea can be transformed into a viable business opportunity. Product prototypes may be required, software developed, and new process designs market-tested. While we can't tell you which ideas will make good business opportunities, we can offer some insights into criteria that potential investors may consider when assessing the viability of the commercialized version of your idea.

SWOT analysis

an examination of strengths, weaknesses, opportunities, and threats to determine the business opportunity viability of an idea

A useful tool in an initial investigation of business feasibility is a **SWOT analysis**. The focus of such an analysis is the strengths (S), weaknesses (W), opportunities (O), and threats (T) of the business, product, or service idea. Figure 2.3

---

[8] For more comprehensive discussions of how business opportunities are identified and developed, see Jeffry A. Timmons, *New Business Opportunities* (Acton, MA: Brick House Publishing, 1989); and Timmons and Spinelli, *New Venture Creation*, chap. 4.

[9] See Anne Fisher, "Ideas Made Here," at http://money.cnn.com/magazines/fortune/fortune_archive/2007/06/11/100061499/index.htm.

FIGURE 2.3   SWOT Analysis for Initially Assessing the Feasibility
of a Business Idea

I. Internal Environment

	Strengths	Weaknesses
High	1. _____	1. _____
	2. _____	2. _____
	3. _____	3. _____
Low	1. _____	1. _____
	2. _____	2. _____
	3. _____	3. _____

II. External Environment

	Opportunities	Threats
High	1. _____	1. _____
	2. _____	2. _____
	3. _____	3. _____
Low	1. _____	1. _____
	2. _____	2. _____
	3. _____	3. _____

---

illustrates a SWOT analysis approach. The strengths and weaknesses assessment focuses on the internal aspects of the idea; the opportunities and threats focus on the external or competitive environment.

The baby boomer population is aging quickly. As people get older, they find it more and more difficult to open food products that have twist-off caps. Consider an entrepreneur who has invented a relatively simple product to make it easier for senior citizens to open food products. Can such an idea be converted to a viable business opportunity? At a minimum, the SWOT analysis should consider the following areas as potential strengths or weaknesses:

1. Unfilled customer need
2. Intellectual property rights
3. First mover
4. Lower costs and/or higher quality
5. Experience/expertise
6. Reputation value

To begin, we ask whether there is an unfilled customer need for the new senior-friendly jar opener. Healthy demand is a strength; unproven or questionable demand is a weakness. Next, we need to determine whether there are any intellectual property rights that might shield the venture from the ravages of immediate competition. For example, can the product be patented? The ability to affordably establish intellectual property protection is a strength; the threat of immediate knock-offs is a definite weakness. By the time it is distributed, will the product be first to market? If so, first-mover advantages can be considerable strengths; if not, there are many challenges in taking a weaker position as second (or even later) to market. High-quality production at low cost is an ideal strength; lower-quality production at any cost is most likely a weakness. Past experience can be a strength or weakness, depending on the amount and context. Reputation can open or close important doors.

The SWOT analysis should, at a minimum, consider the following areas as potential opportunities or threats:

1. Existing competition
2. Market size/market share potential
3. Substitute products or services
4. Possibility of new technologies
5. Recent or potential regulatory changes
6. International market possibilities

Competition in the targeted market is not usually considered a strength, unless it means that the market accepts new entrants (one of which is your venture's product or service). What current products assist in removing twist-off caps on food products? Well-defined existing and potential competitors that can provide comparable products are almost always a threat. Is the market large and waiting for a category killer? If so, there is probably a great opportunity; if not, then death by attrition is a definite threat. What are the substitutes for this new jar-opening technology? It is usually hard to see a large range of substitutes as anything other than a threat. On the other hand, if the product deploys some new technology that sufficiently dominates all existing ones (and is protected), then perhaps the opportunity can overcome competitors' threats involving their substitute products.

What if all existing jar-opening technologies had been deemed dangerous by regulatory authorities, but the venture's technology is fundamentally safer. This would be an important opportunity. On the other hand, if the new technology involves mechanics or materials with unproven safety, there could be a serious regulatory threat. With respect to international opportunities, there are seniors around the world and food jars are almost universal. The possibility for selling internationally might be an important opportunity if the product can be produced cheaply.

Once Figure 2.3 is completed, we should have a better (first-pass) understanding of the potential for the new jar opener to form the basis of a viable business opportunity. Should competition already exist, it would be wise to prepare a similar analysis for each major (potential) competitor. The side-by-side comparison of SWOT analyses provides an important multidimensional view of the new venture's relative competitive position.

- What is meant by a SWOT analysis?

2.6 SCREENING VENTURE OPPORTUNITIES

After passing an initial SWOT analysis, a venture seeking external financing should be subject to more formal feasibility analysis addressing qualitative and quantitative aspects of its expected growth and performance. While there are many variations in the theme of business feasibility analysis, all suggest substantial, more significant investment of time and effort to provide external reference points and data in support (or refutation) of the basic conjectures used in the SWOT analysis.

Venture opportunity screening is the process of creating useful qualitative and quantitative assessments of an idea's commercial potential and its likelihood of producing revenue growth, financial performance, and value. An analogy used in the entrepreneurship literature is that venture screening involves finding "caterpillars" (ideas) that are likely to become "butterflies" (successful business or venture opportunities). When evaluating business opportunities, it is important to consider a number of different factors: industry, market, economics, competitive advantage issues, management team, and so on.[10]

We present a two-stage approach to assessing a venture's viability. The first stage emphasizes a qualitative assessment using a systematic interview with the entrepreneurial team.[11] While an interview can quickly lead to dismissing the idea, in other cases the interview highlights the tasks to be done before more formal planning (i.e., moving from the development stage to the startup stage). The interview, in some cases, provides the first building block for a successful launch. If we assume that the interview indicates a potential "butterfly," our second stage involves applying a more quantitative screen to help determine whether venture investors are likely to fund the metamorphosis.

venture opportunity screening
assessment of an idea's commercial potential to produce revenue growth, financial performance, and value

AN INTERVIEW WITH THE FOUNDER (ENTREPRENEUR) AND MANAGEMENT TEAM: QUALITATIVE SCREENING

Our qualitative screening takes the form of question-and-answer dialogues. While it is possible for the entrepreneur to respond in privacy, we believe that it is much more useful to seek out others to engage in a little role playing. For example, if one can seek out a friend, spouse, or other supportively skeptical party to play the

---

[10] For further discussion of the venture opportunity-screening process, see Timmons and Spinelli, *New Venture Creation*, chaps. 4 and 5.

[11] We have used variations of this approach on many occasions to assist potential entrepreneurs at the very beginning of their process of launching a venture.

role of the interviewer, the screening exercise may generate more useful input than when the entrepreneur answers the questions in isolation. Moreover, if there are other members of the management team in place, each can take the lead responsibility for responding in his areas.[12] The four individual roles are:

- Founder
- Marketing manager
- Operations manager
- Financial manager

In the event that a management team is not in place at the time of the qualitative screening, the entrepreneur or founder may have to play all of the roles.

Figure 2.4 begins the interviewing process with the entrepreneur and is aimed at understanding the big picture. This interview seeks information regarding the intended customers, possible competition, intellectual property, challenges to be faced, and so on. At the conclusion of the interview, the interviewer prepares a subjective assessment and indicates one of the following:

1. High commercial potential
2. Average commercial potential
3. Low commercial potential

Figure 2.5 addresses the marketing. This interview seeks information on who makes the purchase decision for the venture's product or service and who pays for the purchase. Other questions focus on market size and growth, channel and distribution challenges, and marketing and promotion needs. After receiving the responses, the interviewer appraises the venture's marketing aspect as high, average, or low commercial potential.

Figure 2.6 presents a dialogue with the venture's operations manager. Information is sought on the state of the idea in terms of prototypes and whether they have been tested. What risks remain between now and successful market delivery? Are there potential development or production concerns? Again, the interviewer appraises the developmental and operational aspects as high, average, or low commercial potential.

Figure 2.7 focuses on a dialogue with the venture's financial manager. Important questions are: What is the length of time projected before the venture will achieve breakeven? How will the venture be financed? How much outside financing will be needed and when? Again, after the responses have been given, the financial aspects are judged as high, average, or low potential.

We recognize that an entrepreneur may choose to continue to pursue her idea even if the qualitative assessments are not very high. However, if the entrepreneur needs to raise a substantial amount of financial capital from outside investors, the viability of a venture with low qualitative scores should be reassessed. Only ventures receiving at least a majority of "high" assessments are

---

[12] In a classroom or executive retreat context, we like to see group members acting as the skeptical interviewer while the rest of the team formulates the best responses the context will allow.

FIGURE 2.4 Dialogue with Entrepreneur or Founder: The Big Picture

Interviewer:	So, let's start with the 30,000-foot view; what's this all about?
Founder:	…
Interviewer:	OK, it passes my "laugh test" although I'm a little light headed at this altitude. Plunging back down to earth, can you tell me a bit more about your intended customers and what they see as the benefits your venture offers?
Founder:	…
Interviewer:	I can see the potential, but aren't others targeting those same customers? Are none of the existing competitors' offerings similar in use and cost?
Founder:	…
Interviewer:	Granted, it sounds like a promising strategy, but won't others knock you off in relatively short order? Is there anything proprietary in your approach, and if so, do you have a plan to protect the related intellectual property?
Founder:	…
Interviewer:	Intellectual property usually means that something's new and unfamiliar. Will there be significant consumer education issues involved in using your product and services?
Founder:	…
Interviewer:	You're doing pretty well in your current career and one never knows when to take the plunge. So, why start now rather than later?
Founder:	…
Interviewer:	Will you be able to leverage your existing contacts and network? Is your network a strength or weakness relative to the competition?
Founder:	…
Interviewer:	Experience tells us that there's a lot of uncertainty and learning that takes place in a startup. Of course, learning takes time and resources. For your venture, how do you see the relationship between the size or scale of your startup efforts and its ability to progress through the uncertainty about viability or market acceptance? In particular, can the uncertainty be resolved more quickly if you are better financed?
Founder:	…
Interviewer:	Everyone understands that a business plan is outdated by the time it's printed. I'm thinking about the inevitable trade-offs each venture makes regarding things like in-house production versus outsourcing or human crafted versus robotics. What challenges does the venture face in making these decisions and subsequently adjusting them, if necessary, to changing conditions?
Founder:	…
Interviewer:	We look forward to watching your venture grow and prosper. Thank you for taking time out of your hectic schedule so we can look back on today and say, "We knew you when …" [Or: You seem to have an interesting idea; however, our funds are committed at this time.]

FIGURE 2.5   Dialogue with Marketing Manager: Know Thy Customer

Interviewer:	I've noticed in the past that it's pretty important for a new venture to know its customers and how they make buying decisions. Who will write the check for the product or service you intend to sell? Is there a point person or a team that makes the purchase?
Marketing manager:	…
Interviewer:	Do you see these customers as one-timers or repeat buyers?
Marketing manager:	…
Interviewer:	What about add-ons, support, service, and consulting? Are they integral to your product or revenue strategy?
Marketing manager:	…
Interviewer:	As buyers get to know your venture, how does their experience with the product or service translate into reputation for the venture? Is there a lot of word-of-mouth opportunity or risk? Do you have to take a more direct approach to establishing your "brand"?
Marketing manager:	…
Interviewer:	Many early-stage ventures don't have the resources for extensive market research. Nonetheless, everyone agrees that one of the big issues with new ventures is making sure the entrepreneurial team understands the market's needs and how the venture's products and services fit in. Have you conducted any formal market research for the venture? Do you have a good idea what characteristics are important to potential customers?
Marketing manager:	…
Interviewer:	Tell me about the overall market. How fast is it growing? How much of this market can the venture capture in the next five years?
Marketing manager:	…
Interviewer:	Who else currently shares your market? Who will survive the five years of your expansion? How do their products and services compare to yours?
Marketing manager:	…
Interviewer:	What are your channel and distribution challenges?
Marketing manager:	…
Interviewer:	What are you thinking in terms of promoting your products and services?
Marketing manager:	…
Interviewer:	What is your plan for moving ahead? Are you conducting ongoing market research? What customer questions need to be answered for you to take the plunge?
Marketing manager:	…
Interviewer:	It sounds like you have a great opportunity. Thanks for taking the time to provide a glimpse into your world. [Or: You have an interesting idea, but we will be unable to participate at this time. Maybe we can have a further discussion in the future.]

FIGURE 2.6	Dialogue with Operations Manager: Production and Development Challenges
Interviewer:	We've all heard of vaporware and experienced significant delays in products we were told were coming to market. I know it sounds a bit pessimistic, but does the venture have prototypes? Can we kick the tires, as it were?
Operations manager:	...
Interviewer:	What do you see as the big hurdles between where you are now and successful market delivery of the venture's products and services?
Operations manager:	...
Interviewer:	What steps are you planning to take to deal with the risks of development delays and production challenges? Do you have a position on quality standards?
Operations manager:	...
Interviewer:	What are the staffing, outsourcing, and supply challenges in bringing your products to market?
Operations manager:	...
Interviewer:	Where will the business be located and how much square footage are you planning to occupy?
Operations manager:	...
Interviewer:	Are you ready to move in or do you have to renovate first?
Operations manager:	...
Interviewer:	What are your production and headquarters equipment needs? Can you lease this equipment or are you facing a big initial financing challenge?
Operations manager:	...
Interviewer:	Do you have a formal organizational structure? If so, what is it and why did you choose that structure?
Operations manager:	...
Interviewer:	Is there any significant legal work facing the venture (patents, trademarks, licensing, external financing, etc.)?
Operations manager:	...
Interviewer:	Will you be cultivating vertical or horizontal strategic alliances? If so, what is the plan for when and how these alliances will be negotiated and effected?
Operations manager:	...
Interviewer:	It sounds like you've got a good handle on the challenges. We wish you success. Thanks. [Or: You seem to have a good handle on the likely operations challenges for the venture; however, we need to develop a further understanding before considering a commitment.]

FIGURE 2.7   Dialogue with Financial Manager: Financial Fortune Telling

Interviewer:	OK, you're going to have to be patient with me. Typically, I'm a big-picture person, so I'll need to keep it simple. Let's start with profit. Tell me why you think you can make a profit in this business.
Financial manager:	…
Interviewer:	Is there a minimum scale for breaking even and pushing the venture into profitability?
Financial manager:	…
Interviewer:	When you say "profit," does that include paying the entrepreneurial team a competitive wage or are they deferring compensation to foster an earlier appearance of profitability? (More directly, are you expensing those compensation options, at least in how you think of profitability?)
Financial manager:	…
Interviewer:	Do you have projections we can look at for the next few years? I'm interested in how fast you think you will get to a sustainable market position with reasonable margins.
Financial manager:	…
Interviewer:	One of your functions is to help arrange for financing this new venture. On that front, one of your priorities is covering the startup costs. What are these and how do you plan to secure the requisite financing? Do you have a targeted piece of the equity you're planning to sell off?
Financial manager:	…
Interviewer:	About that initial balance sheet: Are you carrying any deadweight from the venture's past?
Financial manager:	…
Interviewer:	Can you give us any idea what your first six months' and year's profit and loss are going to look like?
Financial manager:	…
Interviewer:	How about projected balance sheets to go with them?
Financial manager:	…
Interviewer:	I'm glad to see that the venture team has someone who can see the financial reflections of the venture's future achievements. Have you thought about a little longer horizon, say, five years out?
Financial manager:	…
Interviewer:	What kind of investors are you planning to pitch and how much return (1×, 2×, 5×, etc.) do you expect they will demand to help finance your venture's youthful exuberance?
Financial manager:	…
Interviewer:	Let's say I'm ready to invest. How and when do you plan to get my investment and return back to me?
Financial manager:	…
Interviewer:	Sign me up. Thanks for taking this time. We'll see you at the IPO! [Or: While you have an interesting idea, money is very tight now. Let's talk again in a few months.]

likely to be candidates to "pass" our second-stage quantitative assessment of venture investor interest.[13]

SCORING A PROSPECTIVE NEW VENTURE: QUANTITATIVE SCREENING

Figure 2.8 is a template of a more quantitative approach to assessing a proposed new venture's viability. We call it the **VOS Indicator™**. It contains a checklist to consider when calibrating a new venture's feasibility and attractiveness to venture investors. The approach focuses on four factor categories: industry/market, pricing/profitability, financial/harvest, and management team. For each factor category, there are four specific items. Each item is evaluated as being high, average, or low in terms of potential attractiveness. Assign a point value of 3 for a high rating, 2 for an average rating, and 1 for a low rating. For items where there is insufficient current data to provide a reasonable approximation, an N/A (not available) can be used for a response.[14] Points are totaled for each of the three columns and added together to get the overall total. Calculate an average score by dividing the total points by the number of scored individual items (omitting the N/As in this count). For example, there are sixteen items. With no N/As, a perfect score would produce forty-eight total points with an average score of 3.00, while the lowest score would be sixteen points and an average of 1.00.

Figure 2.9 contains metrics or verbal labels to be used for judging each item in the VOS Indicator™. These response categories will help the evaluator determine how each item adds to the proposed venture's overall appeal.[15] As we are trying to represent a quantitative approach that entrepreneurs and venture investors alike might employ, it should not surprise us to find very high "expectations" for attractive new ventures. For example, for a proposed venture "home run," investors would most likely want the venture to have significant prospects for an industry demand in excess of $100 million where sales growth rates exceed 30 percent annually and the new venture anticipates capturing greater than 20 percent market share in that industry.[16]

VOS Indicator™

checklist of selected criteria and metrics used to screen venture opportunities for potential attractiveness as business opportunities

---

[13] The main purpose of the interviews is to stimulate reasonable and important introspection by the founder or team. Often, the aspiring entrepreneur has a solitary perspective on the viability of the new venture. Completing the dialogues allows impressions and biases to be identified and confirmed, rejected, or, in most cases, subjected to more formal inquiry before proceeding further. While we do not provide sample answers to the questions of Figures 2.4 to 2.7, we believe that the questions themselves, when addressed seriously, will stimulate important insights on the likelihood that a caterpillar will become a butterfly.

[14] Not being able to judge an item may indicate that further due diligence is needed to accurately evaluate the potential attractiveness of the proposed venture. Based on the scores for the other items, further investigation efforts may be warranted.

[15] It is important to understand that the metrics used in Figure 2.9 represent general guidelines in use today but are not cut-and-dried rules. In fact, some of these metrics will probably change over time as economic and operating conditions change.

[16] Venture investors often like to draw analogies between baseball terms and venture performance or attractiveness. For example, a "home run" is an investment that returns at least five times the venture investor's initial investment. Of course, only a few business opportunities will be home runs. A "double" refers to expecting a doubling of the investment. A "single" returns only a portion of the initial investment. A "strikeout" reflects a total loss of the investment. Venture investors need an occasional home run to make up for several strikeouts.

FIGURE 2.8

Venture Opportunity-Screening Guide: The VOS Indicator™

FACTOR CATEGORIES	POTENTIAL ATTRACTIVENESS		
	HIGH	AVERAGE	LOW
Industry/Market			
Market size potential	_____	_____	_____
Venture growth rate	_____	_____	_____
Market share (year 3)	_____	_____	_____
Entry barriers	_____	_____	_____
Pricing/Profitability			
Gross margins	_____	_____	_____
After-tax margins	_____	_____	_____
Asset intensity	_____	_____	_____
Return on assets	_____	_____	_____
Financial/Harvest			
Cash flow breakeven	_____	_____	_____
Rate of return	_____	_____	_____
IPO potential	_____	_____	_____
Founder's control	_____	_____	_____
Management team			
Experience/expertise	_____	_____	_____
Functional areas	_____	_____	_____
Flexibility/adaptability	_____	_____	_____
Entrepreneurial focus	_____	_____	_____
Total points by ranking	_____	_____	_____
Overall total points (OTP)		_____	
Average score (OTP/16)		_____	

Ideas that have the potential to become high-growth, high-performance ventures, or home runs, would be expected to have a preponderance of "highs" indicated on the potential attractiveness scale with an average score in the 2.34 to 3.00 range. An idea/opportunity that scores average (1.67 to 2.33) in terms of potential attractiveness also may be a viable venture opportunity; however, the expectations of the entrepreneur and venture investors for an average opportunity should be equivalent to "hitting a double." If you proceed with such a venture, it is unlikely that it will become a home run; attracting venture investors may be more difficult. If your idea/opportunity generates a low score (1.00 to 1.66) in terms of its potential attractiveness, it is probably wise to abandon the idea/opportunity and seek other ideas that might have greater venture opportunity potential. Later in this chapter, we will provide an example of the application of our VOS Indicator™.

FIGURE 2.9
Classification Guidelines for Completing the VOS Indicator™

FACTOR CATEGORIES	HIGH	AVERAGE	LOW
Industry/Market			
Market size potential	>$100 million	$20–$100 million	<$20 million
Venture growth rate	>30%	10%–30%	<10%
Market share (year 3)	>20% (leader)	5%–20%	<5% (follower)
Entry barriers	Legal protection	Timing/size	Few/none
Pricing/Profitability			
Gross margins	>50%	20%–50%	<20%
After-tax margins	>20%	10%–20%	<10%
Asset intensity	>3.0 turnover	1.0–3.0 turnover	<1.0 turnover
Return on assets	>25%	10%–25%	<10%
Financial/Harvest			
Cash flow breakeven	<2 years	2–4 years	>4 years
Rate of return	>50% per year	20%–50% per year	<20% per year
IPO potential	<2 years	2–5 years	>5 years
Founder's control	Majority	High minority	Low minority
Management team			
Experience/expertise	Industry/market	General/general	Little/none
Functional areas	All covered	Most covered	Few covered
Flexibility/adaptability	Quick to adapt	Able to adapt	Slow to adapt
Entrepreneurial focus	Full team	Founder	None

Column span header: POTENTIAL ATTRACTIVENESS (over HIGH, AVERAGE, LOW)

Notes: Market size potential refers to the expected size of the industry revenues at maturity; venture growth rate and market share are expressed in terms of the venture's revenues. These industry/market items, as well as the items under each of the other three factors, are discussed in the chapter.

Many of the interview questions are "leading," in the sense that one may have a good idea of what constitutes a "good" answer; however, for some of the more quantitative interview questions—and most of the categories involved in VOS™ scoring—some additional explanation of the range of expected answers is needed. While we believe it is sufficient to allow the entrepreneur or investor to grapple with most of the qualitative questions without much guidance, we now digress to expand on some of those more quantitative categories before giving an example of the application of our scoring procedure.

CONCEPT CHECK

- What is meant by a viable venture or business opportunity?

INDUSTRY/MARKET CONSIDERATIONS

The size of the industry, currently and expected, is a critical factor in the likelihood of your venture's becoming a high-growth, high-performance firm in that industry, something very attractive to venture investors. Making generalizations is risky because there are always exceptions, but generalizations do provide benchmarks for appraising the viability of business opportunities. Of course, when exceptions arise, they should be handled qualitatively or strategically with some regard given to why the benchmarks are not relevant.

Your idea may be about an innovative product/service in a well-established industry, an industry that is in its infancy, or an industry that does not yet exist. While there is development variance across industries, we provide the following general industry guidelines for identifying potential high-growth, high-performance ventures. One rule of thumb is that the industry must have potential sales or revenues of more than $100 million to score a "high" in terms of potential attractiveness. For new industries, the projection of industry revenues should generally be for three to five years in the future. Industry revenues or sales also should be growing rapidly. Expected revenue growth during the industry's rapid-growth stage is one comparative benchmark; industries that are growing, or are expected to grow, at compound rates in excess of 30 percent per year are likely to contain high-growth, high-performance ventures. While slower-growth industries are not necessarily bad, firms in these industries are less likely to be able to attract venture capital unless they are substantially changing or consolidating the industry.

Operating in a high-growth industry, however, is not enough. A venture's expected revenue growth rate also must be assessed. High-growth, high-performance potential is generally associated with an expected annual compound growth rate in excess of 30 percent during the venture's rapid-growth stage. Potential high-growth, high-performance ventures also are expected to be industry leaders by the third year of operation. This generally means that such business opportunities will need to garner more than 20 percent market share of the industry's revenues. (Of course, this percentage depends on industry concentration.) What is important is the expectation of becoming a top player in the industry. While being first is preferred, in some industries the third- or even fourth-place firm can still be a successful entrepreneurial venture. In contrast, if the potential venture's market share of industry revenues is expected to be small (e.g., less than 5 percent), the venture will be a follower, and, unless there are other compelling considerations and non-venture sources of capital, serious thought should be given to reformulating or abandoning the idea/opportunity.

For almost all businesses to survive, it is important that they plan to at least match their industry's average growth to avoid the ravages of a declining market share. Entrepreneurial ventures are typically expected, and projected, to achieve revenue growth rates in excess of the relevant industry average. If you expect a revenue growth rate below the industry average, your strategy must include some plan for operating at a competitive disadvantage in terms of economies of scale.[17]

---

[17] Annual sales growing at a rate that is less than the industry average is a warning sign that you may need to reorganize, restructure, or even dissolve the venture. Financial distress, restructuring, and liquidation topics are covered in Chapter 15.

In summary, initial survival and eventual success often depend on a venture's ability to maintain or grow market share over time. Potentially successful entrepreneurial ventures should have revenue growth rates that exceed the industry average growth rate.

One should also consider barriers to entry when evaluating potential business opportunities. We look at the degree to which the proposed venture may be able to inhibit or outpace the competition. When intellectual property rights can be protected through patents, copyrights, trademarks, and so on, the potential for the idea to become a viable business opportunity is greatly enhanced. Protection can be particularly important if the idea is "ahead of its time"—that is, no developed market exists yet. Timing or size can also provide some protection against competitors' entering the proposed market. Being first with the idea, even if the idea cannot be legally protected, provides some competitive advantage that may discourage others from entering the market. Being relatively larger in human capital and financial backing can also inhibit competition. If, however, your venture idea faces current entry barriers and promises no future entry barriers, its potential attractiveness is low (other things being equal). The best situation is when no current barriers inhibit your venture, but barriers to future entrants will protect your venture's future.

CONCEPT CHECK

- What is the rule-of-thumb revenue growth rate for a high-growth venture?

PRICING/PROFITABILITY CONSIDERATIONS

Several pricing and profitability tests or metrics, shown in Figure 2.9, are useful. Seeing future paying customers is not enough, at least for a venture that may need to attract outside investors. In addition to expectations of how much customers are willing to pay for the venture's products and services, it is important to consider the direct costs of producing a product or providing a service: the **cost of goods sold**. Revenue minus the cost of goods sold gives the venture's **gross profit**. However, the dollar amount of gross profit is not a useful metric because it depends on size. Rather, it is more common to calculate the **gross profit margin**, which is gross profit divided by revenues. The magnitude of the gross profit margin is one of the most important measures of a venture's potential. The larger the gross profit margin, the greater the cushion for covering all other business expenses while still being able to provide a sufficient return for investors. A gross profit margin greater than 50 percent indicates an attractive potential. In contrast, a gross profit margin of less than 20 percent is a serious warning sign.

A second measure of profitability is the after-tax or net profit margin. A venture's **net profit** is the dollar profit left after all expenses, including financing costs and taxes, have been deducted from the firm's revenues.[18]

cost of goods sold
direct costs of producing a product or providing a service

gross profit
revenues less the cost of goods sold

gross profit margin
gross profit divided by revenues

net profit
dollar profit left after all expenses, including financing costs and taxes, have been deducted from the revenues

---

[18] Chapter 4 provides a review of basic accounting terms and basic financial statements for readers who need or want to undertake such a review.

net profit margin
net profit divided by revenues

The **net profit margin** is calculated by dividing the expected net profit by the venture's revenues. Typically, after-tax margins greater than 20 percent suggest that the business opportunity has sufficiently attractive potential. The would-be entrepreneur probably should pause and reconsider when the after-tax margin is less than 10 percent, at least if the venture requires external financing.

asset intensity
total assets divided by revenues; the reciprocal of asset turnover

When you are screening business opportunities, it is important to examine the venture's asset intensity. **Asset intensity**, or its reciprocal asset turnover, is a measure of the investment in assets necessary to produce or support the projected revenues. Asset intensity is calculated by dividing the venture's total assets—including cash, receivables, inventories, property, plant, and equipment—by its total revenues. It is the dollar amount of assets necessary to support a dollar of revenue. Firms that require a lot of fixed assets or net working capital (the current assets above the amount funded by current liabilities) have high asset intensity (and therefore low asset turnover). When firms with high asset intensity try to grow rapidly, they are likely to need large amounts of external financial capital, although some types of equipment may be bundled with financing through leasing arrangements. Working capital management, using such approaches as "just-in-time" inventory policies, can help reduce the working capital required to conduct business. In rare cases, supplier trade credit and a fast turnover of inventory may actually be a net source of financing. This happens when current liabilities exceed current assets: The venture is operating with "negative net working capital." Although we can provide numerical benchmarks for investments in net working capital, we caution that many business approaches, including much of e-commerce, may result in low inventories, low fixed assets, and, therefore, extremely high asset turnovers. We suggest as a starting point that a high score for asset turnover (low asset intensity) be associated with a ratio of revenues to total assets exceeding 3 (or asset intensity of 1:3; 1 dollar of assets for 3 dollars of revenue). Asset turnover ratios less than 1 (or asset intensities higher than 1) would get a low score.

return on assets
net after-tax profit divided by total assets

return on assets (ROA) model
return on assets is the product of the net profit margin and the asset turnover ratio

To many, one of the most important measures of efficient use of assets is **return on assets**. It is calculated by dividing the net after-tax profit by the venture's total assets. The return on assets measure can be viewed in the context of the **return on assets (ROA) model**, which expresses the return on assets as the product of the net profit margin and the asset turnover measures. This relationship is:

$$\text{Return on Assets} = \text{Net Profit Margin} \times \text{Asset Turnover}$$
$$\text{Net Profit/Total Assets} = \text{Net Profit/Revenues} \times \text{Revenues/Total Assets}$$

Figure 2.10 depicts the dynamics of the ROA model. Net profit margins are plotted on the vertical axis; asset turnover ratios are plotted on the horizontal axis. In this model, industries that command high profit margins typically face relatively low asset turnovers. That is, substantial asset investments are usually necessary to produce high-margin products or services; if not, the high margins will tend to be decreased by entrants and competition. The computer industry is often used as an example to illustrate the Case 1 and Case 2 situations. The manufacturing and selling of computer mainframes (high margins but low sales volume) is a Case 1 example. Most products and services that are the result

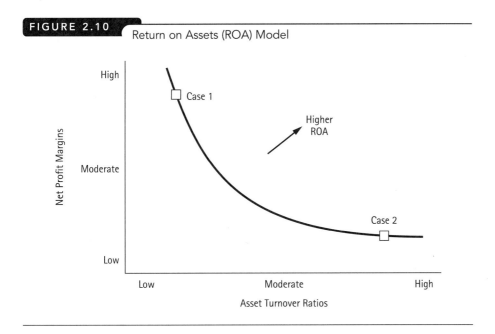

FIGURE 2.10 Return on Assets (ROA) Model

of technological innovations start out as Case 1 examples; this is what most entrepreneurs envision. High margins can be charged because you offer a unique (differentiated) product or service that is valued by consumers. A time-to-market lead over competition also usually allows for higher margins.

Case 2 depicts an opposite extreme whereby the product or service is basically a commodity. Profit margins are low; thus, the only way that a reasonable return on assets can be achieved is by selling the product (or providing the service) in large volumes. In terms of the computer industry, personal computers (PCs) represent an example of the Case 2 situation. Since PCs are sold at low margins, a reasonable return on an investment in assets can be achieved only if a large number of these products are sold. However, because the product is virtually a commodity, demand is often influenced by the condition of the economy—a factor outside the control of PC manufacturers.

The curve passing through Case 1 and Case 2 in Figure 2.10 shows how the same return on assets can be achieved through different combinations of net profit margins and asset turnovers. This curve can be viewed as reflecting an industry average return on assets. Alternatively, the curve can represent a target or benchmark return on assets, the objective being to outperform the benchmark. In this context, the goal would be to try to produce a combination of a net profit margin and an asset turnover that results in a return on assets above and to the right of the curve.

This traditional return on assets business model can be applied to most business models, including e-commerce models. Profit margins are ultimately a critical component. Revenues may be stimulated through advertising or other methods, but in the end, those revenues need to exceed all the relevant costs and lead to profits and cash flows that can be returned to the venture's owners and investors.

If, in an effort to dominate a market, a venture continues to sell products or services at a loss, increasing revenues alone will not result in a positive return on assets or a return to investors.[19]

• What is meant by the ROA model?

FINANCIAL/HARVEST CONSIDERATIONS

We list several criteria under the financial/harvest category in Figure 2.8. One important aspect of this category is the length of time expected for the venture to reach operating cash flow breakeven. It is common practice to consider two types of cash flow. The first is **operating cash flow**, the cash flow associated with producing and selling a product or with providing a service. The operating cash flow is the amount remaining after the cost of goods sold and other business expenses (primarily general and administrative expenses, along with marketing expenses) are subtracted from revenues. Since both the revenues and the expenses reflect an approximation of cash inflows and outflows associated with operations, the residual amount is an approximation of the operating cash flows over a specified time period such as one year.

In accounting terminology, operating cash flow is comparable to the venture's earnings before interest, taxes, depreciation, and amortization, or EBITDA (pronounced ee-bit-dah). As long as the costs associated with operating the venture are higher than the revenues received, operating cash flow is negative and the venture is operating below its cash flow breakeven point. Whether an idea is likely to be viewed as a viable business opportunity depends, in part, on how quickly the venture is expected to reach its operating cash flow breakeven point. Reaching operating breakeven in less than two years would give the proposed venture a high mark in terms of potential attractiveness. If reaching operating breakeven is expected to take more than four years, strong consideration should be given to restructuring or abandoning the venture's approach, particularly if patient external financial capital is not available to help the venture endure this lengthy drought of internal cash flow.

The second type of cash flow to consider is free cash flow. Value creation ultimately depends on the venture's ability to produce cash flow that can be used to pay back investors, that is, free(able) cash flow. **Free cash flow to equity** is the cash available to the entrepreneur and venture investors after deducting other expenses (including debt and tax expenses) and increases in investments, and adding net new debt financing from operating cash flow.[20] Free cash flow to equity

operating cash flow
cash flow from producing and selling a product or providing a service

free cash flow to equity
cash remaining after operating cash outflows, financing and tax cash flows, investment in assets needed to sustain the venture's growth, and net increases in debt capital

---

[19]   Of course, if increased volume lowers the cost of producing a product or providing a service by spreading out fixed costs over more units, profit margins could become positive. We discuss breakeven concepts in Chapter 4.

[20]   In Chapter 1, we presented a less specific but consistent definition of free cash flow to the equity or owners of the venture.

is calculated as the venture's revenues minus operating expenses, minus financing expenses and tax payments, after adjustment for changes in net working capital (NWC), physical capital expenditures (CAPEX) needed to sustain and grow the venture, and net additional debt issues to support the venture's growth. In operational terms, free cash flow to equity = net profit + depreciation charges − ΔNWC − CAPEX + net new debt.[21] Since this is a particularly important concept, we will devote considerable time in later chapters to explaining how and why the free cash flow to equity concept is applied and used. Free cash flow is one of the primary types of valuation cash flows used to value a venture's financial securities.[22]

It is never too early to think about how the proposed venture might be harvested, and how investors will perceive that harvest. Venture investors expect to be compensated with higher-than-average rates of return for investing in the riskier early stages of a venture's existence. The **internal rate of return (IRR)**, which is the most commonly used measure, is the compound rate of return that equates the present value of an investor's projected future cash flows with the initial investment. If your proposed business opportunity offers an IRR greater than 50 percent, potential venture investors will view this as attractive. IRRs in the 20 to 50 percent range will make it more difficult to attract funds. If your idea results in an IRR of less than 20 percent, it will be a significant disadvantage in attracting venture investors unless they have nonfinancial reasons to invest.

One way that venture investors prepare to exit, or cash out, of an investment is by registering their shares to allow them to be sold to the public (called going public), typically through an initial public offering (IPO). Proposed business opportunities that offer a potential IPO within two years merit a high score from venture investors. An average score is given to business opportunities that project an IPO in two to five years after the venture has been started. If the potential IPO is more than five years away, you should expect little venture investor interest.

Venture opportunities are also appraised in terms of the likelihood that the founder/entrepreneur will be able to maintain control of the venture. Sometimes founders lose interest in the venture when they lose voting control. As long as confidence exists in the founder, some potential venture investors won't mind holding minority voting positions. Thus, in instances when the founder has, and is expected to maintain, majority control, the potential attractiveness of a business opportunity gets a high score (high entrepreneur incentive). An average score is associated with the founder's having a high minority stake or position, which is typically characterized by a less than 50 percent position but a higher than 25 percent voting control position. A low minority voting control position— less than 25 percent—receives a low potential attractiveness score (low entrepreneur incentive).

Although not listed separately, the magnitude of external capital necessary to reach breakeven must be considered. When a venture requires substantial external capital before reaching breakeven, the ventures' founders will incur substantial

internal rate of return (IRR)
compound rate of return that equates the present value of the cash inflows received with the initial investment

---

[21]   The Greek character Δ represents "change in."

[22]   We will describe how to calculate the free cash flow to the enterprise in Chapter 13.

dilution and, consequently, face a significant threat to their ability to maintain control. Because ideas can vary widely in terms of financial capital requirements, it is difficult to quantify this dimension. Nonetheless, for many entrepreneurs, the desire to maintain control is strong, and the prospect of losing control in order to raise sufficient funding makes the venture less attractive.

CONCEPT CHECK

• What is meant by a venture's operating cash flow?

MANAGEMENT TEAM CONSIDERATIONS

A sober assessment of the quality of the management team, including the founder(s) and other key personnel, is critical in assessing a proposed business opportunity and moving the venture forward. Figures 2.8 and 2.9 indicate important management team factors to be considered. In determining what the entrepreneurial team brings to the table, there is almost no substitute for experience, expertise, and relevant technological and industry connections. A management team with expertise and experience, with intact networking connections in the proposed industry, merits a high score. A management team that lacks specific industry/market expertise but possesses quality general business experience and expertise receives an average score. Expertise in terms of a technology can offset a lack of related business experience; this simply means that other attributes of the potential business opportunity will need to be great enough to overcome the disadvantage of having inexperienced management or industry outsiders. In instances when the management team has little or no business expertise or experience, the potential attractiveness of the idea as a business opportunity is given a low score. Such a situation will typically make the uphill battle of moving from startup to profitable operations an even longer and less likely prospect. Nonetheless, the lack of experience, by itself, need not doom the idea. In fact, potential venture investors may offer to assist in putting together a stronger management team as a condition to their participating in the venture.

In addition to having management team expertise and experience, coverage of all functional areas is important. Expertise in marketing, operations, and finance is necessary. The founder/entrepreneur may serve as the venture's chief executive officer (CEO) if she has the expertise and desire to do so. There are many examples where the founder chooses to concentrate on marketing the business venture. In other instances, the entrepreneur may wish to concentrate on further research and development. This is often the case with high-technology business ventures. After identifying the management intentions and capabilities of the founder, it is important to put together a comprehensive management team in terms of a CEO and the individuals in charge of the venture's functional areas. A business opportunity that has all the functional areas covered merits a high score. If the management team has few of the functional areas covered, a low score on this attribute would be appropriate.

Venture investors and others assessing the venture's viability will consider the management team's potential to thrive in an entrepreneurial context. It is important to have the entire management team excited about the bumpy ride ahead. While judging this aspect of team competence is an inherently subjective process, enthusiasm about the venture process is a necessity for high scores in the "entrepreneurial focus" characteristic.

CONCEPT CHECK

- Why are management experience and expertise important?

OPPORTUNITY-SCREENING CAVEATS

Predicting which ideas will turn into successful ventures is an art and not a science. Thus, we are reluctant to introduce any scoring device because of the risk that would-be entrepreneurs might expect a guaranteed result; no quantification or interview assessment is infallible in predicting venture success. Venture opportunity-screening guides do not prophesy venture success or failure. Rather, the interview process (assessment) and quantitative approaches such as the VOS Indicator™ are intended to provide some input and direction to the potential entrepreneur's (or investor's) inherently subjective assessment of a new venture's viability.

Most professional venture investors concentrate their investments in high-growth, high-performance ventures operating in industries/markets that offer the potential for high revenues and large future valuations. A relatively high score on the VOS Indicator™ or similar screening guides indicates the likelihood that professional venture investors will be interested in your idea. Of course, the majority of ideas fail to score high in terms of potential attractiveness on a rigorous venture opportunity-screening test. In fact, many ideas should fall in the average potential attractiveness range.

An average score or less-than-stellar interview responses do not necessarily mean that you should immediately abandon the idea. If you are confident in, and committed to, the idea, you may have to retrench, develop alternative approaches, and perhaps bootstrap your way to success (or failure) with a longer horizon. In general terms, bootstrapping refers to the process of minimizing resources. **Financial bootstrapping** involves minimizing the need for financial capital and finding unique sources for financing a new venture.

financial bootstrapping
minimizing the need for financial capital and finding unique ways of financing a new venture

Let's take a look at Water Wonders, a manufacturer of water fountains that probably would not have scored very well on the VOS Indicator™. In 1996, two recently laid-off carpenters, Neil Sater and David Zasloff, while visiting a local greenhouse with a fountain made of monolithic slate, thought there might be commercial potential for relatively light and portable water fountains. They spent $50 on raw materials; a backyard patio became their workplace. The result was a variety of prototypes that combined pieces of furniture with water fountains. In exchange for a fountain, a local photographer agreed to shoot a portfolio of the prototypes. Water Wonders first sold water fountains at art galleries. In early 1997, everything was put on the line when Sater and Zasloff spent $2,500 for a booth at the San Francisco International Gift Show and garnered $50,000 in orders. After total sales of just under $700,000 in 1997, revenues reached $2.8 million in 1998, and projections were $8 to $10 million for 1999. Water fountains now are sold at retail chain stores and galleries, as well as through mail-order catalogs.[23]

The founders of Water Wonders were successful in bootstrapping their way through the development stage and into the startup stage. They were able to move from an idea to product prototypes and initial product sales with minimal financial support. This is an example of financial bootstrapping working to get a new venture set up and operating. Of course, many new ventures will be able to begin operations only if they are able to attract venture investor funds. Thus, the ability to generate reasonable scores on the VOS Indicator™ or other screening guides may be correlated with whether an idea becomes a business opportunity.

While there will be exceptions to almost any rule or guideline, ideas that score low on the VOS Indicator™ probably should be reconsidered; the aspiring entrepreneur might be best served by moving on to other ideas. It is less costly to abandon a poor business idea early rather than later. Stopping during the development stage is much less costly than failing at either the startup or survival life cycle stages, where larger amounts of founder and other investor capital are at risk.

2.7   KEY ELEMENTS OF A BUSINESS PLAN

business plan
written document that describes the proposed product or service opportunity, current resources, and financial projections

If your idea successfully passes the venture opportunity-screening test, it probably deserves further investigation. Movement from the development stage to the startup stage often begins with the preparation of a business plan. A **business plan** is a written document that describes the proposed venture in terms of the product or service opportunity, current resources, and financial projections. It is sometimes said that the business plan sells the excitement, opportunity, and rationale of your business idea to you and other members of your management team, potential investors, and other stakeholders. While time consuming and stressful, the process of writing a business plan is beneficial to the entrepreneur, who must be the first to believe the plan is workable. The entrepreneur must be convinced that starting the business at this time is the right thing to do personally and professionally.

Once you have sold yourself and your management team on the business idea during the development stage, it is important to sell investors, bankers, suppliers, and customers. Investors may include family, friends, and providers of venture capital. Commercial bankers today usually require a written business plan before they will consider lending to an early-stage firm—if they will consider it at all. Rather than expect a bank loan, you might have to rely on borrowing through a home equity credit or bank credit cards. Potential suppliers and customers must be

---

[23]   Donna Fenn, "How to Start a Great Company for $1,000 or Less," *Inc.*, August 1999, pp. 43–50.

convinced that the venture firm will be around to pay its credit purchases and to honor product and other service commitments.

We do not intend for this text to provide details on how to prepare a detailed business plan. Rather, we focus on the key elements found in a typical business plan.[24] A business plan differs from the screening of a venture opportunity in two important ways. First, the business plan is much more detailed than the opportunity assessment in terms of product/service descriptions, marketing plans and strategies, and operations (i.e., producing the product or providing the service). Second, the business plan provides detailed financial plans and forecasts that serve as the initial guide for operating the firm over the next several years. The business plan also identifies the amount and type(s) of funds initially being sought from venture and other investors in the financing section.[25]

Every business plan should begin with a cover page and table of contents, and many business plans also include a confidentiality statement in an attempt to protect proprietary information included in the plan. Figure 2.11 provides an example of an outline of the major sections usually included in a business plan.

COVER PAGE, CONFIDENTIALITY STATEMENT, AND TABLE OF CONTENTS

The cover page of a business plan should identify the company or venture and provide the name, address, and phone number of the entrepreneur or other contact person. Each copy should be numbered, and, if proprietary information is involved, a confidentiality statement may be included as a second page. An example of the wording in such a statement is as follows:

> *This business plan contains information that (the firm) considers proprietary. By accepting this business plan, the recipient acknowledges the proprietary nature of this information contained herein and agrees to keep confidential all such information.*

Wording may be added, and each recipient may be asked to sign the confidentiality statement.[26] The table of contents should include the business plan outline, such as the one depicted in Figure 2.11, and the appropriate page numbers on which each section begins.

---

[24] For readers who wish to learn more details about what goes into a formal business plan, a number of very good sources are available in print or via electronic access. For example, see Timmons and Spinelli, *New Venture Creation*, chap. 6; William D. Bygrave and Andrew Zacharakis, eds., *The Portable MBA in Entrepreneurship*, 3rd ed. (New York: John Wiley & Sons, 2003), chap. 4; and Donald F. Kuratko and Richard M. Hogetts, *Entrepreneurship: Theory, Process, and Practice*, 7th ed. (New York: Thomson/South-Western, 2007), chap. 11. In addition, the Center for Business Planning maintains a comprehensive Web site devoted to the preparation of business plans. See http://www.businessplans.org.

[25] Interest in MBA programs in entrepreneurship has spawned a number of business plan competitions. For example, Moot Corp. is an annual business plan competition, hosted by the University of Texas at Austin, involving student teams from major MBA programs around the world. For a description of what takes place during the business plan competition, see Michael Warshaw, "The Best Business Plan on the Planet," *Inc.*, August 1999, pp. 80–92.

[26] NDAs (nondisclosure agreements), confidentiality statements, and noncompete statements are all well and good, but be warned that VCs will typically not sign them.

FIGURE 2.11

Example of a Typical Business Plan Outline

SECTION I:	**EXECUTIVE SUMMARY**
SECTION II:	**BUSINESS DESCRIPTION**
	A. Description of the product or service
	B. Industry background
	C. Venture or firm background
	D. Goals and milestone objectives
SECTION III:	**MARKETING PLAN AND STRATEGY**
	A. Target market and customers
	B. Competition and market share
	C. Pricing strategy
	D. Promotion and distribution
SECTION IV:	**OPERATIONS AND SUPPORT**
	A. Quality targets
	B. Technology requirements
	C. Service support
SECTION V:	**MANAGEMENT TEAM**
	A. Experience and expertise
	B. Organizational structure
	C. Intellectual property rights
SECTION VI:	**FINANCIAL PLANS AND PROJECTIONS**
	A. Income statements and balance sheets
	B. Statements of cash flow
	C. Breakeven analysis
	D. Funding needs and sources
SECTION VII:	**RISKS AND OPPORTUNITIES**
	A. Possible problems and risks
	B. Real option opportunities
SECTION VIII:	**APPENDIX**
	A. Detailed support for financial forecasts
	B. Time line and milestones

EXECUTIVE SUMMARY

The executive summary is just that—a summary that is an overview of the other sections in the business plan. It provides a brief description of the product or service and market; the marketing plan and strategy; how operations are to be conducted; the management team; and the financial plan, including the dollar amount of financing needs and, in some cases, a potential exit strategy.

Let's take a look at the Companion Systems Corporation (CSC) example (discussed in more detail in the appendix to this chapter). CSC would begin with a summary of its proposed products and market. CSC wants to provide two types of virtual private network (VPN) products as well as dedicated firewall products to businesses operating in the Internet industry. CSC also would provide, in the executive summary, a short description of the materials that follow in each of the sections of the business plan.

BUSINESS DESCRIPTION

Some of the information supplied during the venture assessment on industry/market factors can be included and expanded here. The venture's products and services are described in detail; the description includes proprietary information deemed necessary and relevant for a potential investor to make an informed decision. Industry background information is provided, including the potential market size and projected industry growth rates. The industry characterization is often followed by a description of the venture's background, goals, and milestones for its position in the expanding market. CSC has core expertise from its previously developed software and important existing relationships with ISPs. CSC's goal is to become the leading supplier of networking equipment for small- to medium-sized enterprises and ISPs.

MARKETING PLAN AND STRATEGY

Information from the assessment interview (or scoring exercise) provides a very preliminary example of the type of marketing information that would, ideally, form this section of a business plan. A marketing plan and strategy section might address the specifics of the target market and customers, existing and potential competition, projected market shares, pricing strategies, and plans for promotion and distribution. When possible, all of this would be documented by formal market research.

For CSC, the target market is networking equipment. The market for VPN is expected to grow rapidly due to growth in business use of the Internet, increasing Internet connection speeds, and consolidation of network connections by businesses. CSC intends to target four customer groups: industry end users, original equipment manufacturers, small and medium end users, and ISPs. While at the time of the plan there are no current direct competitors, competition will develop from other VPN startups, firewall software vendors, and established networking companies. CSC expects to capture one-fourth of the market share within three years of operation. Pricing strategies and promotion plans for CSC need to be developed in detail. The plan should specify how CSC will exploit existing distribution channels for selling networking products.

OPERATIONS AND SUPPORT

The business plan should provide details about production methods and service delivery. Quality intentions or targets should be set out in the business plan.[27]

The business plan should provide a discussion of the technology requirements associated with the product or service being proposed. Ideas involving groundbreaking technologies often attract venture investors because of first-mover advantages and inherent scale economies and efficiencies. In such cases, the risk associated with an untested technology may be more than offset by potentially high returns. In contrast, ideas involving existing technologies tend to be less attractive as potential business opportunities; while the risk of substandard operations is lower, so are the expected financial benefits to entrants in an established industry.

The business plan should provide a statement of the venture's philosophy and its intent for customer support, education, and training. In general, the more complex the proposed product or service, the greater must be the commitment to providing service support. The provision of superior support services is a characteristic of successful entrepreneurial ventures.

CSC's VPN products involve state-of-the-art technology. There is some uncertainty regarding whether the products will perform according to specifications. If successful, CSC has the potential to generate large returns. Excellent product quality is essential to the success of CSC's proposed VPN venture. In addition, and perhaps more important, it will be almost impossible to succeed without high-quality service support; the business plan needs to include the resources necessary to establish this support.

MANAGEMENT TEAM

The experience and expertise of the management team can be brought in from the venture assessment materials, if an assessment was conducted. While it is important to "flesh out" the team's information, the essentials are the same. The business plan may be more formal in presenting the organizational structure if the structure is important in establishing credibility. Since many venture investors consider the management team to be the most important characteristic of a new venture, this part of the business plan needs to be crafted to establish the management team's connections and credibility. This does not mean that each member's entire résumé should be presented. Résumés may be included in an appendix. This section is a promotional summary of the relevant highlights from the management team combined with networking information that is not on most résumés.

---

[27] As perceived or real quality goes down, the potential attractiveness of the idea also tends to diminish. This is not to say that no demand exists for low-quality products. Rather, ideas focusing on low quality generally are less attractive to venture investors.

CSC's team is a definite asset, and the challenge will be keeping this section concise and directed. CSC is organized as a corporation and at the time of the business plan does not have patents or trademarks. Nonetheless, CSC had significant intellectual property in the form of proprietary software that would have been granted protection under copyright laws, even without registration.

FINANCIAL PLANS AND PROJECTIONS

As this is a text on entrepreneurial finance, it is reasonable to ask why we have spent so much time on "other things." First, you can rest assured that there is plenty of entrepreneurial finance to come in future chapters. Nonetheless, it is important to stop and disclose our position on financial projections (almost always included in a business plan) and entrepreneurship. Very few entrepreneurs have an irreducibly financial view of the commercial future of their business ideas. Rather, they have a knowledge of the technology, a feeling for the needs of their prospective customers, a knack for doing something better, or some other nonfinancial contribution to make. We see two primary benefits of completing and presenting the financial projections in a business plan. The first is that the process of mapping an entrepreneur's vision into coherent financial statements places a useful structure on many aspects of the business-planning phase. The time lines for acquiring equipment, hiring key employees, testing the market's appetite, and other important parts of the vision have to be formalized in order to produce the financial projections. The process of getting to the financial projections, rather than the actual projections themselves, provides the bulk of this value and certainly helps hold the entrepreneurial team accountable to specific numerical and calendar targets. The second benefit is related but subtler. The absence of coherent financial statements signals a gap in the skill set of the entrepreneurial team. Whether presenting short-term cash budgets to help convince the readers that the venture can manage to stay afloat on a day-to-day basis, or presenting long-term projections to show how value will accumulate as the venture grows and matures, it is the team's ability to produce these quantified versions of the entrepreneur's vision that matters. The absence of financial projections is a costly signal of lack of competence, unwillingness to undertake the effort, or potentially something worse. Everyone knows that the financial projections are no better than the nonfinancial components behind those projections: garbage in–garbage out. Everyone also understands that the business plan is a living document, most likely outdated from the day it's printed. Consequently, while the financial projections contain important information about specifics, they have no credibility apart from the remainder of the business plan; their subservient role is well understood.

With that said, the venture assessment provides a starting point for constructing formal projected financial statements that reflect the venture's vision as presented in the nonfinancial parts of the business plan. In most cases, these initial assumptions (and other, more specific ones) should be transformed into more formal projections: income statements, balance sheets, and statements of cash flows. Chapter 6 introduces techniques for short- and longer-horizon projections that may help the team construct coherent statements.

Projected financial statements also present a formal version of when and how the venture will break even. As we will see, estimating future venture values is a prerequisite to calibrating potential returns for the entrepreneur and venture investors. Projected financial statements also provide an indication of when the venture might have sufficiently attractive financial statistics to conduct a successful initial public offering. Financial statement projections should indicate the size and timing of funding needs, and the business plan should indicate potential sources for acquiring these funds.

CSC will need to provide detailed projected financial statements in its business plan. Presumably, financial projections were made and are consistent with the metrics used in the pricing/profitability factor in the VOS Indicator™ analysis of CSC. Gross profit margins are expected to be 60 percent, and after-tax profit margins are expected to average 15 percent. This latter figure, coupled with an expected asset turnover of two times, indicates an expected return on assets of 30 percent. Cash flow breakeven is expected in less than two years, and venture investors are expected to receive over a 30 percent rate of return on their investments. An IPO is projected as being feasible in three years.

RISKS AND OPPORTUNITIES

The business plan should include a discussion of possible problems. It is a good idea to discuss these before potential venture investors point them out to you. For example, how does the venture's management team expect to react if the industry/market revenues are overestimated or if the target market share in Year 3 is not reached? How does management plan to adjust if competition is fiercer than originally expected and price cutting results? Alternative courses of action should be prepared in the event that such problems arise. The venture should anticipate and have a plan for handling possible risks, such as a delay in implementing new technologies. For example, how does the venture plan to handle product availability or service delivery delays? Potential venture investors want to know that the management team is aware of possible problems and risks and is willing and able to adapt or adjust quickly if the situation warrants action. While signaling that the team is ready to adapt is important, the business plan should maintain a balance and not allow explanations of downside risks and adaptations to swamp the overall optimistic tone that is essential in early-stage ventures.

Potential venture investors are interested in the management team's appraisal of important flexibilities in the business model and market. Finance academics and practitioners sometimes refer to these flexibilities as real options. An option is an opportunity or right, without an obligation, to take a future action. **Real options** involve real or nonfinancial options available to managers as the venture progresses through its life cycle.[28] Examples of real options include growth and scale flexibilities to respond to demand fluctuations, flexibility in manufacturing and design options, and the ability to adapt the venture's strategy to new information,

real options
real or nonfinancial options available to managers as the venture progresses through its life cycle

---

[28] The use of the term "real options" can be traced back to an article involving the discussion of the relationship between strategic planning and finance. See Stewart Myers, "Finance Theory and Financial Strategy," *Interfaces* (January–February 1984): pp. 126–137.

both externally produced (e.g., marketwide) and internally produced (through the venture's "learning by doing" and even by delay and exit options).[29] One can view the movement from development stage to market entry and distribution as a growth option and can view the flexibility in timing this movement as a valuable delay option. If the market that the venture has entered begins to grow rapidly, an initial toehold position may allow the venture to move quickly to capture market growth. Likewise, an investment in a new technology may provide flexibility or learning options with new applications of the technology in the future, or pave the way for an even newer future technology. Exit options allow the entrepreneur the flexibility to discontinue progress when it becomes more lucrative to sell, abandon, or liquidate the venture. Exit options also can relate to deciding when to harvest a successful venture's value.

CSC's business plan needs to include contingencies or adaptations to shortfalls in the economy overall and the Internet sector in particular. CSC should have a contingency plan possibly even including financial statement projections if competition turns out to be fiercer than anticipated and CSC fails to meet its target market share or target dollar revenues. For example, it is possible that market share might still be achieved but only with a significant price reduction. Finally, CSC should point out in its business plan any important flexibilities (real options) that allow CSC to adapt to new information, changing market conditions and technological innovations, or other shocks to the business model and time line.

BUSINESS PLAN APPENDIX

The appendix should contain the detailed assumptions underlying the projected financial statements provided in the financial plans and projections section. A time line and milestones should be included, indicating the amount and size of expected financing needs and when venture investors might expect to be able to exit the venture through an IPO or sale of the venture. Milestones relating to target revenue levels and market share should be noted. The appendix can also contain financial "what if" analyses to address the possible impact of critical factors. For example, backup projected financial statements might show the implications of revenues at 80 percent of initial projections.

Of course, CSC should provide backup financial statement projections, a time line that shows the timing of expected financing needs and sources, and a possible venture exit target. CSC also should provide milestones for dollar revenues and market share.

CONCEPT CHECK

- What are some of the major segments or parts of a business plan?
- What are real options?

---

[29] For a comprehensive, nontechnical treatment of real options, see Martha Amram and Nalin Kulatilaka, *Real Options* (Boston: Harvard Business School Press, 1999). Also see Andrew Metrick, *Venture Capital and the Finance of Innovation* (Hoboken, NJ: John Wiley & Sons, 2007), chap. 21.

SUMMARY

This chapter discussed the process and hurdles involved in moving from an idea through a feasibility analysis toward a viable venture, and the role a business plan can play in that process. In order to be successful, one should have a sound business model: a framework that will generate revenues, produce profits, and eventually provide for a return to the venture's owners and investors, all within an acceptable time period. We defined entrepreneurial ventures, in contrast to salary-replacement firms and lifestyle firms, as being growth driven and performance oriented. We acknowledged that one can learn from studying the best practices of successful entrepreneurial ventures; in particular, there is potential benefit in knowing successful firms' marketing, financial, and management practices. We discussed time to market and other timing considerations affecting the new venture's viability.

Next, we introduced SWOT analysis as a first-pass (or litmus) test for assessing an idea's business viability. We then turned to more formal qualitative and quantitative screening devices that can be useful for entrepreneurial ventures seeking external financing. We provided an example of four "interviews" for a mostly qualitative assessment of a venture's viability and a more quantitative

scoring approach called the VOS Indicator™. Both can be useful in providing founders and investors with some objectivity and encouraging valuable introspection on the likelihood of attracting venture investors and succeeding more generally. We covered industry/market, pricing/profitability, financial/harvest, and management team factors.

During our discussion of pricing/profitability considerations, we introduced the basic ROA model that expresses the venture's return on assets as the product of the net profit margin and the asset turnover. Although the ROA model was originally developed for evaluating brick-and-mortar firms, it is equally important for more modern business models, including firms engaged in e-commerce.

The final section of the chapter discussed the key elements of a business plan. The importance of incorporating financial plans and financial statement projections will become increasingly clear as you progress through this book. In the final part of this chapter, we introduced real options and related them to the risks and opportunities section of the business plan. As we will see in later chapters, there are some important advantages for entrepreneurs who think about their ventures in terms of real options.

KEY TERMS

asset intensity	internal rate of return (IRR)	salary-replacement firms
business plan	lifestyle firms	sound business model
cost of goods sold	net profit	SWOT analysis
entrepreneurial ventures	net profit margin	venture opportunity screening
financial bootstrapping	operating cash flow	viable venture opportunity
free cash flow to equity	real options	VOS Indicator™
gross profit	return on assets	
gross profit margin	return on assets (ROA) model	

DISCUSSION QUESTIONS

1. Identify three types of startup firms.

2. Briefly describe the process involved in moving from an idea to a business plan.

3. What are the components of a sound business model?

4. Describe the differences between entrepreneurial ventures and other entrepreneurial firms.

5. Identify some of the best marketing and management practices of high-growth, high-performance firms.

6. Describe and discuss some of the best financial practices of high-growth, high-performance firms. Why is it also important to consider production or operations practices?

7. Time to market is generally important, but being first to market does not necessarily ensure success. Explain.

8. What is meant by a viable venture opportunity?

9. Describe how a SWOT analysis can be used to conduct a first-pass assessment of whether an idea is likely to become a viable business opportunity.

10. Describe the meaning of venture opportunity screening.

11. An analogy used relating to venture opportunity screening makes reference to "caterpillars" and "butterflies." Briefly describe the use of this analogy.

12. When conducting a qualitative screening of a venture opportunity, whom should you interview? What topics should you cover?

13. Describe the characteristics of a viable venture opportunity. What is the VOS Indicator™?

14. Describe the factor categories used by venture capitalists and other venture investors when they screen venture opportunities for the purpose of deciding to invest.

15. Describe return on assets. Describe the two major ratio components that comprise the venture's ROA model.

16. How do the concepts of operating cash flow and free cash flow to equity differ?

17. What is a business plan? Why is it important to prepare a business plan?

18. What are the major elements of a typical business plan?

19. What are real options? What types of real option opportunities are available to entrepreneurs?

INTERNET ACTIVITIES

1. Access the *Inc.* magazine Web site at http://www.inc.com. Identify a list of recent articles that relate to how business opportunities are evaluated by venture investors and/or articles discussing why venture investors chose not to invest in potential business opportunities.

2. Access the Center for Business Planning Web site at http://www.businessplans.org. The site provides examples of business plans prepared by MBA students from top business schools and presented to panels of investors at recent Moot Corp. competitions hosted by the University of Texas at Austin. Review one of the business plans. Write a brief summary comparing the segments or elements included in the business plan to the key elements of a typical business plan presented in this chapter.

3. Access the Center for Business Planning Web site at http://www.businessplans.org. Find the reference to PlanWrite, which is designed to help an entrepreneur create a business plan. Identify and briefly describe what this software product provides.

EXERCISES/PROBLEMS

1. Following is financial information for three ventures:

	VENTURE XX	VENTURE YY	VENTURE ZZ
After-tax profit margins	5%	25%	15%
Asset turnover	2.0 times	3.0 times	1.0 times

   A. Calculate the return on assets for each firm.
   B. Which venture is indicative of a strong entrepreneurial venture opportunity?
   C. Which venture seems to be more of a commodity-type business?
   D. How would you place these three ventures on a graph similar to Figure 2.10?
   E. Use the information in Figure 2.9 relating to pricing/profitability and "score" each venture in terms of potential attractiveness.

2. In 2008, Jennifer (Jen) Liu and Larry Mestas founded Jen and Larry's Frozen Yogurt Company, which was based on the idea of applying the microbrew or microbatch

strategy to the production and sale of frozen yogurt. They began producing small quantities of unique flavors and blends in limited editions. Revenues were $600,000 in 2008 and were estimated at $1.2 million in 2009. Since Jen and Larry were selling premium frozen yogurt containing premium ingredients, each small cup of yogurt sold for $3, and the cost of producing the frozen yogurt averaged $1.50 per cup. Other expenses, including taxes, averaged an additional $1 per cup of frozen yogurt in 2008 and were estimated at $1.20 per cup in 2009.

A. Determine the number of cups of frozen yogurt sold each year.

B. Estimate the dollar amounts of gross profit and net profit for Jen and Larry's venture in 2008 and 2009.

C. Calculate the gross profit margins and net profit margins in 2008 and 2009.

D. Briefly describe what has occurred between the two years.

3. Jen and Larry's frozen yogurt venture described in Problem 2 required some investment in bricks and mortar. Initial specialty equipment and the renovation of an old warehouse building in lower downtown, referred to as LoDo, cost $450,000 at the beginning of 2008. At the same time, $50,000 was invested in inventories. In early 2009, an additional $100,000 was spent on equipment to support the increased frozen yogurt sales in 2009. Use information from Problem 2 and this problem to solve the following:

A. Calculate the return on assets in both 2008 and 2009.

B. Calculate the asset intensity or asset turnover ratios for 2008 and 2009.

C. Apply the ROA model to Jen and Larry's frozen yogurt venture.

D. Briefly describe what has occurred between the two years.

E. Show how you would position Jen and Larry's frozen yogurt venture in terms of the relationship between net profit margins and asset turnovers depicted in Figure 2.10.

4. Jen Liu and Larry Mestas are seeking venture investors to help fund the expected growth in their Frozen Yogurt venture described in Problems 2 and 3. Use the VOS Indicator™ guidelines presented in Figures 2.8 and 2.9 to score Jen and Larry's frozen yogurt venture in terms of the items in the pricing/profitability factor category. Comment on the likely attractiveness of this business opportunity to venture investors.

5. Assume that you have just "run out of money" and are unable to move your "idea" from its development stage to production and the startup stage. However, you remain convinced that with a reasonable amount of additional financial capital you will be a successful entrepreneur. While your expectations are low, you are meeting with a loan officer of the local bank in the hope that you can get a personal loan in order to continue your venture.

A. As you are about to enter the bank, you see a bank money bag lying on the street. No one is around to claim the bag. What would you do?

B. Now let's assume that what you found lying on the street was a $100 bill. The thought crosses your mind that it would be nice to take your significant other out for a nice dinner—something that you have not had for several months. What would you do?

C. Now, instead of $100 you "find" a $1 bill on the street. The thought crosses your mind that you could buy a lottery ticket with the dollar. Winning the lottery would certainly solve all your financing needs to start and run your venture. What would you do?

SUPPLEMENTAL EXERCISES/PROBLEMS

[Note: These activities are for readers who have an understanding of financial statements.]

6. Refer to the information on the three ventures in Problem 1.
   A. If each venture had net sales of $10 million, calculate the dollar amount of net profit and total assets for Venture XX, Venture YY, and Venture ZZ.
   B. Which venture would have the largest dollar amount of net profit?
   C. Which venture would have the largest dollar amount of total assets?

7. Ricardo Martinez has prepared the following financial statement projections as part of his business plan for starting the Martinez Products Corporation. The venture is to manufacture and sell electronic components that make standard overhead projectors "smart." In essence, through voice commands a projector can be turned on, off, and the brightness of the projection altered. This will allow the user to avoid audience annoyances associated with a bright projection light during periods when no overhead transparency is being used. Venture investors usually screen prospective venture opportunities in terms of projected profitability and financial performance.
   A. Use the following projected financial statements for Martinez Products to calculate financial ratios showing the venture's projected (a) gross profit margin, (b) net profit margin, (c) asset intensity, and (d) return on assets.
   B. The ratios calculated in Part A are found in the venture opportunity-screening guide discussed in the chapter. Rate the potential attractiveness of the Martinez Products venture using the guidelines for the pricing/profitability factor category for the VOS Indicator™.

Martinez Products Corporation Projected Income Statement for Year 1

Sales	$200,000
Cost of goods sold	100,000
Gross profit	100,000
Operating expenses	75,000
Depreciation	4,000
Earnings before interest and taxes	21,000
Interest	1,000
Earnings before taxes	20,000
Taxes (25%)	5,000
Net income	$ 15,000

Martinez Products Corporation Projected Balance Sheet for End of Year 1

Cash	$ 10,000	Accounts payable	$ 15,000
Accounts receivable	20,000	Accrued liabilities	10,000
Inventories	20,000	Bank loan	10,000
Total current assets	50,000	Total current liabilities	35,000
Gross fixed assets	54,000	Common stock	50,000
Accumulated depreciation	4,000	Retained earnings	15,000
Net fixed assets	50,000	Total equity	65,000
Total assets	$100,000	Total liabilities and equity	$100,000

8. Ricardo Martinez, the founder of Martinez Products Corporation (see Problem 7), projects sales to double to $400,000 in the second year of operation.
   A. If the financial ratios calculated for Year 1 in Problem 7 remain the same in Year 2, what would be Martinez's dollar amount projections in his business plan for (a) gross profit, (b) net profit or income, and (c) total assets?
   B. How would your answers change in Part A if the gross profit margin in the second year is projected to be 60 percent, the net profit margin 25 percent, and the asset intensity at five times turnover?
   C. Use the projected ratio information in Part B in the return on assets (ROA) model to determine the projected percentage rate of return on assets.

M I N I   C A S E

LearnRite.com Corporation

LearnRite.com offers e-commerce service for children's edutainment products and services. The word *edutainment* is used to describe software that combines educational and entertainment components. Valuable product information and detailed editorial comments are combined with a wide selection of products for purchase to help families make their children's edutainment decisions. A team of leading educators and journalists provide editorial comments on the products sold by the firm. LearnRite targets highly educated, convenience-oriented, and value-conscious families with children under the age of twelve, estimated to be about 35 percent of Internet users.

The firm's warehouse distribution model results in higher net margins, as well as greater selection and convenience for customers, when compared to traditional retailers. Gross profit margins are expected to average about 30 percent each year. Because of relatively high marketing expenditures aimed at gaining market share, the firm is expected to suffer net losses for two years. Marketing and other operating expenses are estimated to be $3 million in 2009 and $5 million in 2010. However, operating cash flow breakeven should be reached during the third year. Net profit margins are expected to average 10 percent per year beginning in Year 3. Investment in bricks and mortar is largely in the form of warehouse facilities and a computer system to handle orders and facilitate the distribution of inventories. After considering the investment in inventories, the asset intensity or turnover is expected to average about two times per year.

LearnRite estimates that venture investors should earn about a 40 percent average annual compound rate of return and sees an opportunity for a possible initial public offering in about six years. If industry consolidation occurs, a merger might occur sooner.

The management team is headed by Srikant Kapoor, who serves as president of LearnRite .com and who controls about 35 percent of the ownership of the firm. Mr. Kapoor has more than twelve years of experience in high-tech industries, including previous positions with US West and Microsoft. He holds a BS degree in electrical engineering from an Indian technology institute and an MBA from a major U.S. university. Sean Davidson, director of technology, has more than ten years of experience in software development and integration. Walter Vu has almost ten years of experience in sales and business development in the software industry, including positions at Claris and Maxis. Mitch Feldman, director of marketing, was responsible for the marketing communications function and the Internet operations of a large software company for six years. Management strives for continual improvement in ease of user interface, personalized services, and amount of information supplied to customers.

LearnRite.com Corporation (continued)

   The total market for children's entertainment is estimated to be $35 billion annually. Toys account for about $20 billion in annual spending. Summer camps are estimated to generate $6 billion annually. This is followed by children's videos and video games at $4 billion each. Children's software sales currently generate about $1 billion per year in revenues, and industry sales are expected to grow at a 30 percent annual rate over the next several years.
   LearnRite has made the following five-year revenue projections:

	2009	2010	2011	2012	2013
Revenues ($M)	$1.0	$9.6	$30.1	$67.8	$121.4

A. Project industry sales for children's software through 2013.

B. Calculate the year-to-year annual sales growth rates for LearnRite and estimate the compound growth rate over the 2009–2013 time period.

C. Estimate LearnRite's expected market share in each year based on the given data.

D. Estimate the firm's net income (loss) in each of the five years.

E. Estimate the firm's return on assets beginning when the net or after-tax income is expected to be positive.

F. Score LearnRite's venture investor attractiveness in terms of the industry/market factor category using the VOS Indicator™ guide and criteria set out in Figures 2.8 and 2.9. If you believe there are insufficient data, indicate that decision with an N/A.

G. Score LearnRite's venture investor attractiveness in terms of pricing/profitability factors. Follow the instructions in Part F.

H. Score LearnRite's venture investor attractiveness in terms of financial/harvest factors. Follow the instructions in Part F.

I. Score LearnRite's venture investor attractiveness in terms of management team factors. Follow the instructions in Part F.

J. Determine overall total points and an average score for LearnRite as was done for the Companion Systems Corporation in the Appendix. Items where information is judged to be lacking and an N/A is used should be excluded when calculating an average score.

K. Provide a brief written summary indicating how you feel about LearnRite.com as a business opportunity.

Appendix

APPLYING THE VOS INDICATOR™: AN EXAMPLE

Figure 1 provides an application of the VOS Indicator™ using the guidelines described in Figure 2.9 to assess Companion Systems Corporation (CSC).

COMPANION SYSTEMS PROFILE

Companion Systems Corporation's goal is to become the leading supplier of networking equipment for small- to medium-sized enterprises and Internet service providers (ISPs). The firm offers router products that give remote users high-speed, dedicated encrypted access through the Internet to their home servers. This is accomplished by the creation of a virtual private network (VPN) that allows a firm to replace traditional dial-up remote access with secure Internet-based communications links.

MARKET OPPORTUNITY

VPN is an application of the Internet that is expected to grow rapidly over the next few years. Several trends support this view: (1) Business use of the Internet is expected to increase, (2) Internet connection speeds are expected to increase, and (3) businesses are expected to consolidate their network connections using VPN. While the market for VPN equipment is still in its infancy, industry and CSC's revenues are expected to grow at a 50 percent or greater rate over the next several years. Industry revenues are expected to reach the $150 million level in three to five years. At present, there are no known direct competitors for the strategy Companion Systems is pursuing. However, there are three groups of indirect competitors: VPN startups, firewall software vendors, and established networking companies.

Companion Systems' core advantages position the firm to capture early market share for VPN and to be able to capitalize on the explosive growth that is expected to occur. These advantages include internally developed multiprotocol routing and switching software, easy-to-use management software for network devices, distribution channels in place for selling networking products to small/medium businesses, and existing close relationships with several of the top ISPs. The company plans to target four customer groups: high-leverage industry end

---

FIGURE 1 Application of the VOS Indicator™ to Companion Systems Corporation

	POTENTIAL ATTRACTIVENESS		
FACTOR CATEGORIES	HIGH	AVERAGE	LOW
Industry/Market			
Market size potential	3		
Venture growth rate	3		
Market share (year 3)	3		
Entry barriers		2	
Pricing/Profitability			
Gross margins	3		
After-tax margins		2	
Asset intensity		2	
Return on assets	3		
Financial/Harvest			
Cash flow breakeven	3		
Rate of return	3		
IPO potential		2	
Founder's control		2	
Management Team			
Experience/expertise	3		
Functional areas	3		
Flexibility/adaptability		2	
Entrepreneurial focus	3		
Total points by ranking	30	12	0
Overall total points (OTP)		42	
Average score (OTP/16)		2.63	

---

users (seeding program), original equipment manufacturers (OEMs), small and medium end users, and ISPs.

CSC expects to achieve a 25 percent market share within three years of operation. While CSC does not have legal protection (e.g., a patent or trademark), it does have a timing advantage over potential competitors.

PRODUCTS

Companion Systems will provide two types of VPN products: VPN Access and VPN LAN-to-LAN. VPN Access devices allow remote computers to access a corporate network via the Internet. VPN LAN-to-LAN devices provide network-to-network routing services using the Internet. CSC intends to produce top-quality products and to provide superior service support for these products.

The company will also provide dedicated firewall products. Firewalls are used to protect corporate networks from unauthorized access. A firewall is a natural complement to a VPN Access server. Together, they provide a complete method of allowing authorized users to access network services and data (VPN Access server), while protecting the network from unauthorized access (firewall).

Gross profit margins are expected to be 60 percent, and after-tax or net profit margins are expected to average 15 percent. This after-tax margin, coupled with an expected asset turnover ratio of two times, results in an expected return on assets of 30 percent. CSC estimates that it will reach cash flow breakeven in less than two years. The amount of external financing needed for facilities, equipment, and research and development is expected to be moderate.

MANAGEMENT TEAM

The CEO, Mike McDonnell, graduated in 1981 from a major midwestern university with a BS degree in electrical engineering and a BA degree in English. Before founding Companion Systems, McDonnell held engineering, marketing, and sales positions at two different firms, one of which was a fiber-optic data communications company. John Barlow, director of software development and technical support, received a BS in computer science in 1984 and worked as a senior systems analyst for administrative systems for a major university before joining Companion Systems. Gloria Robertson, director of marketing and sales, previously worked for such firms as U.S. West and Prime Computer. In 1974, she received a BA in art history with a minor in marketing from a major university in the Northeast. A director of finance and accounting is being sought but is not in place.

McDonnell owns 40 percent of the equity in CSC. Projections indicate cash flows capable of providing an expected return of at least 60 percent to investors. Furthermore, expectations are that the venture could conduct an initial public offering in approximately three years.

COMPANION SYSTEMS ASSESSMENT

We have made a pass at scoring CSC's descriptive information in Figure 1. An item judged to be high in terms of potential attractiveness gets a 3; an average receives a 2 and a low is assigned a 1. After totaling each of the three columns, we calculate an overall total point score. Finally, an average score is computed by dividing the overall total points by 16. A maximum score of 48 (i.e., 16 items times 3) and an average score of 3.00 are possible. However, as previously stated, the VOS Indicator™ is designed to be a *relative* indicator of the venture's potential attractiveness.

In terms of the industry/market factor category, CSC gets a high score in market size potential, the venture's expected revenue growth rate, and the market share expected in three years. While at the time of this screening there were no known direct competitors, there are no specific barriers to entry; competition would be expected from several sources. We assign an average score to the entry barrier item. Of course, it is important to recognize that, owing to the subjectivity involved in the venture screening process, all evaluators may not come to the same conclusion. We are trying to convey how we believe venture investors, on average, might evaluate the CSC business opportunity proposal.

Turning to the pricing/profitability factor category, CSC gets a high mark in terms of expected gross margins. Both after-tax margins and asset intensity measures fall in the average category. However, since they are on the upper side of the average range, when taken together they produce an expected return on assets that falls in the high potential category.

CSC also receives very good ratings, based on the estimates provided, in terms of the financial/harvest factor category. CSC is expected to reach operating profit breakeven in less than two years; the rate of return on invested equity capital is expected to exceed 50 percent. Of course, venture investors would want to scrutinize the data underlying these estimates. An IPO potential in three years receives an average score, as does the fact that the CEO entrepreneur currently has a high minority stake in CSC.

The management team category also receives generally high marks. A high score is assigned to the experience/expertise item based on descriptive information provided. The functional areas item also receives a high score, although there is still some uncertainty about the coverage of the financial management area. Since flexibility/adaptability is difficult to assess directly, we assign an average score. Supporting arguments for at least an average score would be based on the wide range of job assignments that members of the management team have previously held. This suggests some prior need to be flexible and adaptable. We judge the entrepreneurial focus to be strong and thus give it a high score because of the aggressiveness and desire on the part of the management team to pursue the proposed business opportunity.

The VOS Indicator™ application to CSC in Figure 1 produces overall total points of 42 and an average score of 2.63, which falls in the high potential attractiveness range of 2.34 to 3.00. Also, there were ten high scores and zero low scores. As a result, the CSC scoring would suggest that further investigation of the business opportunity is probably worth pursuing and that venture investors might find an investment in the venture attractive relative to other possible venture investments.

Part 2

ORGANIZING AND OPERATING THE VENTURE

Chapter 3

ORGANIZING AND FINANCING A NEW VENTURE

PREVIOUSLY COVERED

In Chapter 2, we focused on moving from an idea to a business plan. For an idea to become a viable business venture, the entrepreneur must have a sound business model for how the idea will become a product or service for which customers will pay, profits will be realized, and free cash flows will be available to provide a return to the owners and investors, all within an acceptable time frame. We introduced qualitative and quantitative assessment tools and suggested that much of the assessment information could be the seed for the more formal and comprehensive business plan.

LOOKING AHEAD

Chapter 4 provides an introduction to basic accounting and financial statements, their relationships to one another, and their construction. Financial statements help us understand whether a venture is building or burning cash—a critical aspect of the venture's existence and survival. Spending more cash than one takes in from operations means that time must be spent raising external financing. We address the importance of cash and cash flow in two ways—through the statement of cash flows and in the analysis of operating breakeven.

CHAPTER LEARNING OBJECTIVES

In this chapter, we focus on organizing the venture, obtaining and protecting intellectual property, and financing in the early stage. Although an entrepreneur can change the legal form of the venture in the future, her initial choice should carefully consider tax effects, liability implications, and the amount of financial capital needed to begin operating the venture. Typically, entrepreneurs who possess and protect intellectual property increase the chances that their ventures will survive and create value. After completing this chapter, you will be able to:

1. Describe the proprietorship, partnership, and corporate forms of business organization

2. Identify the differentiating characteristics of a limited liability company (LLC)

3. Describe the benefits, risks, and basic tax aspects of various organizational forms

4. Discuss the use of patents and trade secrets to protect intellectual property

5. Discuss the use of trademarks and copyrights to protect intellectual property

6. Describe how confidential disclosure agreements and employment contracts are used to protect intellectual property rights

7. Explain how financing is obtained via financial bootstrapping and through business angels

8. Describe first-round financing sources

To reach the point when formal organization is appropriate, the venture idea should have passed an initial screening (and planning) stage. The enthusiasm and feedback from family, friends, and others provides much of the fuel needed to sustain the entrepreneur's drive. Success is certainly in view! Nonetheless, the arduous task of starting, growing, surviving, and realizing the venture's potential has only just begun. While it is easy to sit back and wish our students success on the road to their new ventures, we believe they expect us to prepare them to face the inevitable challenges. Our response is to set out useful descriptive information, financial methods, and tools to help them organize, formally launch, monitor progress, and set a reasonable course, while watching out for speed bumps.

3.1   PROGRESSING THROUGH THE VENTURE LIFE CYCLE

In Part 1, we introduced entrepreneurial ventures and focused on the development, or first stage, in a successful venture's life cycle. We stressed the importance of screening ideas for their business potential, preparing a business plan, and obtaining seed financing. As the venture progresses through the development stage, there may be occasions when the entrepreneur asks such questions as: "Should we continue with this design, change it, or hang it up altogether? How will our services be delivered? Is this really the best approach? Do we have enough to keep going?"

Part 2 of this book, which we now enter, focuses on the venture's formal launch, issues to be resolved during the startup stage, and the challenges to be overcome in what we term the survival stage—when the venture first experiences the rewards and ravages of commercializing its products and services. During the startup stage in Figure 3.1, the entrepreneur is concerned with choosing the initial organizational form, preparing (or at least understanding) the initial financial statements, and finding ways to obtain startup financing. At this time, the entrepreneur will face important decisions about whether there is a need to regroup, restructure, or even walk away from the venture.

If we assume that the decision is to go forward, the next challenge is the survival stage of Figure 3.1. Unfortunately, while the startup stage is difficult, getting through the survival stage is likely to age one even more rapidly. In this stage, the entrepreneur must monitor financial performance, project the venture's cash needs, and obtain first-round financing. This is usually a time when the venture is burning more money than operations can provide. Financial statements become an

FIGURE 3.1 Life Cycle Approach: Venture Operating and Financial Decisions

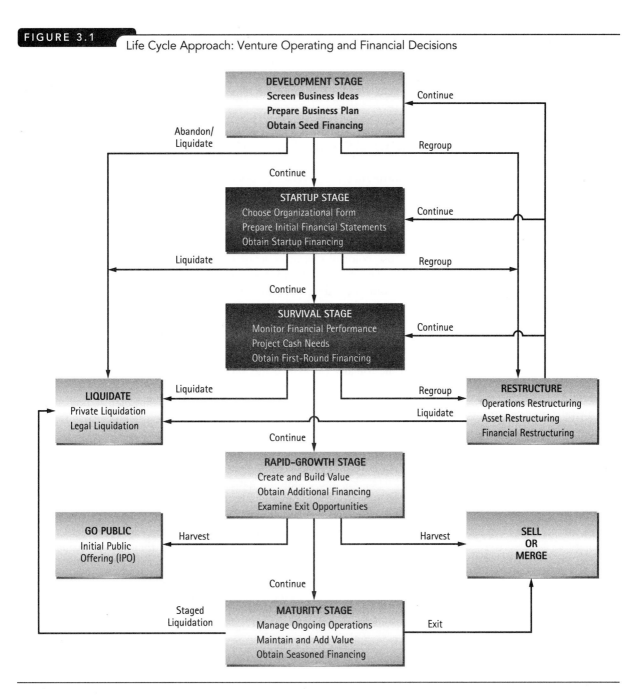

important external (as well as internal) communication device. The ability to obtain adequate financial capital is crucial to venture survival. Many ventures never make the critical jump to credibly communicating with the financial community; consequently, they do not get the necessary funding to continue the entrepreneurial dream.

CONCEPT CHECK

- What are the first three life cycle stages typically encountered by a successful entrepreneurial venture?

3.2   FORMS OF BUSINESS ORGANIZATION

Venture opportunities are diverse. Consider three examples.[1] First, suppose you have an idea for a new and different board game. You grew up playing Scrabble and Pictionary and now you have an idea for a board layout where, depending on which squares you land on, one of several card decks will be activated that requires either "left-brained" (quantitative) or "right-brained" (qualitative) activities. You plan to use colorful character icons that you will protect with trademarks. For reference purposes, we will call this venture idea the BrainGames Company.

Suppose your second venture idea is to manufacture and sell home safety products, including an escape ladder. The ladder will be lightweight, sturdy enough to support someone weighing 200 pounds, and folds down to the size of a small briefcase. You are considering taking a college-level product development course so that you can create a prototype. Once you have a viable prototype, you hope to file for any relevant trademarks and patents. We will call your second venture idea the EasyWayOut Company.

Your third idea involves making miniature devices that can be embedded in athletes' helmets for an unprecedented "up-close" view of the action. During a game, the devices will collect and transmit performance data in real time to a central computer. The computer will transform the raw data into new types of statistics and digital images. For example, you envision a gauge that records the force of a hit or tackle and a stamina gauge that records changes in the speed of a player's movements during a game. The technology is in the late stages of development, and you have applied for two patents. We will call this venture concept the Virtual SportsStats Company.

We explore questions faced by all new ventures as they move through their startup stages: What are the legal organizational forms available when forming a new venture? What factors lead to advantages of a particular form? What intellectual property is involved? What methods of protection are available? What are the available sources of early-stage financing?

The first question addresses legal forms of organization.[2] We specifically consider:

---

[1]   Unfortunately, these ideas are not new. Rather, they are already viable business ventures. Later in the chapter, we will identify the firms pursuing these ideas.

[2]   More detailed discussions of organizational legal issues for startups can be found in legal reference books such as Richard Harroch's *Start-Up Companies: Planning, Financing, and Operating the Successful Business* (New York: Law Journal Seminars-Press, 1993); and Jack Levin's *Structuring Venture Capital, Private Equity, and Entrepreneurial Transactions* (New York: Aspen Publishers, 1997). Both of these texts provide extensive discussion of the issues, and Harroch's text includes several "boilerplate" documents for the startup venture.

- Sole proprietorships
- Partnerships (general and limited)
- Corporations (regular and subchapter S)
- Limited liability companies[3]

Figure 3.2 provides a summary of financial, legal, and tax characteristics one should consider when structuring a new venture. More specifically, these characteristics are:

- Number of owners
- Ease of startup
- Investor liability
- Equity capital sources
- Firm life
- Liquidity of ownership
- Taxation

The first six characteristics are discussed in this section, and the tax implications of various organizational forms are presented in the next section.[4]

- Identify four general types of business organizations.

PROPRIETORSHIPS

A **proprietorship** is a business venture owned by an individual who is personally liable for the venture's debts and other liabilities. The owner or proprietor contributes equity capital and can contract, incur debt, sell products or provide services, and hire employees just like other businesses. A proprietor also has sole responsibility for venture decision making. The primary advantage of a proprietorship is that it allows an entrepreneur to conduct the full range of business activities with almost no organization expenses. In other words, as indicated in Figure 3.2, little time is required to organize a proprietorship, and the associated legal fees are low. The owner also determines the life of the proprietorship. For example, the proprietor can choose to close down or cease operating the venture at any time.

proprietorship
business venture owned by an individual who is personally liable for the venture's liabilities

---

[3] Other, less popular forms of business organizations include joint ventures (treated as general partnerships), joint venture corporations (incorporated joint ventures), syndicates and investment groups (treated as general partnerships unless incorporated), business (Massachusetts) trusts (an arrangement involving property transfer with aspects of a corporation and a limited partnership), incorporated and unincorporated cooperatives (treated like a partnership unless incorporated), and unincorporated associations (treatment depends on the state and the cause for legal action).

[4] For an alternative checklist approach to help in selecting the appropriate organizational form, see John Power and Richard Kolodny, "Initial Decision on Choice of Entity," in *Start-Up Companies: Planning, Financing and Operating the Successful Business*.

FIGURE 3.2   Business Organizational Forms and Selected Financial, Legal, and Tax Characteristics

ORGANIZATIONAL FORM	NUMBER OF OWNERS AND OWNER'S EASE OF STARTUP	INVESTOR LIABILITY	EQUITY CAPITAL SOURCES	FIRM LIFE AND LIQUIDITY OF OWNERSHIP	TAXATION
Proprietorship	One; little time and low legal costs	Unlimited	Owner	Life determined by owner; often difficult to transfer ownership	Personal tax rates
General partnership	Two or more; moderate time and legal costs	Unlimited (joint and several liability)	Partners, families, and friends	Life determined by partners; often difficult to transfer ownership	Personal tax rates
Limited partnership	One or more general and one or more limited partners; moderate time and legal costs	Limited partners' liability limited to their investments	General and limited partners	Life determined by general partner; often difficult to transfer ownership	Personal tax rates
Corporation	One or more, with no limit; long time and high legal costs	Limited to shareholders' investments	Venture investors and common shareholders	Unlimited life; usually easy to transfer ownership	Corporate taxation; dividends subject to personal tax rates
Subchapter S corporation	Fewer than 75 owners; long time and high legal costs	Limited to shareholders' investments	Venture investors and subchapter S investors	Unlimited life; often difficult to transfer ownership	Income flows to shareholders; taxed at personal tax rates
Limited liability company (LLC)	One or more, with no limit; long time and high legal costs	Limited to owners' membership interests	Venture investors and equity offerings to owners	Life set by owners; often difficult to transfer ownership	Income flows to owners; taxed at personal tax rates

unlimited liability
personal obligation to pay a venture's liabilities not covered by the venture's assets

One drawback of a proprietorship is that the personal financial risk is high because the proprietor has an **unlimited liability** or personal obligation to pay the venture's liabilities. In the event that the venture's debts or other obligations cannot be paid from the venture's assets, creditors have recourse to the proprietor's personal assets, including cash, bank accounts, ownership interests in other businesses, automobiles, and real estate. The proprietor of a failed venture with outstanding obligations may be forced into personal bankruptcy to protect personal assets from the venture's creditors.

Other limitations of the proprietorship form of business organization, as noted in Figure 3.2, relate to the fact that it is often difficult to transfer ownership, and capital sources are very limited. While the proprietor can close the venture at will, it is often difficult to find others who are willing to buy the business and keep it operating. For ventures requiring substantial equity capital, the proprietorship form of organization usually does not work well. In a proprietorship, the only source of equity capital is owner's funds.[5]

---

[5] Of course, there is still the potential for loans (debt capital) from friends and family.

In the last chapter, we identified entrepreneurial ventures as the rapid-growth and high-performance subset of all possible entrepreneurial firms. Many entrepreneurial firms that are not concentrating on rapid growth could benefit from being organized as proprietorships because little time and low legal costs are involved in starting the business, and external equity capital is not a priority. Entrepreneurial ventures, in contrast, will in most cases seek to grow at rates that will demand external financing. Because of the implied limitations on how money can be raised, they are less likely to remain organized as proprietorships, even if they start that way.

Rapidly growing ventures emphasizing value creation often incur substantial operating and financial risk to facilitate their growth. In response to these risks, they often desire to limit, when possible, the founders' and other investors' liability. This desire to limit investors' liability is another disadvantage of organizing as a proprietorship.

Returning to the three potential ventures, we can begin to consider the (dis)advantages of different organizational forms. Owing to relatively low production costs and initial sales, the BrainGames Company could be started with limited equity capital supplied by the owner, family, and friends. However, the owner might not wish to risk his personal wealth, beyond that invested in the venture. Initially, EasyWayOut Company and Virtual SportsStats Company are more likely to be capital intensive than the BrainGames Company. They may need financial capital beyond what the entrepreneur, family, and friends can provide. The need for large amounts of financial capital to finance growth, as well as the desire to protect the founder's personal assets, would suggest that neither the EasyWayOut Company nor the Virtual SportsStats Company would be likely to be formed—even initially—as a proprietorship.

CONCEPT CHECK

- What is the owner's liability in a proprietorship?

GENERAL AND LIMITED PARTNERSHIPS

Figure 3.2 shows the financial and legal characteristics of both general and limited partnerships and summarizes how partnerships compare with proprietorships. The term **partnership** refers to a *general* partnership, which is a business venture owned by two or more individuals, called partners, who are each personally liable for the venture's liabilities. Because there are multiple owners, a **partnership agreement** spells out how business decisions are to be made and how profits and losses will be shared. If the partnership agreement does not state otherwise, each general partner has complete managerial discretion over the conduct of business.

Much like proprietorships, equity capital sources for general partnerships are restricted to funds supplied by partners. The costs associated with forming a general partnership are usually moderate in terms of time and legal fees. The partners determine the partnership's life. If one or more partners decide to

partnership
business venture owned by two or more individuals who are jointly and personally liable for the venture's liabilities

partnership agreement
an agreement that spells out how business decisions are to be made and how profits and losses will be shared

transfer their ownership positions to others, the process may be a difficult one. All partners must agree to replace an existing partner with a new partner, and all partners must agree to a sale of a partnership.

joint liability
legal action treats all partners equally as a group

joint and several liability
subsets of partners can be the object of legal action related to the partnership

A general partner's personal financial liability for the venture's obligations mirrors that of the sole proprietor—unlimited. In cases of **joint liability**, legal actions must treat all partners as a group. If the relevant law allows subsets of partners to be objects of legal action related to the partnership, the partners have **joint and several liability**. Joint liability is the norm for partnership debt and contract obligations, although some states hold partners jointly and severally (separately) liable for these. If the conduct of partnership business has wrongfully harmed another party, partners are typically jointly and severally liable. Although a partner's personal liability cannot be altered by the partnership agreement, the agreement can spell out how partners can recover funds from each other.

The body of law normally governing partnerships is the Uniform Partnership Act (UPA).[6] In cases where the partnership agreement is silent, the UPA provides the precedence in general partnership law. Some provisions of the UPA include a set of default partner rights and duties, as shown in Figure 3.3. For example, general partners have a right to participate in profits but a duty to participate in losses. Partners have a right to participate fully in management of the partnership, and each partner is accountable as fiduciary for other partners.[7]

The UPA also specifies default cases in which individuals may be considered partners. When a nonpartner represents herself, or consents to have a partner represent her as a partner, she has the same liability to repay any credit extended on the basis of the representation through a concept called *partnership by estoppel*. The nonpartner and the partner consenting to the representation are estopped (forbidden) from denying liability. If all partners consented to the representation, then the partnership is jointly liable. Parties not otherwise properly organized may be a *deemed partnership*, in which the deemed partners face unlimited personal liability for venture obligations. Under the UPA, receiving a share of the profits can be sufficient to deem the recipient and the payer partners. Participating in profits and losses can result in a deemed partnership, irrespective of the terms used to describe the arrangement.

The UPA also specifies a principle known as *mutual agency*, which states that, even if the partnership agreement restricts a partner's authority, when the restricted partner acts outside the authority with a third party ignorant of the restriction, the partnership is nonetheless obligated. Of course, the restricted partner violating the partnership agreement may incur liability to the other partners for acting outside the partnership agreement. The UPA also specifies the triggering events (like death or incapacity of a partner) that automatically dissolve a

---

6   The UPA has been adopted with minor modifications by all states except Louisiana. It has also been adopted in the District of Columbia, Guam, and the U.S. Virgin Islands.

7   Basic types of violations of fiduciary duty include self-dealing, usurping a partnership business opportunity, competing with the partnership, failure to serve the partnership, taking secret profits, violating confidence, personal use of partnership property, and refusal to be accountable to other partners.

FIGURE 3.3

Rights and Duties of General Partners

RIGHTS	DUTIES
Participation in profits	Participation in losses
Full participation in management	Full liability for partnership obligations
Veto right on new partners	Provision of business information to partners
Reimbursement for expenses	Accountable as fiduciary for other partners
Eventual return of capital	Conformity to partnership agreement
Access to formal account of affairs	Care in transacting partnership business
Access to partnership books	

---

partnership. Partnerships can also be set up to dissolve at a time, or under conditions, specified in the partnership agreement. Under the UPA, each partner has the right to dissolve the partnership at any time, but partners can incur liability for breach of fiduciary duty if they force dissolution in a way that harms the partnership's interests.

In contrast to a general partnership, a **limited partnership** limits certain (limited) partners' liability for venture obligations to the amount paid for partnership interests. A limited partnership is a formal organization governed by state law and, unless the partnership strictly conforms to state restrictions, will be regarded as a general partnership. Structurally, at least one partner must be a general partner and face unlimited liability for firm obligations. This general partner makes the day-to-day business decisions while the limited partners are required, to a great extent, to be passive investors.[8] The formation of a limited partnership usually requires a formal filing with the governing authorities. Just as in a general partnership, it is a good idea to complete and execute an explicit and comprehensive partnership agreement when organizing a limited partnership. Forming a limited partnership usually takes a moderate amount of time and money.

The sources of equity capital for limited partnerships are the funds supplied by the general and limited partners. The total amount of equity funds needed by the limited partnership is typically committed "up front." Thus, growth ventures are not usually set up as limited partnerships. Rather, limited partnerships are often established to purchase income-producing real property when the purchase price is known in advance and operating expenses can be covered with operating income.

With the exception of Louisiana, every state has adopted a version of the Revised Uniform Limited Partnership Act (RULPA).[9] Management of a limited partnership resides with the general partner. Limited partners risk the loss of

limited partnership
certain partners' liabilities are limited to the amount of their equity capital contribution

---

[8] In many cases, the general partner can itself be an entity consisting of limited liability investors. Such a structure, though, requires careful formation and maintenance to avoid loss of the preferential tax treatment and limited liability.

[9] Some version of RULPA has been adopted by forty-nine states, the District of Columbia, and the U.S. Virgin Islands. For more information, see http://www.nccusl.org.

their limitation on liabilities if they become involved in control of the business. Under RULPA, limited partners are allowed to engage in the partnership matters listed in Figure 3.4 without risking their limited liability. RULPA also stipulates that a limited partner may be exposed to creditor liability if his name is used in the name of the partnership, and if the creditor does not know that he is a limited partner. Taking actions other than those listed in Figure 3.4 does not automatically result in a determination that the limited partner has exercised control over the firm and subjected himself to unlimited liability. The general partner has the same type of fiduciary duties toward limited partners as general partners toward one another. Limited partners generally have no fiduciary duties to one another or the general partners. They generally have the same right to access the firm's books, records, and accounting as general partners. Forming limited partnerships takes longer and usually involves legal expenses, including those involved in constructing a partnership agreement.

It is unlikely that the BrainGames, EasyWayOut, or Virtual SportsStats ventures would be organized as either general or limited partnerships. While it may

---

FIGURE 3.4   Permissible Limited Partner Activities (RULPA)

1. Being a contractor for or an agent or employee of the limited partnership or of a general partner or being an officer, director, or shareholder of a general partner that is a corporation

2. Consulting with and advising a general partner with respect to the business of the limited partnership

3. Acting as surety for the limited partnership or guaranteeing or assuming one or more specific obligations of the limited partnership

4. Taking any action required or permitted by law to bring or pursue a derivation action in the right of the limited partnership

5. Requesting or attending a meeting of partners

6. Proposing, approving, or disapproving, by voting or otherwise, one or more of the following matters:
   a. the dissolution and winding up of the limited partnership
   b. the sale, exchange, lease, mortgage, pledge, or other transfer of all or substantially all of the assets of the limited partnership
   c. the incurrence of indebtedness by the limited partnership other than in the ordinary course of its business
   d. a change in the nature of the business
   e. the admission or removal of a general partner
   f. a transaction involving an actual or potential conflict of interest between a general partner and the limited partnership or the limited partners
   g. an amendment to the partnership agreement or certificate of limited partnership
   h. matters related to the business of the limited partnership not otherwise enumerated in this list that the partnership agreement states in writing may be subject to the approval or disapproval of limited partners

7. Winding up the limited partnership in the absence of a general partner to do so

be possible for partners, families, and friends to provide the necessary financial capital (equity and debt) for BrainGames, the unlimited liability associated with a general partnership (say, if a child swallows one of the game's tokens) would likely be a major reason to pursue another form of business organization. Use of a limited partnership arrangement, while limiting the personal liability of limited partners, would not limit the liability of BrainGames' general partners. The need for substantial amounts of equity capital by EasyWayOut and Virtual Sports-Stats probably will preclude organizing as either a general or a limited partnership. Unlimited personal liability for all partners in a general partnership, and for the general partners in a limited partnership, would also be a drawback to organizing as a partnership.

CONCEPT CHECK

- How does a limited partnership differ from a general partnership?

CORPORATIONS

In the United States, business corporations are the dominant form of business organization. Figure 3.2 details some of the comparative financial and legal characteristics of corporations versus the other main forms of business organization. A **corporation** is a legal entity that separates the personal assets of the owners, called shareholders, from the assets of the business. In a more detailed definition, Chief Justice John Marshall stated:

> *A corporation is an artificial being, invisible, intangible, and existing only in the contemplation of law. Being the mere creature of the law, it possesses only those properties which the charter of its creation confers upon it, either expressly, or as incidental to its very existence. These are such as are supposed best calculated to effect the object for which it was created. Among the most important are immortality, and, if the expression may be allowed, individuality; properties by which a perpetual succession of many persons are considered the same, and may act as a single individual.*[10]

State statutes determine the organization and structure of corporations. Thus, one usually makes reference to the state when referring to the firm: "BCS, a Delaware corporation, announced quarterly earnings off 27 percent from expected." Owing to significant differences in the laws dealing with the governance and other aspects of a corporation, the state chosen for incorporation can be an important decision. Delaware is usually regarded as the favorite jurisdiction for incorporating.

As noted in Figure 3.2, corporations raise equity capital from their shareholders through common stock sales or offerings. Like individuals, corporations can own physical capital, borrow from others, and enter into contractual arrangements.

corporation
a legal entity that separates personal assets of the owners, called shareholders, from the assets of the business

---

[10] *Dartmouth College v. Woodward*, 4 Wheaton 518, 636 (1819).

limited liability
creditors can seize the corporation's assets but have no recourse against the shareholders' personal assets

Except in the rare circumstance of a court's "piercing the corporate veil," shareholders have limited liability for the corporation's obligations.[11] **Limited liability** means that creditors can seize the corporation's assets but have no recourse to the shareholders' personal assets if shareholders have not otherwise guaranteed the credit.[12] In contrast to the partnership form of organization, there is no general partner or other individual who retains unlimited liability for the corporation's obligations. The characteristics of a corporation, in addition to a separate standing under the law and limited liability, include the free transferability of shares not otherwise restricted by securities laws, a perpetual existence unless formed otherwise, and a centralized management.

corporate charter
legal document that establishes the corporation

articles of incorporation
basic legal declarations contained in the corporate charter

corporate bylaws
rules and procedures established to govern the corporation

The **corporate charter** is the legal document that establishes the corporation. The **articles of incorporation** are the basic legal declarations contained in the corporate charter. Figure 3.5 shows the usual minimal content of a corporation's articles. For example, each corporation must have a name and an office address, indicate its intended business activities, state the initial size and names of the board of directors, and provide the founders' names and addresses. The **corporate bylaws** are the rules and procedures established to govern the corporation. The bylaws indicate how the corporation will be managed, give the procedures for electing directors, and specify shareholder rights. The bylaws constrain the directors, officers, and shareholders and govern the corporation's internal management structure.

A board of directors, elected by the shareholders, controls a corporation. The board appoints corporate officers to run business operations. Directors and officers have a fiduciary duty to the corporation and its shareholders, not unlike the fiduciary duty a general partner owes other partners. Shareholders generally do not have a fiduciary duty to other shareholders, although there may be exceptions in closely held corporations or when a controlling shareholder is dealing with minority shareholders.

Figure 3.2 indicates that, relative to sole proprietorships and general and limited partnerships, the establishment of corporations usually requires more time to get started and that legal costs are relatively high. However, it is possible to reduce initial legal advising fees by using "boilerplate" examples of articles of incorporation that are widely available and easily modified. Although filing expenses vary from state to state, they include a cost for filing the charter documents, a franchise fee for the right to be a corporation, and other fees and charges associated with incorporation.

The ongoing maintenance costs of organizing as a corporation are generally higher than for the other forms of organization. Once a corporation forms, it must file financial and tax statements with both state and federal government statements. Franchise and other taxes are annual expenses. Director meetings

---

[11] Courts have pierced the corporate veil for failure to observe corporate formalities, domination and control of the corporation by a single shareholder, and failure to be properly capitalized. Failure to maintain separate books and failure to hold director and stockholder meetings are examples of dangerous disregard for corporate formalities.

[12] For small startup corporations, it is common practice for lenders to require major shareholders to cosign before loans are granted. In such instances, if the corporation's assets are inadequate to cover the debt claim, the lender can seize the cosigners' personal assets.

FIGURE 3.5 Articles Typically Required in the Articles of Incorporation

1. Corporation name and initial registered office address
2. Name of the initial registration agent who is served with legal papers on behalf of the corporation
3. Duration of the corporation (usually made perpetual)
4. Intended business activities
5. Share classes, structure of the classes, and authorized shares in each class
6. Indication of whether existing shareholders have a right to maintain their ownership portion in new shares issued
7. Initial size of the board of directors and the initial directors' names
8. Founders' (incorporators') names and addresses

---

must be held and minutes must be taken. Amendments to the articles or bylaws can introduce ongoing legal fees.

One special form of corporate organization is an S corporation (sometimes called a subchapter S corporation). "S corps" are named for the section of the tax code laying out the related requirements. An **S corporation** provides limited liability for its shareholders, while its income is taxed only at the personal level of its shareholders (no corporate taxes).[13] Also, as summarized in Figure 3.2, an S corporation must have fewer than seventy-five shareholders, and no shareholder can be another corporation. The need for more time to organize, and higher legal costs relative to proprietorships and partnerships, is characteristic of S corporations. Furthermore, because of the restriction on the number of shareholders, S corporations may find it more difficult to raise large sums of equity capital and to transfer ownership rights (relative to regular corporations).

Professional corporations (PCs) and service corporations (SCs) are corporate structures that states provide for professionals such as physicians, dentists, lawyers, and accountants. Members of a PC or SC must ordinarily be licensed professionals and are typically shielded only from liability related to contractual and other nonprofessional liability. They remain personally liable for their wrongful professional acts and those of their professional employees.[14]

The BrainGames, EasyWayOut, and Virtual SportsStats ventures all would be good candidates for organizing as corporations. Limiting outside investors' liabilities to their business investments in these ventures would be an important objective and would justify the time and costs required to organize as corporations. The ability to attract large amounts of equity capital and the relative ease of transferring ownership rights suggest additional possible benefits of organizing as corporations. If, however, the need for equity capital is not large and the ease of

S corporation
corporate form of organization that provides limited liability for shareholders; plus, corporate income is taxed as personal income to the shareholders

---

[13] We discuss taxation of the various types of business organizations in the next section.

[14] It is important to note that limited liability usually refers to the status of passive investors in a business. Those who actively engage in wrongful business practice will, in most cases, incur personal liability for their acts, irrespective of their liabilities as investors.

transferring ownership is not that important, one or more of these ventures might opt to organize as a corporation and limit the number of investors to qualify for the IRS's subchapter S status.

CONCEPT CHECK

• What is meant by an S corporation?

LIMITED LIABILITY COMPANIES (LLCs)

limited liability company (LLC)
a company owned by shareholders with limited liability; its earnings are taxed at the personal income tax rates of the shareholders

A **limited liability company (LLC)** provides the owners with limited liability (like a corporation) and passes its income before taxes through to the owners (in a similar manner to a partnership or S corp). Thus, as summarized in Figure 3.2, the LLC combines some of the benefits of both the corporate and the partnership forms of business organization in a manner similar to that for subchapter S corporations. The first LLC was formed in Wyoming in 1977, under special-interest legislation for Hamilton Brothers Oil Company. Since then, all states have passed LLC statutes. The owners of an LLC are called members and are shielded from LLC liability except for their individual acts in connection with the LLC business. An LLC is like a limited partnership with no general partner.[15]

Forming an LLC requires organizational time and legal costs roughly comparable to those of organizing as a corporation. An LLC typically requires the preparation of the following two documents. The *certificate of formation* (Delaware) or the *articles of organization* (California) lay out the LLC's name, address, a formal agent for receiving legal documents, the duration of the firm, and whether members or their appointees will govern the LLC. The *operating agreement* plays the role of the partnership agreement in specifying in more detail how the LLC will be governed, the financial obligations of members, the distribution of profits and losses, and other organizational details. Boilerplates for organizing an LLC are widely available, but competent legal advice is critical in the decision to form an LLC. As these structures are relatively new, the courts are still working out various areas of law related to LLCs, including how they are treated in states other than their formation state.

Equity capital is obtained through equity offerings to owners or members. The life of the LLC is determined by the owners and is generally set for a fixed number of years, in contrast to the unlimited life typical of a corporation. It can be difficult to transfer ownership in an LLC because the consent of the owners or members is required. A major potential advantage of the LLC organization structure, as we will discuss in the next section, relates to the passing through of the LLC's pretax income to the owners who, of course, then will be required to pay taxes at their personal income tax rates on the income received.

---

[15] A limited liability partnership (LLP) is a related but distinct structure, also formed by state law, that is normally affiliated with the provision of professional services. As it is not a common organizational form for entrepreneurial ventures, we do not consider it further.

It is possible that the BrainGames, EasyWayOut, and Virtual SportsStats ventures might choose to organize as limited liability companies, particularly if they also give consideration to organizing as subchapter S corporations. Each venture's decision would undoubtedly be affected by the trade-off between the tax advantages of an LLC and the unlimited life, ease of obtaining additional equity capital, and ease of transferring ownership rights in a regular corporation.

CONCEPT CHECK

- What is the owner's liability in a limited liability company?

3.3   CHOOSING THE FORM OF ORGANIZATION: TAX AND OTHER CONSIDERATIONS

A regular corporation (also known as a C corporation) is taxed as an entity separate from the shareholders who receive payments from the corporation's profits. The corporation pays taxes at the relevant corporate tax rate. Upon receiving payments out of profits, called dividends, shareholders pay an additional layer of taxes at the relevant personal tax rate. C corporation losses accumulate at the corporate level and cannot be passed through to investors to help lower their personal tax bills. The double taxation and the inability to pass losses through put the corporation at a distinct tax disadvantage relative to other organizational forms. Figure 3.2 provides a summary comparison of some of the taxation differences across the various major forms of business organizations.

Figure 3.6 shows the 2007 federal marginal income tax rates relating to both personal and corporate taxable income. Proprietorships and partnerships would be taxed at the personal tax rate, which is likely to be either the rate filing as "single" or that as "married filing jointly." Notice that personal income tax rates increased steadily from 10 up to 35 percent in 2007. Personal income tax rates in the United States are said to be *progressive tax rates* because the percentage of income paid in taxes increases as the dollar amount of income increases. The U.S. corporate tax rate also is progressive, up to a limit. Based on 2006 tax rate schedules, the marginal tax rate increased from 15 to 39 percent for taxable income up to $335,000. For larger amounts of taxable income, the corporate marginal tax rate was 34, 35, or 38 percent.

Let's illustrate the tax liability for a corporation with a taxable income of $100,000.[16] Based on Figure 3.6, the *marginal tax rate*, which is the rate paid on the last dollar of income, would be 34 percent. The *average tax rate* would be

---

[16]   For simplicity, we are ignoring the standard deductions and exemptions that would apply if the amounts represented total annual incomes.

FIGURE 3.6

2007 Personal and Corporate Federal Income Tax Rates

PERSONAL INCOME TAXES

A. MARRIED FILING JOINTLY		B. SINGLE	
TAXABLE INCOME	MARGINAL TAX RATE	TAXABLE INCOME	MARGINAL TAX RATE
$1–15,650	10.0%	$1–7,825	10.0%
15,651–63,700	15.0	7,826–31,850	15.0
63,701–128,500	25.0	31,851–77,100	25.0
128,501–195,850	28.0	77,101–160,850	28.0
195,851–349,700	33.0	160,851–349,700	33.0
Over 349,700	35.0	Over 349,700	35.0

CORPORATE INCOME TAXES

TAXABLE INCOME	MARGINAL TAX RATE
$1–50,000	15.0%
50,001–75,000	25.0
75,001–100,000	34.0
100,001–335,000	39.0
335,001–10,000,000	34.0
10,000,001–15,000,000	35.0
15,000,001–18,333,333	38.0
Over 18,333,333	35.0

determined as the total tax liability divided by the dollar amount of taxable income as follows:

CORPORATE MARGINAL TAX RATE	×	CORPORATE TAXABLE INCOME	=	CORPORATE AMOUNT OF TAXES
.15	×	$ 50,000	=	$ 7,500
.25	×	25,000	=	6,250
.34	×	25,000	=	8,500
		$100,000		$22,250

Dividing the $22,250 in taxes by the $100,000 of taxable income gives an average tax rate of 22.3 percent.

The difference between the $100,000 of taxable income and the $22,250 in income taxes results in an after-tax corporate profit of $77,750. If all this profit were then paid out to a shareholder, with no other personal income, with a filing status of married filing jointly, the additional taxes paid would be:

PERSONAL MARGINAL TAX RATE	×	PERSONAL TAXABLE INCOME	=	PERSONAL AMOUNT OF TAXES
.10	×	$15,650	=	$ 1,565.00
.15	×	48,050	=	7,207.50
.25	×	14,050	=	3,512.50
		$77,750		$12,285.00

Dividing the $12,285.50 in taxes by $77,750 of personal taxable income gives an average tax rate of 15.8 percent. This compares with a personal marginal tax rate of 25 percent.

Under this arrangement, the total federal income taxes paid were $34,535 ($22,250 + $12,285), which, owing to double taxation, results in an average rate of 34.5 percent on the $100,000 of original taxable income. Two layers of taxation can impose a severe tax penalty for entrepreneurs and others who start their own businesses.

Partnerships are treated with *pass-through taxation.* That is, the profits and losses of the enterprise pass directly through to the owners on the basis specified in the partnership agreement. For profits, there is only one layer of taxation at the personal level. For losses, there is an opportunity for partners to immediately lower their personal taxes.[17]

As we mentioned before, the U.S. Internal Revenue Service has a category for closely held corporations that allows them to be taxed on a pass-through basis in a manner similar to a partnership. Qualification for this status, known as an S corporation, is based on three requirements:

1. The corporation cannot have more than seventy-five shareholders all of whom are individuals (other than nonresident aliens) or certain trusts, estates, or tax-exempt organizations.
2. The corporation can have only one class of equity, although certain differences in voting rights and certain option arrangements are allowed.
3. The corporation generally cannot own 80 percent or more of another corporation, except under certain conditions.

Other than how they are taxed and these restrictions, S corporations are the same as C corporations. A firm makes an S corporation election by filing Form 2553 with the IRS.

The restriction on who can be a shareholder in an S corporation will typically interfere with the ability to raise capital from many professionally managed investment funds (like venture capital funds) unless the investment is creatively structured. For example, if a venture capital fund is organized as a partnership, it cannot hold S corporation stock, since it is not an individual. Suppose it agrees to invest in debt that can be converted into equity to avoid being a current holder of S corporation equity. Such a structure is possible under restrictive treasury regulations. However, if the venture fund supplies large amounts of debt capital in this manner, the IRS, under its excessive debt provisions, can treat the debt as equity and disqualify the firm as an S corporation.

In a like manner to a partnership or an S corporation, a limited liability company's profits and losses are passed through to its members. Unlike an S corporation, there is no requirement that members be individuals and no restriction on the number of members. Under the IRS's current "check-the-box" protocol (effective January 1, 1997), a newly formed LLC that is not publicly traded will

---

[17] The ability for limited partners to use losses passed through will be restricted by, among other things, IRS limits on passive activity losses.

be taxed like a partnership unless the LLC affirmatively elects to be taxed as a corporation. State tax treatment of an LLC for the states in which the LLC will do business should be verified prior to organizing as a limited liability company. LLCs can easily accommodate venture capital investments, as long as investors in the venture capital funds are not otherwise restricted from beneficial ownership in an LLC.[18] However, the structure of wage taxation for owners who work for an LLC, and the specific state's tax and fee structures for LLCs (and the alternatives being considered), should be determined. There is no substitute for good legal advice in making this decision for your specific state.

Why should you consider incorporating when LLCs are available? Again, it is important to check the specific conditions of the state in which you will organize. Even with all of those factors weighing in, it may still "pay" to organize as a C corporation. Ultimately, the successful publicly traded entrepreneurial firm almost always ends up with a traditional C corporation structure and will be subject to corporate and personal taxation. For businesses in which investors cannot immediately use loss pass-throughs, the tax cost of incorporating is not great since there is no corporate tax bill when operating at a loss. The ability to maneuver financially, on the other hand, is substantial, and, unlike other organizational forms, no major organizational restructuring is required to raise funds in the public markets. The corporate form also facilitates a tax-free merger into another entity. Consequently, when investors plan to cash in on their success through an initial public offering or a merger, it is usually much easier if the firm is already organized as a corporation. Exiting a partnership or proprietorship may result in dissolving the firm. Exiting an LLC can also prove difficult unless the LLC incorporates first. When organizing, the entrepreneur should consider whether it is best to begin with the form ultimately desired or start with one form and plan for the move to another at the appropriate time.

Although we can't say which or how many of the presented factors were considered when choosing a form of business organization by the three companies that we have been following, we can identify the ventures and report their decisions. BrainGames is actually the Cranium venture founded in 1997 as a corporation. Cranium is also the name of the board game it makes and sells that requires the use of both the left and right sides of the brain. EasyWayOut is the X-It Products venture founded in 1997 as a limited liability company. The company specializes in producing and selling home safety products, including an escape ladder that folds up for easy storage and a fire extinguisher approximately the size of a can of hair spray. The Virtual SportsStats venture is the Trakus venture that was formed as a corporation in 1997. The company specializes in producing miniature devices that are embedded in athletes' helmets and provide real-time statistics such as the force of a tackle or the stamina of a player throughout a game.[19]

---

[18] There is some concern that tax-exempt investors may not be able to invest in venture capital partnerships that subsequently invest in LLCs owing to tax restrictions placed on the tax-exempt investors.

[19] We return to these three ventures when we discuss early-stage financing in the last section of the chapter.

- How is the income earned by regular corporations taxed differently from the income earned by LLCs?

3.4 INTELLECTUAL PROPERTY

Valuable property may take the form of physical assets (bricks and mortar, equipment, inventories, etc.), intangible assets, and human capital. Intangible assets and human capital often are the most important assets held by new ventures. **Intellectual property** refers to a venture's intangible assets and human capital (knowledge in particular). An important subset of intellectual property is the inventions and innovations that can be protected from being freely used or copied by others. Some intangible assets can be protected through patents, trade secrets, trademarks, or copyrights. Intellectual property rights provide an economic incentive for innovation. For example, the decision to spend large amounts on research and development (R&D) often can be justified only if the R&D output can be protected from use by others for a period of time.

As the venture progresses from idea to a viable business opportunity in its startup stage, it is important to identify the venture's valuable intellectual property and protect it wherever possible. In addition to seeking legal protection for an idea or invention, you may find it important to use nondisclosure agreements (NDAs) when seeking new investors or when working with suppliers and, in some cases, potential customers. You may also want to protect your intellectual property with employment contracts (and "noncompete clauses") when hiring key employees.

Intellectual property law is quite complex. It is important to seek legal help when trying to protect your intellectual property. We provide only a basic overview of how intellectual property can be protected.[20]

intellectual property
a venture's intangible assets and human capital, including inventions that can be protected from being freely used or copied by others

PROTECTING VALUABLE INTANGIBLE ASSETS

Intellectual property rights are governed by national laws. Each country establishes its own set of rules to govern intellectual property. This lack of standardized international laws can result in conflicts between governments and companies operating in different countries. Our emphasis is on characteristics of U.S. intellectual property rights. Of course, if you or your competitors are contemplating operating

---

[20] For a more comprehensive overview of intellectual property laws and forms of protection, see Joseph S. Iandiorio, "Intellectual Property," in William D. Bygrave and Andrew Zacharakis, eds., *The Portable MBA in Entrepreneurship*, 3rd ed. (New York: John Wiley & Sons, 2003). Also see Robert D. Door and Christopher H. Munch, *Protecting Trade Secrets, Patents, Copyrights and Trademarks* (New York: John Wiley & Sons, 1990); and Kevin G. Rivette and David Kline, *Rembrandts in the Attic: Unlocking the Hidden Value of Patents* (Boston: Harvard Business School Press, 1999).

in a foreign country, you should explore whether your intellectual property is protected in that country.[21]

WHAT KINDS OF INTELLECTUAL PROPERTY CAN BE PROTECTED?

Examples include a new product, service, or process. You may also be able to protect a new design, package, or marketing promotion. Once you have developed a new idea or business opportunity, the next step is to determine whether and how it might be protected.[22] Four forms of protection, which may be formally recorded as intangible assets for accounting purposes, are available:

- Patents
- Trade secrets
- Trademarks
- Copyrights

An additional form of intellectual property protection was created under the Semiconductor Chip Protection Act in 1984 because of widespread piracy. A "maskwork" (i.e., the three-dimensional design of multilayered chips) can be registered with the U.S. Copyright Office. The owner of a maskwork has the exclusive right to the manufacture of the work.

Patents

patents
intellectual property rights granted for inventions that are useful, novel, and nonobvious

Patents are intellectual property rights granted for inventions that are useful, novel, and nonobvious. The U.S. Patent and Trademark Office grants patents. The application process typically requires reviews and possible changes that can take months, and sometimes even years, to complete. Application fees and legal expenses can run from a few thousand dollars to over $100,000. When a patent expires, the invention passes into the public domain; then anyone can use, make, or sell the invention. Patent law is very complex. If you wish to pursue obtaining a patent, you will most likely need to hire a lawyer who specializes in patent applications.

There are four kinds of patents:

- Utility
- Design

---

[21]   A number of law firms specialize in intellectual property services both domestically and internationally. Front-end costs to register intellectual property in other countries can be high, as can the legal costs of trying to enforce protections internationally. For example, intellectual property protection in Japan is very expensive, while intellectual property rights are only beginning to be considered important in China.

[22]   Intellectual assets should be viewed very broadly and could include customer information, business models, and homegrown processes. Entrepreneurial ventures should attempt to take advantage of all their intellectual assets. For example, see Leigh Buchanan, "Find It. Use It. Here's How to Identify Those Assets and Turn Them into New Business," *Inc.*, May 2007, pp. 93–98. Of course, there are also many counterfeiters who ignore intellectual property rights. One result is the effort to develop increasingly sophisticated methods to thwart counterfeiters. For example, see Eric Schine, "Faking Out the Fakers," *Business Week*, June 4, 2007, pp. 76–80.

- Plant
- Business method

Utility patents cover most inventions pertaining to new products, services, and processes. Most entrepreneurs, when applying for a patent, seek a utility patent. *Design* patents protect the ornamental designs of products. These patents cover the appearances of items such as sports uniforms, electronic products, and automobiles.[23] They are generally easier and less expensive to obtain than are utility patents and provide protection for a maximum of fourteen years. *Plant* patents protect discoveries of asexual reproduction methods of new plant varieties. Included are biotechnically engineered plants that are more weather resistant and higher yielding. Plant patents also cover animal cloning and various human engineering–related efforts.

Business method patents protect a specific way of doing business and the underlying computer codes, programs, and technology. Recent efforts to computerize basic electronic commerce functions, including electronic auctions, video streaming, Web browsing, and so on, have led to record levels of patent applications, an excessive workload for the U.S. patent granting authority, and rapidly growing numbers of lawsuits. For example, some technology licensing firms have acquired large numbers of Internet and electronic commerce business method patents and demand licensing fees from smaller e-commerce firms that cannot afford court defenses.[24] One way to invalidate a patent is to find *prior art* in the form of publicly available documentation relating to a disputed patent.

Utility patents cover mechanical or general inventions, chemical inventions, and electrical inventions. For example, the "Furby" mechanical animal toy, the craze of 1998, was patented. Actually, the words "patent pending" were used on the initial Furbys, which means only that a patent application had been filed. Many consumer and household products also are patented as mechanical or general inventions. Examples of chemical inventions include prescription drugs and new processes or methods for making plastics. Computer software can be patented. Examples include an application program to run an automated production plant and software to provide financial management systems for financial institutions. Most software products, however, such as the Microsoft® Office series, are copyrighted, rather than patented.

Historically, the life of a U.S. utility patent was set at seventeen years from the date when the patent was issued. However, on June 8, 1995, the life of a utility patent was changed to twenty years from the date of the patent application.

What Is the Process for Applying for a Utility Patent?

A new idea by itself cannot be patented. Rather, the idea must be part of an invention that has a physical form, such as a product. The physical form also can exist as a sequence of steps contained in a process or the delivery of a service.

---

[23] An example of a possible design patent infringement was Hain Celestial Group's contention that a rival was using a copycat tea box design. See Susan Decker, "Hain's Celestial Seasonings Sues over Tea Box Design," *Bloomberg News* and *Daily Camera*, October 29, 2002, p. E1.

[24] For example, see Kris Frieswick, "License to Steal?" *CFO*, September 2001, pp. 89–91; and Paul Davidson, "Patents Out of Control?" *USA Today*, January 13, 2004, pp. 1B–2B.

Once an invention has been conceived, you or a registered patent attorney (on your behalf) prepares a patent application. The application then is filed in the U.S. Patent and Trademark Office (PTO). Beginning on June 8, 1995, inventors were permitted to file a provisional patent application. Small entities (individuals, firms with fewer than 500 employees, and universities) are charged a lower filing fee relative to larger entities. Filing dates can be established more quickly and at lower costs since there are fewer requirements compared to the requirements in a regular patent application. Once the provisional patent application has been filed, the inventor is permitted to use the term "patent pending" on the invention. However, it is important to recognize that using the term "patent pending" does not convey any rights or protection to the inventor. Patent rights and protection occur only when a patent is issued.

A provisional patent application requires an invention title and the inventor's name, residence, and address for correspondence. There must be a clearly written description of the invention and drawings to help explain how the invention may be used. The invention's description should allow a "person skilled in the art of the invention's area" to use or practice the invention. The provisional patent application has a life of only twelve months and will be abandoned unless a regular patent application is filed within the yearlong period. In addition to a precise written description of the invention and detailed drawings of how the invention works, the regular patent application requires one or more claims justifying why the invention should be patented. Furthermore, the regular application requires that the inventor indicate the best use or method of practicing or carrying out the invention. An effort to disguise from others the best use of the invention by stressing a secondary use will render any resulting patent invalid.

Why Might Your Patent Application Be Rejected?

The regular patent application requires that your invention be useful. For example, a system of interconnected gears that do nothing is not patentable because it is not useful. Likewise, an inoperable device or machine is not patentable because it lacks utility. The regular patent application must contain one or more claims that the invention is novel and nonobvious. "Novel" means that the proposed invention was not previously produced, described in a publication, or patented. The starting point of any patent application is usually a search of prior patents for the same or similar inventions. The question of whether an invention is obvious depends in part on subjective interpretation. The test is whether the invention would be obvious to a person with ordinary skills in the art of the invention's area or subject. In essence, the test is whether the invention differs enough from prior knowledge to make it nonobvious. An invention that is novel but obvious is not patentable.

Also, the timing of the patent application may render your application unpatentable. The application must be filed within one year of its introduction to the public. This includes offering the invention for sale or even describing the invention in a magazine or in other printed forms that are available to the public. However, because of the difficulty of administering this one-year grace period, it is likely that, in the future, patent law will require that the patent application be filed before any public disclosure or use takes place.

What Does Having a Patent Actually Do for the Inventor?

In a tongue-in-cheek sense, having a patent gives the inventor a license to sue. The government does not enforce your rights. If you are an inventor with a patent, the burden of enforcing the patent is yours. However, legal enforcement is not necessarily easy; records indicate that over one-half of patent infringement suits taken to court are not upheld on behalf of the inventor. Also, others can possibly "design around" your patent. Some argue that the ability to design around an invention is actually aided by the fact that the patent application requires the inventor to disclose so much information about the invention. Please note that we are not suggesting that you refrain from seeking patent protection for your inventions. Rather, we point out that enforcing your patent rights can be costly. Of course, for very valuable inventions, the cost of enforcing patents may be quite worthwhile.

CONCEPT CHECK

- What is a patent?

Trade Secrets

Trade secrets are intellectual property rights in the form of inventions and information (e.g., formulas, processes, customer lists, etc.) not generally known to others. Trade secrets law can, in some circumstances, provide some protection for inventions that have not been patented. Avoiding the detailed disclosure that must be filed with the U.S. Patent and Trademark Office is a common reason that inventors opt out of patent "protection." Another reason for opting out is to try to shield the intellectual property beyond the twenty years granted under a patent. There are no time restrictions on trade secrets. As a classic example, the recipe for Coca-Cola has been a trade secret for more than one hundred years.

What are the possible drawbacks of relying on trade secrets law? In contrast to the patent application process, there is no formal procedure for obtaining protection for an invention or information as a trade secret. Rather, protection under trade secrets law is established by the characteristics of the secret and efforts to protect it. An important point to remember is that an independent replication of the products or services that were previously trade secrets leaves the originator with no legal recourse (if the replication effort is truly independent).

What steps should be taken to protect a trade secret? An ongoing protection program should be in place. Employees and others (consultants, suppliers, etc.) should sign nondisclosure agreements to discourage them from using or disclosing the trade secret. Computer systems, hard-copy files, and other sources containing trade secret information should be secured from third-party access and from employees who have not been cleared. For example, the formula for Coca-Cola is kept in a bank vault in Atlanta and, at any point in time, only a few top executives actually know the secret.

Trade secret misappropriations frequently involve ex-employees. While employed, an employee typically learns a lot about the venture's business and

trade secrets
intellectual property rights in the form of inventions and information, not generally known to others, that convey economic advantages to the holders

perhaps even its trade secrets. Certainly, the acquisition of experience and knowledge makes the ex-employee more valuable to another firm. At issue, however, is whether the employee exits with, and makes use of, his former firm's trade secrets. Some situations are fairly clear. For example, your customer list is likely to be a trade secret and worthy of protection. Thus, you will want to make sure that a sales representative who leaves your firm will not take your customer list with her. Of course, this is easier said than done; proving misappropriations in court may be very costly. Furthermore, knowing that an ex-employee knows your trade secrets does not mean that the knowledge will be conveyed or used by a new employer. Sometimes you don't know until after the fact.[25]

Most countries recognize that individuals and organizations have a contractual right to protect confidential information even though they may not have their own trade secrets laws. In instances when you possess an important trade secret and are contemplating doing business in a foreign country, you may want to explore whether your trade secret may be at risk. For example, Coca-Cola chose not to produce in India when the Indian government required disclosure of the secret formula as a condition for manufacturing in India.

CONCEPT CHECK

- What are trade secrets?

Trademarks

trademarks
intellectual property rights that allow firms to differentiate their products and services through the use of unique marks

Trademarks are intellectual property rights that allow firms to differentiate their products and services through the use of unique marks. These allow consumers easily to identify the source and quality of the products and services. This general definition of trademarks represents an umbrella encompassing four types of marks, which are:

- Trademarks
- Service marks
- Collective marks
- Certification marks

Most trademarks take the form of names, words, or graphic designs. However, trademarks also can be obtained on the shape of packages, colors, odors, and sounds. Technically, the term *trademark* refers only to words, symbols, shapes, and similar items associated with products. *Service marks* refer to services like those provided by Blue Cross/Blue Shield. *Collective marks* cover memberships in groups (e.g., a sorority or a labor union). *Certification marks* provide indications of quality (e.g., the Underwriter's Laboratory seal on electrical appliances).

---

[25] One example of a major trade secrets lawsuit involved Volkswagen (VW) AG and General Motors (GM) Corporation. Volkswagen hired a General Motors director of purchasing and seven other GM employees who supposedly took GM trade secrets with them to VW. Volkswagen agreed to pay $100 million to GM to settle a lawsuit by GM that VW stole its trade secrets when VW hired the GM employees.

For many firms, trademarks are one of the most valuable forms of intellectual property. For example, General Electric's GE trademark may be worth more than the combined value of GE's underlying patents and trade secrets. The value of a new venture's intangible assets, in the form of its trademark, rises rapidly as the venture succeeds. Baskin-Robbins ice cream and Dell computers are examples of recent entrepreneurial success stories. Many ventures and other organizations vigorously defend their trademarks in the courts.[26]

An interesting type of trademark that has grown rapidly in recent years is the registered domain name. The dot-com collapse of the early 2000s reintroduced many previously registered domain names. The market for buying and selling domain names, while still active, has cooled considerably. Many domain names have changed ownership at relatively low prices, at least compared to those observed during the registration scramble of the dot-com era. The domain-name business, however, is probably here to stay. Having a popular Web site involving dollars-per-eyeball ads or pay-per-click routing to other Web sites can still bring in sizable revenues.[27] This entire industry is enabled by the private-sector registration and legal-sector protection of domain names and rights, through what is really the e-commerce extension of the more traditional creation and preservation of trademarks and service marks.

What Should You Consider When Deciding Whether to Claim a Trademark?

The mark should not describe the product since competitors can use the same descriptive term, which means that you cannot get exclusive rights. Rather, your trademark should be suggestive of the product or line of products; for example, "Healthy Choice" is used to refer to a specific line of prepared foods. Before you use a specific trademark, it is important to complete a search to make sure that no one else is using the same or similar trademark. If no search is done, you could end up with a costly situation both in terms of confusion and in terms of legal expenses.

How Do You Obtain or Disclose a Trademark?

There is no formal government procedure for establishing a trademark. Rather, ownership is acquired by being first to use the mark on products. Your rights to a trademark are grounded in common law. You are entitled to keep the trademark so long as you keep using it. A trademark is considered to be abandoned if not used for three years. A trademark also can be lost if the mark becomes a generic term or label. Classic examples of lost trademarks include "aspirin" and

---

[26] For example, the National Football League (NFL) filed a suit against the Coors Brewing Company contending that the firm's effort to promote Coors Light as the "Official Beer of NFL Players" was illegal. The NFL suit claims that the Coors claim was in violation of the NFL's exclusive trademark rights. See "NFL Files Suit Against Coors over Marketing Campaign," Associated Press, June 26, 1999. Another example is the trademarking battle between a woman who owns a ceramics studio named "You're Fired!" and Donald Trump's use of the slogan in the TV show *The Apprentice*. See "Trump in Battle for 'You're Fired!'" http://money.cnn.com/204/03/31/news/midcaps/trump_copyright/index.htm.

[27] For example, see Paul Sloan, "The Man Who Owns the Internet," *Business 2.0*, June 2007, pp. 69–76.

"cellophane." Many trademarks in the form of words or phrases are accompanied by the designation™.

How Do You Register a Trademark?

A trademark may be registered in individual states or with the U.S. Patent and Trademark Office. Federal registration is preferred if you sell your product in more than one state because federal registration applies to all fifty states. For example, if you register your trademark in two states and someone else then registers the same trademark at the federal level, the other person has a valid trademark claim in the other forty-eight states. Federally registered trademarks must be renewed every ten years, even though your rights to the trademark will last as long as you use the trademark. Products with federally registered trademarks show the trademark accompanied by ®. Today, a federal application to register a trademark can be filed before products with the mark are even being sold. Actual use must be shown within six months. Of course, the advantage of filing early ensures your right to the trademark. While a patent can be sold separately from other assets, a trademark is typically transferred along with the sale of a venture as part of the venture's intangible assets, recorded for accounting purposes as goodwill.

CONCEPT CHECK

- What are trademarks?

Copyrights

copyrights
intellectual property rights to writings in printed and electronically stored forms

Copyrights are intellectual property rights to printed and/or electronically stored "writings." The term "writings" is broadly construed. Traditionally, copyrights are associated with books, magazine and journal articles, manuals, and catalogs. Music CDs, movie films, software programs, and databases also can be copyrighted. In a broad sense, copyright law protects the form of expression of an idea, not just words. A copyright covers the life of the author plus at least fifty years thereafter.

How do you establish a copyright? The traditional way is to publish your book or other work accompanied by a copyright notice in the form of the word "Copyright" or the symbol ©. The year when your work was first published and the owner of the copyright should be clearly identified. Many authors do not retain the copyrights to their works. Rather, an author's rights are transferred to the publishing company in lieu of some form of royalty agreement relating to sales of the book.

Today, the copyright notice is not needed to protect published works. The simple fact that a work was "created" is enough to provide copyright protection. However, it is recommended that copyright notice be placed on works deemed to be valuable. You may register your copyright with the U.S. Copyright Office by submitting your work, along with the required forms and fees. A registered copyright provides for an amount of statutory damages that can be recovered without proof of actual damages.

CONCEPT
CHECK

- What are copyrights?

OTHER METHODS FOR PROTECTING INTELLECTUAL PROPERTY RIGHTS

During a new venture's development and startup stages, maintaining confidentiality can be important. This is particularly true during the period before intellectual property protection can be sought in the form of patents, trade secrets, or copyrights. Confidential disclosure agreements and employee contracts are two ways to set the tone for protecting intellectual property rights.

Confidential Disclosure Agreements (Nondisclosure Agreements)

Confidential disclosure agreements are documents used to protect an idea or other forms of intellectual property when disclosed to another individual or organization. For example, in order to launch the venture, you might need to seek funds from potential investors. Your efforts could include building a prototype product for which no patent has been established. Alternatively, your venture might be early in its startup stage and need a supplier to produce important components for your new-but-unpatented invention. A potential large customer could ask for test samples of your new unpatented product. You might seek the advice of a consultant on how to develop your idea or how to market your new product. In each of these instances, others could take your idea or copy your products and make the products themselves. A confidential disclosure agreement or nondisclosure agreement (NDA) will warn those tempted to do so of the potential legal costs.

What should be included in your confidential disclosure agreements? Before receiving confidential information from you, the potential receiver can be asked to sign a written agreement not to disclose any of the confidential information (an NDA). The receiver can agree to limit disclosure of the confidential information to others who need to know the information and can agree to safeguard the information. Often, the agreement specifies a time limit and a provision requiring the return of sensitive materials. In some instances, the receiver may be requested to agree not to compete. It is important to recognize, however, that not everyone the venture may need to approach will be willing to sign an NDA.

Employment Contracts

Employment contracts are agreements between an employer and an employee about the terms and conditions of employment, including the employee's agreement to maintain confidentiality and assign the rights for ideas and inventions to the employer. All ideas, inventions, and other forms of intellectual property developed by the employee that are deemed to be within the scope of the venture's activities should be assigned to the firm. It is important that the assignment include venture-related intellectual property created in a team or alone at any time (twenty-four hours a day) while employed (or possibly even thereafter). The employee should be obligated to disclose promptly new ideas and inventions and, when desired, to

confidential disclosure agreements
documents used to protect an idea or other forms of intellectual property when disclosure must be made to another individual or organization

employment contracts
employer employs the employee in exchange for the employee's agreeing to keep confidential information secret and to assign ideas and inventions to the employer

assist the venture in obtaining patents and copyrights. Of course, an employee's development of intellectual property not related to the venture's scope of business belongs to the employee.

Employment contracts can also consider noncompete clauses. *Noncompete clauses* require employees to abstain from competing directly with the firm during employment and for a specified period thereafter. All confidential information held by employees should be surrendered to the firm at the time of employment termination.[28]

Contracts with consultants represent a special form of employment contract. For example, you may find it necessary to hire a consultant who has expertise in a particular area, such as marketing or production. As with regular employees, you will want the consultant to sign an agreement not to disclose or make use of your firm's intellectual property and to assign to the firm any ideas and inventions that were developed during the consulting contract period. Of course, consultants will also want to protect their own intellectual property rights in the form of knowledge and expertise that they possess. As a result, a consultant contract may be more time consuming and complex to prepare than a more standard employee contract.

CONCEPT CHECK

- What are confidential disclosure agreements and employment contracts?

3.5   SEED, STARTUP, AND FIRST-ROUND FINANCING SOURCES

seed and startup financing
sources of financing available during the development and startup stages of a venture's life cycle

Figure 3.7 shows the financing sources potentially available to the entrepreneur during the early stages of a successful venture's life cycle. **Seed and startup financing** refers to financing sources available during the development and startup stages of a venture's life cycle. Included are the entrepreneur's physical and financial assets, family and friends, and business angels. Other venture investors, including venture capitalists who specialize in investing in startup ventures, may also be sources of financial capital during the early stages of development and operation. First-round financing broadens financing sources to include the majority of venture capitalists, commercial banks, and government assistance programs. During the survival life cycle stage, consideration is also given to funding from the venture's operations, suppliers, and customers.

---

[28] Sometimes litigation results from the hiring away of key employees. For example, Seagate Technology, a major disk drive manufacturer, recently sued SpinVision, Inc., a startup company, for hiring away some of its key employees who held important knowledge of Seagate's business. Seagate alleged that SpinVision's tactic was to speed the development of its own initial products while hampering the progress of Seagate's operations. However, proof by suing firms that former employees are misusing confidential information often is required by judges because they don't want to restrain employees from switching jobs. See Kris Hudson, "SpinVision Raids, Seagate Claims," *Daily Camera*, August 27, 1999, pp. D1–D4.

FIGURE 3.7	Types and Sources of Financing Used During Early Life Cycle Stages	
LIFE CYCLE STAGE	**TYPE OF FINANCING**	**MAJOR SOURCES/PLAYERS**
		Venture Financing
Development stage	Seed financing	Entrepreneur's assets
		Family and friends
Startup stage	Startup financing	Entrepreneur's assets
		Family and friends
		Business angels
		Venture capitalists
Survival stage	First-round financing	Business operations
		Venture capitalists
		Suppliers and customers
		Government assistance programs
		Commercial banks

It is important to recognize the growing role the Internet plays in bringing together entrepreneurs and venture investors. For example, www.garage.com was launched in 1998 to operate as a matchmaker for venture founders and business angel investors or venture capitalists. Not surprisingly, in recent years, the fortunes of venture investor facilitation services have somewhat paralleled the fluctuations of the Internet economy itself.[29]

Figure 3.8 summarizes the early-stage financing employed by four selected startup ventures founded in 2005 and 2006. GreenPrint was founded to make and sell printer software that reduces printer waste in the form of less paper and ink. The founder started GreenPrint with $200,000, which included the founder's savings plus funds from family members and friends. Nanda Home's founder received $80,000 from her family to start a venture to make and sell electronic gadgetry. Ventana Health was started to make and sell an all-natural calorie-free sugar substitute for individuals with special dietary needs. To get up and running, the founder of Ventana Health raised $3.25 million from family and friends. The founder of the TechShop venture, which provides a chain of hands-on industrial arts workshops for inventors and hobbyists, obtained $300,000 from angel investors to get started.

Figure 3.9 provides financing information on another ten ventures started during the latter part of the 1990s. These examples provide a broader view of the types of financing actually taking place during the seed and startup financing stages, as well as examples of first-round and other forms of financing that take place during the survival life cycle stage. We will discuss these venture examples, as well as those ventures mentioned in Figure 3.8, as we progress through this section.

---

[29] For more on Internet-based angel matchmaking services, see Susan Greco, "Get$$$now.com," *Inc.*, September 1999, pp. 35–38. For a guide to online resources for entrepreneurs, also see Harris Collingwood, "The Private-Capital Survival Guide," *Inc.*, March 2003, pp. 100–109.

FIGURE 3.8   Examples of Seed and Startup Financing of Recent New Ventures

VENTURE AND YEAR FOUNDED	IDEAS OR PRODUCTS	SEED AND STARTUP FINANCING
Nanda Home (2005)	Make and sell clever products (i.e., electronic gadgetry) that "humanize technology"	$80,000 from family
TechShop (2006)	Provide a chain of workshops (i.e., hands-on industrial arts) for inventors and hobbyists	$300,000 from angel investors
Ventana Health (2006)	Make and sell an all-natural calorie-free sugar substitute for individuals with special dietary needs	$3.25 million from family and friends
GreenPrint (2006)	Make and sell printer software that reduces printer waste (i.e., less paper and ink)	$200,000 from savings, family, and friends. Venture is seeking to raise an additional $250,000–$500,000

Source: "How to Launch a Cool, Profitable, Start-up," *Inc.*, July 2007, pp. 77–86.

FINANCIAL BOOTSTRAPPING

financial bootstrapping
minimizing the need for financial capital and finding unique ways of financing a new venture

Financial bootstrapping, as defined in Chapter 2, decreases the need for financial capital. In most instances, the financial resources of the entrepreneur are limited, as are those available from family and friends. With this in mind, one way of minimizing the need for financial resources is for the entrepreneur to minimize investment in physical assets and live "on a shoestring" during the development and startup stages. It is often less expensive, at least in the short run, to rent or lease physical assets and start the new venture in the garage or basement.

Once the investment in physical assets is minimized, the entrepreneur should make a list of all of her physical and financial assets. First, in all likelihood, all monies in the form of savings or short-term investments will need to be available to the venture. Second, bond and stock holdings will probably be liquidated to help finance the venture. Third, the entrepreneur should plan on seeking an additional mortgage, usually a second mortgage, on any real property, such as a home. Fourth, it is quite common for entrepreneurs to use financial credit available in the form of cash advances on personal credit cards. Becoming a successful entrepreneur often requires a total commitment of one's physical and financial assets. These are major sacrifices; we don't want to minimize the seriousness of the commitment made to launch most new ventures.[30]

---

[30] For some examples of creative financial bootstrapping, see Donna Fenn, "How to Start a Great Company for $1,000 or Less," *Inc.*, August 1999, pp. 43–50. Also see Emily Barker, "Start with Nothing," *Inc.*, February 2002, pp. 66–73.

FIGURE 3.9   Examples of Early-Stage Financing of Ventures Started During the Latter Part of the 1990s

VENTURE AND YEAR FOUNDED	IDEAS OR PRODUCTS	SEED AND STARTUP FINANCING
Cranium, Inc. (1997)	Make and sell board game that requires use of both sides of the brain	Personal savings of the two cofounders
KaBloom, Ltd. (1998)	Open flower superstores that are much larger than typical U.S. floral shops	$3 million Kestrel Venture Partners, Venture Investment Management Company, and CEO of a major office supply firm. Planned second-round financing of $13 million
Jeremy's MicroBatch Ice Creams (1997)	Make ice cream in small quantities in limited editions (concept patterned after beer microbrewers)	$70,000 raised by the founder's sale of personally owned stock plus $1 million in venture capital from Bluestem Capital Partners
Glow Dog, Inc. (1997)	Sell light-reflective clothing for pets and their owners	$80,000 of founder's capital and $80,000 from outside investors. A $2 million additional round of financing is under way
Net's Best, Inc. (1998)	Create a Sunday newspaper insert for Web sites wanting to advertise offline	$1 million from Stone Investments
SchoolSports Communications Network, LLC (1997)	Advertising-supported media company with Web and print products that focus on high school sports	$850,000 in private equity. Plans are under way to raise $2 million in additional funds
Naut-a-Care Marine Services, Inc. (1998)	Build franchise of custom-designed boats that provide oil-changing and other services for other watercraft	$6,000 each from three founders to start franchise plus $100,000 more from the founders' savings to develop the design of the special boats
X-It Products, LLC (1997)	Make and sell home safety products, including a fold-up escape ladder and a compact fire extinguisher	$500,000 from ten investors
Trakus, Inc. (1997)	Make devices embedded in athletes' helmets that transmit statistical data	$4 million from angels and Venture Investment Management Company in two rounds of financing
Knight-McDowell Labs, Inc. (1997)	Make and sell an effervescent tablet that provides protection in germ-infested airplane cabins	$300,000 in personal savings

Source: "Hot Start-Ups," *Inc.*, July 1999, pp. 35–50.

As noted above, three of the four recent ventures (Nanda Home, GreenPrint, and Ventana Health) presented in Figure 3.8 relied heavily on personal savings and financing provided by family and friends. Figure 3.9 shows that personal savings and other sources of personal wealth were important in the development and startup of Cranium, Jeremy's MicroBatch Ice Creams, Glow Dog, Naut-a-Care Marine Services, and Knight-McDowell Labs. Early-stage financing for Cranium was provided from the personal savings of the two founders, who were former Microsoft executives. While the intellectual effort to develop a new board game may be large, the actual production and marketing expenses of the game board probably would allow two reasonably wealthy individuals to cover the venture's early-stage financing. The founder of Jeremy's MicroBatch Ice Creams raised $70,000 by selling some of his financial assets. The founder of Glow Dog contributed $80,000 in personal savings and financial assets. The three founders of Naut-a-Care Marine Services contributed over $100,000 in collective savings to start their business. The cofounders of Knight-McDowell Labs contributed $300,000 in personal savings to their venture.[31]

Unfortunately, from the data contained in Figure 3.9, it is not possible to separate investments involving family and friends from angels and other venture investors. KaBloom received some of its early-stage financing from the CEO of Staples Corporation, who could have been either a friend or a business angel venture investor. X-It Products obtained $500,000 from a group of ten investors that might have included family, friends, or venture investors. (X-It's two student founders developed their prototype safety escape ladder in a course at Harvard University and began production and marketing within six months.)

Sometimes the financial resources of family and friends can help the entrepreneur get through the development stage and into the startup stage. However, moving through the startup stage and on to the survival stage usually requires the financial help of business angels or other venture investors, including venture capitalists. Glow Dog received $800,000 in early-stage financing from outside investors; SchoolSports Communications Network obtained $850,000 in private-equity funding. The likely providers of these funds are business angels, whom we will discuss next, and venture investors other than professional venture capitalists. That is, some important providers of venture capital are not clearly either business angels or venture capitalists.

CONCEPT CHECK

• What is meant by financial bootstrapping?

BUSINESS ANGEL FUNDING

business angels
wealthy individuals who invest in early-stage ventures in exchange for the excitement of launching a business and a share in any financial rewards

After personal financial resources and those of friends and family have been exhausted, capital-hungry new ventures frequently turn to **business angels,** "wealthy individuals who are willing to pour their money into fledgling companies in exchange for the excitement of launching a business and a share in any financial rewards."[32] It is important for entrepreneurs and founders to recognize the central role that angels play in new venture financing. For example, the TechShop venture mentioned in Figure 3.8 was started with $300,000 from business angels, and the GreenPrint venture was trying to raise an additional $250,000–$500,000 from angels or other venture investors.

---

[31] Information on these and the other ventures discussed in this section is from "Hot Start-Ups," *Inc.*, July 1999, pp. 35–50. For follow-up information on the founders of Cranium, Inc., see Julie Bick, "Inside the Smartest Little Company in America," *Inc.*, January 2002, pp. 54–61.

[32] This definition of angel investors appeared in Anne Field's *Success* article titled "The Angels Among Us," April 1999. The application of the term "angel" derives from its earlier use to describe investors who, at significant risk, back Broadway theatrical productions.

Trakus, mentioned in Figure 3.9, obtained a total of $4 million from a combination of business angels and the Venture Investment Management Company, which is a venture capital firm. Trakus was started by three graduates of MIT who designed a monitoring system affixed to supermarket carts to track the movements of customers. However, they quickly realized that their product was too expensive for grocery businesses to justify. After regrouping, the one remaining cofounder hired two new engineers and developed the Electronic Local Area Positioning System (ELAPS), which was designed to collect performance data on athletes in real time throughout a game. In this example, technology development and infrastructure costs of equipment and computer systems required that the venture find access to a substantial amount of early-stage financing.

Although the size of, and activity level in, the market for angel investing (informal venture capital) is difficult to track (after all, the investments are private), we do have an idea how many angels there are. We also have some idea of the type of people who become angel investors. A 1987 estimate by William Wetzel, Jr., who characterizes angels as "self-made individuals with substantial business and financial experience and with a net worth of $1 million or more," put the number of angel investors at about 250,000 with 100,000 active in a given year.[33] Wetzel estimated the total angel investment portfolio to be about $50 billion (roughly twice the size of professionally managed venture capital at the time of his study). He suggested that angels were involved in funding about 20,000 firms a year (compared to the 2,000 to 3,000 firms a year funded at that time by professional venture capitalists). Wetzel's typical angel-backed venture raised about $250,000 from at least three angels.[34]

While these initial estimates still serve as a starting point for describing this largely unobservable market, there is significant reason to believe that the U.S. angel market today is significantly larger in the size of annual investment and the number of active investors. One recent estimate is that angels are investing at a rate of $20 billion a year (compared to about $12 billion a year during the same time period in professional venture capital).[35] Syndicated angel investing, in which multiple angels participate simultaneously in one funding round, continues to be the norm, although the amount raised per round appears to be growing. One of the most visible groups of angel investors is the Silicon Valley's "Band of Angels," with a 1999 census of about 120 investors.[36]

There is significant evidence that angel investors are the primary ingredients in firms that are introducing new technologies. An early study by Wetzel and John Freear analyzed 284 New England ventures to see how they financed their

---

[33] Wetzel's summary of the angel market can be found in "The Informal Venture Capital Market: Aspects of Scale and Market Efficiency," *Journal of Business Venturing* 2 (1987).

[34] Richard Harrison and Colin Mason argue that angel investors in the United Kingdom are demographically similar to their U.S. counterparts but appear to be older. Their work suggests that, relative to their U.S. counterparts, U.K. angels examine a larger number of deals, invest in a similar numbers of ventures, participate less often in multiple-angel rounds, require higher returns, and have shorter horizons. See "International Perspectives on the Supply of Informal Venture Capital," *Journal of Business Venturing* 7 (1992).

[35] See Field, "The Angels Among Us."

[36] Ibid.

early stages.[37] Of the 284 firms, 107 were launched with no outside equity financing. The remaining 177 firms raised $671 million in 445 rounds of financing. The typical angel round for these firms was less than $500,000, compared to professional venture capital rounds that were typically in the range of $1 to $3 million. In total, the 177 firms raised $76 million from angels and $370 million from professional venture capitalists. Importantly, however, 54 percent of the money raised from angels went to early-stage ventures, compared to 20 percent of the money raised from venture capitalists. Of the 177 ventures, 124 (70 percent) had at least one angel investor round. Wetzel and Freear found that private individuals were the largest source of seed financing, accounting for 48 percent of seed capital funds. Their role declined sharply at the startup stage (20 percent) and again at the first and second stages (8 percent in each stage). Venture capital funds provided almost as much seed capital as private individuals, 46 percent as compared to 48 percent. At the startup stage, venture capital funds were the largest source of capital, providing 45 percent of the capital invested in startup situations. Private individuals provided 76 percent of all rounds of seed financing. Individuals also provided more rounds of startup financing than venture capital funds, 45 percent compared to 31 percent.

The message is quite clear: While professional venture capitalists participate in the funding of early-stage ventures, they concentrate on later-stage investing. An early-stage technology venture is more likely to be funded by angels than by professional venture capitalists. This is not bad news. Angel investors are widely believed to have lower target rates of return than professional venture capitalists.[38] They are also known for making faster-than-VC investment decisions and providing valuable expertise to ventures in which they invest.[39]

Knowing that angels exist is not the same thing as finding them. Research is sparse on who angels are, why some investors become angels while others do not, and where angels can be found. We do have some initial indications, though. The established wisdom is that angel investors maintain important contacts with attorneys, accountants, and university professors, among others, and that securing an introduction through these contacts is a good way to begin your quest for angel capital. Many successful businesses have been funded through angel investments originating with the venture's professional service providers. It is also common for contact with one angel to lead to contact with others.

While U.S. angel investing has existed for a long time, only recently have significant efforts been undertaken to organize angels. Historically, angel organization

---

[37] See William Wetzel and John Freear, "Who Bankrolls High-Tech Entrepreneurs?" *Journal of Business Venturing* 5 (March 1980).

[38] In the April 1999 *Success* article "The Angels Among Us," Tarby Bryant, head of Santa Fe's "Gathering of Angels," suggests angel rates in the 20 to 50 percent range compared with 50 to 60 percent for professional venture capitalists. The lower rates demanded by angels are the basis of much of the discussion in the *Wall Street Journal Interactive Edition's* "Surging Angels' Investing Alters Start-Up Funding," August 13, 1998.

[39] Mary Kay Sullivan and Alex Miller analyze responses from 214 private investors to investigate various possible motivations for angel investing. See "Segmenting the Informal Venture Capital Market: Economic, Hedonistic and Altruistic Investors," *Journal of Business Research* 36 (1996). Sanford Ehrlich et al. examine the comparative roles of angels and professional venture capitalists in their invested ventures in "After the Cash Arrives: A Comparative Study of Venture Capital and Private Investor Involvement in Entrepreneurial Firms," *Journal of Business Venturing* 9 (1994).

has been informal. In 1958, A. H. Rubinstein characterized the angel community as follows:

> *The fraternity of individual backers of small business appears to be rather close-knit, at least on the local level. A good deal of information is passed about by word of mouth. If one investor, who enjoys considerable prestige among his associates, believes a situation to be promising and recommends it to others, his friends may participate merely on the basis of his recommendation.*[40]

In addition to informal networks, national and regional matching services for angels and ventures have been created recently. The U.S. Small Business Administration sponsored the creation of a national listing service called ACE-Net (later renamed to ActiveCapital and on the Web at www.ActiveCapital.org). A good starting point for finding angel matching services is www.allianceofangels.com or www.angelcapitalassociation.org.

Finding angels is not the same as getting them to fund your startup. Reportedly, the Band of Angels requires that, in order to present your business plan, you must be sponsored by at least two members who have already committed to making an investment.[41] One thing is clear: When you do get the introduction to your first angel, you should have a tight business plan summary and a pitch of twenty minutes or less ready to go. Different angels will seek different types of ventures and offer different terms for their investments. Again, while private equity is a difficult area to research, we have some insight into the success factors for early-stage funding. Studying 318 entrepreneurs, Ronald Hustedde and Glen Pulver concluded that it is very important for the entrepreneur to be willing to surrender a large percentage of ownership, to go directly to a number of potential investors, and, perhaps contrary to intuition, not to be too seasoned or late in their entrepreneurial careers.[42]

Even a successful encounter with an angel will take time. So, whatever your contacts and approach, be prepared to take several months in your search for external funding. In addition, success should not be assumed. Even in a banner year for venture funding, the number of externally funded startups is trivial relative to the number of new business organizations.[43] Another important consideration for your startup may be whether you can alter or bootstrap the business plan to avoid having to raise external capital.

CONCEPT CHECK

- Who are business angels?

---

[40] See "Problems in Financing and Managing New Research-Based Enterprises in New England," *Federal Reserve Bank of Boston* (1958).

[41] See Field, "The Angels Among Us."

[42] See "Factors Affecting Equity Capital Acquisition: The Demand Side," *Journal of Business Venturing* 7 (September 1992), pp. 363–374.

[43] See, for example, Amar Bhide's summary of 1987 investing in "Bootstrap Finance: The Art of Start-Ups," *Harvard Business Review* (November–December 1992).

FIRST-ROUND FINANCING OPPORTUNITIES

Figure 3.9 indicates that early-stage funding from venture capitalists was obtained by KaBloom, Jeremy's MicroBatch Ice Creams, and Net's Best from Kestrel Venture Partners, Venture Investment Management Company, Bluestem Capital Partners, and Stone Investments, respectively. The Venture Investment Management Company also provided venture capital funding for Trakus. Professional venture capitalists can be an important source of new venture funding. However, venture capitalists typically concentrate their investing efforts on later-stage companies. Venture capitalists often provide first-round financing and participate in later financing rounds for promising ventures. We will discuss venture capitalists in detail in Chapter 11.

Commercial banks typically do not provide loans to startup ventures. Rather, only after a venture has two or more years of operating history (i.e., has at least shown its ability to survive) will most commercial banks even consider providing loan financing. Furthermore, commercial banks typically concentrate on making business loans to help young ventures finance the working capital (inventories and receivables) associated with seasonal business operations. Such loans are usually paid off through the sale of inventories and the collection of receivables. Commercial banks typically only provide longer-term loans to well-established ventures. Their role as a source of financing for entrepreneurial ventures is discussed further in Chapter 12.

First-round financing may also be available from the Small Business Administration (SBA) and state and local government assistance programs for ventures with some operating history that are still trying to survive. These government-based first-round financing sources are discussed in Chapter 12.

Suppliers can help a young venture get through its survival stage by providing trade credit financing on purchases made by the entrepreneurial venture. Sometimes a venture that produces costly products (or ones that take a long time to manufacture) can garner advance payments from its customers. The survival stage is a time for ventures to seek out all types and sources of financing. Ultimately, the struggling venture must secure sufficient financing and find a way to produce revenues that exceed its operating expenses and continuing investment outlays.

SUMMARY

Chapter 3 is the first of three chapters that form Part 2 of this text, "Organizing and Operating the Venture." Our emphasis in Part 2 is primarily on ventures choosing their business organization forms, preparing financial statements, monitoring financial performance, and obtaining startup and first-round financing, We began this chapter with a discussion of the major forms of business organization: proprietorships, general and limited partnerships, corporations, subchapter S corporations, and limited liability companies. We discussed important issues related to organizational choice, including investor liability, double

taxation, firm life, liquidity of ownership, and the new venture's ability to generate equity capital.

The second section of the chapter focused on intellectual property rights. We discussed the protection of valuable intangible assets through the use of patents, trade secrets, trademarks, and copyrights. We also covered the use of nondisclosure agreements and employment contracts as methods to help protect intellectual property rights.

The last section in the chapter focused on early-stage financing sources. We defined early-stage financing, then provided a discussion of financial bootstrapping and the role of business angels in financing the development and startup stages of a venture's life cycle. We also recognized the importance of venture capitalists as providers of startup and first-round financing and discussed other sources of first-round financing.

KEY TERMS

articles of incorporation	financial bootstrapping	partnership agreement
business angels	intellectual property	patents
confidential disclosure agreements	joint and several liability	proprietorship
copyrights	joint liability	S corporation
corporate bylaws	limited liability	seed and startup financing
corporate charter	limited liability company (LLC)	trade secrets
corporation	limited partnership	trademarks
employment contracts	partnership	unlimited liability

DISCUSSION QUESTIONS

1. Describe the major differences between a proprietorship and a partnership.

2. What is a limited partnership?

3. Briefly describe the corporate form of business organization. What is meant by limited liability?

4. How does a subchapter S corporation differ from a regular corporation?

5. Describe the major characteristics of a limited liability company.

6. Describe the major taxation advantages of a limited liability company or a subchapter S corporation over a regular corporation.

7. What is meant by the term "intellectual property"?

8. Identify and briefly describe the types of patents used to protect valuable intangible assets.

9. What are trade secrets? How are they used to protect valuable intangible assets?

10. What are trademarks? Identify the four types of "marks" used to protect intellectual property.

11. What are copyrights and how are they used?

12. What are confidential disclosure agreements? What are employment contracts?

13. What is seed and startup financing?

14. Describe the meaning of financial bootstrapping.

15. Describe some major characteristics of business angels.

16. What is first-round financing that occurs during the survival life cycle stage?

INTERNET ACTIVITIES

1. Access the *Inc.* magazine Web site at http://www .inc.com. Identify a list of recent articles that relate to how to finance new ventures.

2. Access the http://www.garage.com Web site. Identify the angel matchmaking services that are provided. Determine the site's focus in terms of early-stage versus later-stage financing, as well as the typical range of financing that is provided.

3. Access the Web sites http://www.angeldeals.com, http://www.gatheringofangels.com, and http://www .vcfodder.com. Determine the scope and focus of these sites in terms of matchmaking financing services that are available for entrepreneurs.

EXERCISES/PROBLEMS

1. Assume your new venture, organized as a proprietorship, is in its first year of operation. You expect to have taxable income of $50,000. Use the income tax rate information contained in Figure 3.6 to estimate the amount of income taxes you would have to pay.

   A. Calculate the amount of your income taxes if you were filing as a single individual.

   B. Calculate the amount of your income taxes if you were married and filing jointly.

   C. If your venture had been organized as a standard corporation instead of a proprietorship, calculate your income tax liability.

2. Rework Problem 1 under the assumption that in addition to your venture's taxable income of $50,000, you expect to personally earn another $10,000 from a second job.

3. As your venture has moved from the development stage to the startup stage, a number of trade secrets have been developed along with an extensive client list. You are in the business of developing and installing computer networks for law firms.

   A. Your marketing manager has recently resigned and you are in the process of interviewing new candidates for the position. How might you try to protect your venture's intellectual property since the marketing manager must have access to the trade secrets and client list?

   B. Your operations manager has developed a "new" process and you have heard that he plans to personally apply for a business methods patent. What action(s) would you take?

4. The Capital-Ideas Company is in its development stage and is deciding how to formally organize its business venture. The founder, Rolf Lee, is considering organizing as either a proprietorship or a corporation. He expects revenues to be $2 million next year with total expenses amounting to $1.625 million, resulting in a taxable income of $375,000. Rolf is interested in estimating his federal income tax liability based on the schedules contained in Figure 3.6.

   A. Calculate the amount of federal income tax that Rolf would pay if Capital-Ideas is organized as a proprietorship. What would be the marginal tax rate on the last dollar of taxable income and what would be the average tax rate?

   B. Calculate the amount of federal income tax that the Capital-Ideas Company would have to pay if the venture is organized as a regular corporation. What would be the marginal tax rate on the last dollar of taxable income and what would be the average tax rate?

   C. If the Capital-Ideas Company is organized as a corporation and all after-tax profits are paid out as dividends to Rolf Lee, what additional personal income taxes would be paid? What would be the marginal tax rate and the average tax rate on this personal income received from the corporation?

5. In the second year of operation, the Capital-Ideas Company forecasts revenues to grow to $5 million and expenses, before income tax, to be 70 percent of revenues. Rework Parts A, B, and C of Problem 4 to reflect this new level of revenues and expenses.

6. Rolf Lee is now exploring whether it might be better to organize the Capital-Ideas Company as a subchapter S corporation based on information contained in Problem 4.

    A. Calculate the amount of federal income tax that the Capital-Ideas Company would pay next year.

    B. What would be the marginal tax rate on the last dollar of taxable income and what would be the average tax rate?

7. Rolf Lee is also considering organizing the Capital-Ideas Company as a limited liability company.

    A. Use information contained in Problem 5 to estimate the federal income tax liability in the second year of operation if Capital-Ideas is an LLC.

    B. What would be the marginal tax rate on the last dollar of taxable income and what would be the average tax rate?

8. Phil Young, founder of the Pedal Pushers Company, has developed several prototypes of a pedal replacement for children's bicycles. The Pedal Pusher will replace existing bicycle pedals with an easy-release stirrup to help smaller children hold their feet on the pedals. The Pedal Pusher will glow in the dark and will provide a musical sound as the bicycle is pedaled.

    Phil plans to purchase materials for making the product from others, assemble the products at the venture's facilities, and hire product sales representatives to sell the Pedal Pushers through local retail and discount stores that sell children's bicycles. Phil will need to purchase plastic pedals and extensions, bolts, washers and nuts, reflective material, and a microchip to provide the music when the bicycle is pedaled.

    A. How should Phil organize his new venture? In developing your answer, consider such factors as amount of equity capital needed, business liability, and taxation of the venture.

    B. Phil is concerned about trying to protect the intellectual property embedded in his Pedal Pusher product idea and prototype. How might Phil consider protecting his intellectual property?

9. Francine Delgado, founder of the HairCare Products Company, has developed HairCarePlus, which is a shampoo product containing healthy nutrients that are absorbed through the scalp when the product is used. She also believes that preliminary tests of HairCarePlus show that product residues are environmentally safe.

    A. Francine was wondering whether she might be able to patent the HairCarePlus product. What are the characteristics of patents and what type of patent, if any, might Francine seek?

    B. What other ways, other than through patents, might Francine explore to try to protect the HairCarePlus product?

SUPPLEMENTAL EXERCISES/PROBLEMS

[Note: These activities are for readers who have an understanding of financial statements.]

10. Francine Delgado has developed a business plan for producing and selling a new hair care product that emits nutrients to the scalp when used. The product residues have been judged to be environmentally safe. Following are her projected partial financial statements for the first three years of operation of HairCare Products Company. Francine, however, is unsure whether to organize her business as a proprietorship or a regular corporation.

HairCare Products Company Projected Partial Income Statements & Balance Sheets

	YEAR 1	YEAR 2	YEAR 3
Sales	$200,000	$400,000	$1,800,000
Cost of goods sold	100,000	200,000	800,000
Gross profit	100,000	200,000	1,000,000
Operating expenses	75,000	100,000	200,000
Depreciation	4,000	8,000	20,000
Earnings before interest and taxes	21,000	92,000	780,000
Interest	1,000	2,000	4,000
Earnings before taxes	20,000	90,000	776,000
Taxes	?	?	?
Net income	?	?	?

	YEAR 1	YEAR 2	YEAR 3
Cash and inventories	$ 50,000	$100,000	$500,000
Building and equipment	50,000	100,000	300,000
Total assets	$100,000	$200,000	$800,000

A. Use the tax rate schedules presented in this chapter to estimate the dollar amount of taxes that would have to be paid in each year by HairCare Products Company if the venture is initially formed as a corporation. Also calculate the after-tax net income for each year.

B. Use the tax rate schedules presented in this chapter to estimate the dollar amount of taxes that would have to be paid in each year if HairCare Products Company is organized as a proprietorship and represents Francine's only source of income, and if she is single. Also calculate the after-tax net income for each year.

C. Use ratios from Chapter 2 to calculate the return on assets (ROA) model and its net profit margin and asset intensity ratios.

D. In order to grow sales, HairCare Products will need to invest in assets to support sales growth. How might the venture's assets be financed?

E. Would you recommend that HairCare Products Company be initially formed as a proprietorship or as a corporation? Why? Should Francine consider changing the form of business organization for HairCare Products Company as the firm grows over time?

11. Now let's assume that Francine Delgado (see Problem 10) organizes HairCare Products Company as a proprietorship, is married, and files a joint tax return with her husband, Franco.

A. Calculate the tax liability (using tax tables presented in the chapter) and net income in each of the three years for HairCare Products Company, assuming no other personal income or deductions.

B. For this proprietorship scenario, calculate and make ratio comparisons with the calculations in Part C of Problem 10.

C. Would you recommend that the venture be organized as a proprietorship or as a regular corporation? Why?

D. What other forms of business organization might Francine consider when forming HairCare Products Company? What are their pros and cons?

M I N I   C A S E

Interact Systems, Inc. (Revisited)

Interact Systems, Inc., has developed software tools that help hotel chains solve application integration problems. Interact's application integration server (AIS) provides a two-way interface between central reservations systems (CRSs) and property management systems (PMSs). At least two important trends in the hotel industry are relevant. First, hotels are shifting away from the manual booking of room reservations, and electronic bookings will continue to increase as more bookings are made over the Internet. Second, competitive pressures are forcing hotels to implement yield management programs and to increase customer service. By integrating the CRS and PMS through Interact's AIS, inventories can be better managed, yields improved, and customer service enhanced.

All reservation traffic is routed from the CRS to individual hotel properties. This allows Interact Systems to create a database that can be used to track customers and to facilitate marketing programs, such as frequent-stay or VIP programs, as a way of increasing customer satisfaction. Interact forecasts application integration expenditures in the hospitality industry to exceed $1 billion by 2010.

Greg Thomas founded Interact Systems in 2004 and developed the firm's middleware software and hospitality applications. He has twelve years of systems applications experience and currently is Interact's chief technology officer. Eric Westskow joined Interact in early 2007 as president and CEO. He previously had worked in sales and marketing in the software industry for more than twenty years.

A. What are the advantages of having formed the company as a corporation?

B. What other organizational structures would have been appropriate?

C. Could Interact Systems qualify for S corporation status with the IRS? Why or why not?

D. What is the intellectual property involved in Interact Systems' business model?

E. What methods of protection are available for Interact Systems' intellectual property?

F. What considerations are important in deciding whether to use an employment contract for the newly hired CEO?

M I N I   C A S E

Cooperative Constructs

Part A

Several years ago, Dick and Barbara Harris were asked to attend an organizational meeting for a newly forming neighborhood babysitting cooperative. The idea was simple. Concerned and caring parents would join together in the cooperative and exchange babysitting services. Although they were not particularly interested in committing to trading babysitting favors, as their children were quickly approaching the age where babysitting services would be unnecessary, Dick and Barbara felt socially obligated to attend the meeting with their two children. Eight other families came to the meeting.

continued on next page

Cooperative Constructs (continued)

After a brief period of social exchange, Dick and Barbara listened, as much as possible over the din of children playing, to the organizer, a certified public accountant, explain how the formal accounting for exchanged sitting services would take place. Using specially marked, yet ordinary, poker chips as currency, members of the cooperative would receive an endowment of chips with various colors corresponding to an hour, thirty minutes, and fifteen minutes. When babysitting services were received, payment was required, rounded to the nearest fifteen minutes, in poker chips. Conveniently, no family would need to keep records of whom or how much they owed. With the creation of babysitting currency and some serious remarks about screening other families before allowing them to join, the cooperative was launched—although Dick and Barbara declined to join.

Reflecting on some bad previous experiences with not-for-profit organizations, the couple debated, on the drive home, what could be done to satisfy their concerns. Dick was wondering how the organization could formally barter services among themselves without organizing as a formal barter exchange and recognizing the receipt of poker chips as income. Barbara was more concerned about babysitting for, or by, parents with whom she had only a passing acquaintance. Even if the barter arrangement were shielded from taxation (an item also not discussed), they both contemplated who would be liable in the event of mishaps.

A. What type of an organization is necessary for the babysitting cooperative?

B. Is there potential for liability for members other than those directly involved?

C. What are the nontax differences between exchanging poker chips and charging $4 per hour?

D. What is the difference between exchanging poker chips and charging $4 per hour from the perspective of the IRS?

E. Assuming you had appropriately aged children, would you be willing to join the cooperative?

F. What, if any, are the intellectual property issues in an isolated cooperative?

Part B

The organizers of Dick and Barbara's cooperative had great success and many inquiries from other neighborhoods on how to organize and operate. After the organizers had helped several other groups to form, the time commitment grew to the point that they decided to establish a consulting practice, Cooperative Constructs, and charge fees for providing advice and materials to startup cooperatives. Based on its extensive experiences, Cooperative Constructs had accumulated many stories and experiences and some legal documents. After the practice contracted a videographer to tape one of its organization sessions, a startup package with video and boilerplate agreement documents was ready for distribution.

A. Discuss different organizational structures for Cooperative Constructs and their (dis)advantages.

B. Identify Cooperative Constructs' intellectual property.

C. What intellectual property protection is appropriate for Cooperative Constructs' materials, organization name, and approach?

Chapter 4

MEASURING FINANCIAL PERFORMANCE

PREVIOUSLY COVERED

In Chapter 3, we discussed the alternative forms of business organization the entrepreneur might choose after considering taxes, liability, and the financial capital needed to get started. We also discussed the importance of intellectual property and having a strategy for its protection. We concluded the chapter with an introduction to financial bootstrapping and business angel financing for the early stages in the venture life cycle.

LOOKING AHEAD

Chapter 5 presents financial measures that assist in evaluating a venture's operating and financial performance. Our primary focus is managing and monitoring the venture's liquidity and cash flow, to make sure cash is available to meet creditor obligations. We introduce financial measures that creditors consider when deciding whether to grant credit to the venture. We also present financial measures for tracking venture performance.

CHAPTER LEARNING OBJECTIVES

In this chapter, we introduce basic accounting and financial statements designed to help ventures monitor their progress. We stress the need to understand how cash is built and burned, using financial statements and breakeven analyses. After completing this chapter, you will be able to:

1. Describe the process for obtaining and recording resources needed for an early-stage venture

2. Describe and prepare a basic balance sheet

3. Describe and prepare a basic income statement

4. Explain the use of internal statements as they relate to formal financial statements

5. Briefly describe two important internal operating schedules: the cost of production schedule and the inventories schedule

6. Prepare a cash flow statement and explain how it helps monitor a venture's cash position

7. Describe operating breakeven analysis in terms of EBDAT breakeven (survival) revenues

8. Describe operating breakeven analysis in terms of NOPAT breakeven revenues

After deciding how to organize your business, it is important that you maintain a record of operations. This record provides ongoing feedback for internal decision making and gives creditors and investors necessary information for making sound financial decisions. Every entrepreneur should have a basic understanding of how financial records reflect the venture's initial and developing assets and ownership. An entrepreneur should understand how proper accounting procedures record sales and costs and how this determines whether the venture is making a profit. By using these records to prepare financial statements, the entrepreneur develops an understanding of how cash is generated and depleted. This understanding leads to an ability to interpret important measures of the venture's financial situation (building or burning cash) and project when the venture will reach operating breakeven.[1]

4.1   OBTAINING AND RECORDING THE RESOURCES NECESSARY TO START AND BUILD A NEW VENTURE

Supporting an initial development stage usually requires minimal asset investments such as office furniture and a computer. If the venture will create product prototypes, it may require additional specific machinery and equipment. The initial cash on hand should be adequate to cover expenses such as rent, utilities, and the entrepreneur's subsistence salary. Access to cash beyond what is needed to pay immediate expenses is important since there will likely be no revenues during the development stage. Figure 4.1 illustrates the relationship of gathered resources to their associated financial footprint as a new venture moves from the development stage to the startup stage. The primary venture footprints are seen in its *balance sheet* and *income statement*.

A section of the venture's balance sheet is dedicated to the venture's assets, including its cash holdings. Of course, these assets have to be purchased or placed using financing. Seed financing from the entrepreneur's personal assets, and from funds provided by family and friends, provides the cash to acquire development-stage assets and pay development-stage expenses. Each type of financing provided by the owners (equity) or by lenders (liabilities and debt) has its own place on the venture's balance sheet.

---

[1] Readers who have a knowledge of the content of financial statements and how they are constructed can bypass this chapter without losing any continuity as we progress through the stages of a successful venture's life cycle. However, before deciding to skip this chapter, you should have a firm understanding of how basic financial statements can be used to determine whether the venture is building or burning cash. We cannot overstate the importance of having cash in order to survive the short run and free cash to build value and provide a return to investors over time.

FIGURE 4.1	Obtaining and Recording the Resources Necessary to Start and Build a New Venture

DEVELOPMENT STAGE IN LIFE CYCLE		STARTUP STAGE IN LIFE CYCLE	
BALANCE SHEET	INCOME STATEMENT	BALANCE SHEET	INCOME STATEMENT
Assets:	Revenues:	Assets:	Revenues:
Acquire initial assets (e.g., initial cash, office furniture, computer, etc.)	No sales (consequently no money is coming in)	Acquire production assets (e.g., inventories and equipment to produce products and give credit to customers)	Making sales (money begins flowing in)
Liabilities and Equity:	Expenses:	Liabilities and Equity:	Expenses:
Obtain seed financing (e.g., entrepreneur's assets, family, and friends)	(e.g., rent, utilities, subsistence salary for entrepreneur)	Obtain startup financing (e.g., business angels and venture capitalists in addition to seed financing sources)	(additional expenses to produce and market products and to record business transactions)

The venture's initial expenses leave a footprint on the venture's income statement where revenues and expenses are tallied. The lack of development-stage revenues—while incurring expenses—typically results in an accounting loss (negative net income) during the development stage.

New ventures that succeed in getting to startup and launching a new product, service, or process are to be commended. Many ventures fail prior to this milestone. Along with any congratulations, however, comes the warning that such ventures will soon require additional investments in inventories, equipment, and customer credit. These investments will result in additions to, and changes in, asset accounts on the balance sheet. The related financing, whether from business angels, venture capitalists, or retained earnings, will be recorded as additions to, or changes in, liability and equity accounts on that same balance sheet.

Eventually, the startup will generate revenues to help cover its expenses. The income statement records how the venture is faring in terms of its revenues versus its expenses. Maintaining records of how the venture periodically performs in the constant battle of revenues versus expenses is important in helping set internal direction and communicate with the financial community. Understanding how the venture's expenses are distributed over various categories, such as materials, labor, marketing expenses, and overhead, provides important guidance on how the venture might redeploy resources to gain an edge in the next battle of revenues versus expenses. Perhaps discouragingly, the records of most early battles—as captured in income statements during the startup phase—frequently appear to predict impending defeat: Expenses keep exceeding revenues. However, as the venture gains ground and experience, its income statement and balance sheet footprints can be a misleading measure of progress. During this stage, there are many hidden assets created that dramatically influence the outcome of future battles of much greater magnitude.

Chapter 4 reviews the basic financial statement concepts every venture should master. Chapter 5 introduces techniques for conducting financial analysis based on the venture's data as organized in standard financial statements. With knowledge and proper handling of these basic financial weapons, the venture captures important tactical positioning in future income-versus-expense skirmishes and increases the likelihood the venture will eventually win the war by creating sustainable venture value for its owners.

CONCEPT CHECK

- What resources are generally needed during the development stage of a new venture?

4.2   BUSINESS ASSETS, LIABILITIES, AND OWNERS' EQUITY

Suppose you are working on a venture that will produce and market a personal scanner accessory (PSA) directly attachable to a notebook computer. To date, the venture concept has progressed through the development stage with successful prototype production and test marketing. The PSA quickly scans information on business cards (with a standard 2-inch-by-3.5-inch format) to form customer lists or files. It can also be used to scan small photographs, charts, and other written information (up to a 3-inch-by-5-inch size). The scanner is hand sized and designed for field use by sales personnel. The venture has an existing business plan, has been organized as the PSA Corporation, and now is preparing to manufacture and sell the PSA.

assets
financial, physical, and intangible items owned by the business

Business assets, usually referred to simply as **assets**, are the base on which a venture creates revenue and provides a return to investors. Assets can be tangible, physical items such as cash, property, and equipment; or they can be intangibles such as technological expertise, client lists, patents, and goodwill. Accounting procedures track the acquisition, creation, use, and disposition of assets, and dictate how one prepares financial statements. Accounting procedures and communication typically conform to **generally accepted accounting principles (GAAP)**, the standard for record keeping and communication.[2]

generally accepted accounting principles (GAAP)
guidelines that set out the manner and form for presenting accounting information

accrual accounting
the practice of recording economic activity when it is recognized rather than waiting until it is realized

Accrual accounting is the practice of recording indications of economic activity when they are recognized rather than waiting until they are realized. For example, accrual accounting procedures will recognize (accrue) an expense before the venture has to make the payment. They will also recognize (accrue) sales before the venture receives the associated revenue. Accounting procedures are known for their detail, conservatism, and, according to some, rigidity. Tangible physical assets, with their concrete and verifiable nature, typically become the focus of many day-to-day accounting procedures. The original cost (basis) of such assets plays a central role in GAAP accounting. In contrast, intangible assets, owing to an

---

[2]   We should probably say "should conform" as we have worked with ventures struggling to keep records conforming to any standard. Nonetheless, the struggle was due to lack of familiarity rather than malicious intent.

inherent subjectivity about their perceived value, are generally treated with skepticism and conservatism. For example, GAAP procedures do not track the human capital contributed to a new venture unless it appears in other forms such as patents and recognized intellectual property.[3] This conservative bias usually frustrates aspiring entrepreneurs who correctly perceive themselves as important venture assets. Accounting procedures generally understate the true value of an ultimately successful venture. On the other hand, there is also little doubt that accounting procedures overstate an eventually unsuccessful venture's current value.

Having identified possible biases, we focus on the assets and liabilities that accounting procedures emphasize. The **balance sheet** provides a "snapshot" of a venture's financial position on a specific date. It must be in balance in terms of assets versus liabilities and owners' equity. More specifically, the basic accounting identity is:

$$\text{Total Assets} = \text{Total Liabilities} + \text{Owners' Equity}$$

which is nothing more than an indication that what you have in assets (Total Assets) must have been financed through equity injections (Owners' Equity) or borrowing (Total Liabilities).

Table 4.1 shows what a balance sheet might look like for PSA Corporation on June 30, before scanner production starts. The balance sheet presents a measure of the value of the venture's assets compared to a measure of the value of the venture's liabilities plus any residual value belonging to the venture's owners. The founder contributed $40,000 in cash to start the business; this is the founding equity capital contribution. A friend loaned PSA $10,000 for three years at an annual interest rate of 10 percent. The venture rents space in an industrial building for $1,000 a month to assemble and package products. Recent equipment purchases, including a molding press to make the plastic case housing the scanner, the equipment needed to help assemble electronic components, and other materials for manufacturing PSAs, totaled $20,000. PSA has $10,000 of materials in inventory, but owing to the founder's excellent credit record and personal guarantee, suppliers extended trade credit for the entire inventory, resulting in $10,000 of payables. With this information, we can construct the venture's initial balance sheet.

BALANCE SHEET ASSETS

The balance sheet lists assets in declining order of **liquidity**, or how quickly the asset can be converted into cash. Cash and other assets expected to be converted into cash in less than one year are classified as **current assets**. **Cash** is the amount of coin, currency, and checking account balances available to conduct day-to-day

balance sheet
financial statement that provides a "snapshot" of a business's financial position as of a specific date

liquidity
how quickly an asset can be converted into cash

current assets
cash and other assets that are expected to be converted into cash in less than one year

cash
amount of coin, currency, and checking account balances

---

[3] GAAP procedures do make provision for the acquisition of intangible value in the purchase of a going concern through the formal recognition of accounting goodwill. The accounting recognition of the asset value of the entrepreneur's contribution of human capital to the venture will most likely have to wait until the venture is sold, if ever, to another firm at a price that cannot be justified by tangible assets alone. The failure to reflect the value of human capital is of particular concern to business educators and textbook authors whose jobs are to cultivate this human capital.

TABLE 4.1   Initial Balance Sheet (June 30) for PSA Corporation

ASSETS		LIABILITIES AND EQUITY	
Cash and marketable securities	$30,000	Payables	$10,000
Receivables	0	Accrued wages	0
Inventories	10,000	Bank loans	0
		Other current liabilities	0
Total current assets	40,000	Total current liabilities	10,000
Gross equipment	20,000	Long-term debts	10,000
Less: Accumulated depreciation	0	Capital leases	0
Net equipment	20,000	Total long-term liabilities	10,000
Building	0		
Other long-term assets	0	Owners' equity	40,000
Total assets	$60,000	Total liabilities and equity	$60,000

marketable securities
short-term, high-quality, and highly liquid investments that typically pay interest

receivables
credit sales made to customers

inventories
raw materials, work-in-process, and finished products that the venture hopes to sell

fixed assets
assets with expected lives of greater than one year

depreciation
reduction in value of a fixed asset over its expected life, intended to reflect the usage or wearing out of the asset

accumulated depreciation
sum of all previous depreciation amounts charged to fixed assets

operations. **Marketable securities** are short-term, high-quality, highly liquid investments that usually pay interest. The venture initially holds $2,000 in a checking account and $28,000 in short-term investments. It is common practice to combine cash and marketable securities into a single account for reporting purposes.

Receivables are credit sales made to customers. That is, they are sales not requiring immediate cash payment but, rather, payment by a specified future date. Since PSA Corporation is not yet selling scanners, the accounts receivable account balance is zero. **Inventories** are the products that PSA hopes to sell and the materials to be fashioned into salable products. The inventories account may also include a work-in-process inventory of partially completed products. In late June, PSA ordered $10,000 of materials needed to start scanner production.

Assets with expected lives of greater than one year are **fixed assets**. The $20,000 of equipment is the only fixed asset on the PSA balance sheet. Of course, if PSA had purchased the building instead of renting it, the company would have a balance sheet account for the building. Accounting procedures for estimating the decrease in the value of a fixed asset over time create an expense associated with the purchase price of an asset. For example, the molding press and assembling equipment PSA recently acquired will gradually wear out as they are used to produce scanners. **Depreciation** is a reduction in value of a fixed asset to reflect the asset's decreasing value as it ages. Depreciation guidelines are specified by GAAP and by income tax rules. **Accumulated depreciation** is the sum of all previous depreciation charges against fixed assets. The purchase price of the asset less the accumulated depreciation is the book value of the asset. The book value of all fixed assets is frequently called net fixed assets. Since PSA recently purchased its fixed assets, no depreciation is recorded on the June 30 balance sheet.

Most intangible assets cannot be recorded on the balance sheet. For example, if PSA spent money on research and development, creating new ideas or products, the value of such assets might never show up on a balance sheet. This is not a total loss because the related expenses are immediately deducted from earnings. Of course, immediate recognition of the expenses means that future earnings will be higher than they would be if the idea or product asset (with its future depreciation expense) were placed on the balance sheet. As previously mentioned, an exception to this immediate expensing would be the patent or purchase of intellectual property rights. Then, proper accounting could capitalize a value for the intangible asset and place it in the section for **other long-term assets**. Of course, in this case the expenses associated with the intangible asset would not be deducted immediately from earnings; future depreciation charges would recognize the accounting expense associated with the intangibles' acquisition and use.

other long-term assets
intellectual property rights or intangible assets that can be patented or owned

LIABILITIES AND OWNERS' EQUITY

The other accounts on the balance sheet shown in Table 4.1 are the venture's liabilities and the owners' equity. **Payables** are short-term liabilities to suppliers for materials purchased on credit. The initial balance is the $10,000 for the thirty-day trade credit provided for the purchase of scanner raw materials. **Accrued wages** is an account that reflects liabilities to employees for previously completed work. Firms usually don't pay employees before, or even while, they are doing the compensated work. Rather, they typically pay one or two weeks after the work has been completed. Employees therefore involuntarily provide some of the financial capital needed to finance the business. At the end of June, there were no wages payable since the venture had just hired employees.

payables
short-term liabilities owed to suppliers for purchases made on credit

accrued wages
liabilities owed to employees for previously completed work

The initial balance sheet shows where two additional current liability accounts would be listed. A **bank loan** is, not surprisingly, an interest-bearing loan from a commercial bank. Bankers prefer to make short-term loans (maturities of one year or less) but sometimes lend money for several years. Bank loans for more than one year are recorded as long-term liabilities. New ventures are unlikely to receive bank loans for the first few years because of the lending preferences of most commercial banks.

bank loan
interest-bearing loan from a commercial bank

Although PSA is not currently borrowing short term, it may have such a need in the future. The **other current liabilities** account is a catchall account that includes, for instance, borrowing in the form of cash advances on credit cards. Using credit cards to borrow can be an expensive form of short-term borrowing because of fees and high interest charges; however, there are ways to exploit the initial "teaser" rates offered by credit card providers. It has been estimated that about one-half of all small businesses rely on some credit card financing.[4] PSA has not yet resorted to credit card or other short-term loans.

other current liabilities
catchall account that includes borrowing in the form of cash advances on credit cards

Long-term debts are loans maturing more than one year in the future. The $10,000 loaned to PSA by a friend is an example of a long-term business debt. A substitute for long-term debt on some fixed assets is leasing. If the venture leases, it does not have to buy and borrow. **Capital leases** are long-term, noncancelable leases in which the owner receives lease payments covering (most of) the cost of the equipment plus a return on investment in the equipment. For example, the equipment listed on the balance sheet in Table 4.1 might just as easily come from a capital lease arrangement. If that were the case, the value of the equipment

long-term debts
loans that have maturities of longer than one year

capital leases
long-term, noncancelable leases whereby the owner receives payments that cover the cost of equipment plus a return on investment in the equipment

---

[4] Arthur Andersen/National Small Business United annual survey of small businesses. See "Credit Cards Bank-rolling Small Firms," *Denver Post*, January 17, 1999.

operating leases
leases that provide maintenance in addition to financing and are also usually cancelable

owners' equity
equity capital contributed by the owners of the business

would still be shown as an asset. The capitalized value of the lease payments would then also be shown as a liability. Many firms also make use of **operating leases** that provide maintenance in addition to financing and are also usually cancelable. Computers, copiers, and automobiles often are financed through operating leases. No assets or lease liabilities are recorded on the balance sheet. Operating leases are a major source of off-balance-sheet financing.

The **owners' equity** account at the end of June in the amount of $40,000 reflects the equity capital initially contributed by the owner. As we will see in the next section, the owners' equity account will be adjusted to reflect gains and losses after operations begin. Of course, the owners' equity account will also change when the owner contributes more equity capital (or takes equity capital out) and when part ownership is sold to others, including family members, friends, business angels, or venture capitalists.

CONCEPT CHECK

- What does a balance sheet record or measure?
- Why is it called a balance sheet?

4.3 SALES, EXPENSES, AND PROFITS

PSA Corporation started formal operations on July 1; the venture has been operating for six months. The original estimate of 1,000 scanner sales for the first six months was 200 units less than actual sales. You want to determine whether the venture profited from its first six months of operations. To address the issue of profitability, you need more information and data.

On July 1, PSA hired an employee to operate the molding press and help others assemble the business card scanners. With wages and benefits (payroll taxes, health insurance, etc.), employee costs were substantial but were not a formal liability on July 1. However, now that the workers are employed, wage obligations exist. The founder has concentrated on marketing and distributing the scanners and has been drawing a salary and benefits at a rate of $36,000 per year.

A balance sheet for a given date balances the repositories of accounting value inside a firm (assets) with those promised to creditors (liabilities) and belonging to owners (equity). An **income statement** tracks changes in the value of the various repositories over a given period, with an emphasis on netting those changes to determine the change in the accounting value of ownership. In the absence of equity injections or withdrawals, the accounting value of ownership (the book value of equity) will increase by the amount of net income.

income statement
financial statement that reports the revenues generated and expenses incurred over an accounting period

Table 4.2 displays PSA Corporation's income statement for the first six months of its formal life, July 1 through December 31. To see how the income statement tracks changes in the value of assets and liabilities, consider a cash expense during the period. As cash was depleted to pay the expense, the decrease in the cash account asset was mirrored by an increase in expenses reported in the

TABLE 4.2	PSA Corporation Income Statement for the Six-Month Period Ending December 31	
Net sales		$120,000
−Cost of goods sold		−78,000
Gross earnings		42,000
−Marketing expenses		−12,500
−Administrative expenses		−18,000
−Building rental		−6,000
−Depreciation expense		−1,000
Earnings before interest and taxes		4,500
−Interest		−500
Earnings before taxes		4,000
−Taxes (@ 25%)		−1,000
Net income		$ 3,000

income statement for the period. If the same expense were incurred but funded by trade credit, then the increase in the repository of value represented by payables would be similarly mirrored on the income statement by an increase in expenses for the period. Either way, an income statement expense mirrors the net change in the balance sheet repositories of value (less cash or more liability). Other things being equal, higher expenses diminish net income, and the accounting value of ownership will increase by less than it would have with lower expenses. A similar situation exists for cash and credit sales. Increases in the assets (cash or receivables) would be mirrored by revenue on the income statement and a higher net income's being added to the equity account.[5]

With scanners priced at $100 each, net sales or revenues (after returned scanners were deducted) were $120,000 (i.e., 1,200 units at $100 each). All PSA sales were made on credit, payable in thirty days, to large computer retail chains in the United States, which, in turn, mark up the scanners to sell to the public for $149 each. In December, PSA sold 500 scanners for credit sales of $50,000. Standard procedures require that PSA record these credit sales as revenue, although it won't receive the cash payment until January. In other words, revenue is recorded as having taken place in December, and the value in receivables is increased by the amount of the revenue at the time the sales are made. When the cash arrives in January, the receivables will be decreased and cash will be increased by the amount collected. This is accrual accounting at its heart.

To complete the income statement, PSA must first deduct the cost of producing the scanners from the $120,000 in revenues. The cost of production, or **cost of goods sold**, is the cost of the materials and labor incurred to produce the scanners that were sold. Production and inventory schedules must be maintained separately from the balance sheet and income statement, so that PSA can determine the cost

cost of goods sold
cost of materials and labor incurred to produce the products that were sold

---

[5] While there is some choice for small firms, most will choose to adopt accrual accounting procedures and record sales when made and expenses when incurred, whether or not cash is actually received or disbursed.

gross earnings
net sales minus the cost of production

operating income
also called earnings before interest and taxes (EBIT), the firm's profit after all operating expenses, excluding financing costs, have been deducted from net sales

EBIT
earnings before interest and taxes; also called operating income

net income (or profit)
bottom-line measure of what's left from the firm's net sales after operating expenses, financing costs, and taxes have been deducted

of producing the scanners and properly record the amount of inventories at the end of December. The total production cost for 1,200 scanners was $78,000.

The venture's **gross earnings** are calculated as net sales minus the cost of production. For PSA, gross earnings were $42,000 (i.e., $120,000 – $78,000). Marketing expenses, including shipping and sales calls, were $12,500 during the six-month period. Administrative expenses of $18,000 covered the founder's salary and benefits during the first six months of operation. Other expenses included building rent of $6,000 and depreciation expense of $1,000 on the $20,000 of equipment. The venture's **operating income**, also called **earnings before interest and taxes (EBIT)**, reflects the venture's profit after all operating expenses, excluding financing costs, have been deducted from net sales. PSA's EBIT was $4,500 for the six-month period.

Next, financing charges in the form of interest payments must be deducted from EBIT. Recall that the interest rate on the $10,000 loan from the founder's friend was 10 percent, or $1,000 per year. Thus, the interest expense is $500 for use of the $10,000 during the first six months of operation. After paying taxes at a 25 percent average rate, PSA earned $3,000. The venture's earnings are also known as its **net income** or **net profit**. In the absence of withdrawals, the net income is the increase in equity. PSA, unlike most new ventures, made a profit in its first six months of formal operation. However, before PSA can spend this profit, it is important to remember that the financial statements were prepared using accrual accounting procedures that do not emphasize whether cash is available to spend.

CONCEPT CHECK

• What does an income statement record or measure?

4.4   INTERNAL OPERATING SCHEDULES

Before we can make much use of the income statement, we need to know where the details for the cost of goods sold come from, how the venture records its inventories on hand, and how balance sheets were prepared at the end of an operating period. In the income statement in Table 4.2, production costs were $78,000. Let's examine how these costs were determined. The breakdown of costs is as follows:

	COST PER SCANNER	TOTAL UNITS	TOTAL COSTS
Electronic components	$40	1,200	$48,000
Plastic materials	5	1,200	6,000
Connectors, screws, etc.	5	1,200	6,000
Direct labor	15	1,200	18,000
Total costs	$65	1,200	$78,000

In order to make each scanner, PSA must purchase $40 of electronic components. Plastic materials cost $5; connectors, screws, and other materials cost an additional $5. It took an average of one and one-half worker hours to make the plastic cases and to assemble each scanner. At a rate of $10 per hour (salary and benefits), direct labor was $15 per scanner.

Table 4.3 shows monthly production, cost of goods sold, and inventory schedules for PSA Corporation during its first six months of operation. Two hundred scanners were produced in both July and August. Beginning in September, the scanner production increased to 300 units per month, resulting in 1,600 scanners during the first six months of operation. The cost of goods sold schedule in the table shows that 1,200 scanners were actually sold during the last half of the calendar year. Sales went from zero in July to a peak of 500 units in December. The venture's decision to produce scanners at a monthly rate that exceeded sales (until December) was based on the expectation that sales would continue to grow in the future. Also, at a monthly production rate of 300 scanners, the current workforce was being fully employed. The result of production's exceeding sales was a finished goods inventory of 400 units at the end of December.

TABLE 4.3   PSA Corporation Production and Inventories Schedules

COST OF PRODUCTION SCHEDULE

	COST PER UNIT	JULY	AUG.	SEPT.	OCT.	NOV.	DEC.	TOTAL
Production (units)		200	200	300	300	300	300	1,600
Production costs								
Electronic parts	40	$ 8,000	8,000	12,000	12,000	12,000	12,000	$ 64,000
Plastic materials	5	1,000	1,000	1,500	1,500	1,500	1,500	8,000
Connectors, etc.	5	1,000	1,000	1,500	1,500	1,500	1,500	8,000
Direct labor	15	3,000	3,000	4,500	4,500	4,500	4,500	24,000
Total costs	65	$13,000	13,000	19,500	19,500	19,500	19,500	$104,000

COST OF GOODS SOLD SCHEDULE

	JULY	AUG.	SEPT.	OCT.	NOV.	DEC.	TOTAL
Sales (units)	0	100	100	250	250	500	1,200
Costs @ $65/unit	$ 0	6,500	6,500	16,250	16,250	32,500	$ 78,000

INVENTORIES SCHEDULE

	JULY	AUG.	SEPT.	OCT.	NOV.	DEC.
Beginning finished goods	$ 0	13,000	19,500	32,500	35,750	39,000
Production						
Materials	10,000	10,000	15,000	15,000	15,000	15,000
Direct labor	3,000	3,000	4,500	4,500	4,500	4,500
Additions	13,000	13,000	19,500	19,500	19,500	19,500
Total (beginning + additions)	13,000	26,000	39,000	52,000	55,250	58,500
Less: Cost of goods sold	0	−6,500	−6,500	−16,250	−16,250	−32,500
Ending finished goods	$13,000	19,500	32,500	35,750	39,000	26,000

The $78,000 cost of goods sold from the income statement in Table 4.2 was determined by multiplying the 1,200 units sold by the $65 cost to produce each scanner. The middle of Table 4.3 (cost of goods sold schedule) presents monthly and aggregate costs of goods sold. The lower portion of Table 4.3 (inventories schedule) provides the schedule of inventories. Because PSA first began producing scanners in July, there were no finished goods (scanners) on hand at the time. However, the $10,000 purchase of materials in late June made possible the July production of 200 scanners. After several weeks of operating, PSA found that materials could be ordered early in the same month in which they would be assembled into a scanner.[6] Thus, at the beginning of each month, materials were ordered based on the expected scanner production for that month. It costs $50 in purchased materials (electronic components = $40; plastic materials = $5; and connectors, screws, etc. = $5) to produce one scanner and, therefore, $10,000 in materials to produce 200 scanners (i.e., 200 times $50). No materials were ordered in July; a $10,000 order for materials was placed at the beginning of August. In September, monthly purchases increased to $15,000 per month to reflect the 300 units per month production rate for September and thereafter. Owing to production in excess of sales levels, finished goods inventories at the end of each month increased to a peak of $39,000 (or 600 units at a production cost of $65 per unit) in November. Even after record sales in December, the year-end inventories were still $26,000—the amount recorded as the year-end inventories account balance.

With this additional detail, we can prepare the year-end PSA Corporation balance sheet of Table 4.4. We begin by working down the asset side of the balance sheet. The venture has maintained a $1,000 balance in its checking account, although the original marketable securities were spent several months ago. Credit sales of $50,000 (500 units at $100 each) in December are the year-end receivables. Next, $26,000 is the year-end inventories balance. Current assets grew from $40,000 at the end of June (see Table 4.1) to $77,000 at the end of December.

Turning to fixed assets, the $20,000 gross (predepreciation) amount of equipment remains unchanged from the June 30 balance sheet, since no additional equipment purchases were made. A depreciation charge of $1,000 for one-half of a year implies a net equipment balance of $19,000. Adding the $77,000 of current assets to the $19,000 of fixed assets produces total assets of $96,000. This completes the year-end accounting of the venture's assets.

We next turn to the liabilities and equity side of the balance sheet. Year-end payables amounted to $15,000 from the credit purchases in early December to produce 300 scanners for January of the next year. Direct labor cost was $4,500 in December; administrative wages and benefits were $3,000 (i.e., $36,000 per year divided by 12). Of this $7,500, $3,000 had been earned but not paid and, therefore, represents the year-end accrued wages balance. We will return to the curiously high balance of "Other current liabilities" shortly.

Long-term debt remained at $10,000. The original owners' equity account of $40,000 (see Table 4.1) was increased by the profit of $3,000 (see Table 4.2)

---

[6] By ordering and receiving materials shortly before they are needed for production purposes, the firm has less financial capital tied up in financing materials inventories.

TABLE 4.4   PSA Corporation Balance Sheet for December 31

ASSETS		LIABILITIES AND EQUITY	
Cash and marketable securities	$ 1,000	Payables	$15,000
Receivables	50,000	Accrued wages	3,000
Inventories	26,000	Bank loan	0
		Other current liabilities	25,000
Total current assets	77,000	Total current liabilities	43,000
Gross equipment	20,000	Long-term debts	10,000
Less: Accumulated depreciation	1,000	Owners' equity	43,000
Net equipment	19,000		
Building	0		
Other long-term assets	0		
Total assets	$96,000	Total liabilities and equity	$96,000

earned during the first six months of operation. Thus, the owners' equity account is $43,000 at year end. The sum of financial capital from payables ($15,000), accrued wages ($3,000), long-term debts ($10,000), and owners' equity ($43,000) amounts to $71,000. Since total assets were $96,000 and recorded financial capital is $71,000, there was a shortfall of financial capital of $25,000. That is, PSA did not have enough money from the founder's investment, the initial loan, and trade credit to sustain the first six months of operations. Somewhere PSA borrowed more money to stay afloat, creating a short-term liability. This is a typical problem for new ventures. Even when they are profitable, they may be out of cash and forced to go to extreme measures to fund profitable operations. PSA's founder applied for, and personally guaranteed, two credit cards; together they provided a line of credit of $30,000. Both had introductory rate specials of 0 percent for the first six months (and rising to 12.9 percent thereafter). Once PSA starts paying interest on the carried balances on these credit cards, the income statement will have to reflect the additional interest expenses.

PSA Corporation has now been indoctrinated in accrual accounting. When asked to determine whether a venture has been profitable, there should be some concern whether the question is the relevant one. As it turns out, PSA is profitable but may not survive. For new ventures, a more critical question is whether the venture survives its cash crunches. Not all profitable ventures have access to a quick $25,000 fix using credit cards. What would have happened to PSA if its founder had not unleashed $25,000 of personally guaranteed debt? Would the market have stalled? Would competitors have entered and taken over? Another important question is when the venture will have the cash to pay off the credit cards. For PSA, the $50,000 in January cash receipts for December credit sales will allow the credit cards to be zeroed out. These critical survival questions are best handled by considering cash flow directly. Constructing a statement of cash flows is an easy way to monitor the evolution of PSA's cash position. The importance of this statement justifies treating it in its own section.

4.5   STATEMENT OF CASH FLOWS

One additional financial statement must be described and constructed. The income statement considers flows in and out of asset and liability accounts and their net effect on the flow to the owners' equity account where the accounting value of ownership resides. For most ventures, a more pressing concern is the netting of flows to determine the impact on the venture's cash position. The **statement of cash flows** accomplishes this task for the same period of time as the income statement.

statement of cash flows
financial statement that shows how cash, as reflected in accrual accounting, flowed into and out of a company during a specific period of operation

Table 4.5 presents PSA Corporation's statement of cash flows for the first six months of operation. Cash flows from operating activities begin with the $3,000 in net income during the period. Next, we add back $1,000 in depreciation expense, because depreciation charges are an accounting fiction for approximating a real decrease in the value of fixed assets. They are not a use of cash.

TABLE 4.5   Statement of Cash Flows for PSA Corporation (for the Six-Month Period Ended December 31)

CASH FLOW FROM OPERATING ACTIVITIES		EXPLANATION
Net income	$ 3,000	Other things being equal, net income produces a cash inflow.
+Depreciation	1,000	Depreciation was subtracted to get to net income but was not a cash outflow—add it back.
−Increase in receivables	−50,000	When you extend more trade credit, you use current cash reserves to fund sales in hopes of future cash receipts.
−Increase in inventories	−16,000	Expanding inventories uses cash.
+Increase in payables	5,000	Taking trade credit decreases the cash needed to support inventories.
+Increase in accrued wages	3,000	Borrowing more from employees decreases the amount of cash otherwise needed.
Net cash flow from operations	−54,000	
Cash flow from investing activities		
−Increase in gross equipment	0	You have to get cash from somewhere to pay for new equipment.
CASH FLOW FROM FINANCING ACTIVITIES		
+Increase in other short-term liabilities	25,000	Borrowing increases the venture's currently available cash.
Net change excluding cash account	−29,000	
Beginning cash and marketable securities	30,000	
Ending cash and marketable securities	$ 1,000	The survival bottom line is that the venture's liquid resources went from $30,000 at founding to $1,000 by the end of its first six months and wouldn't be there without $25,000 in new debt.

The associated cash outflow took place when the fixed asset was acquired. Other cash flows related to operations originate in collecting more receivables than those granted during the period and similar net changes in inventories, payables, and accrued wages. For example, PSA had no receivables on June 30 but ended the year with $50,000 in receivables, tying up an additional $50,000 of cash in financing receivables for the first six months of operation.

The concept of cash flow is easier to understand if we examine the inventories account. If inventories decreased between two balance sheets, the cash released from supporting inventory had to go somewhere. If the inventories increased, the cash to support their current level had to come from somewhere. PSA's inventories increased from $10,000 at the end of June to $26,000 at the end of December. There was an inventory-related net use of cash to the tune of $16,000 over the six-month period.

One way to offset the increased use of cash from growing inventories is to use more trade credit. If the entire $16,000 increase in inventories was mirrored by a $16,000 increase in payables, then suppliers would be providing all of the cash necessary to support the new inventory level and the net cash flow effect of growing inventories and trade credit would be zero. For PSA, payables were $10,000 on June 30 and $15,000 on December 31. While the $5,000 increase in payables helps, it does not go far to soften the $16,000 hole created by swelling inventories. Borrowing from employees through accrued wages cuts free an additional $3,000 over the period.

The statement of cash flows makes it clear that selling on credit and increasing inventories are a major threat to PSA's survival. The net result of the cash inflows and outflows from operating activities was –$54,000. That is, PSA spent $54,000 more cash than it generated from operations. Were it not for the $29,000 depletion of cash and marketable securities and the $25,000 of credit card debt, the trade credit and swelling inventories could easily have caused PSA to cease operations. The future still looks bleak if you just freeze on December balances, $1,000 in cash and $35,000 in debt, $25,000 of which is short-term, soon-to-be-high-interest cost, and personally guaranteed by the founder. One can take some solace in the swollen accounts receivable of $50,000, so long as that money can be collected (soon). When it is collected, any net decrease in receivables (because collections exceed new sales on credit) will be a source of cash.

A review of PSA's first six months is in order. As a result of the venture's growth in production and sales, more external financial capital was needed. This occurred primarily because the venture stockpiled inventory and extended credit to customers. PSA was forced to use its cash and marketable securities account balance and borrow significant additional funds ($25,000) in order to stay in business. This is separate from the fact that PSA turned a $3,000 profit, which at this stage may be the least of its concerns.

Another way of looking at the statement of cash flows is in terms of whether the venture is building (generating) or burning (spending) cash. By combining the cash flow from operating activities and the cash flow from investing activities, we can quickly determine this. *Net cash burn* occurs when the sum of cash flows from operations and investing is negative. *Net cash build* exists when the sum of cash flows from operations and investing is positive. If the result is negative, the venture is burning cash. A positive figure indicates a cash build situation for the venture. For PSA, the net cash flow from operating activities is a negative $54,000 while the net cash flow from investing activities is zero. Thus, the netting out of the two figures results in net cash burn of $54,000. To cover this cash burn, PSA drew down (used up) most of its cash and marketable securities account from an initial $30,000 to $1,000.[7] However, PSA would still have been short $25,000 ($54,000 – $29,000) and would have gone into financial distress except for the fact that the venture was able to borrow the $25,000.

CONCEPT CHECK

- Why is an increase in receivables a use of cash?
- What is a statement of cash flows?

4.6   OPERATING BREAKEVEN ANALYSES

Recall from Chapters 1 and 3 that the third stage in a successful venture's life cycle is the survival stage. While some new ventures show profitability during their startup stages, it is more common to have income statement losses until the venture generates adequate revenues to cover expenses. During this stage, the venture is trying to survive—thus the term "survival stage." A venture must measure and monitor financial performance, project cash needs, and obtain first-round financing during its survival stage. In this chapter, we concentrate on determining the level of sales necessary to cover costs, i.e., "break even." In the next chapter, our emphasis shifts to monitoring or evaluating financial performance from the perspective of those providing seed, startup, and first-round financing.

PSA Corporation not only survived its first six months of operation, but also experienced an additional three years of growing sales. Table 4.6 presents PSA's first three years of income statements. Given these data, we can ask important questions about whether PSA is surviving. Operating breakeven analysis is one way to assess this.

To examine whether PSA has been breaking even, we need to compare revenues to cash operating and financing costs. Alternatively, we can look at breakeven by comparing revenues to cash and noncash operating costs, omitting financing costs from the comparison. While both methods are used in practice, the first measure best indicates whether revenues are sufficient to survive.

---

[7]   An alternative approach is to hold cash and marketable securities in two separate accounts. Since marketable securities are short-term investments, the selling of marketable securities is a financing activity, and thus $28,000 could have been recorded as a decrease (financing source) in marketable securities under cash flow from financing activities. In this approach, the $54,000 of net cash burn would have been met by a sale of $28,000 of marketable securities, a loan of $25,000, and a reduction in cash of $1,000.

TABLE 4.6	PSA Corporation's First Three Years of Income Statements		
	YEAR 1	**YEAR 2**	**YEAR 3**
Number of units sold	5,000	15,000	25,000
Revenues	$500,000	$1,500,000	$2,500,000
−Cost of goods sold*	−325,000	−975,000	−1,625,000
Gross profit	175,000	525,000	875,000
−Administrative expenses	−200,000	−200,000	−200,000
−Marketing expenses	−180,000	−180,000	−180,000
EBITDA	−205,000	145,000	495,000
−Depreciation	−25,000	−25,000	−25,000
EBIT	−230,000	120,000	470,000
−Interest expenses	−20,000	−20,000	−20,000
EBT	−250,000	100,000	450,000
−Taxes**	75,000	−30,000	−135,000
Net income	−$175,000	$ 70,000	$ 315,000

*   65% of revenues

**   30% treated on accrued basis

SURVIVAL BREAKEVEN

Expenses or costs that vary directly with revenues are said to be **variable expenses**. The costs of directly producing a product or delivering a service are considered to be variable expenses for most firms. In general terms, this is referred to as the cost of goods sold. Other costs also may be variable. For example, a venture's sales force may be paid a commission or a percentage of the sales that they make. These costs vary with the sales generated; thus, they are variable costs.[8] Ventures that must closely manage their available cash may prefer to pay their sales force on a commission basis. Many other expenses are fixed by managerial operating decisions. **Fixed expenses** or costs are expected to remain constant over a range of revenues for a specific time period, such as a year. General and administrative expenses, including predetermined compensation in the form of base salaries, are largely fixed expenses for most firms. For many venture firms, significant outlays are made for marketing expenditures to acquire customers.[9] For example, a business plan may call for advertising costs to be fixed (i.e., a firm commitment, possibly contractual) over some time period, such as one year.[10]

variable expenses
costs or expenses that vary directly with revenues

fixed expenses
costs that are expected to remain constant over a range of revenues for a specific time period

---

[8]   In actual practice, many costs turn out to be semifixed or semivariable. For example, a sales force may be compensated in the form of base salary (fixed) plus commissions (variable) based on the volume of revenues generated.

[9]   For example, E*Trade, which is an online broker, was able to grow its client list to more than one million accounts. Much of this accomplishment was due to massive advertising campaigns, including the offering of incentives such as sign-up bonuses or frequent-flyer miles on United Airlines.

[10]   In some instances, it may be possible to scale back planned advertising expenditures in midyear, making these commitments semivariable costs. Of course, such actions may accelerate a firm's demise.

EBITDA
earnings before interest,
taxes, depreciation, and
amortization

EBITDA (pronounced ee-bit-dah) is a firm's earnings before interest, taxes, depreciation, and amortization. EBITDA measures a firm's revenues minus its variable operating expenses (such as cost of goods sold) and its fixed operating expenses. General and administrative costs, rental payments, insurance premiums, and possibly all or a portion of marketing costs are generally viewed as being fixed.

However, when considering venture survival, the entrepreneur also must be able to cover financing costs in the form of interest payments.[11] Thus, to break even from a survival viewpoint, the venture's revenues need to cover all expenses. This occurs exactly when earnings before depreciation, amortization, and taxes, **EBDAT** (pronounced eeb-dat), rather than EBITDA, equal zero.[12] We refer to EBDAT = 0 for a given period as **EBDAT breakeven**. Our EBDAT breakeven is a precise version of what venture investors sometime refer to as **cash flow breakeven**. Because venture investors use several working definitions of cash flow, it's a good idea to know what they mean in a particular circumstance. We have chosen to couch our breakeven analysis using a specific type of cash flow (EBDAT) related to survival.[13]

EBDAT
earnings before depreciation, amortization, and
taxes

EBDAT breakeven
amount of revenues (i.e.,
survival revenues) needed
to cover a venture's cash
operating expenses

cash flow breakeven
cash flow at zero for a
specific period (EBDAT = 0)

Traditional capital spending to acquire fixed assets produces known depreciation schedules that are determined by tax laws. While depreciation is considered to be a fixed expense in a given year, it is a *noncash* expense. Asset amortization is handled in a similar fashion. Consequently, we exclude depreciation and amortization from the expenses that revenues need to cover to achieve survival breakeven. We also exclude income tax implications because they would have to be paid only if the venture earned taxable income (which it would not at survival breakeven).

It simplifies things if we rework the income statement to emphasize EBDAT. Table 4.7 shows a reworked before-tax analysis after stripping out noncash items (depreciation and amortization).

Historically, it is easy to examine whether a venture achieved breakeven levels of EBDAT. Just look at (rework) its income statements. PSA Corporation did not achieve breakeven during its first full year (due primarily to ramping up its administrative and marketing expenses). In Year 2, it passed breakeven to achieve a surplus EBDAT of $125,000. Year 3 exhibited even greater success with EBDAT reaching 19 percent of revenues.

It is frequently helpful to provide additional interpretive analysis directly relating the income statement quantities to survival breakeven. For example, PSA's experience did not include a year where it exactly broke even. What level of sales is needed to exactly break even?

---

[11] Borrowing costs in the form of interest payments on loans are easy to identify as deductions below the EBITDA line. However, lease payments are more difficult to classify since they have a component relating to the use of an asset, as well as a financing or interest-related component. In this book, we will treat lease payments as noninterest operating expenses.

[12] Although EBITDA and EBDAT differ in the location of the letter T, this is just for pronunciation's sake. The only difference between EBITDA and EBDAT is that the latter is an after-interest expense (i.e., interest financing costs have been paid).

[13] Venture investors do not use the phrase "cash flow breakeven" to refer to a "free cash flow to equity" of zero. This cash flow would not be related to survival as it includes investment flows that may be optional.

TABLE 4.7	PSA Corporation's Three-Year EBDAT Experience		
	YEAR 1	**YEAR 2**	**YEAR 3**
Number of units sold	5,000	15,000	25,000
Revenues	$500,000	$1,500,000	$ 2,500,000
−Cost of goods sold (65% of revenues)	−325,000	−975,000	−1,625,000
Gross profit	175,000	525,000	875,000
−Administrative expenses	−200,000	−200,000	−200,000
−Marketing expenses	−180,000	−180,000	−180,000
−Leasing and interest expenses	−20,000	−20,000	−20,000
EBDAT	**−$225,000**	**$ 125,000**	**$ 475,000**
Percent of revenues	−45.0%	8.3%	19.0%

To address these types of questions, it is helpful to note that a venture's EBDAT can be expressed as follows:

$$EBDAT = Revenues\ (R) - Variable\ Costs\ (VC) - Cash\ Fixed\ Costs\ (CFC)$$

Cash fixed costs (CFC) include both fixed operating and fixed financing costs. When EBDAT is zero, $R = VC + CFC$, and the firm is at its survival breakeven. We can, in turn, solve for the breakeven level of survival revenues as follows:

1. For our example, the ratio of variable costs to revenues is a constant (VC/R) that we will refer to as VCRR (variable cost revenue ratio). By multiplying this variable cost revenue ratio by the dollar amount of revenues, we obtain the dollar amount of variable costs. Thus, the dollar amount of variable costs for any level of revenue (R) equals:

$$VC = (VCRR)(R) \tag{4.1}$$

2. Working backward from breakeven, we can define **survival revenues (SR)** as the level of revenue just offsetting variable and cash fixed costs:

$$SR = VC + CFC,\ or$$
$$CFC = SR - VC \tag{4.2}$$

survival revenues (SR) amount of revenues just offsetting variable and cash fixed costs (EBDAT breakeven)

3. Next, by substituting SR for R in equation 4.1 into equation 4.2, we have:

$$CFC = SR - (VCRR)(SR) \tag{4.3}$$

4. Rewriting 4.3 gives:

$$CFC = SR[1 - (VCRR)] \tag{4.4}$$

5. Finally, solving for survival revenues (SR) gives the operating revenues necessary for a zero EBDAT (i.e., the earnings before depreciation, amortization, and taxes breakeven point):

$$SR = [CFC/(1 - VCRR)] \tag{4.5}$$

contribution profit margin

portion of the sale of a product that contributes to covering the cash fixed costs

VCRR is a fraction less than 1. That is, the variable costs associated with producing a product must be less than the sales revenues derived from selling that product.[14] The term "1 – VCRR" is referred to as the **contribution profit margin** that the sale of a product contributes toward covering all cash fixed costs (both operating and financing). As long as the contribution margin is positive, more sales will contribute to the firm's ability to reach survival breakeven and possibly even an operating profit. We can use equation 4.5 to solve for a venture's survival breakeven point—the dollar amount of revenues (i.e., survival revenues) needed to produce a zero EBDAT.

By solving for the survival breakeven revenues, we can identify the amount of survival revenues needed to achieve a zero EBDAT. First, the cost of goods sold to revenues ratio was constant at 65 percent and is the only variable cost during the three-year period. Annual cash fixed costs are $400,000, consisting of $200,000 in administrative expenses, $180,000 in marketing expenses, and $20,000 in financing costs. Using equation 4.5, the EBDAT would have been zero at a level of survival revenues (SR) of:

$$SR = \$400{,}000/(1 - .65) = \$400{,}000/.35 = \$1{,}142{,}857, \text{ or } \$1{,}143{,}000 \text{ (rounded)}$$

We can check the accuracy of this calculation as follows:

Survival revenues	$1,143,000
−Cost of goods sold (65%)	−743,000
Gross profit	400,000
−Administrative expenses	−200,000
−Marketing expenses	−180,000
−Interest expenses	−20,000
EBDAT	$ 0

PSA needed survival revenues of $1,143,000 to cover both its variable costs of producing scanners and its cash fixed costs. As a check, the revenues in the two years when PSA exceeded survival breakeven were $1,500,000 and $2,500,000. At a $100 selling price per scanner, PSA needed to produce and sell 11,430 units to produce a zero EBDAT. The unit sales in the same two years were 15,000 and 25,000.

Figure 4.2 illustrates a survival breakeven chart for PSA Corporation. First, we display cash fixed costs of $400,000 as a horizontal line indicating that these costs are fixed over the range of possible unit sales depicted in the graph. Next, the variable operating costs in the form of costs of goods sold are added to the fixed costs to produce the total cash operating costs line (denoted as total costs). Because variable costs move directly with units sold and revenues (at a .65 ratio), the total costs curve increases at a linear rate. The revenue line starts at the intersection of the two axes where zero units sold reflects zero sales revenues. However, as sales are produced, the revenue line is more steeply

---

[14]   If variable costs are greater than the sales price, the entrepreneur would be wise to liquidate or exit the venture immediately. The act of selling more products and increasing the volume of sales will only result in even larger losses.

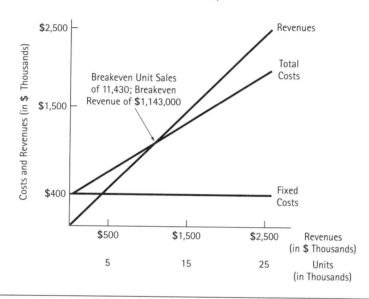

FIGURE 4.2   EBDAT Breakeven Chart for PSA Corporation (Where Variable Costs Are 65 Percent of Revenues)

sloped than the total costs line because sales revenue on an incremental unit exceeds variable costs of that unit. Because cash fixed costs are being spread more thinly as the number of units increases, there will be a point where the total operating costs and revenues lines intersect. This intersection, of course, occurs when the EBDAT is zero. At revenue levels below (to the left of) the intersection point, PSA would have had an operating loss. At revenue levels above (to the right of) the intersection point, PSA would have had positive EBDAT.

CONCEPT CHECK

- What is EBDAT?
- What is meant by EBDAT breakeven in terms of survival revenues?

NOPAT BREAKEVEN

In recent years, a concept called economic value added has swept through the business world. **Economic value added (EVA)** is a measure of a firm's economic profit over a specified time period, usually one year.[15] EVA differs primarily

economic value added (EVA)
measure of a firm's economic profit over a specified time period

---

[15]   Stern Stewart & Company, a consulting firm whose founders developed a proprietary version of the economic profit concept, has an associated registered trademark, EVA®.

from a firm's accounting profit by deducting a charge for the cost of equity capital when calculating EVA.[16] The basic EVA formula is:

EVA = Net Operating Profit After Taxes − After-Tax Dollar Cost of Financial Capital Used

NOPAT
net operating profit after taxes or EBIT times one minus the firm's tax rate

NOPAT is the abbreviation for a firm's net operating profit after taxes and is calculated as the earnings before interest and taxes (EBIT) times one minus the firm's tax rate. In formula terms, it is written as:

NOPAT = EBIT(1 − Tax Rate)

EVA emphasizes the separation of a firm's operations from its financing. A major difference between EVA's NOPAT and the accounting measure of net profit, or net income, is that NOPAT ignores any interest costs of debt financing; it calculates operating after-tax profits by applying the firm's tax rate directly against EBIT. In contrast, we calculate accounting net profit after taxes by first subtracting interest expenses from EBIT and then applying the tax rate to the remaining profit.

The second component of EVA estimates the dollar cost of the amount of financial capital used to support the firm's operations. We will defer discussing the financing cost side of EVA until Chapter 7.

NOPAT breakeven revenues (NR)
amount of revenues needed to cover a venture's total operating costs

NOPAT breakeven revenues (NR) is the amount of revenues needed to cover a venture's total operating costs. NOPAT breakeven considers cash expenses and depreciation (and amortization), but not interest costs.

For EBDAT or survival breakeven, recall that PSA Corporation's three years of experience demonstrate various levels of success. The initial year achieved unit sales of 5,000. The unit sales for the second and third years were 15,000 and 25,000, respectively. Recall that depreciation expenses were $25,000 per year. The effective tax rate for PSA was 30 percent.

Table 4.8 differs from Table 4.7 by excluding interest payments and including depreciation and taxes for the three years. Depreciation, a noncash expense, reflects a cost of production related to the depletion of the economic life of fixed assets such as machinery and equipment.[17]

The 5,000 scanners sold in the first year yielded a NOPAT of −$161,000. For readers closely following this example, it may be disturbing that the NOPAT of −$161,000 appears to be less troubling than the EBIT of −$230,000. The discrepancy lies in the common financial practice of taking tax credits immediately when taxable income is actually a loss. In a sense, we have used PSA's restated Year 1 tax filing, in which the tax loss carryforward created by the first-year loss

---

[16] The process of applying EVA to accounting information may also result in adjustments to research and development costs and depreciation and amortization expenses. Inventories may also be revalued. For further specifics, see G. Bennett Stewart III, *The Quest for Value* (New York: Collins Publishers, 1991). Also see Al Ehrbar, *EVA: The Real Key to Creating Wealth* (John Wiley & Sons, 1998).

[17] By subtracting accounting-based depreciation when calculating NOPAT, we are assuming that the amount written off for accounting and tax purposes is the same as the true economic depreciation. Otherwise, the accounting-based depreciation would need to be adjusted to conform to economic depreciation reflecting the actual wearing out of or using up of the fixed assets.

TABLE 4.8   NOPAT Flows Expected Under Three Possible Revenue Scenarios for Next Year for PSA Corporation

	YEAR 1	YEAR 2	YEAR 3
Number of units sold	5,000	15,000	25,000
Revenues	$500,000	$1,500,000	$2,500,000
−Cost of goods sold (65% of revenues)	−325,000	−975,000	−1,625,000
Gross profit	175,000	525,000	875,000
−Administrative expenses	−200,000	−200,000	−200,000
−Marketing expenses	−180,000	−180,000	−180,000
EBITDA	−205,000	145,000	495,000
−Depreciation expenses	−25,000	−25,000	−25,000
EBIT	−230,000	120,000	470,000
Taxes (at a 30% effective rate)	69,000	−36,000	−141,000
NOPAT	−$161,000	$ 84,000	$ 329,000
Percent of revenues	−32.2%	5.6%	13.2%

is reflected in a positive cash flow from taxes (instead of the usual negative cash flow to taxes).[18]

In the second year, 15,000 scanners were sold, yielding a NOPAT of $84,000. We see that the cash operating income (EBITDA) of $145,000 is reduced by $25,000 in depreciation and $36,000 in taxes. NOPAT as a percent of revenues was 5.6 percent. In the third year, PSA moved into its prime by reaching sales of 25,000 units and NOPAT of $329,000, or 13.2 percent of revenues.

When EBIT is zero, NOPAT is also zero because no taxes are payable. With this relationship between EBIT and NOPAT in mind, we can easily solve for the NOPAT breakeven revenues (NR) necessary for zero NOPAT by following the example shown earlier in terms of the amount of survival revenues needed for zero EBDAT. Total operating fixed costs (TOFC) consist of cash operating fixed costs (excluding interest expenses) plus noncash fixed costs (e.g., depreciation). The bottom line is:

$$NR = TOFC/(1 - VCRR) \tag{4.6}$$

where VCRR, as before, is the venture's (or a comparable venture's) ratio of variable cost to revenues.

While the amount of revenues needed for NOPAT breakeven focuses on the venture's operations, including depreciation, it is the operating breakeven

---

[18] Note that when NOPAT equals zero (breakeven), there is no imputed tax (on NOPAT), and therefore this convention does not change the location of NOPAT breakeven. This convention is actually very close to the way the accrual method of accounting would record the tax implications of a loss. However, concurrent with the raising of net income by tax credit from a loss carryforward, accountants would also require the booking of a deferred tax asset (as a use of the cash "created" by the accruing of the tax benefit).

(EBDAT = 0) that is critical in short-term survival. That is, it is important for the entrepreneur to know the revenues necessary to cover variable, fixed cash operating, and interest costs. The inability to cover these costs is an indication that the venture faces financial distress in the absence of external funding. In contrast, the failure to cover noncash charges associated with depreciation and amortization is not an indication of immediate financial distress.

CONCEPT CHECK

- What is NOPAT?
- What is meant by NOPAT breakeven?

IDENTIFYING BREAKEVEN DRIVERS IN REVENUE PROJECTIONS

It is important for the entrepreneur to identify major drivers for breakeven levels of revenues. A survival-stage venture will be concerned primarily with EBDAT breakeven. For many new ventures, the most important influence (or driver) on the venture's breakeven is its VCRR. We illustrate this influence using a hypothetical change in PSA Corporation's VCRR.

Suppose in Year 2 that, owing to volume purchase discounts, PSA had received a pleasant surprise: lower production costs of $60 per unit (or 60 percent of revenues). While you could rework Table 4.7 and observe the impact of a higher contribution profit margin (40 percent instead of 35 percent) on the venture's EBDAT, directly solving for the new survival breakeven revenues (SR) is enlightening. This can be done as follows:

$$SR = \$400{,}000/(1 - .60) = \$400{,}000/.40 = \$1{,}000{,}000$$

Therefore, at a contribution profit margin of 40 percent, the level of survival revenues needed to have broken even at zero EBDAT would have dropped to $1,000,000. On a per-unit basis, PSA would have needed to sell only 10,000 scanners to have broken even. On a relative basis, a decrease in the VCRR from 65 to 60 percent causes the survival breakeven revenues to drop from $1,143,000 (11,430 units) to $1,000,000 (10,000 units). Stated in percentage change terms, a 7.7 percent [(.60 − .65)/.65] decrease in the variable costs percentage translates into a 12.5 percent [($1,143,000 − $1,000,000)/ $1,143,000)] decline in the survival revenues breakeven point where EBDAT would have been zero.

The importance of the decline in VCRR on survival revenues is depicted in Figure 4.3. The key thing to notice is the slope of the total costs curve (variable costs per unit plus fixed costs) in Figure 4.3 is less steep than the total costs curve in Figure 4.2. This lower slope in Figure 4.3 allows the revenue line to cross the total costs line (i.e., reach EBDAT breakeven) more quickly compared to Figure 4.2.

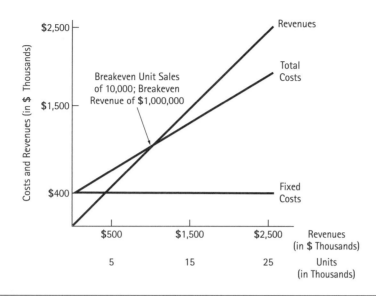

FIGURE 4.3 EBDAT Breakeven Chart for PSA Corporation (Where Variable Costs Are 60 Percent of Revenues)

Not surprisingly, under this hypothetical Year 2 scenario, PSA would have produced a more attractive EBDAT. We can see this as follows:

Survival revenues	$1,500,000
−Cost of goods sold (60%)	−900,000
Gross profit	600,000
−Administrative expenses	−200,000
−Marketing expenses	−180,000
−Interest expenses	−20,000
EBDAT	$ 200,000
EBDAT as a percent of revenues	13.3%

Recall from Table 4.7 that unit sales of 15,000 and a contribution profit margin of 35 percent yield an EBDAT of 8.3 percent of revenue. The hypothetical increase in contribution profit margin to 40 percent yields an EBDAT of 13.3 percent of revenues.

A second key determinant of the revenues that a venture will need to break even is the amount of fixed costs. As a second hypothetical, suppose that the fixed component of Year 2 founder compensation dropped by $50,000. Total administrative expenses would have been only $150,000 and cash fixed costs would have been $350,000 (i.e., $150,000, $180,000, and $20,000 in administrative, marketing, and interest expenses, respectively). This would have led to lower survival revenues (yielding EBDAT = 0). We illustrate this change in conjunction with the original contribution profit margin of 35 percent.

Survival revenues (SR) to produce a zero EBDAT would have been:

$$SR = \$350,000/(1 - .65) = \$350,000/.35 = \$1,000,000$$

Thus, EBDAT breakeven would have been $1,000,000 (or 10,000 units) compared with the $1,143,000 (11,430 units) depicted in Figure 4.1. We see that a $50,000 or 12.5 percent ($50,000/$400,000) decrease in cash fixed costs would have resulted in a comparable 12.5 percent decrease in the amount of survival revenues needed to have broken even [i.e., ($1,143,000 − $1,000,000)/ $1,143,000].

As we can see, two important drivers play critical roles in determining how high revenues must be to contribute to venture survival. Higher VCRR (variable costs to revenue ratio) and higher fixed costs both raise the level of survival revenues necessary to break even at EBDAT equal to zero. Typically, a venture will face a trade-off between fixed and variable costs. This trade-off relates to the venture's leverage.

venture leverage
measure of how changes in top-line revenues relate to changes in EBDAT

Venture leverage is a measure of how changes in top-line revenues relate to changes in a performance measure (e.g., EBDAT). A highly leveraged venture can turn a small increase in revenues into a major increase in EBDAT. When a venture chooses to pay higher up-front fixed costs (to lower variable costs at the time of production), each additional dollar of revenue translates to more EBDAT. As an example, consider two firms each producing 1,000,000 widgets to generate revenues of $1,000,000 from total cash costs (production and financing) of $800,000. Firm A has $600,000 in fixed costs and $200,000 in variable costs at the current production level. Firm B has $200,000 in fixed costs and $600,000 in variable costs. This means that the next widget Firm A produces costs $.20. In contrast, the next widget that Firm B produces costs $.60. Firm A can clearly turn the revenue from an additional unit ($1) into more EBDAT than Firm B can.

CONCEPT CHECK

• What is meant by breakeven drivers?

SUMMARY

In this chapter, we developed a basic understanding about the creation and use of accounting information. We examined three main financial statements (income statement, balance sheet, and statement of cash flows) and their use in diagnosing whether a venture's performance has been contributing to survival. We discussed cash burn and cash build as they can be observed from the statement of cash flows.

The last part of the chapter focused on using accounting information to address venture survival and breakeven levels of revenue and unit sales. First, we described the use of the EBDAT breakeven analysis to help calibrate the level of *survival revenues* (SR) that would have been necessary to cover the venture's variable and cash fixed costs (both operating and financing). Second, we described the use of the NOPAT breakeven analysis to calibrate the level of *NOPAT breakeven revenues* (NR) that would have been necessary to cover the venture's cash and noncash (e.g., depreciation) fixed costs and taxes (but not interest costs). Our final discussion focused on identifying major drivers—the variable costs to revenue ratio (VCRR) and the amount of cash fixed costs—on the amount of revenues that would have been necessary to survive.

KEY TERMS

accrual accounting	EBDAT breakeven	net income or profit
accrued wages	EBIT	NOPAT
accumulated depreciation	EBITDA	NOPAT breakeven revenues (NR)
assets	economic value added (EVA)	operating income
balance sheet	fixed assets	operating leases
bank loan	fixed expenses	other current liabilities
capital leases	generally accepted accounting principles (GAAP)	other long-term assets
cash		owners' equity
cash flow breakeven	gross earnings	payables
contribution profit margin	income statement	receivables
cost of goods sold	inventories	statement of cash flows
current assets	liquidity	survival revenues (SR)
depreciation	long-term debts	variable expenses
EBDAT	marketable securities	venture leverage

DISCUSSION QUESTIONS

1. Describe the types of resources (assets) needed for a new product venture during its development and startup stages. Comment on the likely revenues and expenses during these early life cycle stages.

2. What is meant by the statement that a balance sheet provides a "snapshot" of a venture's financial position as of a point in time? Why must a balance sheet be in balance?

3. Briefly describe the typical types of accounts that are found in the current assets of a new venture.

4. What is meant by the terms "depreciation" and "accumulated depreciation"?

5. What types of liabilities might show up on a venture's balance sheet?

6. What does an income statement measure or track over time?

7. Define the term "EBIT." How does EBIT differ from a firm's net income or net profit?

8. What are the three internal operating schedules that most firms must prepare?

9. Briefly describe what is meant by a statement of cash flows.

10. What is meant by net cash build and net cash burn?

11. Describe the differences between variable expenses and fixed expenses.

12. Define the term "EBITDA."

13. What is a venture's contribution profit margin?

14. Define the term "economic value added (EVA)." What are the two major components of EVA?

15. Define the term "EBDAT" and describe the meaning of EBDAT breakeven and survival revenues.

16. Describe and illustrate how an EBDAT (survival) breakeven chart is constructed.

17. Define the term "NOPAT" and describe the meaning of NOPAT breakeven and NOPAT breakeven revenues.

18. Identify and explain the formula for finding the NOPAT breakeven revenues. Relate this to breakeven in terms of EBIT.

19. What is meant by breakeven drivers? Identify two important drivers affecting the amount of revenues needed for ventures to break even.

INTERNET ACTIVITIES

1. A number of Web sites are available to help young ventures measure their financial performance and to help them when they are growing and "ramping up" revenues. Access the http://money.cnn.com/magazines/business2/ Web site and identify sources helpful to growing firms.

2. Access the http://www.nvst.com Web site and find information on how to choose an accountant and other organizations that will help in measuring a venture's financial performance.

3. Access the Nolo Press Web site at http://www.nolo.com and other publishers' Web sites, and identify software products designed to help the young venture with its legal and accounting problems.

EXERCISES/PROBLEMS

1. Assume you are starting a new business involving the manufacture and sale of a new product. Raw materials costs are $40 per product. Direct labor costs are expected to be $30 per product. You expect to sell each product for $110. You plan to produce 100 products next month and expect to sell 90 products.

   A. Prepare cost of production, cost of goods sold, and inventories schedules for next (the first) month.

   B. During the second month, you plan to produce 110 products but expect sales in the month to be 115 products. Prepare cost of production, cost of goods sold, and inventories schedules for the second month.

2. Assume you have developed and tested a prototype electronic product and are about to start your new business. You purchase preprogrammed computer chips at $70 per unit. Other component costs include plastic casings at $15 per unit and assembly hardware at $5 per unit. Direct labor costs are $15 per hour and three units can be produced per hour. You intend to sell each unit at a 50 percent markup over the total costs of producing each unit. The plan is to produce 500 product units per month in January, February, and March. Sales are expected to be 200 units in January, 400 units in February, and 800 units in March.

   A. Calculate the dollar amount of sales revenue expected in each month (i.e., January, February, and March) and for the first quarter of the year.

   B. Prepare a cost of production schedule for January, February, and March.

   C. Prepare a cost of goods sold schedule for each of the three months and for the first quarter of the year. Using your cost of goods sold estimates and the sales revenues expected in Part A, calculate the gross earnings for January, February, and March, as well as for the first quarter of the year.

   D. Prepare an inventories schedule for January, February, and March.

3. This problem is a continuation of Problem 2. Assume you ramp up production to 1,000 units per month in April, May, and June. Sales are expected to be 800 units in April and 1,100 units in each of May and June. Repeat the calculations requested in Problem 2 for the second quarter of the year (April, May, and June).

4. During its first year of operations, the SubRay Corporation produced the following income statement results:

Net sales	$300,000
Cost of goods sold	−180,000
Gross profit	120,000
General and administrative	−60,000
Marketing expenses	−60,000
Depreciation	−20,000
EBIT	−20,000
Interest expenses	−10,000
Earnings before taxes	−30,000
Income taxes	−0
Net earnings (loss)	−$ 30,000

Costs of goods sold are expected to vary with sales and be a constant percentage of sales. The general and administrative employees have been hired and are expected to remain a fixed cost. Marketing expenses are also expected to remain fixed since the current sales staff members are expected to remain on fixed salaries and no new hires are planned. The effective tax rate is expected to be 30 percent for a profitable firm.

A. Estimate the survival or EBDAT breakeven amount in terms of survival revenues necessary for the SubRay Corporation to break even next year.

B. Estimate the NOPAT breakeven amount in terms of revenues necessary for the SubRay Corporation to break even next year.

C. Assume that the product selling price is $50 per unit. Calculate the EBDAT and NOPAT breakeven points in terms of the number of units that will have to be sold next year.

5. Cindy and Robert (Rob) Castillo founded the Castillo Products Company in 2006. The company manufactures components for personal decision assistant (PDA) products and for other handheld electronic products. Year 2007 proved to be a test of the Castillo Products Company's ability to survive. However, sales increased rapidly in 2008, and the firm reported a net income after taxes of $75,000. Depreciation expenses were $40,000 in 2008. Following are the Castillo Products Company's balance sheets for 2007 and 2008.

Castillo Products Company

	2007	2008
Cash	$ 50,000	$ 20,000
Accounts receivable	200,000	280,000
Inventories	400,000	500,000
Total current assets	650,000	800,000
Gross fixed assets	450,000	540,000
Accumulated depreciation	−100,000	−140,000
Net fixed assets	350,000	400,000
Total assets	$1,000,000	$1,200,000

Accounts payable	$ 130,000	$ 160,000
Accruals	50,000	70,000
Bank loan	90,000	100,000
Total current liabilities	270,000	330,000
Long-term debt	300,000	400,000
Common stock	150,000	150,000
Paid-in capital	200,000	200,000
Retained earnings	80,000	120,000
Total liabilities and equity	$1,000,000	$1,200,000

A. Calculate Castillo's cash flow from operating activities for 2008.

B. Calculate Castillo's cash flow from investing activities for 2008.

C. Calculate Castillo's cash flow from financing activities for 2008.

D. Prepare a formal statement of cash flows for 2008 and identify the major cash inflows and outflows that were generated by the Castillo Products Company.

E. Use your calculation results from Parts A and B to determine whether Castillo was building or burning cash during 2008 and indicate the dollar amount of the cash build or burn.

F. If Castillo had a net cash burn from operating and investing activities in 2008, divide the amount of burn by 12 to calculate an average monthly burn amount. If the 2009 monthly cash burn continues at the 2008 rate, indicate how long in months it will be before the firm runs out of cash if there are no changes in financing activities.

6. The Castillo Products Company described in Problem 5 had a very difficult operating year in 2007, resulting in a net loss of $65,000 on sales of $900,000. In 2008, sales jumped to $1,500,000, and a net profit after taxes was earned. The firm's income statements are shown below.

Castillo Products Company

	2007	2008
Net sales	$900,000	$1,500,000
Cost of goods sold	540,000	900,000
Gross profit	360,000	600,000
Marketing	90,000	150,000
General and administrative	250,000	250,000
Depreciation	40,000	40,000
EBIT	−20,000	160,000
Interest	45,000	60,000
Earnings before taxes	−65,000	100,000
Income taxes	0	25,000*
Net income (loss)	−$ 65,000	$ 75,000

* Includes tax loss carryforward from 2007.

A. Calculate each income statement item for 2007 as a percent of the 2007 sales level. Make the same calculations for 2008. Determine which cost or expense items varied directly with sales for the two-year period.

B. Use the information in Part A to classify specific expense items as being either variable or fixed expenses. Then estimate Castillo's EBDAT breakeven in terms of survival revenues if interest expenses had remained at the 2007 level ($45,000) in 2008.

C. Estimate the dollar amount of survival revenues actually needed by the Castillo Products Company to reach EBDAT breakeven in 2008, given that more debt was obtained and interest expenses increased to $60,000.

7. Salza Technology Corporation increased its sales from $375,000 in 2007 to $450,000 in 2008 as shown in the firm's income statements presented below. LeAnn Sands, chief executive officer (CEO) and founder of the firm, expressed concern that the cash account and the firm's marketable securities declined substantially between 2007 and 2008. Salza's complete balance sheets are also shown. Ms. Sands is seeking your assistance in the preparation of a statement of cash flows for Salza Technology.

A. Prepare a statement of cash flows for 2008 for Salza Technology Corporation.

B. Provide a brief description of what happened in terms of cash flows (both inflows and outflows) for Salza between 2007 and 2008.

Salza Technology Corporation
Annual Income Statements (in $ Thousands)

	2007	2008
Net sales	$375	$450
Less: Cost of goods sold	225	270
Gross profit	150	180
Less: Operating expenses	46	46
Less: Depreciation	25	30
Less: Interest	4	4
Income before taxes	75	100
Less: Income taxes	20	30
Net income	$ 55	$ 70
Cash dividends	$ 17	$ 20

Balance Sheets as of December 31 (in $ Thousands)

	2007	2008
Cash	$ 39	$ 16
Accounts receivable	50	80
Inventories	151	204
Total current assets	240	300
Gross fixed assets	200	290
Less accumulated depreciation	−95	−125
Net fixed assets	105	165
Total assets	$345	$465

Accounts payable	$ 30	$ 45
Bank loan	20	27
Accrued liabilities	10	23
Total current liabilities	60	95
Long-term debt	15	15
Common stock	85	120
Retained earnings	185	235
Total liabilities and equity	$345	$465

C. Use your calculations from Part A for cash flows from operating and investing activities to indicate the extent to which Salza was building or burning cash in 2008.

D. Convert the 2008 annual cash build or cash burn to a monthly rate. If cash flow activities relating to operations and investing for 2008 continue into 2009, indicate (1) how long it will be before Salza runs out of cash (if Salza is burning cash) or (2) the expected 2009 year-end cash account balance if Salza is building cash. Assume no changes in cash flows from financing activities in 2009 for calculation purposes.

8. LeAnn Sands wants to conduct revenue breakeven analyses of Salza Technology Corporation for 2008. Income statement information is shown in Problem 7. For 2008, the firm's cost of goods sold is considered to be variable costs, and operating expenses are considered to be fixed cash costs. Depreciation expenses in 2008 also are expected to be fixed costs.

A. Calculate Salza's EBDAT breakeven in terms of survival revenues for 2008.

B. Calculate Salza's NOPAT breakeven in terms of NOPAT breakeven revenues for 2008.

9. LeAnn Sands has reason to believe that 2009 will be a replication of 2008 except that cost of goods sold is expected to be 65 percent of the estimated $450,000 in revenues. Other income statement relationships are expected to remain the same in 2009 as they were in 2008.

A. Calculate the EBDAT breakeven point for 2009 for Salza in terms of survival revenues.

B. Calculate the NOPAT breakeven point for 2009 for Salza in terms of NOPAT breakeven revenues.

M I N I   C A S E

Jen and Larry's Frozen Yogurt Company

In 2008, Jennifer (Jen) Liu and Larry Mestas founded Jen and Larry's Frozen Yogurt Company, which was based on the idea of applying the microbrew or microbatch strategy to the production and sale of frozen yogurt. (The reader may recall that we introduced this yogurt venture in the problems section at the end of Chapter 2.) Jen and Larry began producing small quantities of unique flavors and blends in limited editions. Revenues were $600,000 in 2008 and were estimated at $1.2 million in 2009.

Since Jen and Larry were selling premium frozen yogurt containing premium ingredients, each small cup of yogurt sold for $3, and the cost of producing the frozen yogurt averaged $1.50 per cup. Administrative expenses, including Jen and Larry's salary and expenses for an accountant and

Jen and Larry's Frozen Yogurt Company (continued)

two other administrative staff, were estimated at $180,000 in 2009. Marketing expenses, largely in the form of behind-the-counter workers, in-store posters, and advertising in local newspapers, were projected to be $200,000 in 2009.

An investment in bricks and mortar was necessary to make and sell the yogurt. Initial specialty equipment and the renovation of an old warehouse building in lower downtown (known as LoDo) occurred at the beginning of 2008. Additional equipment needed to make the amount of yogurt forecasted to be sold in 2009 was purchased at the beginning of 2009. As a result, depreciation expenses were expected to be $50,000 in 2009. Interest expenses were estimated at $15,000 in 2009. The average tax rate was expected to be 25 percent of taxable income.

A. How many cups of frozen yogurt would have to be sold in order for the firm to reach its projected revenues of $1.2 million?

B. Calculate the dollar amount of EBDAT if Jen and Larry's Frozen Yogurt Company achieves the forecasted $1.2 million in sales for 2009. What would EBDAT be as a percent of revenues?

C. Calculate the dollar amount of NOPAT if Jen and Larry's venture achieves the forecasted $1.2 million in sales in 2009. What would NOPAT be as a percent of sales?

D. Jen and Larry believe that under a worst-case scenario yogurt revenues would be at the 2008 level of $600,000 even after plans and expenditures were put in place to increase revenues in 2009. What would happen to the venture's EBDAT and NOPAT?

E. Jen and Larry also believe that under optimistic conditions yogurt revenues could reach $1.5 million in 2009. Show what would happen to the venture's EBDAT and NOPAT.

F. Calculate the EBDAT breakeven point for 2009 in terms of survival revenues for Jen and Larry's Frozen Yogurt Company. How many cups of frozen yogurt would have to be sold to reach EBDAT breakeven?

G. Calculate the NOPAT breakeven point for 2009 in terms of NOPAT breakeven revenues for Jen and Larry's venture. How many cups of frozen yogurt would have to be sold to reach NOPAT breakeven?

H. Show what would happen to the EBDAT breakeven in terms of survival revenues if the cost of producing a cup of yogurt increased to $1.60 but the selling price remained at $3.00 per cup. How would the EBDAT breakeven change if production costs declined to $1.40 per cup when the yogurt selling price remained at $3.00 per cup?

I. Show what would happen to the EBDAT breakeven point in terms of survival sales if an additional $30,000 was spent on advertising in 2009 while the other fixed costs remained the same, production costs remained at $1.50 per cup, and the selling price remained at $3.00 per cup. Also show what would happen to the NOPAT breakeven point in terms of NOPAT breakeven revenues under the just-described situation.

J. Now assume that, owing to competition, Jen and Larry must sell their frozen yogurt for $2.80 per cup in 2009. The cost of producing the yogurt is expected to remain at $1.50 per cup and cash fixed costs are forecasted to be $395,000 ($180,000 in administrative, $200,000 in marketing, and $15,000 in interest expenses). Depreciation expenses and the tax rate are also expected to remain the same as projected in the initial discussion of Jen and Larry's venture. Calculate the EBDAT and NOPAT breakeven points in terms of survival and NOPAT breakeven revenues, respectively.

Chapter 5

EVALUATING FINANCIAL PERFORMANCE

PREVIOUSLY COVERED

Chapter 4 provided a review of historical financial statements, emphasizing the importance of measuring and monitoring a new venture's financial progress. We introduced the important concept of cash flow and breakeven. By examining the venture's historical performance, one can see the influence of certain drivers, including cash fixed costs and the variable-cost-to-revenue ratio.

LOOKING AHEAD

Chapter 6 further explores the centrality of cash flow. We cover short-term and long-term financial planning, including projected monthly and annual financial statements. While short-term projections focus on survival, longer-term projections identify the need for additional funds to support the growth envisioned in the business plan. Projected financial statements usually reflect the financial analysis introduced in the current chapter.

CHAPTER LEARNING OBJECTIVES

In this chapter, we focus on identifying and understanding the financial ratios used to evaluate a venture's financial performance over time. Venture performance and efficiency are important to a variety of constituencies, including lenders and creditors, equity investors, and the entrepreneur. Lenders and creditors want to be repaid in full and on time; investors want a sufficient return on their investments as compensation for the risks they are taking; the entrepreneur initially wants to survive and then build value in the venture. After completing this chapter, you will be able to:

1. Understand important financial performance measures and their users, by life cycle stage

2. Describe how financial ratios are used to monitor a venture's performance

3. Identify specific cash burn rate measures and liquidity ratios and explain how they are calculated and used by the entrepreneur

4. Identify and describe the use and value of conversion period ratios to the entrepreneur

5. Identify specific leverage ratios and explain their use by lenders and creditors

6. Identify and describe measures of profitability and efficiency that are important to the entrepreneur and equity investors

7. Describe limitations when using financial ratios

Now that we have an understanding of how basic financial statements are prepared, we are ready to examine why and how various parties use financial data. Once a venture has survived the initial shock of the startup phase, attention must shift to measuring and monitoring the venture's health. A solid understanding of how financial data are used is critical for understanding how current performance will be analyzed and interpreted by others. Which financial ratios will lenders use to decide whether to extend a loan? Which financial ratios are important to venture investors when they decide whether, and on what terms, to make an investment? For the entrepreneur, financial analysis is as much about dealing with the future as it is about understanding the past.

5.1 USERS OF FINANCIAL PERFORMANCE MEASURES BY LIFE CYCLE STAGE

Figure 5.1 lists important financial performance measures and those who employ them during a successful venture's progression from birth through the rapid-growth stage. Seed financing during the development stage is usually provided by the entrepreneur and willing family and friends. For some ventures, business angels and venture capitalists (VCs) contribute additional startup-stage financing. The financial focus during these two early stages is how quickly the venture uses cash (the cash burn rate) and the venture's ability to meet short-term financial obligations (as measured by liquidity ratios). Closely connected to cash burn and liquidity is the venture's operating cycle—the average time it takes from purchasing materials to collecting cash for products sold. Monitoring cash burn, cash conversion, and liquidity ratios can consume considerable time and energy during these early stages.

Family and friends who provide early-stage financing typically do not get involved in financial monitoring, with or without formal measures and ratios. Their understanding of the venture's financial situation tends to evolve through informal communication during social interactions with the entrepreneur (complete with the inherent biases such occasions provide). However, business angels and venture capitalists do typically want to track relevant financial indicators of the venture's status and progress. Consequently, we turn our attention to the ingredients of early-stage financial analysis, focusing on connecting burn rates, liquidity, and operating cycle.

Figure 5.1 also depicts the importance of monitoring and measuring cash and liquidity through a venture's survival stage. Many ventures continue to rely heavily on external cash and investment during this time. The entrepreneurial

FIGURE 5.1	Measures of Financial Performance by Life Cycle Stage and User		
LIFE CYCLE STAGE	**TYPE OF FINANCING**	**FINANCIAL RATIOS AND MEASURES**	**USERS OF FINANCIAL RATIOS AND MEASURES**
Development and startup stages	Seed financing and startup financing	Cash burn rates and liquidity ratios Conversion period ratios	Entrepreneur Business angels Venture capitalists (VCs)
Survival stage	First-round financing	Cash burn, liquidity, and conversion ratios Leverage ratios Profitability and efficiency ratios	Entrepreneur, angels, and VCs Commercial banks
Rapid-growth stage	Second-round, mezzanine, and liquidity-stage financing	Leverage ratios Profitability and efficiency ratios	Entrepreneur, angels, and VCs Commercial banks Investment bankers

team and external investors begin to focus on profitability and efficiency in addition to liquidity and burn rate. Investors start to wonder whether the venture will eventually provide a return on invested capital. As reasonable multiyear performance data become available during the survival stage, professional debt providers are a more feasible source of external financing. Commercial banks and other creditors carefully consider liquidity and financial leverage ratios as important indicators of the venture's potential to employ and repay debt.

For ventures that enter the rapid-growth stage, external financing needs usually expand dramatically. Commercial banks and other creditors often are asked to increase their financing commitments, making it even more important for the venture to continue monitoring leverage and liquidity ratios. Second-round (and higher-round) financing typically requires additional equity injections from venture capitalists and other investors seeking ownerships positions. Profitability and efficiency ratios become increasingly important to these equity investors. Mezzanine investors who take a part-debt part-equity position in the venture's financing are an excellent example of financiers who are concerned about leverage and liquidity ratios (due to the debt character in part of their financing) and about profitability and efficiency ratios (due to the equity kickers or sweeteners component of their financing).

Investment bankers often play a role in providing liquidity-stage financing for venture equity investors by creating a public market for the venture's equity. This provides an opportunity for the entrepreneur, business angels, and venture capitalists to sell part or even all of their equity holdings. Investment bankers focus primarily on profitability and performance ratios reflecting possible venture values.

Before turning our attention to measures of financial performance, we will discuss how financial ratios are used. We conclude the chapter by emphasizing that, while ratios can provide important diagnostic signals, entrepreneurs need to understand the widely accepted limitations to their application.

- What are the primary types of financial performance measures used by life cycle stage?
- Who are the primary users of financial performance measures at each life cycle stage?

5.2   USING FINANCIAL RATIOS

Financial ratios show the relationships between two or more financial variables or between financial variables and time. They are a useful way to summarize large amounts of financial data in order to simplify comparisons of a venture's performance with itself and other firms over time. While financial ratios may suggest some answers to inquisitors' questions, they are more widely appreciated for suggesting useful questions about a venture's past and potential future performance.

It is often said that "cash is king"; nowhere is it more true than for the entrepreneur. In addition to paying liabilities as they come due, cash fuels the entrepreneur's continuing vision. The absence, or threatened absence, of cash can prove to be a serious distraction from the core mission of a venture. Having to focus on finding survival cash impairs progress and, ultimately, the potential for success.

Financial ratios addressing related venture attributes are often grouped together by financial analysts. The operating and financial performance attributes we examine are captured by ratios representing measures of liquidity (the ability to meet short-term obligations), conversion period (the time taken to convert another asset into a cash receipt), leverage (the use of debt), and profitability and efficiency. The three basic ratio analysis techniques are (1) **trend analysis** (to examine a venture's performance over time), (2) **cross-sectional analysis** (to compare a venture's performance against other specific firms at a similar stage of maturity or in a related industry), and (3) **industry comparables analysis** (to compare a venture's performance against an average for the venture's industry).

For well-established mature industries, comparable data are readily available. Average industry data are provided by organizations, such as Dun & Bradstreet and Robert Morris Associates, and by individual industry trade associations. Consequently, cross-sectional and industry comparables analysis is very common. For entrepreneurial ventures operating in new or emerging industries, comparable data can be hard to locate. If the standard organizational structure for firms in the industry is sole proprietorship, partnership, or closely held corporation, it may not be possible to uncover comparable data; such firms have no obligation to provide public disclosure. Benchmarking can be very informative and lead to drastic changes in a venture's strategy. Even in the absence of comparable data, a venture can be benchmarked against earlier versions of itself. Trends in a venture's ratios over time often provide signs of progress or problems.

financial ratios
relationships between two or more financial variables or between financial variables and time

trend analysis
examination of a venture's performance over time

cross-sectional analysis
comparison of a venture's performance against another firm at the same point in time

industry comparables analysis
comparison of a venture's performance against the average performance of other firms in the same industry

Tables 5.1, 5.2, and 5.3 contain financial statement data for Medical Products Company (MPC), which you are considering purchasing. MPC will serve as the basis for our examples of ratio construction and analysis. Three years of balance sheets and two years of income statements are available. MPC produces and sells a diversified product line of scientific medical instruments that monitor a patient's (user's) vital signs. The venture's medical instruments are used in hospitals,

---

TABLE 5.1

MPC Income Statements for Years Ended 2007 and 2008

	2007	2008
Net sales	$438,000	$575,000
Cost of goods sold	285,000	380,000
Gross profit	153,000	195,000
Administrative expenses	45,000	65,000
Marketing expenses	32,000	39,000
Research and development	20,000	27,000
Depreciation	14,000	17,000
EBIT	42,000	47,000
Interest expense	12,000	20,000
Income before taxes	30,000	27,000
Income taxes (30% rate)	9,000	8,000
Net income	$ 21,000	$ 19,000

TABLE 5.2

MPC Balance Sheets for Years Ended 2006, 2007, and 2008

ASSETS	2006	2007	2008
Cash and marketable securities	10,000	10,000	5,000
Receivables	60,000	75,000	105,000
Inventories	70,000	95,000	140,000
Total current assets	140,000	180,000	250,000
Gross plant and equipment	205,000	205,000	255,000
Less: accumulated depreciation	28,000	42,000	59,000
Net plant and equipment	177,000	163,000	196,000
Total assets	**317,000**	**343,000**	**446,000**
Liabilities and Equity			
Payables	47,000	57,000	84,000
Short-term bank loan	40,000	44,000	110,000
Accrued liabilities	8,000	9,000	10,000
Total current liabilities	95,000	110,000	204,000
Long-term debt	100,000	90,000	80,000
Owners' equity	122,000	143,000	162,000
Total liabilities and equity	**317,000**	**343,000**	**446,000**

TABLE 5.3 MPC Statements of Cash Flow for Years Ended 2007 and 2008		
CASH FLOW FROM OPERATING ACTIVITIES	**2007**	**2008**
Net Income	21,000	19,000
+ Depreciation	14,000	17,000
− Increase in Receivables	−15,000	−30,000
− Increase in Inventories	−25,000	−45,000
+ Increase in Payables	10,000	27,000
+ Increase in Accrued Liabilities	1,000	1,000
Net Cash Flow from Operations	**6,000**	**−11,000**
Cash Flow from Investing Activities		
−Increase in Gross Equipment	0	−50,000
Net Cash Flow from Investing Activities	**0**	**−50,000**
Cash Flow from Financing Activities		
+Increase in Short-Term Bank Loan	4,000	66,000
−Decrease in Long-Term Debt	−10,000	−10,000
Net Cash Flow from Financing	**−6,000**	**56,000**
Net Change Excluding Cash Account	**0**	**−5,000**
Beginning Cash and Marketable Securities	**10,000**	**10,000**
Ending Cash and Marketable Securities	**10,000**	**5,000**

medical clinics, and retirement home facilities. While you believe this venture is promising, you would like to consider the opportunity more thoroughly.

CONCEPT CHECK

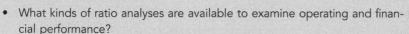

- Why and how are financial ratios useful in analyzing the performance of new ventures?
- What kinds of ratio analyses are available to examine operating and financial performance?

5.3 CASH BURN RATES AND LIQUIDITY RATIOS

The cash burn rate refers to how quickly a venture distributes cash. The cash build rate refers to how quickly it builds cash balances from collections on sales. Liquidity is the ability of a venture to maintain a burn rate high enough to meet its obligations as they come due. Burn rate calculations such as "weeks of cash" remind everyone of the central role that cash, or the lack thereof, plays in a venture's survival. Accounting-oriented measures of a venture's ability to pay (liquidity) are also a traditional approach to assessing a venture's short-term viability. For instance, creditors generally feel safer when current assets exceed current liabilities.[1] When we address the viability of rapidly growing ventures, averages of beginning and ending period accounting values often provide more useful comparisons through time and across firms.

MEASURING VENTURE CASH BURN AND BUILD AMOUNTS AND RATES

Before we assess whether, and how long, a venture can survive on its current capital, it is important to calibrate how fast the venture has been expending cash and consuming capital reserves. For this calibration, the balance sheet and the income statement provide some very useful information. First, we look at a raw measure of how fast the venture is spending cash. To get this number, we need to calculate the actual disbursements of cash over a given period. One approach to calculating cash burn is to start with the cash disbursements related to the income statement's tracking of operating expenses (where we would exclude depreciation and amortization as noncash expenses), interest expenses, and taxes. To these we add increases in the inventories and subtract increases in non-interest-bearing current liabilities accounts (i.e., payables and accrued liabilities). A final adjustment would be to add the amount of capital expenditures (increases in gross fixed assets). In summary, **cash burn** is the cash a venture expends on its operating and financing expenses and its investments in assets. In general, we have:

cash burn

cash a venture expends on its operating and financing expenses and its investments in assets

Cash Burn = Income Statement–Based Operating, Interest, and Tax Expenses
    + Increase in Inventories
    − (Changes in Payables and Accrued Liabilities)
    + Capital Expenditures

cash burn rate

cash burn for a fixed period of time, typically a month

The **cash burn rate** is the cash burn for a fixed period of time, typically a month.

For MPC in 2008 we first calculate cash operating expenses from Table 5.1 as the sum of cost of goods sold ($380,000), administrative expenses ($65,000), marketing expenses ($39,000), and research and development expenses ($27,000) for a total of $511,000. To this we add interest expenses of $20,000 and income taxes of $8,000 for an income statement–related total of $539,000. Changes in the relevant 2007 and 2008 balance sheets are taken from Table 5.2. Inventories increased by $45,000 (from $95,000 to $140,000).[2] Accounts payable increased in 2008 by $27,000 (from $57,000 to $84,000), and accrued liabilities increased in 2008 by $1,000 (from $9,000 to $10,000). Gross fixed assets (capital

---

[1] It is generally expensive for the venture to maintain this posture because it may involve foregoing trade credit from suppliers.

[2] Some analysts prefer to calculate an inventory-related purchases amount by adding the cost of goods sold to the increase in inventories. For MPC in 2008, this would total $45,000 + $380,000 for a total of $425,000. The cash expenditures from the income statement would, in turn, be decreased by the $380,000 down to $231,000 (i.e., $539,000 − $380,000). Since everything else is the same, the cash burn would still be $606,000 for MPC in 2008. Since cost of goods sold includes both labor and materials expenses, this inventory-related purchases calculation is just a rearrangement of the relationship: Ending Inventory = Beginning Inventory + Inventory-Related Purchases − Cost of Goods Sold.

expenditures) increased in 2008 by $50,000 (from $205,000 to $255,000). Using the cash burn equation for MPC, we have:

$$\text{Cash Burn} = 539,000 \text{ (i.e., } 511,000 + 20,000 + 8,000)$$
$$+ 45,000$$
$$- 28,000 \text{ (i.e., } 27,000 + 1,000)$$
$$+ 50,000$$
$$= 606,000$$

On a raw basis, MPC burned $606,000 in cash to pay expenses, build inventory, and buy equipment during 2008.

Cash build is what the venture receives on its sales; that is, **cash build** is net sales less the increase in receivables. In general, we have:

$$\text{Cash Build} = \text{Net Sales} - \text{Increase in Receivables}$$

For MPC in 2008, sales were $575,000 from Table 5.1, and the increase in receivables was $30,000 (from $75,000 to $105,000). Thus, we have an annual cash build for 2008 of:

$$\text{Cash Build} = 575,000 - 30,000 = 545,000$$

The **cash build rate** is the cash build for a fixed period of time, typically a month.

Net cash burn occurs when the cash burn exceeds the cash build in a specified time period. In equation form, we have:

$$\text{Net Cash Burn} = \text{Cash Burn} - \text{Cash Build}$$

For MPC in 2008, we have:

$$\text{Net Cash Burn} = -606,000 + 545,000 = -61,000$$

The **net cash burn rate** is the net cash burn for a fixed period of time, typically a month. Of course, a positive dollar amount would result in a net cash build and a net cash build rate.

As we discussed in Chapter 4, we also can use the statement of cash flows to determine whether a venture was experiencing a net cash burn or build position. If cash flow from operating activities plus cash flow from investing activities is positive, then the venture was building cash. A negative amount would mean a net burn position. Reference to Table 5.3 shows that the cash flow from operating activities for 2008 was −$11,000. Cash flow from investing activities (i.e., the increase in gross fixed assets—plant and equipment) was −$50,000. Thus, for MPC, the net cash burn was:

$$\text{Net Cash Burn} = -11,000 + -50,000 = -61,000$$

Thus, both approaches calculated the net cash burn at −$61,000 for MPC in 2008.

cash build
net sales less the increase in receivables

cash build rate
cash build for a fixed period of time, typically a month

net cash burn
when cash burn exceeds cash build in a specified time period; also cash burn less cash build

net cash burn rate
net cash burn for a fixed period of time, typically a month

For many, the preferred presentation of cash burn and build is on a daily, weekly, or monthly basis. For example, if we divide by 12, we have:

Monthly Burn Rates

Monthly cash burn rate	−606,000 ÷ 12	−50,500.00
−Monthly cash build rate	+545,000 ÷ 12	+45,416.67
Monthly net cash burn rate	−61,000 ÷ 12	−5,083.33

Our net cash burn rate is frequently referred to as simply the venture's (monthly) burn rate.

If we divide the year-end cash balance of $5,000 by the monthly net cash burn rate, we see that MPC had less than a month of cash left at the end of 2008. Concisely, MPC was ".98 months until out of cash."

A typical use for this type of calculation is to approximate an answer to the question, "If I invest $15,000, how long will it be before more external financing is needed?" For MPC in 2008, this number would be about three months. What it would be now could vary significantly from the 2008 experience. Nonetheless, awareness of historical burn rates and monitoring of ongoing burn rate provide important survival information to the new venture.

BEYOND BURN: TRADITIONAL MEASURES OF LIQUIDITY

liquidity ratios
ratios that indicate the ability to pay short-term liabilities when they come due

Burn rates are calculated to deal explicitly with cash use and planning and are central to survival for the new venture. Several alternative measures that attempt to measure a venture's potential to produce and distribute cash are in widespread use among credit analysts. Instead of dealing with the balance of a cash account and the venture's tendency to deplete it over time, these measures, known as **liquidity ratios**, deal with a broader notion of liquidity by comparing assets that can be quickly converted to cash with liabilities that represent near-term needs for cash. Because these measures tend to be used to address longer-term trends (not just surviving this week), they will be presented in versions that average beginning and end-of-period values. The first of these compares all current assets against all current liabilities.

Current Ratio

This ratio is a simple indication of the margin of current assets over current liabilities. MPC's 2008 current ratio was calculated as:

$$\text{Current Ratio} = \frac{\text{Average Current Assets}}{\text{Average Current Liabilities}} = \frac{(250{,}000 + 180{,}000)/2}{(204{,}000 + 110{,}000)/2} = 1.37$$

A current ratio of 1.0 or more indicates that if all current assets could be converted into cash, they would be adequate to pay all current liabilities. Credit analysts believe current ratios above 1.0 indicate a liquidity cushion in the event that some noncash current assets cannot be fully converted into cash. A ratio of 1.37 indicates that current assets provide a 37 percent cushion over and above current liabilities.

Quick Ratio

Among current assets, inventories are viewed as being the least likely to be converted quickly into cash at the values recorded on a venture's balance sheet. Cash and marketable securities plus receivables (or current assets less inventories) comprise the **liquid assets.** The quick ratio measures the ability of liquid assets to pay current liabilities. The 2008 MPC quick ratio is calculated as:

liquid assets
sum of a venture's cash and marketable securities plus its receivables

$$\text{Quick Ratio} = \frac{\text{Average Current Assets} - \text{Average Inventories}}{\text{Average Current Liabilities}}$$
$$= \frac{(250,000 + 180,000)/2 - (140,000 + 95,000)/2}{(204,000 + 110,000)/2}$$
$$= .62$$

A quick ratio of less than 1.0 indicates that the venture's liquid assets would not be adequate to pay off its current liabilities. Since the quick ratio for MPC was .62, a forced payment of the 38 percent gap would require liquidating inventory.

NWC-to-Total-Assets Ratio

An alternative way to calibrate liquidity considers the venture's **net working capital (NWC)**, which is current assets minus current liabilities.[3] NWC is a dollar amount measure of the cushion between current assets and current liabilities. A dollar amount, however, is difficult to interpret unless it is viewed relative to the overall size of the venture. MPC's ratio of average net working capital to average assets was:

net working capital (NWC)
current assets minus current liabilities

$$\text{NWC-to-Total-Assets Ratio} = \frac{\text{Average Current Assets} - \text{Average Current Liabilities}}{\text{Average Total Assets}}$$
$$= \frac{(250,000 + 180,000)/2 - (204,000 + 110,000)/2}{(446,000 + 343,000)/2}$$
$$= .147, \text{ or } 14.7\%$$

The average net working capital for MPC was $58,000. When related to the average total assets of $394,500, the working capital buffer is a little less than 15 percent of the venture's total assets. The higher the percentage is, the greater the liquidity is, other things being equal. An important qualifier on the conclusions drawn from any of the liquidity ratios is that receivables account balances are assumed collectible and inventories (if included in the ratio) are assumed salable.

INTERPRETING CASH-RELATED AND LIQUIDITY-RELATED TRENDS

Now that we know several different ways to examine liquidity, we can consider MPC's cash and liquidity profile. Table 5.4 presents the 2007 and 2008 MPC burn rates and liquidity ratios.

---

[3] When current liabilities are greater than current assets, the firm has negative net working capital and may be technically insolvent. As long as creditor payment obligations are met, though, no payment defaults actually occur, and the firm may prosper from this cheap (free) source of funds. There are many examples of firms with stable cash sales that strive to achieve a negative net working capital position.

TABLE 5.4	MPC Burn Rates and Liquidity Ratios for 2007 and 2008			
RATE OR RATIO	2007	2008	CHANGE	% CHANGE
Cash burn	417,000	606,000	+189,000	+45.3
Monthly cash burn	34,750	50,500	+15,750	+45.3
Cash build	423,000	545,000	+122,000	+28.8
Monthly cash build	35,250	45,417	10,167	+28.8
Net cash burn	−6,000	61,000	+67,000	N/A
Monthly net cash burn rate	−500	5,083	5,583	N/A
Year-end months of cash	N/A	.98	N/A	N/A
Current ratio	1.56	1.37	−.19	−12.2
Quick ratio	.76	.62	−.14	−18.4
NWC-total-assets ratio	.174	.147	−.027	−15.5

The venture's ability both to generate and to consume cash increased in 2008. MPC increased its cash generation by $122,000, or $10,167 per month, an increase of 28.8 percent over 2007. However, MPC's ability to spend cash grew at the significantly faster rate of 45.3 percent. Absent external financing, MPC net-generated cash in 2007 and net-spent it in 2008. Whereas 2007's year-end cash position appeared to be of little concern, 2008 ends with the venture's having less than a month to live (if something doesn't change).

The average monthly cash burn rate for MPC was $50,500 in 2008, compared to $34,750 in 2007. The change represents a 45.3 percent increase in the rate of cash outflow. Consistent with MPC's having filled the financial gap with a $5,000 depletion of cash and $56,000 of net new external debt, the current, quick, and NWC-to-total-assets ratios reflect a significant decline in liquidity during 2008.

Whether increased burn rates and declining liquidity are a problem for MPC cannot be addressed without examining the reasons for the changes. (This is an example of the manner in which financial analysis can lead to asking the right questions.) If the venture is expanding (as its sales and investments in new equipment indicate), the changes may actually represent good fortune. Along these lines, $4,167 of the $5,583 increase in monthly net burn is due to the $50,000 capital expenditure. There were no capital expenditures in 2007. The increase left over is still $1,416 per month and is mostly closely affiliated with another type of investment. MPC's extension of additional trade credit and building of inventories heavily outstripped its ability to take down its own trade credit. Intermittent capital expenditures and increased investment in inventories and the extension of trade credit can easily distort simple comparisons. Nonetheless, however justifiable the cause of the gap, it is a sign of pressing financial needs.

In summary, while MPC's burn rate and liquidity aspects appear to have weakened in 2008, the venture still has a lot going for it. Sales and assets are increasing rapidly and the venture is profitable, albeit at a lower level than in 2007. To enjoy success, MPC needs to take extreme care in supplying the cash needs associated with growth.

- What are the possible causes of an increase in cash burn?
- What are the positive and negative aspects of negative net working capital?

5.4   CONVERSION PERIOD RATIOS

Conversion period ratios measure the average time in days required for noncash current assets and selected current liabilities to create or demand cash. The faster assets can be converted into cash, the greater is the venture's liquidity, other things being equal. Of course, the faster liabilities transform into cash demands, the less liquid the venture is. All of this comes together in a venture's **operating cycle,** which measures the time it takes to purchase raw materials, assemble a product, book the sale, and collect on it. The operating cycle for a simple manufacturing venture is as shown in Figure 5.2.

The **cash conversion cycle** is the amount of time taken to buy materials and produce a finished good (the inventory-to-sale conversion period) plus the time needed to collect sales made on credit (sale-to-cash conversion period) minus the time taken to pay suppliers for purchases on credit (the purchase-to-payment conversion period).

conversion period ratios
ratios that indicate the average time it takes in days to convert certain current asset and current liability accounts into cash

operating cycle
time it takes to purchase required materials, assemble, and sell the product plus the time needed to collect receivables if the sales are on credit

cash conversion cycle
sum of the inventory-to-sale conversion period and the sale-to-cash conversion period less the purchase-to-payment conversion period

FIGURE 5.2   Operating Cycle

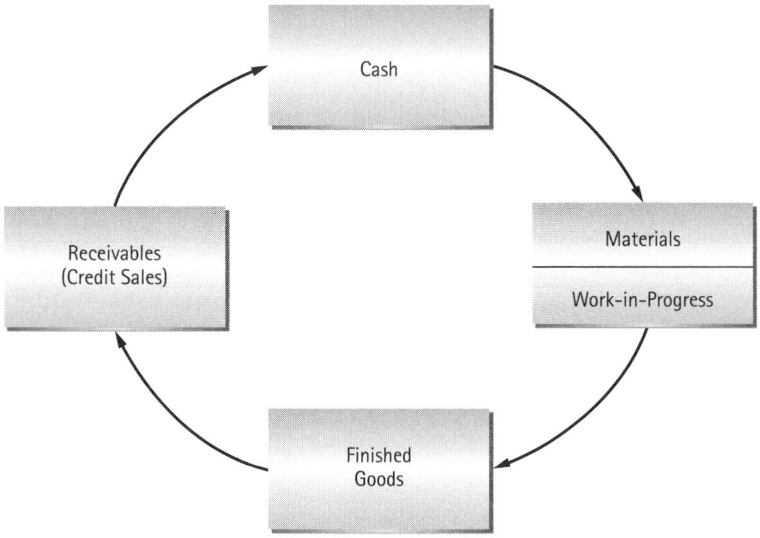

MEASURING CONVERSION TIMES

Inventory-to-Sale Conversion Period

When a venture can decrease the amount of time between the cash outlay for materials and labor and the production of a salable good, fewer dollars get tied up in production costs. With continuing production, there will always be materials in inventory. The cost of inventories is a cost of doing business. For example, if the venture keeps average materials and work-in-progress inventories of $175,000, this is $175,000 that must be financed and cannot be used elsewhere. The cash tied up in these inventories is a deadweight cost of doing business. Decreasing this cost allows the cash to be employed elsewhere (or paid back to creditors and investors).[4]

The inventory-to-sale conversion period is calculated by dividing average inventories by the venture's average daily cost of goods sold. The rationale for this measure is that when materials are purchased and labor is contributed, the associated costs are booked into the cost of inventories. When the products are completed and sold, the associated labor and materials costs are subtracted from the inventory balance and added to the cost of goods sold. If the cost of goods sold (COGS) for an average day's sales is $100 and we have $5,000 in inventories, we say that the venture has fifty days of COGS in inventory. Put differently, the next dollar put into inventories won't be subtracted from inventories and added to COGS until fifty days from now.

As we mentioned before, the average of the beginning and ending levels usually provides a more stable measure for a rapidly growing enterprise. For MPC in 2008, the inventory-to-sale conversion period was:

$$\text{Inventory-to-Sale Conversion Period} = \frac{\text{Average Inventories}}{\text{Cost of Goods Sold}/365}$$
$$= \frac{(140,000 + 95,000)/2}{380,000/365}$$
$$= 112.9 \text{ days}$$

Thus, in 2008, it took an average of almost 113 days for MPC to convert the purchase of materials into a sale of finished goods. Ideally, MPC and other ventures want to have the shortest possible inventory-to-sale conversion period given the characteristics of the products. Production time depends on the complexity of the product and the automation used in assembly, among other things. Each venture must balance the trade-offs between faster production, the quality of production, and the amount spent to automate the process. Sales often depend on having products on hand when customers want them. Each venture, therefore, has to determine how inventory investment is split among the various levels of raw materials, work-in-progress, and finished goods.

---

[4] Firms in the service and merchandising industries generally will have shorter inventory conversion periods because they have little or no production time. Of course, they still carry some finished goods and face purchase-to-payment conversion challenges.

Sale-to-Cash Conversion Period

The sale-to-cash conversion period measures the average days of sales committed to the extension of trade credit. Cash sales impose the least financial burden on a venture because the immediate receipt minimizes the time gap between the sales inflow and the previous outflow for product materials and labor.[5] Of course, it is unlikely that a venture will be able to have all sales paid in cash. If, for instance, competitors extend credit, the venture will find it difficult not to follow suit. The vast majority of ventures will have accounts receivable.

The sale-to-cash conversion period is calculated by dividing the average receivables by the net sales per day. The rationale for this measure is that when a sale is booked as revenue it is done so at the sales price, which is cost plus a profit. Consequently, if the sale is on credit, the accounts receivable entry will be at the sales price. If we divide the accounts receivable balance by an average day's sales, we have a good idea how many days of sales are being supported by trade credit.[6] For MPC in 2008, the sale-to-cash conversion period was:

$$\text{Sale-to-Cash Conversion Period} = \frac{\text{Average Receivables}}{\text{Net Sales}/365}$$
$$= \frac{(105{,}000 + 75{,}000)/2}{575{,}000/365}$$
$$= 57.1 \text{ days}$$

Analysts may refer to this calculation as the "days of sales outstanding" or the "average collection period."[7] MPC takes, on average, fifty-seven days to collect its credit sales. These 57 days, when added to the 113 days needed, on average, to convert inventories into sales, produce an average operating cycle of 170 days.

Purchase-to-Payment Conversion Period

The purchase-to-payment conversion period measures the average time from a purchase of materials and labor to actual cash payment. The ability to delay payment is analogous to borrowing money from suppliers and employees and, therefore, decreases the need for external financing. It is usually considered safe to pay a venture's bills on the last day of the credit period. Many entrepreneurs have found it easier to "stretch" their credit periods (formally or informally) rather than arrange for alternative funding. However, the venture must balance the exploitation of trade credits with the cost and consequences of damaging relationships with suppliers and employees and violating relevant ethical norms.

---

[5] Some firms may even take advances on future sales. In this case, cash may be received prior to the expenditures for the associated materials and labor. Ventures taking advances should formally anticipate lower future cash receipts than if advances are not taken. Standard accounting procedures handle this formal recognition well.

[6] The firm is financing the entire sales price (cost and profit), in the sense that it didn't immediately receive the sales proceeds (cost and profit) it is owed. This is different from the way we view the financing required to keep the same good in finished-goods inventory (cost only) prior to a sale, because there we have no commitment to pay the profit portion.

[7] Since this calculation reflects the collection period on both credit and cash sales (where it is zero), it understates the average days a credit sale will be outstanding. If you wish to estimate the collection (or conversion) period for credit sales only, the denominator of the ratio should be daily average credit sales. For the purpose of calibrating the venture's operating cycle, we want to leave the denominator as total sales per day.

The purchase-to-payment conversion period is calculated by dividing the sum of average payables and operations-related accrued liabilities by the venture's cost of goods sold per day.[8] For MPC in 2008, the purchase-to-payment conversion period was:

$$
\begin{aligned}
&\text{Purchase-to-Payment Conversion Period} \\
&= \frac{\text{Average Payables} + \text{Average Accrued Liabilities}}{\text{Cost of Goods Sold}/365} \\
&= \frac{(84{,}000 + 57{,}000)/2 + (10{,}000 + 9{,}000)/2}{380{,}000/365} \\
&= 76.8 \text{ days}
\end{aligned}
$$

Thus, MPC had almost seventy-seven days of the costs of production financed by trade credit and accrued wages and liabilities.

Cash Conversion Cycle

The cash conversion cycle (also known as C^3) indicates the average time it takes a venture to complete its operating cycle less a deduction for the days supported by trade credit and delayed payroll financing. It is the number of days of operation that must be externally financed. It also represents the time from a dollar outlay on raw materials to a dollar receipt on sales (because it includes the delay in the payment of the dollar through the purchase-to-payment delay and the delay in receipt through the sale-to-cash delay).

As a target, the typical venture should try to keep its cash conversion cycle as close to zero as possible. This would indicate that production was fully internally financed. The typical venture, however, will not accomplish financing-neutral operations. The cash tied up in inventory and receivables will almost always exceed the cash supplied by creditors and accrued liabilities.

One calculates the cash conversion cycle by adding the inventory-to-sale conversion period to the sale-to-cash conversion period and subtracting the purchase-to-payment conversion period. For 2008, the MPC cash conversion cycle was:

$$
\begin{aligned}
\text{Cash Conversion Cycle} =\ & \text{Inventory-to-Sale Conversion Period} \\
& + \text{Sale-to-Cash Conversion Period} \\
& - \text{Purchase-to-Payment Conversion Period} \\
=\ & 112.9 \text{ days} + 57.1 \text{ days} - 76.8 \text{ days} = 93.2 \text{ days}
\end{aligned}
$$

Thus, it takes ninety-three days, on average, for MPC to complete its cash conversion cycle. To produce and sell its inventories takes an average of 113 days plus another 57 days to collect receipts on sales and arrive at the average operating cycle of 170 days. However, because MPC's suppliers and employees support an average seventy-seven days through voluntary or involuntary credit, the cash conversion cycle is reduced to ninety-three days.

---

[8] Ventures frequently rely on delayed payroll as a source of financing. This is not as common in mature companies. Consequently, in traditional analysis, financing through accruing wages and other liabilities is typically ignored and omitted from the numerator.

- How is the cash conversion cycle (C^3) calculated?
- How does the C^3 represent the time from a dollar outlay on raw materials to a dollar receipt on the related revenue?

INTERPRETING CHANGES IN CONVERSION TIMES

Table 5.5 shows MPC's conversion period ratio performance for 2007 and 2008. The inventory-to-sale conversion period increased by almost nine days between 2007 and 2008. The time required to produce finished goods could have increased due to production bottlenecks (e.g., skilled labor shortages, materials order delays, or quality problems), or MPC may have carried finished-goods inventories for longer periods. A change in the venture's product mix toward more complex and time-consuming products could also account for the longer inventory conversion period. (Ratio analyses rarely provide answers; they suggest questions that need answers.)

While it is normal for inventories to increase with sales, inventories that increase more rapidly than sales saddle the venture with the need for added financial capital. For example, the average inventories account balance was $82,500 [($70,000 + $95,000)/2] in 2004 and $117,500 [($95,000 + $140,000)/2] in 2008. This represents an increase of 42.4 percent [($117,500 − $82,500)/$82,500]. At the same time, the venture's cost of goods sold increased by 33.3 percent [($380,000 − $285,000)/$285,000]. If the inventories account had increased by the same rate as cost of goods sold, the inventories account balance would have been only $110,000 ($82,500 × 1.333). This breakout allows us to separate the actual change in the average inventories account balance into the portion due to a change in cost of goods sold and that due to a longer inventory-to-sale conversion period:

Actual 2008 average inventories	$117,500
Forecast based on COGS growth	−110,000
Equals: Amount due to longer conversion period	7,500

We also could have seen the impact of a longer inventory-to-sale conversion period by using the inventory-to-sale conversion period formula. Here we use the

---

TABLE 5.5   MPC Conversion Period Performance

CONVERSION PERIOD RATIO	2007	2008	INDICATED IMPACT ON CASH CONVERSION CYCLE
Inventory-to-sale	105.7 days	112.9 days	+7.2 days (lengthens C^3)
Sale-to-cash	56.3 days	57.1 days	+.8 days (lengthens C^3)
Purchase-to-payment	77.5 days	76.8 days	+.7 days (lengthens C^3)
Cash conversion cycle (C^3)	84.5 days	93.2 days	+8.7 days (longer C^3)

"daily cost of goods sold" information for 2008 but solve for what the average inventories account balance would have been, had the conversion period remained at 105.7 days. This is done as follows. Because

$$\text{Inventory-to-Sale Conversion Period} = \frac{\text{Average Inventories}}{\text{COGS}/365}$$

we can rearrange to get:

$$\begin{aligned}\text{Average Inventories} &= \text{Inventory-to-Sale Conversion Period} \times (\text{COGS}/365)\\ &= 105.7 \times \$1{,}041\\ &= \$110{,}000 \text{ (rounded)}\end{aligned}$$

The result is that MPC, even after correcting for growth, is carrying an extra $7,500 in inventories in 2008. At a financing cost of, say, 10 percent, this is an extra $750 of lost profit before taxes.

Table 5.5 shows that the sale-to-cash conversion period increased slightly (.8 days) between 2007 and 2008. This indicates slightly slower average payment practices by MPC's customers. Even though this is a small change, some ongoing monitoring of the sale-to-cash conversion period would be in order to assure that future increases do not go unnoticed and that remedial action, if appropriate, is taken.[9]

The purchase-to-payment conversion period shows a decrease of slightly less than one day and increases MPC's cash conversion cycle (other things being equal). MPC has most likely been slightly increasing the speed at which it pays suppliers. Faster payment to suppliers means a longer C^3, other things being equal. Payables credit is a particularly important source of financial capital for growing ventures, and securing longer credit terms is an added benefit that frequently justifies the cost of searching. An analysis of changes in receivables and payables could have been conducted in the same way that we analyzed the impact of a change in the inventory-to-sale conversion period.

Overall, the cash conversion cycle has increased by almost nine days. The result is an increased burden on external financing. As we have seen, the primary reason for the increase was a longer inventory-to-sale conversion period. Now we turn our attention to examining how MPC has acquired external financing in support of the longer cash conversion cycle.

CONCEPT CHECK

- How does the increase in MPC's cash conversion cycle relate to its increase in net cash burn rate?

---

[9] Of course, the change in ratio will also reflect a net change of cash customers into credit customers. While this change may not indicate any collection problems, it may indicate that the venture's credit terms are also attracting customers that traditionally paid cash.

5.5   LEVERAGE RATIOS

Leverage ratios indicate the extent to which the venture has used debt and its ability to meet debt obligations. When a venture takes out a loan or otherwise formally borrows money, it generally promises to repay the amount borrowed and an additional amount of interest. The **loan principal amount** is the dollar amount borrowed. **Interest** is an additional dollar amount paid to the lender in return for lending money to the venture. By borrowing, the venture gives the lender a superior claim on venture income and assets. Straight debt lenders, almost without exception, get paid before founders and venture investors. Many venture-financing arrangements have elements of debt and equity and, therefore, may not fall conveniently into categories that permit analysis. Nonetheless, it is good to start with the traditional counterpoint of debt versus equity.

MEASURING FINANCIAL LEVERAGE

Total-Debt-to-Total-Assets Ratio

By comparing a venture's total debt (current liabilities plus long-term debt) to its total assets, we can construct a quick picture of how much of the venture has been pledged to debtholders and how much is supported by equity. The more that has been pledged, the higher is the risk that a pledge will be broken. Subsequent to the broken pledge, the debtholders will control the enterprise. We will calculate the total-debt-to-total-assets ratio using beginning and ending period averages for current liabilities, long-term debt, and total assets. MPC's debt-to-total-assets ratio in 2008 was:

$$
\begin{aligned}
\text{Total-Debt-to-Total-Assets Ratio} &= \frac{\text{Average Total Debt}}{\text{Average Total Assets}} \\
&= \frac{(204{,}000 + 110{,}000)/2 + (80{,}000 + 90{,}000)/2}{(446{,}000 + 343{,}000)/2} \\
&= .6134, \text{ or } 61.34\%
\end{aligned}
$$

According to the accounting notion of (book) value, about 61 percent of MPC was pledged to debtholders and other creditors, leaving 39 percent to equity holders.

An interesting conceptual viewpoint adopted by some academics is that the venture has really been sold to the debtholders, in return for proceeds of the loans and an option to buy the venture back for the amounts specified in the debt agreement. If the venture owners can marshal enough cash to pay interest and principal obligations on time, then the option to buy back the venture is considered exercised, and the venture is reowned by the holders of its equity. While this viewpoint has some advantages in emphasizing the potential loss of control and ownership associated with debt financing, by law, the owners are in control of the venture's operating and financing decisions until debt obligations are breached and formal legal proceedings have placed control elsewhere.

Frequently, entrepreneurs have the impression that debt financing is the best method because they retain control. While this argument has merit, when financial

leverage ratios
ratios that indicate the extent to which the venture has used debt and its ability to repay its debt obligations

loan principal amount
dollar amount borrowed from a lender

interest
dollar amount paid on the loan to a lender as compensation for making the loan

difficulties arise, the venture would almost always be better off dealing with a few equity investors who have voting rights rather than with debtholders who have re-course to court bankruptcy actions affecting the control of the enterprise. As we will discuss later, it is not uncommon for venture investors to buy equity and, thereby, precommit to forego the legal protection offered to debtholders through federal and state bankruptcy statutes.

Equity Multiplier

This ratio summarizes the venture's debt position from a different vantage point, total assets divided by owners' equity. It shows the magnification of equity injec-tions into amount of assets. For MPC in 2008, the equity multiplier was:

$$\text{Equity Multiplier} = \frac{\text{Average Total Assets}}{\text{Average Owners' Equity}}$$
$$= \frac{(446,000 + 343,000)/2}{(162,000 + 143,000)/2}$$
$$= 2.587 \text{ times}$$

A value of 2.0 would mean that one-half of the book value of the venture's assets was financed by (the book value of) debt financial capital. Since MPC had a ratio of about 2.6 times, the interpretation is that more assets are supported by debt than by equity. This is not surprising, since the equity multiplier is just an-other way of reporting the total-debt-to-total-assets ratio. When calculating the equity multiplier directly from total debt to total assets, note that the equity mul-tiplier equals 1 ÷ (1 − total debt to total assets). We will return to the equity multiplier when we examine how some of the different types of ratios are linked together.

Debt-to-Equity Ratio

A direct comparison of debt and equity gives yet another view of the same scen-ery. For a total-debt-to-total-assets ratio of .5, we get an equity multiplier of 2 and a debt-to-equity ratio of 1. The debt-to-equity ratio equals total debt to total assets ÷ (1 − total debts to total assets).

CONCEPT CHECK

- What is the debt-to-equity ratio for a venture having total debt to total assets of .75 (or an equity multiplier of 4)?

Current-Liabilities-to-Total-Debt Ratio

While a debt snapshot is useful, survival is about current debt obligations. Ac-counting rules have simplified this determination by requiring that the current portion of long-term debt obligations (that which is due soon) be classified as a current liability. The percent of total debt held in current liabilities therefore is a reasonable glimpse of the venture's reliance on debt that will soon require cash outflow. Other things being equal, the greater the ratio of current liabilities to total debt, the more quickly the venture faces payment or restructure of its outstanding debt. We calculate the current-liabilities-to-total-debt ratio for MPC in 2008 as:

$$\text{Current-Liabilities-to-Total-Debt Ratio} = \frac{\text{Average Current Liabilities}}{\text{Average Total Debt}}$$
$$= \frac{(204{,}000 + 110{,}000)/2}{(284{,}000 + 200{,}000)/2}$$
$$= .6488, \text{ or } 64.88\%$$

MPC had nearly 65 percent of its debt in the form of current liabilities. A high total-debt-to-total-assets ratio coupled with a high current-liabilities-to-total-debt ratio makes it more likely that the venture will encounter debt repayment problems.

Interest Coverage

Interest payments represent the most frequent type of debt flow facing a borrower. As long as interest payments are made, the principal amount frequently can be rolled over with an existing or new lender. A reasonable question is: How big is the cushion between a venture's ability to generate cash to pay interest and its interest obligations?

To calculate interest coverage, we divide a venture's earnings before interest, taxes, depreciation, and amortization (EBITDA) by the annual interest payment.[10] Interest is paid before taxes, and since depreciation and amortization do not involve the outflow of cash, we use earnings prior to both taxes and depreciation (and, of course, before interest). For MPC in 2008, the interest coverage was:

$$\text{Interest Coverage} = \frac{\text{EBITDA}}{\text{Interest}}$$
$$= \frac{47{,}000 + 17{,}000}{20{,}000}$$
$$= 3.20 \text{ times}$$

This means that MPC's income before depreciation, interest, and taxes could have fallen to one-third of its current level without affecting MPC's ability to pay interest.

Fixed-Charges Coverage

Interest payments often are not the only payments that need to be made to creditors. For instance, if a venture decides to rent or lease equipment or buildings, periodic (often monthly) payments must be made. Missing payment on these types of fixed charges has similar consequences to missing interest payments. Also, many debt arrangements stipulate that a portion of a loan's principal amount or balance must be regularly repaid. One example is a commercial bank's term loan's requiring periodic payments of interest and principal.[11] Even

---

[10] Accounting amortization for intangible assets is a noncash expense analogous to depreciation.

[11] These loans have a similar structure to car and home loans and other loans where the principal is repaid gradually (amortized).

sinking-fund payments
periodic repayments of a
portion of debt principal

when businesses borrow long term by publicly selling bonds, they often are required to make **sinking-fund payments** that can be used to retire their bonds
gradually.

Rental or lease payments should be listed on the income statement before the
tax line. It is easy for venture *insiders* to get data on the scheduled payments
for debt. For venture *outsiders* who are looking at MPC, as we are, these data
may not be readily available and can pose a significant challenge to calculating a
proper accurate fixed-charges coverage ratio. To calculate MPC's fixed-charges
coverage for MPC, we divide the venture's EBITDA plus lease payments by the
sum of interest payments, rental or lease payments, and the before-tax amount of
earnings needed to make after-tax debt repayments.[12] According to Table 5.1,
MPC had interest expenses in 2008 but no rental or lease payments. We can
now calculate MPC's fixed-charges coverage for 2008 as:

$$
\text{Fixed-Charges Coverage}
$$
$$
= \frac{\text{EBITDA} + \text{Lease Payments}}{\text{Interest} + \text{Lease Payments} + [\text{Debt Repayments}/(1 - \text{Tax Rate})]}
$$
$$
= \frac{64{,}000 + 0}{20{,}000 + 0 + [10{,}000/(1 - .30)]}
$$
$$
= 1.87 \text{ times}
$$

MPC had adequate earnings to meet its fixed charges. Earnings before interest, taxes, and depreciation could have fallen to $35,000 without affecting
MPC's ability to pay fixed charges.[13]

CONCEPT CHECK

- What do leverage ratios indicate or measure?

INTERPRETING CHANGES IN FINANCIAL LEVERAGE

Table 5.6 reports the leverage ratio performance for MPC for both 2007 and
2008. Total debt to total assets increased from about 60 to 61 percent. Coupled
with the fact that current liabilities to total debt increased from 53 to about
65 percent, we see that MPC has increased its financial leverage and its financial
risk. Larger borrowing amounts increase the likelihood that a venture will have
increased difficulties in paying interest and repaying debt principal. The risk of
not being able to repay debt when it comes due is further increased by the fact
that MPC relied heavily on short-term borrowing.

---

[12] An after-tax payment is changed to its equivalent before-tax amount by dividing the after-tax amount
($10,000 for MPC) by the value of 1 minus the firm's income tax (1 − .30 for MPC). The result is a before-tax
amount of $14,286 needed to pay an after-tax debt repayment of $10,000.

[13] As with many ratios, there are many variants of the fixed-charges coverage ratio.

TABLE 5.6	MPC Leverage Ratio Performance		
LEVERAGE RATIO	**2007**	**2008**	**IMPACT ON LEVERAGE RISK**
Total debt/total assets	59.8%	61.3%	Increase
Equity multiplier	2.491	2.587	Increase
Current liabilities/total debt	52.9%	64.9%	Increase
Interest coverage	4.67	3.20	Increase
Fixed-charges coverage	2.13	1.87	Increase

The pattern of MPC's interest and fixed-charges coverage provides some additional insight. Interest coverage declined between 2007 and 2008, partly owing to the increase in interest expense from $12,000 to $20,000. Even so, the interest coverage continued to exceed 3.0 times in 2008. Fixed-charges coverage is off from its 2007 level, again mostly owing to the increase in interest expense.

In order to keep from diluting ownership, it is common for rapidly growing ventures to seek debt financing even though they may not have the track record or the profile to succeed in the search. When they do succeed, it is usually with short-term borrowing that imposes an interactive and relatively close relationship with the debt providers. This can provide good incentives for the new venture to manage its operations and finances carefully. It can also be a nuisance. Depending on the balance, there may be good reason to opt for dealing with voting equity investors instead of short-term lenders.

5.6 PROFITABILITY AND EFFICIENCY RATIOS

Profitability and efficiency ratios indicate how efficiently a venture controls its expenses and uses its assets. Growth is of little value if it does not lead to higher profits. We treat profitability ratios last because they measure the bottom-line consideration for owners: rates of returns on sales, assets, and equity. These accounting-based measures of profitability are a standard starting point for examining venture value. However, we will see in later chapters that valuation is more complex and forward looking than these simple ratios suggest.

profitability and efficiency ratios
ratios that indicate how efficiently a venture controls its expenses and uses its assets

INCOME STATEMENT MEASURES OF PROFITABILITY

Gross Profit Margin

Do the venture's revenues exceed the cost of the goods being sold? For many new and high-growth ventures, the answer to this question is "no." The potential offered by growth ventures can be a temporary excuse, but eventually the venture will have to create more revenues from a product than the costs to produce it, or the venture will collapse.[14] The venture's gross profit margin (or earnings margin) is calculated by dividing the gross profit (i.e., net sales minus cost of goods sold) by the venture's net sales or revenues. For 2008, MPC's gross profit margin was:

$$\text{Gross Profit Margin} = \frac{\text{Net Sales} - \text{Cost of Goods Sold}}{\text{Net Sales}}$$

$$= \frac{195,000}{575,000}$$

$$= .3391, \text{ or } 33.91\%$$

MPC spends about 66 percent of its sales covering costs of production. This 34 percent gross profit margin, in turn, must be adequate to cover all other expenses if the venture is to be profitable.

Operating Profit Margin

The operating profit margin is calculated by dividing the venture's operating income, measured as the earnings before interest and taxes (EBIT), by the venture's net sales. MPC's operating profit margin for 2008 was:

$$\text{Operating Profit Margin} = \frac{\text{EBIT}}{\text{Net Sales}}$$

$$= \frac{47,000}{575,000}$$

$$= .0817, \text{ or } 8.17\%$$

Thus, MPC earned a little more than 8 percent operating profit margin on its sales after covering production and other operating costs. If a venture can also cover financing costs (primarily interest expenses) and pay the tax bill, it will experience a net profit.

Net Profit Margin

The 2008 bottom line for MPC's owners is whether MPC made a profit after all expenses have been taken into account. As a venture matures, a net profit or net income is an increasingly critical source of financing. Remember that net profit is the first source of cash found in the statement of cash flows. MPC's 2008 net profit margin was:

$$\text{Net Profit Margin} = \frac{\text{Net Profit}}{\text{Net Sales}}$$

$$= \frac{19,000}{575,000}$$

$$= .0330, \text{ or } 3.30\%$$

Thus, MPC averaged earnings of a little more than 3¢ on each dollar of sales.

---

[14] We have been careful to use the phrase "create more revenues from a product" to emphasize the indirect revenues that come with product sales, which by themselves may be at a loss. Many computer software products are given away for free but lead directly to revenue generation other than from sales of the software.

NOPAT Margin

Directly comparing bottom lines between two ventures with different amounts of financial leverage can lead to tax-related distortions in relative performance. The tax deductibility of interest creates an **interest tax shield** equal to the tax rate times the interest payment. This part of profit is merely a government gift for using debt instead of equity. One approach to leveling the playing field is to find the profit each firm would have had in the absence of financial leverage—that is, after restating taxes to what they would be if interest were not tax deductible. Accordingly, MPC's NOPAT margin for 2008 was:

interest tax shield
proportion of a venture's interest payment that is paid by the government because interest is deductible before taxes are paid

$$\text{NOPAT Margin} = \frac{\text{EBIT}(1 - \text{Tax Rate})}{\text{Net Sales}}$$
$$= \frac{47,000(1 - .30)}{575,000}$$
$$= .0572, \text{ or } 5.72\%$$

If one is interested in operating performance in the absence of financial leveraging, MPC's NOPAT margin of 5.72 percent may be a better ratio to compare with other ventures taking different approaches to the use of financial leverage.

EFFICIENCY AND RETURN MEASURES

Sales-to-Total-Assets Ratio

Ideally, it would be great for MPC to be able to generate revenues without having to invest in any assets. Growth would be uninhibited, and financing needs would be trivial. Unfortunately, such firms are few and far between, irrespective of what the latest infomercial told you. Running a business with no money down is rare. It is far easier to think of examples of industries that require massive asset deployments before generating a single dollar of revenue. An electric utility company undertakes phenomenal investments in assets to generate the first dollar of revenue. Nuclear energy production is perhaps one of the most extreme examples of the lag between cash outlay and revenues. There are industries that do not require large investments in assets; a travel agency is a good example. Unfortunately, the travel agency industry, because of low required asset investment, is wide open to other newcomers. Large required asset investments are a blessing and a curse. The same thing that makes it difficult for you to enter prohibits others from entering. Ultimately, for a given industry, the objective is to use assets as efficiently as possible within the range of discretion provided by the industry.

The sales-to-total-assets ratio is calculated as net sales or revenues divided by average total assets. It is particularly important to use average assets because growing ventures can add significantly to the asset base in a period, and if not taken into account, this will distort the apparent efficiency of asset utilization. MPC's sales-to-total-assets (asset turnover or intensity) ratio for 2008 was:

$$\text{Sales-to-Total-Assets Ratio} = \frac{\text{Net Sales}}{\text{Average Total Assets}}$$

$$= \frac{575{,}000}{(446{,}000 + 343{,}000)/2}$$

$$= 1.458 \text{ times}$$

MPC was able to create 2008 sales of about 1.5 times the asset base.

Some analysts also calculate a number of efficiency ratios (something over net sales) for specific current assets, including receivables and inventories. We have chosen to measure the efficient use of receivables and inventories within the context of the cash conversion cycle discussed earlier. Since cash production and depletion is the key to a new venture's survival, we believe it is best to examine the efficient use of receivables in that context. Note that the sale-to-cash conversion period can easily be interpreted as a measure of the efficiency of receivables in generating sales.

OPERATING RETURN ON ASSETS

Every venture must be able to generate profits from operations if it is to survive. Previously, we calculated the operating profit margin as EBIT divided by net sales to measure the venture's profitability from operations (before financing costs and tax payments). We can also calculate the operating return on average assets, which is sometimes called the venture's *basic earning power*. The MPC calculation for 2008 is:

$$\text{Operating Return on Assets} = \frac{\text{EBIT}}{\text{Average Total Assets}}$$

$$= \frac{47{,}000}{(446{,}000 + 343{,}000)/2}$$

$$= .1191, \text{ or } 11.91\%$$

MPC earned nearly 12 percent on the average assets outstanding in 2008. The higher the venture's basic earning power, the more easily it can cover interest expenses, pay its taxes, and produce profits for its owners.

It is important to note that the owners of the venture benefit from the use of borrowed funds as long as the effective interest rate is less than the venture's operating return on assets. For example, MPC's interest costs in 2008 were $20,000. Average short-term debt was $77,000 [($110,000 + $44,000)/2], and average long-term debt was $85,000 [($80,000 + $90,000)/2] for total average interest-bearing debt of $162,000. This gives an average effective interest rate of 12.35 percent ($20,000/$162,000). Since this rate was higher than the venture's basic earning power, the owners of the venture were worse off because they used debt to increase their scale when their earning power didn't even cover the increased debt costs. MPC's resulting net profit margin was only 3.30 percent.

Return on Assets (ROA)

A third ratio combining data from the income statement and the balance sheet relates net income to average assets. This ratio has the useful property that it can be treated as the product of net profit margin and sales to total assets. The direct calculation of return on assets is net profit divided by average total assets. MPC's 2008 ROA was:

$$\text{Return on Assets} = \frac{\text{Net Profit}}{\text{Average Total Assets}}$$
$$= \frac{19,000}{(446,000 + 343,000)/2}$$
$$= .048, \text{ or } 4.8\%$$

MPC earned a little less than 5 percent on its asset base in 2008.

Rather than calculate the return on assets directly, we can indirectly calculate the ratio using the **ROA model**, where ROA decomposes into the product of the net profit margin and the sales-to-total-assets ratio:

$$\text{Return on Assets} = \frac{\text{Net Profit}}{\text{Net Sales}} \times \frac{\text{Net Sales}}{\text{Average Total Assets}}$$
$$= \frac{19,000}{575,000} \times \frac{575,000}{(446,000 + 343,000)/2}$$
$$= .0330 \times 1.458 = .048$$

ROA model
the decomposition of ROA into the product of the net profit margin and the sales-to-total-assets ratio

The advantage of this breakout is that it simultaneously presents the venture's return on assets as the joint outcome of two distinct aspects of the venture's operations—the ability to create sales from assets and the ability to carve a profit out of those sales.

Return on Equity (ROE)

Ultimately, the entrepreneur and other equity investors are interested in the rate of return they have earned on their investment. At this time, we calculate single-period returns using accounting information.[15] The return on owners' equity is calculated as the net income or profit divided by the average owners' equity. The MPC calculation for 2008 is:

$$\text{Return on Equity} = \frac{\text{Net Income}}{\text{Average Owners' Equity}}$$
$$= \frac{19,000}{(162,000 + 143,000)/2}$$
$$= .1246, \text{ or } 12.46\%$$

MPC earned a return of about 12.5 percent on its 2008 average equity investment.

---

[15]　In later chapters when we examine a venture's market value, we will calculate periodic market rates of return that may or may not resemble accounting rates of return.

Notice that the ROE is larger than the ROA. With the use of debt, the venture can purchase more assets than it could with equity alone. Any additional return on these assets enhances the total return and improves the ROE. Similarly, any losses on these additional assets decrease the total return and harm the ROE. This is the basic magnifier effect of financial leverage. Good returns are better. Bad returns are worse. The ratio of ROE to ROA gives the equity multiplier view of financial leverage. For MPC in 2008, the equity multiplier was .1246/.0482, or 2.59 times. A useful relationship between the ROA model and a related **ROE model**, in which ROE decomposes into the product of net profit margin, sales-to-total-assets ratio, and the equity multiplier, is:

ROE model
the decomposition of ROE into the product of the net profit margin, the sales-to-total-assets ratio, and the equity multiplier

$$\text{ROE} = \underbrace{\text{Net Profit Margin} \times \text{Asset Turnover}}_{\text{ROA}} \times \text{Equity Multiplier, or}$$

Using the previously calculated ratios for MPC for 2008, we have:

$$\text{ROE} = 3.3\% \times 1.46 \times 2.59 = 12.5\%$$

INTERPRETING CHANGES IN PROFITABILITY AND EFFICIENCY

Table 5.7 shows a comparison of several profitability and efficiency ratios for MPC for 2007 and 2008. All profitability measures declined between the two years. The gross profit margin declined from about 35 percent to about 34 percent, indicating that MPC's cost of production increased 1 percent from 65 to 66 percent.

The operating profit margin declined sharply from about 9.6 percent to 8.2 percent, indicating that some or all of the operating expenses (administrative, marketing, and research and development) increased more quickly than sales. We can examine this lapse in greater detail by considering each expense as a percent of

TABLE 5.7   MPC's Profitability, Efficiency, and Return Measures

RATIO	2007	2008	INDICATED IMPACT ON PROFITABILITY/EFFICIENCY
Gross profit margin	34.93%	33.91%	Lower
Operating profit margin	9.59%	8.17%	Lower
Net profit margin	4.79%	3.30%	Lower
NOPAT margin	6.71%	5.72%	Lower
Sales to total assets	1.327	1.458	Higher
Operating return on assets	12.73%	11.91%	Lower
Return on assets	6.36%	4.82%	Lower
Return on owners' equity	15.85%	12.46%	Lower

sales and comparing it to 2007 levels. MPC's operating expenses as a percent of sales in both years were:

| | PERCENT OF SALES | |
	2007	2008
Administrative expenses	10.3	11.3
Marketing expenses	7.3	6.8
Research and development	4.6	4.7
Total	22.2	22.8

Thus, in addition to the increase in the COGS as a percent of sales (reflected in a decreased gross profit margin), the overall operating profit margin suffered from an additional increase in administrative expenses as a percent of sales. The margin decline would have been even more dramatic except for a decline in marketing expenses (as a percent of sales).

On the positive side, MPC's sales to total assets increased in 2008 from 1.33 to 1.46. However, the decline in the net profit margin, from about 4.8 to 3.3 percent, more than offset the improvement in utilization of assets, causing the return on assets to drop to 4.8 from 6.4 percent. The increase in financial leverage, reflected in the increased equity multiplier, was not enough to prevent a decline in MPC's ROE (from 15.9 to 12.5 percent).

5.7 INDUSTRY COMPARABLE RATIO ANALYSIS

Up to this point, we have stressed the use of trend analysis to examine and monitor the financial health of new and growing ventures. Table 5.8 shows selected average ratios for existing firms operating in MPC's industry. As previously indicated, industry data are sometimes difficult to find and may be incomplete. This is particularly true for new industries where we often find intense entrepreneurial activity. For MPC, however, we have industry data; MPC compares poorly with the industry averages for 2007 and 2008.

We showed earlier that cash burn rates could be calculated directly from the income statement, balance sheet, and statement of cash flows. To provide comparables on burn rate, we would need to find those statements for competitors in the industry. For the other standard financial ratios, finding comparable data is usually less difficult because industry associations and accounting firms frequently track the standard ratios. Table 5.8 presents cash conversion cycle data for MPC's industry. MPC takes an average of nearly thirteen days longer to complete inventory-to-sale conversions. MPC's sale-to-cash conversion period is about two days slower than the industry average. MPC took more than two days longer than the industry average to pay for its purchases.

MPC's total-debt-to-total-assets ratio is a little higher than the industry average of 60 percent. Consistent with this, the venture's interest coverage is below the industry average. Profitability ratios indicate that MPC was underperforming

TABLE 5.8	MPC Industry Comparables Analysis		
	2008	2008 INDUSTRY AVERAGE	COMPARISON WITH INDUSTRY
Liquidity Ratios			
Current ratio	1.37	1.80	Lower
Quick ratio	.62	.80	Lower
Conversion Period Ratios			
Inventory-to-sale conversion period	112.9 days	100.0 days	Higher +12.9 days
Sale-to-cash conversion period	57.1 days	55.0 days	Higher +2.1 days
Purchase-to-payment conversion period	76.8 days	74.1 days	Higher +2.7 days
Cash conversion cycle	93.2 days	80.9 days	Higher +12.3 days
Leverage Ratios			
Total debt to total assets	61.3%	60.0%	Higher
Interest coverage	3.20	4.00	Lower
Profitability Ratios			
Gross profit margin	33.91%	35.00%	Lower
Operating profit margin	8.17%	10.00%	Lower
Net profit margin	3.30%	4.50%	Lower
NOPAT margin	5.72%	6.00%	Lower
Efficiency and Return Ratios			
Sales to total assets	1.458	1.500	Lower
Operating return on assets	11.91%	15.00%	Lower
Return on assets	4.82%	6.30%	Lower
Return on equity	12.46%	15.00%	Lower

relative to the industry average for 2008. MPC's apparently higher cost of production and other expenses led to an operating profit margin significantly below the industry average of 10 percent.

Lower profits from operations and a lower utilization of assets (as reflected in the sales to total assets and cash conversion cycle) contribute to the relatively lower return on assets for MPC. MPC's return on equity lagged behind the average return to owners of other firms in the industry.

CONCEPT CHECK

- How are industry comparative data used, and what are some of the possible problems that can occur when using this approach to ratio analysis?

5.8   A HITCHHIKER'S GUIDE TO FINANCIAL ANALYSIS

Fortunately, or unfortunately as the case may be, familiarity with financial ratios pays. As a venture matures, ratios become an increasingly important platform for communicating with outsiders. Public companies have no choice but to be concerned with the ratios that are important to equity analysts, bond-rating firms, and banks. Restrictive bond covenants frequently are stated in terms of financial ratios. Anyone who has applied for a mortgage or car loan knows that debt ratios are central to the process of creating a personal credit profile. Ratios are here to stay. As with many other aspects of entrepreneurial finance, it is best to buckle up early in the venture's life and prepare for the ride ahead. Make peace (or, better yet, an alliance) with financial ratio analysis and you won't regret it.

It is not feasible to introduce all of the ways financial ratios can be combined and analyzed. With N accounts presented on financial statements, there are $N^2 - N$ ratios that can be built by dividing one account balance by another. If we allow the sums of subsets of account balances to be divided by sums of other subsets, the number rises to $(2^N)^2 - 2^N$.[16] You can easily create a previously unknown financial ratio and name it after yourself. This will be much less difficult than finding a new star or planet. The hard part will be convincing the rest of the world that the ratio is useful in diagnosing a venture's problems and predicting its future.

You may find the sheer proliferation of measures frustrating. Automobiles have only a few controls and gauges. Sometimes it feels as if financial ratio analysis more closely resembles the cockpit controls of a Boeing 747. You may wonder how we settled on a set of ratios to include. After all, knowing which ratios are in vogue with venture investors could be important. Ratio fashion consciousness, however, is not an important goal for most entrepreneurs.[17] *Answers* to the questions suggested by thoughtful ratio analysis are far more important. Therein lies most, if not all, of the value that ratio analysis offers new and growing ventures. Whatever the controls and gauges you ultimately decide to use, some general warnings are in order.

Although we have spent a substantial amount of time discussing the role of financial ratios in monitoring and evaluating venture performance, care must be taken when constructing ratio-oriented views of a growing venture. Entrepreneurs may own more than one venture and move assets back and forth between ventures. Accounting procedures may be nonstandard, incorrect, or even nonexistent.[18] Even with properly structured accounting, a venture may, in aggressively avoiding taxes, structure business flows in a way that makes traditional trend or industry-comparable analysis difficult. Besides, some of the most important assets

---

[16] For N = 30, we have $N^2 - N = 870$ and $(2^N)^2 - 2^N = 1.153 \times 10^{18}$.

[17] It is also not high on finance professors' priority lists. Nonetheless, it is amazing how much devotion specific ratios receive.

[18] Imagine confusing a speedometer with a fuel gauge.

(knowledge, experience, creativity, and existing business relationships) are not recorded anywhere. Financial ratios, at best, indirectly reflect the value contributed by such assets.

Industry comparisons can be misleading for a number of reasons. Of particular concern for a new venture in an old industry is the difference in firm age. A smaller, rapidly growing venture might benefit from *not* emulating large, mature firms. Rather than using industry averages, it might be better to compare the young venture against other young ventures in the same, or a related, industry. When comparing ratios, one should also be careful to ensure that ratios are calculated the same way for the venture and its comparable firms. Using other firms' data as benchmarks for venture performance is still a good idea, even when the match is not perfect. The questions that arise when the venture departs markedly from benchmark firms are usually worth addressing.

Seasonal factors can distort ratio comparisons. If a firm sells a large proportion of its products during the year-end holiday season, it is important to make comparisons at the same point in time each year. When comparing fiscal-year data against industry averages, it is usually better to consider benchmark firms with the same fiscal year. For example, if industry data are based on fiscal years ending in March and a venture's fiscal year ends in December, seasonal sales patterns may distort comparisons across firms.

Although standard accounting procedures eliminate a great deal of discretion in preparing financial statements, firms still have some financial reporting choices. While inventories are typically recorded at cost, there are cases when market values are used. Firms also may differ in terms of off-the-balance-sheet financing through the use of operating leases. They may differ substantially in how they repay principal on long-term debt. Inflation tends to complicate long-term trend analysis because of the heavy emphasis traditional financial statements place on historical costs. For real estate holdings (buildings and land) and inventory, current and historical values can differ substantially.

One should avoid looking at only one or two ratios. A full set of ratios viewed in concert will provide a more complete view of the venture. It is always possible that the venture or comparable firms are "window dressing" one or two ratios; a firm wishing to improve its current and quick ratios could borrow long term (for longer than one year) and hold the proceeds in cash and marketable securities. The result would be improved liquidity ratios. However, if we examine leverage ratios, it will be immediately obvious that the firm has created this liquidity by shifting into longer-term debt.

One must be cautious in stating whether a specific ratio is good or bad. "Goodness" is frequently a matter of perspective or strategy. Having a high current ratio indicates liquidity that implies a low probability of financial distress or bankruptcy. However, the high current ratio may reflect a high accounts receivable balance and collection difficulty. It also could reflect an inability to secure trade credit. In any case, while creditors might like a high current ratio, the venture may be incurring high financing costs to support investments in inventories and accounts receivable. Whether this is good or bad depends on where you're sitting, and how the situation relates to the venture's strategy. With proper care, ratio analysis can provide important gauges for monitoring whether the venture needs to apply the brake or the accelerator.[19] Differences in ratios over time, or apparent weakness relative to competitors, can suggest important questions about a venture's vitality and viability. While you may begin as a hitchhiker on the ratios we (or others) suggest, ultimately you need to develop and monitor ratios that are meaningful for your specific venture.

CONCEPT CHECK

- What are some of the concerns or cautions that need to be considered when conducting ratio analysis?

SUMMARY

This chapter covered the use of ratio analysis to monitor the progress of an entrepreneurial venture. We examined four ratio categories: cash burn and liquidity ratios, conversion period ratios, leverage ratios, and profitability and efficiency ratios. We also discussed how to interpret the impact of ratios using trend and industry comparables analysis of a venture's operating and financial performance. We concluded with warnings to keep in mind when constructing and interpreting a ratio profile of new and growing ventures.

KEY TERMS

cash build	industry comparables analysis	net cash burn rate
cash build rate	interest	net working capital (NWC)
cash burn	interest tax shield	operating cycle
cash burn rate	leverage ratios	profitability and efficiency ratios
cash conversion cycle	liquid assets	ROA model
conversion period ratios	liquidity ratios	ROE model
cross-sectional analysis	loan principal amount	sinking-fund payments
financial ratios	net cash burn	trend analysis

DISCUSSION QUESTIONS

1. Describe the types of financial ratios and other financial performance measures that are used during a venture's successful life cycle. Who are the users of financial performance measures?

2. What are financial ratios and why are they useful?

3. What are the three types of comparisons that can be made when conducting ratio analyses?

4. What are the meanings of the terms "cash build" and "cash burn"? How do we calculate net cash burn rates?

---

[19] By way of extending the analogy, note that some cars add "idiot lights" in case the driver misses the signals being communicated by gauges. While there may not be a perfect example of a venture idiot light, there are some bankers and venture capitalists who could suggest a few.

5. How is the current ratio calculated and what does it measure? How does the quick ratio differ from the current ratio?

6. Describe how a firm's net working capital (NWC) is measured and how the NWC-to-total-assets ratio is calculated. What does this ratio measure?

7. What is meant by a venture's operating cycle? Also, describe the cash conversion cycle.

8. What are the three components of the cash conversion cycle? How is each component calculated?

9. Briefly explain how changes in the conversion times of the components of the cash conversion cycle can be interpreted.

10. What is the meaning of leverage ratios? What ratios are used for relating total debt to a venture's assets and/or its equity?

11. What is the importance of the relationship between a venture's current liabilities and its total debt?

12. Describe the two types of coverage ratios that are typically calculated when trying to assess a venture's ability to meet its interest payments and other financing-related obligations.

13. What are four measures used to indicate how efficient the venture is in generating profits on its sales? Describe how each measure is calculated.

14. Identify and describe four efficiency/return ratios that combine data from both the income statement and the balance sheet.

15. Identify and describe the two components of the ROA model both in terms of what financial dimensions they measure and how they are calculated.

16. What are the three ratio components of the ROE model? How is each calculated and what financial dimensions do they measure?

17. Indicate some of the concerns or cautions that need to be considered when conducting ratio analysis.

INTERNET ACTIVITIES

1. Go to the Hoovers business online Web site at http://www.hoovers.com and click on "Companies A–Z." Identify a firm such as Google, Inc. (ticker symbol: GOOG) or Applebee's International, Inc. (ticker symbol: APPB).

    A. Obtain the most recent three years of income statements and balance sheets. Analyze the changes in operating and financial performance, if any, by applying the ratio analyses covered in this chapter.

    B. Estimate the length of the cash conversion cycle over the two most recent years of available data. What changes have occurred, if any?

    C. Identify the industry that the firm being studied resides in and the major competitors. Obtain financial statement information for one or more competitors and conduct a ratio analysis of each competitor analyzed.

EXERCISES/PROBLEMS

1. Bike-With-Us Corporation, a specialty bicycle parts replacement venture, was started last year by two former professional bicycle riders who had substantial competitive racing experience, including the Tour de France. The two entrepreneurs borrowed $50,000 from members of their families, and each put up $30,000 in equity capital. Retail space was rented and $60,000 was spent for fixtures and store equipment. Following is the abbreviated income statement and balance sheet information for the Bike-With-Us Corporation after one year of operation.

Bike-With-Us Corporation

Sales	$325,000
Operating costs	285,000
Depreciation	10,000

Interest	5,000
Taxes	6,000
Cash	$ 1,000
Receivables	30,000
Inventories	50,000
Fixed assets, net	50,000
Payables	11,000
Accruals	10,000
Long-term loan	50,000
Common equity	60,000

A. Prepare an income statement and a balance sheet for the Bike-With-Us Corporation using only the information provided above.

B. Calculate the current ratio, quick ratio, and NWC-to-total-assets ratio.

C. Calculate the total-debt-to-total-assets ratio, debt-to-equity ratio, and interest coverage.

D. Calculate the net profit margin, sales-to-total-assets ratio, and the return on assets.

E. Calculate the equity multiplier. Combine this calculation with the calculations in Part D to show the ROE model with its three components.

2. Use the financial statement data for the Bike-With-Us Corporation provided in Problem 1 to make the following calculations:

A. Calculate the operating return on assets.

B. Determine the effective interest rate paid on the long-term debt.

C. Calculate the NOPAT margin. How does this compare with the results for the net profit margin? Did the owners benefit from the use of interest-bearing long-term debt?

3. Following are two years of income statements and balance sheets for the Munich Exports Corporation.

Munich Exports Corporation

	2007	2008
Cash	$ 50,000	$ 50,000
Accounts receivable	200,000	300,000
Inventories	450,000	570,000
Total current assets	700,000	920,000
Fixed assets, net	300,000	380,000
Total assets	$1,000,000	$1,300,000
Accounts payable	130,000	$ 180,000
Accruals	50,000	70,000
Bank loan	90,000	90,000
Total current liabilities	270,000	340,000
Long-term debt	400,000	550,000
Common stock ($1 par)	50,000	50,000
Paid-in-capital	200,000	200,000

continued on next page

Retained earnings	80,000	160,000
Total liabilities and equity	$1,000,000	$1,300,000

	2007	2008
Net sales	$1,300,000	$1,600,000
Cost of goods sold	780,000	960,000
Gross profit	520,000	640,000
Marketing	130,000	160,000
General and administrative	150,000	150,000
Depreciation	40,000	55,000
EBIT	200,000	275,000
Interest	45,000	55,000
Earnings before taxes	155,000	220,000
Income taxes (40% rate)	62,000	88,000
Net income	$ 93,000	$ 132,000

A. Calculate the cash build, cash burn, and net cash burn or build for Munich Exports in 2008.

B. Assume that 2009 will be a repeat of 2008. If your answer in Part A resulted in a net cash burn position, calculate the net cash burn monthly rate and indicate the number of months remaining "until out of cash." If your answer in Part A resulted in a net cash build position, calculate the net cash build monthly rate and indicate the expected cash balance at the end of 2009.

4. Two years of financial statement data for the Munich Export Corporation are shown in Problem 3.

A. Calculate the inventory-to-sale, sale-to-cash, and purchase-to-payment conversion periods for Munich Exports for 2008.

B. Calculate the length of Munich Exports' cash conversion cycle for 2008.

5. The Castillo Products Company was started in 2006. The company manufactures components for personal decision assistant (PDA) products and for other handheld electronic products. A difficult operating year, 2007, was followed by a profitable 2008. However, the founders (Cindy and Rob Castillo) are still concerned about the venture's liquidity position and the amount of cash being used to operate the firm. Following are income statements and balance sheets for the Castillo Products Company for 2007 and 2008.

Castillo Products Company

	2007	2008
Net sales	$900,000	$1,500,000
Cost of goods sold	540,000	900,000
Gross profit	360,000	600,000
Marketing	90,000	150,000
General and administrative	250,000	250,000
Depreciation	40,000	40,000
EBIT	−20,000	160,000
Interest	45,000	60,000
Earnings before taxes	−65,000	100,000

	0	25,000
Income taxes	0	25,000
Net income (loss)	−$ 65,000	$ 75,000

	2007	2008
Cash	$ 50,000	$ 20,000
Accounts receivable	200,000	280,000
Inventories	400,000	500,000
Total current assets	650,000	800,000
Gross fixed assets	450,000	540,000
Accumulated depreciation	− 100,000	− 140,000
Net fixed assets	350,000	400,000
Total assets	$1,000,000	$1,200,000
Accounts payable	$ 130,000	$ 160,000
Accruals	50,000	70,000
Bank loan	90,000	100,000
Total current liabilities	270,000	330,000
Long-term debt	300,000	400,000
Common stock	150,000	150,000
Paid-in-capital	200,000	200,000
Retained earnings	80,000	120,000
Total liabilities and equity	$1,000,000	$1,200,000

A. Use year-end data to calculate the current ratio, the quick ratio, and the NWC-to-total-assets ratio for 2007 and 2008 for Castillo Products. What changes occurred?

B. Use Castillo Products' complete income statement data and the changes in balance sheet items between 2007 and 2008 to determine the firm's cash build and cash burn for 2008. Did Castillo Products have a net cash build or a net cash burn for 2008?

C. Convert the annual cash build and cash burn amounts calculated in Part B to monthly cash build and cash burn rates. Also indicate the amount of the net monthly cash build or cash burn rate.

6. Castillo Products Company, described in Problem 5, improved its operations from a net loss in 2007 to a net profit in 2008. While the founders, Cindy and Rob Castillo, are happy about these developments, they are concerned about how long the firm took to complete its cash conversion cycle in 2008. Use the financial statements from Problem 5 to make your calculations. Balance sheet items should reflect the averages of the 2007 and 2008 accounts.

A. Calculate the inventory-to-sale conversion period for 2008.

B. Calculate the sale-to-cash conversion period for 2008.

C. Calculate the purchase-to-payment conversion period for 2008.

D. Determine the length of Castillo Products' cash conversion cycle for 2008.

7. Use the financial statement data for Castillo Products presented in Problem 5.

A. Calculate the net profit margin in 2007 and 2008 and the sales-to-total-assets ratio using year-end data for each of the two years.

B. Use your calculations from Part A to determine the rate of return on assets in each of the two years for Castillo Products.

C. Calculate the percentage growth in net sales from 2007 to 2008. Compare this with the percentage change in total assets for the same period.

D. Express each expense item as a percentage of net sales for both 2007 and 2008. Describe what happened that allowed Castillo Products to move from a loss to a profit between the two years.

8. Safety-First, Inc., makes portable ladders that can be used to exit second-floor levels of homes in the event of fire. Each ladder consists of fire-resistant rope and high-strength plastic steps. A lightweight fire-resistant cape with a smoke filter is included with the Safety-First ladder. Each ladder and cape, when not in use, is rolled up and stored in a pouch the size of a backpack and can easily be taken on trips and vacations.

Jan Smithson founded Safety-First after graduating from a private liberal arts college in the Northwest three years ago. After struggling for the first year, the venture seemed to be growing and producing profits. Following are the two most recent years of financial statements, expressed in thousands of dollars, for Safety-First, Inc.

Safety-First, Inc.

INCOME STATEMENTS (IN $ THOUSANDS)

	2007	2008
Net sales	$3,750	$4,500
Cost of goods sold	2,250	2,700
Gross profit	1,500	1,800
Operating expenses	670	860
Interest	30	40
Income before taxes	800	900
Income taxes	250	300
Net income	$ 550	$ 600

BALANCE SHEETS (IN $ THOUSANDS)

	2007	2008
Cash	$ 400	$ 150
Accounts receivable	500	800
Inventories	1,450	2,000
Total current assets	2,350	2,950
Gross fixed assets	2,000	2,800
Less accumulated depreciation	−950	−1,250
Net fixed assets	1,050	1,550
Total assets	$3,400	$4,500

	2007	2008
Accounts payable	$ 300	$ 400
Bank loan	150	250
Accrued liabilities	100	150
Total current liabilities	550	800
Long-term debt	150	150
Common stock	850	1,100
Retained earnings	1,850	2,450
Total liabilities and equity	$3,400	$4,500

A. Using year-end data, calculate the inventory-to-sale conversion period, the sale-to-cash conversion period, and the purchase-to-payment conversion period for 2007 and 2008.

B. Determine the cash conversion cycle for each year and discuss the changes, if any, that took place.

9. Return to the financial statement data provided in Problem 8 for Safety-First, Inc.

A. Calculate the net profit margin, the sales-to-total-assets ratio, and the equity multiplier for both 2007 and 2008 using year-end (rather than average) balance sheet data.

B. Use the results from Part A to calculate the venture's return on equity in each year.

C. Describe what happened in terms of the financial performance of Safety-First, Inc., between 2007 and 2008.

10. Make use of the financial statement data provided in Problem 8 for Safety-First, Inc.

A. Calculate the operating profit margins and the NOPAT margins in 2007 and 2008 for Safety-First, Inc. What changes occurred?

B. Calculate the operating return on assets (or the venture's basic earning power) using year-end balance sheet information for both 2007 and 2008. Describe what happened in terms of operating return performance.

C. Did the venture benefit from using interest-bearing debt in the form of bank loans and long-term debt in 2007 and 2008?

M I N I   C A S E

Scandi Home Furnishings, Inc.

Kaj Rasmussen founded Scandi Home Furnishings as a corporation during mid-2005. Sales during the first full year (2006) of operation reached $1.3 million. Sales increased by 15 percent in 2007 and another 20 percent in 2008. However, profits, after increasing in 2007 over 2006, fell sharply in 2008, causing Kaj to wonder what was happening to his "pride-and-joy" business venture. After all, Kaj has continued to work as closely as possible to a 24/7 pace beginning with the startup of Scandi and through the first three full years of operation.

Scandi Home Furnishings, located in eastern North Carolina, designs, manufactures, and sells Scandinavian-designed furniture and accessories to home furnishings retailers. The modern Scandinavian design has a streamlined and uncluttered look. While this furniture style is primarily associated with Denmark, both Norwegian and Swedish designers have contributed to the allure of Scandinavian home furnishings. Some say that the inspiration for the Scandinavian design can be traced to the elegant curves of art nouveau from which designers were able to produce aesthetically pleasing, structurally strong modern furniture. Danish furnishings and the home furnishings produced by the other Scandinavian countries—Sweden, Norway, and Finland—are made using wood (primarily oak, maple, and ash), aluminum, steel, and high-grade plastics.

Kaj grew up in Copenhagen, Denmark, and received an undergraduate degree from a technical university in Sweden. As is typical in Europe, Kaj began his business career as an apprentice at a major home furnishings manufacturer in Copenhagen. After learning the trade, he quickly moved into a management position in the firm. However, after a few years, Kaj realized that what he really wanted to do was to start and operate his own Scandinavian home furnishings business. At the same time, after traveling throughout the world, including the United States, he was sure that he

continued on next page

Scandi Home Furnishings, Inc. (continued)

wanted to be an entrepreneur in the United States. Kaj moved to the United States in early 2005. With $140,000 of his personal assets and $210,000 from venture investors, he began operations in mid-2005. Kaj, with a 40 percent ownership interest and industry-related management expertise, was allowed to operate the venture in a way that he thought was best for Scandi. Four years later, Kaj is sure he did the right thing.

Following are the three years of income statements and balance sheets for Scandi Home Furnishings. Kaj felt that in order to maintain a competitive advantage that he would need to continue to expand sales. After first concentrating on selling Scandinavian home furnishings in the Northeast in 2006 and 2007, he decided to enter the West Coast market. An increase in expenses occurred associated with identifying, contacting, and selling to home furnishings retailers in California, Oregon, and Washington. Kaj Rasmussen hopes that you can help him better understand what has been happening to Scandi Home Furnishings from both operating and financial standpoints.

Scandi Home Furnishings, Inc.

INCOME STATEMENTS

	2006	2007	2008
Net sales	$1,300,000	$1,500,000	$1,800,000
Cost of goods sold	780,000	900,000	1,260,000
Gross profit	520,000	600,000	540,000
Marketing	130,000	150,000	200,000
General and administrative	150,000	150,000	200,000
Depreciation	40,000	53,000	60,000
EBIT	200,000	247,000	80,000
Interest	45,000	57,000	70,000
Earnings before taxes	155,000	190,000	10,000
Income taxes (40%)	62,000	76,000	4,000
Net income	$ 93,000	$ 114,000	$ 6,000

Scandi Home Furnishings, Inc.

BALANCE SHEETS

	2006	2007	2008
Cash	$ 50,000	$ 40,000	$ 10,000
Accounts receivable	200,000	260,000	360,000
Inventories	450,000	500,000	600,000
Total current assets	700,000	800,000	970,000
Fixed assets, net	300,000	400,000	500,000
Total assets	$1,000,000	$1,200,000	$1,470,000
Accounts payable	$ 130,000	$ 170,000	$ 180,000
Accruals	50,000	70,000	80,000
Bank loan	90,000	90,000	184,000
Total current liabilities	270,000	330,000	444,000

Scandi Home Furnishings, Inc. (continued)

Long-term debt	300,000	400,000	550,000
Common stock ($10 par)*	300,000	300,000	300,000
Capital surplus	50,000	50,000	50,000
Retained earnings	80,000	120,000	126,000
Total liabilities and equity	$1,000,000	$1,200,000	$1,470,000

* Thirty thousand shares of common stock were issued to Kaj Rasmussen and the venture investors when Scandi Home Furnishings was incorporated in mid-2005.

A. Kaj was particularly concerned by the drop in cash from $50,000 in 2006 to $10,000 in 2008. Calculate the average current ratio, the quick ratio, and the NWC-to-total-assets ratio for 2006–2007 and 2007–2008. What has happened to Scandi's liquidity position?

B. An analysis of the cash conversion cycle should also help Kaj understand what has been happening to the operations of Scandi. Prepare an analysis of the average conversion periods for the three components of the cash conversion cycle for 2006–2007 and 2007–2008. Explain what has happened in terms of each component of the cycle.

C. Kaj should be interested in knowing whether Scandi has been building or burning cash. Compare the cash build, cash burn, and the net cash build/burn positions for 2007 and 2008. What, if any, changes have occurred?

D. Creditors, as well as management, are also concerned about the ability of the venture to meet its debt obligations as they come due, the proportion of current liabilities to total debt, the availability of assets to meet debt obligations in the event of financial distress, and the relative size of equity investments to debt levels. Calculate average ratios in each of these areas for the 2006–2007 and 2007–2008 periods. Interpret your results and explain what has happened to Scandi.

E. Of importance to Kaj and the venture investors is the efficiency of the operations of the venture. Several profit margin ratios relating to the income statement are available to help analyze Scandi's performance. Calculate average profit margin ratios for 2006–2007 and 2007–2008 and describe what is happening to the profitability of Scandi Home Furnishings.

F. Kaj and the venture investors are also interested in how efficiently Scandi is able to convert its equity investment, as well as the venture's total assets, into sales. Calculate several ratios that combine data from the income statements and balance sheets and compare what has happened between the 2006–2007 and 2007–2008 periods.

G. An ROA model consisting of the product of two ratios provides an overview of a venture's efficiency and profitability at the same time. An ROE model consists of the product of three ratios and simultaneously shows an overview of a venture's efficiency, profitability, and leverage performance. Calculate ROA and ROE models for the 2006–2007 and 2007–2008 periods. Provide an interpretation of your findings.

H. Kaj has been able to obtain some industry ratio data from the home furnishings industry trade association of which he is a member. The industry association collects proprietary financial information from members of the association, compiles averages to protect the proprietary nature of the information, and provides averages for use by individual trade association members. Over the 2006–2007 and 2007–2008 periods, the inventory-to-sale conversion

continued on next page

Scandi Home Furnishings, Inc. (continued)

period has averaged 200 days, while the sale-to-cash conversion period (days of sales outstanding) for the industry has averaged sixty days. How did Scandi's operations in terms of these two components of the cash conversion cycle compare with these industry averages?

l. Trade association data for the home furnishings industry show an average net profit margin of 6.5 percent, a sales-to-assets ratio of 1.3 times, and a total-debt-to-total-assets ratio of 55 percent over the 2006–2007 and 2007–2008 periods. Compare and contrast with the industry average in terms of the ROA and ROE models. Make sure you compare the components of each model as well as the product of the components.

P a r t 3

PLANNING FOR THE FUTURE

Chapter 6

FINANCIAL PLANNING: SHORT TERM AND LONG TERM

PREVIOUSLY COVERED

In Chapter 5, we introduced financial ratios to measure an early-stage venture's progress and compare its success to other firms. We began with financial measures relating to a venture's cash position: burn rates, liquidity ratios, and the cash conversion cycle. We identified ratios often considered by potential lenders and creditors and discussed profitability and efficiency measures tracked by entrepreneurs and venture investors.

LOOKING AHEAD

In Chapter 7, we describe how one obtains and pays for financial capital. We relate the cost of debt to the stated interest rate for a loan or bond. We relate the cost of equity to the dividends and capital gains investors expect to receive. We discuss how venture capitalists calibrate the rates of return they apply to venture investments.

CHAPTER LEARNING OBJECTIVES

In this chapter, we focus on how the venture quantifies its vision of the future: projected financial statements—short term and long term. The availability of cash drives an entrepreneurial venture. Inadequate cash constrains its ability to grow, is a primary cause of financial distress, and can lead to bankruptcy even in the presence of accounting profits. After introducing Part 3, we discuss cash budgeting. Preparing a cash budget and projecting financial statements helps the entrepreneur anticipate cash shortfalls. After completing this chapter, you will be able to:

1. Construct a cash budget

2. Describe how projected statements of cash flows relate to cash budgets

3. Explain why projected statements of cash flows are important to the entrepreneur

4. Understand the concept of a sustainable sales growth rate

5. Understand the process of identifying the quantity and timing of additional funds needed to support the venture's sales forecasts

6. Connect sales growth rates to the amount and timing of additional funds needed

7. Describe the percent-of-sales method for preparing financial plans

Financial planning usually begins with a forecast of sales. For short-term financial planning, monthly forecasts are customary. Although projecting monthly revenues and cash flow is common for all ventures, it is especially critical for startups and for ventures enduring their survival stages. For ventures at all stages, longer-term financial planning involves three to five years of forecasts for annual levels of many variables such as revenues, profits, and investments in property, plant, equipment, and working capital.

6.1 FINANCIAL PLANNING THROUGHOUT THE VENTURE'S LIFE CYCLE

If it sounds as though financial planning pervades all stages of a venture's life cycle, then our point is hitting home. Figure 6.1 displays the venture life cycle. Part 1 of this book introduced useful financial measures and tools for screening and feasibility assessment during a venture's development stage. Part 2 focused on getting the venture organized and operating. During this stage, implementing a financial (accounting) system to measure and evaluate performance is crucial. Using that system to monitor cash burn rates, liquidity ratios, and the cash conversion cycle is particularly important as the venture moves from the startup stage through its survival stage.

Part 3 emphasizes relatively formalized forward-looking financial tools, the application of which pervades all the life cycle stages—projected income statements, balance sheets, and statements of cash flows.[1] Most new ventures project annual sales three to five years into the future and prepare the related financial statements.[2] The horizon of these forecasts usually takes the successful venture from startup, through survival, and well into its rapid-growth stage. These annual projections provide valuable indicators of the quantity and timing of required additional financing.

Long-run planning is of little value if the venture does not survive the short run. It is equally important—if not more important—to construct short-term

---

[1] Of course, successful ventures won't always have additional financing needs. While financing needs are highly likely during the development, startup, survival, and early part of the rapid-growth stages, after ramping up to support rapid growth in sales, the successful venture begins generating excess or free cash during the latter part of its rapid-growth stage and throughout its maturity stage.

[2] Industry ratio benchmark data are the basis of most forecasted individual accounts on the income statement and balance sheet. If the venture is creating a new industry, benchmark ratios are taken from industries perceived to be similar in their operations. For a venture with an operating history, the venture's own historical ratios and account relationships are typically used as benchmarks for new projections.

FIGURE 6.1 Life Cycle Approach: Venture Operating and Financial Decisions

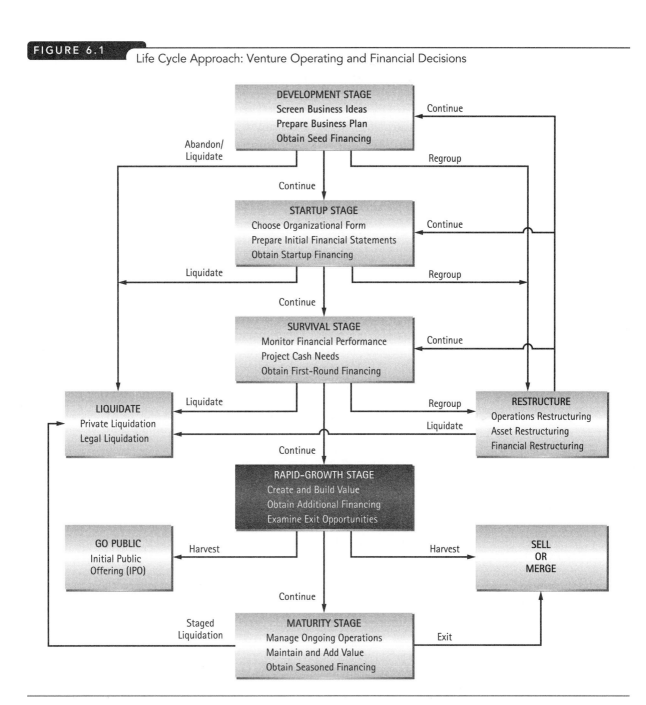

(one- to two-year) forecasts of cash requirements. Entrepreneurs can break down annual sales projections into monthly projections to consider the impact of any seasonality in sales. Other accounts can be tied to the sales forecasts using the benchmark ratios taken from the venture's (or its industry's) operating history. Short-term financial planning is critical during the survival stage because operations not yet turning a profit and the associated cash burn often lead to a venture's inability to pay its maturing liabilities. Short-term financial planning is also very important during a venture's rapid-growth stage—but for a different reason. Cash shortages during this stage frequently derive from the lack of operating profits to fund the investments in working capital and fixed assets necessary to continue on the growth trajectory. While this is not the same type of dilemma that unprofitable early operations pose, it is still a threat to a venture's achieving its projected leadership in its markets.

6.2   SURVIVING IN THE SHORT RUN

Cash is the lifeblood of an entrepreneurial venture. Without sufficient cash, a venture dies. Even ventures that survive can experience cash crunches that inflict mental and physical trauma, with lifelong consequences for the entrepreneur. While we cannot ensure that reading this chapter (or any other one) will keep your venture from experiencing financial distress, we do provide a framework for anticipating cash flow shortages. Knowing that a crunch is coming gives you time to minimize, if not avoid, any associated trauma.

Short-term financial planning usually involves projecting monthly financial statements and concentrating on a venture's cash needs. Most initial business plans contain monthly projected (pro forma) financial statements for at least one year, and sometimes for two or more years. These short-horizon forecasts directly address whether a venture is expected to generate—or otherwise obtain—the required cash to meet its coming obligations. Firms of all sizes, at all stages, wonder whether cash supply will meet cash demand. With solid banking relationships and access to short-term lending markets, a sophisticated Fortune 500 cash manager can assure that cash requirements are met precisely and that no dollar is left idle. By moving in and out of short-term lending arrangements, the cash manager can hedge the cash flow impacts of predictable and unexpected swings in a firm's operations. For such firms, the joy of unexpected success, which almost invariably involves materials and labor outflows before collections, is not replaced by the panic of a cash crunch.

Unfortunately, young and growing entrepreneurial ventures seldom, if ever, have access to these markets and cash management techniques. Consequently, short-term planning is critical for early-stage ventures; such a plan maps out how a given venture expects to survive its startup and survival stages. A young venture—restricted in its access to bank credit lines, limited in its access (if any) to short-term lending markets, and faced with months of preparation and negotiation before the next financing round—can easily choke on its own success. For many new ventures, getting from one cash injection to the next will be more challenging than designing, developing, and manufacturing a new product.

One of entrepreneurial finance's distinguishing features is that chronic cash requirements tend to be treated with acute cash injections. Figure 6.2 graphically depicts a jagged path for an entrepreneurial venture. In a very young venture,

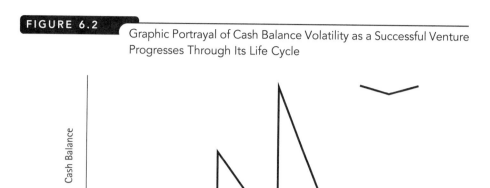

FIGURE 6.2 Graphic Portrayal of Cash Balance Volatility as a Successful Venture Progresses Through Its Life Cycle

when there is frequently no visible source of cash, a founder's initial funds are conserved by changing diet, losing sleep (working longer), and foregoing a salary. Cash conservation through these and other measures makes the descent from the initial cash peak relatively gentle. After an intense phase of attempting to preserve ownership and control by avoiding fundraising, many ventures realize that resistance is futile and involves an unacceptably high risk of missing a window of opportunity. For many startups, seeking funds from family, friends, and acquaintances is a first choice for external financing. This initial external financing creates the next cash peak, but the new cash is frequently spent more rapidly as the venture surrenders the notion of complete independence through internal funding. For a high-growth venture, the descents from cash peaks remain steep until the venture is a prominent player in the targeted market. This can happen long after the venture becomes a public company.

For an early-stage venture, when a cash fix (a vertical line pushing the venture up from zero) is sought during a panic, the venture is at a distinct bargaining disadvantage. The financial terms offered and accepted will reflect this. In addition, the cash panic seriously detracts from the venture's primary and more long-term goal of creating value through product innovation, development, manufacturing, and sales. Avoiding cash panics is the primary goal of cash planning; the primary tool is the cash budget, which we introduce below by way of example.

CONCEPT CHECK

- Why is considering cash so important in entrepreneurial ventures?

6.3   SHORT-TERM CASH-PLANNING TOOLS

Pamela, Dharma, and Constance, upon completing their undergraduate degrees, decided to start their own venture. They were able to acquire exclusive North American distribution rights for a new type of interior wall paint product, New-Age Paint, which emits a light fragrance when interior temperature changes and conveys a subtle color alteration as the mix of lighting changes from primarily solar to primarily incandescent (as a day matures). Several different fragrances can be embedded in the paint; the fragrance has an expected useful life of five years with annual wipe-down of a "revitalizer." Pamela, Dharma, and Constance have formed the PDC Company to own the distribution rights. The founders believe they have a unique new product that can introduce a recurring revenue business model where none has previously existed.

PDC inventories NewAge Paint that it plans to sell shortly after having received the paint. It is currently March 31, 2008, and the sales force has provided the following projected sales:

April	$115,000	July	$115,000
May	$184,000	August	$ 92,000
June	$138,000		

Table 6.1 presents PDC's initial balance sheet. PDC is buying a used delivery truck on April 1 for $6,900 cash. PDC expects to pay miscellaneous cash expenses equal to 5 percent of the current sales and rent of $4,600 per month, and it records insurance expense at $460 per month, although it writes a check to the insurance company for a year at a time. PDC plans to draw the prepaid insurance account balance down to zero before cutting the next check to the insurance company. Depreciation expense is $1,150 per month, including the truck, and PDC anticipates a zero tax rate. Wages are paid twice a month with $5,750 per month fixed and 15 percent of sales (assumed to be uniform throughout a month) as a variable commission. Wages are paid a half month after they are earned. As an example, the

---

TABLE 6.1   PDC Company Initial Balance Sheet (March 31)

ASSETS		LIABILITIES AND EQUITY	
Current Assets		**Current Liabilities**	
Cash	23,000	Accounts payable	38,640
Accounts receivable	36,800	Accrued wages	9,775
Paint inventory	110,400	**Total current liabilities**	48,415
Prepaid insurance	4,140		
Total current assets	174,340		
Property, plant, and equipment			
Gross property, plant, and equipment	85,100	**Equity**	181,585
Accumulated depreciation	−29,440		
Net property, plant, and equipment	55,660		
Total assets	230,000	**Total liabilities and equity**	230,000

expected and realized sales of $92,000 for March are responsible for the $9,775 [(.5 × $5,750) + (.5 × .15 × $92,000)] currently in the accrued wages account.

PDC's inventory policy is to begin a month with sufficient inventory to cover 80 percent of the sales for the month plus a $46,000 cushion. Previous inventory balances have conformed to the current policy, and sales forecasts have been accurate. The cost of goods sold amounts to 70 percent of sales. For example, sales are forecasted to be $115,000 in April. The corresponding desired inventory level (end of March and beginning of April) is estimated as $64,400 ($115,000 × .8 × .7) + $46,000 = $110,400. The beginning of month inventory amount (e.g., for April) is also the inventory amount at the end of the prior month (e.g., March). The venture takes all deliveries on account and pays half in the current month and half in the following month.

PDC's sales are 60 percent cash and 40 percent on accounts receivable collected in the following month. It has no currently overdue accounts and anticipates none in the near future. For example, 40 percent of the $92,000 sales made in March were credit sales and show up as $36,800 in accounts receivable on the balance sheet at the end of March.

PDC's only available credit line is from a founder who agreed (in return for a piece of the equity) to lend the company money at 1.5 percent interest per month for the next two years. The agreement with this founder stipulates a $23,000 minimum cash balance in the venture's checking account. PDC borrows from, and repays, the founder only at the end of the month. Interest is therefore the previous month's ending balance multiplied by .015.

Our goal is to project PDC's cash balance at the end of each of the next four months and to create a set of projected financial statements congruent to the projections. We break this daunting task down into smaller pieces.

Task 1: Budget PDC's cash and borrowing position for the next four months (through July 31).

Implementation Plan: (a) Use the sales forecast to determine the monthly cash collections from the current month's cash sales and collections of receivables on the previous month's credit sales, (b) use the inventory policy to determine the inventory expenses and schedule for their payments, (c) schedule the wages payments according to the semimonthly pay arrangements, and (d) put these items together with the other assumptions and determine cash needs before financing, and complete the cash budget by determining the necessary borrowing and repayment provisions, including interest payments, ensuring that $23,000 is available in the checking account.

Table 6.2 presents each step of this plan for PDC. In Part A, we first prepare a sales schedule for each month that includes the sales forecast and cash collections. Cash sales are collected in the month the sales occur. Credit sales are collected in the month following when sales occur. For example, in April cash sales are expected to be 60 percent of $115,000, or $69,000. Accounts receivable of $36,800 at the end of March (from credit sales made during March) are added to the $69,000 in expected April cash sales for total collections of $105,800 expected in April.

Next, in Part B of Table 6.2, we prepare a purchases schedule for each month that includes estimating the amount of purchases and the payment or disbursement

TABLE 6.2 PDC Company Operating Schedules and Cash Budget

(A) SALES SCHEDULE

	MARCH	APRIL	MAY	JUNE	JULY	AUGUST	APRIL TO JULY
Schedule 1: Sales Forecast	92,000	115,000	184,000	138,000	115,000	92,000	552,000
Credit sales, 40%	36,800	46,000	73,600	55,200	46,000		
Cash sales, 60%	55,200	69,000	110,400	82,800	69,000		
Schedule 2: Cash Collections							
Cash sales this month		69,000	110,400	82,800	69,000		
100% of last month's credit sales		36,800	46,000	73,600	55,200		
Total collections		105,800	156,400	156,400	124,200		

(B) PURCHASES SCHEDULE

	MARCH	APRIL	MAY	JUNE	JULY	APRIL TO JULY
Schedule 3: Purchases						
Ending inventory	110,400	149,040	123,280	110,400	97,520	
Cost of goods sold	64,400	80,500	128,800	96,600	80,500	386,400
Total needed	174,800	229,540	252,080	207,000	178,020	
Beginning inventory	−97,520	−110,400	−149,040	−123,280	−110,400	
Purchases	77,280	119,140	103,040	83,720	67,620	
Schedule 4: Purchase Disbursements						
50% of last month's purchases		38,640	59,570	51,520	41,860	
50% of this month's purchases		59,570	51,520	41,860	33,810	
Disbursements for purchases		98,210	111,090	93,380	75,670	

(C) WAGES AND COMMISSIONS SCHEDULE

	MARCH	APRIL	MAY	JUNE	JULY	APRIL TO JULY
Schedule 5: Wages and Commissions						
Wages, all fixed	5,750	5,750	5,750	5,750	5,750	
Commissions (15% of current sales)	13,800	17,250	27,600	20,700	17,250	
Total	19,550	23,000	33,350	26,450	23,000	105,800
Schedule 6: Disbursements— Wages and Commissions						
50% of last month's expenses		9,775	11,500	16,675	13,225	
50% of this month's expenses		11,500	16,675	13,225	11,500	
Total		21,275	28,175	29,900	24,725	

TABLE 6.2 PDC Company Operating Schedules and Cash Budget (*continued*)

	(D) CASH BUDGET			
	APRIL	MAY	JUNE	JULY
Beginning cash balance	23,000	23,000	23,000	23,000
Cash receipts:				
Collections from customers	105,800	156,400	156,400	124,200
Total cash available for needs				
before financing	128,800	179,400	179,400	147,200
Cash disbursements:				
Merchandise	98,210	111,090	93,380	75,670
Wages and commissions	21,275	28,175	29,900	24,725
Miscellaneous expenses	5,750	9,200	6,900	5,750
Rent	4,600	4,600	4,600	4,600
Truck purchase	6,900	0	0	0
Total disbursements	136,735	153,065	134,780	110,745
Minimum cash balance desired	23,000	23,000	23,000	23,000
Total cash needed	159,735	176,065	157,780	133,745
Excess of total cash	−30,935	3,335	21,620	13,455
Financing				
New borrowing	30,935	0	0	0
Repayments		2,871	21,199	6,865
Loan balance	30,935	28,064	6,865	0
Interest	0	464	421	103
Total effects of financing	30,935	−3,335	−21,620	−6,968
Cash balance	23,000	23,000	23,000	29,487

---

of funds to pay for the purchases. Paint inventory on hand at the end of March was $110,400 and represents the beginning inventory for April. Target ending inventory for April is $149,040. The reader should be able to verify this amount based on our earlier discussion of PDC's inventory policy. However, the process is probably worth repeating here. First forecast May's sales at $184,000. Eighty percent of sales or $147,200 ($184,000 × .8) is the target inventory coverage. Multiplying $147,200 by .7 converts sales into a "cost" basis of $103,040. Adding a safety stock cushion of $46,000 produces an ending inventory target for April of $149,040. Actual cost of goods sold for April is $80,500 ($115,000 × .7). Adding $149,040 and $80,500 produces total needed inventory of $229,540 for April. Subtracting the beginning inventory (amount remaining from March) of $110,400 results in the need to purchase $119,140 of paint to meet April's ending inventory target.

Purchases are made on account with net 15-day credit terms such that 50 percent of the purchases made in a specific month are paid in that month. The other 50 percent of a month's purchases are paid the following month. To complete the purchases schedule, a purchases disbursement schedule must be completed. For April, PDC pays the $38,640 in accounts payable existing at the end of March ($77,280 March cost of goods sold times .5) and also pays $59,570 ($119,100 × .5) for April purchases for total April disbursements for purchases of $98,210.

In Part C of Table 6.2, we prepare a wages and commissions schedule. As previously discussed, fixed monthly wages are projected at $5,750. PDC also pays commissions amounting to 15 percent of the current month's sales. Based on April forecasted sales of $115,000, commissions are estimated at $17,250 ($115,000 × .15) for total wages and commissions of $23,000 ($5,750 + $17,250). However, because there is a one-half month lag between when wages and commissions are earned and when they are paid, actual dollar disbursements are 50 percent of last month's wage and commission expenses and 50 percent of the current month's expenses. For April, 50 percent of March's wages and commissions were $9,775 ($19,550 × .5) and 50 percent of April's expenses ($23,000 × .5) for a total monthly disbursement of $21,275. The three internal operating schedules (sales schedule, purchases schedule, and wages and commissions schedule) now are used to prepare a fourth schedule indicating the flow of cash through a venture.

cash budget

a venture's projected cash receipts and disbursements over a forecast period

A **cash budget** shows a venture's projected cash receipts and disbursements over a forecast period. Cash budgets often are estimated monthly for up to a one-year period. Part D of Table 6.2 illustrates a cash budget for PDC covering the April through July period. Cash on hand from the March balance sheet is $23,000, and PDC wants to maintain this cash level in each of the forecast months. Projected cash receipts for April of $105,800 (taken from the sales schedule) are added to the beginning cash for total cash of $128,500 before disbursements and financing. Total cash disbursements in April amount to $136,735, which reflects in part the sum of disbursements for purchases (merchandise) of $98,210 from the purchases schedule and $21,275 from the wages and commissions schedule. As noted earlier, miscellaneous cash expenses are forecasted at 5 percent of the current month's sales, or $5,750 for April ($115,000 × .05). Rent was projected to be $4,600 per month and an annual insurance bill of $6,900 ($460 × 12) was to be paid in April.

Total cash needed in April is $159,735 ($136,735 + $23,000). Cash needed exceeds cash generated by $30,935 ($159,735 − $128,600), making it necessary to borrow $30,935 so that PDC can meet its target cash balance of $23,000. Cash receipts are projected to exceed cash disbursements (including the desired $23,000 cash balance) by $3,335 ($179,400 − $176,065) in May. This extra cash will be used to pay interest of $464 ($30,935 × .015) and loan repayments of $2,871. By the end of July, the loan will be repaid in full and PDC will have an ending cash balance of $29,487, which is $6,487 greater than the target ending cash balance of $23,000.

6.4   PROJECTED MONTHLY FINANCIAL STATEMENTS

Another common way to express the venture's anticipated cash needs is to project the balance sheet and income statement into the future and produce the statement of cash flows. This is easiest to do when we have already calculated the interest expenses for the four months.

Task 2: Prepare PDC's pro forma income statement for the four months.

Implementation Plan: Use the summaries of the revenue and expense items to create four months of income statements that include the interest expenses determined in Task 1. Table 6.3 presents these income statements.

Task 3: Prepare PDC's pro forma balance sheet for July 31.

Implementation Plan: (a) Adjust the initial balance sheet, excluding the cash account, for each of the four months of changes; (b) make sure the equity account reflects each month's net income; (c) calculate the cash account balance, which is consistent with total assets = total liabilities + equity; and (d) ascertain that the resulting cash account balance agrees with that from the cash budget.

Table 6.4 presents the projected balance sheets.

Task 4: Prepare PDC's statements of cash flows for the four-month period.

Implementation Plan: (a) Refer to our discussion of the construction of the statement of cash flows in Chapter 4 and the presentation of cash flow statements in Chapter 5; (b) apply the cash flow from operations, investing activities, and financing activities to the data for PDC; and (c) ascertain that the resulting ending cash flow agrees with the cash budget and the cash account balance on the pro forma balance sheets.

Table 6.5 presents the projected statements of cash flows. Cash flows from operations are projected to be −$24,035 in April. This amount, coupled with cash flows from investing activities of −$6,900, produces a total cash shortage of −$30,935 before financing activities in April. However, the required loan of $30,935 in April is projected to be paid off in full by July. In addition to repaying

---

TABLE 6.3   PDC Company Projected Income Statements

BUDGETED INCOME STATEMENTS	MARCH	APRIL	MAY	JUNE	JULY	APRIL TO JULY
Sales	92,000	115,000	184,000	138,000	115,000	552,000
Cost of goods sold	−64,400	−80,500	−128,800	−96,600	−80,500	−386,400
Gross margin	27,600	34,500	55,200	41,400	34,500	165,600
Operating expenses						
Wages and commissions	−19,550	−23,000	−33,350	−26,450	−23,000	−105,800
Rent	−4,600	−4,600	−4,600	−4,600	−4,600	−18,400
Miscellaneous expenses	−4,600	−5,750	−9,200	−6,900	−5,750	−27,600
Insurance	−460	−460	−460	−460	−460	−1,840
Depreciation	−1,150	−1,150	−1,150	−1,150	−1,150	−4,600
Total operating expenses	−30,360	−34,960	−48,760	−39,560	−34,960	−158,240
Income from operations	−2,760	−460	6,440	1,840	−460	7,360
Interest expense	0	0	−464	−421	−103	−988
Net income	−2,760	−460	5,976	1,419	−563	6,372

TABLE 6.4 PDC Company Projected Balance Sheets

BALANCE SHEET	MARCH	APRIL	MAY	JUNE	JULY
Current assets					
Cash	23,000	23,000	23,000	23,000	29,487
Accounts receivable	36,800	46,000	73,600	55,200	46,000
Merchandise inventory	110,400	149,040	123,280	110,400	97,520
Prepaid insurance	4,140	3,680	3,220	2,760	2,300
Total current assets	174,340	221,720	223,100	191,360	175,307
Plant					
Equipment, fixtures, and other	85,100	92,000	92,000	92,000	92,000
Accumulated depreciation	−29,440	−30,590	−31,740	−32,890	−34,040
Net property, plant, and equipment	55,660	61,410	60,260	59,110	57,960
Total assets	230,000	283,130	283,360	250,470	233,267
Current liabilities					
Accounts payable	38,640	59,570	51,520	41,860	33,810
Accrued wages and commissions payable	9,775	11,500	16,675	13,225	11,500
Loan	0	30,935	28,064	6,865	0
Total current liabilities	48,415	102,005	96,259	61,950	45,310
Owners' equity	181,585	181,125	187,101	188,520	187,957
Total liabilities and equity	230,000	283,130	283,360	250,470	233,267

the loan, PDC will accumulate $6,487 in surplus cash beyond the target balance of $23,000.

As a consequence of such an exercise, you should be convinced of the following fact: Indirectly projecting cash balances (or deficits) through pro forma balance sheets and income statements (and using a statement of cash flows) gives the same answer as direct calculation of receipts and disbursements (as long as you have magically included the correct amount of interest expense). In fact, the adjustments made in the cash flow statement are *exactly* those necessary to calculate the net impact on the cash account. Delays in receipts and disbursements from the associated accounting revenues and expenses are incorporated through changes in the associated accounts in the cash flow statement. To finalize this insight, try the fastest method of communicating cash projections.

6.5 CASH PLANNING FROM A PROJECTED MONTHLY BALANCE SHEET

Task 5: Calculate the change in the cash account balance in a spreadsheet that uses only the beginning and ending balance sheets and net income.

Implementation Plan: (a) Create a spreadsheet with the balance sheets for 3/31 and 7/31 as columns; (b) difference the columns and adjust the sign to reflect the

TABLE 6.5 PDC Company Projected Statements of Cash Flows

ACCOUNTING STATEMENT OF CASH FLOWS	APRIL	MAY	JUNE	JULY
Cash flows from activities				
Net income	−460	5,976	1,419	−563
Adjustments to net income for CF				
+ Depreciation expense	1,150	1,150	1,150	1,150
− Change in A/R	−9,200	−27,600	18,400	9,200
− Change in inventory	−38,640	25,760	12,880	12,880
− Change in prepaid Insurance	460	460	460	460
Change in A/P	20,930	−8,050	−9,660	−8,050
+ Change in accrued liabilities	1,725	5,175	−3,450	−1,725
Total adjustments	−23,575	−3,105	19,780	13,915
Net cash flow from operations	−24,035	2,871	21,199	13,352
Cash flows from investing				
Capital expenditures (CAPEX)	−6,900	0	0	0
Net cash used by investments	−6,900	0	0	0
Cash flows from financing				
Equity issues	0	0	0	0
Dividends	0	0	0	0
Debt issues	30,935	−2,871	−21,199	−6,865
Net cash flows from financing	30,935	−2,871	−21,199	−6,865
Net change in cash	0	0	0	6,487
Beginning cash balance	23,000	23,000	23,000	23,000
Ending cash balance	23,000	23,000	23,000	29,487

change in cash flow, placing these signed differences in a third column; and (c) sum the third column to calculate the change in PDC's cash position directly.

Table 6.6 presents this method for PDC.

When projecting a venture forward into the future, there are several ways to complete the exercise. If the planner is not particularly concerned with maintaining a strategic level of cash, he or she can let the cash account take up the slack to balance the balance sheets. If the venture has overspent, the balance will be negative at an amount representing the minimum level of cash necessary to function according to projections (excluding financing costs on the funds used to offset the negative balance). This balancing cash must come from somewhere, and the cash balance should not really be thought of as negative (unless, perhaps, the plan is to overdraw the venture's checking account). If the venture must strategically hold a certain amount of cash, it is better to project the cash account to contain that strategic amount of cash and then formally modify an existing, or add a new, liability to provide the balancing cash inflow (including the financing expenses). If the planner balances by increasing the liability and the cash, he should not forget that the increase in the liability is not usually a done deal. Most early-stage ventures have serious difficulties locating debt arrangements.

TABLE 6.6   PDC Company's Balance Sheet Method for Determining Cash Flows

BALANCE SHEETS	MARCH	JULY	CHANGE	
Current assets				
Cash	23,000	29,487		
Accounts receivable	36,800	46,000	−9,200	Use of cash
Merchandise inventory	110,400	97,520	12,880	Source of cash
Prepaid insurance	4,140	2,300	1,840	Source of cash
Total current assets	174,340	175,307		
Plant				
Equipment, fixtures, and other	85,100	92,000	−6,900	Use of cash
Accumulated depreciation	−29,440	−34,040	4,600	Source of cash
Net property, plant, and				
equipment	55,660	57,960		
Total assets	230,000	233,267		
Current liabilities				
Accounts payable	38,640	33,810	−4,830	Use of cash
Accrued wages and				
commissions payable	9,775	11,500	1,725	Source of cash
Loan	0	0	0	No four-month effect
Total current liabilities	48,415	45,310		
Owners' equity	181,585	187,957		
Total equities	230,000	233,267	115	Total balance sheet cash impact
			6,372	Net income—dividends
			6,487	Accounting four-month cash flow

6.6   BEYOND SURVIVAL: SYSTEMATIC FORECASTING

Forecasting for firms with operating histories is generally much easier than forecasting for early-stage ventures. Difficulty, however, is no defense for new ventures; forecasts are a necessary ingredient in business plans, particularly if the venture wishes to attract external financing. There is something to be said for taking a small step in the light before leaping into the darkness that is new venture forecasting. Accordingly, we begin with the forecasting for a seasoned firm and use the insights it offers as guideposts for a useful approach to new venture forecasting.

FORECASTING SALES FOR SEASONED FIRMS

Forecasting sales or revenues for a seasoned firm usually begins with a review of the firm's sales for the past several years, typically five years. Samsing Corporation, a manufacturer of electrical components for industrial air-conditioning control systems, has eight years of operating history. The past five years of sales were:

YEAR	SALES ($ MILLIONS)	PERCENT CHANGE
2004	$20.00	
2005	22.00	+10%
2006	23.76	8
2007	26.14	10
2008	29.27	12
		Average = 10%

As you can see, sales growth has been relatively stable, ranging from 8 to 12 percent annually during this period.

Sales forecasts usually are based on either a single specific scenario or weighted averages of several possible realizations. A first step for Samsing would be to forecast future sales growth rates for several possible scenarios and to gauge the likelihood of each scenario. For example, three economic scenarios— slow economic growth, average economic growth, or rapid economic growth— might provide a basis for Samsing's projections. Based on Samsing's historical experience and market outlook, the marketing team suggests:

ECONOMIC SCENARIO	PROBABILITY OF OCCURRENCE	×	SALES GROWTH RATE	=	COMPONENT WEIGHT
Rapid growth	.20	×	12%	=	2.4%
Average growth	.60	×	10	=	6.0
Slow growth	.20	×	8	=	1.6
	1.00		Expected value	=	10.0%

The **expected value** is the weighted average of a set of scenarios or possible outcomes. Because of the symmetry of the above distribution, the 10 percent growth rate for "average growth" is the same as the three-scenario expected growth rate.

Figure 6.3 shows a plot of Samsing's historical sales, and what future sales levels would be if sales were to continue to grow at a 10 percent annual rate. The figure also displays sales growth rates of 8 percent (slow growth) and 12 percent (rapid growth). At a 10 percent annual growth, Samsing's sales would be about $47 million dollars in 2013. However, if sales were to grow at 8 percent, the 2013 level would be $43 million. If sales grow at 12 percent, the 2013 level would exceed $51.5 million.

A second step is to corroborate Samsing's projected sales growth rates with industry growth rates and Samsing's past market share. This method is frequently referred to as a "top-down" or market-share-driven approach to sales forecasting. For example, suppose that evidence shows that industry sales grew at an average 10 percent over the past five years. Demand at the industry level is expected to grow at an average rate of 10 percent over the next five years, with a range from 8 to 12 percent, depending on the economy. Furthermore, Samsing's sales have averaged 15 percent of industry sales during the past five years. Unless there are compelling reasons to believe that Samsing will increase its market share, it is reasonable to project that its sales will grow in lockstep with the industry (at an average rate of 10 percent).

The third step used to validate the sales forecast is through direct contact with existing and potential customers (market research). This is a "bottom-up" or

expected value
weighted average of a set of scenarios or possible outcomes

FIGURE 6.3

Historical Sales Levels and Sales Projections for Samsing Corporation (Millions of Dollars)

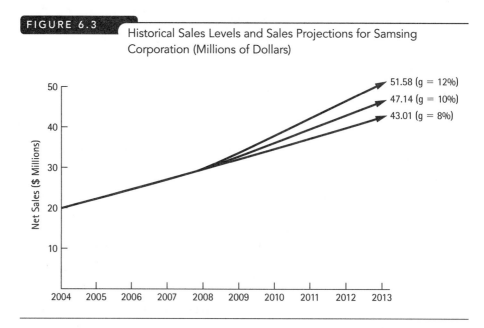

customer-driven approach to forecasting sales. Samsing sells electronic components to firms that manufacture wall units for controlling industrial air-conditioning systems. Likely sales to each of Samsing's major customers over the next five years are added to potential expected sales to new customers over the same period. This sum is then compared to the initial forecast, if any, and adjustments are negotiated. For example, upon closer inspection, Samsing may find that its customers plan to increase their orders at a rate of 8 percent next year because of a slowing economy. Because of a rapid economic recovery expected by the end of next year, the following year those same customers will bounce back to support a 12 percent growth. On balance, Samsing may conclude that a 10 percent annual growth rate over the next five years is reasonable.

A fourth and final step considers the likely impact of major operating changes. For example, major research and development investments may provide significant lead-time advantages over competitors and an increased market share for Samsing. In addition, the impact of changes in pricing policies, credit policies, and major advertising and promotional campaigns must be considered. Finally, it is important for forecasters to include the effects of inflation and to use nominal dollar estimates. That is, inflation in input and output prices should be incorporated in all projections. While general price levels may increase, a specific venture's ability to pass increases in input prices to its customers depends on how competitors respond and on the elasticity of demand for the firm's products.

Samsing is not planning any major changes in research and development or advertising expenditures. No change in pricing is anticipated (although Samsing will forcefully respond to any price cutting initiated by competitors). Inflation is expected to remain at about 3 percent. As a result, Samsing is comfortable with projecting a 10 percent sales growth rate for the next five years. However, for the next two years, it will use 8 and 12 percent, respectively.

FORECAST YEAR	SALES ($ MILLIONS)	PERCENT CHANGE
2009	$31.61	+8% (from 2008 level)
2010	35.40	12
2011	38.95	10
2012	42.84	10
2013	47.12	10
		Average = 10%

Serious consequences can result when sales forecasts are grossly inaccurate. For example, if inadequate sales forecasts are used to set Samsing's production capacity, the firm may not be able to respond to market demand. Market share will be lost as customers are serviced by competitors. On the other hand, when sales forecasts are excessive, cash-burning inventories will tend to swell and outlays for capacity increases are wasted.

CONCEPT CHECK

- What is the usual starting point for forecasting sales for seasoned firms?

FORECASTING SALES FOR EARLY-STAGE VENTURES

Early-stage ventures are those in the development stage, startup stage, survival stage, or just entering into their rapid-growth stage. The HandPilot Company, formed at the end of 2007, is in its startup stage. The venture developed and produces a handheld electronic device, the HandPilot, that controls kitchen appliances (i.e., adjusts settings, as well as turns them on and off) from remote distances. HandPilot's sales are expected to be $1 million in 2008, which is about to come to a close. Rapid sales growth is expected over the next five years, and HandPilot wishes to prepare five years of sales forecasts for potential investors. How should the forecasts be made?

early-stage ventures firms in their development stage, startup stage, survival stage, or just entering their rapid-growth stage

As an emerging venture, HandPilot doesn't have the luxury of extrapolating from past sales data. In these circumstances, a top-down, market-driven approach is useful. First, HandPilot estimates the next five years' overall market demands. Contracted market research estimates market demand of $20 million in 2009. It also suggests that the most likely scenario is a subsequent four-year market growth rate of 50 percent (reaching $101 million by 2013). HandPilot has decided to give this scenario a 40 percent weight and assess 30 percent weights on 40 percent and 60 percent growth rates:

INDUSTRY SALES SCENARIO	PROBABILITY OF OCCURRENCE	×	SALES GROWTH RATE	=	COMPONENT WEIGHT
Optimistic forecast	.30	×	60%	=	18.0%
Most likely forecast	.40	×	50	=	20.0
Pessimistic forecast	.30	×	40	=	12.0
	1.00		Expected value	=	50.0%

HandPilot has several competitors that have completed test marketing and are set to sell their own versions of kitchen appliance controllers; there are three potential rivals that, as far as HandPilot knows, have not yet decided to design or market a similar device. HandPilot's management is confident that successful business plan execution will yield a 25 percent market share throughout the five-year planning horizon. With the 2009 market size at $20 million, this implies initial sales of $5 million for HandPilot.

Figure 6.4 illustrates HandPilot's "hockey stick" sales pattern, typical for a new and successful high-growth venture. At a 50 percent growth rate, HandPilot's sales will reach $25 million in 2013. Figure 6.4 also displays the trajectory for 60 percent and 40 percent growth rates. Sixty percent growth leads to HandPilot sales of $32 million (actually $31.77 million) in 2013; 40 percent growth leads to $19.21 million.

HandPilot needs to validate its sales forecast by contacting existing and potential customers. Since there were initial orders and sales leads in 2008, these customers and leads can provide critical information for the successful execution of HandPilot's business plan and realization of its sales projections. Finally, HandPilot should ensure that projections incorporate realistic expectations about price trends, if any, owing to market competition and inflation. For planning purposes, HandPilot has adopted the 50 percent growth rate scenario:

FORECAST YEAR	SALES ($ MILLIONS)	PERCENT CHANGE
2009	$5.00	
2010	7.50	50%
2011	11.25	50
2012	16.88	50
2013	25.31	50
		Average = 50%

FIGURE 6.4

Historical Sales Levels and Sales Projections for the HandPilot Corporation (Millions of Dollars)

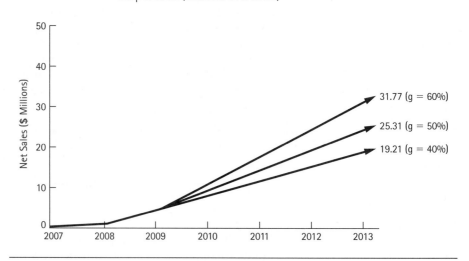

Of no small consequence, the $5 million projected for 2009 reflects a 400 percent increase $[([\$5 - \$1]/\$1) \times 100]$ over the realized sales of $1 million in 2008. HandPilot is entering its rapid-growth stage.

Before we move on, a caveat is in order. It is natural, and in most cases even desirable, for entrepreneurs to exhibit extreme optimism about sales and expense forecasts. Venture capitalists and other seasoned investors know that forecasting sales usually gets easier as a firm matures. Figure 6.5 illustrates this relationship between life cycle stage and forecasting accuracy with appropriate financing for each stage. Difficulty in accurately forecasting and rationalizing financial projections has traditionally been a sign that private equity fundraising is more appropriate than public equity fundraising. Developing and rationalizing forecasts for Samsing Company would be relatively straightforward. In contrast, HandPilot's forecasts call for an immediate 400 percent growth followed by four years of 50 percent growth. These forecasts are highly subjective and may involve "leaps of faith" rather than cold, hard, rational expectations. Consequently, we shouldn't be surprised to see Samsing seeking public financing while HandPilot negotiates for private equity financing.

One way that venture investors adjust for optimism and forecasting difficulties is by revising an entrepreneur's sales forecasts downward (and expenses upward).[3] For example, a venture capitalist might alter the range of sales growth

FIGURE 6.5   General Relationship Between a Firm's Life Cycle Stage and the Ability to Accurately Forecast Sales

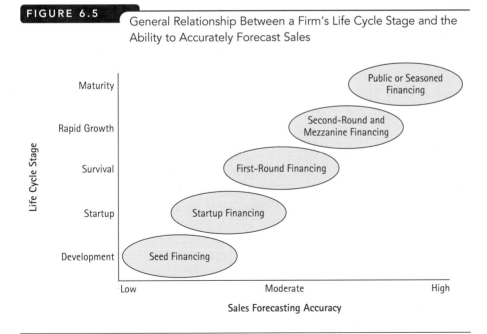

---

[3] An alternative method of adjusting for greater risk in forecasting sales and cash flows for early-stage ventures relative to more mature firms is to use higher discount rates to discount the venture's cash flows when evaluating investment in early-stage ventures. We will discuss this risk-adjusted discount rate approach in the next chapter.

rates, particularly on the down side, or assign different weights. In the HandPilot example, the 40 percent rate forecast probably is too unrealistically high to be considered "pessimistic." Perhaps 10 percent is more appropriate. Although the investor may like the 60 percent growth rate, perhaps this optimistic scenario deserves only a 20 percent weight (rather than 30 percent), with the weight shifted over to the pessimistic scenario (increasing it to 40 percent). These revisions would imply:

INDUSTRY SALES SCENARIO	PROBABILITY OF OCCURRENCE	×	SALES GROWTH RATE	=	COMPONENT WEIGHT
Optimistic forecast	.20	×	60%	=	12.0%
Management forecast	.40	×	50	=	20.0
Pessimistic forecast	.40	×	10	=	4.0
	1.00		Expected value =		36.0%

Thus, the venture investor's revised projections would be based on a growth rate of 36 percent rather than 50 percent. Note that the previous "most likely forecast" has been relabeled a "management forecast" and now carries the same weight as the pessimistic forecast.

With a 36 percent growth rate, the next five years' projections are as follows:

FORECAST YEAR	SALES ($ MILLIONS)	PERCENT CHANGE
2009	$ 5.00	
2010	6.80	36%
2011	9.25	36
2012	12.58	36
2013	17.11	36
		Average = 36%

The result is that sales are projected to reach only $17 million by 2013, rather than the $25 million HandPilot is forecasting (using 50 percent growth rates).

Furthermore, as the HandPilot venture was in its development stage in 2007, one could defend slashing the growth rates even further. If an investor were to believe that only two scenarios, equally weighted, were relevant, the following might result:

VENTURE'S SALES SCENARIO	PROBABILITY OF OCCURRENCE	×	SALES GROWTH RATE	=	COMPONENT WEIGHT
Management forecast	.50	×	50	=	25.0%
Pessimistic forecast	.50	×	0	=	0.0
	1.00		Expected value =		25.0%

Clearly, there are many possible scenario-weighting combinations, some of which are valid views of HandPilot's possible future. It is important to remember that one of our entrepreneurial finance principles is that "New venture financing involves search, negotiation, and privacy." Different beliefs give rise to different scenarios and weights, which lead to different projected growth rates and to different prices paid for the venture's securities. The process of new venture fundraising is centered on finding a workable compromise between founder and investor beliefs (and the related venture projections and values) that enables the venture to pursue its business plan.

Working toward a compromise involves an inherent dilemma. On the one hand, venture investors don't want to curtail the entrepreneur's optimism; formally adjusting the entrepreneur's forecasts downward to reflect more reasonable expectations may be taken as a lack of confidence or even as an insult to the entrepreneur's expertise. It can also set up motivating or dysfunctional "I'm going to show you" situations, depending on the personalities involved. This is one of the main reasons that many venture investors will work with founders' optimistic-scenario business plans (without much adjustment for other scenarios) and alter their valuation approaches accordingly. In the next chapter, we consider how venture investors accommodate optimistic-scenario projections by using optimistic-scenario returns on their securities to determine the price at which they will buy a venture's securities.

CONCEPT CHECK

- What process might be used to estimate sales for early-stage ventures?
- What is the dilemma faced by venture capitalists when it comes to estimates of sales forecasts by early-stage ventures?

6.7   ESTIMATING SUSTAINABLE SALES GROWTH RATES

To increase value, most ventures need to increase their scale. Revenue growth in isolation, however, does not assure increasing value. Incremental sales must lead to incremental overall profits and free cash flows. There are several potential impediments to a lockstep relationship between incremental sales and incremental cash flows. First, the incremental sales must be sold at prices that cover all incremental costs (capacity and variable costs). This may not be so easy if the venture, like most firms, faces downward-sloping demand (with lower prices required to sell more units). Second, the revenues from additional unit sales must cover increases in working capital investments (inventory and accounts receivable) required to support those incremental sales. Only when sales revenues cover all of these costs are there free cash flows that can give rise to an increase in venture value. When a venture requires external funds to support expansion, the venture must consider whether its margins allow it to pay its costs and still provide the type of return demanded by venture investors. Some ventures will conclude that slower growth from internal funding is a better way to go. Others will seek out external capital in a costly but total commitment to rapid growth.

internally generated funds

net income or profits (after taxes) earned over an accounting period

sustainable sales growth rate

rate at which a firm can grow sales based on the retention of profits in the business

A firm's net income or profit after taxes, also referred to as its **internally generated funds,** can be distributed to owners or reinvested to support growth. The portion retained in the business becomes an increase in retained earnings. The **sustainable sales growth rate** is the rate supported without external equity capital (through the retention of profits). If a firm can scale itself up without changing its strategy and margins, the firm can increase its sales at the growth rate of its book value of equity:[4]

$$
\begin{aligned}
g &= \frac{\text{Ending Equity} - \text{Beginning Equity}}{\text{Beginning Equity}} \\
&= \frac{\text{Change in Equity}}{\text{Beginning Equity}} \\
&= \frac{\Delta E}{E_{beg}}
\end{aligned}
\tag{6.1}
$$

where g is the annual percentage growth rate in equity, ΔE is the change in equity during the year, and E_{beg} is the equity at the beginning of the year.

Assuming that the venture does not raise new external equity (or retire existing equity), we see that its equity only changes by earnings retention. The change in equity can be expressed as:

$$
\Delta E = \text{Net Income} \times \text{Retention Rate} = NI \times RR
\tag{6.2}
$$

where RR is the proportion of net income retained in the firm. For early-stage ventures, the retention rate will be 100 percent. More mature firms may use some of their income to fund a dividend; the retention rate is one minus the dividend payout percentage, $1 - DPO\%$.

Dividing both sides of equation 6.2 by the beginning equity gives:

$$
\Delta E/E_{beg} = (NI/E_{beg}) \times RR
\tag{6.3}
$$

By substituting g in the left side of equation 6.3, we get:

$$
g = (NI/E_{beg}) \times RR
\tag{6.4}
$$

Note that NI/E_{beg} is the return on beginning equity. We could have used ROE as in Chapter 5's treatment of performance measurement as long as we are careful to consider the venture's equity base prior to any dividend or retention during the current period. For clarity, we emphasize that sustainable growth analysis considers the earnings created by the stock of equity in place throughout the time interval, with no intermediate changes.

For concreteness, assume that the venture started the year with $10 million in book value of equity. It plans no intermediate equity injections or withdrawals

---

[4] For a more detailed discussion of sustainable sales growth, see Robert C. Higgins, *Analysis for Financial Analysis*, 8th ed. (New York: McGraw-Hill/Irwin, 2007), chap. 4; and Gordon Donaldson, *Managing Corporate Wealth* (New York: Praeger, 1984). Learning Supplement 10A of this text also provides an expanded treatment of sustainable growth and its relationship to price-earnings ratios.

and projects net income of $2 million for the year. It will pay a $500,000 (25 percent) dividend at the beginning of the next period and retain $1,500,000 (75 percent). Assuming it will scale up with the same margins, we see that the venture will grow by:

$$g = (\$2,000,000/\$10,000,000) \times .75 = .20 \times .75 = .15, \text{ or } 15\%$$

The venture's maximum sustainable growth rate is at 100 percent retention, where $g_{max} = 20$ percent (.20 times 1).

If the firm projects growth in excess of 20 percent, it must raise external equity capital, have some scaling advantage leading to improved asset efficiency, and have lower incremental variable costs or some other organic change (including increased use of nonequity financing). In Chapter 5, we defined the return on equity (ROE) model as:

$$\text{ROE} = \text{Net Profit Margin} \times \text{Asset Turnover} \times \text{Equity Multiplier}$$

In equation form, this was:

$$\text{ROE} = \frac{\text{NI}}{\text{CE}} = \frac{\text{NI}}{\text{NS}} \times \frac{\text{NS}}{\text{TA}} \times \frac{\text{TA}}{\text{CE}} \qquad \textbf{(6.5)}$$

where NI is net income and NS is net sales for an accounting time period, usually one year; CE is common equity; and TA is total assets. Again, when conducting sustainable growth analysis for a period with no new capital infusions or withdrawals, we want to use beginning-of-period measures. Assuming that all equity is treated as common equity (e.g., "as converted" if the venture has convertible preferred), we can insert equation 6.5 into equation 6.4 as follows:

$$g = \frac{\text{NI}}{\text{NS}} \times \frac{\text{NS}}{\text{TA}} \times \frac{\text{TA}}{\text{CE}_{beg}} \times \text{RR} \qquad \textbf{(6.6)}$$

A venture's maximum sustainable growth rate, g_{max}, is its return on beginning equity, which decomposes into the product of net profit margin, asset turnover ratio, and the firm's equity multiplier ratio. When the venture retains less than 100 percent of the net income, this maximum sustainable growth rate must be adjusted downward to the venture's projected sustainable growth rate (g) by multiplying g_{max} by the retention ratio (RR).

The GameToy Company has recently introduced a new home video game. GameToy has a projected sales growth rate of 30 percent per year. Sales in the first full year of operation were $1.6 million. These sales were supported by an investment in assets of $1 million and produced a net income of $160,000. Equity at the beginning of last year was $800,000. Management intends to retain all profits in the venture. Assuming the components of the ROE model scale remain constant with growth, the sustainable sales growth rate from equation 6.6 is:

$$g = \frac{\$160,000}{\$1,600,000} \times \frac{\$1,600,000}{\$1,000,000} \times \frac{\$1,000,000}{\$800,000} \times 1.00$$
$$= .10 \times 1.60 \times 1.25 \times 1.00 = .20, \text{ or } 20\%$$

GameToy can grow its sales at 20 percent each year as long as profit margins, asset turnovers, and financial leverage ratios remain constant during the increases, and all net income (profit) is retained.

Another way to look at sustainable growth is to separate the firm's operating performance and financial policy. Recall from Chapter 5 that a firm's return on assets (ROA) is the product of its net profit margin (NI/NS) and its asset turnover (NS/TA); it measures the firm's operating performance over a specified time period. The first two right-hand-side components of equation 6.6 provide the ROA measure of operating performance. The product of the financial leverage or equity multiplier component (TA/CE_{beg}) and the retention rate (RR, or $1 - DPO\%$) reflects the firm's financial policy (FP). Sustainable growth is:

$$g = \text{Operating Performance} \times \text{Financial Policy, or}$$
$$g = \text{ROA} \times \text{FP} \tag{6.7}$$

To illustrate, we return to the GameToy venture. Recall that the equity multiplier was 1.25 ($1,000,000/$800,000), using beginning-of-period equity, and retention is 100 percent. Accordingly, the financial policy factor is 1.25 (i.e., 1.25×1.00), and its sustainable growth rate is:

$$g = \text{ROA} \times (1.25 \times 1.00) = \text{ROA} \times 1.25$$

Sustainable growth varies linearly with the venture's return on assets as long as the financial policy (financial leverage and retention of profits decisions) remains stable.[5] Figure 6.6 presents a graphic representation of this linear relationship. When GameToy's ROA is 16 percent, sustainable growth is 20 percent ($.16 \times 1.25$). The solid line depicts sustainable growth at various ROAs. Growth rates above the line, such as the 30 percent target sales growth rate, are not feasible without operating improvements, changes in financial policy, or external equity capital. Owing to market capture considerations, many early-stage ventures will not want to limit growth to the sustainable level.

Improvements in profit margins and/or asset turnovers, leading to improved ROA, can pave the way for some growth beyond the current sustainable level. For example, we can solve for the ROA operating performance that GameToy would need in order to achieve 30 percent sustainable growth:

$$.30 = \text{ROA} \times 1.25, \text{ or}$$
$$\text{ROA} = .30/1.25 = .24, \text{ or } 24\%$$

To achieve a sustainable growth of 30 percent, GameToy would have to improve its return on assets from 16 percent to 24 percent—a 50 percent improvement, an unlikely prospect. Debt is notoriously scarce and most likely already would have been used to the extent possible. If GameToy had been funding part of its

---

[5] An alternative approach is to use return on invested capital (i.e., total assets less current liabilities) instead of return on assets to measure operating performance. For this approach, see Donaldson, *Managing Corporate Wealth*, chap. 4.

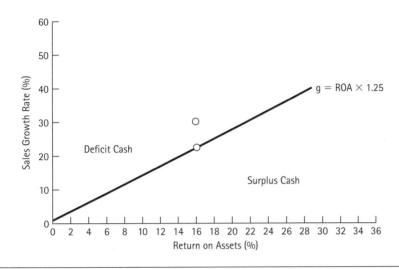

FIGURE 6.6

Sustainable Growth for GameToy Company as a Function of ROA (Holding Financial Policies Stable)

assets with debt, the sustainable growth rate of 20 percent *already incorporates* the benefit of continuing the debt strategy (as a percent of assets). To enable additional growth, GameToy must borrow even more per dollar of assets than it currently borrows. As GameToy probably has exhausted all avenues for improving operating efficiency and expanding debt, external equity capital markets become the only viable path to realizing its growth ambitions.

CONCEPT CHECK

- What is meant by a sustainable sales growth rate?
- What are the major components used to estimate a sustainable sales growth rate?

6.8 ESTIMATING ADDITIONAL FINANCING NEEDED TO SUPPORT GROWTH

While it is useful to understand a new venture's growth prospects in the absence of new external equity, projected growth rates in the business plan almost invariably exceed the sustainable rate even after efficiency improvements, maximum retention, and exploitation of all debt avenues. Predicting the magnitude and timing of the shortfall becomes an important process for the rapidly growing venture.

Figure 6.7 shows the major funding sources available to ventures that have successfully reached their survival or rapid-growth life cycle stages. Business

FIGURE 6.7	Type and Sources of Financing by Selected Life Cycle Stage	
LIFE CYCLE STAGE	**TYPE OF FINANCING**	**MAJOR SOURCES/PLAYERS**
Survival stage	First-round financing	Business operations
		Venture capitalists
		Suppliers and customers
		Government assistance programs
		Commercial banks
Rapid-growth stage	Second-round financing	Business operations
	Mezzanine financing	Suppliers and customers
	Liquidity-stage financing	Commercial banks
		Investment bankers

operations become an increasingly important source for growth funding. More than just producing revenues, growth ventures need to earn and retain profits. It is important for rapidly growing ventures to employ supplier trade credit to help fund the increasing volume of goods and services needed for expansion. Recall that this type of financing typically results in short-term accounts payables. Employees and the government provide spontaneous short-term financing. Wages payable financing arises because employees are paid only after a delay (one week to a month) between their labor (with the booking of the associated expense) and the payroll check for that labor. The government provides short-term financing in the form of taxes payable because actual tax payments typically lag the recognition of the amount owed to the government (the tax expense).

In the event that a growing venture's investment in assets is not financed by profits from business operations plus spontaneous financing from suppliers, employees, and the government, additional funds will be needed. These additional funds will need to come from external parties, including venture capitalists, venture investors that provide mezzanine financing, government assistance programs, commercial banks, and investment banks. It is important for the entrepreneurial team to estimate any shortfall in financing and negotiate for additional financing well in advance. We now will turn to a review of a "back-of-the-envelope" method for estimating the amount of additional financing needed to support revenue growth.

THE BASIC ADDITIONAL FUNDS NEEDED EQUATION

financial capital needed (FCN)
funds needed to acquire assets necessary to support a firm's sales growth

spontaneously generated funds
increases in accounts payables and accruals (wages and taxes) that accompany sales increases

additional funds needed (AFN)
gap remaining between the financial capital needed and that funded by spontaneously generated funds and retained earnings

Financial capital needed (FCN) is the additional funding required to support a firm's projected growth. Some of this funding gap will be covered by trade credit and other current liabilities that increase spontaneously with sales. **Spontaneously generated funds** are increases in accounts payables and accruals (wages and taxes) that accompany sales increases. For example, when sales increase, credit purchases from suppliers should also increase, leading to lockstep increases in accounts payable. If the venture is profitable and scaling up without margin changes, its increase in profits, when retained, helps meet a firm's FCN. **Additional funds needed (AFN)** is the gap remaining between the financial capital needed and that funded by spontaneously generated funds and retained earnings:

$$\text{AFN} = \text{Required Increase in Assets} - \text{Spontaneously Generated Funds} - \text{Increase in Retained Earnings}$$

In equation form this becomes:

$$\text{AFN} = \frac{TA_0}{NS_0}(\Delta NS) - \frac{AP_0 + AL_0}{NS_0}(\Delta NS) - (NS_1)\frac{NI_0}{NS_0}(RR_0) \qquad \textbf{(6.8)}$$

where TA is the total assets, NS is the net sales, ΔNS is the change in net sales expected between the current year and next year, AP is the accounts payable, AL is the accrued liabilities, NI is the net income, RR is the retention rate as previously defined, and the subscripts "0" and "1" represent the current year and the forecast for next year, respectively.

Notice the similarity to the sustainable sales growth rate equation. First, to determine the required increase in assets, we need to establish the percentage relationship between total assets and net sales. Instead of using the asset turnover ratio (NS/TA) directly, we take the inverse to get a percentage. This percentage then is multiplied by the change in net sales to obtain the required increase in assets (financial capital needed). The change in net sales reflects the projected growth in sales. The third term, the increase in retained earnings, is the projected internally generated funds (next year's sales times the prevailing net profit margin) multiplied by the retention rate.

However, the sustainable growth rate and the additional funds needed (AFN) equations differ. The AFN recognizes spontaneously generated funds (the second term in the equation) and does not assume that financial policy (leverage) is proportional as is the case with the sustainable growth calculation. The AFN focuses on determining the total funding gap, allowing management to decide whether debt or equity will bridge the gap.[6]

Recall that GameToy's last year's sales were $1.6 million and were supported by a $1 million investment in assets. The sales produced a net income of $160,000. We will calculate the AFN assuming GameToy contemporaneously had current assets of $520,000, fixed assets of $480,000, accounts payable of $48,000, and accrued liabilities of $32,000. At a 30 percent growth rate, next year's sales will reach $2.08 million ($1.6 million × 1.3), a change of $480,000 ($2.08 million − $1.6 million). Equation 6.8 gives:

$$
\begin{aligned}
\text{AFN} &= \frac{\$1,000,000}{\$1,600,000}(\$480,000) - \frac{\$80,000}{\$1,600,000}(\$480,000) \\
&\quad - (\$2,080,000)\frac{\$160,000}{\$1,600,000}(1.00) \\
&= .625(\$480,000) - .05(\$480,000) - \$2,080,000(.10)(1.00) \\
&= \$300,000 - \$24,000 - \$208,000 \\
&= \$68,000
\end{aligned}
$$

---

[6] The AFN equation, like the sustainable sales growth equation, does not include amortization- and depreciation-generated sources of funds. This is because these equations assume that depreciation and amortization funds are used to replace existing assets and thus are not available to finance new sales growth.

GameToy will need $300,000 in additional financial capital to acquire the assets needed to achieve the projected 30 percent growth in sales. The company projects $24,000 to come from spontaneously generated funds (liabilities to suppliers, employees, and the government) and $208,000 from retained earnings. The remaining AFN of $68,000 must be raised from new external financiers (debt and/or equity).

Panel A in Figure 6.8 illustrates the $300,000 increase in GameToy's assets necessary to support next year's 30 percent growth. Notice that the percentage change in assets is the same as the percentage change in sales, since the AFN model assumes that the past relationship between assets and sales remains stable (scaling with no margin change). Panel B depicts how the $300,000 in additional assets will be financed.

As previously discussed, management has only three choices to consider when the achievable sales growth rate is constrained by inadequate financing:

FIGURE 6.8   Projected Balance Sheet Changes for GameToy Company

Panel A: Increase in Assets Needed to Support a 30 Percent Increase in Sales

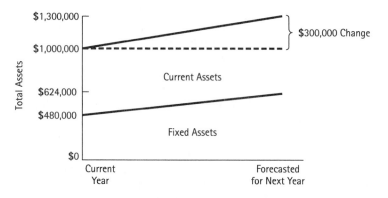

Panel B: Financial Capital Provided and Additional Funds Needed to Finance Increase in Assets

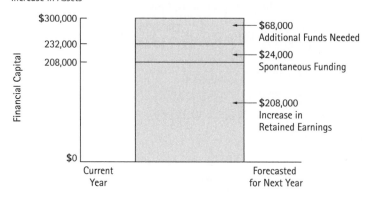

(1) improvements in operating performance, (2) changes in financial policy (debt and payout), or (3) sale of part ownership through equity fundraising. Of course, the venture should also consider moderating the projected growth rate. For GameToy, there are no known paths to reliable performance improvement, profit retention is at 100 percent, and sufficient debt is not available. That leaves two choices: Sell ownership or change the business plan trajectory to one of slower growth. The former involves negotiating with venture investors and potential loss of control; the latter involves organic changes in the firm's strategy, approach, and market penetration. Just as in other situations when a balance sheet doesn't balance (i.e., total assets exceed total liabilities plus equity), the venture must either alter its asset strategy or alter its liabilities and equity strategy. The entrepreneurial team should contemplate the associated trade-offs carefully.

CONCEPT CHECK

- What is meant by financial capital needed?
- What are the major components of the additional funds needed (AFN) model?

IMPACT OF DIFFERENT GROWTH RATES ON AFN

While $68,000 may not be a substantial gap for some ventures, the AFN usually grows linearly with sales growth rates. For example, consider how GameToy's AFN rises when sales are projected to grow at 50 percent. Sales would reach $2,400,000 ($1,600,000 × 1.50), an increase of $800,000. If we asssume that the other financial relationships remain the same, the new AFN from equation 6.8 is:

$$\text{AFN} = \frac{\$1,000,000}{\$1,600,000}(\$800,000) - \frac{\$80,000}{\$1,600,000}(\$800,000)$$
$$- (\$2,400,000)\frac{\$160,000}{\$1,600,000}(1.00)$$
$$= .625(\$800,000) - .05(\$800,000) - \$2,400,000(.10)(1.00)$$
$$= \$500,000 - \$40,000 - \$240,000$$
$$= \$220,000$$

If sales are projected to grow at 50 percent (rather than 30 percent), the AFN rises to $220,000 from $68,000, a greater than threefold increase.

Figure 6.9 graphs the AFN for GameToy at sales growth rates ranging from 20 to 60 percent for next year. We hold the venture's operating performance and financial policy stable over the entire range of possible sales growth rates. Of course, in actual practice, operating performance and financial policies are unlikely to be the same at very low and very high sales growth rates. An important point is that, with no change in asset or liability strategy, the AFN is likely to increase linearly with sales growth rates. For GameToy, the AFN increases by

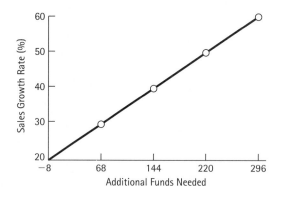

FIGURE 6.9

Illustration of How the Amount of Additional Funds Needed Might Increase as Sales Growth Increases for GameToy Company

$76,000 for each ten-percentage-point increase in sales growth.[7] During rapid sales growth, the venture should be prepared (and willing) to sell ownership in exchange for the AFN implied by the business plan.

ESTIMATING THE AFN FOR MULTIPLE YEARS

Although we have used one year as the projection period for our examples, the length of time for an AFN calculation is arbitrary. For example, if GameToy expects sales to grow at 30 percent per year for each of the next two years, we can calculate the total two-year AFN. All we need to do is plug two-year changes in sales into equation 6.8. After two years of 30 percent sales growth, sales will reach $2,704,000 ($1,600,000 × 1.30 × 1.30). Total two-year sales will be $4,784,000 ($2,080,000 + $2,704,000), reflecting a two-year change in sales of $1,104,000 ($2,704,000 − $1,600,000). Inserting our numbers into equation 6.8 gives a two-year AFN of:

$$
\begin{aligned}
\text{AFN} &= \frac{\$1,000,000}{\$1,600,000}(\$1,104,000) - \frac{\$80,000}{\$1,600,000}(\$1,104,000) \\
&\quad - (\$4,784,000)\frac{\$160,000}{\$1,600,000}(1.00) \\
&= .625(\$1,104,000) - .05(\$1,104,000) - \$4,784,000(.10)(1.00) \\
&= \$690,000 - \$55,200 - \$478,400 \\
&= \$156,400
\end{aligned}
$$

---

[7] The interested reader may note that the sustainable growth rate for sales is a little less than 20 percent in terms of the AFN equation since at a 20 percent growth rate the AFN is −$8,000. Thus, while not exactly the same, owing to some slight variations in the sustainable sales growth and additional funds needed equations, they typically produce very similar estimates of sales growth rates that can be sustained without generating additional financial capital.

GameToy needs to raise $156,400 over the next two years. Since we have already calculated that the one-year forward AFN is $68,000, the additional amount to be raised to support the second year of growth is $88,400 ($156,400 − $68,000).

- What changes need to be made in the AFN model when forecasting sales for more than one year?

6.9 PERCENT-OF-SALES PROJECTED FINANCIAL STATEMENTS

Sustainable growth and AFN calculations are useful for understanding how financial measures interact and relate to future financing needs. Ultimately, however, the goal is to create a set of projected financial statements that quantify the venture's view of the future. The **percent-of-sales forecasting method** projects account balances by assuming that most expenses and balance sheet items can be expressed as a percent of sales. For example, if a venture's cost of goods sold varies proportionately with sales (i.e., they are variable costs as defined earlier in the text), they represent a constant percent of sales. If the cost of goods sold last year was 60 percent of sales, it will be forecasted to remain 60 percent of sales next year.

Similarly, if assets were 66.7 percent of sales last year, they will be forecasted to be 66.7 percent of sales next year. If sales are expected to grow by 30 percent next year, assets also are forecasted to grow at a rate of 30 percent to sustain 66.7 percent of sales next year. In general, if a cost or balance sheet item is expected to remain at the same percentage of sales from year to year, then it will grow at the same rate as sales. Using a *constant* percent of sales in projections results in constant ratios and is one way to implement a **constant-ratio forecasting method**. Of course, if one keeps the ratios constant for all years, or one keeps the percents of sales constant for all years, the two approaches coincide.

The financial forecasting process used to project financial statements is:

1. Forecasted sales
2. Project the income statement
3. Project the balance sheet
4. Project the statement of cash flows

We continue to use the GameToy example to illustrate how percent-of-sales forecasting, in its constant-ratio variant, is applied in forecasting financial statements.

percent-of-sales forecasting method
forecasting method that makes projections based on the assumption that most expenses and balance sheet items can be expressed as a percentage of sales

constant-ratio forecasting method
variant of the percent-of-sales forecasting method that projects selected cost and balance items at the same growth rate as sales

- What is meant by the percent-of-sales forecasting method and how is it related to the constant-ratio forecasting method?

FORECASTING SALES

We start the financial forecasting process by first forecasting sales. Since this is the "top-line" projection and sales forecasts drive the preparation of projected financial statements, the ability to project sales accurately is crucial to the venture's financial health. We recognize that forecasting early-stage ventures, particularly development-stage ventures, is inherently more difficult than forecasting more mature firms. Nonetheless, having some idea of the financial future beats complete ignorance, particularly when one is negotiating for external financing. To provide a perspective on the potential ramifications of missing projections, the venture can produce projections under a variety of possible sales and expense scenarios and maintain a spreadsheet version that automatically revises the entire set of financials as things change.

We prepare GameToy's financial statement projections using a projected 30 percent sales increase from a base of $1,600,000 in 2008. Thus, sales are expected to be $2,080,000 (i.e., $1,600,000 × 1.30) in 2009, an increase of $480,000 over 2008. While all of our projected financial statements use the expected 30 percent sales growth rate, GameToy should also consider the financial ramifications of higher (optimistic) and lower (pessimistic) growth rates.

PROJECTING THE INCOME STATEMENT

Table 6.7 provides a reasonably detailed income statement for 2008. Sales of $1.6 million led to $160,000 in net income, a 2008 net profit margin of 10 percent ($160,000/$1,600,000). Recall that the AFN model holds this net profit

TABLE 6.7	GameToy Company Income Statements (Actual for 2008 and Projected for 2009)		
	ACTUAL 2008	**FORECAST BASIS**	**FORECAST 2009**
Sales	$1,600,000	1.3 × 2008 sales	$2,080,000
Cost of goods sold	960,000	.600 × 2009 sales	1,248,000
Gross profit	640,000		832,000
Marketing expenses	160,000	.100 × 2009 sales	208,000
General and administrative	152,000	Fixed costs	152,000
Depreciation	48,000	.030 × 2009 sales	62,400
EBIT	280,000		409,600
Less interest	13,300	Initially fixed	13,300
Earnings before taxes	266,700		396,300
Less taxes (40% rate)	106,700	40% of EBT	158,500
Net income	160,000		237,800
Less cash distributions	0		0
Added retained earnings	$ 160,000		$ 237,800

margin constant when projecting next year's net income. This, of course, is an oversimplification and would hold only if all costs were variable—and would be expected to vary directly with sales. However, as we previously noted, most firms will have some costs that are fixed, or at least semivariable, over a range of sales. The percent-of-sales forecasting method, and its constant-ratio variant, attempts to simplify projecting a firm's income statement.

Cost of goods sold was 60 percent of sales ($960,000/$1,600,000) and, for 2009, is forecasted to be 60 percent of sales, $1,248,000 (.60 × $2,080,000). The cost of goods sold is judged to be a variable cost and could equally well have been projected by multiplying the 2008 level of $960,000 by 1.30 (to reflect a 30 percent growth rate) to get $1,248,000.

Marketing expenses also are expected to vary with sales, since the venture is planning to increase its advertising budget and other marketing expenses in proportion to the expected increase in sales. Because marketing expenses were 10 percent of sales in 2008 ($160,000/$1,600,000), they are projected to be 10 percent of the 2009 sales, or $208,000. The marketing expenses could also have been projected by multiplying the 2008 amount of $160,000 by 1.3 to get $208,000.

General and administrative expenses are considered to be fixed for 2008 and 2009 and thus are expected to remain at their current $152,000 level. That is, even though sales are expected to grow rapidly, management does not intend to increase expenditures for existing staff employees and does not plan to expand the size of its present staff. Depreciation expenses were 3 percent of sales ($48,000/$1,600,000) and 10 percent of plant and equipment ($48,000/$480,000) in 2008. If fixed assets are expected to increase with sales, as would be the case if there were no excess production capacity at the end of 2008, depreciation expenses would be expected to increase proportionally with sales. Depreciation is projected to remain at the 3 percent of sales level for 2009. Alternatively, the $48,000 in depreciation could have been multiplied by 1.3 to get the 2009 level of $62,400. Of course, if the venture has excess production capacity and the increase in sales can be supported without an increase in fixed assets, depreciation expenses would remain constant or fixed at the $48,000 level.

It is common to produce a first-pass projection, omitting any costs of additional financing. Accordingly, in this first estimation projection, the 2008 interest expense of $13,300 carried forward to 2009, and we have not yet determined the amount of additional funds that will be needed (if any) and have not decided how we will obtain any needed funds, debt, or equity.

By applying a 40 percent tax rate to the estimated earnings before taxes for 2009, we project GameToy's net income to be $237,800, a 2006 net profit margin of 11.4 percent ($237,800/$2,080,000). The reasons that the net profit margin for this first pass has increased from 10 percent in 2008 are: (1) general and administrative expenses are not scaling up with sales, and (2) additional financing costs are ignored. Recall that the AFN model estimated the increase in retained earnings to be $208,000, or 10 percent of the forecasted 2009 sales of $2,080,000. Our more detailed analysis using projected financial statements shows that the spreading of fixed costs over increased sales lowers the actual AFN (from the "model AFN") through an increase in retained earnings.

- How does the mix between variable and fixed operating costs affect the amount of internally generated funds when sales are growing?

PROJECTING THE BALANCE SHEET

Table 6.8 shows the first pass at the 2009 balance sheet. The approach taken here coincides with asset requirements from the AFN model ($300,000). Initially, we expect that all assets will vary or increase with sales. Recall from the AFN model that total assets as a percent of net sales in 2008 were 62.5 percent ($1,000,000/$1,600,000). Notice that, by expressing each asset item as a percent of sales in 2008, the total sums to 62.5 percent. In this first-pass estimation, the existing asset-to-sales relationship is projected to hold for 2009. For example, inventories were 20 percent of sales in 2008 and are estimated to be 20 percent of 2009 sales, $416,000 (.20 × $2,080,000). Of course, the change in inventories could just as easily have been projected by multiplying the 2008 level by 1.3 ($320,000 × 1.3 = $416,000). After all asset items are projected for 2009, the total increase in assets is projected to be $300,000 ($1,300,000 − $1,000,000) for 2009, the same dollar estimate produced by the AFN model.

The liabilities and equity side of the balance sheet recognizes spontaneous funding and the retention of earnings. Remember that spontaneously generated funds come from suppliers (accounts payable) and employees and the government (accrued liabilities). Because these current liability accounts are expected to

TABLE 6.8   GameToy Company Balance Sheets (Actual for 2008 and Projected for 2009)

	ACTUAL 2008	FORECAST BASIS	FORECAST 2009
Cash	$ 16,000	.01 × 2009 sales	$ 20,800
Accounts receivable	184,000	.115 × 2009 sales	239,200
Inventories	320,000	.200 × 2009 sales	416,000
Total current assets	520,000	.325 × 2009 sales	676,000
Net plant and equipment	480,000	.300 × 2009 sales	624,000
Total assets	$1,000,000	.625 × 2009 sales	$1,300,000
Accounts payable	$ 48,000	.03 × 2009 sales	$ 62,400
Accrued liabilities	32,000	.02 × 2009 sales	41,600
Bank loan	120,000		120,000
Total current liabilities	200,000		224,000
Common equity	800,000	+237,800*	1,037,800
Additional funds needed	0		38,200**
Total liabilities and equity	$1,000,000		$1,300,000

*   Increase in retained earnings estimated for 2009 taken from Table 6.7.

** The AFN is a "plug" amount that makes the total assets balance with the total liabilities and equity.

increase proportionally with sales, they are projected to remain at their current percentage of sales and grow at the same rate as sales. In Table 6.8, we project the accounts payable balance at 3 percent of the 2009 sales, or $62,400, an increase of $14,400 (a 30 percent increase) over 2008's $48,000. Similarly, accrued liabilities are projected at 2 percent of $2,080,000 or $41,600, a $9,600 increase over 2008. Total spontaneous funding is $24,000 ($14,400 + $9,600), or 5 percent of the 2009 sales of $2,080,000. Notice that this $24,000 of spontaneously generated funds is also the same amount estimated using the AFN model.

Up to now, our projected balance sheet calculations project the necessary increase in assets ($300,000) to support a 30 percent sales increase and project spontaneously generated funding ($24,000). The second, and frequently most important, source for financing the necessary asset growth is retained earnings. For GameToy, the projected $237,800 increase in retained earnings, when added to the venture's existing $800,000 in equity in 2008, brings the total retained earnings to $1,037,800 for 2009.

When we prepare a projected balance sheet, the additional funds needed become a "plug" amount that makes the total liabilities and equity equal to the firm's total assets. We start with the estimated $1,300,000 in total assets for 2009 and subtract the projected total current liabilities of $224,000 and the equity of $1,037,800. The result is a gap of $38,200. This gap becomes the AFN that balances the balance sheet.

CONCEPT CHECK

- Why is the amount of additional funds needed (AFN) considered to be a "plug" figure when preparing a projected balance sheet?

FORECASTING THE STATEMENT OF CASH FLOWS

Preparing a projected statement of cash flows (Table 6.9) serves as check on the projected income statement and projected balance sheet. Since the cash account was projected to remain at 1 percent of projected sales, the statement of cash flows is prepared last. We begin, as described in Chapter 5, with the cash flows from operations, starting with net income. We add back noncash items, such as depreciation. After adjustments for incremental investments in receivables and inventories, and incremental financing from increases in current liabilities accounts, the resulting surplus cash from operations is $173,000.

Expenditures for necessary plant and equipment, projected at $206,400, create a projected shortfall of $33,400. Furthermore, since the cash needed to conduct operations is forecasted to increase by $4,800 to $20,800, the total amount of additional financing is $38,200. The statement of cash flows provides a check on the other two financial statements and another way of looking at the projected gap in funding.

It is important to note that, while we don't recommend it, the statement of cash flows can be used as a dynamic statement for estimating future cash needs rather than merely as a check of the income statement and balance sheets. For example, instead of fixing cash as a percentage of next year's estimated sales, a minimum target

GameToy Company Statement of Cash Flows (Projected for 2009)

	FORECAST 2009
Operating Activities	
Net income	$237,800
Depreciation	62,400
Increase in accounts receivable	−55,200
Increase in inventories	−96,000
Increase in accounts payable	14,400
Increase in accrued liabilities	9,600
Net cash from operating activities	173,000
Long-Term Investing Activities	
Increase in fixed assets*	−206,400
Net cash from long-term investing activities	−206,400
Financing Activities	
Additional funds needed	38,200
Net cash from financing activities	38,200
Summary	
Net change in cash	4,800
Cash at beginning of year	16,000
Cash at end of year	20,800

* This entry should show the increase in gross fixed assets, which is the sum of the increase in net plant and equipment of $144,000 and the 2009 depreciation of $62,400.

cash amount might be established, with additional funds needed to make sure the minimum is met. For example, assume that GameToy's management believes that it needs to maintain a minimum cash balance of $14,000 to cover day-to-day operations. In this case, we would first project the income statement and then the balance sheet minus two account amounts—cash and additional funds needed.

The statement of cash flows then would be prepared. We would begin with cash from operations. Then, as before, we would estimate investment requirements in fixed assets. Cash from financing operations for the GameToy example would be zero, since no specific plans have yet been made. The cash account then would be adjusted to reflect that it could be reduced to its target minimum. The balancing variable, if needed, would be the change in the balance sheet account AFN required to keep the cash account at its target minimum. Following is a summary of the statement of cash flow components for GameToy:

Cash from operating activities	$173,000
Cash from long-term investment activities	−206,400
Cash from financing activities	0
Net cash flow	−33,400
Plus beginning cash	16,000
Less target minimum cash	−14,000
Change in additional funds needed	$ 31,400

The balance sheet would be completed by entering $14,000 in the cash account. Since cash would be reduced by $6,800 from the original target of $20,800, total assets would be $1,293,200 instead of $1,300,000. The AFN plug, which then makes the balance sheet "balance," would be only $31,400 (yielding a change in AFN of $31,400 from the 2008 level of zero).

However, while the projected cash flow statement can be used as a dynamic forecasting financial statement, most long-term financial planning efforts set cash as a percentage of sales or as a fixed dollar amount for planning purposes. Thus, the statement of cash flows is primarily used as a "checking" statement. The important point, however, is that in our new venture context, the three statements involve a redundancy. A complete balance sheet and income statement mechanically imply a working statement of cash flows. Similarly, if we use the statement of cash flows to solve for an increase in a liability or equity account to "plug" (change in AFN), then that change in liability or equity must be posted to the balance sheet. You should either plug the balance sheet and derive the statement of cash flows or plug the statement of cash flows and post that plug directly into the balance sheet. Don't use separate "plugs" in the balance sheet and statement of cash flows.

FINANCING COST IMPLICATIONS ASSOCIATED WITH THE NEED FOR ADDITIONAL FUNDS

The cost of obtaining additional funds may involve projected expenses, such as additional interest expenses for borrowed AFN. Interest expenses show up directly on the projected income statement and, in turn, alter the AFN shown on the balance sheet. In contrast, added costs for equity sources of AFN need not involve projected expenses since much of the cost is in the form of a projected increase in the value of securities sold. If GameToy obtains the $38,200 in AFN from additional equity investments, there is no adjustment to the projected financial statements.[8]

If the $38,200 is borrowed, the interest costs will eat into the firm's internally generated funds and increase the AFN. That is, GameToy needs to borrow the initial AFN and any associated (after-tax) interest costs. Many ventures prepare second-pass projected financial statements that incorporate additional financing costs. If GameToy faces a 12 percent interest rate, it will incur about an incremental $4,600 (.12 × $38,200) interest expense to get the necessary AFN. The second-pass income statement would be:

EBIT	$409,600
Interest ($13,300 + $4,600)	−17,900
Earnings before taxes (EBT)	391,700
Taxes (40% of EBT)	−156,700
Net income	$235,000

---

[8] Of course, the proportional interests of existing equity investors in the income and assets of the firm will be diluted if they don't purchase a proportional amount of the additional equity capital being raised.

As a result of financing costs on the AFN, net income (and retained earnings) will be only $235,000 instead of the first-pass projection of $237,800. This $2,800 difference means that the AFN plug or balancing amount on the projected balance sheet needs to increase by $2,800 to a total of $41,000 ($38,200 plus $2,800).[9]

CONCEPT CHECK

- How do implicit financing costs in the form of additional interest payments affect the AFN estimate?

SUMMARY

This chapter emphasized projecting financial statements, a common component of business plans. Entrepreneurs can greatly benefit from taking the time to prepare short- and long-term financial plans. While long-term financial planning is critical to creating and building the venture's wealth, the venture first must survive. Short-term cash planning is necessary to avoid being surprised by short-term cash needs. Monthly cash budgets are the starting point for detecting likely cash shortages. If one expects a cash shortage, the monthly cash budget predicts the timing and magnitude. A year's worth of monthly cash budgets will indicate the duration of, and recovery from, the cash shortfall. If no recovery is in sight, the shortfall should lead to changes in the long-term financial plan.

Long-term financial planning signals to the entrepreneur if, and when, additional funds will be needed, along with their expected magnitude. Successful long-term financial planning and execution will provide the financing necessary for the working capital and fixed assets needed to support revenue growth.

Long-term financial planning begins with a forecast of sales. While forecasting sales is generally easier for seasoned firms because of existing historical sales data, early-stage ventures also must make sales forecasts as accurate as possible. Early-stage ventures usually begin with an estimate of the overall industry or market demand. Next, they use a market share percentage of industry sales to estimate the sales for the new venture. Finally, they fine-tune the forecast by working with existing and potential customers to determine purchasing intentions. Even before the venture completes a detailed long-term financial plan, the analysis of the venture's sustainable growth rate provides important information about the growth rate that can be achieved without external financial capital. The additional funds needed approach complements the sustainable-growth approach for ventures anticipating growth in excess of the sustainable level.

KEY TERMS

additional funds needed (AFN)	expected value	spontaneously generated funds
cash budget	financial capital needed (FCN)	sustainable sales growth rate
constant-ratio forecasting method	internally generated funds	
early-stage ventures	percent-of-sales forecasting method	

---

[9] Technically, GameToy will need a little more than $41,000 since interest will also have to be paid on the additional $2,800 of borrowed funds. However, because this additional impact is relatively small, usually additional estimations are not made. Rather, a slightly larger loan such as $42,000 would be requested.

DISCUSSION QUESTIONS

1. Provide a description of the financing cash implications associated with a venture's need for additional funds.

2. What is meant by a cash budget? Describe how a cash budget is prepared.

3. Besides the cash budget, what additional financial statements are projected monthly in conjunction with short-term financial planning?

4. Why is it usually easier to forecast sales for seasoned firms in contrast with early-stage ventures?

5. Explain how projected economic scenarios can be used to help forecast a firm's sales growth rate.

6. Identify and describe the four-step process typically used to forecast sales for seasoned firms.

7. What are the three steps typically used to forecast sales for early-stage ventures?

8. Describe the general relationship between the life cycle stage and the ability to accurately forecast sales for a firm.

9. How do venture investors adjust for the belief that entrepreneurs tend to be overly optimistic in their sales forecasts?

10. What is meant by a sustainable sales growth rate?

11. Identify and describe the two equations that can be used to estimate a firm's sustainable growth rate.

12. Describe the basic additional funds needed (AFN) equation.

13. List the major sources of funds typically available to ventures that have successfully entered into their rapid-growth life cycle stage.

14. Explain how the AFN equation can be used to forecast the amount of funds that will be needed over a several-year period.

15. What is the percent-of-sales forecasting method?

16. After forecasting sales, describe how the income statement is projected.

17. Describe how balance sheets are projected once a sales forecast has been made.

INTERNET ACTIVITIES

1. Access the U.S. Census Bureau Web site at http://www.census.gov. Find relevant information for trends in U.S. population growth for a specific business idea. Comment on the manufacturing statistics and regional or national statistics relevant for that business.

2. For a specific business idea, find labor wage data for the types of employees who will be involved. Examples of relevant Web sites include the Bureau of Labor Statistics Web site at http://www.bls.gov and career information sites like http://www.wetfeet.com.

EXERCISES/PROBLEMS

1. Short-term financial planning for the PDC Company was described earlier in this chapter. Refer to the PDC Company's projected monthly operating schedules in Table 6.2. PDC's sales are projected to be $80,000 in September 2008.
   A. Prepare PDC's sales schedule, purchases schedule, and wages schedule for August 2008.
   B. Prepare a cash budget for August 2008 for PDC and describe how the forecast affects the end-of-month cash balance.

2. Short-term financial planning for the PDC Company was described earlier in this chapter. Refer to the PDC Company's projected monthly operating schedules in Table 6.2. PDC's sales are projected to be $80,000 in September 2008.
   A. Prepare PDC's projected income statement for August.
   B. Prepare PDC's projected balance sheet for August.
   C. Prepare PDC's projected statement of cash flow for August.

    D. Compare your balance sheet at the end of August with the balance sheet in Table 6.1 and apply the balance sheet method to determine cash flows over the March–August period.

3. Rework Problem 1 based on the assumption that, because of an unexpected order, PDC's sales are forecasted to be $160,000 for September 2008.

4. Rework Problem 2 based on the assumption that, because of an unexpected order, PDC's sales are forecasted to be $160,000 for September 2008.

5. Petal Providers Corporation opens and operates "mega" floral stores in the United States. The idea behind the superstore concept is to model the U.S. floral industry after its European counterparts, whose flower markets generally have larger selections at lower prices. Revenues were $1 million with net profit of $50,000 last year when the first Petal Providers floral outlet was opened. If the economy grows rapidly next year, Petal Providers expects its sales to grow by 50 percent. However, if the economy exhibits average growth, Petal Providers expects a sales growth of 30 percent. For a slow economic growth scenario, sales are expected to grow next year at a rate of 10 percent. Management estimates the probability of each scenario occurring to be rapid growth (.30), average growth (.50), and slow growth (.20). Petal Providers' net profit margins are also expected to vary with the level of economic activity next year. If slow growth occurs, the net profit margin is expected to be 5 percent. Net profit margins of 7 and 10 percent are expected for the average- and rapid-growth scenarios, respectively.

    A. Estimate the average sales growth rate for Petal Providers for next year.

    B. Estimate the dollar amount of sales expected next year under each scenario, as well as the expected value sales amount.

    C. Estimate the dollar amount of net profit expected next year under each scenario, as well as the expected value net profit amount.

6. Petal Providers Corporation, described in Problem 5, is interested in estimating its sustainable sales growth rate. Last year, revenues were $1 million, net profit was $50,000, investment in assets was $750,000, payables and accruals were $100,000, and equity at the end of the year was $450,000 (i.e., beginning-of-year equity of $400,000 plus retained profits of $50,000). The venture did not pay out any dividends and does not expect to pay dividends for the foreseeable future.

    A. Estimate the sustainable sales growth rate for Petal Providers based on the information provided in this problem.

    B. How would your answer to Part A change if economic growth is average and Petal Providers' net profit margin is 7 percent?

    C. If Petal Providers' sales are expected to grow at a rate of 30 percent next year, what would be your estimate of the additional funds needed next year based on the information provided? (Note: Ignore the information in Part B.)

7. Artero Corporation is a traditional toy products retailer that recently started an Internet-based subsidiary that sells toys online. A markup is added on goods the company purchases from manufacturers for resale. Swen Artero, the company president, is preparing for a meeting with Jennifer Brown, a loan officer with First Banco Corporation, to review year-end financing requirements. After discussions with the company's marketing manager, Rolf Eriksson, and finance manager, Lisa Erdinger, sales over the last three months of 2008 are forecasted to be:

MONTH	SALES FORECAST ($000)
October 2008	$1,000
November	1,500
December	3,000

Artero's balance sheet as of the end of September 2008 was as follows:

Artero Corporation

BALANCE SHEET AS OF SEPTEMBER 30, 2008 (IN $ THOUSANDS)

Cash	$ 50	Accounts payable	$ 0
Accounts receivable	700	Notes payable	800
Inventories	500	Long-term debt	400
Net fixed assets	750	Total liabilities	1,200
		Equity	800
Total assets	$2,000	Total	$2,000

All sales are made on credit terms of net 30 days and are collected the following month. No bad debts are anticipated. The accounts receivable on the balance sheet at the end of September thus will be collected in October, the October sales will be collected in November, and so on. Inventory on hand represents a minimum operating level (or safety stock), which the company intends to maintain. Cost of goods sold averages 80 percent of sales. Inventory is purchased in the month of sale and paid for in cash. Other cash expenses average 7 percent of sales. Depreciation is $10,000 per month. Assume taxes are paid monthly and the effective income tax rate is 40 percent for planning purposes.

The annual interest rate on outstanding long-term debt and bank loans (notes payable) is 12 percent. There are no capital expenditures planned during the period, and no dividends will be paid. The company's desired end-of-month cash balance is $80,000. The president hopes to meet any cash shortages during the period by increasing the firm's notes payable to the bank. The interest rate on new loans will be 12 percent.

A. Prepare monthly pro forma income statements for October, November, and December and for the quarter ending December 31, 2008.

B. Prepare monthly pro forma balance sheets at the end of October, November, and December 2008.

C. Prepare both a monthly cash budget and pro forma statements of cash flows for October, November, and December 2008.

D. Describe your findings and indicate the maximum amount of bank borrowing that is needed.

SPREADSHEET EXERCISES/PROBLEMS

[Note: The following activities are for students with spreadsheet software skills.]

8. Short-term financial planning for the PDC Company was described earlier in this chapter. Refer to the PDC Company's projected monthly operating schedules in Table 6.2. PDC's monthly sales for the remainder of 2008 are expected to be:

September	$ 80,000
October	$100,000
November	$130,000
December	$160,000

A. Prepare PDC's sales schedule, purchases schedule, and wages schedule for each of the last four months of 2008.

B. Prepare cash budgets for each of the last four months of 2008 for the PDC Company and describe how the forecast affects the end-of-month cash balances.

C. Prepare PDC's projected monthly income statements for the August–December period.

D. Prepare PDC's projected monthly balance sheets for the August–December period.

E. Prepare PDC's projected monthly statements of cash flows for the August–December period.

F. Compare your balance sheet at the end of December with the balance sheet in Table 6.1 and apply the balance sheet method to determine cash flows over the March–December period.

9. Artero Corporation, discussed in Problem 7, is a retailer of toy products. The firm's management team recently extended the monthly sales forecasts that were prepared for the last three months of 2008 for an additional six months in 2009. These forecasts were presented to Swen Artero, the firm's president, as follows:

MONTH	SALES FORECASTS
October 2008	$1,000,000
November	1,500,000
December	3,000,000
January 2009	1,500,000
February	1,000,000
March	700,000
April	700,000
May	700,000
June	700,000

A. Use the income statement data and the balance sheet information from Problem 7 to prepare monthly income statements, balance sheets, and statements of cash flows for October through December 2008. What is the maximum amount of bank borrowing that would be needed?

B. Prepare monthly income statements, balance sheets, and statements of cash flows for the first six months of 2009. Assume the information and data relationships from Problem 7 will continue to hold for the first six months of 2009. Indicate if, and when, the additional bank borrowing needed during the last three months of 2008 can be repaid.

C. Based on your financial statement projections for the first six months of 2009, indicate whether new bank borrowing will be needed.

10. Artero Corporation, discussed in Problems 7 and 9, is a retailer of toy products. This is a continuation of Problem 9. The firm's management team recently extended the monthly sales forecasts through the last six months of 2009. Artero expects to spend $100,000 on fixed assets in July 2009 and depreciation charges will increase to $12,000 per month beginning in August 2009.

MONTH	SALES FORECASTS
July	$ 900,000
August	1,100,000
September	1,400,000
October	1,700,000
November	2,800,000
December	4,000,000

A. Prepare monthly income statements, balance sheets, and statements of cash flows for the last six months of 2009.

B. Based on your financial statement projections for the last six months of 2009, indicate (1) whether new bank borrowing will be needed to finance the seasonal sales pattern and (2) if a loan is needed, when does the need start occurring and what is the maximum amount needed?

C. Assume that sales are forecasted for the first three months of 2010 as follows: January = $3 million, February = $2 million, and March = $1 million. Will Artero be able to pay off any bank borrowing that is needed in 2009? Based on your analyses, what type(s), if any, of bank loan(s) will be needed in 2009?

M I N I   C A S E

Pharma Biotech Corporation

The Pharma Biotech Corporation spent several years working on developing a DHA product that can be used to provide a fatty-acid supplement to a variety of food products. DHA stands for docosahexaenoic acid, an omega-3 fatty acid found naturally in cold-water fish. The benefits of fatty fish oil have been cited in studies of the brain, the eyes, and the immune system. Unfortunately, it is difficult to consume enough fish to get the benefits of DHA, and most individuals might be concerned about the taste consequences associated with adding fatty fish oil to eggs, ice cream, or chocolate candy. To counter these constraints, Pharma Biotech and several competitors have been able to grow algae and other plants that are rich in DHA. The resulting chemical compounds then are used to enhance a variety of food products.

Pharma Biotech's initial DHA product was designed as an additive to dairy products and yogurt. For example, the venture's DHA product was added to cottage cheese and fruit-flavored yogurts to enhance the health benefits of those products. After the long product development period, Pharma Biotech began operations in 2006. Income statement and balance sheet results for 2007, the first full year of operations, have been prepared.

Pharma Biotech, however, is concerned about forecasting its financial statements for next year because it is uncertain about the amount of additional financing of assets that will be needed as

continued on next page

Pharma Biotech Corporation (continued)

the venture ramps up sales. Pharma Biotech expects to introduce a DHA product that can be added to chocolate candies. Not only will consumers get the satisfaction of the taste of the chocolate candies, but they will also benefit from the DHA enhancement. Since this is anticipated to be a blockbuster new product, sales are anticipated to increase 50 percent next year (2008), even though the new product will come online in midyear. An additional 80 percent increase in sales is expected the following year (2009).

Pharma Biotech Corporation

INCOME STATEMENT FOR DECEMBER 31, 2007
(THOUSANDS OF DOLLARS)

Sales	$ 15,000
Operating expenses	−13,000
EBIT	2,000
Interest	−400
EBT	1,600
Taxes (40%)	−640
Net income	960
Cash dividends (40%)	−384
Added retained earnings	$ 576

Pharma Biotech Corporation

BALANCE SHEET AS OF DECEMBER 31, 2007
(THOUSANDS OF DOLLARS)

Cash and marketable securities	$ 1,000	Accounts payable	$ 1,600
Accounts receivable	2,000	Bank loan	1,800
Inventories	2,200	Accrued liabilities	1,200
Total current assets	5,200	Total current liabilities	4,600
		Long-term debt	2,200
		Common stock	2,400
Fixed assets, net	6,800	Retained earnings	2,800
Total assets	$12,000	Total liabilities and equity	$12,000

A. Estimate the additional funds needed (AFN) for 2008, using the formula method based on percent-of-sales relationships.
B. Estimate the AFN for Pharma Biotech for 2009.
C. Prepare pro forma income and balance sheet statements for 2008 before obtaining any additional financing. Why does the AFN from the spreadsheet projections differ from the AFN estimated in Part A?
D. Prepare a second iteration of your pro forma financial statements for 2008 if the initial AFN estimate is to be financed by additional long-term funds at an interest rate of 10 percent.
E. Prepare pro forma financial statements for 2009 that build on the pro forma results obtained in Part D.

Pharma Biotech Corporation (continued)

[Note: The following activities are for students with spreadsheet software skills.]

F. Prepare projected income statements, balance sheets, and statements of cash flows for Pharma Biotech for 2008 and 2009 before obtaining any additional financing. What are the amounts of additional funds needed?

G. Assume that sales are expected to grow at 100 percent in 2010 (over the 2009 sales level), 50 percent in 2011, and 20 percent in 2012. Extend your projected financial statements prepared in Part E to include 2010, 2011, and 2012. What will be the maximum amount of additional funds needed during your five-year forecast?

H. Assume that you will acquire the amount of funds needed in Part F by selling or issuing more common stock and by borrowing from lenders at an interest rate of 10 percent. Prepare a second round of projected five-year financial statements showing that the initial financing needed will be obtained equally each year by issuing new stock (50 percent) and by borrowing from lenders (50 percent).

Chapter 7

TYPES AND COSTS OF FINANCIAL CAPITAL

PREVIOUSLY COVERED

In Chapter 6, we emphasized projecting short-term and long-term financial statements. Inadequate cash constrains a profitable venture's ability to grow and fosters financial distress. Preparing projected financial statements forces an entrepreneurial team to estimate (and anticipate) required additional financing and helps the venture avoid financial distress.

LOOKING AHEAD

Chapter 8 introduces specific aspects of securities law related to new venture fundraising. We review the major laws, regulations, and exemptions facing a new venture seeking funding from venture investors and the public. Since ignorance of securities laws and regulations is no defense, even a basic understanding helps entrepreneurs avoid costly fundraising mistakes.

CHAPTER LEARNING OBJECTIVES

In this chapter, we characterize financial markets and discuss how one obtains, and pays for, financial capital. Without adequate capital, even the best ideas and ventures fail. The cost of debt is relatively easy to understand because it is closely associated with periodic interest payments. The cost of equity is a more difficult concept. One typically pays only a small part, if any, of the cost of equity through periodic payments (dividends). Typically, most, if not all, of equity's recurring cost is that investors expect future increases in their value ownership (e.g., capital gains on their shares). When a venture sells part of its ownership, failure to increase the venture's value creates investor dissatisfaction and related fallout. After completing this chapter, you will be able to:

1. Understand some basic characteristics of the financial markets

2. Understand how risk-free securities prices reflect risk-free borrowing rates

3. Explain how corporate debt prices reflect higher interest rates when a borrower may default

4. Explain investment risk

5. Estimate the cost of publicly traded equity capital (e.g., exchange-listed common stocks)

6. Estimate the cost of private equity capital

7. Explain how capital costs combine into a weighted average cost of capital (WACC)

8. Understand venture investors' target returns and their relation to capital costs

Entrepreneurs, and other members of the founding team, must understand that they will not remain in control of an externally funded venture when they produce only enough cash to pay explicitly billed and due expenses. A very real and relevant cost is the "rent" due on the financial capital venture investors provide. While this expense may not present itself for periodic explicit payment, inadequate or untimely coverage for this cost can be as fatal as missing or delaying payments to suppliers and lenders.

7.1 IMPLICIT AND EXPLICIT FINANCIAL CAPITAL COSTS

We argued earlier that cash flow, rather than accrued revenues, accrued expenses, or other accounting measures, is a new venture's lifeblood. This is the first of two major differences between the finance and accounting perspectives. The second is that the finance perspective demands that, where possible, the cost of financial capital be explicitly incorporated in evaluations, projections, and strategy. While accountants recognize that financial capital has a cost and recommend its complete inclusion in performance appraisal and decision making, historical accounting for this cost is incomplete, at least in formal financial statements. Unlike debt, much of equity's cost is not an expense in a traditional accounting sense (with documentation); only a part of this cost (e.g., dividends) is reflected in historical financial statements. There is virtually no historical accounting for the nondividend component of equity's cost, even though is it clear that the nondividend cost component increases with cuts in dividends.

Some have attempted to supplement historical accounting data with imputed line-item costs for the cost of *all* financial capital, including equity. One of the more recent adjusted accounting approaches has been dubbed "economic profit" or "economic value added" (EVA). Rather than a criticism of accounting, approaches like economic profit or EVA highlight that, even though there is no precisely observable accounting transaction, these costs are real.

There is an important link between the cost of capital and the value a new venture is striving to create. Quite generally, the value of a financial claim varies inversely with the cost of that type of capital. We can learn a lot about the cost of financial capital by studying how prices form and change in the financial markets. For example, a bond's price is related to its promised payments by an interest rate (yield) representing the rental rate for using that type of capital. If you want to borrow from similar investors on similar terms, you should expect to pay a similar (competitive) rate on your promised payments. A publicly traded firm's historical stock price behavior provides evidence about the rental rate for equity capital invested in that type of firm. Financial markets continually provide information about the costs of renting financial capital from investors.

- How does the cost of debt and equity differ from the perspective of accounting measures?

7.2 FINANCIAL MARKETS

public financial markets
markets for the creation, sale, and trade of liquid securities having standardized features

Figure 7.1 summarizes the use of interest-bearing debt and equity financing through the venture life cycle. **Public financial markets** are those involving the issuance, buying, and trading of standardized liquid securities such as stocks, bonds, and options. Successful well-established corporations are the most common issuers of these public market securities, although the Internet Age has changed maturity expectations for some issuers. An initial public offering (IPO) of common stock, usually accomplished with the aid of investment bankers, can provide liquidity-stage financing as a successful corporate venture moves deep into its rapid-growth stage.

FIGURE 7.1 Types of Interest-Bearing Debt and Equity Financing, Financing Sources, and Business Riskiness by Life Cycle Stage

LIFE CYCLE STAGE	TYPES OF FINANCING	MAJOR DEBT AND EQUITY SOURCES	VENTURE'S RISKINESS: POOR PERFORMANCE OR FAILURE
	1. VENTURE FINANCING		
Development stage	Seed financing	Entrepreneurs	Very high
Startup stage	Startup financing	Entrepreneurs	Very high
		Business angels	
		Venture capitalists	
Survival stage	First-round financing	Venture capitalists	High
		Commercial banks	
Rapid-growth stage	Second-round financing	Investment bankers	High to moderate
	Mezzanine financing	Venture lenders/investors	
	Liquidity-stage financing	Commercial banks	
	2. SEASONED FINANCING		
Maturity stage	Issuing stock	Investment bankers	Low
	Issuing bonds	Commercial banks	
	Obtaining bank loans		

Public financial markets and financial institutions become the most common sources of financing during a successful venture's maturity stage. Financial institutions become more willing to lend to the venture for several years at a time. Investment bankers are available to assist maturity-stage corporations in raising financial capital by selling the firm's stocks and bonds to the public, to institutional investors, and even to other operating companies. While individual maturity-stage firms can exhibit poor performance—or even fail—as a group they are still considered to have low business risk. At this point in the life cycle, equity investors are typically willing to accept target annual rates of return of less than 20 percent.

Early-stage ventures in the development, startup, survival, or (early) rapid-growth stage usually cannot tap public financial markets. **Private financial markets** involve the issue and sale of illiquid, less standardized financial contracts and securities. Bank loans and privately placed debt (sold to financial institutions and venture lenders) are examples of private debt transactions. Although there are exceptions, bank loans become a likely funding source only after a few successful years of operations. For equity financing, early-stage ventures typically rely on private equity financing from the entrepreneur and her friends or family, from business angels, and from professional venture capitalists. Only in later stages does tapping the public equity (stock) markets become feasible. By then, it may even be essential.

Many development-stage ventures are unlikely to succeed. Investors see such ventures as belonging to a group containing some that will succeed and some (more) that will fail. Consequently, a development-stage venture's business plan needs to make the case for potentially achieving very high returns. In Figure 7.1, we depict development-stage ventures as having very high business risk. Target expected annual rates of return at 40 percent and above for equity investments are common. Startup-stage ventures also have very high business risk and are considered to be only slightly less risky than they were in the development stage. Survival-stage firms continue to have high business risk, and, accordingly, their investors continue to seek high annual rates of return. Rapid-growth firms are perceived as remaining highly risky during the early part of this stage, although their business risk decreases to moderate levels as they successfully emerge from rapid growth. Target annual rates of return exceeding 20 percent are common for rapid-growth-stage ventures.

One of the goals of this chapter is to provide a framework for assessing the types of returns that a venture's business plan needs to suggest for investors providing the financing in various stages of a venture's life cycle. Entrepreneurial finance focuses on early-stage ventures. Corporate finance focuses on more mature firms (typically, corporations) operating late in their rapid-growth or maturity stages. Early-stage ventures usually have access only to private capital markets. Mature corporations have access to private and public capital markets. Ultimately, however, the private, public, and even government security markets compete with each other for much of the capital available for investment. Depending on the risk and returns offered, investors move their investing attention from category to category. Accordingly, it helps if we start with financial markets more broadly in order to develop a unified perspective on how expected returns are determined, whether it be for early-stage or Fortune 500 companies.

private financial markets
markets for the creation, sale, and trade of illiquid securities having less standardized negotiated features

- How do public and private financial markets differ?
- What are the primary providers or sources of early-stage capital?

7.3   DETERMINING THE COST OF DEBT CAPITAL

interest rate
price paid to borrow funds

Typically, one bears the cost of debt by making periodic payments equal to an **interest rate** multiplied by the amount borrowed and by repaying the amount borrowed. In this arrangement, the interest rate determines the cost of debt capital. In debt markets, the supply and demand for funds determines the interest rate new borrowers must agree to pay.

Figure 7.2 graphically illustrates the market determination of interest rates. In Panel A, equilibrium (Q_1) in borrowed and loaned funds occurs when supply (S_1) intersects demand (D_1). The result is an interest rate we will call "r" depicted as 8 percent.[1] Panel A also shows the interest rate for higher demand (D_2) due to factors like overall economic expansion. Notice that the quantity of funds borrowed and loaned increases to Q_2 as the interest rate rises to 10 percent.

default risk
risk that a borrower will not pay the interest and/or principal on a loan

In addition to understanding that supply and demand interact to set interest rates, it is important to realize that riskier debt costs more. The risk that a borrower may not make an interest or principal payment is **default risk**. Lenders expect to be compensated for such risk. Panel B in Figure 7.2 depicts two possible supply/demand relationships, one for low-default-risk debt and one for high-default-risk debt. Note that the equilibrium interest rate for high-default-risk debt is higher than that for low-default-risk debt. We have depicted the quantity demanded and supplied for low-risk debt as being greater than that for high-risk debt. This represents the normal case. The distance between the two interest rates depends on the relative demand for the two types of debt and lenders' willingness to lend at various interest rate differentials between the two types of debt. For example, when the economy is growing, the willingness to lend (supply) to higher-risk borrowers usually increases. Boom-time lenders may accept a smaller risk premium (an interest rate closer to low-risk rates) when lending to high-risk borrowers. During a recession, lenders may be more conservative and demand high-risk premiums. Consequently, recession-time lenders may demand very high interest rates from high-risk borrowers or not lend to them at all.

DETERMINANTS OF MARKET INTEREST RATES

nominal interest rate
observed or stated interest rate

An observed or stated interest rate, such as the rate on a bank loan, is referred to as the **nominal interest rate**. It is common practice to state interest rates on an

---

[1] While we use "r" to denote the cost of financial capital in this chapter, different textbooks may use "i" when referring to interest rates or "k" for "kapital" costs. All of these can be used interchangeably.

FIGURE 7.2 Interest Rates Determined by the Supply and Demand for Borrowed Funds

Panel A: Impact of a Shift in Demand on the Price of Borrowing

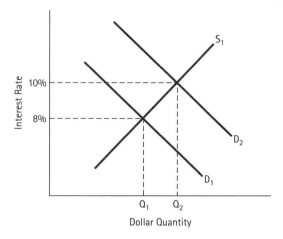

Panel B: Low-Default-Risk and High-Default-Risk Loans

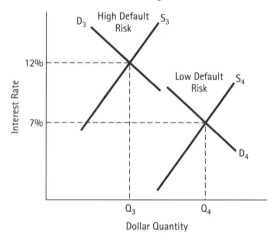

annual or annualized basis. For example, the interest rates depicted in Figure 7.2 are annual nominal interest rates. Recall that Panel B displays possible interest rates for low and high default risk. In addition to default risk, other factors—inflation expectations, marketability, and the life span of the debt instrument—play important roles in determining the supply and demand of funds and, therefore, equilibrium interest rates.

Economists like to reference a baseline, stripped-down interest rate. The **real interest rate (RR)** is an abstract notion of the interest rate one would face in the absence of inflation, risk, illiquidity, and any other factors determining the

real interest rate (RR) interest one would face in the absence of inflation, risk, illiquidity, and any other factors determining the appropriate interest rate

applicable interest rate.[2] One estimate of the real rate of interest (transferring consumption from today to next year) is in the neighborhood of 3 percent.[3] Since it excludes such factors as inflation and risk, this is the closest estimate we have to the pure time value of money. Borrowers must pay more than the real rate (RR) to compensate the lender (supplier of debt funds) for an inflation premium (IP), a default risk premium (DRP), a marketability or liquidity premium (LP), and a maturity premium (MP). We can express these relationships in equation form as follows:

$$r_{debt} \text{ or } r_d = RR + IP + DRP + LP + MP \qquad \textbf{(7.1)}$$

CONCEPT CHECK

- What is meant by the real interest rate?

RISK-FREE INTEREST RATE

risk-free interest rate
interest rate on debt that is virtually free of default risk

inflation
rising prices not offset by increasing quality of the goods or services being purchased

It is possible to find debt that is virtually free of default risk. The observed interest rate on such debt securities is called the **risk-free interest rate**, which we will denote as r_f. Most investors consider U.S. Treasury securities to have almost no default risk and value them using risk-free rates. **Inflation** occurs when rising prices are not offset by increases in the quality of the goods or services being purchased. The result is a lower purchasing power for the same amount of money. During inflationary times, to offset erosion in money's purchasing power, even risk-free securities are priced using higher interest rates. The result is an inflation premium that is added to the real rate. The resulting *nominal* risk-free rate is:

$$\text{Risk-Free Rate or } r_f = RR + IP \qquad \textbf{(7.2)}$$

---

[2] Here we simplify by using "real interest rate" to denote what is more accurately a real *risk-free* interest rate. This abstraction for a baseline interest rate is dubbed a "real" interest because it attempts to measure an increase in real consumption (as distinct from an increase in prices). The usefulness of the abstraction is easiest to grasp in a simple single good economy having only one tangible physical (real) asset and no financial assets. As long as the economy has only oranges, then the amount of future oranges produced by investing current oranges provides the "orange interest rate" or the "real interest rate" for the orange consumption economy. Of course, for an economy with many different types of productive investment technologies, the real interest rate is more of an abstraction about the rate at which one can lend current consumption in exchange for future consumption. The Learning Supplement in Chapter 9 provides a more detailed treatment of the introduction of financial contracting to orange production economies. Needless to say, in the real (noneconomist) world, it is oxymoronic to term the abstract notion of a baseline rate a real rate.

[3] Of course, observing a real interest rate is not possible as the notion is an abstract one. Nonetheless, the U.S. Treasury recently introduced Treasury Inflation-Protected Securities (TIPS) containing an inflation adjustment formula for preserving the consumption value of the principal. Since the principal is hedged against inflation, such securities bear interest rates highly correlated with the unobservable real interest rate. How high the correlation is depends on how well one believes the consumer price index (CPI) calibrates the inflation adjustment necessary to preserve the consumption value of the principal.

where the **inflation premium (IP)** reflects the expected inflation that will occur during the risk-free loan.[4]

To illustrate, consider a lender whose time value of money (real rate) is 3 percent per year. The lender might be a relative wishing to buy a better hot tub next year by earning interest on your loan or a financial intermediary or bank representing other ultimate lenders. In either case, the ultimate lender gives up current consumption and expects to receive a higher future consumption in return. If we believe that hot tub (and general) price levels will rise 3 percent during the year of the loan, then to assure a 3 percent higher consumption from spending the funds next year, the nominal rate on the loan will need to be approximately 6 percent. Using equation 7.2, we have:

$$r_f = 3\% + 3\% = 6\%$$

In the case where zero inflation is expected, the risk-free interest rate would be equal to the real interest rate, 3 percent in our example.

Because they relate to the exchange of real products and services across time, many investors and academics believe that it is reasonable to assume that real interest rates are relatively stable. This leaves inflation expectations as the explanation for changes in risk-free interest rates. During periods of very high inflation expectations, risk-free interest rates tend to be high. The important point is that risk-free interest rates shift up and down with inflation expectations. In our context, and in finance practice, it is common to start directly with nominal risk-free rates, taking the market's appraisal of real rates and expected inflation (rather than trying to project them). The prices of Treasury securities and the related nominal risk-free rates are easy to find. All we need to do is consider how our specific application changes when we introduce default risk. Starting with nominal risk-free rates, we can write the default return equation as:

$$r_d = r_f + DRP + LP + MP \qquad \textbf{(7.3)}$$

It is important to remember that it is conventional practice to refer to the risk-free interest rate as being free from default risk, and not free from inflation risk. A venture must promise to pay substantially more than the risk-free rate to obtain debt financing. Investors expect some compensation for bearing the venture's financial risk.

inflation premium (IP)
average expected inflation rate over the life of a risk-free loan

CONCEPT CHECK

- What is meant by a risk-free interest rate?
- What is meant by an inflation premium?

---

[4] To be technically correct, there is a cross-product interaction between RR and IP. That is, the risk-free rate is more accurately thought of as $[(1 + RR)(1 + IP)] - 1$. In our example, we would have $[(1.03)(1.03)] - 1 = 1.0609 - 1 = .0609$. However, it is common to view these two components of the nominal risk-free interest rate as additive since the other components of "r" are treated similarly.

DEFAULT RISK PREMIUM

**default risk premium
(DRP)**

additional interest rate
premium required to com-
pensate the lender for the
probability that a borrower
will default on a loan

The **default risk premium (DRP)** is the additional interest rate premium required
to compensate the lender for the probability that a borrower will not pay the
promised interest and principal payments. The higher the quality of the loan or
debt security, the lower the default risk premium—and, therefore, the lower the
nominal interest rate. Borrowers with very low default risk may need to pay less
than 1 percent more than the risk-free rate. Riskier borrowers of investment-
grade quality typically pay about 2 percent more than the risk-free rate. High-
default-risk borrowers may pay many points over, or even multiples of, the risk-
free rate. In extreme cases or severe market conditions, these borrowers may not
have any access to debt capital.

Suppose the current risk-free rate is 6 percent, and a mature venture expects
a two-percentage-point default risk premium. Assuming no liquidity or maturity
risk premium, we would have the following inputs to equation 7.3:

$$r_d = 6\% + 2\% + 0\% + 0\% = 8\%$$

This mature venture would expect to pay an 8 percent interest rate when the
U.S. government is borrowing at 6 percent. An early-stage venture might have to
pay 11 percent (i.e., 6 percent of r_f plus 5 percent of DRP) or more. Actually,
lenders often like to talk in "basis points," where one percentage point is 100 basis points. The early-stage venture would face a rate 500 basis points above the
prevailing risk-free rate.

prime rate

interest rate charged by
banks to their highest-
quality (lowest default risk)
business customers

Banks have their own terminology for borrowers. Banks do not generally lend
to the government and, thus, make only risky loans. For their highest-quality
(lowest default risk) business customers, banks typically charge a **prime rate**.
This prime rate establishes a benchmark rate for loans to riskier customers.
Also, banks like to quote rates to riskier customers as "prime plus." That is,
some percentage point interest rate premium is added to the prevailing prime
rate. For example, a moderately risky customer might get a "prime plus 2 percent" loan. If the prime rate is 7 percent, this translates to a 9 percent borrowing rate (i.e., 7 percent + 2 percent). Early-stage ventures, when they can get
bank loans, might pay "prime plus 5 percent" or 12 percent when the prime
rate is 7 percent. Even the prime rate, however, is not as low as the government's risk-free rate.

It is important to understand that the default risk premium for a given class
of firms and the risk-free interest rate change over time with changes in expectations about economic activity. Figure 7.3 depicts the impact of some of these
changes. In Panel A, the slope of the risk premium curve is held constant while
the risk-free interest rate shifts upward and downward on the vertical axis to
reflect changes in inflation expectations. As previously suggested, the risk-free
rate will be high when inflation expectations are high because we add the inflation premium to a reasonably stable real interest rate (of about 3 percent). When
inflation is expected to be 7 percent or higher annually, the risk-free rate will be
at the double-digit level. In contrast, a low inflation rate of 2 percent suggests a
risk-free rate of about 5 percent.

FIGURE 7.3

Shifts in Risk-Free Interest Rates and Default Risk Premiums Required by Borrowers

Panel A: Impact of Changes in Inflation Expectations

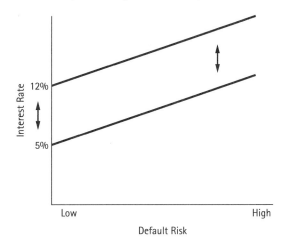

Panel B: Impact of Changes in Economic Expectations

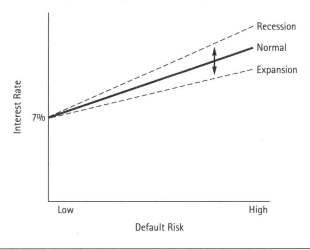

Panel B of Figure 7.3 holds the risk-free rate constant and depicts changes in the slope of the default risk premium with changes in expectations about the economy. When investors expect an expanding economy, they may believe that a given class of firms (such as startups) will exhibit decreased default rates and that investors will demand lower default risk premiums for debt issued by this class of ventures. This is depicted by a less steep default risk premium curve related to the lower likelihood of borrower default. When investors expect a recessionary economy, investors (lenders) require larger default risk premiums.

bond rating
an assessment that reflects the default risk of a firm's bonds as judged by a bond-rating agency

For larger mature corporations, differences in default risk premiums are often captured by bond ratings. A **bond rating** reflects the default risk of a firm's bonds as judged by a bond-rating agency such as the Standard & Poor's Corporation (S&P) or Moody's. Scores are used to indicate the default risk class for a given firm. Firms with the lowest default risk are assigned AAA ratings by S&P. This rating is followed by AA, A, and BBB for increasing class levels of default risk. The default risk for BBB bonds is considered low enough to remain *investment grade*. However, lower ratings (BB, B, CCC, and D) are frequently referred to as *high-yield* or *junk* bonds. AAA-rated bonds usually require a default risk premium of less than one percentage point above the rate on Treasury bonds. Even BBB-rated bonds typically require only about a two-percentage-point premium over Treasuries. Junk bonds are considered very high default risk and often require a premium of an additional 5 percent or more. Early-stage ventures must pay rates comparable to junk-bond rates for access to debt capital, if they have access at all.

Movements in inflation and economic expectations are not necessarily independent. While Figure 7.3 separately considers changes in expected inflation (Panel A) and expected economic conditions (Panel B), these expectations may interact. For example, at the beginning of the 1980s, risk-free rates were very high owing to double-digit inflation. The default risk premium curve was quite steep because the U.S. economy was in recession. In contrast, at the end of the 1990s, risk-free rates were low because of low inflation (below 3 percent) and the expectation of high real growth rates, resulting in a flattened default risk premium curve. In the context of borrowing costs, the U.S. economy went from what some would say was possibly the worst situation at the beginning of the 1980s to possibly the best situation by the end of the 1990s. The decline in the cost of financial capital paralleled the rapid rise of U.S. entrepreneurial activities.

From an entrepreneur's perspective, it can be more difficult to undertake new business ventures as interest rates rise. When higher interest rates reflect higher inflation expectations, it is often difficult to sustain profitability. If the venture cannot easily pass price increases on to its customers, the venture faces eroded demand at the new higher prices or lower margins on existing demand. In either case, profitability declines or even vanishes. Many who watch markets claim that, when the default risk premium curve steepens, we should expect an economic slowdown or, possibly, even a recession. In addition to rising interest rates for new ventures, there can be a serious negative impact on existing ventures' revenues. In such instances, new ventures face increased capital costs and decreased profitability. Most new ventures will have a tougher time surviving periods of high risk-free interest rates and steeply sloped default risk premium curves.

CONCEPT CHECK

- What is meant by a default risk premium?
- What is a prime rate?

LIQUIDITY AND MATURITY RISK PREMIUMS

In addition to inflation and default expectations, liquidity and maturity horizon may influence the nominal interest rate on a venture's debt. A **liquidity premium (LP)** is charged when a loan or other debt instrument cannot be sold quickly at its existing value.[5] Investment-grade debt and prime loans usually can sell quickly at little, if any, discount to their true values. In contrast, higher-risk loans and junk bonds may require significant lead time and/or discount from true value to be sold quickly. Although we usually think of default risk and liquidity premiums as moving together, one can observe different liquidity premiums for financial securities with similar default risk and maturity.

A **maturity premium (MP)** is an added interest rate charge for long-horizon debt contracts. Many think of this as compensation for additional interest rate risk in the long term. For example, while the inflation realized over the next year will probably be close to its expected level of, perhaps, 3 percent, it becomes increasingly risky to extend a fixed-rate loan (of, say, 7 percent) for ten or even twenty years when inflation could vary widely from current expectations. Investors' tastes for lending, default risk premiums, and the overall economic climate are more uncertain over long time intervals. Depending on how uncertainty is perceived to compound over time, it is possible that the annualized maturity premium (rate per year) might increase with the lending horizon. If so, holding other factors constant, we would expect to see nominal interest rates rise with maturity.

The relationship between nominal interest rates and time to maturity, when default risk is held constant, is referred to as the **term structure of interest rates**. A **yield curve** is a graph of the term structure of interest rates. Figure 7.4 shows a typical upward-sloping yield curve for U.S. Treasury securities. Because Treasuries are treated as essentially default free at all maturities, we know that lenders are requiring (and the Treasury is paying) maturity premiums. Notice that the maturity risk premium over the one-year Treasury rate is 1 percent (7 percent − 6 percent) for five-year, 2 percent (8 percent − 6 percent) for ten-year, and 3 percent (9 percent − 6 percent) for twenty-year Treasuries. In general, yield curves flatten out after maturities reach about ten years. That is, the incremental annual maturity risk premium typically decreases (to zero) after maturities of about ten years. Note that although the incremental annual maturity premium goes to zero, maturity premiums are applied every year. Consequently, the total dollar amount of maturity premium (as opposed to the annual rate) rises with maturity, and a compounding effect remains. While some suggest that this decline in annual increments (or constant annual maturity premium) beyond ten years indicates that much of this risk plays out in the first ten years, it is better to view the absence of additional annual increment as an indication that the risk per year has stabilized even though total risk continues to rise with each year on the loan.

When we examine yield curves to calibrate maturity risk premiums, a caveat is in order. The supply and demand for funds at each maturity determines how

liquidity premium (LP)
premium charged when a debt instrument cannot be converted to cash quickly at its existing value

maturity premium (MP)
premium that reflects increased uncertainty associated with long-term debt

term structure of interest rates
relationship between nominal interest rates and time to maturity when default risk is held constant

yield curve
graph of the term structure of interest rates

---

[5] Actually, the premium or added interest rate is for a lack of liquidity. However, convention has led users to call this a liquidity premium rather than an "illiquidity" premium.

FIGURE 7.4 Yield Curve Representation of the Term Structure of Interest Rates

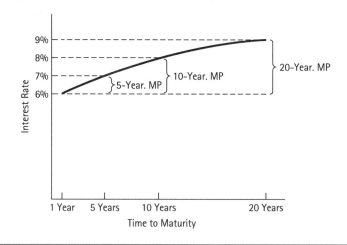

the current term structure slopes. Supply and demand are affected by the factors we have discussed and an important one we haven't—the Federal Reserve. U.S. monetary policy is implemented by the Federal Reserve, primarily through a variety of activities that can shift the supply and demand of Treasury securities at various maturities. Consequently, it is not unusual to observe flat, humped, or even downward-sloping yield curves as the authorities conduct monetary policy manipulations in an attempt to influence the U.S. (and global) economy. Complicating the rather straightforward supply-and-demand effects of Federal Reserve purchases is the fact that long-term inflation expectations are closely related to public perceptions of the attitude of the monetary authorities. Fed actions can therefore have direct and indirect supply-and-demand effects. As an example, when the Fed is attempting to raise short-term interest rates to slow down the expansion rate of an allegedly overheated economy, it may have a direct effect on short-horizon supply and demand (higher interest rates). If it communicates by its actions that long-run inflation will be controlled, long-term interest rates may drop. The result is a torquing of the term structure toward flatness or, possibly, even an inversion (downward sloping). When examining the term structure for maturity premiums, it is important to keep in mind all of the factors of supply and demand, including current monetary policy.

We now estimate the cost of borrowed financial capital by returning to equation 7.3. Assume that the risk-free rate is 6 percent, based on a 3 percent inflation expectation and a 3 percent real interest rate. An entrepreneur is expecting to pay a five-percentage-point cost for default risk in order to obtain borrowed funds for five years. The loan will be difficult to resell, and market norms dictate a three-percentage-point liquidity premium. Finally, given the prevailing shape of the yield curve, the maturity premium will average two percentage points over the life of the five-year loan. The venture's cost for this debt capital is:

$$r_d = 6\% + 5\% + 3\% + 2\% = 16\%$$

Debt issues may be secured or unsecured. A debt issue is secured by pledging a venture's specific assets (plant, equipment, and/or working capital) to be used in the event of default in satisfaction of at least a portion of the debt. Debt secured by a venture's assets is typically called **senior debt**. Unsecured debt is typically referred to as **subordinated debt**, owing to the inferiority of its claim relative to the senior debt's specific claim on venture assets. Subordinated debt has more severe concerns upon default and, consequently, carries a higher interest rate. Early-stage firms have little, if any, senior debt because the value of salvageable assets is negligible. In general, early-stage ventures with no profitable operating history will not be candidates for traditional debt. They may, however, use debt capital originating in the founders' ability to borrow on personal credit or with a personal guarantee through mortgages, personally guaranteed bank loans, and credit cards.[6]

While relating expected returns to the degree of default risk has intuitive appeal, in practice, many debt issues are not rated solely for default risk. A generalization of default risk is variability in the payment of returns. Nonpayment is certainly a form of variability (from expectations). Thinking about risk in terms of variability of payment extends to other securities where there is no legal obligation to pay. The prime example of such a security is a venture's equity. When we view each security's risk in terms of the variability of the payments it can make to investors, we get a broader definition of investment risk.

senior debt
debt secured by a venture's assets

subordinated debt
debt with an inferior claim (relative to senior debt) to venture assets

CONCEPT CHECK

- What is meant by (a) a liquidity premium and (b) a default risk premium?
- What is meant by the term structure of interest rates?

A WORD ON VENTURE DEBT CAPITAL

It is possible that a venture may be able to borrow money at below-market rates from family members and friends. Such investors' primary interests in the venture may very well be nonfinancial. They may also have other ways of achieving nonfinancial returns. Additionally, state and local government assistance programs (also having interests beyond the venture's success) may provide subsidized debt financing.[7] However, entrepreneurs and their teams need to understand that unaffiliated, nonsubsidizing lenders are motivated primarily by expected and realized financial returns on the financing they provide; they demand a competitive rent for the use

---

[6] Although personal borrowing by the founders is common, in practice in startups involving multiple founders, personal debt may fund what amounts to an equity investment by the individual founders. That is, it is possible that the venture's culture will treat the debt as the individual founder's problem and never really assume the debt service burden as its own. On the upside, when the venture succeeds, it will help the founder relieve the personal debt burden. Unfortunately, as the venture fails, the debt service may be left to the individual founder faced with what amounts to forced additional investment in a struggling venture. Accordingly, it is probably better to think of personally guaranteed debt and investment funded by personal debt as partly or entirely equity (and correspondingly due the higher returns expected for equity).

[7] We devote Chapter 12 to an extensive introduction to such sources.

of their funds. The business angels, venture capitalists, and (rarely) banks that provide unaffiliated capital expect to earn an overall return comparable to that available elsewhere for investments of similar risk. "Renting" their capital to the venture has an immediate cost of not "renting" it elsewhere. In the long run facing the surviving venture, it is the private and public financial markets that determine the appropriate target return for the venture's debt. Subsidized borrowing can provide some important early advantages, but the financial advantages themselves are short lived, and the available financing is inadequate to meet a successful venture's long-term financing needs.

Some venture debt that appears to bear below-market rates may not be subsidized even though, at first, it appears to be. Venture lenders and investors that provide mezzanine financing to successful ventures in their rapid-growth stages may achieve part of their target return by participating in the venture's equity success when, and if, it occurs. The part of the lender's return that is conditioned on the value of the venture's equity is usually structured by adding warrants (see Chapter 13) to the venture loan. Together, the target return from loan principal and interest and that from the warrant's payoff will still be kept in check by competition in the financial markets.

7.4   WHAT IS INVESTMENT RISK?

The word "risk" comes from the early Italian word *risicare* and means "to dare."[8] Dictionary definitions refer to risk as being a peril or hazard that results in exposure to loss or injury. For example, the decision to ride a bicycle in automobile traffic involves the chance (risk) of suffering bodily injury. Likewise, the decision to start a business, or to invest in someone else's venture, involves the possibility (risk) of financial or monetary loss. **Investment risk of loss** is the chance, or probability, of financial loss on one's venture investment. Debt, equity, and founding investors all assume investment risk of loss.

investment risk of loss
chance or probability of financial loss from a venture investment

MEASURING RISK AS DISPERSION AROUND AN AVERAGE

Perceived variation in possible venture returns is a widely accepted notion of venture investment risk. Returns include any interest or dividends received, plus any change in the value of the investment (appreciation or depreciation) over the period of the investment. For example, assume that you are contemplating making a $100 investment in the HiTec Company. You expect that at the end of one year you will receive $10 in cash flow in the form of dividends and expect the investment's value to be $110. Thus, the return would be $20 ($10 in cash dividends and $10 in capital appreciation) on the initial $100 investment. Typically,

---

[8]   Peter L. Bernstein, *Against the Gods: The Remarkable Story of Risk* (New York: John Wiley & Sons, 1996), p. 8. Bernstein provides a comprehensive discussion of how the understanding of risk developed through history, how to measure risk, and how to weigh the consequences of taking on risk.

this would be couched as an expected return of 20 percent.[9] In equation form, we have:

$$\% \text{ Rate of Return} = \frac{\text{Cash Flow} + (\text{Ending Value} - \text{Beginning Value})}{\text{Beginning Value}} \times 100 \qquad \textbf{(7.4)}$$

For our example, we then have:

$$\% \text{ Rate of Return} = \frac{\$10 + (\$110 - \$100)}{\$100} \times 100 = \frac{\$20}{\$100} \times 100 = 20.0\%$$

Thus, the rate of return is expected to be 20 percent.

Now assume that the 20 percent return is expected for the HiTec Company only if normal economic conditions prevail next year. The economy, however, could be either in a recession or growing rapidly. If a recession occurs, no cash dividend is expected from the investment, and the investment's value is expected to fall to $80. On the other hand, if the economy grows rapidly, the dividend is expected to be $20 with the investment's value expected to rise to $140. The returns expected under each scenario for HiTec would be:

Recession:

$$\% \text{ Rate of Return} = \frac{\$0 + (\$80 - \$100)}{\$100} \times 100 = \frac{-\$20}{\$100} \times 100 = -20\%$$

Rapid growth:

$$\% \text{ Rate of Return} = \frac{\$20 + (\$140 - \$100)}{\$100} \times 100 = \frac{\$60}{\$100} \times 100 = 60\%$$

An **expected rate of return** is a probability-weighted average of all possible rates of return. Given only these three possible rates of return, and assuming that the high and low returns occur 30 percent of the time and that the normal return occurs the remaining 40 percent of the time, the expected rate of return for the HiTec Company investment is:

expected rate of return
probability-weighted average of all possible rates of return

ECONOMIC CLIMATE	PROBABILITY OF OCCURRENCE	×	RATE OF RETURN	=	WEIGHTED RETURN
Rapid growth	.3	×	60%	=	18.0%
Normal	.4	×	20	=	8.0
Recession	.3	×	−20	=	−6.0
	1.0		Expected return	=	20.0%

The expected rate of return, given the estimated probabilities for each of the three scenarios, is 20 percent. In other words, the probability-weighted mean or average expected return is 20 percent.

We know, however, that the realized return for the HiTec Company may be as low as −20 percent or as high as 60 percent. The deviation, or dispersion, of outcomes around the expected return of 20 percent, typically quantified by the **standard deviation**, is a commonly used measure of an investment's risk.

standard deviation
measure of the dispersion of possible outcomes around the expected return of an investment

---

[9] For many, it is easier to compare different investments by considering their expected rates of return. While this is not an infallible way to compare investments of differing initial investment or having intertwining investment and return phases, it is usually a reasonable starting point.

The tighter the dispersion, the smaller the standard deviation and the lower the investment risk. It is common practice to use the symbol σ, pronounced "sigma," to indicate the standard deviation. The standard deviation for HiTec is:

OUTCOME MINUS EXPECTED RETURN	DIFFERENCE SQUARED	×	PROBABILITY OF OUTCOME	=	WEIGHTED SQUARED DEVIATIONS
60% − 20% = 40%	1,600	×	.3	=	480.0
20% − 20% = 0	0	×	.4	=	0.0
−20% − 20% = −40	1,600	×	.3	=	480.0
	Variance	=	σ^2	=	960.0
	Standard Deviation	=	$\sqrt{\sigma^2}$	=	31.0%

In words, we calculate standard deviations as follows:

1. Calculate the expected rate of return on an investment based on estimates of possible returns and the probabilities associated with those returns.
2. Subtract the expected value from each outcome to determine deviations from the expected value.
3. Square each difference or deviation.
4. Multiply each squared deviation by the probability of the outcome and sum the weighted squared deviations to get the variance (σ^2).
5. Calculate the square root of the variance to get the standard deviation (σ).

In actual practice, an investment is likely to have more than three possible outcomes. If we increase the number of possible outcomes substantially and assign probabilities that reflect similar probabilities for similar returns, in many cases it will be advantageous to think of the returns as belonging to a continuous probability distribution. Panel A in Figure 7.5 depicts an example of such a distribution for the HiTec Company. Panel A also displays the expected return and the dispersion of returns for the BioTec Company. Notice that while BioTec has the same expected return as HiTec (20 percent), it has a much tighter distribution around its expected value. This is graphical representation of BioTec's smaller standard deviation and lower investment risk. Given investor risk aversion, when considering two otherwise identical investments, investors will prefer the investment with a smaller dispersion of outcomes (lower standard deviation).

In actual practice, investor choices are more complex than depicted in Panel A of Figure 7.5, where two investments had the same expected returns but different standard deviations. Most of the time, investors face trade-offs involving higher expected return for assuming greater risk (standard deviation). Panel B of Figure 7.5 shows the continuous probability distributions of possible returns for the LoTec and HiTec Companies. The expected rate of return for LoTec is 10 percent. However, the dispersion of possible outcomes is much tighter for LoTec, an investment having significantly less investment risk.

Which opportunity would investors choose? The answer is not obvious. It depends on the risk tolerance or risk aversion of each investor. We can standardize the relationship between the expected rate of return and the standard

Continuous Probability Distributions of Rates of Return

Panel A: Rates of Return for the HiTec and BioTec Companies

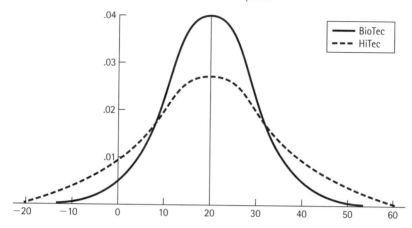

Panel B: Rates of Return for the HiTec and LoTec Companies

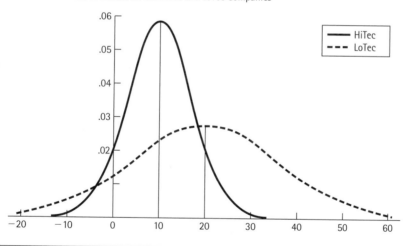

deviation. One way to standardize is by considering the ratio of standard deviation to expected return, a ratio known as the **coefficient of variation**:

$$\text{Coefficient of Variation} = \text{Standard Deviation/Expected Return} \qquad \textbf{(7.5)}$$

coefficient of variation
measure of the dispersion risk per unit of expected rate of return

Assume that even after we have added more outcomes for HiTec, the standard deviation of returns remains at 31 percent. Assume that the standard deviation for LoTec is 12 percent. Using equation 7.5, we have:

LoTec: Coefficient of Variation = 12%/10% = 1.20
HiTec: Coefficient of Variation = 31%/20% = 1.55

We see that the LoTec Company offers a lower dispersion per unit of expected return. Does this mean that all investors would rationally choose LoTec over HiTec? No! Highly risk-averse investors would almost certainly choose the LoTec investment over the HiTec investment.[10] In contrast, investors with a higher tolerance for risk might choose to invest in HiTec because of its expected 20 percent return. Of course, they will assume more risk (dispersion) in the possible outcomes. The potential for higher return is sufficient to entice these investors into taking greater risks.

CONCEPT CHECK

- What is investment risk of loss?
- What is meant by an expected rate of return?
- Explain the terms "standard deviation" and "coefficient of variation."

HISTORICAL RETURN VERSUS RISK RELATIONSHIPS

It is one thing to talk about the trade-off between risk and return in statistical terms. However, if not validated over time, the concept will not be very useful in helping us understand the cost of financial capital. Fortunately, the long-term historical record supports the expectation that investments with higher dispersion risks provide higher average rates of return over time.

Ibbotson Associates compiles and reports average annual return data and standard deviations on investments in bonds and stocks for long periods of time. Table 7.1 shows the annual average total returns and their standard deviations for the 1926 through 2006 period.[11] We have included data on average annual rates of inflation and added coefficients of variation.

The average annual return on an intermediate-term U.S. government bond (i.e., a one-bond portfolio with a maturity of five years) was 5.5 percent over the eighty-one-year (1926–2006) period. The standard deviation was 5.7 percent, resulting in a relatively low coefficient of variation of 1.0 (5.7/5.5). This represents a low-risk–low-return investment example. While this is a default risk–free investment, changes in market interest rates from one year to the next can cause a bond's price (and, therefore, its investment return) to change over its life. Because the government will honor its interest and principal payments, the investor will receive her contracted return over the life of the bond.

For illustration, assume that the government issues a two-year $1,000 bond with a current 6 percent market interest rate. Also assume that interest is paid annually.[12] A bond's price would be set as follows:[13]

---

[10]   In fact, highly risk-averse investors may opt to invest in U.S. government securities and not in equities.

[11]   *Stocks, Bonds, Bills, and Inflation: 2007 Yearbook* (Chicago: Morningstar, Inc., 2007).

[12]   It is standard practice in the United States to pay interest semiannually on bonds with maturities greater than one year. In this example, however, we are assuming annual payments to simplify the example.

[13]   For readers unfamiliar with discounted cash flows, this example uses the methods covered in detail in Chapter 9.

TABLE 7.1	Annual Rates of Return: Inflation, Bonds, and Stocks (1926–2006)		
SECURITY TYPE AND INFLATION	AVERAGE ANNUAL RETURN	STANDARD DEVIATION	COEFFICIENT OF VARIATION
Intermediate-term government bonds	5.4%	5.7%	1.0
Long-term government bonds	5.8	9.2	1.6
Long-term corporate bonds	6.2	8.5	1.4
Large-company stocks	12.3	20.1	1.6
Small-company stocks	17.4	32.7	1.9
Inflation	3.1	4.3	1.4

Source: *Stocks, Bonds, Bills, and Inflation: 2007 Yearbook* (Chicago: Morningstar, Inc., 2007).

$$\text{Bond Price} = \frac{\text{Interest in Year 1}}{(1 + r_d)^1} + \frac{\text{Interest in Year 2}}{(1 + r_d)^2} + \frac{\text{Principal Repayment}}{(1 + r_d)^2} \qquad \textbf{(7.6)}$$

For our example, we would have:

$$\text{Bond Price} = \frac{\$60}{(1.06)^1} + \frac{\$60}{(1.06)^2} + \frac{\$1,000}{(1.06)^2} = \frac{\$60}{1.06} + \frac{\$1,060}{1.1236}$$
$$= \$56.60 + \$943.40$$
$$= \$1,000$$

If the interest rate on similar-maturity government bonds increases to 7 percent before the first interest payment has been made on this two-year bond, its price will fall as follows:

$$\text{Bond Price} = \frac{\$60}{(1.07)^1} + \frac{\$1,060}{(1.07)^2} = \frac{\$60}{1.07} + \frac{\$1,060}{1.1449}$$
$$= \$56.07 + \$925.85$$
$$= \$981.92$$

The investment return for the first year, assuming the bond price is $981.92, would be:

$$\% \text{ Investment Return} = \frac{\text{Interest} + \text{Ending Price} - \text{Beginning Price}}{\text{Beginning Value}} \times 100$$
$$= \frac{\$60 + \$981.92 - \$1000}{\$1000} \times 100$$
$$= \frac{\$41.92}{\$1000} \times 100$$
$$= .0419 \times 100, \text{ or } 4.19\%$$

Thus, instead of an expected return of 6 percent, the sale of the bond at market value ($981.92) after one year would bring a realized return of only 4.19 percent. Of course, if the bond is held the full two years, the realized return will be 6 percent; the government will make the two $60 interest payments and return the $1,000 principal amount. Nonetheless, owing to changes in interest rates, the value of the bond fluctuates during the two-year period.

Fluctuations in bond prices, deriving from changes in interest rates, increase with the life or maturity of the bond. Long-term bonds have greater annual price changes or fluctuations than do intermediate-term bonds. Historical data illustrate this difference very clearly. While the standard deviation on five-year government bonds has been 5.7 percent, the standard deviation for long-term government bonds (a one-bond portfolio with a twenty-year maturity) averaged 9.4 percent over the 1926–2006 period. This greater variability occurred even though the annual average return was only 5.8 percent (i.e., only three-tenths of a percent higher than the intermediate-term bond rate), resulting in a coefficient of variation of 1.6. This is the type of difference one would expect to observe for bonds with a four times longer maturity (twenty years versus five years). This much greater volatility derives from the inherent changes in interest rates accompanying periods of war, low and high inflation, recession and a major depression, and rapid economic growth.

From Table 7.1, it is easy to see that returns on bonds have been lower than those earned on equity investments. The returns on long-term corporate bonds are from an index of high-grade corporate bonds with an approximate maturity of twenty years. Large-company stock returns are from the Standard & Poor's 500 composite stock index since 1957 and on the Standard & Poor's 90 stock index prior to then. The common stock returns assume the reinvestment of dividends. The average premium in the return of large corporate stocks over corporate bonds for the 1926–2006 period was 6.2 percent (12.4 percent − 6.2 percent). Over the same period, the standard deviation was 8.6 percent for the corporate bond index and was 20.4 percent on large-company stocks.

The cost of equity capital should be higher than the cost of debt capital. This is true for a given venture and, on average, across all companies. Debtholders have a prior (to equity) claim on a venture's operating income and any liquidation proceeds. Interest must be paid to debtholders before cash dividends can be paid to equity investors. In addition, debtholder returns are paid primarily through interest (and principal) and tend to be relatively stable other than when default takes place. Returns to equity holders come from a combination of cash dividends and expected equity value or price appreciation.

Notice in Table 7.1 that the average annual return for small-company stocks has been 5.1 percent (17.5 percent − 12.4 percent) above the average return on large-company stocks. Small-company stocks were defined as those in the smallest market capitalization quintile on the New York Stock Exchange (NYSE) for the period through 1981. More recent returns are based on the Dimensional Fund Advisors Small Company Fund. The standard deviation of 33.3 percent for small-company stocks (versus 20.4 percent for large-company stocks) also produces a coefficient of variation of 1.9 for small-company stocks (versus 1.6 for large-company stocks). This confirms our a priori expectations that small-company stock investments are riskier than large-company stock investments. Of course, the uncertainty of returns is particularly great for new venture equity investors since virtually all future returns will derive from price appreciation in the equity security. Relative to small public company stocks, venture investments should produce even higher expected returns.

- Describe the average annual relative long-run returns on long-term bonds versus stocks.

7.5 ESTIMATING THE COST OF EQUITY CAPITAL

Equity investors, like debt investors, expect to be compensated for the risk of the investment. Equity investors may be private equity investors or publicly traded stock investors. **Private equity investors** are owners of proprietorships, partners in partnerships, and owners in closely held corporations, who would include entrepreneurs, business angels, venture capitalists, and other private equity investors. **Closely held corporations** are corporations whose stock is not publicly traded. **Publicly traded stock investors**, as the name implies, are equity investors in firms whose stocks trade in public secondary markets—either in the over-the-counter market or on organized securities exchanges. Equity capital is considered to be private until a venture's stock is traded in public markets.

An **organized securities exchange** typically has a specific location with a trading floor where trades take place under rules set by the exchange. The most-cited example of an organized securities exchange is the NYSE. An **over-the-counter (OTC) market** is a network of brokers and dealers that interact electronically without having a formal location. The NASDAQ, which is a system for trading stocks, is the most visible example of the OTC market. An organized securities exchange frequently uses specialists who facilitate trade in specific stocks. In contrast, the NASDAQ has dealers who will execute your trades but also buy and sell securities for their own account. Recently, electronic trading services have become quite popular and provide yet another trading venue for publicly traded securities.

In order to buy and sell securities on an organized exchange, an investor contacts his broker, who then sends the order to the exchange floor where it is executed at the specialist station for that stock. To trade an OTC stock, the investor contacts his broker, who checks a computer listing for dealers in the specified security and their bid-ask prices. After confirming the dealer with the best price, the broker contacts that dealer and executes the trade.

Securities must first be listed before they can be traded on the New York Stock Exchange. In order to qualify for listing on the NYSE, a corporation must meet certain profitability and equity value requirements. Many ventures that successfully complete an initial public offering (IPO) of their stock have their shares traded on the OTC market. It should be noted that while the OTC market specializes in trading securities of smaller, rapidly growing firms, some very large

private equity investors
owners of proprietorships, partners in partnerships, and owners in closely held corporations

closely held corporations
corporations whose stock is not publicly traded

publicly traded stock investors
equity investors of firms whose stocks trade in public markets such as the over-the-counter market or an organized securities exchange

organized securities exchange
a formally organized exchange typically having a physical location with a trading floor where trades take place under rules set by the exchange

over-the-counter (OTC) market
network of brokers and dealers that interact electronically without having a formal location

and successful firms continue to have their securities traded on the NASDAQ. Two examples are Intel and Microsoft.

Private firms have only private equity investors. That is, if any part of a firm's equity trades publicly, we do not consider that firm to be "private." Nonprivate or "public" firms have at least a portion of their equity traded in public markets. A firm's **market capitalization** (or **"market cap"**) is its current stock price multiplied by the number of outstanding shares. A firm with ten million shares outstanding, with prevailing market price per share of $20, has a market cap of $200 million. It is common to refer to public firms as small cap, medium cap, or large cap. While the definition changes over time with growth in stock prices, an example of these categories would be: small cap for less than $1 billion, medium cap for $1 billion to $20 billion, and large cap for greater than $20 billion. The very largest cap firms (e.g., General Electric, Intel, and Microsoft) have capitalization values at times approaching $500 billion.

market capitalization (or "market cap")
a firm's current stock price multiplied by the number of shares that are outstanding

COST OF EQUITY CAPITAL FOR PUBLIC CORPORATIONS

Attitudes about how investors should be rewarded for investment risk taking have changed dramatically over the past sixty years. The idea that investment risk can be reduced by holding securities in diversified portfolios blossomed during the 1950s and 1960s. Finding "efficient" portfolios—in which returns are as high as possible for a given level of standard deviation—became an investment focal point. Perhaps the most successful application of this perspective on how investors *should* be rewarded was the capital asset pricing model (CAPM) developed during the 1960s and 1970s. Whether the markets actually *do* reward investors in a manner consistent with the CAPM remains a subject of ongoing research decades after its development.

The cost of equity capital has components similar to those in the cost of debt capital. The cost of common equity (r_e) is determined by a risk-free interest rate (r_f) plus an equity risk premium (IRP):

$$r_e = r_f + IRP = RR + IP + IRP \qquad (7.7)$$

where r_f decomposes into a real rate (RR) plus an inflation premium (IP). The **investment risk premium (IRP)** is the additional return investors expect when investing in publicly traded common stock. As with the cost of debt capital, the cost of equity capital starts with a baseline of the default risk–free rate and adds premiums for various factors. However, rather than add a maturity premium (MP) and default risk premium (DRP), equity's cost lumps these together in the investment risk premium. We will return to the notion of a separate liquidity premium (LP) when we discuss the cost of private equity capital.

The CAPM can be used to estimate the cost of equity capital for firms that have previously gone public. Specifically, the CAPM suggests an expected rate of

investment risk premium (IRP)
additional return that investors can expect to earn when investing in a risky publicly traded common stock

return for a stock investment related directly to the stock's contribution to a specific well-diversified portfolio—the overall market.[14]

The expected rate of return on a venture's equity (r_e) using the CAPM's security market line (SML) is:

$$r_e = r_f + [r_m - r_f]\beta \qquad (7.8)$$

where r_f is the risk-free interest rate, r_m is the expected rate of return on the overall stock market for the same time period, and β (called "beta") is a measure of the stock's risk contribution to a well-diversified portfolio (the overall market portfolio). By construction, the beta for the overall market is 1.00. In practice, equation 7.8 is calibrated using annual rates.

The usual practice in this calibration exercise is to use a historical estimate of $(r_m - r_f)$ and current interest rates for r_f. In this exercise, the **market risk premium (MRP)** is the excess average annual return of common stocks over government bonds. We can emphasize this approach by rewriting the SML equation as:

$$r_e = r_f + [MRP]\beta \qquad (7.9)$$

market risk premium (MRP)

excess average annual return of common stocks over long-term government bonds

The product of the market risk premium and the individual security's beta is the investment risk premium (IRP) in equation 7.7.

From Table 7.1, we can see that large-company stocks have provided average annual excess returns of 6.6 percent (i.e., 12.4 percent − 5.8 percent) over long-term government bonds for the 1926–2006 period. In fact, over most historical periods of twenty years or more, this excess return has averaged 6.5 to 7.5 percent. If we believe that this average historical spread between large-company stocks and long-term government bonds is a good estimate of what will happen in the future, we can substitute this spread for MRP.

For example, if we assume that the current risk-free interest rate on long-term government bonds is 6 percent, and we use 7 percent as reflecting the expected market risk premium, our expected average annual rate of return on large-company stocks would be:

$$r_e = 6\% + [7\%]1.00 = 6\% + 7\% = 13\%$$

A reasonable expected rate of return on large-company stocks would be about 13 percent. The expected average annual rate of return would, of course, be affected by the prevailing base (risk-free) interest rates and expectations about the future market risk premium. When risk-free rates or market risk premiums are relatively low, expected returns for large-company stocks also would be low.

---

[14] For the reader interested in understanding the current application of these concepts in corporate finance, graduate-level texts in investments and corporate finance will provide substantial detail. For those interested in a nonmathematical discussion of the development of financial economics relating to security returns and prices, see Peter L. Bernstein, *Capital Ideas* (New York: The Free Press/Simon & Schuster, 1993).

From Table 7.1, we also can see that small-company stocks provided average annual excess rates of return of 11.7 percent (i.e., 17.5 percent − 5.8 percent) over long-term government bonds for the 1926–2006 period. Relative to large-company stocks, small-company stocks historically averaged 5.1 percent (17.5 percent − 12.4 percent) higher returns.

If we estimate a future market risk premium of 12 percent for small-company stocks owing to an additional 5 percent MRP (above the 7 percent MRP for large-company stocks) and use a 6 percent long-term government bond rate, the result is:

$$r_e = 6\% + [7\% + 5\%]1.00 = 6\% + [12\%]1.00 = 6\% + 12\% = 18\%$$

CONCEPT CHECK

- What is meant by an investment risk premium?
- What is meant by a market risk premium?

COST OF EQUITY CAPITAL FOR PRIVATE VENTURES

Historically, venture capital returns have exceeded those of broad groups of publicly traded small stocks. Recently, Venture Economics and the National Venture Capital Association reported the historical venture investing experiences shown in Table 7.2.

For the period ending December 2006, the long-run (twenty-year) return on all of the venture capital investments tracked (16.6 percent) exceeds the long-run (twenty-year) small stock performance number (13.2 percent).[15] While similar in nature, venture investments appear to offer slightly higher returns at a higher risk than small public companies. There have been periods when venture returns were extraordinary (in both directions).[16] As shown in Table 7.2, five-year (2002–2006) rates of return for all ventures averaged only 1 percent, reflecting the "bust" during the early years of this decade. In contrast, the three-year holding period (2004–2006) produced a compound average return of 9.1 percent for all ventures. For the most recent ten years (1997–2006), the compound rate of return for all ventures was 20.3 percent. While venture investing offers important risk-return opportunities not easily available elsewhere, there is no strong case

---

[15] The 16.6 and 13.2 percents are both geometric averages (like IRR). The 13.2 percent is the small stock return tracked by Ibbotson Associates for 1987–2006. See *Stocks, Bonds, Bills, and Inflation: 2007 Yearbook* (Chicago: Morningstar, Inc., 2007).

[16] For example, we reported in the second edition of this textbook that three-year returns (2001–2003) for all venture investments tracked were −18.9 percent. Five-year returns (1999–2003) for seed/early-stage investing were 54.9 percent. For an academic view of venture investing returns that does not include the beginning of the current decade's downturn, see John Cochrane, *The Risk and Return of Venture Capital*, National Bureau of Economic Research, Working Paper No. 8066 (January 2001).

TABLE 7.2					
Venture Capital Holding Period Returns Ending December 2006					
	1 YEAR	3 YEARS	5 YEARS	10 YEARS	20 YEARS
Early/seed	9.90	6.50	–3.00	36.40	20.50
Later-stage VC	25.20	9.40	3.70	9.00	14.00
All ventures	**16.40**	**9.10**	**1.00**	**20.30**	**16.60**

Source: Thomson Financial/National Venture Capital Association.

Note: The Private Equity Performance Index is based on the latest quarterly statistics from Thomson Financial's Private Equity Performance Database analyzing the cash flows and returns of over 1,860 U.S. venture capital and private equity partnerships with a capitalization of $678 billion. Sources are financial documents and schedules from limited partner investors and general partners. All returns are calculated by Thomson Financial from the underlying financial cash flows. Returns are net to investors after management fees and carried interest.

for claiming that venture investing offers a superior risk return to other, more widely available investments.

For mature publicly traded companies, analysts can consider a rich collection of historical data to help produce unbiased projections. The host of analysts digesting the diverse—but related—information provides some assurance that the projections are reasonable. Because the firms have lengthy histories, the projections will be less prone to the type of overconfidence or **venture hubris** exhibited in the financial projections of many business plans.

New ventures provide little or no historical data on which to base credible projections. About the only projections we have are those in the business plan. Fortunately, we have the insider's vision and prophecy set down in print; unfortunately, it is bad that those projections seldom represent objective views of the venture's future. When we look at a business plan and see 70 percent projected returns to investors, we need to understand their relationship to long-term expected venture returns of approximately 20 percent. First, 70 percent is not an unconditional expected return. It is a conditional expected return. That is, finding successful ventures that returned 70 percent is not hard. However, finding a diversified pool of successful and failed ventures returning 70 percent over long periods of time is virtually impossible. When you hear about 70 percent expected returns, understand that these are for the subset of ventures that have great success, not for ventures drawn at random.

We are left with an important question about financial customs and manners in venture investing: Why use the 70 percent number when the true expected return is closer to 20 percent? The answer is straightforward. By concentrating on returns conditional on venture success, we get a good idea how high returns have to be for winners in the portfolio—because there will be losers (some at 100 percent loss) and they have to average to 20 percent overall. As all entrepreneurs' business plans project success, we must compare investors' projected returns with benchmarks for successful ventures (not expected returns). The "manners" aspect of using a high target rate like 70 percent is that most venture investors prefer not

venture hubris
optimism expressed in business plan projections that ignore the possibility of failure or underperformance

to dampen venture drive by telling the entrepreneur that all the numbers are "pie in the sky" and should be redone to incorporate an 80 percent chance of failure. It is much easier to let the entrepreneurial team "breathe their own exhaust" and use a conditional-on-success metric to assess the adequacy of projected returns. In most cases, margins will be reasonably projected; but sales, time to market, and competition will be subject to relatively large biases from entrepreneurial hubris.

In summary, it is useful to examine historical venture capital returns, or current and future venture industry returns using statistical samples and unbiased expected returns, to get numbers like 20 percent. However, for business plan projections and new venture analysis, it is often more convenient to compare projected returns to success-scenario returns (50, 70, or even 100 percent).[17]

Venture investors are frequently the source of consulting and advice for the venture. In some cases, venture capitalists take an active position in a venture's operations or management. Typically, these positions receive below-market compensation, if any at all. When a "value-adding" investor contributes these under-compensated services, he typically expects to make greater financial returns on his investments. This is quite different from a stock market investor who buys a blue-chip stock and renders no services. We will refer to the compensation for these services, when loaded into the return expectations, as an advisory premium (AP). Venture investors buy securities that are not publicly traded and, therefore, bear the liquidity risk to which we referred earlier. Incorporating a premium for this liquidity risk (LP), recognizing that compensation for advisory services is loaded into return expectations, and allowing a hubris projections premium (HPP) when dealing with hubris-influenced business plan projections, we can see that the rate of return venture investors seek is:

$$
\begin{aligned}
r_v &= r_f + IRP + AP + LP + HPP \\
&= r_e + AP + LP + HPP
\end{aligned}
\tag{7.10}
$$

While we have seen that CAPM's SML allows us to estimate the cost of equity for publicly traded firms, estimating the cost of equity for ventures that are not publicly traded is much more difficult. We begin by recognizing that private equity investors require additional expected compensation for taking on added risk. IRP and therefore r_e will generally be higher for private equity investments. Private equity investors typically find it very difficult and costly to sell their positions. This leads to a potentially large liquidity premium (LP). On top of this, depending on the situation, venture investors may also increase their target return for advisory services (AP) and overly optimistic business plan projections (HPP).

---

[17] For the astute finance legalist, it may be disturbing to see that we are advocating the use of inflated projections and inflated return expectations. After all, this is certainly not the usual asset-pricing practice in which unbiased expected cash flows are compared to unbiased expected returns (unbiased in the sense of incorporating all possible venture eventualities). Nonetheless, this venture investor practice is well grounded elsewhere in finance. In particular, when we extract an internal rate of return on promised bond payments from one bond and use it to value the promised payments from another bond, we have done precisely the same thing. Promised bond payments are the maximum that will ever be paid. They are certainly not an unbiased expectation of what will be paid (taking into account the possibility of default). Bond valuation conducted in this manner uses success cash flows and success rates of return in precisely the same way as using 70 percent expected return with success-scenario business plans.

SOURCES AND COSTS OF VENTURE EQUITY CAPITAL

The founding entrepreneurial team, business angels, and venture capitalists are the primary sources of early-stage capital. While the entrepreneurial team's investment motives may be complicated, business angels and venture capitalists seek venture returns commensurate with venture risk taking. In almost all cases, any stated interest on a venture investment, if any, is only a small part of the higher return that is truly expected. For example, if a venture investor buys a bond that can be converted into shares of equity, the stated bond interest rate will be a minor part of the total expected return, including any capital gain realized upon conversion.

Even more commonly in the United States, venture capitalists may choose to invest in convertible preferred stock, which can provide better liquidation claims (compared to common stock), have a claim to periodic payments similar to interest, and possess the same voting rights as common stock.[18] The realized return on the convertible security will not be known until its conversion (into common stock) and sale (or liquidation). Since the payments, if any, received during the investment will be small and certainly inadequate to compensate for the risk, most of the return comes in the form of appreciation in the value of the security (capital gain) over time. Even though there is no formal accounting recognition of the accumulating, but at risk, rent for using investors' capital, the cost is real. Founders and managers who cannot provide liquidation proceeds sufficient to meet these accumulated costs can face significant restrictions on their future access to capital. More immediately, as venture investors realize that the future proceeds will be inadequate, they will be almost overwhelmed by the urge to make management changes to improve the likelihood of higher future proceeds. Again, it is important when dealing with venture investors to remember that competition with other ventures for investors' funds restricts entrepreneurs' abilities to avoid such costs. Competition among potential investors is equally important. Such competition restricts an individual investor's ability to buy venture securities "on the cheap" and target above-market returns on their investments in your venture.

Typically, competition among venture equity investors results in stage-specific target rates. Recall that in Figure 7.1 we characterized ventures' risks of underperformance and failure as very high, high, moderate, and low. There is a natural progression from very high risk to low risk as a successful venture progresses from its development stage to its maturity stage and beyond. Figure 7.6 displays graphically how the expected target annual rates of return decrease along with these decreases in risk. The highest target annual rates of return are associated with equity seed financing during a venture's development stage. Target rates of return sought by startup investors also are very high but, on average, less than those sought by seed equity investors. Target rates of return continue to decline as venture investors provide first- and second-round financing. Equity investors expect the lowest annual rates on seasoned equity investments sold to the public.

---

[18] We discuss the design of venture investors' securities, including convertible bonds and preferred stock, in more detail in Chapter 13.

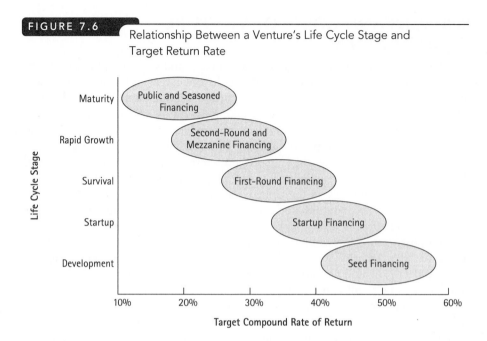

FIGURE 7.6

Relationship Between a Venture's Life Cycle Stage and Target Return Rate

Figure 7.7 presents a rough estimate of targeted annual returns and typical realized return ranges by stage in the life cycle.[19] Empirical data on returns earned by publicly traded corporations indicate that large capitalization stocks tend to provide annual rates of return in the low double digits while successful small capitalization stocks provide annual rates of return in the high teens. A representative target rate of 15 percent and a range of 12 to 18 have been historically reasonable for maturity-stage corporations.

At the other extreme, ventures in their development life cycle stage have the highest risk of not succeeding, and we have indicated a representative target rate of 50 percent with a typical range of 40 to 60 percent. We are aware that some venture investors claim to use target expected rates of return of 100 percent or even higher. While many ventures have realized returns well in excess of 100 percent, such outcomes are not representative of what venture investors set as a target return to use in evaluating an early-stage business plan. A representative target rate of 40 percent, with a range of 30 to 50 percent, is more reasonable for returns suggested by early-stage financial projections. Survival-stage ventures, also highly risky, face target returns a little lower than those faced by startups. Ventures in their rapid-growth stage actually vary in risk according to where they are in that stage. Early in the rapid-growth stage, business risk remains high as reflected in a representative target return of 30 percent per year with a range of 25 to 35 percent. Late rapid-growth-stage ventures become less

19   For one study providing ranges of target returns for different venture rounds, see Burton Dean and Joseph Giglierano, "Multistage Financing of Technical Start-Up Companies in Silicon Valley," *Journal of Business Venturing* 5 (November 1990): pp. 375–389.

FIGURE 7.7 Target Return Rates and Typical Rate Ranges by Life Cycle Stage

LIFE CYCLE STAGE	REPRESENTATIVE TARGET RATE	TYPICAL RANGE
Maturity	15%	12%–18%
Rapid growth		
Late rapid growth	25%	20%–30%
Early rapid growth	30%	25%–35%
Survival	35%	25%–45%
Startup	40%	30%–50%
Development	50%	40%–60%

risky and the representative target rate declines to 25 percent with a typical range being 20 to 30 percent.

While we have tried to give indicative target rates by maturity stage, it is important to remember that many individual ventures result in 100 percent loss and others provide only low-single-digit annual rates of realized return. To counterbalance these poor outcomes, venture investors have to restrict attention to firms that, when successful, offer returns well in excess of target rates. One of the characteristics of venture investing is high returns on some investments and −100 percent on others. Professional venture investing depends on having above-target winners offset losers. We explore professional venture investment more thoroughly in Chapter 11.

CONCEPT CHECK

- What is venture hubris?

7.6 WEIGHTED AVERAGE COST OF CAPITAL

The **weighted average cost of capital (WACC)** is simply a weighted average of the cost of the individual components of interest-bearing debt and common equity capital. The cost of debt is the interest rate the venture pays for borrowed funds, adjusted for the fact that interest is tax deductible.

Suppose we have a $1 venture that has issued $.50 of debt and $.50 of equity to capitalize the $1 value. If the interest rate on debt is 10 percent, the tax rate is 30 percent, and the required return on equity is 20 percent, the after-tax weighted average cost of capital is 13.5 percent. To see this, we can plug the numbers into the formula:

weighted average cost of capital (WACC)
weighted average of the cost of the individual components of interest-bearing debt and common equity capital

$$\text{After-Tax WACC} = (1 - \text{Tax Rate}) \times (\text{Debt Rate}) \times (\text{Debt to Value})$$
$$+ \text{Equity Rate} \times (1 - \text{Debt to Value})$$
$$= (.70 \times .10 \times .5) + (.20 \times .5)$$
$$= .135, \text{ or } 13.5\%$$

How Earning After-Tax WACC Satisfies All Investors

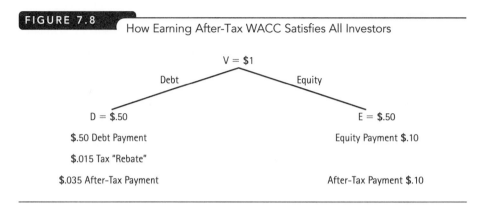

If this is a bit opaque, Figure 7.8 provides a graphical depiction equivalent to the mathematical formula. Each side of the tree in Figure 7.8 calculates the amount of money (on an after-tax basis) required to keep the investor happy.

A LIFE CYCLE–BASED WACC EXAMPLE

Although most early-stage financing is equity capital, the opportunity to use debt increases as a successful venture progresses through its life cycle. Development-stage ventures typically rely on equity seed capital from the entrepreneur, friends, and family. If the product or process development requires a long time and is expensive, the venture may need outside venture investors to provide additional equity capital.

We examine the debt-financing possibilities for a typical venture through its life cycle stages. Beta Omega Corporation was launched to develop chemical nutrients for food enhancement. Because of the development time and facilities required to grow algae-rich nutrients, Beta Omega needed external venture financing to supplement the equity capital provided by the entrepreneur, Joann So. She raised a total of $500,000 from venture investors who appraised the prospective investment using a target rate of return of 50 percent.

After developing a process to extract an oil-based nutrient from the algae, Beta Omega began marketing and selling enriched multivitamins. The nutrient additive was designed to increase a user's metabolism. Although the venture faced several struggles and product redevelopments, it moved into its survival stage, received an additional $500,000 in venture financing, and was about to enter its rapid-growth stage. Somewhat surprisingly, there was a definite seasonality in sales. (Sales peaked during the winter holiday season.) As a consequence, in order to produce and make credit sales to retailers, Beta Omega sought short-term financing from a local bank.

A bank loan of one year or less shows up on a venture's balance sheet as a note payable and may be in the form of an informal line of credit or a formal revolving-credit agreement. Both types of loans usually have cleanup clauses requiring the loan balance to be reduced to zero sometime during the year. These types of loans are sometimes called "self-liquidating loans." Beta Omega was able to borrow $100,000 at a 9 percent interest rate.

To help finance a growth in sales and accommodate sales seasonality, Beta Omega raised $500,000 in debt financing at an interest cost of 14 percent. At this point, Beta Omega's financial capital consisted of $600,000 in interest-bearing debt capital and $1 million in common equity capital. The effective tax rate for the venture was 30 percent. So wondered what had happened to Beta Omega's cost of capital as the venture transitioned from its development stage to its early rapid-growth stage. Since Beta Omega had both debt and equity in its financial structure, the venture's cost of capital was an average of the debt and equity components.

Beta Omega's estimated WACC started with the after-tax interest costs on the two outstanding loans. Since the venture had a 30 percent income tax rate, the effective after-tax cost of the 9 percent bank loan was 6.3 percent [9 percent × (1 − .30)]. Likewise, the 14 percent before-tax cost on the long-term debt implied an after-tax cost of 9.8 percent.

As previously discussed, the cost of equity capital is an implicit cost (expected capital gains). For firms with publicly traded stocks, we use methods like the CAPM to estimate the cost of equity capital. For private equity ventures, we must start with normal equity returns and add premiums for illiquidity, uncompensated advisory services, and venture hubris (in business plan projections). The previous section introduced representative rates reflecting these adjustments. At the time, So estimated Beta Omega's cost of venture equity capital to be 25 percent.

With this preparation, So was set to calculate her venture's weighted average cost of capital. We can replicate her analysis by determining the total amount of interest-bearing and equity capital. We can determine the percentage weight of each component. Next, we will need to multiply the after-tax cost of each component times its percentage weight and sum these products. The result is her venture's WACC. For Beta Omega, the calculations are:

FINANCIAL CAPITAL	DOLLAR AMOUNT	PERCENTAGE WEIGHT	×	AFTER-TAX COST	=	COMPONENT COST
Note payable	$ 100,000	6.25%	×	.063	=	.39%
Long-term debt	500,000	31.25	×	.098	=	3.06
Equity	1,000,000	62.50	×	.250	=	15.63
	$1,600,000	100.00%		WACC	=	19.08%

The 19 percent (rounded) WACC is much lower than Beta Omega's cost of capital (all equity) in its development stage (50 percent). The decline in the venture's capital costs (and access to debt) was due to gaining an operating history and the perception that Beta Omega had significantly reduced its risk (with less venture hubris reflected in its financial projections). This progress and realism, along with the tax deductibility of interest payments, led to the 19 percent WACC.

USING WACC TO COMPLETE THE CALIBRATION OF EVA

We can use the WACC information to calculate a venture's economic value added (EVA). Recall in Chapter 4 that we defined EVA as:

$$\text{EVA} = \text{Net Operating Profit After Taxes}$$
$$- \text{After-Tax Dollar Cost of Financial Capital Used}$$

where net operating profit after taxes, or NOPAT, is:

$$\text{NOPAT} = \text{EBIT}(1 - \text{Effective Tax Rate})$$

Assume that Beta Omega had $4 million in revenues with earnings before interest and taxes (EBIT) of $500,000. Its NOPAT was $350,000 [$500,000 × (1 − .30)]. To calculate the EVA-imposed financial capital cost, we need to determine the amount of financial capital used. Recall that the sum of the interest-bearing debt and common equity capital was $1.6 million and that the WACC was 19 percent. Taking the product of these two gives the cost of the financial capital used:

$$\text{After-Tax Dollar Cost of Financial Capital Used} = \$1,600,000 \times .19 = \$304,000$$

EVA then is estimated to be:

$$\$350,000 - \$304,000 = \$46,000$$

To summarize, Beta Omega's operations generated $350,000 of NOPAT. In doing so, Beta Omega incurred explicit and implicit financing costs in the amount of $304,000. Beta Omega's NOPAT exceeded the dollar cost of financial capital used. In particular, it generated a positive EVA of $46,000 for the year. EVA is one measure of the amount of economic gain accomplished during that year.

CONCEPT CHECK

- What is meant by the weighted average cost of capital?

SUMMARY

The main conceptual purpose of this chapter is to impress upon entrepreneurs that a new venture must pay its explicit bills (expenses) and its implicit bills (cost of financial capital). Failure to provide a return for investors will almost certainly result in the lack of access to capital to fund the current venture. It is also likely that the entrepreneur will have difficulty raising funds for the next venture she wishes to launch; as investors note the lack of an adequate return, they will look elsewhere for leadership capable of providing such a return.

To get a better idea of the total implicit and explicit capital costs, we introduced the cost of debt capital (interest and principal payments) and the cost of equity capital (dividends and capital gains). We modified our basic approach to the cost of equity with a discussion of the role of venture hubris and how venture investors set target return rates for their investments in your venture. We completed our discussion of financial capital costs by combining the various costs to get the venture's weighted average cost of capital.

KEY TERMS

bond rating
closely held corporations
coefficient of variation
default risk
default risk premium (DRP)
expected rate of return
inflation
inflation premium (IP)
interest rate
investment risk of loss
investment risk premium (IRP)
liquidity premium (LP)

market capitalization
(or "market cap")
market risk premium (MRP)
maturity premium (MP)
nominal interest rate
organized securities exchange
over-the-counter (OTC) market
prime rate
private equity investors
private financial markets
public financial markets
publicly traded stock investors

real interest rate (RR)
risk-free interest rate
senior debt
standard deviation
subordinated debt
term structure of interest rates
venture hubris
weighted average cost of capital
(WACC)
yield curve

DISCUSSION QUESTIONS

1. Describe how the costs of debt and equity differ from the perspective of accounting measures.

2. How do private and public financial markets differ?

3. Briefly describe venture debt capital and venture equity capital.

4. What is an interest rate? What is default risk?

5. What is a meant by a nominal interest rate? Describe a risk-free interest rate and a real rate of interest.

6. Define "inflation." What is meant by an inflation premium?

7. Define the term "default risk premium."

8. What is meant by a prime rate?

9. What is a bond rating?

10. What is a liquidity risk premium? What is a maturity risk premium?

11. What is meant by the term structure of interest rates? What is a yield curve?

12. Describe the differences between senior debt and subordinated debt.

13. Explain the meaning of investment risk of loss and describe how risk can be defined relative to an average value.

14. Describe the following: (a) expected rate of return, (b) standard deviation, and (c) coefficient of variation.

15. Describe the historical average annual return relationships among long-term U.S. government bonds, corporate bonds, small-firm common stocks, and large-firm common stocks.

16. What is the difference between private equity investors and publicly traded stock investors?

17. How does an organized securities exchange differ from an over-the-counter market?

18. What is meant by an investment risk premium? What is a market risk premium?

19. What rates of return at various horizons have venture capitalists earned, on average, in recent years? How do these returns compare with the average venture capital returns over the past twenty years?

20. How do we estimate the cost of equity capital for private ventures? In developing your answer describe the major components that are considered when estimating the rates of return required by venture investors.

21. What discount rates are typically used for development-stage, startup-stage, survival-stage, and early-growth-stage ventures?

22. What is meant by the weighted average cost of capital or WACC?

INTERNET ACTIVITIES

1. Access the Federal Reserve Board of Governors Web site at http://www.federalreserve.gov/releases/ to find current interest rates (and foreign exchange rates) relevant to your business venture.

2. Access http://www.bloomberg.com for interest rates and financial market news. Summarize the current financial market conditions.

3. Access http://www.pwcmoneytree.com for a summary of recent venture capital investment performance. Summarize the return experience for the various venture-investing rounds.

EXERCISES/PROBLEMS

1. Voice River, Inc., provides media-on-demand services via the Internet. Management has been studying current interest rates. A lender is willing to make a two-year loan to Voice River at a 12 percent annual interest rate. The U.S. government is currently paying 8 percent annual interest on its two-year securities.
   A. If the real rate of interest is expected to be 3 percent annually, what is the inflation premium expected at this time?
   B. What is the amount of the total risk premium that Voice River will have to pay?
   C. If a 1 percent liquidity premium is built into the 12 percent rate, what is the default risk premium on the loan?

2. Following is interest rate information currently being observed by the Electronic Publishing Corporation:

One-year U.S. government securities	4.5%
One-year bank loans	6.0
Five-year U.S. government securities	7.0
Five-year bank loans	9.5

   A. What is the amount of the maturity risk premium on one-year versus five-year U.S. government securities?
   B. What is the amount of the maturity risk premium on one-year versus five-year bank loans?
   C. What is the default risk premium on one-year bank loans and on five-year bank loans?

3. A venture investor, BKAngel, is considering investing in a software venture opportunity. However, the rate of return to be realized next year is likely to vary with the economic climate that actually occurs. Following are three possible economic outcomes, the probability that each one will occur, and the rate of return projected for each outcome:

ECONOMIC CLIMATE	PROBABILITY OF OCCURRENCE	RATE OF RETURN
Recession	.25	−20.0%
Normal	.50	15.0
Rapid growth	.25	30.0

A. What is the expected rate of return on the software venture?

B. Calculate the variance and standard deviation of the rates of return for the software venture.

C. Calculate the coefficient of variation of the rates of return for the software venture. If the coefficient of variation of the rates of return for BKAngel's prior venture investments is 1.5, would the software venture be considered as being less or more risky?

4. A potential venture investment has the following possible outcomes:

PERFORMANCE OUTCOME	PROBABILITY OF OCCURRENCE	RATE OF RETURN
Home run (success)	.15	500.0%
Breakeven	.35	15.0
Strikeout (failure)	.50	−100.0

A. What is the expected rate of return on the venture?

B. Calculate the variance and standard deviation of the rates of return for the venture.

C. Calculate the coefficient of variation of the rates of return for the venture. If the coefficient of variation of the rates of return for your prior venture investments is 4.0, would the new venture be considered as being less or more risky?

5. Three venture investments previously made by BKAngel, a venture investor, achieved the following outcomes for the year just completed:

VENTURE OPPORTUNITY	INITIAL VALUE	CASH FLOW	ENDING VALUE
Venture 1	$300,000	$75,000	$600,000
Venture 2	$400,000	$50,000	$300,000
Venture 3	$300,000	−$60,000	$360,000

A. Calculate the percentage rate of return for each of the venture investments.

B. Calculate the expected rate of return for a portfolio of these three venture investments weighted by each venture's investment share of a total $1 million investment.

C. Calculate the variance and standard deviation of the rates of returns for the portfolio investment.

D. Calculate the coefficient of variation of the rates of returns for the portfolio investment. Is this portfolio investment less or more risky than another investment opportunity with a coefficient of variation of 1.5?

6. Refer to Problem 5. Assume that BKAngel's initial investments in the three ventures had been Venture 1 = $500,000, Venture 2 = $300,000, and Venture 3 = $200,000, with each investment having achieved the same cash flows and ending values shown in Problem 5.

A. Calculate the percentage rate of return for each of the venture investments.

B. Calculate the expected rate of return for a portfolio of these three venture investments weighted by each venture's investment share of a total $1 million investment.

C. Calculate the variance, standard deviation, and coefficient of variation of the rates of returns for the portfolio investment.

7. Jerry's Tree Services is trying to raise debt funds from a prospective venture investor, SureWay LLC. SureWay indicated to Jerry Lau that the annual interest rate on risky venture loans is currently 15 percent. Jerry is seeking a three-year loan with annual payments. He is willing to pay back $100,000 at the end of three years. However, because of cash flow problems, he can afford to pay interest at only a 12 percent annual rate.

   A. Calculate the dollar amount that SureWay venture investors would lend to Jerry's Tree Services.

   B. What would be the dollar amount of the loan if the loan is made for only two years?

8. Refer to Problem 7. Show how your answer to Part A of Problem 7 would change if Jerry were willing to pay 16 percent annual interest and a principal payment of $100,000 at the end of three years.

9. Following is the rate-of-return component information for FirstVenture investors:

RATE COMPONENT	RETURN COMPONENT
Liquidity premium	5.5%
Risk-free rate	6
Advisory premium	9
Investment risk premium	11.5
Target rate of return	40

   A. Calculate the expected rate of return before considering premiums for illiquidity, advisory activities, and hubris projections.

   B. Estimate the hubris projections premium for this FirstVenture investment.

10. Use the following information to estimate the VentureBanc investors' target rate of return:

RATE COMPONENT	RETURN COMPONENT
Liquidity premium	5%
Risk-free rate	6
Advisory premium	9
Market risk premium	7.5
Hubris projection premium	15

   A. VentureBanc uses a systematic risk measure of 2.0. Based on the information shown, estimate VentureBanc's investment risk premium. Then estimate the cost of equity capital for VentureBanc.

   B. Determine the rate components and their returns that a venture investor like VentureBanc would require to be covered beyond a traditional cost-of-equity estimate.

   C. What overall venture investment discount rate would be used by VentureBanc?

11. Kareem Construction Company has the following amounts of interest-bearing debt and common equity capital:

FINANCING SOURCE	DOLLAR AMOUNT	INTEREST RATE	COST OF CAPITAL
Short-term loan	$200,000	12%	
Long-term loan	$200,000	14%	
Equity capital	$600,000		22%

   Kareem Construction is in the 30 percent average tax bracket.

A. Calculate the after-tax weighted average cost of capital (WACC) for Kareem.

B. Determine the after-tax dollar cost of financial capital used by Kareem.

C. Kareem's earnings before interest and taxes (EBIT) was $300,000. Calculate Kareem's net operating profit after taxes (NOPAT).

D. Calculate Kareem's economic value added (EVA). Did the venture build or destroy value?

12. Refer to the Kareem Construction Company example in Problem 11.

A. Show how Kareem's WACC would change if the tax rate dropped to 25 percent and the estimated cost of equity capital were based on a risk-free rate of 7 percent, a market risk premium of 8 percent, and a systematic risk measure or beta of 2.0.

B. Also assume that Kareem's EBIT was only $240,000. Calculate the venture's economic value added and indicate whether the Kareem Construction Company was building or destroying value.

13. Voice River, Inc., has successfully moved through its early life cycle stages and now is well into its rapid-growth stage. However, by traditional standards this provider of media-on-demand services is still considered to be a relatively small venture. The interest rate on long-term U.S. government securities is currently 7 percent. Voice River's management has observed that, over the long run, the average annual rate of return on small-firm stocks has been 17.3 percent, while the annual returns on long-term U.S. government securities has averaged 5.7 percent. Management views Voice River as being an average small-company venture at its current life cycle stage.

A. Determine the historical average annual market risk premium for small-firm common stocks.

B. Use the capital asset pricing model (CAPM) to estimate the cost of common equity capital for Voice River.

14. Voice River, Inc., is interested in estimating its weighted average cost of capital (WACC) now that it is in its rapid-growth stage. Voice River has a $500,000, 10 percent interest, short-term bank loan; a $1.5 million, 12 percent interest, long-term debt issue; and $42 million in common equity. The venture is in the 35 percent income tax bracket.

A. Determine the after-tax costs of the bank loan and the long-term debt issue.

B. Calculate the WACC for Voice River, Inc., using the cost of common equity capital estimated in Problem 13.

15. Refer to Problem 14 for Voice River, Inc.

A. Estimate the WACC if the cost of common equity capital is 20 percent.

B. Estimate the WACC if the cost of common equity capital is at the representative target rate of 25 percent for typical ventures in their late rapid-growth life cycle stage.

M I N I   C A S E

Alpha One Software Corporation

The Alpha One Software Corporation was organized to develop software products that would provide Internet-based firms with information about their customers. As a result of initial success, the venture's premier product allows firms with subscriber bases to predict customer profiles, retention, and satisfaction.

continued on next page

Alpha One Software Corporation (continued)

Arlene Io received an undergraduate degree in computer science and information systems from a major northeastern university four years ago. The Omega Subscriber Software Product was developed and test-marketed with the help of two of her classmates; Alpha One Software Corporation was up and running within one year. Venture capital was obtained to start up operations; a second round of venture financing helped Alpha One to move through its survival stage. Product success in the marketplace has allowed the venture to achieve such rapid sales growth that it now is able to get bank loans and to issue long-term debt. The interest rate on the bank loan is 10 percent. An effective cost for the long-term debt will need to be determined; the cost of common equity was estimated using a risk-free rate of 7 percent and a risk premium of 13 percent.

Arlene Io has now reached the point of being able to consider whether Alpha One is adding economic value in terms of its net operating profit after taxes (NOPAT) and its weighted average cost of capital (WACC). Based on the most recent years' financial statements, Io was interested in answering the following:

A. What is Alpha One's NOPAT? Why does the NOPAT differ from the earnings after taxes?
B. Estimate the effective before-tax cost of the long-term debt.
C. Estimate the effective after-tax cost of the bank loan and the long-term debt.
D. Estimate the cost of common equity capital.
E. Determine the financial structure weights for the two interest-bearing debt components and the common equity.
F. What is Alpha One's WACC?
G. Determine the dollar cost of financial capital used.
H. Estimate Alpha One's economic value added (EVA).

Alpha One Software Corporation

INCOME STATEMENT	2007
Net sales	$1,500,000
Cost of goods sold	−850,000
Gross profit	650,000
General and administrative expenses	−250,000
Marketing	−206,000
Depreciation	−50,000
Earnings before interest and taxes	144,000
Interest	−84,000
Earnings before taxes	60,000
Income taxes (40% rate)	−24,000
Earnings after taxes	$ 36,000

Alpha One Software Corporation

BALANCE SHEET	2007
Cash	$20,000
Accounts receivable	250,000
Inventories	350,000
Total current assets	620,000

Alpha One Software Corporation (continued)

Fixed assets, net	480,000
Total assets	$1,100,000
Accounts payable	$ 125,000
Accrued liabilities	125,000
Notes payable	100,000
Total current liabilities	350,000
Long-term debt	500,000
Common stock (20,000 shares)	100,000
Retained earnings	150,000
Total liabilities and equity	$1,100,000

Chapter 8

SECURITIES LAW CONSIDERATIONS WHEN OBTAINING VENTURE FINANCING

PREVIOUSLY COVERED

Chapter 7 covered the types and costs of financial capital. We discussed how different financial securities have risk characteristics associated with market-determined required returns for those who bear the risks and explained why venture investors seek relatively high expected returns on their investments.

LOOKING AHEAD

In Part 4, we shift our focus to creating and recognizing venture value. Chapter 9 covers the fundamentals of financial valuation from an equity perspective. We show how the venture's current value derives from its ability to generate future cash flows that can be disbursed to investors. We focus on the value created when the venture completes its rapid-growth stage and enters maturity. Venture capital valuation methods are discussed in Chapter 10.

CHAPTER LEARNING OBJECTIVES

It is often necessary to comply with securities laws when raising external financial capital. In this chapter, we introduce several major legal aspects of fundraising for the new venture. We discuss the central role of the Securities Act of 1933 and the exemptions available to ventures seeking to issue securities without having to register them with the Securities and Exchange Commission. After completing this chapter, you will be able to:

1. Identify four relevant components of the federal securities laws

2. Explain what is meant by blue-sky laws

3. Define "security" according to the Securities Act of 1933 and explain why such a designation matters

4. Describe what is involved in registering securities with the Securities and Exchange Commission (SEC)

5. Identify some of the securities that are exempt from registration with the SEC

6. Identify some transaction exemptions granted under the Securities Act of 1933

7. Describe and discuss how the SEC's Regulation D serves as a securities registration "safe harbor"

8. Explain how Rules 504, 505, and 506 of Regulation D differ from one another

9. Describe Regulation A and explain how and when it is used

You have finished your initial feasibility study and started your business plan. Finding yourself in the typical position, you realize that the venture will quickly deplete all present and potential personal financial resources. You must consider how and when to use other people's money. We want you to realize that, at such a point, you stand at the doorway to the complex, confusing, rewarding, and hazardous world of financial securities. While most of this textbook deals with the financial aspects of venture securities markets, the advantage of familiarity with the legal aspects of those same markets cannot be overemphasized. Your business plan must allow the time and money necessary to secure proper legal advice from attorneys who specialize in tracking, interpreting, and applying the ever-changing securities laws.

Selling securities to the general public to raise financial capital is time consuming and may cost hundreds of thousands of dollars in accounting, legal, and investment banking fees. As a consequence, most ventures attempt to raise financial capital from business angels, venture capitalists, or other private investors through sales of securities that are exempt from federal registration requirements. It is essential that entrepreneurs understand and comply with both federal and state securities laws when raising financial capital.[1] Noncompliance may lead to fines, damage penalties, and even prison time.

8.1 REVIEW OF SOURCES OF EXTERNAL VENTURE FINANCING

During the development and startup stages, an entrepreneur is likely to be focused on identifying, developing, and bringing a product, service, or process to the market. Little consideration is usually given to the amounts and number of "rounds" of financing needed to get the venture successfully through its

---

[1] While we discuss the basics of securities law as it relates to the public and private offerings of securities, it is important to understand that we are not providing legal advice. When you contemplate the issuing of securities, it is advisable to hire a securities law specialist. There are a number of references that will further help you understand securities law basics. For example, see Constance E. Bagley, *Managers and the Legal Environment*, 4th ed. (New York: West/Thomson Learning, 2002), chap. 24.

rapid-growth stage. Figure 8.1 presents the external venture financing typically needed during the development, startup, survival, and rapid-growth stages. As we have said before, seed financing during the development stage is generally provided by the entrepreneur's assets and by family and friends. Some ventures survive with an initial amount of financing and grow only as fast as the funds generated from business operations will allow.

In other cases, the entrepreneur's own finances and those of friends and family are inadequate. This leads the entrepreneur to seek financing from business angels and venture capitalists. Business angels generally want some kind of ownership claim (not straight debt) structured as common stock or as a security that can be converted into common stock. Venture capitalists also seek equity positions in the venture and, at least in the United States, have a strong tendency to structure their investments as preferred stock (see Chapters 10 and 13) that is convertible into common stock.

Ventures in the survival stage need what is often referred to as first-round financing. While some venture capitalists provide startup financing, it is more common for professional venture capital firms to begin investing in a venture during this "first round." Most venture capitalists will plan to participate in subsequent rounds for the same venture. Chapter 11 discusses professional venture capital firms and their operations. Since commercial banks usually require that a venture demonstrate financially successful operations before lending to that venture, they are not usually expected to be a source of financing at this stage.

Rapid-growth-stage firms with large financing needs typically seek second-round funding from existing and new venture capitalist investors. Commercial banks become potential providers of debt financing. Mezzanine financing to build working capital investments in receivables and inventories arises during this stage. Such financing is frequently a hybrid of debt and equity. During the latter part of a venture's rapid-growth stage, investment bankers facilitate liquidity-stage financing

---

FIGURE 8.1   Types and Sources of External Venture Financing by Life Cycle Stage

LIFE CYCLE STAGE	TYPE OF VENTURE FINANCING	MAJOR SOURCES	TYPICAL BUSINESS ORGANIZATION
Development stage	Seed financing	Entrepreneur Family and friends	Proprietorship, partnership, LLC, or corporation
Startup stage	Startup financing	Entrepreneur Family and friends Business angels Venture capitalists	Proprietorship, partnership, LLC, or corporation
Survival stage	First-round financing	Venture capitalists Commercial banks	LLC or corporation
Rapid-growth stage	Second-round financing Mezzanine financing Liquidity-stage financing	Venture capitalists Commercial banks Venture lenders/investors Investment bankers	Corporation

by orchestrating a venture's initial public offering. Alternatively, they may be involved in arranging the venture's sale to an acquirer that can provide further funding for the venture's expansion.

In Figure 8.1, we associate four forms of business organizations—proprietorship, partnership, limited liability company (LLC), and corporation—with venture life cycles. During the first two life cycle stages adequate external financing may be possible with all of the standard business structures: a proprietorship (if none of the external financing is equity), a partnership, a limited liability company (LLC), or a corporation. However, as ventures reach the survival stage and expand in the rapid-growth stage, larger financing sources and rounds necessitate a more flexible structure, like that typically available for a corporation. This listing of business structures, however, should not be perceived as suggesting that ventures evolve their structures as they grow. Changing organizational structure (e.g., from proprietorship to corporation) can involve very costly legal and accounting fees. Some thought (with competent legal counsel) should be given to whether there is any advantage to starting with a structure that is likely to be changed as the venture grows.

Figure 8.2 reviews selected financial and legal characteristics for proprietorships (partnerships are similar), LLCs, and corporations. These factors, as well as tax considerations and future ambitions, influence the initial choice of business organization. By definition, a proprietorship has a single owner, which means that additional venture funds must be in the form of debt or borrowings typically from family and friends. If the entrepreneur projects the need for a single, reasonably small infusion of outside equity (ownership) capital, the proprietorship may need to transition into a general or limited partnership. While a proprietorship requires little time and low legal costs to get started and many times exists by default, recall from our discussion in Chapter 3 that a moderate amount of time and legal costs should be incurred to form a partnership.

Ventures in the rapid-growth stage often find it desirable, or even necessary, to seek new investors through large private or public offerings. To conserve on accounting and legal hassles in these later stages, it's important for new, ambitious

FIGURE 8.2   Selected Business Organizational Forms, Financial Considerations, and Legal Characteristics

ORGANIZATIONAL FORM	NUMBER OF OWNERS AND OWNER'S EASE OF STARTUP	INVESTOR LIABILITY	EQUITY CAPITAL SOURCES	FIRM LIFE AND LIQUIDITY OF OWNERSHIP
Proprietorship	One; little time and low legal costs	Unlimited	Owner, family, and friends	Life determined by owner; often difficult to transfer ownership
Limited liability company (LLC)	One or more, with no limit; time consuming and high legal costs	Limited to owners' investments	Venture investors and equity offerings to owners	Life set by owners; often difficult to transfer ownership
Corporation	One or more, with no limit; time consuming and high legal costs	Limited to shareholders' investments	Venture investors and common shareholders	Unlimited life; usually easy to transfer ownership

ventures to be aware of this eventuality and plan accordingly. Anticipation often leads such ventures to incur the costs of organizing as a corporation (or possibly an LLC) at the very beginning of, or at least very early in, the life cycle.

A business angel typically invests in the equity of an LLC or a nonpublic (subchapter S or C) corporation. The investment decision involves a direct negotiation between the entrepreneur and the business angel, who usually wants a substantial ownership interest for a specified investment amount. Venture capitalists also prefer equity investments in nonpublic corporations with the contractual arrangements spelled out in "term sheets," as well as in legal contracts. We cover the contents of term sheets in Chapter 11 when we discuss professional venture capital firms. While equity investments by business angels and venture capitalists require the preparation of legal ownership and investment documents, they avoid some of the more onerous provisions of federal and state securities laws.

CONCEPT CHECK

- What are the major sources involved in providing external venture financing?
- Identify some of the financial and legal differences across several forms of business organization.

8.2 OVERVIEW OF FEDERAL AND STATE SECURITIES LAWS

These concepts are at the heart of securities laws: (1) Prospective investors should have all relevant information necessary to make informed investment decisions; (2) investors in securities available to the general public should not be permitted to benefit from nonpublic or inside information; and (3) deceived investors should receive relief in the event of securities fraud. Securities creations, transactions, issuers, and advisers are regulated by federal and state laws. Figure 8.3 shows the regulatory objectives and the federal laws passed to achieve those objectives. We will discuss them in the sequence given.

SECURITIES ACT OF 1933

Securities Act of 1933
main body of federal law governing the creation and sale of securities

The main body of federal law governing the creation and sale of securities is the **Securities Act of 1933**. Passed in response to abuses thought to have contributed to the Great Depression, the core principles of the law have remained substantially the same as when originally enacted. The most important aspects of the law relate to securities fraud, requirements to register securities formally with the federal government, and the nature and authority of the Securities and Exchange Commission where such registrations are filed. Most of this chapter deals with this act, its interpretation, and the current SEC rules governing securities issues.

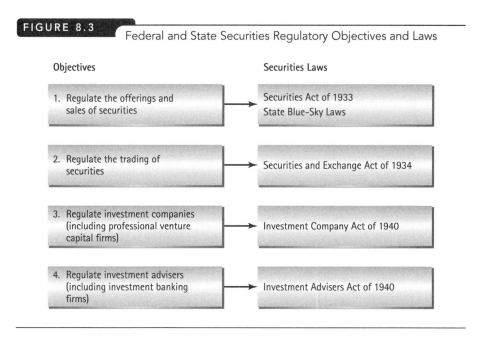

FIGURE 8.3 Federal and State Securities Regulatory Objectives and Laws

SECURITIES EXCHANGE ACT OF 1934

It is important to understand that the federal securities laws were originally passed in two installments, the Securities Act of 1933, and the **Securities Exchange Act of 1934**, which deals with the mechanisms and standards for public securities trading. In the 1934 act's own wording, the act is:

> *To provide for the regulation of securities exchanges and of over-the-counter markets operating in interstate and foreign commerce and through the mails, to prevent inequitable and unfair practices on such exchanges and markets, and for other purposes.*

The provisions of the act involve many important aspects of securities law, including insider trading and buying on margin. Because the 1934 act primarily relates to the exchange of publicly traded securities, it is of less immediate interest to early-stage ventures than the 1933 act. The 1934 act's restrictions and provisions will be important for a late-stage venture issuing securities to the public, particularly when those securities will be listed on a national securities exchange.

INVESTMENT COMPANY ACT OF 1940

The **Investment Company Act of 1940** provides a definition of an "investment company." Investment companies have very specific regulations that must be carefully followed. They are excluded from using some of the registration exemptions originating in the 1933 act. Recall that venture capital firms are formed for the sole purpose of pooling together investor funds used to provide venture capital. Professional venture capital firms are investment companies, and any attempt

Securities Exchange Act of 1934
federal law that deals with the mechanisms and standards for public security trading

Investment Company Act of 1940
federal law that defines an "investment company"

to structure one requires conformity with the provisions of the Investment Company Act of 1940.

INVESTMENT ADVISERS ACT OF 1940

Investment Advisers Act of 1940

federal law that focuses on people and organizations that seek to provide financial advice to investors and defines "investment adviser"

The **Investment Advisers Act of 1940** (as amended) addresses people and organizations that seek to provide financial advice to investors. It also defines important terms like "investment adviser":

> *"Investment adviser" means any person who, for compensation, engages in the business of advising others, either directly or through publications or writings, as to the value of securities or as to the advisability of investing in, purchasing, or selling securities, or who, for compensation and as part of a regular business, issues or promulgates analyses or reports concerning securities; but does not include (A) a bank, or any bank holding company as defined in the Bank Holding Company Act of 1956 which is not an investment company; (B) any lawyer, accountant, engineer, or teacher whose performance of such services is solely incidental to the practice of his profession; (C) any broker or dealer whose performance of such services is solely incidental to the conduct of his business as a broker or dealer and who receives no special compensation therefore; (D) the publisher of any bona fide newspaper, news magazine or business or financial publication of general and regular circulation; (E) any person whose advice, analyses, or reports relate to no securities other than securities which are direct obligations of or obligations guaranteed as to principal or interest by the United States, or securities issued or guaranteed by corporations in which the United States has a direct or indirect interest which shall have been designated by the Secretary of the Treasury, pursuant to section 3(a)(12) of the Securities Exchange Act of 1934, as exempted securities for the purposes of that Act; or (F) such other persons not within the intent of this paragraph, as the Commission may designate by rules and regulations or order.*

One of the major requirements in Section 203(a) of this act is that:

> *Except as provided in subsection (b) and section 203A, it shall be unlawful for any investment adviser, unless registered under this section, to make use of the mails or any means or instrumentality of interstate commerce in connection with his or its business as an investment adviser.*

Investment banking firms advise and assist corporations on the structure, timing, and costs of issuing new securities and facilitate the sale of firms. Many investment banks also provide brokerage services and investment advice to prospective investors. Most investment banking firms must register under the Investment Advisers Act of 1940.

Again, our primary purpose here is to discuss a growing venture's fundraising through the issue of securities. While this process will almost certainly bring the venture into contact with registered investment advisers, such a designation will be of more concern for the financial experts (e.g., investment bankers) working with the venture or for those trying to "pitch" the venture's securities to their clients. For completeness, we have introduced four major components or acts to federal securities laws. However, our main interest lies with the Securities Act of 1933, which focuses on the regulation of the offerings and sales of securities.

STATE SECURITIES REGULATIONS: "BLUE-SKY" LAWS

In addition to being concerned about complying with the federal restrictions, issuers must consider restrictions imposed by the various states. These state laws are known as **blue-sky laws,** which are designed to protect individuals from investing in fraudulent security offerings.[2] While most state restrictions are designed to regulate the offerings and sales of securities, much like the Securities Act of 1933, sometimes state laws differ from federal ones. Thus, an issuer seeking exemption from federal registration will also need to seek state-by-state exemptions for all states in which the issuer and any offerees reside. There are current efforts to get states to adopt some version of the North American Security Administrator Association's Uniform Limited Offering Exemption, but these efforts have not yet resulted in uniform exemptions; therefore, security issuers still need to concern themselves with the particulars of each state's exemptions.

The Capital Markets Efficiency Act was passed in 1996 in part to provide more uniformity between federal and state securities laws. In general, states cannot require more filing detail than is required by the SEC. State registration requirements also are preempted in most initial public offerings registered with the SEC. Of course, while our emphasis is on federal laws, it is important that entrepreneurs not overlook appropriate state laws when contemplating the issuing of securities.

blue-sky laws
state laws designed to protect individuals from investing in fraudulent security offerings

CONCEPT
CHECK

- What are the four main acts of U.S. securities laws?
- What are blue-sky laws?

8.3 PROCESS FOR DETERMINING WHETHER SECURITIES MUST BE REGISTERED

Once an entrepreneur has decided that additional outside financial capital is needed to achieve the venture's sales growth and performance objectives, it is important to determine whether securities must be registered with the SEC. Figure 8.4 presents a decision tree related to SEC registration requirements. Our discussion follows this

---

[2] The term "blue-sky laws" apparently derived from unscrupulous individuals who tried to sell potential investors what amounted to nothing more than a "piece of the blue sky."

FIGURE 8.4 Process to Determine Whether Securities Must Be Registered with the SEC

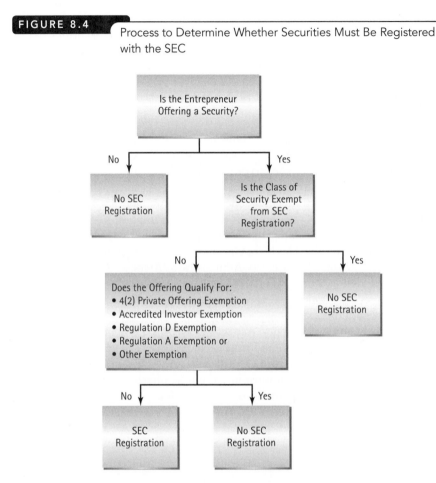

diagram. We start with the question: Is the entrepreneur offering a security? To answer this question, we need to see how the 1933 act treats the terms "offer," "sale," and "security."

OFFER AND SALE TERMS

The first two terms are defined in Section 2(3) of the 1933 act. The term "offer" (including "offer to sell" or "offer for sale") is "every attempt or offer to dispose of, or solicitation of an offer to buy, a security or interest in a security, for value." The term "sale" or "sell" includes "every contract of sale or disposition of a security or interest in a security, for value."

Section 2(3) further states:

The terms defined in this paragraph and the term "offer to buy" as used in subsection (c) of Section 5 shall not include preliminary negotiations or agreements between an issuer ... and any underwriter or among underwriters who are or are to be in privity of contract with an issuer.... Any security given or delivered with, or as a bonus on account of, any purchase of securities or any other thing, shall be conclusively presumed to constitute a part of the subject of such purchase and to have been offered and sold for value....

In most cases, venture financing involves an offer to sell some kind of financial contract for value. The key question will therefore be: Is the financial contract being offered a security?

WHAT IS A SECURITY?

The 1933 act gives quite broad latitude in what can constitute a security. In addition to traditional structures such as stocks and bonds (debentures), structures such as an investment contract, profit-sharing agreement, preorganization certificate or subscription, put, and call are included in the noncomprehensive listing.

According to Section 2(1) of the 1933 act:

The term "security" means any note, stock, treasury stock, bond, debenture, evidence of indebtedness, certificate of interest or participation in any profit-sharing agreement, collateral-trust certificate, preorganization certificate or subscription, transferable share, investment contract, voting-trust certificate, certificate of deposit for a security, fractional undivided interest in oil, gas, or other mineral rights, any put, call, straddle, option, or privilege on any security, certificate of deposit, or group or index of securities (including any interest therein or based on the value thereof), or any put, call, straddle, option, or privilege entered into on a national securities exchange relating to foreign currency, or, in general, any interest or instrument commonly known as a "security," or any certificate of interest or participation in, temporary or interim certificate for, receipt for, guarantee of, or warrant or right to subscribe to or purchase, any of the foregoing.

Given this very broad definition of what constitutes a "security," it is important to determine whether the financial contract offered is a security and therefore subject to securities regulation. Choosing to organize as a debt-free proprietorship allows the entrepreneur to be exempt from securities regulation. Recall from Figure 8.2 that a proprietorship requires little time and low legal costs to get started. The downside is that the owner has unlimited liability and is the only legal provider of equity capital, and it is often difficult to transfer ownership. A general partnership, where all partners are "active" participants in business operations, would most likely not be subject to securities regulation. A partnership's financial and legal characteristics are very similar to those for a proprietorship. A general partnership has two or more owners (partners), and its establishment requires only a moderate amount of time and legal costs to start. Recall from Chapter 3 that general partner liability is unlimited (i.e., there is joint and several liability), and equity capital can be provided only by the general partners. As in a proprietorship, it is often difficult to transfer ownership in a general partnership.

The SEC and most states consider ownership interests in limited liability companies (LLCs) to be securities. As previously noted, limited partnerships consist of one or more general partners and one or more limited partners. Since the limited partners are "passive" investors, who also have limited liability, limited partnership offerings are considered securities. Furthermore, court cases have shown that even a general partnership can, in specific circumstances, constitute a security when the partner is expected to be passive.[3]

Investments or instruments in the form of stocks and bonds of public and private firms are easily identifiable as securities. Investment contracts or instruments can also be considered securities if money is invested in a common enterprise where profits are dependent on the efforts of others. Promissory notes and other instruments of indebtedness may (or may not) be securities, depending on the facts of each case.[4] Thus, unless you're dreaming of someone just giving you the money, almost any way you can think of raising financing from an outside passive investor probably involves the creation and sale of a security.

It is also important to recognize that, under current law, one need not actually sell a security to trigger the securities laws; one need only offer to sell the security. All this can make an entrepreneur a little nervous (as it should) about picking up the phone and calling an old friend three states away to see if she wants to invest in the venture.

Now that we have a better idea what constitutes a security under the Securities Act of 1933, we can return to the decision tree in Figure 8.4 and answer the question: Is the entrepreneur offering a security? If the answer is "no" (which is rare), there is no SEC registration requirement. As an example, selling a general partnership interest where the partner is active won't usually involve the issue of a security as defined under the 1933 act. For the vast majority of venture offerings that involve securities, we advance to the next question: Is the class of security exempt from registration? For early-stage ventures, the answer is most likely "no," and we will have to advance to the final question of whether the structure of the offering allows it to be exempted from SEC registration. Before discussing exempt types of securities and exempt structures for the offerings, it is useful to examine more closely the federal registration requirement.

CONCEPT CHECK

- What is a security?
- When might a partnership investment involve a security?

---

[3]　See, for example, the list of cases given by Richard Harroch in "Federal Securities Law Considerations of Raising Capital," *Start-Up Companies: Planning, Financing, and Operating the Successful Business* (New York: Law Journal Seminars-Press, 1993).

[4]　For a discussion of the types of "tests" applied by the courts to determine whether an investment contract or instrument is a security, see Bagley, *Managers and the Legal Environment*.

8.4 REGISTRATION OF SECURITIES UNDER THE SECURITIES ACT OF 1933

In general—and there are exceptions—public offerings of securities in the United States must be registered with the Securities and Exchange Commission. The process of registration requires the filing of a description of the business and the security being offered, information about the management, and audited financial statements with the SEC, as well as distribution of that information to prospective investors through the issuance of a *prospectus*. It is important to note that the SEC does not judge the merits of the securities offering, but rather focuses on the accuracy and completeness of the information disclosed in the registration form filings and prospectus.

Section 5 of the 1933 act states:

(a)   *Unless a registration statement is in effect as to a security, it shall be unlawful for any person, directly or indirectly:*

   (1)   *To make use of any means or instruments of transportation or communication in interstate commerce or of the mails to sell such security through the use or medium of any prospectus or otherwise; or*

   (2)   *To carry or cause to be carried through the mails or in interstate commerce, by any means or instruments of transportation, any such security for the purpose of sale or for delivery after sale.*

(b)   *It shall be unlawful for any person, directly or indirectly:*

   (1)   *To make use of any means or instruments of transportation or communication in interstate commerce or of the mails to carry or transmit any prospectus relating to any security with respect to which a registration statement has been filed under this title, unless such prospectus meets the requirements of Section 10; or*

   (2)   *To carry or to cause to be carried through the mails or in interstate commerce any such security for the purpose of sale or for delivery after sale, unless accompanied or preceded by a prospectus that meets the requirements of subsection (a) of Section 10.*

(c)   *It shall be unlawful for any person, directly or indirectly, to make use of any means or instruments of transportation or communication in interstate commerce or of the mails to offer to sell or offer to buy through the use or medium of any prospectus or otherwise any security, unless a registration statement has been filed as to such security, or while the registration statement is the subject of a refusal order or stop order or (prior to the effective date of the registration statement) any public proceeding or examination under Section 8.*

To summarize, securities cannot be sold to the public before the securities are registered with the SEC. Registration involves filing the required forms (Form S-1 or Form SB-1 for small businesses), preparation of a prospectus, and the completion of a waiting period until the registration becomes effective with the SEC.

As previously noted, registering your securities with the SEC is a costly and time-consuming process and is usually done with the assistance of investment banking professionals in coordination with your venture's legal counsel.[5] We will discuss the initial public offering process and the role of investment bankers in Chapter 14, where we cover the harvesting of successful ventures.

Preparing the firm's historical accounting records and other disclosures for submission to the SEC can be a tedious process, particularly if the venture has not been accumulating registration-related information along the way. The extent of exposure a venture faces when registering an offering is significant. Appendix A to this chapter presents the thirty-two separate areas of disclosure specified in the 1933 act (as amended).

There have been many cases where securities issuers did not register and were subsequently found not to be exempt. The downside in this scenario can be significant. For example, one of the more common remedies for a fouled-up securities offering is a rescission of the offering, when all funds are returned to the investors. You can see how this unpleasant circumstance tends to hit your venture when it is already down. If your venture is solid and the future is a great place, your investors probably will not be interested in filing any complaints. Even if SEC problems were to arise, the investors probably would want to reinvest their funds after the legal details were worked out.

In contrast, if your venture is on the way down, many (if not all) of the investors will be thinking about whether your securities were properly issued. Complaints are not difficult or costly to file. An order to rescind the offering would leave you with a failing venture that cannot easily attract new investors and, usually, an obligation on your part (as a principal) to use your own funds to return the illegal offering's proceeds. One way to think about offerings that are both nonregistered and nonexempt is that such offerings extend free options to all of your investors. When the firm is prosperous, the put option (right to sell) given to investors is not exercised and the investors keep the securities (or reinvest after the mess is cleaned up). When the firm falters, the investors exercise the put and make you buy back the securities. To avoid packaging these unintended free put options in your securities offerings, either register or make sure you're exempted from registration. After all, you promise attractive upside returns in return for investors' willingness to sustain losses if things don't work out. However, you should not be in the business of providing investors with a poorly defined and unexpected money-back guarantee.

As an example of the way this asymmetric process works in the real world, consider the difficulties Lloyd's of London encountered with some of its investors.[6] Lloyd's, a U.K. insurance company known for its unique and sometimes bizarre insurance policies, raised money from U.S. investors, known as "names." Lloyd's has always considered the Lloyd's names as having liability like general partners, meaning that when a really bad year hits, any financial obligations not funded out of reserves held at Lloyd's could be collected from the names. In

---

[5] For a presentation of the process involved in conducting an initial public offering, see Constance E. Bagley and Craig E. Dauchy, *The Entrepreneur's Guide to Business Law* (New York: West/International Thomson Publishing, 1998), chap. 15.

[6] The *Rocky Mountain News* gives an excellent recounting of how Colorado's state securities regulators dealt with Lloyd's and the Colorado "names." "Names Behind the 'Names' Exclusive Report," *Rocky Mountain News*, October 6, 1996, p. 1B.

profitable years, the names received profit distributions for their willingness to invest and assume this role. For these years, the names did rather well and enjoyed the upside benefits of their investment in Lloyd's.

A few years back, Lloyd's financial condition headed south after some amazing losses on its insurance policies. Lloyd's started trying to collect from the U.S. names, who almost immediately went to state securities authorities, claiming that Lloyd's had issued nonexempt securities to the public without registration. While most of the disputes were settled without Lloyd's paying back the money originally invested by the U.S. names, to keep the legal matters from getting worse, Lloyd's in many cases agreed not to seek the additional funds to which it was entitled under the terms of the investment agreement. While not a totally free option, it is clear that Lloyd's lack of rigor in dealing with U.S. (and state) securities laws unintentionally softened investors' downsides.

In addition to the possibility that security regulators will alter your investment agreement to the benefit of the investors, the Securities Act of 1933 gives the SEC broad civil and some criminal procedures to use in enforcement. In securities law, it is important to remember the old saying "Ignorance is no defense." It is worth your time to investigate whether your venture can somehow issue the necessary securities under an exemption from the registration requirement.

Before we turn our attention to the classes of securities that are exempt from registration, a few words are in order about securities fraud. Section 17A of the 1933 act states:[7]

(a) *It shall be unlawful for any person in the offer or sale of any securities by the use of any means or instruments of transportation or communication in interstate commerce or by the use of the mails, directly or indirectly:*

   (1) *To employ any device, scheme, or artifice to defraud, or*

   (2) *To obtain money or property by means of any untrue statement of a material fact or any omission to state a material fact necessary in order to make the statements made, in the light of the circumstances under which they were made, not misleading, or*

   (3) *To engage in any transaction, practice, or course of business which operates or would operate as a fraud or deceit upon the purchaser.*

(b) *It shall be unlawful for any person, by the use of any means or instruments of transportation or communication in interstate commerce or by the use of the mails, to publish, give publicity to, or circulate any notice, circular, advertisement, newspaper, article, letter, investment service, or communication which, though not purporting to offer a security for sale, describes such security for a consideration received or to be received, directly or indirectly, from an issuer, underwriter, or dealer, without fully disclosing the receipt, whether past or prospective, of such consideration and the amount thereof.*

(c) *The exemptions provided in Section 3 shall not apply to the provisions of this section.*

---

[7] The federal laws frequently are predicated on some offending behavior affecting more than one state (fraudulent interstate transactions) owing to "states-rights" traditions and the notion that an infraction confined to one state is a state, not federal, matter.

Note point (c)'s declaration that there are no exemptions from these fraud provisions, even for securities otherwise exempted (from registration) in the act.

CONCEPT CHECK

• Why does it matter whether an investment is a security or not?

8.5   SECURITY EXEMPTIONS FROM REGISTRATION UNDER THE 1933 ACT

Now that we have introduced the 1933 act's registration requirements and restrictions, we return to the second question in the decision tree in Figure 8.4: Is the class of security exempt from registration? If the answer is "yes," we say that a "security exemption" is available and there will be no SEC registration requirement. If the answer is "no," then we face the final and most complicated of all of the questions in that tree. It asks if there is a "transaction exemption" available for the offering. First, we consider security exemptions.

Section 3 of the Securities Act of 1933 provides for certain classes of securities to be exempt from registration. Among the securities exempted in the 1933 act are:

1. Government securities (federal, state, and subdivisions thereof)
2. Securities issued by banks, savings and loans, and similar regulated thrifts
3. Certain securities issued by insurance companies
4. Certain not-for-profit organizations' securities
5. Certain securities involved in bankruptcy proceedings
6. Certain securities exchanged by issuers with existing security holders
7. Securities that are a part of an issue and sold only to persons resident within a single state or territory, where the issuer of such security is a person resident and doing business within, or, if a corporation, incorporated by and doing business within, such state or territory

So, for example, borrowing money from a bank does not create any securities registration responsibilities. Likewise, U.S. Treasury securities do not have to be registered with the SEC nor do the debt instruments issued by state and local governments. Furthermore, securities issued and sold only to residents of a single state where the issuer is also a resident of the same state do not have to be registered with the SEC.

From time to time, you can observe offerings seeking to be exempt based on the intrastate offering exemption. As we have already mentioned, the federal law leaves room for states to regulate their internal securities markets. The key here, of course, is "internal." To make effective use of this exemption, the issuer must ensure that offerees and purchasers are in the issuer's home state. While satisfying all of the restrictions on such an offering can be difficult and present serious problems in staged financing unless investors are committed not to move out of the issuer's state, there are some success stories involving intrastate offerings. A high-profile example of such success is Ben & Jerry's, which sold shares directly to the Vermont public in an exempted intrastate offering.

Some clarifications of the qualifications implied by phrases used in the intrastate exemption are available in SEC Rule 147. For example, regarding the nature of the issuer:

The issuer of the securities shall at the time of any offers and the sales be a person resident and doing business within the state or territory in which all of the offers, offers to sell, offers for sale and sales are made.

1. *The issuer shall be deemed to be a resident of the state or territory in which:*

    i. *it is incorporated or organized, if a corporation, limited partnership, trust or other form of business organization that is organized under state or territorial law;*

    ii. *its principal office is located, if a general partnership or other form of business organization that is not organized under any state or territorial law;*

    iii. *his principal residence is located, if an individual.*

2. *The issuer shall be deemed to be doing business within a state or territory if:*

    i. *the issuer derived at least 80 percent of its gross revenues and those of its subsidiaries on a consolidated basis*

        A. *for its most recent fiscal year, if the first offer of any part of the issue is made during the first six months of the issuer's current fiscal year; or*

        B. *for the first six months of its current fiscal year or during the twelve month fiscal period ending with such six month period, if the first offer of any part of the issue is made during the last six months of the issuer's current fiscal year from the operation of a business or of real property located in or from the rendering of services within such state or territory; provided, however, that this provision does not apply to any issuer which has not had gross revenues in excess of $5,000 from the sale of products or services or other conduct of its business for its most recent twelve month fiscal period;*

    ii. *the issuer had at the end of its most recent semi-annual fiscal period prior to the first offer of any part of the issue, at least 80 percent of its assets and those of its subsidiaries on a consolidated basis located within such state or territory;*

    iii. *the issuer intends to use and uses at least 80 percent of the net proceeds to the issuer from sales made pursuant to this rule in connection with the operation of a business or of real property, the purchase of real property located in, or the rendering of services within such state or territory; and*

    iv. *the principal office of the issuer is located within such state or territory.*

Rule 147 also provides some guidance on the issuer's responsibilities to be diligent in assuring that the offerees are in state and that the securities don't move across state lines:

1. *The issuer shall, in connection with any securities sold by it pursuant to this rule:*

    i. *Place a legend on the certificate or other document evidencing the security stating that the securities have not been registered under the Act and setting forth the limitations on resale contained in paragraph (e);*

ii. *Issue stop transfer instructions to the issuer's transfer agent, if any, with respect to the securities, or, if the issuer transfers its own securities, make a notation in the appropriate records of the issuer; and*

iii. *Obtain a written representation from each purchaser as to his residence.*

2. *The issuer shall, in connection with the issuance of new certificates for any of the securities that are part of the same issue that are presented for transfer during the time period specified in paragraph (e), take the steps required by subsections (f)(1)(i) and (ii).*

3. *The issuer shall, in connection with any offers, offers to sell, offers for sale or sales by it pursuant to this rule, disclose, in writing, the limitations on resale contained in paragraph (e) and the provisions of subsections (f)(1)(i) and (ii) and subparagraph (f)(2).*

The classes of securities relating to the government and specific industries (banking, insurance, and not-for-profit) listed above are unlikely to be sources of early-stage venture financing. Securities involved in bankruptcy proceedings or securities exchanges also would not be primary sources of venture funds. However, some entrepreneurs who have their ventures organized and operating in a specific state may find it useful to take advantage of the intrastate offering exemption under the 1933 act. If you choose to obtain venture financing through an intrastate offering, be sure you and your legal counsel extensively discuss the restrictions introduced by such an exemption. While not regulated by federal law, intrastate securities offerings are closely regulated by state securities laws.

To summarize, if you make only a qualifying intrastate securities offering, the offering is exempt from federal (SEC) registration. The other exempt classes of securities are not likely to be used by entrepreneurs trying to raise venture funding. Returning to Figure 8.4, it is not likely that an early-stage venture's securities fall within a class allowing exemption from SEC registration. We therefore continue on to the transactions exemptions.

CONCEPT CHECK

- What classes of securities are exempt from registration with the SEC?
- What is an intrastate offering?
- What is the purpose of SEC Rule 147?

8.6   TRANSACTION EXEMPTIONS FROM REGISTRATION UNDER THE 1933 ACT

The final question in Figure 8.4 asks: Does the offering qualify for...? and then lists several common transaction exemptions. Since early-stage ventures are likely to try to raise funds by issuing a nonexempt security, this is usually the most relevant question.

Figure 8.5 compares and contrasts several of the common transaction exemptions. There are three basic types of exemptions: (i) Section 4 exemptions,

FIGURE 8.5

Selected Limits and Other Characteristics by Type of SEC Registration Exemption

SEC EXEMPTION	AMOUNT OF OFFERING	NUMBER OF INVESTORS	QUALIFICATIONS OF INVESTORS
Section 4(2)	No limit	Small number	Must be sophisticated investors
Section 4(6)	$5 million limit	No limit on number of accredited investors	Must be accredited investors
Reg D: Rule 504	$1 million limit (in a 12-month period)	No limit	No specific qualifications
Reg D: Rule 505	$5 million limit (in a 12-month period)	35 unaccredited investors; no limit on accredited investors	No specific qualifications for unaccredited investors
Reg D: Rule 506	No limit	35 unaccredited investors; no limit on accredited investors	Unaccredited investors must have financial knowledge
Regulation A	$5 million limit (in a 12-month period)	No limit	No specific qualifications

(ii) Regulation D exemptions, and (iii) the Regulation A exemption. The primary Section 4 exemptions are the private offering exemption and the accredited investor exemption.

PRIVATE OFFERING EXEMPTION

The most widely used of the so-called transaction exemptions granted in the 1933 act is Section 4(2)'s "transactions by an issuer not involving any public offering," known as the private placement or offering exemption. While Section 4(2) introduces the notion that private offerings are not the target of SEC regulation, it also provides no definition of what constitutes a public offering. As is customary, the courts and experimental issuers were left to try to find the boundaries between public and private offerings. Although our present purpose is not to dive into the history of U.S. securities litigation, there are a couple of important cases that help shed some light on how we got to where we are today.[8]

In *SEC v. Ralston Purina* (1953), the U.S. Supreme Court took an important step toward defining a private (nonpublic) offering for the purposes of Section 4(2). The case involved the issue of securities to key employees of Ralston Purina. The Court found that, because Ralston Purina's offer included clerks and baker foremen who would not necessarily have access to the appropriate type of information, the offering did not fall within the exemption. Following in this vein, the courts and the SEC have continued to interpret the private placement exemption as applying to "sophisticated" offerees and purchasers who have access to the type of information a company would be compelled to disclose in a registration filing. In a concept we will see again, "sophisticated" investors having such information are assumed to be experienced and capable of watching out for their own financial interests.

---

[8] For a more detailed listing of related securities law precedents, see Harroch, "Federal Securities Law Considerations of Raising Capital."

A 1980 Ninth Circuit Court of Appeals decision (*SEC v. Murphy*) stated four considerations in determining an offering to be a private placement:

1. The number of offerees must be limited.
2. The offerees must be "sophisticated."
3. The size and the manner of the offering must not indicate widespread solicitation.
4. Some relationship between the offerees and the issuer must be present.

This decision included some discussion of these factors and highlighted that the restrictions apply to offerees, not just purchasers. It also argued that an issuer seeking this exemption had a burden of proof regarding the restricted number of offerees and the issuer's procedure to ensure that the offerees are sophisticated. As we will see, the practical implication of this ruling is that, almost without exception, private placement offering materials are numbered and given only to suitability-screened offerees. To ensure that these screened investors have access to the appropriate information, these materials typically come together in a *private placement memorandum*. Much like the prospectus in a public securities offering, the private placement memorandum document serves to help sell the securities as well as provide adequate disclosure of descriptive and financial information.

The *SEC v. Murphy* decision also stated that the issuer may not stand alone in terms of liability. Others who are responsible for the distribution of unregistered securities can incur liability along with the issuer. It is important to note that, since the early 1960s, the SEC has reaffirmed the importance of the purchasers' buying for their own portfolio without intent to redistribute the securities.

A final aspect in which the *SEC v. Murphy* decision provided an important precedent involves how and when one begins and ends counting investors for a given offering. Because the case involved a sequence of related offerings (same sponsor, general purpose, financing plan, class of security, and consideration) and resulted in a total of 400 purchasers, the decision addressed the question of whether sequential offerings, otherwise exempted, can be integrated into one non-exempt offering. The court concluded in this case that separation in time was not sufficient to keep the offerings from being integrated. While the cases that have followed have not set a maximum number of offerees for exemption under Section 4 (2), it is clear that, other things being equal, the greater the number of offerees, the greater the chance that the offering will not be Section 4(2) exempt.

ACCREDITED INVESTOR EXEMPTION

Section 4(6) provides that offers and sales of securities to accredited investors are exempt from SEC registration. There is no limit to the number of accredited investors so long as the offering amount does not exceed $5 million and there is no advertising or public solicitation involved in the offering. The (amended) 1933 act's definition is:

2(a)(15) The term "accredited investor" shall mean:

(i) A bank as defined in Section 3(a)(2) whether acting in its individual or fiduciary capacity; an insurance company as defined in paragraph (13) of this subsection;

an investment company registered under the Investment Company Act of 1940 or a business development company as defined in Section 2(a)(48) of that Act; a Small Business Investment Company licensed by the Small Business Administration; or an employee benefit plan, including an individual retirement account, which is subject to the provisions of the Employee Retirement Income Security Act of 1974, if the investment decision is made by a plan fiduciary, as defined in Section 3(21) of such Act, which is either a bank, insurance company, or registered investment adviser; or

(ii) Any person who, on the basis of such factors as financial sophistication, net worth, knowledge, and experience in financial matters, or amount of assets under management qualifies as an accredited investor under rules and regulations which the Commission shall prescribe.

Accredited investors are not the types of investors that the act seeks to protect. They are assumed to have sufficient financial expertise and wherewithal to make an intelligent, informed investment decision. Of course, just because these investors are not the object of SEC protection in the form of required securities registration does not mean that they lose protection under the fraud provisions of the 1933 act. The accredited investor exemption in Section 4(6) concerns

Transactions involving offers or sales by an issuer solely to one or more accredited investors, if the aggregate offering price of an issue of securities offered in reliance on this paragraph does not exceed the amount allowed under Section 3(b) of this title, if there is no advertising or public solicitation in connection with the transaction by the issuer or anyone acting on the issuer's behalf, and if the issuer files such notice with the Commission as the Commission shall prescribe.

The amount referred to in Section 3(b) is presently $5 million. For most ventures, the accredited investor exemption has few, if any, advantages over other exemptions and does not appear to be frequently used. The remainder of our discussion will center on the Regulation D exemptions where we will also encounter provisions relating to accredited investors.

CONCEPT CHECK

- What is meant by a private placement exemption?
- What is meant by an accredited investor exemption?
- From what are "exempted" securities exempted?

8.7 SEC'S REGULATION D: SAFE-HARBOR EXEMPTIONS

A second category of possible transaction exemptions in Figure 8.4 comprises the Reg D (or Regulation D) exemptions. Due to lingering uncertainty about what constitutes a nonpublic offering, the SEC was pressured to provide some

Regulation D
regulation that offers a safe
harbor from registration of
securities with the SEC

"safe-harbor" conditions that, when met, result in guaranteed exemption as a private placement.

Regulation D (or Reg D for short), which took effect on April 15, 1982, although modified several times since, remains a centerpiece of U.S. securities law. Reg D's structure is somewhat complex, with many definitions and conditions. Plowing through Reg D brings home many of the principles currently reflected in securities law (even at the state level). In the federal regulations' internal numbering system, Reg D's rule numbers are preceded by "230," the regulation number for Regulation D. For example, Regulation D's Rule 501 is numbered "§230.501."

Reg D's first part, consisting of Rules 501–503 (§230.501–503), is devoted almost entirely to definitions and disclosure. For example, Rule 501 expands the definition of an "accredited investor" that was presented in the Securities Act of 1933. Rule 502 focuses on four conditions of a Reg D offering: (a) integration (when multiple issues count as one), (b) information (what you need to disclose when you must formally disclose), (c) solicitation (what you can't do when promoting the offering), and (d) resale (restrictions limiting resale). Rule 503 requires insurers of securities that are exempted under Reg D to file a form (called a Form D) with the SEC. Rule 507 (§230.507) provides disqualifications from using Reg D, and Rule 508 (§230.508) comments on the efficacy of Reg D's safe harbor even when an issuer has insignificant deviations from its provisions. Discussion materials relating to Rules 501–503, 507, and 508, as well as Rule 144, which restricts the resale of privately placed unregistered securities, are presented in Appendix B of this chapter.[9]

Rules 504, 505, and 506 (§230.504–506) are the specific private placement exemptions under Reg D and are the focus of this section. Figure 8.5 provides information on various exemption methods in terms of dollar limits, number and types of investors, and qualifications of investors. In the last section, we discussed Section 4(2) exemptions (private offerings or placements) and Section 4(6) exemptions (accredited investors). Section 4(2) exemptions are not limited in terms of size of offerings but are generally limited to a small number of sophisticated investors. Section 4(6) exemptions have offering limits of $5 million but can have an unlimited number of accredited investors. Figure 8.5 summarizes dollar limits, investor limits, and investor qualification requirements separately for Reg D's 504, 505, and 506 exemptions.

RULE 504: EXEMPTION FOR LIMITED OFFERINGS AND SALES OF SECURITIES NOT EXCEEDING $1 MILLION

Recent changes in the Rule 504 exemption have been quite important. Before the February 1999 changes, Rule 504 placed no explicit restrictions on general

---

[9] It is possible to omit the contents of Appendix B and still develop a basic understanding of securities law complexities as they relate to the raising of venture capital. However, at some time it will be important for an entrepreneur attempting to raise venture funds to understand the definition of an "accredited investor" under Reg D (Rule 501); Rule 502's coverage of integration, information, solicitation, and resale topics; and Rule 144's restrictions on the resale of unregistered securities. We encourage the interested reader to explore the securities law subject matter presented in Appendixes A, B, and C.

solicitation and advertising or reselling. Owing to some early and more recent abuse of Rule 504's rather liberal tone, the SEC appeared to want a more restrictive use of Rule 504. The current solution involves leaning a bit more on state registration, or lack thereof, to be able to generally solicit and resell. [See §230.504(b) below.] There is continuing pressure on the SEC to reconsider (soften) the current structure.[10]

Figure 8.5 shows that a Reg D 504 offering cannot exceed $1 million in a twelve-month period. However, a Rule 504 exemption has no limit in terms of the number and qualifications of investors.

§230.504

(a) *Exemption. Offers and sales of securities that satisfy the conditions in paragraph (b) of this §230.504 by an issuer that is not:*

    (1) *subject to the reporting requirements of section 13 or 15(d) of the Exchange Act;*

    (2) *an investment company; or*

    (3) *a development stage company that either has no specific business plan or purpose or has indicated that its business plan is to engage in a merger or acquisition with an unidentified company or companies, or other entity or person, shall be exempt from the provisions of section 5 of the Act under section 3(b) of the Act.*

(b) *Conditions to be met.*

    (1) *General conditions. To qualify for exemption under this 230.504, offers and sales must satisfy the terms and conditions of 230.501 and 230.502 (a), (c) and (d), except that the provisions of 230.502(c) and (d) will not apply to offers and sales of securities under this 230.504 that are made:*

        (i) *Exclusively in one or more states that provide for the registration of the securities, and require the public filing and delivery to investors of a substantive disclosure document before sale, and are made in accordance with those state provisions;*

        (ii) *In one or more states that have no provision for the registration of the securities or the public filing or delivery of a disclosure document before sale, if the securities have been registered in at least one state that provides for such registration, public filing and delivery before sale, offers and sales are made in that state in accordance with such provisions, and the disclosure document is delivered before sale to all purchasers (including those in the states that have no such procedure); or*

        (iii) *Exclusively according to state law exemptions from registration that permit general solicitation and general advertising so long as sales are made only to "accredited investors" as defined in 230.501(a).*

    (2) *The aggregate offering price for an offering of securities under this §230.504, as defined in §230.501(c), shall not exceed $1,000,000, less the aggregate offering price for all securities sold within the twelve months before*

---

[10] The "Final Report of the SEC Government-Business Forum on Small Business Capital Formation" (available at http://www.sec.gov) contains a brief history of the recent Rule 504 debate and its relationship to current initiatives by, among others, the North American Securities Administrators Association.

the start of and during the offering of securities under this §230.504, in reliance on any exemption under section 3(b), or in violation of section 5(a) of the Securities Act.

Note 1: The calculation of the aggregate offering price is illustrated as follows:

If an issuer sold $900,000 on June 1, 1987 under this §230.504 and an additional $4,100,000 on December 1, 1987 under §230.505, the issuer could not sell any of its securities under this §230.504 until December 1, 1988. Until then the issuer must count the December 1, 1987 sale towards the $1,000,000 limit within the preceding twelve months.

Note 2: If a transaction under §230.504 fails to meet the limitation on the aggregate offering price, it does not affect the availability of this §230.504 for the other transactions considered in applying such limitation. For example, if an issuer sold $1,000,000 worth of its securities on January 1, 1988 under this §230.504 and an additional $500,000 worth on July 1, 1988, this §230.504 would not be available for the later sale, but would still be applicable to the January 1, 1988 sale.

RULE 505: EXEMPTION FOR LIMITED OFFERS AND SALES OF SECURITIES NOT EXCEEDING $5 MILLION

Figure 8.5 indicates that a Reg D 505 offering cannot exceed $5 million in a twelve-month period. However, while a 505 exemption has no limit in terms of the number of accredited investors, the offering is limited to thirty-five unaccredited investors.

§230.505

(a) *Exemption. Offers and sales of securities that satisfy the conditions in paragraph (b) of this §230.505 by an issuer that is not an investment company shall be exempt from the provisions of section 5 of the Act under section 3(b) of the Act.*

(b) *Conditions to be met.*

   (1) *General conditions. To qualify for exemption under this section, offers and sales must satisfy the terms and conditions of §§230.501 and 230.502.*

   (2) *Specific conditions.*

      (i) *Limitations on aggregate offering price. The aggregate offering price for an offering of securities under this §230.505, as defined in §230.501(c), shall not exceed $5,000,000, less the aggregate offering price for all securities sold within the twelve months before the start of and during the offering of securities under this §230.505 in reliance on any exemption under section 3(b) of the Act or in violation of section 5(a) of the Act.*

   Note: The calculation of the aggregate offering price is illustrated as follows:

   Example 1. If an issuer sold $2,000,000 of its securities on June 1, 1982 under this §230.505 and an additional $1,000,000 on September 1, 1982, the issuer would be permitted to sell only $2,000,000 more under this §230.505 until June 1, 1983. Until that date the issuer must count both prior sales towards the $5,000,000 limit. However, if the issuer made its third sale on June 1, 1983, the issuer could then sell $4,000,000 of its securities because the June 1, 1982 sale would not be within the preceding twelve months.

Example 2. If an issuer sold $500,000 of its securities on June 1, 1982 under §230.504 and an additional $4,500,000 on December 1, 1982 under this §230.505, then the issuer could not sell any of its securities under this §230.505 until June 1, 1983. At that time it could sell an additional $500,000 of its securities.

(ii) *Limitation on number of purchasers. There are no more than or the is-suer reasonably believes that there are no more than 35 purchasers of se-curities from the issuer in any offering under this section §230.505.*

Note: See §230.501(e) for the calculation of the number of purchasers and §230.502(a) for what may or may not constitute an offering under this section.

(iii) *Disqualifications. No exemption under this section shall be available for the securities of any issuer described in §230.262 of Regulation A, except that for purposes of this section only:*

   (A) *The term "filing of the offering statement required by §230.252" as used in §230.262(a), (b) and (c) shall mean the first sale of securi-ties under this section;*

   (B) *The term "underwriter" as used in §230.262(b) and (c) shall mean a person that has been or will be paid directly or indirectly remuner-ation for solicitation of purchasers in connection with sales of secu-rities under this section; and*

   (C) *Paragraph (b)(2)(iii) of this §230.505 shall not apply to any issuer if the Commission determines, upon a showing of good cause, that it is not necessary under the circumstances that the exemption be denied. Any such determination shall be without prejudice to any other action by the Commission in any other proceeding or matter with respect to the issuer or any other person.*

RULE 506: EXEMPTION FOR LIMITED OFFERS AND SALES WITHOUT REGARD TO DOLLAR AMOUNT OF OFFERING

Figure 8.5 shows that a Reg D 506 offering has no limit in terms of the dollar amount of the offering. Rule 506 places no limit on the number of accredited in-vestors. However, a 506 offering is limited to thirty-five unaccredited investors, each of whom must have sufficient financial knowledge to be able to evaluate the investment opportunity.

§230.506.

(a) *Exemption. Offers and sales of securities by an issuer that satisfy the conditions in paragraph (b) of this §230.506 shall be deemed to be transactions not involving any public offering within the meaning of section 4(2) of the Act.*

(b) *Conditions to be met.*

   (1) *General conditions. To qualify for exemption under this section, offers and sales must satisfy all the terms and conditions of §§230.501 and 230.502.*

   (2) *Specific conditions.*

(i) *Limitation on number of purchasers. There are no more than or the issuer reasonably believes that there are no more than 35 purchasers of securities from the issuer in any offering under this §230.506.*

Note: See §230.501(e) for the calculation of the number of purchasers and §230.502(a) for what may or may not constitute an offering under this section 230.506.

(ii) *Nature of purchasers. Each purchaser who is not an accredited investor either alone or with his purchaser representative(s) has such knowledge and experience in financial and business matters that he is capable of evaluating the merits and risks of the prospective investment, or the issuer reasonably believes immediately prior to making any sale that such purchaser comes within this description.*

A few final remarks on the use of Reg D are in order. The SEC interpretive comments (available from the SEC) are quite useful for those thinking about structuring a Reg D offering. For example, many private offerings have "all or nothing" or other contingent offering provisions. In such offerings, the SEC comments indicate that supplemental disclosure may be required when an insider is willing to stand by and complete any stipulated minimum for the offer to be completed. In any case, shares should probably be escrowed if there is a chance the offer will not be consummated. These comments also deal with the possibility of extending the deadline for the offering. As you discuss the structure of an offering with your legal counsel, you would be wise to became familiar with these structural issues. You should also remember that not conforming to the safe harbor of Regulation D does not mean that you have violated any securities laws or given up your rights to seek general protection under 4(2) of the 1933 act. An attempted compliance with the provisions of Reg D is not an exclusive election.

CONCEPT CHECK

- What are the monetary limits on Rule 504 and Rule 505 offerings?
- When does the issuer need to make sure the offerees are sophisticated?
- What is the major difference between Rules 505 and 506?

8.8   REGULATION A SECURITY EXEMPTION

Regulation A is another method used by entrepreneurs to offer securities that are exempt from SEC registration. Regulation A is acknowledged in Figure 8.4, and some of its offering size and investor characteristics are presented in Figure 8.5. However, anyone who has filed the requisite paperwork would probably tell you it is basically a registration, albeit a shorter and simpler one than the full registration normally required. Reg A offerings are limited to $5 million, but they do not have limitations on the number or sophistication of offerees (see Figure 8.5 for a comparison with other exemption methods). They are public offerings rather than private placements. The securities issued generally can be resold freely.[11] Up to $1.5 million of the securities can be secondary sales of shares already owned by current security holders.

Reg A cannot be used by SEC reporting companies, investment companies, or "blank check" companies (without a specific business plan) and requires that an offering statement be filed with the SEC. There are also some prohibitions on issuers with tainted records in the securities business.

Reg A issuers are allowed to "test the waters" before preparing the offering circular (unlike almost all other security offerings). The right to test the waters requires filing a statement with the SEC specifying the content of the issuer's pitch for interest. Upon filing such a statement, the issuer can communicate with potential investors orally, in writing, by advertising in newspapers, on radio and on television, or in the mail to determine investor interest. The issuer cannot, of course, take any commitments or funds. In fact, there is a formal delay (of twenty calendar days) before sales can be made. If the interest level is not sufficient, the potential issuer can drop the idea of a Reg A placement without the full expense of a Reg A filing. If there is sufficient interest, the issuer must submit an "offering statement" (or circular) on Form 1-A for qualification by the SEC. The delivery of an offering statement is required forty-eight hours before confirmation of the sale of any securities. Some Reg A offerings can be found on the Internet as one form of a "direct public offering." (Reg D 504 provides the exemption for most of the other direct public offerings.) Reg A has insignificant deviation and substantial good-faith compliance clauses very similar to Reg D.

CONCEPT CHECK

- What is meant by the term "testing the waters"?

SUMMARY

The four relevant components of the federal securities laws are the Securities Act of 1933, the Securities and Exchange Act of 1934, the Investment Company Act of 1940, and the Investment Advisers Act of 1940. To avoid violating federal securities laws, if an issuer's offering is not somehow exempt, it must be registered with the SEC, a costly process in time and money.

It is important to understand when securities must be registered with the SEC. Figure 8.4 provides a decision tree for addressing the question of whether an SEC registration is required. We first ask if the issuer is trying to sell securities. If so, we next ask if the securities are exempt based on the type or class of securities (as with an

intrastate securities offering). If not, we then ask if there is a transactions exemption available under Section 4 of the 1933 act, under Reg D, or under Reg A (or other available transactions exemptions like those listed in Appendix C). In almost all cases for early-stage ventures, it is this last question that will be the most important and the most difficult.

Many entrepreneurs at some time during their venture's life cycle are likely to try to raise venture financing by issuing nonexempt securities. Familiarity with the securities law's structure and restrictions can be an important factor in avoiding securities law problems associated with fundraising.

---

[11] No affiliate resales are permitted, however, if the issuer has not had net income from continuing operations in at least one of its last two fiscal years.

KEY TERMS

blue-sky laws	Investment Company Act of 1940	Securities Act of 1933
Investment Advisers Act of 1940	Regulation D	Securities Exchange Act of 1934

DISCUSSION QUESTIONS

1. Briefly define the (a) Securities Act of 1933 and (b) Securities Exchange Act of 1934.

2. Briefly discuss the (a) Investment Company Act of 1940 and (b) Investment Advisers Act of 1940.

3. What is meant by the term "blue-sky laws" and how do these laws apply when issuing securities?

4. Describe the meaning of a "security" in terms of the Securities Act of 1933.

5. Why does it matter if an investment is, or is not, viewed as being a "security"?

6. Briefly describe what is meant by the statement "registering securities with the SEC is a costly and time-consuming process."

7. Identify some of the types of securities that are "exempt" from registration with the SEC.

8. Briefly describe what is meant by an "intrastate" offering. What are the major difficulties in assuring that an offer is "intrastate"?

9. Identify and briefly describe two basic types of transactions that are exempt from registration with the SEC.

10. What does the term "accredited investor" mean in terms of the Securities Act of 1933? Why does the designation matter?

11. Briefly describe the importance of the 1953 *SEC v. Ralston Purina* case in terms of securities registration requirements.

12. What is the purpose of the SEC's Regulation D?

13. What are the restrictions on general solicitation and advertising covered in Rule 504?

14. How do Rules 504, 505, and 506 of Reg D differ from one another?

15. Provide a brief description of the use of Regulation A when issuing securities.

[Note: The following questions relate to the material presented in Appendixes B and C.]

16. Briefly describe how the SEC's Regulation D expanded the original Securities Act of 1933 definition of an "accredited investor."

17. What are the income and net worth requirements for being an accredited investor? What in the requirements for designation as an accredited investor relates to the level of sophistication? Do the criteria act as good proxies for sophistication?

18. What are the four conditions of a Reg D offering that are covered under Rule 502?

19. What is "integration" as it applies to securities offerings and why does it matter?

20. What types of information need to be disclosed to offerees under Reg D?

21. What is a "restricted" security? Why does this designation matter? What types of buyers must the owner of restricted securities find?

22. Briefly describe the purpose of Rule 144 of Reg D.

23. Briefly describe Rule 508 of Reg D.

24. Briefly describe the types of exemptions from registration of securities covered under Rules 701 and 1001.

INTERNET ACTIVITIES

1. Access the Securities and Exchange Commission Web site at http://www.sec.gov. Identify recent developments and changes in Rule 504 of the SEC's Regulation D.

2. In 1995, the Office of Advocacy of the Small Business Administration created the Angel Capital Electronic Network (ACE-Net), which has evolved into Active Capital at http://www.activecapital.org. Active Capital

brings investors and entrepreneurs together through an Internet database. Determine how Active Capital is structured and how it works for investors, entrepreneurs, and securities attorneys.

3. Access the Nolo Press Web site at http://www.nolo .com. Develop a list of legal references relating to securities laws.

EXERCISES/PROBLEMS

1. The NetCare Company, which operates assisted-living facilities, is planning to issue or sell shares of stock to accredited investors. Briefly explain whether each of the following individuals would qualify as an "accredited investor" under the SEC's Regulation D. [Note: Materials in Appendix B are useful in answering this exercise.]
   A. Amy Smith is the chief executive officer (CEO) of NetCare Company.
   B. Bruce Jones, who has a net worth of $750,000, is planning to purchase shares of stock to be issued by NetCare Company.
   C. Jean Wu also is considering purchasing shares of stock that will be issued by NetCare Company. Jean's annual income has been $250,000 in each of the past two years and she expects to have a comparable amount of income next year.
   D. James Shastri is a software programmer for NetCare Company.
   E. Julie Kukoc recently inherited some financial assets and now has a net worth of $2 million with an annual income of $35,000.

2. The CareAssist Company, a Web-based provider of information for the elderly, is planning to sell $4 million in securities. Management is trying to decide which, if any, securities laws must be complied with. For each of the following situations, describe the securities laws that might apply:
   A. A private placement
   B. An interstate public offering
   C. An intrastate public offering

M I N I   C A S E

The VirtualStream Company

The VirtualStream Company has developed proprietary server and control software for providing communication and media-on-demand services via the Internet. The company is in the process of collecting prerecorded video and audio content from clients and then digitally transferring and storing the content on network servers. The content then is available for replay by customers via the Internet. VirtualStream's mission is to provide the most dependable and user-friendly multimedia streaming service worldwide.

The Internet technology service industry is characterized by rapid revenue growth, with industry revenues predicted to exceed $300 billion in three years. Market participants include companies engaged in video and audio teleconferencing, corporate training, computer-based training, and distance learning. VirtualStream is attempting to focus on helping large companies to communicate more effectively, using both archived and live communications content, via the Internet. Video and audio content is digitally stored in a central location and is available on demand to clients. This approach will save time and money required to duplicate and ship materials. The company also offers a service that enables transmission of live broadcasts via the Internet.

continued on next page

The VirtualStream Company (continued)

VirtualStream raised $500,000 in the form of founder's capital last year. The firm is now seeking additional financial capital from investors by issuing or selling securities in the form of stock in the firm. The firm is planning to obtain $750,000 as soon as possible from private investors.

A. Discuss whether you would recommend registering these securities with the Securities and Exchange Commission.
B. Some securities are exempt from the SEC registration requirement. Is it likely that VirtualStream's stock would qualify for such an exemption? Why or why not?
C. Would you recommend that the initial $750,000 be obtained through an intrastate offering? Explain.
D. Briefly describe the two basic types of transaction exemptions that may be available to VirtualStream that would allow the firm not to have to register its securities with the SEC.
E. The Securities and Exchange Commission's Regulation D offers a "safe-harbor" exemption to firms from having to register their securities with the SEC. Describe how the VirtualStream Company could use Reg D for issuing $750,000 in stock to private investors. In developing your answer, describe the Reg D rules that would likely apply to this security issue.
F. Now assume VirtualStream also is planning to issue an additional $2 million in stock toward the end of the year. Would this decision have an impact on the Reg D rules that would govern the issuance of the firm's securities? Describe. [Note: The material in Appendix B may be helpful in developing an answer to this question.]
G. The other alternative is to seek to raise the total $2,750,000 amount now by selling securities to investors. Which Reg D rules and/or other securities laws would be triggered by such a plan? Describe why and how.

Appendix A

SCHEDULE A
(Securities Act of 1933, as Amended)

REQUIREMENTS FOR REGISTRATION OF SECURITIES OTHER THAN A SECURITY ISSUED BY A FOREIGN GOVERNMENT OR POLITICAL SUBDIVISION THEREOF

(1) *The name under which the issuer is doing or intends to do business;*

(2) *The name of the state or other sovereign power under which the issuer is organized;*

(3) *The location of the issuer's principal business office, and if the issuer is a foreign or territorial person, the name and address of its agent in the United States authorized to receive notice;*

(4) *The names and addresses of the directors or persons performing similar functions, and the chief executive, financial and accounting officers, chosen or to be chosen if the issuer be a corporation, association, trust or other entity; of all partners, if the issuer be a partnership; and of the issuer, if the issuer be an individual; and of the promoters in the case of a business to be formed, or formed within two years prior to the filing of the registration statement;*

(5) *The names and addresses of the underwriters;*

(6) *The names and addresses of all persons, if any, owning of record or beneficially, if known, more than 10 per centum of any class of stock of the issuer, or more than 10 per centum in the aggregate of the outstanding stock of the issuer as of a date within 20 days prior to the filing of the registration statement;*

(7) *The amount of securities of the issuer held by any person specified in paragraphs (4), (5) and (6) of this schedule, as of a date within 20 days prior to the filing of the registration statement, and, if possible, as of one year prior thereto, and the amount of the securities, for which the registration statement is filed, to which such persons have indicated their intention to subscribe;*

(8) *The general character of the business actually transacted or to be transacted by the issuer;*

(9) *A statement of the capitalization of the issuer, including the authorized and outstanding amounts of its capital stock and the proportion thereof paid up, the number and classes of shares in which such capital stock is divided, par value thereof, or if it has no par value, the stated or assigned value thereof, a description of the respective voting rights, preferences, conversion and exchange rights, rights to dividends, profits, or capital of each class, with respect to each other class, including the retirement and liquidation rights or values thereof;*

(10) *A statement of the securities, if any, covered by options outstanding or to be created in connection with the security to be offered, together with the names and addresses of all persons, if any, to be allotted more than 10 per centum in the aggregate of such options;*

(11) *The amount of capital stock of each class issued or included in the shares of stock to be offered;*

(12) *The amount of the funded debt outstanding and to be created by the security to be offered, with a brief description of the date, maturity, and character of such debt, rate of interest, character of amortization provisions, and the security, if any, therefor. If substitution of any security is permissible, a summarized statement of the conditions under which such substitution is permitted. If substitution is permissible without notice, a specific statement to that effect;*

(13) *The specific purposes in detail and the approximate amounts to be devoted to such purposes, so far as determinable, for which the security to be offered is to supply funds, and if the funds are to be raised in part from other sources, the amounts thereof and the sources thereof, shall be stated;*

(14) *The remuneration, paid or estimated to be paid, by the issuer or its predecessor, directly or indirectly, during the past year and ensuing year to: (a) the directors or persons performing similar functions, and (b) its officers and other persons, naming them wherever such remuneration exceeded $25,000 during any such year;*

(15) The estimated net proceeds to be derived from the security to be offered;

(16) The price at which it is proposed that the security shall be offered to the public or the method by which such price is computed and any variation therefrom at which any portion of such security is proposed to be offered to any persons or classes of persons, other than the underwriters, naming them or specifying the class. A variation in price may be proposed prior to the date of the public offering of the security, but the Commission shall immediately be notified of such variation;

(17) All commissions or discounts paid or to be paid, directly or indirectly, by the issuer to the underwriters in respect of the sale of the security to be offered. Commissions shall include all cash, securities, contracts, or anything else of value, paid, to be set aside, disposed of, or understandings with or for the benefit of any other persons in which any underwriter is interested, made, in connection with the sale of such security. A commission paid or to be paid in connection with the sale of such security by a person in which the issuer has an interest or which is controlled or directed by, or under common control with, the issuer shall be deemed to have been paid by the issuer. Where any such commission is paid, the amount of such commission paid to each underwriter shall be stated;

(18) The amount or estimated amounts, itemized in reasonable detail, of expenses, other than commissions specified in paragraph (17) of this schedule, incurred or borne by or for the account of the issuer in connection with the sale of the security to be offered or properly chargeable thereto, including legal, engineering, certification, authentication, and other charges;

(19) The net proceeds derived from any security sold by the issuer during the two years preceding the filing of the registration statement, the price at which such security was offered to the public, and the names of the principal underwriters of such security;

(20) Any amount paid within two years preceding the filing of the registration statement or intended to be paid to any promoter and the consideration for any such payment;

(21) The names and addresses of the vendors and the purchase price of any property, or good will, acquired or to be acquired, not in the ordinary course of business, which is to be defrayed in whole or in part from the proceeds of the security to be offered, the amount of any commission payable to any person in connection with such acquisition, and the name or names of such person or persons, together with any expense incurred or to be incurred in connection with such acquisition, including the cost of borrowing money to finance such acquisition;

(22) Full particulars of the nature and extent of the interest, if any, of every director, principal executive officer, and of every stockholder holding more than 10 per centum of any class of stock or more than 10 per centum in the aggregate of the stock of the issuer, in any property acquired, not in the ordinary course of business of the issuer, within two years preceding the filing of the registration statement or proposed to be acquired at such date;

(23) The names and addresses of counsel who have passed on the legality of the issue;

(24) Dates of and parties to, and the general effect concisely stated of every material contract made, not in the ordinary course of business, which contract is to be executed in whole or in part at or after the filing of the registration statement or which contract has been made not more than two years before such filing. Any management contract or contract providing for special bonuses or profit-sharing arrangements,

and every material patent or contract for a material patent right, and every contract by or with a public utility company or an affiliate thereof, providing for the giving or receiving of technical or financial advice or service (if such contract may involve a charge to any party thereto at a rate in excess of $2,500 per year in cash or securities or anything else of value), shall be deemed a material contract;

(25) *A balance sheet as of a date not more than 90 days prior to the date of the filing of the registration statement showing all of the assets of the issuer, the nature and cost thereof, whenever determinable, in such detail and in such form as the Commission shall prescribe (with intangible items segregated), including any loan in excess of $20,000 to any officer, director, stockholder or person directly or indirectly controlling or controlled by the issuer, or person under direct or indirect common control with the issuer. All the liabilities of the issuer in such detail and such form as the Commission shall prescribe, including surplus of the issuer showing how and from what sources such surplus was created, all as of a date not more than 90 days prior to the filing of the registration statement. If such statement be not certified by an independent public or certified accountant, in addition to the balance sheet required to be submitted under this schedule, a similar detailed balance sheet of the assets and liabilities of the issuer, certified by an independent public or certified accountant, of a date not more than one year prior to the filing of the registration statement, shall be submitted;*

(26) *A profit and loss statement of the issuer showing earnings and income, the nature and source thereof, and the expenses and fixed charges in such detail and such form as the Commission shall prescribe for the latest fiscal year for which such statement is available and for the two preceding fiscal years, year by year, or, if such issuer has been in actual business for less than three years, then for such time as the issuer has been in actual business, year by year. If the date of the filing of the registration statement is more than six months after the close of the last fiscal year, a statement from such closing date to the latest practicable date. Such statement shall show what the practice of the issuer has been during the three years or lesser period as to the character of the charges, dividends or other distributions made against its various surplus accounts, and as to depreciation, depletion, and maintenance charges, in such detail and form as the Commission shall prescribe, and if stock dividends or avails from the sale of rights have been credited to income, they shall be shown separately with a statement of the basis upon which the credit is computed. Such statement shall also differentiate between any recurring and non-recurring income and between any investment and operating income. Such statement shall be certified by an independent public or certified accountant;*

(27) *If the proceeds, or any part of the proceeds, of the security to be issued is to be applied directly or indirectly to the purchase of any business, a profit and loss statement of such business certified by an independent public or certified accountant, meeting the requirements of paragraph (26) of this schedule, for the three preceding fiscal years, together with a balance sheet, similarly certified, of such business, meeting the requirements of paragraph (25) of this schedule of a date not more than 90 days prior to the filing of the registration statement or at the date such business was acquired by the issuer if the business was acquired by the issuer more than 90 days prior to the filing of the registration statement;*

(28) *A copy of any agreement or agreements (or, if identical agreements are used, the forms thereof) made with any underwriter, including all contracts and agreements referred to in paragraph (17) of this schedule;*

(29) A copy of the opinion or opinions of counsel in respect to the legality of the issue, with a translation of such opinion, when necessary, into the English language;

(30) A copy of all material contracts referred to in paragraph (24) of this schedule, but no disclosure shall be required of any portion of any such contract if the Commission determines that disclosure of such portion would impair the value of the contract and would not be necessary for the protection of investors;

(31) Unless previously filed and registered under the provisions of this title, and brought up to date: (a) a copy of its articles of incorporation, with all amendments thereof and of its existing by-laws or instruments corresponding thereto, whatever the name, if the issuer be a corporation; (b) a copy of all instruments by which the trust is created or declared, if the issuer is a trust; (c) a copy of its articles of partnership or association and all other papers pertaining to its organization, if the issuer is a partnership, unincorporated association, joint-stock company, or any other form of organization; and

(32) A copy of the underlying agreements or indentures affecting any stock, bonds, or debentures offered or to be offered. In case of certificates of deposit, voting trust certificates, collateral trust certificates, certificates of interest or shares in unincorporated investment trusts, equipment trust certificates, interim or other receipts for certificates, and like securities, the Commission shall establish rules and regulations requiring the submission of information of a like character applicable to such cases, together with such other information as it may deem appropriate and necessary regarding the character, financial or otherwise, of the actual issuer of the securities and/or the person performing the acts and assuming the duties of depositor or manager.

Appendix B

SELECTED SEC REGULATION D MATERIALS

Regulation D's "Preliminary Notes"

1. The following rules relate to transactions exempted from the registration requirements of section 5 of the Securities Act of 1933 (the "Act") [15 U.S.C. 77a et seq., as amended]. Such transactions are not exempt from the antifraud, civil liability, or other provisions of the federal securities laws. Issuers are reminded of their obligation to provide such further material information, if any, as may be necessary to make the information required under this regulation, in light of the circumstances under which it is furnished, not misleading.

2. *Nothing in these rules obviates the need to comply with any applicable state law relating to the offer and sale of securities. Regulation D is intended to be a basic element in a uniform system of federal-state limited offering exemptions consistent with the provisions of sections 18 and 19(c) of the Act. In those states that have adopted Regulation D, or any version of Regulation D, special attention should be directed to the applicable state laws and regulations, including those relating to registration of persons who receive remuneration in connection with the offer and sale of securities, to disqualification of issuers and other persons associated with offerings based on state administrative orders or judgments, and to requirements for filings of notices of sales.*

3. *Attempted compliance with any rule in Regulation D does not act as an exclusive election; the issuer can also claim the availability of any other applicable exemption. For instance, an issuer's failure to satisfy all the terms and conditions of Rule 506 shall not raise any presumption that the exemption provided by section 4(2) of the Act is not available.*

4. *These rules are available only to the issuer of the securities and not to any affiliate of that issuer or to any other person for resales of the issuer's securities. The rules provide an exemption only for the transactions in which the securities are offered or sold by the issuer, not for the securities themselves.*

5. *These rules may be used for business combinations that involve sales by virtue of Rule 145(a) (17 CFR 230.145(a)) or otherwise.*

6. *In view of the objectives of these rules and the policies underlying the Act, Regulation D is not available to any issuer for any transaction or chain of transactions that, although in technical compliance with these rules, is part of a plan or scheme to evade the registration provisions of the Act. In such cases, registration under the Act is required.*

7. *Securities offered and sold outside the United States in accordance with Regulation S need not be registered under the Act. See Release No. 33-6863. Regulation S may be relied upon for such offers and sales even if coincident offers and sales are made in accordance with Regulation D inside the United States. Thus, for example, persons who are offered and sold securities in accordance with Regulation S would not be counted in the calculation of the number of purchasers under Regulation D. Similarly, proceeds from such sales would not be included in the aggregate offering price. The provisions of this note, however, do not apply if the issuer elects to rely solely on Regulation D for offers or sales to persons made outside the United States.*

RULE 501: DEFINITIONS AND TERMS USED IN REGULATION D

As previously noted, an "accredited investor" was defined in the Securities Act of 1933. This definition was expanded in Rule 501 of Reg D to include eight categories of accredited investors. Following is the text from Section 4(6) of Rule 501 relating to the accredited investor exemption:

§230.501(a) Accredited investor. "Accredited investor" shall mean any person who comes within any of the following categories, or whom the issuer reasonably believes

comes within any of the following categories, at the time of the sale of the securities to that person:

(1) Any bank as defined in section 3(a)(2) of the Act, or any savings and loan association or other institution as defined in section 3(a)(5)(A) of the Act whether acting in its individual or fiduciary capacity; any broker or dealer registered pursuant to section 15 of the Securities Exchange Act of 1934; any insurance company as defined in section 2(13) of the Act; any investment company registered under the Investment Company Act of 1940 or a business development company as defined in section 2(a)(48) of that Act; any Small Business Investment Company licensed by the U.S. Small Business Administration under section 301(c) or (d) of the Small Business Investment Act of 1958; any plan established and maintained by a state, its political subdivisions, or any agency or instrumentality of a state or its political subdivisions, for the benefit of its employees, if such plan has total assets in excess of $5,000,000; any employee benefit plan within the meaning of the Employee Retirement Income Security Act of 1974 if the investment decision is made by a plan fiduciary, as defined in section 3(21) of such Act, which is either a bank, savings and loan association, insurance company, or registered adviser, or if the employee benefit plan has total assets in excess of $5,000,000 or, if a self-directed plan, with investment decisions made solely by persons that are accredited investors;

(2) Any private business development company as defined in section 202(a)(22) of the Investment Advisers Act of 1940;

(3) Any organization described in section 501(c)(3) of the Internal Revenue Code, corporation, Massachusetts or similar business trust, or partnership, not formed for the specific purpose of acquiring the securities offered, with total assets in excess of $5,000,000;

(4) Any director, executive officer, or general partner of the issuer of the securities being offered or sold, or any director, executive officer, or general partner of a general partner of that issuer;

(5) Any natural person whose individual net worth, or joint net worth with that person's spouse, at the time of his purchase exceeds $1,000,000;

(6) Any natural person who had an individual income in excess of $200,000 in each of the two most recent years or joint income with that person's spouse in excess of $300,000 in each of those years and has a reasonable expectation of reaching the same income level in the current year;

(7) Any trust, with total assets in excess of $5,000,000, not formed for the specific purpose of acquiring the securities offered, whose purchase is directed by a sophisticated person as described in §230.506(b)(2)(ii); and

(8) Any entity in which all of the equity owners are accredited investors.

Preliminary Note (7) also gives the conditions under which foreign investors would not be counted (because they are included in a legally separate offering that won't be integrated with the Reg D offering). Of particular interest are categories (5) and (6), which provide individual wealth and income levels necessary for a person to be categorized as an accredited investor. Regulation D's qualifications for accredited investor status are important because, as we will see in the exemptions of Rules 505 and 506, one does not have to count accredited investors when meeting the thirty-five investor limit (when it applies). Specifically:

§230.501(e) Calculation of number of purchasers. For purposes of calculating the number of purchasers under §§230.505(b) and 230.506(b) only, the following shall apply:

(1) The following purchasers shall be excluded:

(i) Any relative, spouse or relative of the spouse of a purchaser who has the same principal residence as the purchaser;

(ii) Any trust or estate in which a purchaser and any of the persons related to him as specified in paragraph (e)(1)(i) or (e)(1)(iii) of this §230.501 collectively have more than 50 percent of the beneficial interest (excluding contingent interests);

(iii) Any corporation or other organization of which a purchaser and any of the persons related to him as specified in paragraph (e)(1)(i) or (e)(1)(ii) of this §230.501 collectively are beneficial owners of more than 50 percent of the equity securities (excluding directors' qualifying shares) or equity interests; and

(iv) Any accredited investor.

(2) A corporation, partnership or other entity shall be counted as one purchaser. If, however, that entity is organized for the specific purpose of acquiring the securities offered and is not an accredited investor under paragraph (a)(8) of this section, then each beneficial owner of equity securities or equity interests in the entity shall count as a separate purchaser for all provisions of Regulation D (§§230.501–230.508), except to the extent provided in paragraph (e)(1) of this section.

(3) A non-contributory employee benefit plan within the meaning of Title I of the Employee Retirement Income Security Act of 1974 shall be counted as one purchaser where the trustee makes all investment decisions for the plan.

Note: The issuer must satisfy all the other provisions of Regulation D for all purchasers whether or not they are included in calculating the number of purchasers. Clients of an investment adviser or customers of a broker or dealer shall be considered the "purchasers" under Regulation D regardless of the amount of discretion given to the investment adviser or broker or dealer to act on behalf of the client or customer.

In category (4), executive officers are also considered to be "accredited" investors for securities issued by their firms.[12] More specifically:

§230.501(f) Executive officer. "Executive officer" shall mean the president, any vice president in charge of a principal business unit, division or function (such as sales, administration or finance), any other officer who performs a policy making function, or any other person who performs similar policy making functions for the issuer. Executive officers of subsidiaries may be deemed executive officers of the issuer if they perform such policy making functions for the issuer.

---

[12] There are a few other definitions, such as "purchaser representative," that we do not cover here. They can be found at the SEC Web site at http://www.sec.gov.

RULE 502: GENERAL CONDITIONS TO BE MET

Rule 502 (§230.502) deals with four conditions of a Reg D offering: integration (when multiple issues count as one), information (what you need to disclose when you must formally disclose), solicitation (what you can't do when promoting the offering), and resale (serious restrictions).

INTEGRATION

Rules 504 (§230.504) and 505 (§230.505) have limits on the dollar amount of money that can be raised. It is therefore important to understand when multiple Reg D offerings will not be integrated (combined) into one offering that might exceed the dollar limits. The easiest way to ensure nonintegration of offers is to make sure the surrounding twelve months is free and clear of other Reg D offerings of the same type of security. Specifically, Rule 502 (§230.502) gives this safe harbor as:

> *§230.502 (a) Offers and sales that are made more than six months before the start of a Regulation D offering or are made more than six months after completion of a Regulation D offering will not be considered part of that Regulation D offering, so long as during those six month periods there are no offers or sales of securities by or for the issuer that are of the same or a similar class as those offered or sold under Regulation D, other than those offers or sales of securities under an employee benefit plan as defined in Rule 405 under the Act [17 CFR 230.405].*

Outside this safe harbor, things get a little vaguer:

> *Note: The term "offering" is not defined in the Act or in Regulation D. If the issuer offers or sells securities for which the safe harbor rule in paragraph (a) of this §230.502 is unavailable, the determination as to whether separate sales of securities are part of the same offering (i.e., are considered "integrated") depends on the particular facts and circumstances. Generally, transactions otherwise meeting the requirements of an exemption will not be integrated with simultaneous offerings being made outside the United States in compliance with Regulation S. See Release No. 33-6863.*
>
> *The following factors should be considered in determining whether offers and sales should be integrated for purposes of the exemptions under Regulation D:*
> *(a) whether the sales are part of a single plan of financing;*
> *(b) whether the sales involve issuance of the same class of securities;*
> *(c) whether the sales have been made at or about the same time;*
> *(d) whether the same type of consideration is being received; and*
> *(e) whether the sales are made for the same general purpose.*
>
> *See Release No. 33-4552 (November 6, 1962) [27 F.R. 11316].*

When issuing outside the safe harbor, thus risking having the integrated current and past offerings jointly lose Reg D exemption, the current offering disclosure probably (if not certainly) needs to disclose the possible liabilities that may arise from the loss of the exemptions.

INFORMATION

Rule 502 (§230.502) also specifies when formal disclosure information must be furnished to investors and the minimal content of that disclosure. If any investor is not accredited, then the issuer, in order to keep a 505 (§230.505) or 506 (§230.506) safe harbor, must furnish to that investor specific information (usually in a private placement memorandum) at a "reasonable time prior to sale." A 504 (§230.504) exemption does not require any specific disclosure document, but disclosure of "material" information is still mandated by the antifraud provisions of the 1933 act. Although the issuer is not required to provide a disclosure document to accredited investors, the regulation does have the following note:

> *Note: When an issuer provides information to investors pursuant to paragraph (b)(1), it should consider providing such information to accredited investors as well, in view of the anti-fraud provisions of the federal securities laws.*

When required, the type of information to be disclosed varies by the venture's status and size:

§230.502(b)(2) Type of information to be furnished.

> (i) *If the issuer is not subject to the reporting requirements of section 13 or 15 (d) of the Exchange Act, at a reasonable time prior to the sale of securities, the issuer shall furnish to the purchaser, to the extent material to an understanding of the issuer, its business, and the securities being offered:*
>
> > (A) *Non-financial statement information. If the issuer is eligible to use Regulation A (§230.251–263), the same kind of information as would be required in Part II of Form 1-A (§239.90 of this chapter). If the issuer is not eligible to use Regulation A, the same kind of information as required in Part I of a registration statement filed under the Securities Act on the form that the issuer would be entitled to use.*
> >
> > (B) *Financial Statement Information.*

> (1) *Offerings up to $2,000,000. The information required in Item 310 of Regulation S-B (§228.310 of this chapter), except that only the issuer's balance sheet, which shall be dated within 120 days of the start of the offering, must be audited.*
>
> (2) *Offerings up to $7,500,000. The financial statement information required in Form SB-2 [§239.10 of this chapter]. If an issuer, other than a limited partnership, cannot obtain audited financial statements without unreasonable effort or expense, then only the issuer's balance sheet, which shall be dated within 120 days of the start of the offering, must be audited. If the issuer is a limited partnership and cannot obtain the required financial statements without unreasonable effort or expense, it may furnish financial statements that have been prepared on the basis of Federal income tax requirements and examined and reported on in accordance with generally accepted auditing standards by an independent public or certified accountant.*

(3)   Offerings over $7,500,000. The financial statement as would be required in a registration statement filed under the Act on the form that the issuer would be entitled to use. If an issuer, other than a limited partnership, cannot obtain audited financial statements without unreasonable effort or expense, then only the issuer's balance sheet, which shall be dated within 120 days of the start of the offering, must be audited. If the issuer is a limited partnership and cannot obtain the required financial statements without unreasonable effort or expense, it may furnish financial statements that have been prepared on the basis of Federal income tax requirements and examined and reported on in accordance with generally accepted auditing standards by an independent public or certified accountant.

This section contains additional requirements (that we have not presented) for foreign private issuers and for reporting companies under the Securities Exchange Act of 1934.[13] Reporting companies will have to supply various kinds of disclosure documents, many of which they must regularly produce. We have focused on nonreporting companies to reinforce the emphasis on "entrepreneurial finance" where the disclosure work will represent a greater burden and perhaps even induce a culture shock.

Two-way communication with investors is required when the safe harbor dictates disclosure:

§230.502(b)(2)(v) The issuer shall also make available to each purchaser at a reasonable time prior to his purchase of securities in a transaction under §230.505 or 230.506 the opportunity to ask questions and receive answers concerning the terms and conditions of the offering and to obtain any additional information which the issuer possesses or can acquire without unreasonable effort or expense that is necessary to verify the accuracy of information furnished under paragraph (b)(2)(i) or (ii) of this §230.502.

CONCEPT CHECK

• What is integration as it applies to securities offerings?
• What types of information need to be disclosed to offerees?

SOLICITATION

With the exception of certain Rule 504 (§230.504) offerings, general advertising and soliciting are strictly forbidden:

§230.502(c) Limitation on manner of offering. Except as provided in §230.504(b)(1), neither the issuer nor any person acting on its behalf shall offer or sell the securities by any form of general solicitation or general advertising, including, but not limited to, the following:

---

[13] Reporting companies under the 1934 act typically would meet one of three tests: (1) have a security traded on a national exchange, (2) have consolidated gross assets of at least $10 million and more than 500 equity holders, or (3) have a 1933 act registered public offering that has not been deregistered.

(1)   *Any advertisement, article, notice or other communication published in any newspaper, magazine, or similar media or broadcast over television or radio; and*

(2)   *Any seminar or meeting whose attendees have been invited by any general solicitation or general advertising.*

Provided, however, that publication by an issuer of a notice in accordance with #167; 230.135c shall not be deemed to constitute general solicitation or general advertising for purposes of this section.

While these limitations are clear, the SEC has, through a number of comments and no-action letters, helped to clarify some of the practical marketing implications.[14] In most, if not all, of the private offerings we have seen, one finds conformity to the following basic restrictions. The number of offers (offerees) is limited and, when possible, concentrated on investors with sufficient prior relationship to the issuer to ensure that the investors are suitable. When there is no prior relationship, the issuer thoroughly examines investor suitability, usually through an investor suitability questionnaire. There is no public advertising. Word of mouth and networking are about the only way the word gets out. The offering is tracked by numbering the private placement memoranda and logging each one given out. A Regulation D compliance officer is appointed to ensure that all the information is properly collected and stored. Serious education about the nature and restrictions of private placements takes place inside the issuing firm to make sure that an exemption is not forfeited due to unauthorized employee actions.

These offerings don't take place without substantial competent legal advice from securities law specialists. Pay now or pay later. As an example of how important context-specific legal advice can be, one of our students recently took a brochure about his startup to a venture capital conference. While the student was not officially on the program to present to the VCs (and others in the audience), he did have a small spot at a table in the refreshments area where, in addition to making his brochures available, he assisted the conference attendees in scheduling conference-related activities. According to the student, who had already spent a sizable sum on securities-related legal counsel, the use of the phrase "prospective investor" in the brochure was the point of serious debate and negotiation with company counsel. The point here is that this concern was over brochures being handed out primarily to venture investors, who were almost certainly qualified (accredited). However, without a prior relationship, one can't really know, can one? A brochure isn't an offering, is it? Does the brochure have to contain formal disclosure and have to be numbered and logged? Is the solicitation of interest at such a meeting a "general" solicitation? Lest you think that the student became bogged down in the mire of such questions, he did not. He took the legal counsel and ran with it. His venture was completely funded within a few weeks of graduation. This is the true purpose of the current chapter: to familiarize you with the process so that you can move ahead without fear of having your venture vexed with legal problems related to fundraising.

---

[14]   For one list of SEC comments and no-action letters, see Harroch, "Federal Securities Law Considerations of Raising Capital."

RESALE

The purpose of a private placement exemption is to make the path easy for non-public securities to be placed. Restricting resale opportunities is consistent with the goal of keeping the placement private:

> *§230.502(b)(2)(vii) At a reasonable time prior to the sale of securities to any purchaser that is not an accredited investor in a transaction under §230.505 or §230.506, the issuer shall advise the purchaser of the limitations on resale in the manner contained in paragraph (d)(2) of this section. Such disclosure may be contained in other materials required to be provided by this paragraph.*

The specific resale restrictions to which this disclosure requirement refers are:

> *§230.502(d) Limitations on resale. Except as provided in §230.504(b)(1), securities acquired in a transaction under Regulation D shall have the status of securities acquired in a transaction under section 4(2) of the Act and cannot be resold without registration under the Act or an exemption therefrom. The issuer shall exercise reasonable care to assure that the purchasers of the securities are not underwriters within the meaning of section 2(11) of the Act, which reasonable care may be demonstrated by the following:*
>
> *(1) Reasonable inquiry to determine if the purchaser is acquiring the securities for himself or for other persons;*
>
> *(2) Written disclosure to each purchaser prior to sale that the securities have not been registered under the Act and, therefore, cannot be resold unless they are registered under the Act or unless an exemption from registration is available; and*
>
> *(3) Placement of a legend on the certificate or other document that evidences the securities stating that the securities have not been registered under the Act and setting forth or referring to the restrictions on transferability and sale of the securities.*
>
> *While taking these actions will establish the requisite reasonable care, it is not the exclusive method to demonstrate such care. Other actions by the issuer may satisfy this provision. In addition, §230.502(b)(2)(vii) requires the delivery of written disclosure of the limitations on resale to investors in certain instances.*

CONCEPT CHECK

- What are the restrictions on general solicitation and advertising?
- What is a restricted security and why does this designation matter?
- What types of buyers must the owner of restricted securities find?

RULE 503: FILING OF NOTICE OF SALES

Rule 503 (§230.503) dictates that for all Reg D exemptions, a Form D should be filed within fifteen days after the first sale of securities. For 505 exemptions, signing Form D also indicates that the issuer is willing to furnish to the SEC, upon the written request of its staff, the Rule 502 information furnished by the issuer to any nonaccredited investor. Failure to file a Form D within fifteen days does not result in automatic loss of the Reg D safe harbor but can restrict the issuer's future ability to use Reg D through Rule 507.

- What are the reporting requirements on a Reg D offering?

RULE 507: REG D DISQUALIFICATION PROVISIONS

Rule 507 (§230.507) prohibits the use of Reg D exemptions "for an issuer if such issuer, any of its predecessors or affiliates have been subject to any order, judgment, or decree of any court of competent jurisdiction temporarily, preliminarily or permanently enjoining such person for failure to comply with §230.503" (filing of Form D). The disqualification can be waived for good cause by the SEC.

RULE 508: REG D INSIGNIFICANT DEVIATIONS CLAUSE

Rule 508 (§230.508) allows for "insignificant" deviations from the exemptions' requirements without necessarily losing the safe harbor altogether. The deviation must (1) not be from a term, condition, or requirement directly intended to protect the investor for whom the exemption is claimed; (2) must be insignificant with respect to the offer as a whole; and (3) must not be with respect to restrictions on general advertising and solicitation, amounts issued, or the investors count. In addition, the issuer must have made a "good faith and reasonable attempt" to comply with all the requirements for the Reg D exemption claimed. This rule also notes that even when safe harbor from registration is granted under this rule, the SEC retains its authority (under Section 20 of the 1933 act) to sanction the issuing firm for noncompliance.

With the context provided by Rules 501–503, 507, and 508, we can more easily understand the actual exemptions found in Rules 504, 505, and 506. While we will present the exemptions more formally, the basic choice in exemptions trades off the number and exclusiveness of investors against the amount of money raised. Rule 504 permits only a $1 million offering but has no restrictions on the number of investors and, as we have already seen, can avoid restrictions on general advertising and resales. (More detail on the avoidance is coming.) Rule 505 applies to offerings of up to $5 million but caps the number of investors who must be counted (nonaccredited, etc.) at thirty-five. Rule 506 has no monetary limit but limits investors who must be counted to thirty-five and requires that they be "sophisticated." (The actual exemption text is, of course, more obtuse.)

RULE 144 (§230.144)

The primary exemption from the prohibition of resale of unregistered securities (including, but not limited to, securities safely harbored in Rules 505 and 506 offerings) is Rule 144. This rule is designed to make sure that privately placed securities are resold to the public only when adequate current information is publicly available, and to make sure that the market is not suddenly flooded with the venture's unregistered securities. The SEC makes clear in a preliminary note that this rule is not for use by underwriters buying securities with intent to resell. A lot of the legal language revolves around the concept of a security distribution, which is what the exempted reselling needs to avoid. Some insight is available in the following comments from the preliminary note:

> In determining when a person is deemed not to be engaged in a distribution several factors must be considered.
>
> First, the purpose and underlying policy of the Act to protect investors requires that there be adequate current information concerning the issuer, whether the resales of securities by persons result in a distribution or are effected in trading transactions. Accordingly, the availability of the rule is conditioned on the existence of adequate current public information.
>
> Secondly, a holding period prior to resale is essential, among other reasons, to assure that those persons who buy under a claim of a Section 4(2) exemption have assumed the economic risks of investment, and therefore are not acting as conduits for sale to the public of unregistered securities, directly or indirectly, on behalf of an issuer. It should be noted, that there is nothing in Section 2(11) which places a time limit on a person's status as an underwriter. The public has the same need for protection afforded by registration whether the securities are distributed shortly after their purchase or after a considerable length of time.
>
> A third factor, which must be considered in determining what is deemed not to constitute a "distribution," is the impact of the particular transaction or transactions on the trading markets. Section 4(1) was intended to exempt only routine trading transactions between individual investors with respect to securities already issued and not to exempt distributions by issuers or acts of other individuals who engage in steps necessary to such distributions. Therefore, a person reselling securities under Section 4(1) of the Act must sell the securities in such limited quantities and in such a manner as not to disrupt the trading markets. The larger the amount of securities involved, the more likely it is that such resales may involve methods of offering and amounts of compensation usually associated with a distribution rather than routine trading transactions. Thus, solicitation of buy orders or the payment of extra compensation are not permitted by the rule.
>
> In summary, if the sale in question is made in accordance with all of the provisions of the rule, as set forth below, any person who sells restricted securities shall be deemed not to be engaged in a distribution of such securities and therefore not an underwriter thereof. The rule also provides that any person who sells restricted or other securities on behalf of a person in a control relationship with the issuer shall be deemed not to be engaged in a distribution of such securities and therefore not to be an underwriter thereof, if the sale is made in accordance with all the conditions of the rule.

As this note suggests, Rule 144's restrictions relate primarily to: (i) holding period (currently one year); (ii) adequacy of public information (SEC filing of reports or similar information available otherwise); and (iii) the somewhat complex rule that describes allowable volume:

§230.144(e)

1. Sales by affiliates. If restricted or other securities sold for the account of an affiliate of the issuer, the amount of securities sold, together with all sales of restricted and other securities of the same class for the account of such person within the preceding three months, shall not exceed the greater of

    i. one percent of the shares or other units of the class outstanding as shown by the most recent report or statement published by the issuer, or

    ii. the average weekly reported volume of trading in such securities on all national securities exchanges and/or reported through the automated quotation system of a registered securities association during the four calendar weeks preceding the filing of notice required by paragraph (h), or if no such notice is required the date of receipt of the order to execute the transaction by the broker or the date of execution of the transaction directly with a market maker, or

    iii. the average weekly volume of trading in such securities reported through the consolidated transaction reporting system contemplated by Rule 11Aa3-1 under the Securities Exchange Act of 1934 during the four-week period specified in subdivision (ii) of this paragraph.

2. Sales by persons other than affiliates. The amount of restricted securities sold for the account of any person other than an affiliate of the issuer, together with all other sales of restricted securities of the same class for the account of such person within the preceding three months, shall not exceed the amount specified in paragraphs (e)(1)(i), (1)(ii) or (1)(iii) of this section, whichever is applicable, unless the conditions in paragraph (k) of this rule are satisfied.

For an interesting example of a recent attempt to use Rule 144 in new territory, consider the recent listing of Rule 144 shares on eBay, the online person-to-person auction service.[15] Although eBay withdrew its initial approval for the listing because it did not in any way want to be cast as a securities broker or dealer, the owner of these securities and his legal counsel have introduced some very interesting questions about the relationship between Rule 144 and the Internet. Rule 144 resales must be reported to the SEC:

§230.144(h) Notice of proposed sale. If the amount of securities to be sold in reliance upon the rule during any period of three months exceeds 500 shares or other units or has an aggregate sale price in excess of $10,000, three copies of a notice on Form 144 shall be filed with the Commission at its principal office in Washington, D.C.; and if such securities are admitted to trading on any national securities exchange, one copy of such notice shall also be transmitted to the principal exchange on which such securities are so admitted. The Form 144 shall be signed by the person for whose account the securities are to be sold and shall be transmitted for filing concurrently with either the placing with a broker of an order to execute a sale of securities in reliance upon this rule or the execution directly with a market maker of such a sale. Neither

---

[15] See, for example, Matt Krantz, "Stock Listing On eBay Stirs Controversy," *USA Today*, August 20, 1999.

the filing of such notice nor the failure of the Commission to comment thereon shall be deemed to preclude the Commission from taking any action it deems necessary or appropriate with respect to the sale of the securities referred to in such notice. The requirements of this paragraph, however, shall not apply to securities sold for the account of any person other than an affiliate of the issuer, provided the conditions of paragraph (k) of this rule are satisfied.

When reselling restricted securities to other institutions in the venture investing business, it is more common to rely on the exemption written specifically for such resales, Rule 144A. The provisions of this rule allow resales in a less (volume and time) restricted manner to qualified institutional buyers. There are still significant requirements on the adequacy and currency of the information available to the buyer.

CONCEPT CHECK

- What is the purpose of Rule 144?
- To what do Rule 144's restrictions relate?

Appendix C

OTHER FORMS OF REGISTRATION EXEMPTIONS AND BREAKS

In this section, we cover two other forms of registration exemptions. The first applies to issuing securities as part of the compensation package for key employees, while the second describes an effort by the state of California to provide a more general version of an accredited investor at its state level.

RULE 701

Almost all ventures will want to have a compensation scheme that includes some issue of equity or equity-related securities to key employees. If all such issues were in need of registration, it would impose a huge burden on fast-growth ventures wanting to attract talented team members. A full investigation of Rule 701's provisions would take us too far afield, and its text is widely available. We will summarize the rule by noting that a typical early-stage venture that is not an investment company and that takes the time to have written compensation agreements or a written benefit plan can typically structure compensation-related securities issues so they are exempt from SEC registration requirements. The aggregate sales price or amount of securities sold in reliance on this exemption during any consecutive twelve-month period:

must not exceed the greatest of the following: i) $1,000,000; ii) 15% of the total assets of the issuer (or of the issuer's parent if the issuer is a wholly-owned subsidiary and the securities represent obligations that the parent fully and unconditionally guarantees), measured at the issuer's most recent annual balance sheet date (if no older than its last fiscal year end); or iii) 15% of the outstanding amount of the class of securities being offered and sold in reliance on this section, measured at the issuer's most recent annual balance sheet date (if no older than its last fiscal year end).

Supplemental disclosure is required if the aggregate issue during any twelve-month period reaches $5 million. Resale of the securities is restricted (as in Rule 144) in a manner similar to the way other nonregistered securities are.

RULE 1001

Recently, California has taken a position of leadership in trying to formulate a more general accredited investor exemption at the state level. The current California exemption uses "qualified purchaser" in place of the Reg D notion of "accredited investor." Sales can be made only to a "qualified purchaser" who buys more than $150,000 of the offering by committing less than 10 percent of her net worth. In exchange for this slightly tougher standard (Reg D accredits investors having a net worth of $1 million and allows for up to thirty-five nonaccredited investors), the California exemption, like Regulation A (discussed in Section 8.8), allows "testing the waters." That is, investors can be asked if they have any interest before a full filing with regulatory authorities. In a supportive move, the SEC has granted these California-exempt offerings an accompanying federal exemption. The SEC exemption has become known as Regulation CE and may soon become available in other states that follow California's lead in establishing state-accredited investor exemptions. Securities issued under the California exemption are restricted in the sense of Rule 144.

REGULATION SB

Normal full-blown registrations are governed by SEC Regulation C and usually involve the complicated and time-consuming submission of Form S-1. For small business issuers, there are two alternative simplified registration forms: SB-1 and SB-2. Note that we are now talking about small business compliance with, not exemption from, the 1933 act's registration requirements. The intent of Regulation SB is to simplify the registration process for small businesses seeking modest capital from the public markets.

§228.10 (Item 10).

(a) *Application of Regulation S-B. Regulation S-B is the source of disclosure requirements for "small business issuer" filings under the Securities Act of 1933 (the "Securities Act") and the Securities Exchange Act of 1934 (the "Exchange Act").*

  (1) *Definition of small business issuer. A small business issuer is defined as a company that meets all of the following criteria:*

    (i)   *has revenues of less than $25,000,000;*

    (ii) *is a U.S. or Canadian issuer;*

    (iii) *is not an investment company; and*

    (iv) *if a majority owned subsidiary, the parent corporation is also a small business issuer.*

  Provided however, that an entity is not a small business issuer if it has a public float (the aggregate market value of the issuer's outstanding securities held by non-affiliates) of $25,000,000 or more.

  Note: The public float of a reporting company shall be computed by use of the price at which the stock was last sold, or the average of the bid and asked prices of such stock, on a date within 60 days prior to the end of its most recent fiscal year. The public float of a company filing an initial registration statement under the Exchange Act shall be determined as of a date within 60 days of the date the registration statement is filed. In the case of an initial public offering of securities, public float shall be computed on the basis of the number of shares outstanding prior to the offering and the estimated public offering price of the securities.

The standard filing form for an SB registration is SB-2. The requirements for disclosure and even guidelines on including management forecasts are provided by Regulation SB. An alternative, simpler registration form, SB-1, is available to small business issuers who seek to raise not more than $10 million in a twelve-month period and take only cash as consideration.

CONCEPT CHECK

- What must be the purpose of securities issued under Rule 701?
- Which state's accredited investor exemption is recognized by Rule 1001?

Part 4

CREATING AND RECOGNIZING VENTURE VALUE

Chapter 9

VALUING EARLY-STAGE VENTURES

PREVIOUSLY COVERED

In Chapter 8, we discussed securities law considerations faced by entrepreneurs when obtaining venture financing. Our intent was to provide an introductory discussion of federal laws, and to a lesser extent state laws, related to financing and therefore likely to be important to an entrepreneur. Since acquiring outside financial capital by issuing securities is a "must" for virtually every entrepreneur, we provided a brief discussion of the Securities Act of 1933. A particularly important focal point was the use of Regulation D as a "safe harbor" from the cost and time involved in registering securities with the Securities and Exchange Commission.

LOOKING AHEAD

Chapter 10 simplifies this chapter's equity valuation methods to focus on the division of ownership for ventures requiring multiple-stage financing. The simplified methods are often termed "venture capital methods" because of their rather widespread adoption among professional venture capitalists.

CHAPTER LEARNING OBJECTIVES

In this chapter, we introduce basic concepts of valuation, the process of estimating values. We consider the owner of a growing business who is beginning negotiations with a potential investor. We introduce the mechanics of valuation and some mathematical simplification that can be used to value the venture. By dividing the venture's future into an explicitly forecasted period and a subsequent constant growth period, we can greatly simplify the valuation problem faced by the venture's entrepreneur. We discuss two valuation methods that differ in how projected financial statements are created and when credit for creating surplus cash is granted. After completing this chapter, you will be able to:

1. Explain how the time pattern of cash flows relates to venture value

2. Describe how valuation incorporates projections of near- and long-term success

3. Extract the necessary valuation data from projected financial statements

4. Understand the relationship between dividends and equity valuation cash flow

5. Put the pieces together for a unified treatment of financial projections and valuation

Part 4 of this text introduces the concepts and mechanics of venture valuation. One of the most important indicators of venture progress is an increase in the venture's value. At each stage, we would hope that there is a measurable increase. In the early stages, when there is little or no operating experience, the process is especially subjective. Nonetheless, when the venture is raising money, there is tangible evidence of value—investors buy shares at a commonly agreed-upon price. Later in the venture's life cycle, it becomes more important to quantify the value being created even in the absence of intervening financing. The process becomes less subjective and more accurate.

9.1   WHAT IS A VENTURE WORTH?

present value (PV)
value today of all future cash flows discounted to the present at the investor's required rate of return

Every entrepreneur wants to turn an opportunity into a viable business, grow the business, and harvest the resulting value. It is not appropriate simply to sum all future returns to determine a venture's value; there is a time value or cost of having to wait for future cash flows. A venture's **present value (PV)** is the value today of all future cash flows discounted to the present at the rate of return required by investors.

We begin with Jim, the owner-manager of the FrothySlope microbrewery and restaurant in a small Colorado ski town, who has recently been the object of potential investor attention. The success of his first brewpub and the local popularity of his microbrews have resulted in a direct offer to invest $100,000 in ongoing operations and a desire to consider bottling and broader distribution. Although Jim has a business degree, complete with introductory exposures to accounting and finance, he is most comfortable overseeing the production of his handcrafted honey wheat ale. While he welcomes the eager investor, he also has no feeling for how much ownership he should be willing to sell in exchange for the $100,000 investment.

DOES THE PAST MATTER?

After some thought, Jim structures his approach as follows:

1. I have $50,000 of my own cash in the brewpub and one and a half years of seventy-hour weeks.

2. I have taken only a small amount of cash out of the business for my living expenses, certainly not equal to a reasonable wage.

3. In college, I worked at a brewpub for $10 an hour, but that college degree ought to be worth at least $5 more per hour.

4. It seems like I have about $131,900 [$50,000 + (78 × 70 × $15)] of cash and sweat in this brewpub.

5. $100,000 + $131,900 = $231,900, and 100,000/231,900 is about 43 percent.

6. I can take the $100,000, remain the majority owner, and take a shot at the big time. Done . . . I think.

Before signing the deal, he decides to run his thinking by an acquaintance more closely connected with the financial aspects of business valuation and investment . . . you.

QUESTIONS

1. What are the advantages and disadvantages of Jim's approach to determining the investor's percent ownership?

2. What role, if any, do the $50,000 cash and the $81,900 sweat equity play in determining the postfinancing ownership structure? Would the investor want less ownership if there had been two years of history rather than a year and a half?

3. How will the investor make a return on the $100,000 investment? Does this relate to the existing investment?

4. How would you structure an approach to answering Jim's question regarding how much the new investor should own in exchange for the $100,000 investment?

5. Comment on the casual remark, "Investors pay for the future; entrepreneurs pay for the past."

LOOKING TO THE FUTURE

One difficulty in dealing with Jim's framing of the ownership structure, which is really a valuation question, is that he is intimately familiar with the struggle and the sacrifice of the past. Accordingly, he is not in the mood to be told that the value of his business is not directly related to the quantity of his past efforts in cash or sweat. While accounting for the past is all well and good, an investor seeks to quantify and value the future. To the extent that the quantity and quality of Jim's historic efforts have laid the foundation for a lucrative future, new investors will compensate him. Ineffective or irrelevant past efforts are the entrepreneur's sunk costs. They are not the basis of investor willingness to pay.

What really matters in the valuation question is whether these past efforts resulted in a product or brand that can be the basis for future profits to repay the investor. Jim should be structuring his approach to address such issues as (1) the future customer base, consumption, and sales behavior; (2) distribution and quality issues in growing outside the small Colorado town; (3) the scope for the business—local, regional, national, or international; (4) the growth plan for any additional brewpubs; (5) whether the presence of one of his brewpubs is integral to marketing his ales in other towns; and (6) the margins on the various follow-on products sharing the same brand. With an eye to the future, 43 percent may vastly exceed the amount Jim needs to sell to justify the $100,000 investment. On the other hand, Jim's future might be so limited that the investor would be justified in demanding 75 percent. In either case, the future, not the past, is the basis of value. Different perceptions of the future will undoubtedly result in different valuations and ownership structures, even when launching from the same past.

> - What is sweat equity? How does it influence the task of valuing a venture?
> - When is sweat equity valuable? When is it worthless?

VESTED INTERESTS IN VALUE: INVESTOR AND ENTREPRENEUR

Once Jim understands that his past efforts contribute to value only indirectly, through their influence on the ability of the business to generate future profits (and returns to investors), he sees the importance of business planning. To communicate effectively with potential investors he will need to formalize—and, to the extent possible, quantify—his vision and objectives.

If Jim had wished to remain local and sell only through the restaurant, a certain clientele of investors would have been willing to join him, vesting their hopes in the single brewpub. On the other hand, because his plan is to market his craft brewing nationally through normal retail stores and a chain of brewpubs, a different clientele of investors will consider partaking in the risk and return of the grander vision. Ascertaining the type of investor offering the $100,000 investment is critical. Communicating his vision effectively and attracting compatible investors (who share the same, or a highly correlated, view of the future) is one of the central purposes of a formal written business plan.

It is clear that investors are not going to share all of Jim's personal objectives for owning and operating a chain of brewpubs. For instance, in addition to having a national consumer base, Jim may wish to locate pubs in towns he likes to visit or where his relatives reside. He may want to employ a relative as chief financial officer. Similarly, Jim will not share all of his investors' objectives. It is common for upstream suppliers and downstream distributors to invest in order to solidify strategic relationships. Some of the objectives of strategic relationship investors may be at odds with Jim's objectives.

In this and other investment contexts, however, there is a financial objective that, other things being equal, both Jim and his potential investor can support—increasing the value of the ownership of Jim's operations. Rarely do investors and founders agree on exactly how to increase value. Nevertheless, there is almost always an unwritten agreement that, whatever the strategy (purchasing, operations, marketing, management), from the venture's viewpoint the fundamental criterion for evaluation is the strategy's contribution (directly or indirectly) to firm value. If Jim wants to appoint Dad as CFO, he will be asked to explain to the other investors why this enhances value relative to other choices for CFO. If the venture's hops supplier has invested and wants the business to increase its hops inventory holdings, someone will have to explain why this is a net financial advantage.

Jim and his potential investor have been debating two expansion strategies. Jim believes that, in order to affiliate his crafted ales with the brewpub experience, early customers should continue to purchase his ales primarily at a company pub. Such belief dictates that pub operations be expanded relatively rapidly or that licenses be granted to existing pubs with the proper atmosphere to sell his draft ale. Jim's potential investor thinks it is better to go with a few destination pubs, no licensed pubs, and extensive advertising to create a brewpub affiliation as bottled versions of his crafted ales are distributed through normal distribution channels. While it is not clear how this debate will be resolved, it is obvious that one important criterion by which the strategies will be judged will be the bottom-line impact on the value of Jim's venture. Valuation is how visions of the future are translated, quantified, interpreted, and made relevant to *current* investor negotiations.

For those who are interested in why economists, finance professionals, and academics focus on the present value of owners' wealth to choose a firm's strategic direction, Learning Supplement 9A (at the end of this chapter) presents a nontraditional treatment of the traditional microeconomics argument for maximizing firm value as a unifying theme when evaluating investments. In such a context, it is easy to see how financial markets unify investor objectives for the firm without denying important differences in the way investors perceive a firm's investment (and harvest) opportunities. Recognizing the role of financial market signals, and incorporating them into decision making, can provide an important financial framework for investors and founders to use when evaluating the advantages and disadvantages of different expansion strategies. Agreement on an evaluation criterion is a first step toward agreement on the strategy itself.

CONCEPT CHECK

- How are Jim's and the investor's objectives related to venture value?
- Is creating a larger value something about which they would always agree?
- Why is increasing value a reasonable venture objective?

9.2 BASIC MECHANICS OF VALUATION: MIXING VISION AND REALITY

While our previous remarks concentrated on valuation as a quantification of a future vision, we have spent no time connecting the entrepreneur's (or investor's) vision with reality. Valuation always involves a tension between observable history, observable present, and unobservable—yet envisioned—future. There are two major contact points with the observable reality. These contact points become clearer if we review basic valuation as taught in introductory finance courses.

PRESENT VALUE CONCEPT

We begin with the simplest valuation problem—a known payment at a known future date. Suppose you can invest in risk-free U.S. Treasury securities so that a $1 investment generates a $1.05 payment from the Treasury one year from now. It should be clear that the Treasury markets are offering you a 5 percent annual return. (Ignore, for now, that the same Treasury will be taking some of this money back as tax.) That is, one dollar grows into one dollar and five cents over the process of a year. Put differently, the U.S. government is willing to pay you five cents to rent your money for a year. Just as important, you are demanding that the U.S. government compensate you for having the use of your money for a year. Your supply of funds and the Treasury market's demand for funds are meeting at an interest rate of five cents for the year:

$$(1) \times (1.05) = 1.05 \quad \text{therefore} \quad \frac{1.05}{(1.05)} = 1$$

If there were a Treasury security for a dollar that paid only four cents in interest, you would do better to put your dollar in one of the five-cent-a-year securities. You might, however, offer to pay the holder of the Treasury security less for the security paying only four cents of interest. How much less? This is the valuation question. For this simple problem, the solution is also simple: If a dollar expands at 5 percent a year, a comparable price this year for the four-cent payer is the value "?" from which an expansion at 5 percent gives the payoff of $1.04:

$$(?) \times (1.05) = 1.04 \quad \text{therefore} \quad \frac{1.04}{(1.05)} = (?)$$

As you can see, this value is determined by dividing the payment 1.04 by one plus the market-determined rate of return on a one-year investment in Treasury securities. In this example, ? = .9905. You must pay less than $1 to be making 5 percent with only a 4 percent interest payment. Price adjusts downward to achieve the 5 percent target.

Generalizing this to a multiyear investment is straightforward. Suppose two-year Treasuries are currently priced to guarantee a rate of 5.499 percent, and we are considering buying a Treasury that pays $.06 each year for the next two years and then returns a dollar (for each dollar invested). This Treasury must be priced so that the amount of money initially invested will expand to $1.05499 \times 1.05499 = 1.113$ per dollar invested. This is what it means to be priced to make 5.499 percent per year. The flows on this investment are $.06 at the end of the first year and $1.06 at the end of the second year. You will have to do something with the $.06 at the end of the first year. In orderly markets, the only way one-year Treasuries can promise 5 percent, and two-year Treasuries can promise 5.499 percent per year, is if interest rates to use your money for that second year are higher than 5 percent. In fact, simple arbitrage trading restrictions imply that 5.499 percent must be a (geometric) average of the first-year rate of 5 percent and a second-year rate of 6 percent:

$$(1.05) \times (1.06) = (1.05499)^2 = 1.113$$

With this information, we know how much we can make on the $.06 you get a year from now and can add it to the $1.06 you get at the end of the second year:

$$(?) \times (1.05)(1.06) = .06 \times (1.06) + 1.06 \quad \text{therefore} \quad \frac{.06}{(1.05)} + \frac{1.06}{(1.05)(1.06)} = (?)$$

In this example, the amount you would be willing to pay is ? = 1.00952381. You must pay a premium (more than one dollar per dollar of principal) to assure that this six-cent payer only makes 5.499 percent. Again, prices adjust to make sure that market-determined returns are made. This is the essence of valuation: Find a price that allows an investor to make the same as she would make in other comparable investment opportunities. In this example, $1.00952381 is the price that allows you to make 5.499 percent per year on a two-year committed investment. It is the present value (PV) of the six-cent payer security.

Let's return to our comment that valuation exercises must have two contact points with reality. We have discovered the first. Given a set of future payments, a proper valuation considers investors' other real present investment opportunities. While a venture's payment stream will not be as certain as a Treasury bond's, we still will want to determine what alternative uses there are for the investors' funds. Valuation will treat the opportunity cost imposed by these other investments as a hurdle to be cleared. Applying our approach to finding the value represented by "?", we can see that, for Jim's brewpub venture, the numerators will relate to his (or the potential investor's) expected payments (returns on investment), whereas the denominators will be derived from the current terms set in the market for venture investments of a similar profile. In this sense, vision is in the numerator and reality is in the denominator. The second point of a valuation's contact with reality is when we benchmark the vision with recent venture history, market research, and comparable firms' behaviors, a process to which we will often return.

We are now in a position to consider Jim's potential investor who summarized his offer as, "I am willing to invest $100,000 but expect to make a 50 percent return on my investment." Is 50 percent appropriate and fair? Where did it come from? Would the investor really get 50 percent elsewhere? Does Jim really have to pay that much? As long as markets exist and comparisons can be made, one at least has the hope that some objectivity may be introduced into the negotiations.

CONCEPT CHECK

- What is meant by "vision is in the numerator and reality is in the denominator"?

IF YOU'RE NOT USING ESTIMATES, YOU'RE NOT DOING A VALUATION

Finance academics (and, by association, finance students) have always been comfortable studying stock returns, dividend streams, and business successes and failures, and applying usable data from their observations to the analysis of an investment initiative. Not surprisingly, but perhaps disappointingly, their comparative advantage becomes the denominator of the valuation equation. They have little or nothing to say about the visions represented by the numerators, other than "garbage in, garbage out."

Consequently, it is not surprising that many students of entrepreneurial finance never really make peace with the type of fiction required in a business plan. Their comfort levels drop even lower as their best guesses at revenues, expenses, timing, and investment requirements end up in the numerator of some valuation. In the rehearsal sessions for a recent venture capital conference, we observed a seasoned entrepreneur providing what appeared to be inadequate estimates of where he saw the venture and its market heading. When questioned about the lack of numbers after the first year, he replied that he wasn't comfortable projecting any further. The venture capitalists at the rehearsal pointed out that his firm was supposed to have some comparative advantage in predicting the future of his venture and its market. He responded by saying that any numbers he provided publicly would be taken as a commitment to which investors would hold him. One of the venture capitalists responded by noting that this drawback was part of the point of the exercise.

One of the first signs that an entrepreneur (or student) has failed in an approach to valuation is that only historical numbers have been used. Accounting for the past is, in our experience, far simpler than projecting the firm into the future. Historically, money was made and spent, and there are good rules and guidelines about how the associated activities are to be recorded. Balancing a balance sheet is really a matter of knowing what happened. Assets have to equal liabilities plus equity, right?

The process of projecting financial statements into the future is not so narrowly confined. Money will be made. How? Money will be spent. Where? When? Financing will be required. How much? What kind? When? On what terms? Almost invariably, projected balance sheets never initially balance, and, without more comprehensive thought, they probably shouldn't. Projecting the assets forward with an operations mentality does not address how the liabilities are to be projected. We all know that assets, liabilities, and equity are connected. Many users of accounting don't fully grasp accounting's essence until they (1) make up an entirely fictitious future, (2) balance the associated projected balance sheet, (3) square the balance sheet with the projected income statement, and (4) produce solely from the other two financial statements a projected statement of cash flows displaying the correct cash account balance.

While predicting a venture's future is a dreadful process for some, projecting the venture into the future is nonetheless necessary. It is more useful for the trip to be planned, and unanticipated excursions encountered, than to start with no plan and never admit that the pothole-laden side road was a detour from the planned route. As for whether it is feasible to peer into the future in high-tech industries, one need look no further than the pharmaceutical industry's "orphan drugs" to know that R&D-intensive industries have some formal feeling for the possibility that future revenues will never justify current development costs. Valuation and strategic planning require some vision of the future. In addition, valuation asks that it be quantified to the extent possible.

As we hope we have made clear, valuation is inherently about the future. The past matters only insofar as it influences the expectations and realizations of future economic events. When considering your venture, remember: *If you're not using estimates, it's not a valuation.* Get accustomed to making up the numbers, good numbers. Not all fiction is equally meritorious. It is true that you may be constructing the bomb by which your venture, or at least your position in the venture, will be destroyed. If this is your fear, consider Dr. Strangelove's adaptation: "How I learned to stop worrying and love the bomb."

CONCEPT CHECK

- Is it adequate to project financial statements into the future based solely on the use of historical information?

DIVIDE AND CONQUER WITH DISCOUNTED CASH FLOW

Because investors look to the future for streams of cash they expect to receive, proper investment valuation begins with projected future performance. A venture's ability to pay investors future cash streams depends on its future performance (in sales and expenses). Although we will take greater care later in this chapter when defining what is meant by valuation cash flow (VCF), valuation is a connection between a venture's ability to generate future cash and an investor's willingness to provide the funds necessary to achieve those future cash flows.

In their simplest form, most basic valuation techniques calibrate a security's value by estimating future cash flows and discounting them for risk and delay. The total found when adding up all the discounted values is the venture's value. Valuations employing this approach are referred to as **discounted cash flow (DCF)** valuations. The resulting estimated value is known as the present value (PV) of the future cash flows. Beginning our discussion of valuation procedures with DCF PV has the added advantage of providing a solid foundation for interpreting other, more ad hoc methods to value securities.

A DCF valuation should incorporate all of the cash that will flow to a given security. To provide tractability and expositional advantages, evaluators commonly partition the future into an **explicit forecast period** of two to ten years and a terminal value. In our main approach to calculating the venture's **terminal (or horizon) value** at the end of the explicit period, the venture is modeled as growing smoothly at a reasonable long-term rate. A smooth venture is one that has matured to the point where its margin, profit, operating ratios, capital needs, and other business aspects grow in proportion to revenues. Such smoothness is certainly not characteristic of a startup but may be a reasonable approximation to the venture's character five to ten years down the road. When the venture is no longer venturesome, there are some convenient mathematical simplifications for calibrating DCF values.[1]

discounted cash flow (DCF)
valuation approach involving discounting future cash flows for risk and delay

explicit forecast period
two- to ten-year period in which the venture's financial statements are explicitly forecast

terminal (or horizon) value
the value of the venture at the end of the explicit forecast period

---

[1] All of the supernormal growth, efficiency improvements, and learning-curve advances are treated in the non-smooth explicit forecast period. Of course, the length of the explicit forecast period, the terminal growth rate, and the operating ratios will be critical assumptions in any DCF valuation.

Suppose the venture is growing smoothly, maintaining normal operating ratios, and providing a growing (at rate g) stream of payments to its investors. How would the investors assess the venture's DCF value at this mature stage and time? With the firm growing at a constant rate and maintaining its operating ratios, we can treat the cash flow in the terminal value period as a growing perpetuity. The current value of a growing perpetuity is the next period's cash flow (VCF_T) divided by the spread between the assumed constant discount (r_∞) and growth (g) rates:

$$\text{Terminal Value} = \frac{VCF_T}{r_\infty - g} \qquad \textbf{(9.1)}$$

capitalization (cap) rate
the spread between the discount rate and the growth rate of cash flow in the terminal value period

The spread between the discount rate and the growth rate is referred to as the **capitalization (cap) rate** for the terminal flows. When using this formula, the calibrated value is as of time $T - 1$.

Learning Supplement 9B, at the end of this chapter, provides a formal derivation of this result and demonstrates how this simple formula captures the value of an infinite future stream of cash flows.

A few warnings are in order. The most common error in this approach to terminal value is an improper year T flow (VCF_T). We sometimes refer to year T as the **stepping-stone year**, to remind everyone that it is the first step into the infinite future. The impact of an error in the stepping-stone year affects all of eternity and can be quite large. It is important, therefore, to make sure that year T's flows are representative of the proper margins and ratios and that the growth from year $T - 1$ to T preserves those margins and ratios while accomplishing the intended smooth growth rate. We will return to these precautions in the following chapters when we more carefully analyze the type of cash flow being discounted.

stepping-stone year
first year after the explicit forecast period

We now have the tools for the divide-and-conquer approach to DCF valuation. Because our terminal value is a time $T - 1$ value, we can add it to the explicit flow for $T - 1$ and have one spreadsheet with a finite number of columns. We denote the discount rate over the explicitly projected years (before the terminal years) by r_v, to foreshadow the fact that the venture investor discount rate (r_v) can be quite different from the mature firm discount rate (r_∞).

Time 0 Valuation	**1**	**2**	$\cdots$	**T − 1**
DCF PV (= row sum)	$\dfrac{VCF_1}{1 + r_v}$	$\dfrac{VCF_2}{(1 + r_v)^2}$	$\cdots$	$\dfrac{VCF_{T-1} + \text{Terminal Value}}{(1 + r_v)^{T-1}}$
Or				
DCF PV (= row sum)	$\dfrac{VCF_1}{1 + r_v}$	$\dfrac{VCF_2}{(1 + r_v)^2}$	$\cdots$	$\dfrac{VCF_{T-1} + \dfrac{VCF_T}{r_\infty - g}}{(1 + r_v)^{T-1}}$
Or				
DCF PV (= row sum)	$\dfrac{VCF_1}{1 + r_v}$	$\dfrac{VCF_2}{(1 + r_v)^2}$	$\cdots$	$\dfrac{VCF_{T-1}}{(1 + r_v)^{T-1}} + \dfrac{VCF_T}{(r_\infty - g)(1 + r_v)^{T-1}}$

reversion value
present value of the terminal value

This last version separates the present value of the final explicit period flow, $VCF_{T-1}/(1 + r_v)^{T-1}$, from the present value of the flows in the terminal value period $VCF_T/(r_\infty - g)(1 + r_v)^{T-1}$, which is known as the venture's **reversion value**. This reversion value (the time-zero present value of the terminal value) plays an important role in the pervasive venture capital methods of valuation extensively covered in Chapter 10.

As we are sure these symbols are a bit dense and their application somewhat distant, it is time to return to the valuation of Jim's brewpub. In order to conquer his problem, we divide the future into five years of explicitly forecasted cash flows and a continuing (terminal value) period for Year 6 and beyond. Jim provides us with his best guess for what his venture would have left over after all operating expenses and reinvestments in the first five years: $0 this year, $0 next year, $0 the third year, $2,500,000 the fourth year, and $3,000,000 the fifth (= T − 1 in this example) year. In the sixth year, he believes that the mature venture would have a surplus (after reinvestment) of about $3,500,000, and this would be expected to grow at roughly 6 percent per year after Year 6. He believes that his potential investor (and he) should expect to make about 40 percent on a five-year investment; his investor has other equally risky investment alternatives that would provide a similar return if successful. Jim can't see investors (himself included) expecting to make more than about 20 percent a year for a mature brewpub and distribution operation; he backs this up with some data on a similar, but older, venture that is now publicly traded.

We can now map Jim's best guesses for the symbols we have been using: $T = 6$, $r_v = .40$, $r_\infty = .2$, $g = .06$, $VCF_1 = VCF_2 = VCF_3 = 0$, $VCF_4 = 2,500,000$, $VCF_5 = 3,000,000$, $VCF_T = 3,500,000$.

$$\text{DCF PV} \quad \frac{0}{1.4} \quad \frac{0}{(1.4)^2} \quad \frac{0}{(1.4)^3} \quad \frac{2,500,000}{(1.4)^4} \quad \frac{3,000,000 + 3,500,000/(.2 - .06)}{(1.4)^5}$$
$$\text{BREWPUB}$$

Adding up all of the columns gives a current valuation of $5,856,935 for the FrothySlope venture. This value, before including the money injected by the new investor, is referred to as a **pre-money valuation**. While these calculations are relatively simple to do by hand, in practice the actual calculations are frequently done using a spreadsheet function (e.g., Excel®'s NPV function). The valuation section in the spreadsheet would look like the following:

pre-money valuation present value of a venture prior to a new money investment

	A	B	C	D	E	F	G	H
1		Time 0	Yr 1	Yr 2	Yr 3	Yr 4	Yr 5	Year 6 = T
2	Annual Cash Flow		0	0	0	2,500,000	3,000,000	3,500,000
3	Terminal Value						25,000,000	
4	Total Flow to Discount		0	0	0	2,500,000	28,000,000	
5	Present Value	$5,856,935						

In Excel®, the formula for this cell is "=NPV (0.4,C4:G4)."

In Excel®, the formula for this cell is "=H2/(.2 − .06)."

A **post-money valuation** is the pre-money valuation plus the new investment. If we add the $100,000 new investment to the pre-money amount of $5,856,935, we have FrothySlope's post-money valuation of $5,956,935. So now we can say something about the amount of the venture that Jim would be willing to sell for $100,000 of new financing. We divide the new $100,000 investment by the post-money valuation of $5,956,935 and get 1.68 percent. This approximate 2 percent (rounded) is a far cry from the 43 percent Jim discussed when he considered how much sweat and cash he had put into the FrothySlope brewpub venture. To see why the 2 percent is reasonable, ignore the flows in the explicit period. There's a projected $25,000,000 going concern five years from now. Two percent of $25,000,000 is $500,000, a factor of five on the $100,000 investment.

post-money valuation pre-money valuation of a venture plus money injected by new investors

net present value (NPV)
present value of a set of
future flows plus the current
undiscounted flow

For this example, we have used Excel®'s NPV function. The **net present value (NPV)** is the present value of a set of future flows plus the current (first) undiscounted flow. It is a present value that is net of the current flow (outflow). For some reason, Excel® adopted for its NPV function the convention that the first flow is discounted. Accordingly, its NPV function is really a PV function since the first flow is assumed to be in the future. When using a spreadsheet program's intrinsic functions, it is important to know the assumptions involved. Excel®'s NPV function can be easily adjusted to a traditional NPV by adding the current undiscounted flow to the Excel® NPV of the future cash flows.

CONCEPT CHECK

- What is a terminal value?
- What is the difference between a reversion value and a terminal value?
- How does a pre-money valuation differ from a post-money valuation?

9.3   REQUIRED VERSUS SURPLUS CASH

We begin with the most straightforward type of DCF valuation—discounting the flows to equity, also known as the equity method. As normally executed, it results in a pre-money valuation and would be used like the above pre-money valuation for Jim's brewpub. Although it was quite informal, when Jim first entertained an investment in his brewing operations he considered how much cash would be left over in future periods to pay out to all of the venture's owners. Wherever the new money comes from, the venture should expect it to provide a fair (market) return. Consequently, we must determine whether the future holds enough promise to justify the $100,000, irrespective of its source. This is the essence of pre-money valuation. The structure and providers of current and future financing should be expected to make a fair return on their investments in the venture. Investments that earn fair returns enable the venture to survive but, in themselves, neither add nor detract from venture value. They're "fair" or "zero NPV." It is not necessary to incorporate zero NPV investments when conducting valuation. We can value the venture ignoring the origin and timing of financing. It is important, however, to realize that we will value how the money is *spent*, just not its timing or origin. The timing and origin will be assumed to result in zero NPV financing. In Chapter 10, we will further address post-money valuations, popular with venture capital investors.

To determine precisely what pre-money flows are available to pay to the holders of the venture's equity, we will be a little more formal than in our quick look at Jim's brewpub. In particular, this time we want to start with a statement of cash flows that, as it turns out, contains almost all of the information needed to conduct a formal valuation. In Chapter 6 (Table 6.5), we created the PDC Company's statement of cash flows for April to July (repeated in Table 9.1).

PDC's change in cash balance is $0 for each of April, May, and June and $6,487 for July. The dividends line is zero for all months. In this projection, no

TABLE 9.1   PDC's Statement of Cash Flows, April 1 to July 31

ACCOUNTING STATEMENT OF CASH FLOWS	APRIL	MAY	JUNE	JULY
Cash flows from activities				
Net income	−460	5,976	1,419	−563
Adjustments to net income for CF				
+ Depreciation expense	1,150	1,150	1,150	1,150
− Change in A/R	−9,200	−27,600	18,400	9,200
− Change in inventory	−38,640	25,760	12,880	12,880
− Change in prepaid insurance	460	460	460	460
+ Change in A/P	20,930	−8,050	−9,660	−8,050
+ Change in accrued liabilities	1,725	5,175	−3,450	−1,725
Total adjustments	−23,575	−3,105	19,780	13,915
Net cash flow from operations	−24,035	2,871	21,199	13,352
Cash flows from investing				
Capital expenditures (CAPEX)	−6,900	0	0	0
Net cash used by investments)	−6,900	0	0	0
Cash flows from financing				
Equity issues	0	0	0	0
Dividends	0	0	0	0
Debt issues	30,935	−2,871	−21,199	−6,865
Net cash flows from financing	30,935	−2,871	−21,199	−6,865
Net change in cash	0	0	0	6,487
Beginning cash balance	23,000	23,000	23,000	23,000
Ending cash balance	23,000	23,000	23,000	29,487

payments to PDC's investors are scheduled for the four-month period. PDC has not been in a position to pay out any cash and, in fact, has been borrowing to maintain the required cash balance of $23,000. **Required cash** is the amount of cash necessary to cover a venture's day-to-day operations. **Surplus cash** is cash in addition to required cash that is left over after all operating expenses and reinvestments have been projected. PDC has surplus cash of $6,487 in July.

What may not be immediately obvious is that a valuation should treat the $6,487 surplus cash and the $23,000 required cash quite differently. The $23,000 is an investment analogous to an investment in inventory: This cash inventory has built up during startup, but, more importantly, it remains tied up during the venture's operations. It is not free to be used elsewhere by the venture or its investors. Cash tied up in the normal course of business cannot be paid as a dividend or invested in marketable securities. The maximum possible July dividend is therefore $6,487, not $6,487 + $23,000 = $29,487.

Whether or not the $6,487 is actually paid as a dividend, an argument can be made that equity valuation should treat it as a cash flow available to equity. It has been freed up and can be (at least temporarily) invested elsewhere. It is not currently supporting the venture's operations. Once it is freed from the venture's

required cash
amount of cash needed to cover a venture's day-to-day operations

surplus cash
cash remaining after required cash, all operating expenses, and reinvestments are made

operations, it should be treated as though separated from the venture. It is a separate project with a separate risk and value. It neither creates nor destroys additional venture value until it is invested to support the venture's operations. At that time, the related investment outlays it supports will themselves enter the cash flow negatively. In contrast, the $23,000 is not free and cannot be separated, even conceptually, from the firm, and is really invested in required non-interest-bearing cash. Summarizing, from the information contained in the statement of cash flows, we can discern that the cash flow available to be paid to investors is dividends (and repurchases) plus initial surplus cash. For PDC, this is $6,487. We begin with the easiest equity valuation method. It discounts a dividend stream of the absolute maximum possible dividends the venture could pay while still implementing the business plan.

CONCEPT CHECK

- If PDC had paid a $6,487 dividend to the equity holders on the last day of July rather than keeping it as retained earnings, what would have happened to the statement of cash flows?

9.4   EQUITY VALUATION: THE MAXIMUM DIVIDEND METHOD

maximum dividend method (MDM)
valuation method involving explicitly forecasted dividends to provide surplus cash of zero

We now assume that four months (April, May, June, and July) were on track; it is currently August 1. A potential venture investor is considering buying some of the venture's equity. We need to get a good approximation of PDC's value to facilitate the negotiation of investment terms.

We begin by projecting financial statements for an industry standard T = 5 years, starting 8/1/Y0 and ending 7/31/Y5, where Y0 and Y5 simply indicate year zero and year five.[2] What makes this pre-money valuation method the **maximum dividend method (MDM)** is that we project the venture so that all surplus cash is stripped out in formally projected dividends. That is, dividends are maximized. Using the best available information, Tables 9.2 to 9.4 (see pages 361–362) present PDC's projected statements that, in addition to sales and expense forecasts, reflect PDC's belief that it will eventually finance partly with debt (bearing an interest rate of 10 percent) and will begin to face taxation (30 percent rate). Growth rates for the first two years range from 20.8 to 40 percent. In Years 4 and 5, the projections are forced to adapt to what PDC believes is its long-term growth rate of 6 percent. Long-term debt is added in Year 4 to bring the venture to a more

---

[2] For our current purposes, we treat the projections as given. We assume that the entrepreneurial team has produced this set of coherent projected financial statements. For the interested reader, the maximum dividend financial statements strategically set the level of dividends so that the surplus cash (the balance sheet "plug" account) is set equal to zero. Chapter 6 discusses the projection of coherent financial statements.

TABLE 9.2

PDC's Projected Income Statements with Yearly Surplus Cash Paid as a Dividend

	4/1/Y0– 7/31/Y0	YEAR 1 8/1/Y0– 7/31/Y1	YEAR 2 8/1/Y1– 7/31/Y2	YEAR 3 8/1/Y2– 7/31/Y3	YEAR 4 8/1/Y3– 7/31/Y4	YEAR T = 5 8/1/Y4– 7/31/Y5
Sales	552,000	1,656,000	2,000,000	2,800,000	2,968,000	3,146,080
(growth rates)			20.8%	40.0%	6.0%	6.0%
Income Statements	Historical	Projected	Projected	Projected	Projected	Projected
Sales	552,000	1,656,000	2,000,000	2,800,000	2,968,000	3,146,080
− COGS	−386,400	−1,159,200	−1,400,000	−1,960,000	−2,077,000	−2,202,256
− Wages and commissions	−105,800	−317,400	−383,333	−536,667	−568,867	−602,999
− Rent, miscellaneous, and insurance	−47,840	−111,780	−135,000	−189,000	−200,340	−212,360
− Depreciation	−4,600	−5,796	−5,630	−6,800	−9,520	−10,091
Earnings before interest and taxes (EBIT)	7,360	61,824	76,036	107,533	111,673	118,374
− Interest expense	−988	0	0	0	0	−22,664
Earnings before taxes	6,372	61,824	76,036	107,533	111,673	95,709
− Taxes	0	−18,547	−22,811	−32,260	−33,502	−28,713
Net income	6,372	43,277	53,225	75,273	78,171	66,997
− Dividends	−6,487	−65,403	−20,125	0	−288,649	−63,460
Retained earnings	−115	−22,126	33,100	75,273	−210,477	3,537

TABLE 9.3

PDC's Projected Balance Sheet with Yearly Surplus Cash Paid as a Dividend

PROJECTED BALANCE SHEETS	TODAY 7/31/Y0	EOY 1 7/31/Y1	EOY 2 7/31/Y2	EOY 3 7/31/Y3	EOY 4 7/31/Y4	EOY 5 = T 7/31/Y5
Current assets	(after $6,487 stripped out)					(Debt ratio at long-term rate)
Required cash	23,000	24,840	30,000	42,000	44,520	47,191
Surplus cash	0	0	0	0	0	0
Accounts receivable	46,000	46,000	55,556	77,778	82,444	87,391
Merchandise inventory	97,520	82,800	100,000	140,000	148,400	157,304
Prepaid insurance	2,300	2,300	2,778	3,889	4,122	4,370
Total current assets	168,820	155,940	188,333	263,667	279,487	296,256
Net property, plant, and equipment	57,960	56,304	68,000	95,200	100,912	106,967
Total assets	**226,780**	**212,244**	**256,333**	**358,867**	**380,399**	**403,223**
Current liabilities						
Accounts payable	33,810	41,400	50,000	70,000	74,200	78,652
Accrued wages and commissions	11,500	11,500	13,889	19,444	20,611	21,848
Total current liabilities	45,310	52,900	63,889	89,444	94,811	100,500
Long-term debt	0	0	0	0	226,643	240,241
Owner's equity	181,470	159,344	192,444	269,422	58,945	62,482
Total liabilities and equity	**226,780**	**212,244**	**256,333**	**358,867**	**380,399**	**403,223**

TABLE 9.4   PDC's Projected Statement of Cash Flow with Yearly Surplus Cash Paid as a Dividend

ACCOUNTING STATEMENT OF CASH FLOWS	YEAR 1 8/1/Y0– 7/31/Y1	YEAR 2 8/1/Y1– 7/31/Y2	YEAR 3 8/1/Y2– 7/31/Y3	YEAR 4 8/1/Y3– 7/31/Y4	YEAR T = 5 8/1/Y4– 7/31/Y5
Cash flows from activities					
Net income	6,372	43,277	53,225	75,273	78,171	66,997
Adjustments to net income for cash flow					
+ Depreciation expense	4,600	5,796	5,630	6,800	9,520	10,091
− Change in prepaid insurance	1,840	0	−478	−1,111	−233	−247
+ Change in accrued liabilities	1,725	0	2,389	5,556	1,167	1,237
− Change in inventory	12,880	14,720	−17,200	−40,000	−8,400	−8,904
+ Change in accounts payable	−4,830	7,590	8,600	20,000	4,200	4,452
− Change in accounts receivable	−9,200	0	−9,556	−22,222	−4,667	−4,947
Total adjustments	7,015	28,106	−10,614	−30,978	1,587	1,682
Net cash flow from operations	13,387	71,383	42,611	44,296	79,758	68,678
Cash flows from investing					
Capital expenditures	−6,900	−4,140	−17,326	−34,000	−15,232	−16,146
Net cash from investing	−6,900	−4,140	−17,326	−34,000	−15,232	−16,146
Cash flows from financing					
+ Equity issues	0	0	0	1,704		0
− Dividends	−6,487	−65,403	−20,125	0	−288,649	−63,460
(= −net dividend)	−6,487	−65,403	−20,125	1,704	−288,649	−63,460
+ Debt issues	0	0	0	0	226,643	13,599
Net cash flows from financing	−6,487	−65,403	−20,125	1,704	−62,006	−49,861
Net change in cash and equivalents	0	1,840	5,160	12,000	2,520	2,671
Beginning cash balance	23,000	23,000	24,840	30,000	42,000	44,520
Ending cash balance	23,000	24,840	30,000	42,000	44,520	47,191

reasonable long-term debt ratio (30 percent market debt-to-value). Chapter 13 provides more details on this future recapitalization.[3]

PDC's potential venture investors are looking for a relatively modest 25 percent annual rate of return on all the money they invest in PDC. Two points are in order. The first is simple: If PDC makes it to Year 5, its risk will be lower. We assume that everyone agrees that, by that time, PDC's investors (whoever they are) would only demand 18 percent returns. The second point is perhaps a little obscure when studying firms in a textbook but is immediately evident in real-world contexts. PDC would prefer not to have to pay the 25 percent if it isn't

---

[3]   In Chapter 13, where we introduce the enterprise method, the origin of the debt issue for the fifth year will become more apparent. For the purposes of this chapter, the 419,991 of debt issued in Year 5 should be taken as given. An integrated set of spreadsheets for PDC's valuation (equity and enterprise methods) is available on the course Web site.

currently using the money to support venture operations. If PDC takes the money early, it will merely park the surplus in marketable securities or an interest-bearing checking account, yielding, say, 5 percent, until the money is needed for venture operations. By taking the money before it needs it and keeping it longer than needed (and consenting to a valuation that uses the 25 percent required return), PDC's calibrated value erodes.

If we think of the positive (negative) net payments to equity investors as positive (negative) net dividends, we have projected PDC's "maximum dividends"—paying out as much as possible and raising as little as possible. These payments (and issues when needed) are the substance of the line "Net Dividend" we have inserted in the accounting statement of cash flows. PDC's maximum dividend projections allow us to avoid a surplus cash penalty of assessing a 25 percent required return on surplus cash held in bank accounts or marketable securities (both NPV = 0 investments). We value the venture as though we strip out surplus cash as soon as feasible and then re-raise it just as it's needed to be invested in the venture's other assets.

The maximum dividend method (MDM) treats equity investments like a line of credit that is drawn down when needed for investment in other assets and repaid immediately when it is no longer needed. For valuation purposes, it is as though cash distributions to, and cash injections from, equity investors happen "just in time." That this works for valuation is not because the venture will actually have a just-in-time equity investor. Such an investor would be a rare find. It works because surplus cash, even if not paid out, is treated as though it is invested in some NPV = 0 financial arrangement (interest-bearing bank account or marketable securities). Such investments of surplus cash neither add to, nor detract from, venture value. Consequently, we get the same venture value whether we think of the venture as (i) paying out surplus cash to a just-in-time investor and then re-raising the money when it needs to be spent on other venture assets or (ii) retaining surplus cash on the venture's balance sheet and incorporating all the interest and returns on its NPV = 0 usage. Method (ii) is extremely tedious for valuation because of fluctuations in the risk borne, and therefore the returns deserved, by venture investors. Since method (i) gives the same venture value and does so by simplifying the projections rather than making them almost intractable, all valuation methods introduced in this chapter value the venture as though it employed just-in-time equity capital. Approaches to valuation that treat surplus cash as though it were raised only when necessary, and paid back when idle, are known as "free cash flow valuation methods." Chapter 10 details some alternative discounted cash flow valuation techniques that treat all cash as necessary with no surplus or "free" cash. As you might guess, these will typically result in a lower calibration of venture value.

For MDM financial statements, "Net Dividend" in the statement of cash flows is the flow we want to discount. From the projected maximum net dividend/issue stream in Table 9.4, where we have changed the sign to reflect an investor's viewpoint (receiving dividends, paying for issues), we can get the following:

$$\text{PDC's Equity NPV} = 6,487 + \frac{65,403}{1.25} + \frac{20,125}{(1.25)^2} + \frac{-1,704}{(1.25)^3} + \frac{288,648}{(1.25)^4} + \frac{\frac{63,460}{.18-.06}}{(1.25)^4}$$

$$= 405,657$$

$$\text{PDC's Equity NPV} = \frac{65,403}{1.25} + \frac{20,125}{(1.25)^2} + \frac{-1,704}{(1.25)^3} + \frac{288,648}{(1.25)^4} + \frac{\frac{63,460}{.18-.06}}{(1.25)^4} = 399,170$$

In these projections, PDC's equity owners are scheduled to receive dividends in the first two years and then pay back some of those dividends through reissues in Year 3. Since cash raised by issuing is immediately spent on assets and operations, you can see that this works like an equity line of credit. While the cash is treated as outside the firm, the valuation is just imposing NPV = 0 wherever that cash is invested. The only thing that enhances or detracts from the venture's value is what happens to the cash when it is used inside the firm.

The NPV calculation involves the following flows to (+) and from (−) investors: $6,487 immediately, $65,403 at the end of Year 1, $20,125 at the end of Year 2, −$1,704 (a reinvestment) at the end of Year 3, and, finally, $288,648 + $528,833 in Year 4. The Year 4 (= T − 1) flow is 288,648 by itself. The $528,833 is the terminal value or going concern value. It is a Year 4 (= T − 1) value because the perpetuity's first cash flow ($63,460) is a year after the date for which we are calculating a terminal value. It equals the Year 5 (= T) flow divided by the cap rate (63,460/(.18 − .06)). The valuation is for the entire set of investors that, as a group, experiences these flows. This valuation does not tell us which shareholders get what portion of that total pie. The investors' equity in totality has a value of $405,657 if they have claim to the first $6,487 and $399,170 if they do not. The MDM method demonstrates that the normal cash flow used to value equity is nothing more than the dividend and issue flows the equity holders would experience if they provided a just-in-time equity line of credit.

For valuation, the most relevant present values are typically those at the start of the financial projections ($405,657 and $399,170) when we are considering taking on new investors. Table 9.5 also displays calibrated values for all of the future dates appearing in the financial projections (e.g., NPV = $498,962 and PV = $433,560 at the end of Year 1). The Year 4 present value (rather than the *net* present value) is $528,833. This is just the terminal value calculated using the $63,460 as the start of a perpetuity growing at 6 percent and discounted by the

---

TABLE 9.5   Equity Valuations Using the MDM Method

VALUATION DATE	TODAY 7/31/Y0	EOY 1 7/31/Y1	EOY 2 7/31/Y2	EOY 3 7/31/Y3	EOY 4 7/31/Y4	EOY 5 = T 7/31/Y5
PV Equity (Excluding Current Equity VCF)	399,170	433,560	521,825	653,985	528,833	560,563
Capital gain on market equity		8.6%	20.4%	25.3%	−19.1%	6.0%
Dividend yield on market equity		16.4%	4.6%	−0.3%	44.1%	12.0%
Total return on market equity		25.0%	25.0%	25.0%	25.0%	18.0%
NPV Equity (Including Current Equity VCF)	405,657	498,962	541,949	652,281	817,481	624,023

mature venture's 18 percent required return for equity (= $63,460/(.18 − .06)). In Table 9.5, we also provide a breakout of how the investors are projected to receive their return. As an example, in year 2, the investors are projected to make a 25 percent total return. This is a combination of a 20.4 percent capital gain (= 521,825/433,560 − 1) and a 4.6 percent dividend yield (= 20,125/433,560). You can see that the equity investors are projected to earn 25 percent in every year, but the way they earn it differs from year to year. Importantly, by the terminal year 5, the capital gain on market equity is growing at 6 percent—the same rate as sales. This growth rate in the market value of equity confirms that everything has smoothed out, making the application of a smooth-growth perpetuity appropriate from year T = 5 forward.

WHAT'S BEHIND OUR MDM PROJECTIONS

To understand how to value the venture using the static financial statements in Tables 9.2 to 9.4, it is really not necessary to know where those financial statements originated. They work and are internally consistent. They specify a dividend and issue pattern that can be plugged directly into a valuation as we did above. However, it has been our experience that many students want to obtain, digest, and master fast and flawless ways to produce custom projections that are directly pluggable into an NPV. They want to alter a sales figure or the timing of an investment and have the spreadsheet update and automatically produce consistent financial statements and a new valuation. For such students (and entrepreneurs), there is no substitute for building one's own dynamic spreadsheet that fuses projections and valuation. The "value added" that spreadsheet programs bring in terms of real-time instantaneous updating, projecting, and valuation is substantial.

As a start down this road, if you would like to reproduce these MDM financial statements, you need some additional information on how we built the projections. We started with the historical experience displayed in the first column and added the following assumptions for the five projected years: (i) COGS is 70 percent of sales; (ii) wages are 19.167 percent of sales; (iii) rent, insurance, and miscellaneous are 6.75 percent of sales; (iv) depreciation is 10 percent of beginning-of-year net fixed assets; (v) required cash is 1.75 percent of sales; (vi) accounts receivable are 2.8 percent of sales; (vii) merchandise inventory is 5 percent of sales; (viii) prepaid insurance is .139 percent of sales; (ix) net PP&E is 3.4 percent of sales; (x) accounts payable are 2.5 percent of sales; (xi) accrued wages and commissions are .694 percent of sales; and (xii) starting in Year 4, the firm takes on the debt levels we have specified. (In Chapter 13, we demonstrate that those are the exact levels of debt that result in the venture's having a 30 percent market debt-to-value ratio.) Taking these assumptions and applying them to the given sales forecasts, making sure that the current year's equity balance is equal to the previous year's balance plus resulting retained earnings and new issues, forcing total assets to equal total liabilities, and, finally, calculating surplus cash as total assets minus all other assets gets the job done. The product is a working (adapting) set of financial statements that, with the addition of a discount rate (or two), produces an NPV.

In the absence of any projected dividends or issues, the initial balance sheet constructed from these assumptions will, at first, display a nonzero surplus cash line. This is because the spending and financing are not constrained to be in harmony. The inadequacy or overabundance ends up in this surplus cash line. The only reason the surplus cash line appears in our MDM projections is to balance the balance sheet mechanically. For a given level of all other balance sheet accounts, there is one and only one surplus cash balance that results in the equality of total assets to total liabilities plus equity, TA = TL + E. We have "one equation and one unknown." With the other accounts on the balance tied down by projection assumptions or accounting rules, the surplus cash balance is the only unknown in the accounting identity equation. Surplus cash is merely a device for forcing the balance sheet to balance in order to avoid the irony (and credibility risk) of presenting a balance sheet that doesn't, in fact, balance. However, for MDM valuation, nonzero surplus cash account balances are a to-do list waiting to be done. MDM surplus cash balances must ultimately disappear.

It is true in a sense that we are recommending surplus cash as the "plug" to balance the balance sheet. While this is true mechanically, for MDM projections, it is a bit misleading logically since the surplus cash balance must end up at zero. Dividends and equity issues are the amounts we will manipulate in MDM projections to zero out surplus cash when that surplus cash balance is forced (by using a spreadsheet cell formula) to be equal to total assets less all other assets (and total assets is forced by a spreadsheet cell formula to be equal to total liabilities and equity), thereby balancing the balance sheet. To see how this plays out, we move from the initial financial statements having nonzero surplus cash balances and start increasing dividends or equity issues until surplus cash balances zero out. It is important to do this zeroing while the formulas for the surplus cash balances force them to equal total assets less all other assets (for their respective years). Of course, the financial statements must be dynamically linked for this to work easily. Specifically, the formula for this year's equity account has to set it equal to last year's equity plus this year's retained earnings (net income less dividends) plus new issues—whatever those numbers are. When we change a dividend, for example, the financial statements need to perpetuate that change automatically by updating the retained earnings, the current equity balance, the total liabilities and equities, the total assets, and, finally, the surplus cash necessary to remain in balance.

For PDC's spreadsheet, we start in the Year 0 columns, where we can see that dividends have to rise to $6,487 for the surplus cash account to be zero while balancing the balance sheet. Mechanically, as we increase the dividends, the equity account balance falls through the depletion of retained earnings. This leads to an equal-amount decrease in the total liabilities and equity side of the balance sheet (since all the liability accounts are tied down). To balance, total assets will have to fall by an amount equal to that by which total liabilities and equity fell. Since all of the other asset accounts are tied down, this can only happen if surplus cash falls by that same amount. When we make the time-zero dividend exactly $6,487 in the statement of cash flows, the initial balance sheet in Table 9.3 has a zero surplus cash account balance. Of course, all future surplus cash balances will change because of this initial dividend. Moving on to the Year 1 columns, Year 1 dividends will have to rise to $65,403 for the surplus cash account to be zero while balancing the first year's (actually year end's) balance sheet, and so on. When we get to what has, in the interim, become a negative surplus cash balance in Year 3 (column 4), we will need to project equity issues of $1,704 to raise the surplus cash account to zero while balancing the third year's balance sheet. The issues act just like a negative dividend. This process continues from left to right (in columns) until all surplus cash balances are zeros and we have our maximum dividends. This is the process used to create all of the financial projections in Tables 9.2 to 9.4. Note that, other than the dividends and issues lines, the statement of cash flow numbers are tied down by income statement entries or by changes in balance sheet numbers. The dividends and issues lines appear to be the only remaining discretion in the statement of cash flows. But this discretion is illusory for MDM projections. These numbers are dictated by the fact that they are required to be a specific level to zero out the surplus cash account.

While it's true that the surplus cash account is acting as a mechanical adjustment to satisfy the accounting identity (keeping the balance sheet balanced), throughout this process the MDM procedures are selecting specific dividends and issues in order to result in a surplus cash account balance of zero. In doing this, the MDM adjustments are actually a "dividends as plug" approach to producing coherent projected financial statements. The valuation advantage of this method should be pretty clear. With the MDM, preparation for a valuation is almost a completely unintentional byproduct of projecting coherent financial statements. When the projections are dynamically connected, we can easily see and make the MDM adjustments that are needed to zero out each surplus cash balance. Getting to valuation from there is a snap. There are no mysterious working capital calculations or additional cash flow formulas to memorize and apply. All that remains is applying a discount rate to the net dividends line (dividends − issues). Doing so gives the values $405,657 (NPV) and $399,170 (PV) displayed above. The MDM method lays the groundwork for more complicated valuation formulas that produce the same valuation. That value is the "fundamental value" found by discounting the maximum dividends that could be paid if the venture had a just-in-time equity line of credit.

Unfortunately, while the MDM sets up a fast and easy valuation, anyone who uses the resulting financial projections will have a lot of explaining to do when showing them to an investor or banker. It is almost certain that the dialogue will hang, possibly fatally, on those dividends in the statement of cash flows. After all, what kind of growth venture projects dividends so high they have to do an issue in the next year? While this almost simultaneous payment of dividends and new issue of equity may occur for some mature firms maintaining a high dividend payout, it is certainly not wise for growth-stage companies. Therefore, we need to devise an approach to financial projections and valuation that reflects the almost certain reality that no dividends will be paid in those early years (even when the venture temporarily has surplus cash), but still gets the fundamental value right. This is the goal of our next method. Finance practitioners and academics usually refer to our next approach as valuation by discounting the "free cash flows" that represent the potential dividends the venture could afford, although no one expects the venture to pay them. This allows us to value the venture as though it had a just-in-time equity capital line of credit, thereby avoiding surplus cash penalties when the venture parks surplus cash in zero-NPV interest-bearing accounts or in marketable securities. Importantly for presentations, the PDM (unlike the MDM) accomplishes this with dividend-free financial projections. As we will see, the resulting "free cash flows," or "pseudo dividends" as we will call them, are exactly the same as the net dividends in the MDM projections. The coincidence of maximum and pseudo dividends assures that we will arrive at the same venture value but without the offending dividends line in the statement of cash flows. We need some background first.

9.5   ACCOUNTING VERSUS EQUITY VALUATION CASH FLOW

A comparison of cash flow for accounting and equity valuation purposes can help reinforce some important connections and distinctions. As we discussed at length in Chapter 6, the statement of cash flows demonstrates that traditional balance sheets and income statements contain all of the data necessary to calculate exactly the same cash flow as that found in a cash budget of receipts and disbursements. This future glimpse of the cash account balance is critical for the short-term survival and management of any venture, new or old. The accounting statement of cash flows organizes accounting information in a way that assists in conducting valuation using our next method.

ORIGINS OF ACCOUNTING CASH FLOWS

A statement of cash flows combines the flows from an income statement with the flows implied by changes in balance sheet accounts. More specifically, the income statement depicts operating and financing flows inside the firm, including sales, cost of sales, and interest expense. The balance sheet depicts the level of certain stocks or stores of value (assets and liabilities) for the same firm.[4] The cash flow statement nets the operating and financing flows with those required to increase or decrease the asset and liability accounts. The result is a comprehensive and unified view of the cash effect of a firm's investing and operating activities. Figure 9.1 graphically demonstrates how income statement flows are combined with changes in balance sheet stocks to arrive at a statement of the venture's cash flow. The

---

[4]   In this text, we use the word "stock" to refer to a store of value. We use the word "equity" to refer to ownership positions in the venture. For example, we will use the term "preferred equity" rather than "preferred stock" to avoid confusion in our use of the word "stock" as a store of value.

FIGURE 9.1 The Accounting Statement of Cash Flows

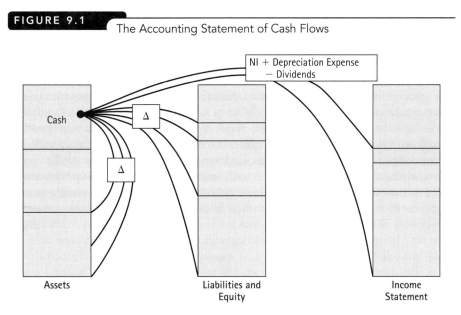

The accounting statement of cash flows nets the cash impact of all other balance sheet and income accounts to focus on the cash account as the repository of any remaining cash flow.

focus of a statement of cash flows is the cash account. All other account changes are netted together to treat the cash account as the residual for anything (cash) left over.

- What is the focal point of the statement of cash flows?
- How does the statement accomplish the goal of deriving the cash account balance by using the balance sheet?

FROM ACCOUNTING TO EQUITY VALUATION CASH FLOWS

While a single (required + surplus) cash account view is made to order for cash planning, as we hope our four-month treatment of PDC has made clear, cash flow for valuation purposes is about how much could be paid out ($6,487), not how much actually will be ($0 for growing entrepreneurial ventures). Unlike the accounting statement of cash flows, we do not want to treat the cash account as a residual for surplus cash. Increases in surplus cash need to be treated as though they flow through to investors (whether they do or not). To accomplish this, we need to project required cash (as we did with the MDM) like any other inventory investment. Then we will construct an equity valuation cash flow that reflects the contribution to value represented by the growth in surplus cash, whether it's paid out or retained.

For PDC's valuation, the required cash of $23,000 is treated as a required inventory of cash. Additional investment in required cash, just like other investments in inventory, decreases the amount of residual flow available to the venture's equity holders. The asymmetric treatment of surplus cash (as if flowing through to shareholders) and required cash (as stopped inside the venture) contrasts with the symmetric treatment of all cash in the accounting statement of cash flows. Figure 9.2 graphically depicts the treatment of required cash as an asset investment with the flow to equity (potential dividends) as the residual. For the accounting statement of cash flows, the residual is the cash account. Flows that don't get diverted anywhere else end up becoming part of the change in cash at the bottom of the accounting statement of cash flows. For equity valuation cash flows, we can think of the change in required cash as an inventory investment like the other inventory investments. With diversion for required cash already considered, the bottom line of this altered accounting statement of cash flows becomes the change in surplus cash (rather than the change in total cash). If we combine that bottom-line change in surplus cash with the equity flows earlier in the accounting statement of cash flows (projected dividends and issues), the sum is the equity valuation cash flow to be discounted when valuing equity.

While it may seem a bit confusing at first, valuing the firm as though all changes in surplus cash are combined with projected equity flows in order to get a grand-total equity valuation flow causes no problems with future flows, so long as the valuation doesn't mistakenly try to strip out accumulated surplus cash balance in the future. That is, the valuation strips out incremental surplus cash as it

---

FIGURE 9.2   Equity Valuation Cash Flows

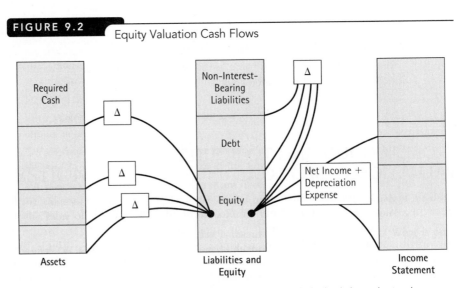

The calculation of equity valuation cash flows nets the cash impact of all other balance sheet and income accounts to focus on the equity account as the repository of any remaining cash flow.

becomes available, even though it appears to remain on the balance sheet. The most important implication is that the balance of the surplus cash account cannot be added to the terminal value as a lump sum in the future (even though many are tempted to do this). For valuation purposes, all but the last year's addition to surplus cash balance is incorporated in the valuation when it first becomes a part of the surplus cash account (and since then has been assumed to be invested at NPV = 0).

A direct calculation that extracts the relevant information from the balance sheet and income statement is available. Its structure mirrors a reorganized accounting statement of cash flows. Dividends, issues, and changes in surplus cash are combined as one bottom-line residual equity valuation cash flow (replacing the change in total cash). This **equity valuation cash flow** is the cash flow that can be used directly to value a venture's equity. For most ventures, calculating the equity valuation cash flow starts with net income and (1) adds noncash expenses like depreciation and amortization; (2) subtracts increases in **net operating working capital** (defined as current assets other than surplus cash less non-interest-bearing current liabilities); (3) subtracts capital expenditure outlays (CAPEX) for plant and equipment; and (4) adds net debt issues (issues less retirements):[5]

equity valuation cash flow
cash flow used for valuing equity

net operating working capital
current assets other than surplus cash less non-interest-bearing current liabilities

> Equity Valuation Cash Flow
> = Net Income + Depreciation and Amortization Expense
>   − Change in Net Operating Working Capital (Excluding Surplus Cash)
>   − Capital Expenditures
>   + Net Debt Issues

To check the formula, we first examine changes in the balance sheet accounts that contribute to the change in net working capital. Table 9.6 displays the calculation of PDC's change in net operating working capital for the historic period 4/1/Y0 to 7/31/Y0. With this calculation of the change in net operating working capital (excluding surplus cash), the calibration of the time-zero equity VCF (the netting of all other accounts to give an equity effect) is straightforward:

Net Income	6,372
+ Depreciation and Amortization Expense	+4,600
− Change in Net Operating Working Capital	+2,415
− Capital Expenditures	−6,900
+ Net Debt Issues	+0
= Equity Valuation Cash Flow	6,487

This $6,487 is exactly the same as the maximum dividend that we projected for Year 0 in the MDM. This is not an accident and will work for the remaining years in the project. Calculating this equity valuation cash flow for each year and discounting it leads to our second equity valuation method, which we call the "pseudo dividend method."

---

[5] We have assumed that the net income projection assesses the cash flow from taxes at the time the tax burden is incurred. If the net income projection is based on accrued taxes, then the cash flow calculation should include an addition (subtraction) for the increase in deferred taxes.

TABLE 9.6 Calculation of Change in Net Operating Working Capital

Current assets	
July balance	175,307
March balance	−174,340
Change in current assets	967
Surplus cash	
July amount	6,487
March amount	−0
Change in surplus cash	6,487
Current liabilities	
July amount	45,310
March amount	−48,415
Change in current liabilities	−3,105
Change in net operating working capital	
(= 967 − 6,487 + 3,105)	−2,415

CONCEPT CHECK

- How do finance and accounting concepts of cash flow differ?

9.6 EQUITY VALUATION: THE PSEUDO DIVIDEND METHOD

Even though financings for most high-potential new ventures are staged, in part, to avoid dangerous gluts of surplus cash, equity investors usually don't provide equity investments that adjust like a line of credit; one wouldn't really contemplate paying out surplus cash that has been raised but not yet employed. Most new ventures are not free to pay, nor do they desire to pay, real cash dividends. No one wants to see them in the venture's projected financial statements like those in the MDM projections. Additionally, for cash-planning purposes, it would be better to have more accurate financial statements rather than ones with expected cash balances that have been artificially depleted by hypothetical MDM dividends. While they are convenient for understanding the nature of equity valuation (as discounting dividends to get fundamental value), the MDM projections are a convenient fiction *only* for valuation purposes. That same fiction is inconvenient in almost all other uses of a venture's financial statement.

The pseudo dividend method has the advantage of presenting the appropriate financial statements for cash budgeting (with actual projected venture balances) while avoiding discounting investments in low-risk surplus cash at the venture's high-risk discount rate. We start by projecting the venture as paying no dividends. Tables 9.7 to 9.9 (pages 373–374) present those statements. While these

TABLE 9.7

PDC's Projected Income Statements with Retained Surplus Cash

	4/1/Y0– 7/31/Y0	YEAR 1 8/1/Y0– 7/31/Y1	YEAR 2 8/1/Y1– 7/31/Y2	YEAR 3 8/1/Y2– 7/31/Y3	YEAR 4 8/1/Y3– 7/31/Y4	YEAR T = 5 8/1/Y4– 7/31/Y5
Sales	552,000	1,656,000	2,000,000	2,800,000	2,968,000	3,146,080
(growth rates)			20.8%	40.0%	6.0%	6.0%
Income Statements	Historical	Projected	Projected	Projected	Projected	Projected
Sales	552,000	1,656,000	2,000,000	2,800,000	2,968,000	3,146,080
– COGS	–386,400	–1,159,200	–1,400,000	–1,960,000	–2,077,600	–2,202,256
– Wages and commissions	–105,800	–317,400	–383,333	–536,667	–568,867	–602,999
– Rent, miscellaneous, and insurance	–47,840	–111,780	–135,000	–189,000	–200,340	–212,360
– Depreciation	–4,600	–5,796	–5,630	–6,800	–9,520	–10,091
Earnings before interest and taxes (EBIT)	7,360	61,824	76,036	107,533	111,673	118,374
– Interest expense	–988	0	0	0	0	–22,664
Earnings before taxes	6,372	61,824	76,036	107,533	111,673	95,709
– Taxes	0	–18,547	–22,811	–32,260	–33,502	–28,713
Net income	6,372	43,277	53,225	75,273	78,171	66,997
– Dividends	0		0	0	0	0
Retained earnings	6,372	43,277	53,225	75,273	78,171	66,997

TABLE 9.8

PDC's Projected Balance Sheet with Retained Surplus Cash

PROJECTED BALANCE SHEETS	TODAY 7/31/Y0	EOY 1 7/31/Y1	EOY 2 7/31/Y2	EOY 3 7/31/Y3	EOY 4 7/31/Y4	EOY 5 = T 7/31/Y5
Current assets						
Required cash	23,000	24,840	30,000	42,000	44,520	47,191
Surplus cash	6,487	71,890	92,015	90,310	378,959	442,419
Accounts receivable	46,000	46,000	55,556	77,778	82,444	87,391
Merchandise inventory	97,520	82,800	100,000	140,000	148,400	157,304
Prepaid insurance	2,300	2,300	2,778	3,889	4,122	4,370
Total current assets	175,307	227,830	280,348	353,977	658,446	738,675
Net property, plant, and equipment	57,960	56,304	68,000	95,200	100,912	106,967
Total assets	**233,267**	**284,134**	**348,348**	**449,177**	**759,358**	**845,641**
Current liabilities						
Accounts payable	33,810	41,400	50,000	70,000	74,200	78,652
Accrued wages and commissions	11,500	11,500	13,889	19,444	20,611	21,848
Total current liabilities	45,310	52,900	63,889	89,444	94,811	100,500
Long-term debt	0	0	0	0	226,643	240,241
Owner's equity	187,957	231,234	284,459	359,733	437,904	504,900
Total liabilities and equity	**233,267**	**284,134**	**348,348**	**449,177**	**759,358**	**845,641**

TABLE 9.9   PDC's Projected Statement of Cash Flow with Retained Surplus Cash

ACCOUNTING STATEMENT OF CASH FLOWS	YEAR 1 8/1/Y0– 7/31/Y1	YEAR 2 8/1/Y1– 7/31/Y2	YEAR 3 8/1/Y2– 7/31/Y3	YEAR 4 8/1/Y3– 7/31/Y4	YEAR T = 5 8/1/Y4– 7/31/Y5
Cash flows from activities					
Net income	6,372	43,277	53,225	75,273	78,171	66,997
Adjustments to net income for cash flow					
+ Depreciation expense	4,600	5,796	5,630	6,800	9,520	10,091
+ Change in accrued liabilities	1,725	0	2,389	5,556	1,167	1,237
− Change in inventory	12,880	14,720	−17,200	−40,000	−8,400	−8,904
+ Change in accounts payable	−4,830	7,590	8,600	20,000	4,200	4,452
− Change in accounts receivable	−9,200	0	−9,556	−22,222	−4,667	−4,947
Total adjustments	7,015	28,106	−10,614	−30,978	1,587	1,682
Net cash flow from operations	13,387	71,383	42,611	44,296	79,758	68,678
Cash flows from investing					
Capital expenditures	−6,900	−4,140	−17,326	−34,000	−15,232	−16,146
Net cash from investing	−6,900	−4,140	−17,326	−34,000	−15,232	−16,146
Cash flows from financing					
+ Equity issues	0	0	0	0	0	0
− Dividends	0	0	0	0	0	0
(=−net dividend)	0	0	0	0	0	0
+ Debt issues	0	0	0	0	226,643	13,599
Net cash flows from financing	0	0	0	0	226,643	13,599
Net change in cash and equivalents	6,487	67,243	25,285	10,296	291,169	66,131
Beginning cash balance	23,000	29,487	96,730	122,015	132,310	423,479
Ending cash balance	29,487	96,730	122,015	132,310	423,479	489,610

pseudo dividend method (PDM)
valuation method involving zero explicitly forecasted dividends and an adjustment to working capital to strip surplus cash

avoid the MDM projection's distortions of the venture's real (versus fictional) projected future cash balances, many would still claim that it is unfair to apply high-venture discount rates to cash balances invested in marketable securities or interest-bearing checking accounts. In the **pseudo dividend method (PDM)**, we avoid this unfair penalty by valuing "pseudo dividends" that could be paid but are retained inside the venture.

These pseudo dividends will not appear on any projected financial statements but will be created by using the approach taken in Table 9.6 for calculating working capital with surplus cash stripped out. As anticipated, the valuation cash flow is exactly the same as in the net dividend from the MDM, because the surplus cash flow is not stopped in the working capital calculation, but is allowed to flow through to the equity valuation cash flow through the calculated changes in net working capital excluding surplus cash. To see this, we can duplicate the calculations in Table 9.6 for one of the years in this valuation, say Year 2:

Current assets	
Year 2 balance	280,348
Year 1 balance	−227,830
Change in current assets	52,518
Surplus cash	
Year 2 amount	92,015
Year 1 amount	−71,890
Change in surplus cash	20,125
Current liabilities	
Year 2 amount	63,889
Year 1 amount	−52,900
Change in current liabilities	10,989
Change in net working capital	
(= 52,518 − 20,125 − 10,989)	21,404

This calculation treats changes in the surplus cash as a pseudo dividend.[6] As suggested earlier, a risk of the pseudo dividend method, in retaining surplus cash for balance sheet projections while letting it flow through for valuation purposes (as we have done in the PDM projections and valuation), is that one will be tempted to strip the ending cash balance ($442,419) again. Usually, the argument goes something like this: "What's the value of a house with $442,419 in the basement? It's the value of the house plus the $442,429, right? So, why do you value the venture while ignoring all that wonderful cash in the basement? Why don't you add that Year 5 cash account balance to the terminal value in Year 5?" While the basement cash analogy poses a good question, the user of the pseudo dividend method must remember that the valuation has treated the basement cash as leaking out to investors all along. Although the balance sheet may suggest otherwise, for valuation purposes the only surplus cash left in the basement in Year 5 is that last change in surplus cash from Year 4. All previous changes have already been incorporated.

Table 9.10 presents PDM valuations for each of the years in the projections. They coincide in all years with those found using the MDM.

Summarizing, we have covered two approaches to valuing a venture's equity:

1. **Maximum Dividend Method (MDM):** Formally project all cash surpluses as being paid out as dividends. The balance sheet will have zeros for all surplus cash balances. The venture's equity can be valued directly using the dividends/ issue line in the statement of cash flows (or by the equity VCF method, which gives the same amount). There is no excess cash in the end, and the balance sheet says so.

2. **The Pseudo Dividend Method (PDM):** Formally retain all cash surpluses in a surplus cash account. Project all dividends at zero. Value the venture's equity using the equity VCF with working capital calculations that omit surplus cash.

---

[6] In practice, others may refer to the pseudo dividend method as the "free cash flow to equity" method. As the term "free cash flow" has different meanings to different people, we have chosen a more specific terminology.

Remember that the projected balance sheets indicate surplus cash balances that have been treated by the valuation as already having been paid. These balances cannot be added to a terminal value or otherwise stripped out again.

The maximum dividend method is the cleanest for valuation purposes (permitting directly discounting the net dividend line in the statement of cash flows), but it involves financial statements that can create more problems than they solve. The financial statements display eyebrow-raising dividends that will most likely not be paid as scheduled. For appearance and other reasons, these investor returns are accumulated for payment at a later date. The MDM's dividend-laden financial statements can dramatically understate the amount of cash the firm actually has in its possession and may needlessly attract investors' negative attention. It is primarily a pedagogical device for showing how simple valuation can be (once financial statements are constructed) and serves as a straw man for introducing the PDM method. Perhaps the most appealing feature of the MDM is that the calibrated venture value is simply the fundamental value found by discounting the venture's projected dividends.

The pseudo dividend method, with its accurate financial projections, no dividends, and the exact same valuation, is the cleanest for cash-planning and outside presentation purposes. One drawback is that you cannot value the venture by discounting the dividends in the accounting statement of cash flows (as you can with the MDM). You must use the mechanical and seemingly disconnected equity VCF calculation to determine cash flows to be discounted. Observers may never see how this flow relates to the financial statements. You must omit surplus cash from the working capital calculations and remember not to add the accumulated surplus cash in the final explicit forecast year to the exit value since the valuation has

TABLE 9.10   Spreadsheet for Equity Valuation Cash Flows and Value

EQUITY VALUATION	4/1/Y0– 7/31/Y0	YEAR 1 8/1/Y0– 7/31/Y1	YEAR 2 8/1/Y1– 7/31/Y2	YEAR 3 8/1/Y2– 7/31/Y3	YEAR 4 8/1/Y3– 7/31/Y4	YEAR T = 5 8/1/Y4– 7/31/Y5
Net income	6,372	43,277	53,225	75,273	78,171	66,997
+ Depreciation and amortization	4,600	5,796	5,630	6,800	9,520	10,091
− Capital expenditures	−6,900	−4,140	−17,326	−34,000	−15,232	−16,146
− Change in net working capital	2,415	20,470	−21,404	−49,778	−10,453	−11,081
+ Debt proceeds	0	0	0	0	226,643	13,599
Equity VCF (valuation cash flow)	6,487	65,403	20,125	−1,704	288,649	63,460
(vs. dividends − equity issues)	0	0	0	0	0	0
VALUATION DATE	TODAY 7/31/Y0	EOY 1 7/31/Y1	EOY 2 7/31/Y2	EOY 3 7/31/Y3	EOY 4 7/31/Y4	EOY 5 = T 7/31/Y5
PV Equity (Excluding Current Equity VCF)	399,170	433,560	521,825	653,985	528,833	560,563
Capital gain on market equity		8.6%	20.4%	25.3%	−19.1%	6.0%
Dividend yield on market equity		16.4%	4.6%	−0.3%	44.1%	12.0%
Total return on market equity		25.0%	25.0%	25.0%	25.0%	18.0%
NPV Equity (Including Current Equity VCF)	405,657	498,962	541,949	652,281	817,481	624,023

already stripped out all but the last increment in surplus cash. These manipulations and caveats can be difficult to explain and may confuse even those familiar with valuation concepts and procedures. Nonetheless, the PDM is consistent with the theoretical and conceptual foundations of financial valuation (in its treatment of risk and return) and still provides financial statements useful for cash planning.

CONCEPT CHECK

- How does the working capital calculation create a pseudo dividend?
- Why does the direct method for determining valuation cash flows give the same valuation as in the maximum dividend method?
- What characteristics of the projected financial statements would signal that a pseudo dividend method valuation would be appropriate?

SUMMARY

We have discussed, at length, the equity approach to valuing a new venture. We have seen how the equity valuation cash flows (equity VCFs) are determined and have considered their relationship to the treatment of surplus cash. We related these flows to the accounting statement of cash flows and discussed the merits of each. We enumerated the advantages and disadvantages of two approaches to combining projected financial statements with a valuation. We concluded that the best approach combines dividend-free financial statements with a valuation that gives credit for surplus cash when it is first created, the PDM method. We applied both approaches to the PDC venture to arrive at identical valuations.

KEY TERMS

capitalization (cap) rate	net operating working capital	required cash
discounted cash flow (DCF)	net present value (NPV)	reversion value
equity valuation cash flow	post-money valuation	stepping-stone year
explicit forecast period	pre-money valuation	surplus cash
maximum dividend method (MDM)	present value (PV)	terminal (or horizon) value
	pseudo dividend method (PDM)	

DISCUSSION QUESTIONS

1. What is a venture's present value? Does the past matter?

2. Describe what is meant by the statement "If you're not using estimates, you're not doing a valuation."

3. Define the terms (a) "explicit forecast period" and (b) "terminal or horizon value" as they relate to a venture's discounted cash flow valuation.

4. What is meant by a capitalization (or cap) rate in reference to calculating a terminal value? What other types of terminal values might be appropriate (i.e., other than smooth growth procedures)?

5. What is a venture's reversion value?

6. What is meant by a stepping-stone year? Why is it important in determining a venture's value?

7. Explain the difference between pre-money valuation and post-money valuation.

8. Define (a) required cash and (b) surplus cash. Why does it matter how we treat surplus cash for valuation purposes?

9. Describe the maximum dividend method (MDM) of valuation.

10. What is meant by net operating working capital?

11. Identify and describe the major components that are used to calculate the equity valuation cash flow.

12. Describe the pseudo dividend method (PDM) of valuation.

13. What is the main difference between the maximum dividend method and the pseudo dividend method?

14. What is the relationship between equity valuation cash flows and dividends?

15. Why do the numerical examples in this chapter involve a large dividend in the last year of the explicit forecast period?

16. Why do net income and cash flow in the numerical examples in this chapter both grow at the same rate (g) in the terminal value period? Why is this important?

INTERNET ACTIVITIES

1. Web-surfing exercise: Find a fast-growth publicly traded firm with financial statements posted on the firm's Web page. Relate that firm's financial statements to those of the examples in this chapter. Formulate the process by which you would project that firm's financial statements into the future in order to conduct a valuation.

2. Using a free stock quoting and research site on the Web (e.g., http://www.bloomberg.com or http://money.cnn.com), examine the current price for an Internet company. Relate the financial data you can find on the firm to the current stock price.

EXERCISES/PROBLEMS

1. Assume you sell for $100,000 a 10 percent ownership stake in a future payment one year from now of $1.5 million.
   A. What are you saying about the implied return for the 10 percent owner?
   B. What is the present value of the entire $1.5 million, using the implied return from Part A?
   C. What is 10 percent of the value determined in Part B?
   D. Does it matter whether you grow the $100,000 at 50 percent to $150,000 and note it is 10 percent of $1.5 million, or discount the $1.5 million at 50 percent to get $1 million and note that $100,000 is 10 percent of this present value?

2. The TecOne Corporation is about to begin producing and selling its prototype product. Annual cash flows for the next five years are forecasted as:

YEAR	CASH FLOW
1	−$ 50,000
2	−$ 20,000
3	$100,000
4	$400,000
5	$800,000

   A. Assume annual cash flows are expected to remain at the $800,000 level after Year 5 (i.e., Year 6 and thereafter). If TecOne investors want a 40 percent rate of return on their investment, calculate the venture's present value.

B. Now assume that the Year 6 cash flows are forecasted to be $900,000 in the stepping-stone year and are expected to grow at an 8 percent compound annual rate thereafter. Assuming that the investors still want a 40 percent rate of return on their investment, calculate the venture's present value.

C. Now extend Part B one step further. Assume that the required rate of return on the investment will drop from 40 to 20 percent beginning in Year 6 to reflect a drop in operating or business risk. Calculate the venture's present value.

D. Let's assume that TecOne investors have valued the venture as requested in Part C. An outside investor wants to invest $3 million in TecOne now (at the end of Year 0). What percentage of ownership in the venture should the TecOne investors give up to the outside investor for a $3 million new investment?

3. Assume the forecasted cash flows presented in Problem 2 for the TecOne Corporation venture also hold for the LowTec venture. However, investors in LowTec have an expected rate of return of 30 percent on their investment until Year 6 when the rate of return is expected to drop to 18 percent. The perpetuity growth rate for cash flows after Year 6 is expected to be 7 percent.

A. Determine the present value for the LowTec venture.

B. If an outside investor offers to invest $1.5 million today, what percentage ownership in LowTec should be given to the new investor?

4. Ben Toucan, owner of the Aspen Restaurant, wants to determine the present value of his investment. The Aspen Restaurant is currently in the development stage but hopes to "begin" operations early next year. After-tax cash flows during the next five years are expected to be as follows: Year 1 = 0, Year 2 = 0, Year 3 = 0, Year 4 = $2.5 million, and Year 5 = $3 million. Cash inflows are expected to be $3.18 million in Year 6 and are expected to grow at a 6 percent annual rate thereafter. Recall from Chapter 7 that venture investors often use different discount rates when valuing ventures at various stages of their life cycles. For example, target discount rates by life cycle stage are: development stage, 50 percent; startup stage, 40 percent; survival stage, 35 percent; and early rapid-growth stage, 30 percent. As ventures move from their late rapid-growth stages and into their maturity stages, a 20 percent discount rate is often used.

A. Determine the Aspen Restaurant's terminal or horizon value at the end of five years, assuming the venture will be entering its maturity stage.

B. What is the present value of the Aspen Restaurant, assuming that it is a development-stage venture?

C. What percent ownership interest should Ben Toucan be willing to give today to a venture investor, Sherri Isitar, for her $1 million investment?

D. Let's assume that the Aspen Restaurant was started early last year and, thus, is in its startup stage and has the same future cash flow expectations as indicated above. Using a typical startup-stage required rate of return or discount rate, calculate the present value of the Aspen Restaurant.

E. Owning a restaurant is often considered to be a risky investment, in that restaurants often are continuously moving into and out of their survival stages. Assume that a typical survival-stage required rate of return is applied to all future cash flows estimated for the Aspen Restaurant. Calculate the venture's present value.

5. Refer to the FrothySlope microbrewery example at the beginning of this chapter.

A. How does the $500,000 piece of the terminal value relate to the future value of the $100,000? That is, the brewpub investor was looking for a 40 percent return. The five-year-out future value of $100,000 growing at 40 percent is $100,000 \times (1.4)^5 = \$537,824$, slightly more than $500,000. Does this mean the investor is not really expected to make 40 percent on the $100,000, even though we used that discount rate to arrive at the initial $5,856,935 valuation? (*Hint:* What about explicit forecast period flows?)

B. Returning to the brewpub spreadsheet with all flows included, how much more of the venture's ownership of surplus cash flows would have to be sold for the $100,000 if the investor expected to make 70 percent (given Jim's utopian vision of his future)?

C. What percentage of the brewpub's present value is contained in the present value of the terminal value (the venture's reversion value)?

D. How much ownership of the brewpub cash flows would need to be sold to an investor demanding 40 percent, but agreeing that the mature brewpub venture would terminally grow at a rate of 8 percent with a risk profile requiring a discount rate of 16 percent? What if the terminal growth rate were 10 percent and the discount rate 18 percent?

6. Following are financial statements (historical and forecasted) for the Global Products Corporation.

Global Products Corporation

	2007	FORECAST 2008
Cash	$ 50,000	$ 60,000
Accounts receivable	200,000	290,000
Inventories	450,000	570,000
Total current assets	700,000	920,000
Fixed assets, net	300,000	380,000
Total assets	$1,000,000	$1,300,000
Accounts payable	140,000	$ 180,000
Accruals	50,000	70,000
Bank loan	80,000	90,000
Total current liabilities	270,000	340,000
Long-term debt	400,000	550,000
Common stock ($1 par)	50,000	50,000
Capital surplus	200,000	200,000
Retained earnings	80,000	160,000
Total liabilities and equity	$1,000,000	$1,300,000

	2007	FORECAST 2008
Net sales	$1,300,000	$1,600,000
Cost of goods sold	780,000	960,000
Gross profit	520,000	640,000
Marketing	130,000	160,000
General and administrative	150,000	150,000
Depreciation	40,000	55,000
EBIT	200,000	275,000
Interest	45,000	55,000
Earnings before taxes	155,000	220,000
Income taxes (40% rate)	62,000	88,000
Net income	$ 93,000	$ 132,000

A. Assume that the cash account includes only required cash. Determine the dollar amount of equity valuation cash flow for 2008.

B. Now assume that Global Products' required cash is set at 3 percent of sales. Any additional cash would be surplus cash. Re-estimate the dollar amount of equity valuation cash flow for 2008.

C. Let's assume that investors in Global Products want to estimate the venture's present value at the end of 2007. Forecasted financial statements reflect the stepping-stone year. Cash flows are expected to grow at a perpetual 8 percent annual rate beginning in 2009. Assume that all cash is required cash as was done in Part A. What is Global Products' present value if investors want an annual rate of return of 25 percent?

D. Work with the assumptions in Part B about Global Products' required cash being 3 percent of sales. Calculate the present value of the Global Products venture at the end of 2007 if investors want an annual rate of return of 25 percent and cash flows are expected to grow at a perpetual 8 percent annual rate beginning in 2009.

7. Return to the discussion of the FrothySlope venture at the beginning of the chapter. Formulate an answer for each of the five questions that are posed under the heading "What Is a Venture Worth?"

Spreadsheet Valuation Problem

8. The Biometrix Corporation has been in operation for one full year (2007). Financial statements follow. Biometrix's management is interested in determining the value of the venture as of the end of 2007. Sales are expected to grow at a 20 percent annual rate for each of the next three years (2008, 2009, and 2010) before settling down to a long-run growth rate of 7 percent annually. The cost of goods sold is expected to vary with sales. Operating expenses are expected to grow at 75 percent of the sales growth rate (i.e., be semi-fixed) for the next three years before again growing at the same rate as sales beginning in 2011. Individual asset accounts are expected to grow at the same rate as sales. Depreciation can be forecasted either as a percentage of sales or as a percentage of net fixed assets (since net fixed assets are expected to grow at the same rate as sales growth). Accounts payable and accrued liabilities are also expected to grow with sales.

Biometrix's management is interested in determining the equity value of the venture as of the end of 2007. Because Biometrix is in its startup life cycle stage, management and venture investors believe that 40 percent is an appropriate discount rate until the firm reaches its long-run or perpetuity growth rate. At that time it will have survived and will become a more typical firm with an estimated cost of equity capital of 20 percent.

A. Project the financial statements for the next four years (2008–2011).

B. Calculate the valuation cash flow for each year.

C. Determine Biometrix's equity value at the end of 2007.

Biometrix Corporation

INCOME STATEMENT FOR DECEMBER 31, 2007
(THOUSANDS OF DOLLARS)

Sales	$20,000
Cost of goods sold	− 10,000
Gross profit	10,000
Operating expenses	−7,500

continued on next page

Depreciation	−400
EBIT	2,100
Interest	−100
EBT	2,000
Taxes (40%)	−800
Net income	$ 1,200

BALANCE SHEET AS OF DECEMBER 31, 2007
(THOUSANDS OF DOLLARS)

Cash	$ 1,000	Accounts payable	$ 1,500
Accounts receivable	2,000	Accrued liabilities	1,000
Inventories	2,000	Bank loan	1,000
Total current assets	5,000	Total current liabilities	3,500
Gross fixed assets	5,400	Common stock	5,300
Accumulated depreciation	400	Retained earnings	1,200
Net fixed assets	5,000	Total equity	6,500
Total assets	$10,000	Total liabilities and equity	$10,000

M I N I   C A S E

SoftTec Products Company

The SoftTec Products Company is a successful small, rapidly growing, closely held corporation. The equity owners are considering selling the firm to an outside buyer and want to estimate the value of the firm. Following is last year's income statement (2007) and projected income statements for the next four years (2008–2011). Sales are expected to grow at an annual 7 percent rate beginning in 2012 and continuing thereafter.

	ACTUAL	PROJECTED			
[$ THOUSANDS]	2007	2008	2009	2010	2011
Net sales	$ 150.0	$ 200.0	$ 250.0	$ 300.0	$ 350.0
Cost of goods sold	−75.0	−100.0	−125.0	−150.0	−175.0
Gross profit	75.0	100.0	125.0	150.0	175.0
SG&A expenses	−30.0	−40.0	−50.0	−60.0	−70.0
Depreciation	−7.5	−10.0	−12.5	−15.0	−17.5
EBIT	37.5	50.0	62.5	75.0	87.5
Interest	−3.5	−3.5	−3.5	−3.5	−3.5
EBT	34.0	46.5	59.0	71.5	84.0
Taxes (40% rate)	−13.6	−18.6	−23.6	−28.6	−33.6
Net income	$ 20.4	$ 27.9	$ 35.4	$ 42.9	$ 50.4

Selected balance sheet accounts at the end of 2007 were as follows. Net fixed assets were $50,000. The sum of the required cash, accounts receivable, and inventories accounts was $50,000. Accounts payable and accruals totaled $25,000. Each of these balance sheet accounts was expected to grow with sales over time. No changes in interest-bearing debt were projected, and there were no plans to issue additional shares of common stock. There are currently 10,000 shares of common stock outstanding.

SoftTec Products Company (continued)

Data have been gathered for a comparable publicly traded firm in the same industry that Soft-Tec operates in. The cost of common equity for this other firm, Wakefield Products, was estimated to be 25 percent. SoftTec has survived for a period of years. Management is not currently contemplating a major financial structure change and believes a single discount rate is appropriate for discounting all cash flows.

A. Project SoftTec's income statement for 2012.
B. Determine the annual increases in required net working capital and capital expenditures (CAPEX) for SoftTec for the years 2008 to 2012.
C. Project annual operating free cash flows for the years 2008 to 2012.
D. Estimate SoftTec's terminal value cash flow at the end of 2011.
E. Estimate SoftTec's equity value in dollars and per share at the end of 2007.
F. SoftTec's management was wondering what the firm's equity value (dollar amount and on a per-share basis) would be if the cost of equity capital were only 20 percent. Recalculate the firm's value using this lower discount rate.
G. Now assume that the $35,000 in long-term debt (and therefore interest expense at 10 percent) is expected to grow with sales. Recalculate the equity using the original 25 percent discount rate.

M I N I   C A S E

RxDelivery Systems, Inc.

RxDelivery Systems is an R&D venture specializing in the development and testing of new drug delivery technologies. Driving factors behind this growth include efforts to reduce drug side effects through site-specific delivery, the need to maintain the activity of new biopharmaceutical compounds, and the extension of drug patent life. Improved drug delivery methods are expected to reduce the number of surgical interventions and the length of hospital stays and improve patient compliance in taking prescribed drugs.

The world market for biopharmaceuticals (including peptide, protein, RNA, and DNA drugs) was about $50 billion in 2004. Sales of polymer-based drug delivery systems are forecasted to reach $1.4 billion in 2011. Pulmonary delivery systems currently account for one-third of the drug delivery market and sales are projected to reach $22 billion by 2011.

RxDelivery Systems believes it can compete effectively in both the polymer-based and the pulmonary drug delivery areas. The venture's delivery technology is expected to utilize hydrophobic ion pairing and supercritical carbon dioxide precipitation to incorporate water-soluble drug molecules into biodegradable controlled-release microspheres. The resulting microspheres will take the form of dry powders and will contain drug molecules small enough to allow for intravenous, intranasal, or pulmonary delivery. It is anticipated that this technology will be incorporated into products for controlled-release applications, including treatment of cancer, infectious diseases, and gene therapy.

RxDelivery Systems, through an agreement with its pharmaceutical parent, a major drug company, will initially operate as an independent corporation but will be merged into the parent at the end of its second year. At that time, RxDelivery Systems' entrepreneurial team will be paid a lump sum of $2.5 million as the terminal value for the venture.

continued on next page

RxDelivery Systems, Inc. (continued)

Following are limited financial statement projections for the next two years for RxDelivery Systems:

First-year revenues	$12,500
Second-year revenues	$16,000
Expenses (including depreciation)	$125,000 per year
Initial time-zero (net) fixed assets	$50,000
Depreciation	10% of beginning-of-year net fixed assets
Accounts payable (Years 1 and 2)	$750
Inventories (Years 1 and 2)	$0
Corporate marginal tax rate	30%
Accounts receivable (Years 1 and 2)	$0
Accrued expenses (Years 1 and 2)	$300
Required cash	$3000
Debt (all years)	$0

A. Construct the venture's income statements for Years 1 and 2.
B. Construct the venture's balance sheets at startup and at the end of Years 1 and 2. Put initial fixed asset investments in Year 0 and initial working capital investments in Year 1. Assume the initial $50,000 is equity financed.
C. Construct the pseudo dividend method (PDM) equity valuation cash flow, including the $2,500,000 terminal payment.
D. Using a 30 percent discount rate for the first two years and a $2,500,000 terminal value, what is the value of the venture at its launch?

Learning
Supplement 9A

VALUE MAXIMIZATION AND THE FIRST ENTREPRENEURIAL TEAM

A FICTIONAL RECOLLECTION OF *HOMO ECONOMICUS* AND PARADISE LOST

It has become received wisdom that long ago the benevolent Supreme Being (hereafter, God) created a garden and placed in it the first human inhabitant, Adam, who was to take care of the garden. In the garden, were two orange trees (apples, while not actually mentioned anywhere in the story, usually get the blame). God commanded that no oranges be eaten from the orange tree in the middle of the garden. Such oranges must be allowed to return to the ground. Eating forbidden oranges would result in death, an event not totally clear to Adam. All oranges from any present or future tree other than the one in the middle of the garden were fair game for consumption. God named the forbidden tree "The Tree of the Knowledge of Economics."

God reasoned that it was not good for Adam to be alone and that a suitable helper would be in order. As no suitable helper could be found, God created a second human garden inhabitant named Eve. The permissible orange tree provided the pair with more than enough oranges and, consistent with Adam's seniority and disposition, initially no thought was given to the restriction on oranges from the forbidden tree. Adam enjoyed Eve's companionship but was somewhat concerned about noticeable differences in their temperaments.

One day as Eve was eating the last permissible ripe orange (although several would ripen the next day) a worm perched on the orange.

Worm:	*Indeed, has God said, "You shall not eat from any tree of the Garden."*
Eve:	*From the fruit of the trees of the garden we may eat; but from the fruit of the tree which is in the middle of the garden God has said, "You shall not eat from it or touch it, lest you die."*
Worm:	*You surely shall not die! For God knows that in the day you eat from it your eyes will be opened, and you will be like God, knowing Economics. You will be able to decide how many oranges should be let go to seed and how many can be consumed today. You can decide how much to invest, instead of having God dictate it to you.*

The potential to share in God's Knowledge of Economics exhilarated Eve, who hesitated at first, but saw no reason, other than God's edict, to abstain. Seeing that the forbidden oranges were good for food and pleasing to the eye, and knowing that consuming one and observing the outcome would prove useful as an experiment in gaining the Knowledge of Economics, Eve took a forbidden orange and ate some of it. Eve then handed the remaining fruit to Adam, who noted that it was an exceptionally fine orange and, more important, that Eve had not died. Having been named appropriately, Adam finished off the remaining fruit.

Immediately, their eyes were opened, and they knew that they had overconsumed and suboptimally invested. They felt intellectually naked. It was clear that they had eaten the orange without considering the adverse impact on the growth rate of orange crops. They were horrified when they thought about the effect of their decision on the millions of descendants who would eventually starve because of their momentary indulgence in consumptive excess. There would be underforestation, hunger, disease, and an unbelievably large hole in the ozone layer. How could they have been so naive about the long-term impact of small changes in initial conditions? What chaos. They were hopelessly inadequate in their economic reasoning and were ashamed.

Realizing that they could not bear such shame, they began to attempt a full-scale economic analysis with graphs and math symbols. Shortly thereafter, God came walking through the garden. The pair knew their economic rationalization for consuming the forbidden orange was ridiculously simple and incomplete, so they hid their work under some leaves.

God:	*(as if He didn't know) Where are you?*
Adam:	*I heard the sound of Thee in the garden and I was afraid because we had no economic justification for our consumption and investment behavior; so I hid myself and my work.*
God:	*Who told you that you invested suboptimally? Have you eaten from the tree which I commanded you not to eat?*
Adam:	*Eve gave me from the tree and I ate.*

| God: | *What is this you have done?* |
| Eve: | *The worm deceived me and I ate.* |

After this interchange, God cursed the worm to eat dust all of the days of its life and threw the gardeners out of the garden. Just before throwing them out, God harvested a large tree and turned it into reams of paper on which He recorded a complete economic analysis of the consumption-investment problem as it would have applied to them in the garden. The gardeners were not surprised to see that God's prohibition had not been a whim, but appeared to be fully rational.

Thus it was in rebellion against external unsubstantiated (albeit optimal) investment constraints that economics analysis entered the world. The gardeners were sent out of the garden with the ten ripe oranges that remained and an overwhelming urge to analyze the consumption-investment decision for the ten oranges. Frustration set in as they realized that they would not be able to reconstruct God's analysis, which had been removed from the earth. They would have to go forth and optimize with only vague impressions of what a proper economic analysis should contain. Nonetheless, they had great faith that their newly acquired Knowledge of Economics (albeit somewhat less than divine) would apply, for better or worse, to the more important decisions they would have to make in their earthly life.

They knew they had been rash in consuming too many of the oranges in the garden and were depressed as they considered the possible long-term effects of their actions:

Adam:	*We've done it now. In our brief moment of consumptive ecstasy we have succeeded in eradicating paradise and endangering the future survival of oranges and all of civilization as we know it.*
Eve:	*We really should have considered evolutionary stability before we acted so hastily.*
Adam:	*Do we believe in evolution? Never mind. We have the more immediate problem of what to do with the remaining ten oranges.*
Eve:	*Great. We've wrecked the world and all you can think about is ten lousy oranges.*
Adam:	*They appear to be rotting. How long do you think we'll survive on ten rotting oranges?*
Eve:	*That's odd. I don't recall any rotten oranges in the garden.... Anyway, with ten oranges, I could last at least the square root of five, and no more than x days.*
Adam:	*What does square root mean? Don't you think you've made a few too many simplifying assumptions—like that no one else exists so you get to eat all ten oranges?*
Eve:	*I'm sorry. It's not me talking. It's this damned Knowledge of Economics.*
Adam:	*We will have to make some simplifying assumptions, and I guess yours are a start.*
Eve:	*I think we should start by ignoring others.*
Adam:	*Why not? Where would they come from, anyway?*
Eve:	*Who knows, but they're not here so let's not worry.*
Adam:	*I think it would be easier if we thought of our consumption of oranges as taking place over discrete time intervals.*
Eve:	*Like youth and old age. I agree. The tractability this introduces is important.*

Adam:	It seems important not to eat all of the oranges in youth, leaving none for old age.
Eve:	Not with the current state of the Social Security system.
Adam:	What's that?
Eve:	I'm not sure.
Adam:	I don't think we'll make it to old age if we don't eat some now.
Eve:	Do you think we should try to characterize these assumptions mathematically? I've always preferred graphical analysis.
Adam:	What do you mean always? Your Knowledge of Economics is less than a week old.
Eve:	For me, it seems like an eternity.
Adam:	Your enterprising and impatient nature got us into this fix to start with.
Eve:	No one forced you to eat the forbidden orange. You would have done it eventually. I'm just more decisive than you.
Adam:	Did God use graphs or mathematics in His analysis?
Eve:	I don't recall. Let's start with graphs. We can put some math bones on it later when Calculus has been developed.
Adam:	Calculus?

They set out separately to conduct the graphical analyses that resulted in the three curves of Exhibit 1.

EXHIBIT 1

The Consumption-Investment Decision for the Gardeners

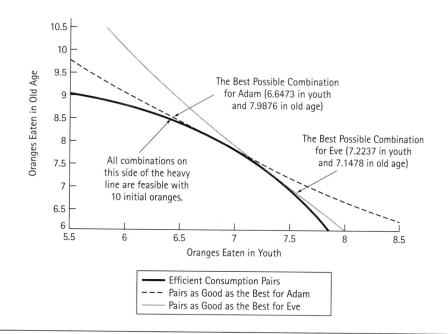

The Best Possible Combination for Adam (6.6473 in youth and 7.9876 in old age)

The Best Possible Combination for Eve (7.2237 in youth and 7.1478 in old age)

All combinations on this side of the heavy line are feasible with 10 initial oranges.

Oranges Eaten in Old Age

Oranges Eaten in Youth

—— Efficient Consumption Pairs
– – – Pairs as Good as the Best for Adam
—— Pairs as Good as the Best for Eve

The area underneath the bold curve was taken to represent the possible combinations of current and future orange consumption that could be obtained by varying current consumption. They concluded that the bold line itself must be the only relevant part because anything below it required wasting either current or future oranges.

The light solid and dashed lines connect combinations of current and future orange consumption that would evoke as much enthusiasm from Eve and Adam (respectively) as they would have for the best among the feasible pairs. Anything to the northeast of these lines would be better, but not feasible; anything to the southwest is feasible but inferior. But a new problem arose which they could not simply ignore.

It was clear that God had created them to work as a team and, ideally, to commune with each other in such a way that the two would be an indissoluble partnership. Such a fusion would certainly have fostered some commitment to working out their differences. However, their intended unity must have been in some philosophical or theological respect rather than an economic one. Being the typical postgarden partnership, each claimed that his or her preference was the only rational one and that the other's was silly. They resolved that their differences were irreconcilable and appealed to God for dissolution (although common-law partnership had yet to be defined).

God knew that the Knowledge of Economics would bring much sorrow and division in the world. After telling the gardeners that disunity and disharmony were not the original intent, He permitted a trial separation so that, this time, the gardeners would more carefully consider the long-run consequences of their actions. Equally dividing the oranges, the first property rights were established. As they went their separate ways, the gardeners reflected again on their consumption-investment problem, but without concern for one another and from a stock of five oranges. A mild remorse set in as they realized that, as a couple, they could have achieved all that they would achieve separately and possibly more. They always had the option of investing as though they were separate. Weren't the gains to collusion always positive? Their initial analyses had not even considered the possibility of dividing the investments into two. Separately, they cursed the Knowledge of Economics and their haste but took some comfort in knowing that true *Homo economici* ignore collusion unless (1) it is the best response to others' actions or (2) legally binding contracts can be written. The gardeners weren't sure what all this meant but felt sure it justified ignoring the benefits of collusion. Their separate but correlated reflections led to the graphs of Exhibit 2.

Motivated by this graphical analysis, Adam ate 2.9159 oranges and Eve ate 3.3584. All remaining orange parts were planted in their respective gardens. As they ate their oranges, their minds wandered to new topics to which they could apply their Knowledge of Economics, including poverty in capitalistic economies with a taxing authority, inefficiency in bartered transactions for trades involving more than two parties, whether God can construct an economy He cannot regulate, whether an increase in the angelic minimum wage would influence the number of angels that could be hired to sit on the head of a pin, and whether there should be a Nobel Prize in economics. Fortunately, just as Malthusian introspection was leading Adam into suicidal depression over the hopeless plight of future hungry masses, the seventh day arrived and they rested.

FINANCIAL MARKETS AND TRADE—PARADISE REGAINED? NOT EXACTLY

Although we have no written account of the events that followed, tradition holds that one day, while off considering their predicament, Eve came upon the idea that the ability to borrow and lend oranges might lead the gardeners to a more efficient consumption-

EXHIBIT 2   Separate Consumption and Investment with Five Oranges Each

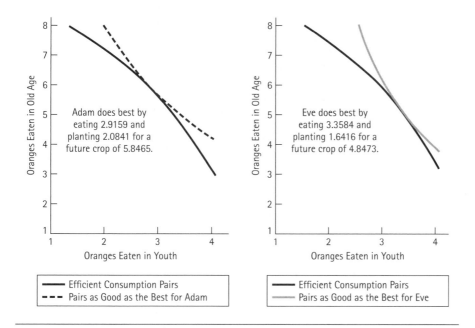

Adam does best by eating 2.9159 and planting 2.0841 for a future crop of 5.8465.

— Efficient Consumption Pairs
- - - Pairs as Good as the Best for Adam

Eve does best by eating 3.3584 and planting 1.6416 for a future crop of 4.8473.

— Efficient Consumption Pairs
— Pairs as Good as the Best for Eve

investment arrangement. Eve could form an orange venture and invest oranges borrowed from Adam and repay the borrowing with future orange interest.

Perhaps in an economy having these financial enhancements all venture partners might agree on the number of oranges to be planted. While Eve was not sure how such an economy might come into existence, such an idea had to be shared; but with whom? After brooding a few days, Eve went in search of Adam, who was contemplating the advantages of using fiat money instead of taking seignorage on full-bodied coins.

Eve:	*Hello, Adam. Long time no see.*
Adam:	*Doesn't seem so long to me. You never were really big on waiting.*
Eve:	*Let's not get into that again.*
Adam:	*Doesn't* Homo economicus *have a sense of humor?*
Eve:	*I don't ever remember including it in my analysis. An interesting point. I'll pursue it later.*
Adam:	*You came for something?*
Eve:	*I was just thinking . . .*
Adam:	*As if there were anything else to do now that the oranges have been planted.*
Eve:	*If investors in an economy could borrow and lend oranges in a market at a fixed rate, then it might be possible for investors with different time preferences to agree on the amount of oranges to be planted.*
Adam:	*(after short pause) Er . . . Well . . . that's . . . obvious.*

Eve:	*If it's so obvious, why didn't you mention it before.*
Adam:	*It's been so long since I covered that topic that I have forgotten most of the important results.*
Eve:	*We've only been out of the garden a little over a week. Some memory.*
Adam:	*I've had more important things on my mind. Give me a day and I'll see if I can reproduce my earlier work.*
Eve:	*If you say so. So we can compare notes, let's start by assuming that each future orange costs .4430 current oranges. The seller of a future orange receives the .4430 paid by the buyer. Of course, this correlates to a rather steep interest rate of 126 percent.*
Adam:	*Where in the world did you get that number? You haven't been smoking the oranges, have you? Didn't God say something about a usury taboo? We don't have any VCs around to take the heat, you know.*
Eve:	*A small voice suggested that I try it.*
Adam:	*Have you been talking to that worm again? I suppose .4430 is OK for a starting point. After all, it's just a theoretical exercise and you'll be the one paying the implied 126 percent interest. Too bad there's no taxing authority to let you take it as a tax deduction. I don't think it's deductible for sacrifice purposes.*
Eve:	*I wait for your analysis.*
Adam:	*Not as patiently as I do.*

They parted, confident that a tractable analysis was forthcoming. The next day they met and compared graphs that have been combined into Exhibit 3.

Adam:	*I've completed my graphical analysis.*
Eve:	*As have I.*
Adam:	*The ability to borrow and lend oranges does make a difference to me. Instead of planting about 2, I would plant just over 1.8 if I could loan oranges at 126 percent.*
Eve:	*Instead of planting 1.6416, I would plant 1.8637, which I calculate to be a more precise statement of the amount you would also plant. As I suspected, and you quickly claimed is obvious, the introduction of a financial market in oranges unifies our investment decision. Aggregate planting rises from 3.7257 to 3.7274, a 17-basis-point increase.*
Adam:	*Basis point? What's that? A way to make something small sound big?*
Eve:	*You should know. Such marketing is not exactly my original sin. Back to the point, it looks like we'll run our orchard operations exactly the same. I could run yours and I'd invest exactly the amount you'd want.*
Adam:	*Hold on a minute. We haven't gotten there yet. We need a structure for the enterprise, an appropriate objective, and adequate incentives for you to carry out my wishes. You might recall that your last managerial endeavor proved less than satisfactory to the owner of the agricultural complex we until recently inhabited. If an all-seeing, all-knowing deity didn't provide strong enough incentives to keep you on the straight and narrow there, the problem must not be that easy for recently mere mortals to solve.*
Eve:	*Forgive and forget, eh?*
Adam:	*I'm just trying to be constructive.*

EXHIBIT 3

Consumption and Production with Borrowing and Lending

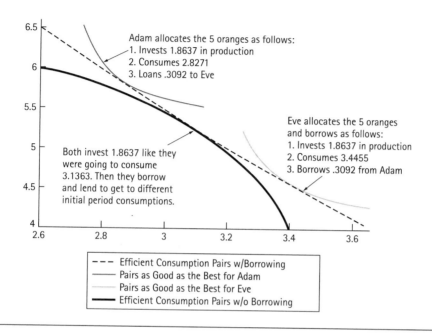

Adam allocates the 5 oranges as follows:
1. Invests 1.8637 in production
2. Consumes 2.8271
3. Loans .3092 to Eve

Eve allocates the 5 oranges
and borrows as follows:
1. Invests 1.8637 in production
2. Consumes 3.4455
3. Borrows .3092 from Adam

Both invest 1.8637 like they
were going to consume
3.1363. Then they borrow
and lend to get to different
initial period consumptions.

--- Efficient Consumption Pairs w/Borrowing
—— Pairs as Good as the Best for Adam
—— Pairs as Good as the Best for Eve
—— Efficient Consumption Pairs w/o Borrowing

Eve: Orchard production translates current oranges into future oranges, but
            lending oranges is a competing way to do the same. These two transla-
            tion rates have to be in equilibrium.

Adam: Equilibrium? I'm with you, but could we cut the physics jargon?

Eve: The orchard firm manager should plant oranges until the product of
            the last orange part planted produces output that, upon conversion at fi-
            nancial market rates back into today's oranges, is the amount planted.
            To plant more is worse than lending the increase; to plant less is worse
            than borrowing the decrease.

Adam: You seem to be claiming that, in arriving independently at 1.8637 as the
            appropriate planting, we have magically maximized the financial market
            value of future production. That should be easy enough to check. Speak-
            ing of checking, I meant to ask you how you're getting these precise four
            decimal numbers? You've been eyeballing those graphs pretty accurately.

Eve: Intuition comes in all sizes, and in this case, accuracies. Investing 1.8637
            maximizes the orchard's value of investment over and above the cost of
            investment. The value is 5.3651 future oranges or, at 126 percent, about
            2.37 presently valued oranges.

Adam: I don't suppose your left and right brain could communicate and give
            me a written objective for the orchard's investment plan to follow.

Eve: No problem: Maximize $f(O)/(1 + 126\%) - O$, where, I believe in our
            context, $f(O) = 3.5 \times O - (O^2)/3$ is appropriate where O is the amount

of oranges planted. Having realized you might ask and wishing to accommodate your more graphics-oriented approach, I have plotted this net present value function. (See Exhibit 4.)

Adam: *It's all coming back to me. I told you it had been awhile since I had fully analyzed this topic. I now recall that rather than doing all of this analysis, the proper orchard manager could just use market interest rates and maximize the value of production. Therefore, a proper maximizing manager invests exactly as I would. However, this fact still doesn't address my concerns that you will not manage the orchard in my best interests. You have had a tendency to eat the investment when the boss has explicitly dictated otherwise.*

Eve: *I see why God thought you needed help. However, I'm not really in the mood to start a tutoring session on how additional derivative markets, in particular options markets, would introduce instruments that provide proper incentives for the orchard manager. I don't want to work for you but am willing to consider ending our trial separation.*

Adam: *Really?*

They next time they encountered God they told him that they understood that financial markets could help impersonalize their investment perspective and thereby restore some level of harmony in their relationship. Their intent was to maintain separate orchards but share the same house and financial markets. Their difference in time preference wasn't an irreconcilable difference that would be the basis of a permanent separation. Knowing that their budding Knowledge of Economics was being tamed but still only a distant second best to what had been intended, God agreed to permit them to return to living together. As the official ceremony was about to be concluded, God asked if anyone knew of a reason why the two should not be rejoined.

Eve: *Why should borrowers and lenders pay the same rate?*

EXHIBIT 4   Net Present Values of Orange Production Opportunities

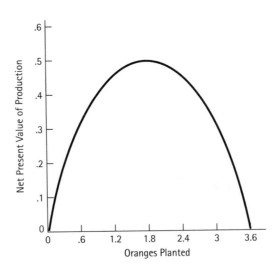

If you remember nothing else from this entire anecdote, remember three things:

1. The compelling arguments behind most classical economic analyses almost always involve an individual acting in his best economic interests. More than an economic statement this is a psychological, or perhaps even a theological, statement.

2. Net present value (NPV) is the finance profession's method for reflecting market prices and interest rates in the value of a proposed investment.

3. A variety of investors, managers, and entrepreneurs can use financial market signals to provide unity in financial objectives. Maximizing the firm's market value is certainly not the only possible firm objective. Nonetheless, it may be the only financial objective various venture participants would agree to pursue.

Regarding the last two points, even the most adamant opponents of present value methods would most likely admit that bond and stock prices contain relevant information for anyone raising money in the financial markets. But, on second thought, there are probably those who would argue that the market price of shampoo is not relevant to Procter & Gamble.

Learning
Supplement 9B

DISCOUNTING GROWING PERPETUITIES

We begin by assuming that a smooth growth assumption seems to be a reasonable approximation after year T (beginning with year $T + 1$). The time line for valuation cash flows (VCFs) growing at a constant rate g after time T is:

$T - 1$	T	$T + 1$	...	$T + t$	...
VCF_{T-1}	VCF_T	VCF_{T+1} $= VCF_T(1 + g)$		VCF_{T+t} $= VCF_T(1 + g)^t$	

Now we discount each flow in the infinite future back to time $T - 1$ (the last time before the terminal period) at a constant rate of r_∞ per period and load an infinite spreadsheet with the results. The first column of the spreadsheet is just a label for the sum of the entries in that row. That is, the sum of the entries in the row equals the time $T - 1$ terminal value for flow in years T and beyond:

$T - 1$	$T \rightarrow T - 1$	$T + 1 \rightarrow T - 1$		$T + t - 1 \rightarrow T - 1$	$T + t \rightarrow T - 1$	$T + t + 1 \rightarrow T - 1$	
Terminal Value (= row sum)	$\dfrac{VCF_T}{(1 + r_\infty)}$	$\dfrac{VCF_T(1 + g)}{(1 + r_\infty)^2}$	...	$\dfrac{VCF_T(1 + g)^{t-1}}{(1 + r_\infty)^t}$	$\dfrac{VCF_T(1 + g)^t}{(1 + r_\infty)^{t+1}}$	$\dfrac{VCF_T(1 + g)^{t+1}}{(1 + r_\infty)^{t+2}}$	...

Note that discounting back to time $T - 1$ is accomplished by dividing each cell by $(1 + r_\infty)^{t+1}$, where r_∞ is the terminal value constant discount rate and t is the number of periods since T. Noting that the exponent on the $(1 + g)$ is one less than the exponent on the $(1 + r_\infty)$, we can multiply by $(1 + g)$ to create a new row that has equal exponents. We can also create a new row with equal exponents by multiplying by $(1 + r_\infty)$:

	$T - 1$	$T \to T - 1$	$T + t \to T - 1$	$\ldots$	$T + t - 1 \to T - 1$	$T + 1 \to T - 1$	$T + t + 1 \to T - 1$	
Terminal Value $\times (1 + g)$ (= row sum)		$\dfrac{VCF_T(1 + g)}{(1 + r_\infty)}$	$\dfrac{VCF_T(1 + g)^2}{(1 + r_\infty)^2}$	$\ldots$	$\dfrac{VCF_T(1 + g)^t}{(1 + r_\infty)^t}$	$\dfrac{VCF_T(1 + g)^{t+1}}{(1 + r_\infty)^{t+1}}$	$\dfrac{VCF_T(1 + g)^{t+2}}{(1 + r_\infty)^{t+2}}$	$\ldots$
Terminal Value $\times (1 + r_\infty)$ (= row sum)	VCF_T	$\dfrac{VCF_T(1 + g)}{(1 + r_\infty)}$	$\ldots$		$\dfrac{VCF_T(1 + g)^{t-1}}{(1 + r_\infty)^{t-1}}$	$\dfrac{VCF_T(1 + g)^t}{(1 + r_\infty)^t}$	$\dfrac{VCF_T(1 + g)^{t+1}}{(1 + r_\infty)^{t+1}}$	$\ldots$

Because of the transformation of future cash flows into time $T - 1$ values (indicated by the $T - 1$ in the column headings), we can combine numbers from any of the columns in the spreadsheet. (They are all time $T - 1$ values.) We shift the first row right one column and subtract it from the second row for the result:

	$T - 1$ Value	$T - 1$ Value	$T - 1$ Value		$T - 1$ Value	$T - 1$ Value	$T - 1$ Value	
$-$Terminal Value $\times (1 + g)$ (= row sum)			$\dfrac{-VCF_T(1 + g)}{(1 + r_\infty)}$	$\ldots$	$\dfrac{-VCF_T(1 + g)^{t-1}}{(1 + r_\infty)^{t-1}}$	$\dfrac{-VCF_T(1 + g)^t}{(1 + r_\infty)^t}$	$\dfrac{-VCF_T(1 + g)^{t+1}}{(1 + r_\infty)^{t+1}}$	$\ldots$
$+$Terminal Value $\times (1 + r_\infty)$ (= row sum)	VCF_T	$\dfrac{VCF_T(1 + g)}{(1 + r_\infty)}$	$\ldots$		$\dfrac{VCF_T(1 + g)^{t-1}}{(1 + r_\infty)^{t-1}}$	$\dfrac{VCF_T(1 + g)^t}{(1 + r_\infty)^t}$	$\dfrac{VCF_T(1 + g)^{t+1}}{(1 + r_\infty)^{t-1}}$	$\ldots$
Terminal Value $\times (r_\infty - g)$ (= row sum)	VCF_T	0	0	0	0	0	0	0

Taking the row sum for this last row gives Terminal Value $\times (r_\infty - g) = VCF_T$. Solving gives time $T - 1$ terminal value $= VCF_T/(r_\infty - g)$.

Chapter 10

VENTURE CAPITAL VALUATION METHODS

PREVIOUSLY COVERED

In Chapter 9, we introduced a formal valuation method relating a venture's value to the future cash that the venture can return to equity investors. We demonstrated that valuation is straightforward once someone has produced a properly projected set of financial statements. We provided two different approaches to mixing financial statements with a valuation: the maximum dividend method (MDM) and the pseudo dividend method (PDM).

LOOKING AHEAD

Part 5 introduces important features of the market for venture capital. Chapter 11 discusses the history of professional venture capital, its role in supporting emerging technologies and business, and, importantly for entrepreneurs seeking venture capital, the fundraising-investment cycle faced by most professional venture capital firms. Chapter 12 discusses alternative sources of capital for early and growing ventures, including regional and national programs that can assist in the quest for investment capital.

CHAPTER LEARNING OBJECTIVES

In this chapter, we present several variations on the simplified valuation procedures and rules of thumb frequently grouped under the designation "venture capital methods." We introduce a three-scenario approach to examining the value of different possible future venture outcomes. After completing this chapter, you will be able to:

1. Relate venture capital methods to more formal equity valuation methods

2. Understand how valuation and percent ownership are related

3. Calculate the amount of shares to be issued to secure a fixed amount of funding

4. Understand the impact of subsequent financing rounds on the structure of the current financing round

5. Construct multiple-scenario valuations and unify them in a single valuation

Now that Chapter 9 has introduced two formal processes for valuing ventures by discounting the cash flows available to pay venture investors, we are ready to investigate the advantages and disadvantages of some popular shortcuts. In many venture investing contexts, the shortcuts are useful to determine whether a venture investment is worth pursuing further. One of the key justifications for the shortcut methods we consider is recognizing that finding the market value (MV) of a venture's assets is the same as finding the market value of its liabilities and equity:

$$MV(Assets) = MV(Liabilities) + MV(Equity)$$

10.1   BRIEF REVIEW OF BASIC CASH FLOW–BASED EQUITY VALUATIONS

The MDM and PDM of Chapter 9 focused on a venture's assets (and operations) to the point where they don't really consider much about the venture's liabilities and equity structure. You could say that the methods in Chapter 9 value the following rearrangement of the market value (MV) version of the accounting identity:

$$MV(Total\ Assets - Total\ Liabilities) = MV(Equity)$$

Working toward finding the left-hand-side value, we built a cash flow for each projected year that was "free" after implementing the ending balance sheet and income projections for that year. For example, the initial maximum or pseudo dividend (both equal to the equity valuation cash flow or VCF) that we calculated for PDC was:

Net income	6,372
+ Depreciation and amortization expense	+4,600
− Change in net operating working capital	+2,415
− Capital expenditures	−6,900
+ Net debt issues	+0
= Equity valuation cash flow	6,487

Recognizing that the flows behind the left-hand side [i.e., MV(total assets − total liabilities)] had to be exactly equal to the flows behind the right-hand side [MV(equity)], we discounted combinations of operating, asset, and liability flows (like this $6,487) using an appropriate equity discount rate and arrived at an estimate of the market value of equity. We started with the business plan, considered its operations, investments, and debt financing (if any), and netted them all together to see what was projected to be left over for equity holders. The logic flowed from implementing the business plan's operations and strategy to what's left to repay owners.

Recall from Chapter 9 that we developed the following cash flows and determined PDC's equity NPV to be:

$$\text{PDC's Equity NPV} = 6{,}487 + \frac{65{,}403}{1.25} + \frac{20{,}125}{(1.25)^2} + \frac{-1{,}704}{(1.25)^3} + \frac{288{,}648}{(1.25)^4} + \frac{\frac{63{,}460}{.18 - .06}}{(1.25)^4}$$

$$= 405{,}657$$

The NPV calculation involved the following flows to (+) and from (−) investors: $6,487 immediately, $65,403 at the end of Year 1, $20,125 at the end of Year 2, −$1,704 (a reinvestment) at the end of Year 3, and, finally, $288,648 + $528,833 in Year 4. The $528,833 is the going concern value and was determined as the Year 5 (= T) $63,460 flow divided by the cap rate (.18 − .06). The valuation is for the entire set of investors that, as a group, experiences these flows. This valuation does not tell us which shareholders get what portion of that total pie. The investors' equity in totality has a value of $405,657 if they have claim to the first $6,487.

Recall that these numbers came from the operating assumptions in the business plan and reflected free cash flows to repay equity investors. What if we had not prepared the financial statement projections in Chapter 9, but rather had magically been given the $6,487 and all the other equity valuation cash flows? Couldn't we just discount them and not use formal financial statements? Yes! However, it's going to be pretty hard to guess the $6,487 and the other years' numbers without seeing the financial statement projections. It's going to be even harder to see how those guesses are related to operating the venture.

There is a simplification usually considered by those who wish to conjecture the equity flows directly (rather than from projecting operations, assets, and liabilities). Suppose that (i) there won't be any free cash flowing from the venture before the fourth year and (ii) we have a good guess from somewhere how big the equity flow will be in Year 4 (our "exit" or terminal year for valuation purposes). Then we could just work directly with the single exit year terminal equity flow, that is, the Year 4 NPV of $817,481 ($288,648 annual cash flow plus $528,833 of going concern value) for PDC. This will give us a quick approximation of the equity value. For PDC, the present value of this Year 4 NPV is $334,840 [= $817,481/(1.25)^4]. This is 82.5 percent (= 334,840/405,657) of the total value from the MDM and PDM methods. This is not bad for just using the Year 4 NPV (terminal value and flow). So, this shortcut is fast and not too far off once someone has given us the $334,840 terminal value. Good luck guessing that $334,840 without any financial projections!

Venture capital shortcuts (VCSCs) usually adopt variations on this approach. That is, most VCSCs concentrate on directly conjecturing flows to equity rather than deriving free cash flows resulting from the business plan's projected assets and operations. Venture investors understand that their returns depend on the venture's ability to generate appropriate future cash flows, or at least show the promise of such flows, so that an acquirer is willing to buy the firm. They know that a venture's future typically involves many unexpected twists and turns. Current detailed projections will almost certainly miss the mark. In emerging industries, valuations may be done quickly and amount to little more than informed speculation about possible return bottom lines and a keen sense of one's bargaining position. How much value there is to projecting a venture's future accurately is certainly worthy of debate. Nonetheless, while a venture's well-documented potential to generate cash at some point in the future may not *appear* to be at the forefront in VCSCs, the basic approach is still one of discounting future flows (periodic and/or terminal) to get present values much like we did in Chapter 9.[1]

CONCEPT CHECK

- Why should discounting the flows from a venture's assets give the same value as discounting the flows to providers of financial capital (debt and equity)?

10.2 BASIC VENTURE CAPITAL VALUATION METHOD

venture capital (VC) method

a valuation method that estimates a venture's value by projecting only a terminal flow to investors at the exit event

We begin our treatment of VCSCs with the simplest of the shortcuts, a procedure sometimes known as the venture capital method. The basic **venture capital (VC) method** estimates the venture's value by projecting only a terminal flow to investors at the exit event (say, in four or five years). Modifications of this basic VCSC will allow us to consider additional rounds and incentive compensation. We will conclude our discussion of VCSCs by extending the basic method to reintroduce intermediate cash flows and incorporate scenario extensions. As an example, we will present a "three-scenario" venture valuation with intermediate flows.

The basic VCSC approach is simple: (1) cash investment today, (2) cash return at some future exit time, (3) discount this entire return flow back at the venture investors' target return, (4) divide today's cash investment by the venture's post-money present value, and you get (5) the percent ownership to be sold in order to expect to provide the venture investors' target return. An example of this simple procedure will help clarify its structure.

Lynda Chen founded a new venture last year with $10,000 in equity capital for which she received 2,000,000 shares of common stock. The venture is now moving into its startup stage and needs an additional $1,000,000 to carry out the business plan. If Lynda had $1,000,000 to invest, she could retain 100 percent ownership of the venture. However, because Lynda does not have additional equity funds to invest, she is negotiating with a venture investor who is willing to invest $1,000,000 for an ownership position in the firm in the form of newly issued shares of common stock. The investor and the founder agree that the horizon (time to exit) for the investment should be five years. The investor expects a 50 percent compound annual rate of return for the entire five years.

---

[1] A note of caution is in order. Even if venture investors directly project and discount some bottom-line payment that they expect to be their return, it does not mean that the venture will escape criticism for failing to provide a formal set of projected financial statements.

We need to value the venture based on a five-year exit and determine how many shares to issue to the investor for the $1,000,000.

Looking ahead five years, we can say that the successful venture is expected to produce $1,000,000 per year in income at that time. We also know that a similar venture recently sold shares to the public for $20,000,000 (denoted P below) and that its last twelve months of income was $2,000,000 (denoted E below). We infer from this that the going price per dollar of income in this technology sector is $10 ($20,000,000/$2,000,000) and estimate the venture's exit value five years from now.[2] Multiplying 10 dollars per dollar of income by the $1,000,000 of projected fifth-year income gives a venture exit value of $10,000,000. Discounting the $10,000,000 exit value by 50 percent per year for five years gives a present value of $1,316,872 or $10,000,000/(1.5)^5$.

Figure 10.1 depicts the $10,000,000 future value "exit pie" as well as the $1,316,872 present value of the exit pie. We can "work" the VC valuations using either form of the exit pie. For initial purposes, we will begin with the present value exit pie, which is consistent with applying the discounted cash flow valuation methods in Chapter 9 whereby we discount future cash flows back to the present.

To apply the VC shortcut method, one must first calculate the percent ownership to be sold and then calculate the shares necessary to achieve that ownership. Equations 10.1 and 10.2 implement the VC method. Using I for the investment, E_5 for the venture's earnings or net income in Year 5, P/E for the comparable price per dollar of earnings or net income, m for existing shares, n for new shares to be issued, and r for the expected or demanded rate of return, we have:

$$
\begin{aligned}
\text{Acquired \% of Final Ownership} &= \frac{I}{\left(\dfrac{P}{E} \times E_5\right) \Big/ (1+r)^5} \\
&= \frac{1,000,000}{\left(\dfrac{10}{1} \times 1,000,000\right) \Big/ (1+.5)^5} \\
&= 75.9375\%
\end{aligned}
\tag{10.1}
$$

$$
\begin{aligned}
\text{Shares to Be Issued} = n &= \frac{m \times (\text{Acquired \%})}{1 - \text{Acquired \%}} \\
&= \frac{2,000,000 \times (.759375)}{.240625} \\
&= 6,311,688
\end{aligned}
\tag{10.2}
$$

In equation 10.1, we have an investment (numerator) of $1,000,000. The denominator gives the venture's $10,000,000 future value (i.e., $1,000,000 in net

---

[2] This approach also is frequently referred to as identifying and applying a price-earnings multiple for valuation purposes. The implicit assumption is that the price per dollar of income is expected to be at the same level at the end of five years. This assumption is common when using current multiples to project future values. We are emphasizing the use of price-earnings multiples and earnings projections to estimate terminal value. Other comparison ratios are frequently used to estimate terminal value. Examples include price to cash flow, price to revenue, and price to customers. The procedure is the same: Find a recent ratio and multiply it by the venture's projected performance on that dimension (e.g., price to revenue multiplied by projected revenue).

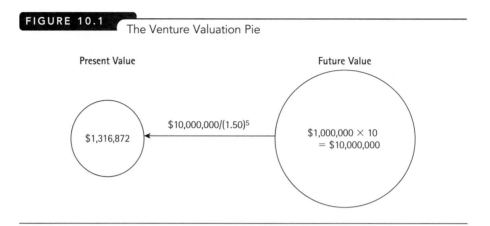

FIGURE 10.1 The Venture Valuation Pie

income times the P/E multiple of 10) discounted back to the present using $(1.50)^5$. The result is $1,000,000/$1,316,872, which equals .759375 or 75.9375 percent, the equity ownership percentage that must be given to the $1,000,000 investor to get the deal done. Equation 10.2 calculates the number of shares to be issued to the new investor so that he can achieve his stated expected compound annual rate of return of 50 percent. The new shares to be issued can be found by dividing 1,518,750 by .240625, which equals 6,311,688. The total number of shares that will be outstanding after the investment will be 8,311,688 (i.e., 2,000,000 original shares plus 6,311,688 new shares). Dividing 6,311,688 by 8,311,688 gives the 75.9375 percent ownership acquired by the new investor. Likewise, the founder will own 2,000,000/ 8,311,688 or 24.065 percent of the venture after the $1,000,000 new investment.

Although it is common practice to calibrate investment decisions using present values, ventures often require more than one round of financing and also may have an incentive ownership round. Since these additional financing rounds are likely to occur sometime in the future up to the venture exit, venture capital shortcut methods sometimes work directly with future exit values instead of their present values. We can easily change the reference time frame from present values ($1,000,000 investment and $1,316,872 present venture value) to Year 5 values ($7,593,750 future value of the $1,000,000 investment and $10,000,000 future venture value). We will get the same answer:

$$\text{Acquired \% of Final Ownership} = \frac{I \times (1+r)^5}{\frac{P}{E} \times E_5}$$

$$= \frac{1,000,000 \times (1+.5)^5}{\frac{10}{1} \times 1,000,000}$$

$$= 75.9375\% \tag{10.3}$$

Equation 10.3's numerator would be $7,593,750, which is equal to $1,000,000 inflated by $(1.50)^5$. The denominator is the same $10,000,000 exit value (i.e., $1,000,000 net income times the P/E of 10) as before. Dividing the future value of the investment by the future exit value also suggests granting a 75.9375 percent ownership position to the new investor. Although the result is the same whether the calculations take place in present or future values, it is important to always compare present (future) values to present (future) values.

Panel A of Figure 10.2 shows that the founder could retain 100 percent ownership if she (Lynda Chen) could make the $1,000,000 investment herself. At exit, she then would own all of the $10,000,000 future value. However, since this is not feasible, Panel B illustrates what would happen to Lynda's ownership position assuming a new $1,000,000 (needed to carry out the business plan) whereby the investor expects a 50 percent compound annual rate of return. After the $1,000,000 capital infusion, the founder would have only a .240625 (1 − .759375) ownership position or 24.0625 percent of the venture. In other words, the ownership percentage for the founder drops from 100 percent ownership as follows:

Founder % Between Financing and Exit = 2,000,000/8,311,688 = 24.0625%
Investor % Between Financing and Exit = 6,311,688/8,311,688 = 75.9375%

With our equations, it is easy to calculate deal parameters commonly used in discussing venture investments. First, we calculate the issue share price:

$$\text{Issue Share Price} = \frac{\$1,000,000}{6,311,688 \text{ shares}} = \$.15843622 \text{ per share}$$

Venture investors sometimes refer to pre-money and post-money valuations. The **pre-money valuation** is the value of the existing venture and its business plan without the proceeds from the contemplated new equity issue. The **post-money valuation** is the pre-money valuation plus the proceeds from the contemplated new equity issue.[3]

pre-money valuation
present value of a venture prior to a new money investment

post-money valuation
pre-money valuation of a venture plus money injected by new investors

Using Present Values

Pre-Money Present Valuation = 2,000,000 shares × $.15843622 per share = $316,872
Post-Money Present Valuation = 8,311,688 shares × $.15843622 per share = $1,316,872

Put differently, the pre-money present valuation of $316,872 plus the proceeds of $1,000,000 results in a post-money present valuation of $1,316,872. It is important to recognize that both the pre-money and the post-money present valuations depend on executing the business plan and its necessary $1,000,000 investment.

Using Future Values

Pre-Money Future Valuation = 2,000,000 shares × $.15843622 per share × $(1.50)^5$
= $2,406,250
Post-Money Future Valuation = 8,311,688 shares × $.15843622 per share × $(1.50)^5$
= $10,000,000

---

[3] Much traditional valuation on the asset side is pre-money, where new financing is not explicitly projected on the financial statements, where it does not affect valuation cash flows, and where share prices are calculated by dividing the pre-money value by current shares outstanding. These pre-money methods are easily adapted to post-money by formally including the proceeds on the balance sheet, adjusting the valuation flows, and calculating share value using the sum of outstanding and to-be-issued shares. A more detailed discussion can be found in Learning Supplement 10B.

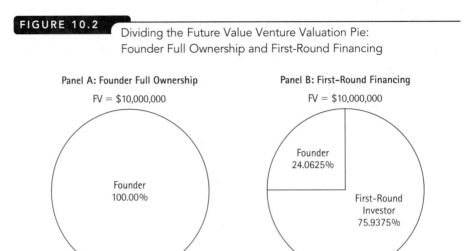

FIGURE 10.2   Dividing the Future Value Venture Valuation Pie:
Founder Full Ownership and First-Round Financing

The pre-money future valuation of $2,406,250 plus the future value of the $1,000,000 investment of $7,593,750 results in a post-money future valuation of $10,000,000.

Both the present and the future value versions of the VCSC ignore all potential or actual intermediate cash flows to, or from, existing or future investors. As we mentioned in Chapter 9, the associated surplus cash penalty is partially diminished by providing financing in sequences of rounds, called **staged financing**. Before we modify our example to include two rounds of financing, we first digress to consider the quick method we have used for calculating an exit value ($10,000,000 here) and how it relates to the terminal values found by discounting perpetual cash flows like we did in Chapter 9.

staged financing
financing provided in sequences of rounds rather than all at one time

CONCEPT CHECK

- What is the role played by the existing shares in determining the number of new shares to be issued for the current financing round?
- How does one derive the post-money valuation from a given pre-money valuation?
- What is the role of the terminal value in venture capital shortcuts?

10.3   EARNINGS MULTIPLIERS AND DISCOUNTED DIVIDENDS

The application of an earnings multiplier to projected earnings to get a projected terminal value is intuitive. After all:

$$\frac{P}{E} \times E = P$$

This is the essence of the earnings multiple conversion of earnings into terminal price. We take a price-earnings ratio (multiple), apply it to earnings, and get price. This method doesn't get interesting until we give the price-earnings ratio (P/E) and the earnings (E) a separate existence and forget their rather direct relationship displayed here. For example, suppose we take a price-earnings ratio from another current venture's prices and earnings when selling shares to the public and apply the ratio to projected earnings for our venture five years in the future. The resulting estimated terminal value is no longer identically the price (as in the equation above). It is an estimated future price:

$$\frac{P_{Current}^{Other\ Firms}}{E_{Current}^{Other\ Firms}} \times E_{Year\ 5}^{Venture} \approx P_{Year\ 5}^{Venture} \tag{10.4}$$

A direct application of a price-earnings ratio to venture earnings is sometimes known as the **direct comparison** method. We are really just comparing other firms' characteristics to a venture's expected characteristics to get a glimpse at possible values for the venture. This type of comparison is similar to examining dollars per square foot to estimate comparable values for real estate. For our current purpose of relating earnings-oriented and dividends-oriented terminal value methods, we focus on (variations of) the earnings multiplier. We get an idea of what's coming by rewriting the multiplier equation as:

direct comparison
valuation by applying a direct comparison ratio to the related venture quantity

$$\frac{E_{Year\ 5}^{Venture}}{E_{Current}^{Other\ Firms}/P_{Current}^{Other\ Firms}} \approx P_{Year\ 5}^{Venture} \tag{10.5}$$

This is sometimes referred to as the **direct capitalization** method. Displaying the multiplier relationship this way hints that we may be doing something like discounting a perpetuity of E at a rate E/P. E/P looks like a return on an investment of P. It is like an accounting rate of return except that we have used price instead of book value per share.

direct capitalization
valuation by capitalizing earnings using a cap rate implied by a comparable ratio

Returning to our previous valuation example, we used a projected earnings in Year 5 of $1,000,000 and a comparable venture P/E multiple of 10. The Year 5 value was calibrated (as in equation 10.4) to be:

$$\frac{P_{Current}^{Other\ Firms}}{E_{Current}^{Other\ Firms}} \times E_{Year\ 5}^{Venture} = \frac{20,000,000}{2,000,000} \times 1,000,000$$

$$= 10 \times 1,000,000 = 10,000,000 \approx P_{Year\ 5}^{Venture}$$

To reinterpret this valuation under the direct capitalization method, we note that a P/E ratio of 10 is a capitalization rate of .10:

$$\frac{E_{Year\ 5}^{Venture}}{E_{Current}^{Other\ Firms}/P_{Current}^{Other\ Firms}} = \frac{1,000,000}{2,000,000/20,000,000}$$

$$= \frac{1,000,000}{.10} = 10,000,000 \approx P_{Year\ 5}^{Venture}$$

To examine more carefully the relationship (between price ratios and discounted perpetuities) suggested by the direct capitalization method, we can derive a representation for P/E (and E/P) when price equals the present value of future dividends. Denoting per-share values of earnings, dividends, and prices as E, D, and P, respectively, we know from the terminal value calculation (Chapter 9, equation 9.1) that the time 5 value (and assumed price) of a growing perpetuity of dividends, starting with a dividend of D_6, is:

$$P_5 = \frac{D_6}{r - g}$$

where r is the discount rate and the dividends grow at rate g. In a constant growth (smooth growth) mode, dividends are equal to the earnings multiplied by a constant payout ratio, D/E. The payout ratio equals one minus the plowback ratio of $b = (E - D)/E$. The plowback ratio (b) is also known as the retention ratio (RR). We can therefore write:

$$P_5 = \frac{E_6 \times (1 - b)}{r - g}$$

Rearranging gives:

$$\frac{P_5}{E_6} = \frac{1 - b}{r - g}$$

Using the smooth-growth assumption, we can write:

$$\frac{P_5}{E_6} = \frac{P_5}{E_5(1 + g)} = \frac{1 - b}{r - g}$$

$$\frac{P_5}{E_5} = \frac{(1 - b) \times (1 + g)}{r - g} \tag{10.6}$$

Note that these formulas help confirm the intuition that, other things being equal, investors will pay more for a stock with higher growth (g) and lower required return (r).[4]

Now that we have an idea what multiplying by a price-earnings ratio is analogous to—adjusting the flow by $(1 - b) \times (1 + g)$ and applying the cap rate $(r - g)$—it is possible to analyze ventures that grow only by retaining earnings and those that grow through both internal and external funding. Learning Supplement 10A provides a detailed examination of several such cases.

CONCEPT CHECK

- Why is the cap rate increasing in g and decreasing in r?
- What types of growth rates are reasonable to use in (r − g)?
- What is the direct comparison method?
- What is the direct capitalization method?

---

[4] As we show in Learning Supplement 10A, even when we are careful to incorporate the fact that b depends on (is a function of) g, we can confirm these basic intuitions about the relationship of price-earnings ratios to growth and discount rate.

10.4 ADJUSTING VCSCs FOR MULTIPLE ROUNDS

As we mentioned in Chapter 9, venture financing is usually staged in rounds. If additional rounds of financing are needed to achieve the Year 5 projected earnings in our current example, the accompanying dilution must be considered in the current round. Failure to do so will result in the investor's not receiving an adequate number of shares to ensure the necessary percent ownership at the time of exit. Suppose the first-round investor believes that Lynda Chen's venture cannot reach the E_5 projection without an additional $1,000,000 infusion in Year 3 from a second-round investor expecting a 25 percent compound annual rate of return on the money contributed at that time.

In essence, the first-round investor is suggesting that he doesn't really buy the original business plan's optimism about getting to the $10,000,000 exit having spent only as much as that plan allowed. He's arguing that there's another $1,000,000 of expenses to be covered to get to that same $10,000,000 exit. By the exit, the $10,000,000 pie will therefore have to be split among three parties: the founders, the first-round investors, and the second-round investors. Since the first- and second-round investors will pay share prices that allow for their 50 percent and 25 percent expected returns, all of the loss in ownership resulting from the second round will be borne by the founder.

As before, we calculate the acquired percent (of the same exit or terminal value) for the second-round investor to be [$1,000,000 × $(1.25)^2$]/$10,000,000 = $1,562,500/$10,000,000 = 15.625 percent. The first round's acquired percent remains at 75.9375 percent. This leaves only 8.4375 percent for the existing 2,000,000 shares. At the terminal period, the total number of shares outstanding will therefore be 2,000,000/.084375 = 23,703,704 shares. We must therefore issue .759375 × 23,703,704 = 18,000,000 shares in round 1 and .15625 × 23,703,704 = 3,703,704 shares in round 2. Note that, at the first round, the initial percent ownership sold to the round-one investors is much higher than the 75.9375 percent ultimate ownership. It is (18,000,000)/20,000,000 = 90 percent. A total of 84.375 percent (1 − .15625) of the investors' ownership fraction will be maintained through the subsequent financing. The reasoning behind this example easily extends to multiple subsequent rounds.

The equations for two rounds would be:

$$\text{Second-Round Acquired \%} = \frac{I \times (1+r)^T}{\dfrac{P}{E} \times E_5} = \frac{1,000,000 \times (1+.25)^5}{\dfrac{10}{1} \times 1,000,000} = 15.625\%$$

$$\text{First-Round Acquired \%} = \frac{I \times (1+r)^T}{\dfrac{P}{E} \times E_5} = \frac{1,000,000 \times (1+.5)^5}{\dfrac{10}{1} \times 1,000,000} = 75.9375\%$$

$$\text{Founder's Remaining \%} = 1 - .15625 - .759375 = .084375$$

$$\text{Total Shares After Financing} = \frac{2,000,000}{.084375} = 23,703,704$$

First Round

Shares Issued $= .759375 \times 23{,}703{,}704 = 18{,}000{,}000$

Share Price $= \$1{,}000{,}000/18{,}000{,}000 = \$.0555556$ per share

Pre-Money Valuation $= \$.0555556 \times 2{,}000{,}000 = \$111{,}111$

Post-Money Valuation $= \$.0555556 \times 20{,}000{,}000 = \$1{,}111{,}111$

Founder % Between First and Second Rounds $= 2{,}000{,}000/20{,}000{,}000 = 10\%$

First-Round Investor % Between First and Second Rounds $=$
  $18{,}000{,}000/20{,}000{,}000 = 90\%$

Second Round

Shares Issued $= .15625 \times 23{,}703{,}704 = 3{,}703{,}704$

Share Price $= \$1{,}000{,}000/3{,}703{,}704 = \$.2700$ per share

Pre-Money Valuation $= \$.2700 \times 20{,}000{,}000 = \$5{,}400{,}000$

Post-Money Valuation $= \$.2700 \times 23{,}703{,}704 = \$6{,}400{,}000$

Founder % Between Second Round and Exit $= 2{,}000{,}000/23{,}703{,}704 = 8.4375\%$

First-Round Investor % Between Second Round and Exit $=$
  $18{,}000{,}000/23{,}703{,}704 = 75.9375\%$

Second-Round Investor % Between Second Round and Exit $=$
  $3{,}703{,}704/23{,}703{,}704 = 15.625\%$

Panel C of Figure 10.3 depicts this further sharing of the exit value pie among the founder, the first-round investor, and the second-round investor. Notice that the first-round investor retains his 75.9375 percent ownership interest and does not suffer ownership dilution associated with the second-round investor.

FIGURE 10.3   Dividing the Future Value Venture Valuation Pie: Adding Second-Round Financing and an Incentive Ownership Round

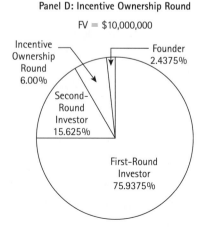

Panel C: Second–Round Financing

FV = $10,000,000

Founder 8.4375%

Second-Round Investor 15.625%

First-Round Investor 75.9375%

Panel D: Incentive Ownership Round

FV = $10,000,000

Incentive Ownership Round 6.00%

Founder 2.4375%

Second-Round Investor 15.625%

First-Round Investor 75.9375%

Unfortunately, the founder (Lynda Chen) suffers the loss in ownership position from 24.0625 percent down to 8.4375 percent, or a difference of 15.625 percent, which goes to the second-round investor.

- What is the effect of a second round of financing on the ownership percentages of the founders and the initial first-round investors?
- How and why does the first-round investors' ownership percentage change between rounds 1 and 2?
- How and why does the founder's ownership percentage change between rounds 1 and 2?

10.5 ADJUSTING VCSCs FOR INCENTIVE OWNERSHIP

For most early-stage ventures, there are at least two strong motives for having an equity component in employee compensation. The usual reason is that the expected deferred and tax-preferred compensation allows the venture to pay a lower current compensation, thereby lowering the current need for external financing. The potentially more significant reason for the equity component is the substantial impact it can have in motivating employees toward the founders' and venture investors' shared goal of a high value for the company's equity. Almost without exception, professional venture investors demand that some equity (or deferred equity) compensation be formally anticipated and structured into any valuation. Some of the shares allocated to equity-based incentive compensation will be for current employees, and some will be for those added as the venture grows. In any case, the portion of final (exit year) value to be distributed as incentive compensation must be considered in valuing each round. As you might guess, this portion of ownership really comes from the entrepreneurs' and founders' stakes. That is, given a fixed exit value and fixed demanded returns for venture investors, the only place from which it can come is the dilution of existing (pre-external financing) ownership.

Perhaps our example venture has agreed to set aside 6 percent of exit-time ownership for use as incentive compensation. The shares will be distributed through a stock option plan and are expected to generate $200,000 in exercise proceeds when the options are exercised (at the end of Year 5). Importantly, we assume that the use of the $200,000 in proceeds has already been included in the projected financial statements, so that we do not need to add it to the $10,000,000 exit valuation. (The valuation we seek is post-money and post-exercise.)

For simplicity, we will treat the 6 percent issue as occurring in Year 5. In many respects, this issue is just another financing round. Proceeding as we did before, the relevant calculations are:

$$\text{Founder's Remaining \%} = 1 - .759375 - .15625 - .06 = .024375$$

$$\text{Total Shares After Financing and Incentive Options} = \frac{2,000,000}{.024375} = 82,051,282$$

First Round

Shares Issued $= .759375 \times 82,051,282 = 62,307,692$

Share Price $= \$1,000,000/62,307,692 = \$.01604938$ per share

Pre-Money Valuation $= \$.01604938 \times 2,000,000 = \$32,099$

Post-Money Valuation $= \$.01604938 \times 64,307,692 = \$1,032,099$

Founder % Between First and Second Rounds $= 2,000,000/64,307,692 = 3.11\%$

First-Round Investor % Between First and Second Rounds $=$
   $62,307,692/64,307,692 = 96.89\%$

Second Round

Shares Issued $= .15625 \times 82,051,282 = 12,820,513$

Share Price $= \$1,000,000/12,820,513 = \$.078$ per share

Pre-Money Valuation $= \$.078 \times 64,307,692 = \$5,016,000$

Post-Money Valuation $= \$.078 \times 77,128,205 = \$6,016,000$

Founder % Between Second Round and Exit $= 2,000,000/77,128,205 = 2.5931\%$

First-Round Investor % Between Second Round and Exit $=$
   $62,307,692/77,128,205 = 80.7846\%$

Second-Round Investor % Between Second Round and Exit $=$
   $12,820,513/77,128,205 = 16.6223\%$

Incentive Ownership Round

Shares Issued $= .0600 \times 82,051,282 = 4,923,077$

Founder % After Incentive Compensation Issue $= 2,000,000/82,051,282 = 2.4375\%$

First-Round Investor % After Incentive Compensation $=$
   $62,307,692/82,051,282 = 75.9375\%$

Second-Round Investor % After Incentive Compensation $=$
   $12,820,513/82,051,282 = 15.625\%$

Employee % After Incentive Compensation $= 4,923,077/82,051,282 = 6.00\%$

Now we can see, numerically, how the outside investors are protected against the 6 percent incentive ownership dilution, the burden of which is borne entirely by the founders. Anticipation of the 6 percent dilution causes the first- (second-) round investor's necessary initial percent ownership to rise from 90 (15.6250 percent) to 96.89 percent (16.6223 percent). Simultaneously, the founders' ownership percent after round 1 (2) declines from 10 (8.4375 percent) to 3.11 percent (2.5931 percent). When we look at the difference between a single round and two rounds with incentive ownership, it is startling that nonfounder shares issued rise from 6,311,688 for one $1,000,000 round to 21,703,704 for two $1,000,000 rounds, to 80,051,282 for two rounds and 6 percent incentive ownership.

Panel D of Figure 10.3 illustrates what happens to the ownership positions of the investors and the founder after accounting for the incentive ownership round. Notice that the "buy-in" ownership positions of the first-round investor and the second-round investor remained at their initial levels of 75.9375 percent and 15.625 percent, respectively. Again, the ownership dilution associated with the 6.00 percent incentive ownership round was borne by the venture's founder. The result is that the founder now has only a 2.4375 percent ownership position in the exit valuation pie.

The price per share in the first $1,000,000 round drops from a little less than $.16 per share with one round to less than $.06 per share with two rounds to less than $.02 per share with two rounds and 6 percent incentive ownership. Such is the impact of dilution. Every entrepreneur should understand the principles and mechanics of dilution before negotiating any type of external financing.

CONCEPT CHECK

- From whose ownership share are incentive shares taken when the need for incentive shares is anticipated in the current round?
- Why is it important to incorporate incentive shares in a venture's valuation?

10.6 ADJUSTING VCSCs FOR PAYMENTS TO SENIOR SECURITY HOLDERS

In many cases, a venture, before the exit period, will issue debt and other alternative securities—convertible debt or (participating) preferred equity—having senior claims to the venture's wealth. If we think of a venture's exit value as a pie, the purchasers of these securities must be served their dessert before the founders and (common) equity investors get theirs. It is important that the valuation shortcuts (and other methods) appropriately carve senior claims out of the pie prior to dividing the remainder among the venture's (common) equity investors.

Traditional valuation methods (including the MDM and PDM methods of Chapter 9) calculate a dividend (or equity VCF) as the cash remaining after all debt obligations (principal and interest) are paid. This is evident from the statement of cash flows and the direct calculation of equity VCF. Debtholders have been paid before we get to equity VCF; the capitalized value (terminal value) of equity VCF is, therefore, free and clear of debt obligations. When using VCSC, we need a similar understanding of who has been paid.

Our current example calibrates the exit value by multiplying earnings (net income) by 10 (to get a $10,000,000 exit valuation). Because we don't have a formal set of financial projections, it is difficult to know how much, if any, of the $10,000,000 other security holders will eat before equity investors. Of course, we only want the value of the equity investors' portion. Do we have to set any part of the $10,000,000 aside to satisfy debtholders? No! Earnings are after interest, but not after principal. While it is not obvious from the simple application of an equity multiplier (P/E $\times$ E = P) that the $10,000,000 is free and clear of debt obligations, perpetuity interpretations of the multipliers make it clear. A growing venture targeting a fixed debt-to-value ratio will issue more debt each period than it retires. (Check the Year 5, 6, and 7 cash flows in the PDC valuation in Chapter 9.) The amount of outstanding debt grows at the same rate as everything else in the venture. The entire $10,000,000 belongs to the venture's equity investors. No net debt deductions, other than those already in the calculation of earnings, are necessary.

What about other types of equity or hybrid securities that can be converted into equity? While we reserve the details of how senior equity securities are structured until the next chapter, modifying the VCSC to recognize senior equity claims on the venture's exit value is quite simple. As an example, we consider equity that has a preferred payment senior to other equity holder payments and that is not included in the venture's projected earnings (net income). For clarity, suppose that our example venture issues a security that, in addition to granting a one-share (common) equity claim, promises the purchaser a full return of the purchase price before the (common) equity investors get a cent. That is, if the security is purchased for $1, the investor would be entitled to a return of the $1 first and then entitled to a one-share claim on what's left. One can see that the $1 is not anywhere in the earnings or equity VCF. Consequently, the $10,000,000 exit value would be partially claimed by all those that hold this senior security. Issuing these securities makes the proceeds a deduction from the exit value before we divide the remainder.

Suppose the first round in our current venture example involved such securities. We must subtract the $1,000,000 proceeds of the first round from the terminal value before dividing up the remainder. We could redo all of the foregoing analyses with an exit value of $9,000,000 instead of $10,000,000. Mechanically, this gets the job done but lacks some realism. Granting first-round senior claims on the exit value can, and probably will, change second-round negotiations. Consequently, any suggestion that the fix for granting $1,000,000 seniority to first-round investors is to cut the (common) equity claim to $9,000,000 and proceed as before is potentially misleading. When second-round investors see that first-round investors have been given a senior $1,000,000 claim on exit value, would they not ask for the same or demand higher returns if not given equal status? Reducing the exit value to $9,000,000, while keeping future discount rates the same, sets up all of the necessary mathematical translations but misses the point. Granting seniority shifts risk from those that get seniority onto those that grant it.

There are two important questions to ask when dealing with senior claims on the exit "pie": (1) Who has already eaten? (2) Of the remaining claimants, who is scheduled to eat before we do? You must make sure senior claims are properly staked in your analysis. A more subtle additional point is that (expected) seniority in the current or a subsequent round changes negotiations throughout. Recognize the value claimed by senior investors and remember that granting seniority complicates future fundraising.

- How does this senior claim on the first $1,000,000 change the risk sharing between founders and investors?

10.7   INTRODUCING SCENARIOS TO VCSCs

Thus far, we have considered only one terminal value, $10,000,000, equal to a price-earnings ratio of 10 multiplied by a projected earnings of $1,000,000. As long as we're in conjecture mode, why not think a little more about what happens to the venture in a few different scenarios? Experience tells venture investors that many ventures result in a 100 percent loss. We refer to such firms as "black holes."[5] Other ventures wander around breakeven for years providing minimal, if any, returns to venture investors. We tag such firms the "living dead." A few ventures hit the big time and provide phenomenal returns. We refer to these big hitters as "venture utopias." A venture investor's return on a portfolio of investments averages these returns.[6]

UTOPIAN APPROACH

Before we can know how to mix these three (or more) possible outcomes with discount rates to create a present value, we must first look a little more closely at the type of discount rates we have been applying. Financial valuation techniques generally use one of two approaches to combining flows and discount rates—utopia approaches and mean approaches. Up to this point, we have been using utopia flows and utopia rates. When a business plan's (utopia) numbers are used for valuation, we have completely ignored two of the three scenarios we have just mentioned (black-hole and living-dead outcomes). The proper interpretation of the discounting process is that the venture investor has determined that when the venture and investor wake up in venture utopia, the investor had better be making 50 percent, 70 percent, or the like on *realized* returns. The investor is not particularly concerned about the realized returns earned in the other two (or more) scenarios. The investor's return concerns are completely expressed in required returns in the one scenario. This type of communication has some serious advantages. Everyone knows that the business plan reflects an idealized scenario. We could try to make the business plan more realistic by presenting, or even averaging, all three scenarios and then applying a lower discount rate (because the cash flows have been knocked down). However, this could have serious

---

[5] We use "black hole" here for two reasons: (1) to draw an analogy to the celestial objects from which not even light—much less cash—can escape and (2) as an indirect reference to one of the biblical characterizations of hell as "outer darkness" where "there shall be weeping and gnashing of teeth."

[6] While we adopt these three labels for this chapter where we consider three-scenario valuation, earlier in Chapter 2 where we considered more variety in the possible outcomes, we used the baseball analogies of strike out, single, double, and home run.

motivational consequences or could break down negotiations entirely. It is usually easier just to take the utopian character of the numbers as given and then discount them at a utopian rate.

One drawback, when the method is not properly understood, is that the use of high discount rates on success-scenario flows can introduce some bargaining friction that is reflected in pejorative phrases such as "vulture capitalist." While venture investors may discount your business plan flows at seemingly obscene rates, you need only look at their portfolio returns (e.g., 25 percent, not much different from the returns on publicly traded small capitalization stocks) to realize that there is nothing particularly nefarious or "vulture" about their business. When a $100 million venture fund invests 20 percent at a total loss, 60 percent at breakeven, and 20 percent at 70 percent annualized returns with liquidity at two years on all outcomes, the annualized portfolio return is:[7]

$$\left(\frac{0 + \$60,000,000 + \$20,000,000 \times (1.7)^2}{\$100,000,000} \right)^{1/2} - 1 = 8.536\%$$

While the utopian outcomes (70 percent) deliver, the portfolio return remains unacceptably low.

Most, if not all, entrepreneurs produce utopian business plans. Venture investors must apply high discount rates when using the business plan's utopian flows. An interesting point here is that venture investors, who do not generally claim to be valuation experts, have structured this process to accommodate an inability to determine which ventures will become venture utopias. With a 20, 60, and 20 percent distribution, assuming we knew which firms were in each category, the valuations for the 20 percent failure and 60 percent living dead would be too high; the valuations for the 20 percent utopias would be too low. The utopia discount process (flows and rates) allows venture investors to invest without knowing a venture's category and to count on diversification to make sure that the portfolio of venture investments achieves an adequate return. Perhaps more important, the **utopia discount process** allows the venture investors to value their investment using only the business plan's explicit forecasts.

utopia discount process
valuation by discounting utopian projections at utopian required returns

While utopia discounting is common in venture valuation, it certainly did not originate there. In valuing the most basic financial instrument—a bond—one easily finds utopia discounting. When practitioners and academics discount the promised coupon and principal from a corporate bond using a comparable yield, they are using utopia discounting. The coupon and principal are the most the bond will ever pay; it will never pay more. It doesn't get any better. Actual expected payments would include some probability of default and would have to be lower than the promised payments. Using the yield from a comparable bond as the discount rate applied to the promised payments for some other bond is a perfect example of the utopia discounting approach. The comparable bond's yield is calculated from its maximum payments and applied to the other bond

---

[7] Gross return is calculated as the gross payment received at the end of the two years [0 + $60,000,000 + $20,000,000 × (1.7)²] divided by the initial investment ($100,000,000). The annualized return for the two-year period is the square root of this gross return minus 1. For three years, we would use the cube root, and so on.

maximum payments. You can't really get more utopian than the bond's achieving its maximum payments. While we do not claim that a business plan's projections are the maximum they could possibly be, the venture valuation methods we have discussed still fall squarely into utopia methods by applying a success-scenario rate to success-scenario flows. There is nothing particularly innovative or heretical here, just good old-fashioned financial valuation viewed from a different perspective.

CONCEPT CHECK

- What is meant by "discount utopian flows at a utopian rate"?

MEAN APPROACH

The alternative to a utopian approach is a mean approach; here we fully intend for the word "mean" to be taken in both common definitions: (1) unkind and (2) the center of a random distribution (statistical mean). We will have to be mean to the business plan numbers in order to produce a (statistical) mean cash flow that gets discounted at a rate representing the expected (mean) return for similar investments. Typical corporate finance capital budgeting and Wall Street equity analyst valuations tend to be mean oriented and avoid utopian approaches. They adjust cash flows down from utopian levels, to expected (mean) levels, and discount with the best proxy available for what investors expect to get in return (the mean or expected return).

While venture investment returns have varied widely over time and across industries, an expected (mean) return on a portfolio of venture investments would be around 22 percent. To use a number in this range, we will have to average flows and values by considering multiple scenarios involving significant downsides not quantified, or even suggested, in the business plan. As one example of how the traditional corporate finance/equity analyst (mean) approach can be adapted to venture valuation, we consider a three-scenario breakout on cash flows.[8]

Consider a $1,000,000 investment in a new twist on an existing technology. The potential venture investors believe that the venture has a 20 percent chance of being a black hole, a 60 percent chance of becoming the living dead, and a 20 percent chance of achieving venture utopia. Having done some homework, they project the black-hole scenario as a total loss in a third-year liquidation. The living-dead scenario is projected at $200,000 in earnings and a price-earnings

---

[8] While the idea of a valuation incorporating multiple scenarios (even more than three) is nothing new, the specific application of a three-scenario approach to valuing venture capital investments is usually credited to Stanley Golder for his work while at First Chicago Corporation. This three-scenario approach has become known in venture investing circles as the "First Chicago Method." See, e.g., Jane Morris, "The Pricing of a Venture Capital Investment," *Pratt's Guide to Venture Capital Sources*, 10th ed. (Wellesley, MA: Venture Economics, 1986). The titles we use for the various scenarios (black hole, living dead, venture utopia) replace the less colorful ones usually encountered (e.g., failure, sideways, success in Morris's article).

ratio of 7 for a seventh-year exit at $1,400,000. The venture utopia scenario is $2,000,000 in earnings and a price-earnings ratio of 20 for a fifth-year exit at $40,000,000.

To show how the method handles intermediate cash flows, we assume that the $1,000,000 investment entitles the investor to a yearly (preferred) dividend of $2,000 only when the venture has the resources to pay (i.e., the dividend does not accumulate) and before exit. Our analysis in Table 10.1, Part A, introduces an algebraic approach to determining the "acquired percentage of final ownership," which is more general than the simple formulas we introduced at the beginning of this chapter. The dividend never appears in the discounted flows for the black-hole scenario; it appears in Years 5 to 7 for the living-dead scenario and in Years 2 to 5 for venture utopia. We begin by calculating expected (mean) cash flows to the venture investors for the seven years. We use the symbol γ (gamma) to represent the acquired percentage of final ownership of the venture sought by the investor (as in equation 10.1). The main point of our exercise is to determine the value of γ. The scenario-specific flows and their means by year (three-scenario mean flow) are shown in Table 10.1, Part A.

If 22 percent is an appropriate discount rate for the venture investor's mixture of dividends and terminal flows, the algebra problem taken directly from the last row of this table is to solve for γ in:

$$1,000,000 = \frac{0}{(1.22)^1} + \frac{400}{(1.22)^2} + \frac{400}{(1.22)^3} + \frac{400}{(1.22)^4} + \frac{8,000,000 \times \gamma + 1,600}{(1.22)^5}$$
$$+ \frac{1,200}{(1.22)^6} + \frac{840,000 \times \gamma + 1,200}{(1.22)^7}$$

Simple algebra shows that γ is about 31.49689 percent. Sometimes, rather than solve this equation the old-fashioned way, it is faster to use a spreadsheet as in Table 10.1, Part B, and solve ("goal seek") for the answer.

Note that this spreadsheet automatically calculates the investors' payments upon exit (in the 2,521,351 and 265,774) and verifies that the PV of the investment (at 22 percent) is $1,000,000. In contrast to the simple VC shortcuts, the current procedure (like the maximum and pseudo dividend methods in Chapter 9)

TABLE 10.1   Part A: Basic Cash Flows

	PROBABILITY	YEAR 1	YEAR 2	YEAR 3	YEAR 4	YEAR 5	YEAR 6	YEAR 7
Black hole	.2	0	0	0	0	0	0	0
Living dead	.6	0	0	0	0	2,000	2,000	1,400,000 $\times \gamma + 2,000$
Venture utopia	.2	0	2,000	2,000	2,000	40,000,000 $\times \gamma + 2,000$	0	0
Three-scenario mean flow		0	400	400	400	8,000,000 $\times \gamma + 1,600$	1,200	840,000 $\times \gamma + 1,200$

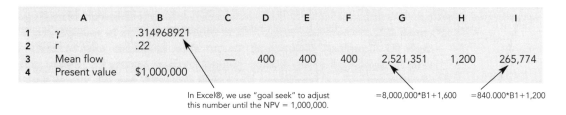

TABLE 10.1 Part B: Spreadsheet Implementation

	A	B	C	D	E	F	G	H	I
1	γ	.314968921							
2	r	.22							
3	Mean flow		—	400	400	400	2,521,351	1,200	265,774
4	Present value	$1,000,000							

In Excel®, we use "goal seek" to adjust this number until the NPV = 1,000,000.

=8,000,000*B1+1,600   =840.000*B1+1,200

incorporates intermediate investor cash flows. Their contribution to value diminishes the amount of final ownership needed to satisfy the investor.[9] While we appreciate the convenience of the earlier formulas for the acquired percentage of final ownership, it may be simpler and more flexible in complicated contexts to use a spreadsheet and a "goal seeking" or "solver" function to determine percent ownership.

An alternative equivalent approach to treating the valuation of multiple scenarios is commonly known as **expected PV**. Previously, we found the expected value of periodic cash flows, then discounted to get a PV. Owing to the mathematical structure of PV, we can take the PVs, as long as we use the one rate (22 percent), and then calculate their expected value to get the same answer as before. This approach to scenario valuation has long been in widespread use outside venture valuation. See Table 10.2.

expected PV
valuation method calculating PVs for each scenario, applying probabilities, and summing

We have arrived at the same percent ownership (31.496892 percent) by calculating a weighted average flow and directly discounting it, and by discounting scenario flows (to scenario PV) and taking weighted average PV. Both approaches give the same answer because of the mathematical structure of PV (multiplication distributes over addition) when the discount rate used is constant across scenarios.

One word of caution is in order. When using these methods, you should always combine P/E and E before averaging (which we have done in all of the preceding analysis). If you average P/Es and Es separately and then multiply the averages, generally you will not get the right answer. As an example, consider the current example reduced to only fifth-year exit flows for both the living-dead (P/E = 7, E = $200,000) and the venture utopia (P/E = 20, E = $2,000,000) scenarios. The living-dead terminal value is $1,400,000, and the venture utopia terminal value is $40,000,000. Using the .6 and .2 weights, respectively, we see that the expected fifth-year terminal flow is $8,840,000. For our purposes, this is the appropriate way to average terminal flows. Note how different the answer

---

[9] Of course, we could return to the methods in Chapter 9 that were built specifically to handle intermediate cash flows, take averages across multiple scenarios, and calculate PV with lower (expected) discount rates rather than the utopian rates we used there. If we were careful, everything would turn out the same.

TABLE 10.2	Three-Scenario Expected PV Approach								
	A	B	C	D	E	F	G	H	I
1	γ	.314968921							
2	r	.22							
3		Y0	Y1	Y2	Y3	Y4	Y5	Y6	Y7
4	Black Hole	0	0	0	0	0	0	0	0
5	**PV BH**	**$.00**							
6	Living Dead	0	0	0	0	0	2,000	2,000	442,956
7	**PV LD**	**$111,460**							
8	Venture Utopia	0	0	2,000	2,000	2,000	12,600,757	0	0
9	**PV VU**	**$4,665,619**							
10									
11	**(Expected) PV**	**$1,000,000** = .2*PV BH + .6*PV LD + .2*PV VU							

would be if we averaged the P/E ratios (.6 × 7 + .2 × 20 = 8.2) and earnings (.6 × 200,000 + .2 × 2,000,000 = 520,000) separately and then combined them (to get 4,264,000 = 8.2 × 520,000).[10] Remember to multiply P/E and E before averaging.

It is true that some professional venture investors and professors believe that venture capital valuation shortcuts are somehow less demanding and better adapted to valuing venture investments; however, in Chapter 9 we saw that traditional valuation is quite simple, given a set of properly projected financial statements. Mechanically, the VCSC offers little in the way of simplification.[11] In all cases, a projection of future flows and payments is discounted to get a present value. The burden shared by all who use discounting-related procedures (VCSC or not) is that formal numerical visions are hard to come by. How formal one is in developing that quantified vision (whether with explicit projected financial statements or a wild guess about a future buyout price) is up to the evaluator. Fortunately or unfortunately, the credibility of calibrated value, shortcut or not, is no higher than the credibility of input ("garbage in, garbage out").

Let us return to whether 22 percent is an appropriate target discount rate for the three-scenario valuation; some warnings are in order. First, the realized rate of return on a venture investment may be quite different from the target because

---

[10] From basic probability, we know that the expectation of a product is only equal to the product of the expectation if the product involves uncorrelated quantities. The P/E and the E in this example are positively correlated: when one is high, the other tends to be high.

[11] Claims that existing financial valuation techniques are somehow specifically unsuitable to valuing high-growth private ventures, and that the VCSC overcomes this unsuitability, reflect (at a minimum) a lack of appreciation for the scope and variety of techniques used to value public high-growth companies. One can easily find publicly traded firms possessing enormous growth opportunities while bleeding red ink so badly that it would appear impossible to justify prevailing public equity prices. As with many new ventures, however, the justification for these public firms' equity prices is the promise of future profitability far removed from the firms' current financial conditions. The point here is that there is nothing unique about the valuation challenges facing entrepreneurs and venture investors. Financial valuation techniques applicable to new ventures are used elsewhere when the situation warrants their use.

the actual cash inflows to the venture investors may differ from the mean flow. In fact, the realization most likely will not be any of the projected flows under the three specific scenarios. When one draws a random number between 1 and 5, the expected outcome is 3. However, drawing a 1 is just as likely as drawing a 2 or a 5. The outcome of the draw is not the same as its mean. The mean is just a representation of what might be expected to be the average outcome after several draws. It is sometimes referred to as a "central tendency," as some draws will be above and some below.

We find the actual realized rate of return by calculating the **internal rate of return (IRR)**, which equates the discounted cash flows realized from the venture investment with the initial investment. That is, we solve for a discount rate that produces a zero net present value (NPV). For example, the initial investment, the weighted mean flows calculated from Table 10.1, and actual cash flow results were:

internal rate of return (IRR)

compound rate of return that equates the present value of the cash inflows received with the initial investment

YEAR	EXPECTED (MEAN) FLOWS	REALIZED FLOWS
0	$(1,000,000)	$(1,000,000)
1	0	0
2	400	400
3	400	400
4	400	400
5	2,521,351	2,200,000
6	1,200	1,200
7	265,774	250,000
IRR	22.00%	18.90%

Notice that the realized rate of return was 18.9 percent rather than the target rate of return of 22.0 percent. When investors use a target discount rate (e.g., 22 percent), they are valuing the venture in an average sense. The realized return on their investment can, of course, be quite different from what they expect to happen on average.

Second, while we examine only three possible outcomes, in reality, there are many other possible outcomes. We are hoping that the three scenarios result in an unbiased valuation. For example, if we are trying to determine the expected number in a random draw from 1 to 5, we can construct an unbiased three-scenario experiment. In particular, we can place 1, 3, and 5 in a hat and draw. The mean is 3 for this three-scenario draw. Of course, a more time-consuming experiment is to place 1, 2, 3, 4, and 5 in the hat. The mean draw would still be 3. The point here is that the number of scenarios is not what determines whether there is a valuation bias. Both of these have the correct mean of 3. In contrast, if we put only 3, 4, and 5 in the hat, the mean draw is 4; this is not "mean enough," as it biases the valuation upward. When the choice of scenario breakouts results in a positive valuation bias using the real expected return (22 percent), the target rate will be adjusted upward, probably to at least 30 percent, to help eliminate the upward valuation bias. Of course, as some of the downside is reflected in the pessimistic scenarios, we would expect the target rate applied to the three-scenario flows to be substantially less than the rate (say, 40 to 70 percent) investors would apply to the pure utopian business plan projected flows.

As long as the scenarios are fair to the venture's upside and downside, we would expect a relatively low target rate close to the returns realized on average for venture investing. If, however, the scenarios preserve the bias inherent in most business plans, we would expect higher three-scenario target rates—although not as high as the rate one would apply to the single-scenario utopian flows.

CONCEPT CHECK

- How would you implement a five-scenario expected PV valuation?
- What would you use for a discount rate to apply to the expected cash flows across the five scenarios?

SUMMARY

We have introduced several variations on the venture capital method of valuation for venture investments. These variations incorporate multiple financing rounds, incentive compensation, and intermediate cash flows with the ultimate goal of determining how many shares must be sold in the current financing round.

We also introduced multiple-scenario valuation techniques for traditional financial valuation and its expected PV counterpart. By explicitly considering different possible venture outcomes (e.g., black hole, living dead, or venture utopia), the valuation exercise sheds light on a venture's upside and downside. Venture capitalists can complete the valuation exercise by applying their subjective beliefs about the probabilities of each scenario and calculating a weighted average.

KEY TERMS

capitalization (cap) rate	internal rate of return (IRR)	utopia discount process
direct capitalization	post-money valuation	venture capital (VC) method
direct comparison	pre-money valuation	
expected PV	staged financing	

DISCUSSION QUESTIONS

1. What is meant by "finding the value of a venture's assets is the same as finding the value of a venture's debt plus equity"?

2. Describe the basic venture capital (VC) method for estimating a venture's value.

3. Describe the process for estimating the percentage of equity ownership that must be given up by the founder when a new equity investment is needed.

4. How does a present value venture valuation pie differ from a future value venture valuation pie?

5. What is meant by pre-money valuation? What is post-money valuation?

6. What is staged financing? Describe how the capitalization (cap) rate is calculated.

7. How is multiplying a projected earnings by a P/E ratio similar to discounting a perpetuity of earnings starting at that level?

8. How would one expect P/E ratios to vary with a venture's risk and growth opportunities?

9. What are the common ways to estimate a terminal value for a venture?

10. What is the difference between the direct comparison method and the direct capitalization method?

11. Describe two important motives for having an equity component in employee compensation.

12. Describe the following terms from the perspective of venture performance: (a) black hole, (b) living dead, and (c) venture utopia. In what sense is the typical business plan utopian?

13. What is meant by the utopia discount process? Describe how expected PV is calculated.

14. Discuss the type of data and the procedural changes necessary to implement a five-scenario expected PV valuation for a venture investment.

15. What is the difference between discounting expected cash flows from multiple scenarios at a constant rate and averaging the scenarios' PVs calculated with that single discount rate?

INTERNET ACTIVITIES

1. Web-surfing exercise: Using a particular industry as a focus, find an industry report that covers several ventures having various levels of maturity and/or performance. Compare their performances in recent years. Develop a model of how you would conduct a multiple-scenario valuation for a newcomer in that industry. What type of discount rate would be appropriate for your approach?

2. Visit one of the venture economics data collection services (e.g., http://www.pwcmoneytree.com) and examine a recent report on the short- and long-term performance of venture capital funds. Relate what you find to a typical discount rate of 50 percent.

EXERCISES/PROBLEMS

1. Calculate the discount rate consistent with a cap rate of 12 percent and a growth rate of 6 percent. Show how your answer would change if the cap rate dropped to 10 percent while the growth rate declined to 5 percent.

2. A venture investor wants to estimate the value of a venture. The venture is not expected to produce any free cash flows until the end of Year 6, when the cash flow is estimated at $2 million, and is expected to grow at a 7 percent annual rate per year into the future.
   A. Estimate the terminal value of the venture at the end of Year 5 if the discount rate at that time is 20 percent.
   B. Determine the present value of the venture at the end of Year 0 if the venture investor wants a 40 percent annual rate of return on the investment.

3. A venture capitalist wants to estimate the value of a new venture. The venture is not expected to produce net income or earnings until the end of Year 5 when the net income is estimated at $1.6 million. A publicly traded competitor or "comparable firm" has current earnings of $1,000,000 and a market capitalization value of $10 million.
   A. Estimate the value of the new venture at the end of Year 5. Show your answer using both the direct comparison method and the direct capitalization method. What assumption are you making when using the current price-to-earning relationship for the comparable firm?

    B. Estimate the present value of the venture at the end of Year 0 if the venture capitalist wants a 40 percent annual rate of return on the investment.

4. Ratchets.com anticipates that it will need $15 million in venture capital to achieve a terminal value of $300 million in five years.

    A. Assuming it is a seed-stage firm with no existing investors, what annualized return is embedded in its anticipation?

    B. Suppose the founder wants to have a venture investor inject $15 million in three rounds of $5 million at times 0, 1, and 2 with a time 5 exit value of $300 million. If the founder anticipates returns of 70 percent, 50 percent, and 30 percent for rounds 1, 2, and 3, respectively, what percent of ownership is sold during the first round? During the second round? During the third round? What is the founder's Year 5 ownership percentage?

    C. Assuming the founder will have 10,000 shares, how many shares will be issued in rounds 1, 2, and 3 (at times 0, 1, and 2)?

    D. What is the second-round share price derived from the answers in Parts B and C?

    E. How does the answer to Part D change if 10 percent of total equity in Year 5 is set aside for incentive compensation? How many total shares are outstanding (including incentive shares) by Year 5?

5. Suppose a venture fund wishes to base its required return (used in discounting future terminal values) on its historical experience and suggests merely averaging the rates on the last three concluded deals. These deals realized total returns of −67 percent at the end of two years, 50 percent at the end of five years, and 70 percent at the end of three years, respectively.

    A. Assuming no intermediate flows before the terminal payoff, verify that the associated annualized rates are −42.55 percent, 8.45 percent, and 19.35 percent.

    B. What is the equally weighted average annualized return?

    C. Does it make sense to use this as a single discount rate to apply across scenarios involving different durations?

6. Rework the two-stage example of Section 10.5 with 1,000,000 initial founders' shares (instead of the original 2,000,000 shares). What changes?

7. Rework the two-stage example of Section 10.5 with first- and second-round required returns of 55 percent and 40 percent (instead of the original 50 percent and 25 percent). Interpret your results as they relate to the founders' ownership and the feasibility of the financing.

8. Suppose you are considering a venture conducting a current financing round involving an issue of 100,000 new shares at $3. The existing number of shares outstanding is 200,000. What are the related pre-money and post-money valuations?

9. A venture capitalist firm wants to invest $1.5 million in your NYDeli dot-com venture that you started six months ago. You do not expect to make a profit until Year 4 when your net income is expected to be $3 million. The common stock of BioSystems, a comparable firm, currently trades in the over-the-counter market at $30 per share. BioSystems' net income for the most recent year was $300,000 and the firm has 150,000 shares of common stock outstanding.

    A. Apply the VC method to determine the value of the NYDeli at the end of four years.

    B. If VCs want a 40 percent compound annual rate of return on similar investments, what is the present value of your NYDeli venture?

C. What percentage of ownership of the NYDeli dot-com venture will you have to give up to the VC firm for its $1.5 million investment?

10. Vail Venture Investors, LLC, is trying to decide how much percent equity ownership in Black Hawk Products, Inc., it will need in exchange for a $5 million investment. Vail Venture Investors has a target compound rate of return of 25 percent on venture investments like Black Hawk Products. Depending on the success of products currently under development, Vail Venture's investment in Black Hawk could turn out to be a complete failure (black hole), barely surviving (living dead), or wildly successful (venture utopia). Vail Venture assigns probabilities of .20, .50, and .30, respectively, to the three possible outcomes. Following are the three cash flow scenarios or outcomes for the Black Hawk Products investment that Vail Venture expects to exit at the end of five years.

OUTCOME	YEAR 1	YEAR 2	YEAR 3	YEAR 4	YEAR 5
Black hole	0	0	0	0	$ 0
Living dead	0	0	0	0	$10 million
Venture utopia	0	0	0	0	$50 million

PART A

A. Calculate the present value of each scenario or outcome for Black Hawk Products.
B. Calculate the weighted average of the present values for the three scenarios. What is the total equity value for the Black Hawk Products venture?
C. Determine the acquired percentage of final ownership of Black Hawk Products that Vail Venture Investors would need for its $5 million proposed investment.

PART B

Now assume under the venture utopia scenario that, in addition to the $50 million cash inflow in Year 5, there will be an annual $1 million preferred dividend (to be paid to Vail Venture Investors but not other equity investors). Vail Venture expects to receive this $1 million dividend under the venture utopia scenario in each of the five years that the Black Hawk investment will be maintained. No preferred annual cash flows are expected under either the black-hole or the living-dead scenario.

D. Calculate the acquired percentage of final ownership of Black Hawk Products that Vail Venture Investors would need to earn a 25 percent compound rate of return on its investment. Use the mean-flow method described in the chapter. (*Hint:* Use "goal seek" in a spreadsheet software program to find the necessary percentage ownership.)
E. Use the expected present value (PV) method described in the chapter when solving for the acquired percentage of final ownership in Black Hawk that Vail Venture needs to earn its 25 percent target rate of return.

11. Vail Venture Investors, LLC, has recently acquired a 40 percent equity ownership in Black Hawk Products, Inc., in exchange for a $5 million investment. Vail Venture Investors is interested in estimating an expected compound rate of return on its investment. Depending on the success of products currently under development, Vail Venture's investment in Black Hawk could turn out to be a complete failure (black hole), barely

surviving (living dead), or wildly successful (venture utopia). Vail Venture has assigned probabilities of .20, .50, and .30, respectively, to the three possible outcomes. Following are the three cash flow scenarios or outcomes for the Black Hawk Products investment that Vail Venture expects to exit at the end of five years.

OUTCOME	YEAR 1	YEAR 2	YEAR 3	YEAR 4	YEAR 5
Black hole	0	0	0	0	$ 0
Living dead	0	0	0	0	$10 million
Venture utopia	0	0	0	0	$50 million

PART A

A. Calculate the internal rate of return (IRR) for each scenario or outcome for Black Hawk Products.
B. Calculate the weighted average of the IRRs for the three scenarios. What is the expected IRR for the Black Hawk Products venture?
C. What would be Vail Venture Investors' expected IRR if its $5 million investment in Black Hawk Products bought only a 35 percent interest in the venture?
D. Show how your answer in Part C would change if Vail Ventures received a 51 percent ownership stake in the Black Hawk Products venture for $5 million.

PART B

Now assume under the venture utopia scenario that, in addition to the $50 million cash inflow in Year 5, there will be an annual $1 million preferred dividend (to be paid to Vail Venture Investors but not other equity investors). Vail Venture expects to receive this $1 million dividend under the venture utopia scenario in each of the five years that the Black Hawk investment will be maintained. No preferred annual cash flows are expected under either the black-hole or the living-dead scenario.

E. Calculate the revised internal rate of return for the venture utopia scenario if Vail Venture's equity ownership stake in Black Hawk Products is 40 percent.
F. What would be Vail Venture's expected IRR on the Black Hawk Products venture?

M I N I   C A S E

R.K. Maroon Company

R.K. Maroon is a seed-stage Web-oriented entertainment company with important intellectual property. RKM's founders, all technology experts in the relevant area, are anticipating a quick leap to dot-com fortune and believe that their unique intellectual property will allow them to achieve a subsequent (Year 3) $100 million venture value with a one-time initial $2 million in venture financing.

In contrast, similar dot-commers in their niche are currently seeking multistage financing amounting to $10 million to achieve comparable results. The founders have organized with one million shares and are willing to grant venture investors a 100 percent return on their business plan projections.

R.K. Maroon Company (continued)

A. What percent of ownership must be sold to grant the 100 percent three-year return?
B. What is the resulting configuration of share ownership (starting from the one million founders' shares)?
C. Suppose the venture investors don't buy the business plan predictions and want to price the deal assuming a second round in Year 2 of $8 million with a 40 percent return. What changes?
D. Suppose the venture investors agree with the founders' assessment, price the deal accordingly (as in Part B), and turn out to be wrong (an additional $8 million at 40 percent must be injected for the final year).
   1. What is the impact on the founders' and round-one investors' final ownership assuming the second round is funded by outsiders?
   2. Compare these to your results for Part C.
   3. Who bears the dilution from an anticipated round?
   4. Who bears the dilution from an unanticipated round?

E. Suppose that the deal is priced assuming the second round (as in Part C) and it turns out to be unnecessary. Comment on the final ownership percentages at exit (Year 3). What do you conclude about the impact of anticipated but unrealized subsequent financing rounds?

Learning Supplement 10A

SUSTAINABLE GROWTH

We first consider a venture that anticipates no equity financing rounds during the smooth growth period and is therefore limited to a growth rate supported by retention of earnings. For the constant growth period, retained earnings must provide the equity base for increases in the venture's assets.

In economics jargon, we assume that the venture's constant growth period is driven by a "constant returns to scale" technology. That is, we assume that a 1 percent increase in each of the components of the asset and liability bases creates a 1 percent increase in all of the possible bottom lines (earnings, dividends, cash flows, etc.). During this period, the venture's growth rate equals the portion (percent) of the accounting return [earnings divided by book value of equity (BVE)] that gets plowed back into new assets, $g = b \times E/BVE$. To see this, substitute $(E - D)/E$ for b in $g = b \times E/BVE$:

$$g = \frac{E - D}{E} \times \frac{E}{BVE} = \frac{E - D}{BVE}$$

where g is the increase in (the book value of) the asset base the firm uses to produce earnings (and dividends). With our constant returns to scale assumption (on the book value of assets), when the firm secures no external equity financing (and maintains its debt-equity mix), growth is limited to $g = b \times E/BVE$, sometimes referred to as the venture's (internally) *sustainable growth rate.*

CASE 1: INTERNALLY SUSTAINED ZERO NET PRESENT VALUE GROWTH

Growth for the sake of growth is the ideology of the cancer cell.
—Edward Abbey

One can build some important intuition by considering what happens to the P/E ratio decomposition when the return on book equity (E/BVE) just equals the required return r. This is the case of zero-NPV growth. Since, for this case, $b = g/r$, growth drops out of the capitalization rate (denominator):

$$\frac{P_5}{E_5} = \frac{(1 - g/r)\,(1 + g)}{(r - g)} = \frac{\frac{(1 + g)}{r}(r - g)}{(r - g)} = \frac{(1 + g)}{r}$$

The absence of g in the denominator merely reflects the fact that growth providing just the required return on the reinvested capital (r = E/BVE) neither creates nor destroys value. The firm is just keeping its head above water on the reinvested amounts. The venture's investors are indifferent to growth because it only provides them the same return they can make elsewhere. You might as well take all the earnings out of the firm as dividends (E = D) and not grow (g = 0). In this case, the growing venture is worth the same (per dollar of earnings) as the no-growth venture.

Note that applying the price-earnings ratio to Year 5 earnings is exactly the same as discounting the dividend stream at rate r or discounting the earnings stream starting in Year 6 [at $(1 + g) \times E_5$] at discount rate r:

$$\frac{D_6}{r - g} = P_5 = \frac{P_5}{E_5} \times E_5 = \frac{(1 + g)E_5}{r} = \frac{E_6}{r} \quad \text{for } r = \frac{E}{BVE}$$

Our objective is to relate the VCSC's conversion of earnings into a terminal value to the MDM's and PDM's conversion of dividends (or pseudo dividends) into a terminal value. For this case, we have now done exactly that. Directly manipulating the last equation, we see that for the internally funded venture with growth opportunities just meeting the required returns (r = E/BVE), the summary of the relationship is that the discount rate on the dividend stream (r) is the reciprocal of the earnings multiplier:

$$\frac{P}{E} = \frac{1}{r} \quad \text{for } r = \frac{E}{BVE}$$

This is how many people think about earnings multipliers—as the reciprocal of a discount rate. Of course, our assumption that growth was net present value zero (r = E/BVE) allowed us to simplify the more complex, but more general, relationship to which we now return.

CASE 2: INTERNALLY SUSTAINED NONZERO NET PRESENT VALUE GROWTH

The more general formula relating price-earnings ratios to growth and discount rates is:

$$\frac{P_5}{E_5} = \frac{(1 - b) \times (1 + g)}{r - g} = \frac{\left(1 - \dfrac{g}{E/BVE}\right) \times (1 + g)}{r - g}$$

As you can see, applying this multiplier to fifth-year earnings is equivalent to adjusting fifth-year earnings and then capitalizing the stream at cap rate r − g. However, inverting the price-earnings ratio no longer gives something as neat and clean as the discount rate r. We can say something about what increases this multiplier. Lower discount rates (r) and higher returns on book equity (E/BVE), other things being held constant, relate to higher price-earnings multiples. Although it is not obvious, higher growth rates, other things being held constant, also relate to higher price-earnings multiples.[12]

CASE 3: NONSMOOTHIES (NONCONSTANT GROWTH TERMINAL PERIODS)

To see that no P/E ratio approach universally applies to all high-growth externally funded firms, look at the active players in almost any emerging technology. Many such firms have (consistently) negative earnings while selling securities to the market (initially and even for more than one round). As earnings for most (if not all) of the sector are negative, we shouldn't expect to get an appropriate value estimate by multiplying prevailing price-earnings ratios (negative ones) by the firm's current or future earnings (negative or positive).

The relationship among price-earnings ratios, discount rates (r), growth opportunities (g), and the profitability (E/BVE) for smooth-growth ventures provides some guidance on how we might expect multipliers to vary for nonsmooth-growth ventures. To generalize the connections between venture characteristics and an appropriate equity multiplier for such firms, we need to back up a bit and reexamine, from a different perspective, how growth adds to a smooth-growth firm's value.

For simplicity, we consider a firm that grows by reinvesting all of its earnings. The value contributed from current operations (as if there were no reinvestment) is D/r (= E/r). Each year's 100 percent reinvestment creates a new project, the net effect of which is an annihilation of the current dividend D in return for the hope of higher future periods' dividends (than without reinvestment). The net present value of the reinvestment is the net effect of the two changes. Examining the logic in Table 10A.1 may help clarify this process. The example assumes E/BVE = .25, b = .4, and therefore the growth rate implied is g = (E/BVE) × b = .1.

The last cell in Table 10A.1 has the value of the firm broken into the sum of the current earnings capitalized at rate r (25/r) and the *net* present value of the entire future of growth reinvestments (a perpetuity starting at NPV_1 and growing at rate g).

From this perspective, it is clear that we can think of the smooth-growth venture's value as the value of the earnings generated by current operations plus the *net* present value of future growth (re)investments:

$$P_5 = \frac{EPS_6}{r} + \text{Net Present Value of Future Growth (Re)investments}$$

[12] When we had not yet substituted g/(E/BVE) for b, it was easy to suggest, but not really prove, that the price-earnings ratio is increasing in g. Here the same result is not so easy to see, but probably true nonetheless. Using ROE = E/BVE > 0, the derivative of the price-earnings ratio in g (now appearing three times in the price-earnings ratio) has the same sign as $g^2 - 2gr - r + ROE + rROE$, and our current case has ROE > r > g > 0. Adding and subtracting r^2 gives $g^2 - 2gr + r^2 - r^2 - r + ROE + rROE$. This rearranges to $(g - r)^2 - r^2 - r + ROE + rROE$, which, in turn, rearranges to $(g - r)^2 + (ROE - r) + (rROE - r^2)$, where each term is positive. Therefore the total derivative of the price-earnings ratio in g is positive, implying that the price-earnings ratio is increasing in g.

TABLE 10A.1 Adding the Value of Current Operations to the Value Created by Growth

	E_1	E_2	E_3	...	NPV_t
Existing assets	25.00	25.00	25.00		$NPV_0 = 25/r$
First reinvestment	−10.00	2.50	2.50		$NPV_1 = −10 + 2.5/r$
Second reinvestment		−11.00	2.75		$NPV_2 = 11 + 2.75/r = (1.1)NPV1$
Third reinvestment			−12.0		$NPV^3 = (1.1)^2 \times NPV_1$
...					
Dividends	15.00	16.50	18.15		$25/r + NPV_1/(r − .1) = 15/(r − .1)$

While we have generated this breakout by analyzing smooth growth, the dichotomy applies equally well to other ventures. Unfortunately for such ventures, when we divide both sides of this last equation by E_6, we have no simple interpretation for the resulting price-earnings ratio representation:

$$\frac{P_5}{E_6} = \frac{1}{r} + \frac{NPV(growth)}{E_6}$$

Nonetheless, as most ventures (hope to) have substantial contributions to value embedded in their (smooth or nonsmooth) growth opportunities, users of price-earnings multipliers should understand the factors that move the multipliers up (growth opportunities and their profitability) and down (risk and therefore required return r).

We have now examined the impact of zero- and positive-NPV smooth- and non-smooth-growth opportunities on the price-earnings ratio used to convert terminal earnings into a terminal value. What changes if the venture is expected to sell some equity to support a growth rate beyond that which is internally sustainable? We confine our discussion to the case of positive-NPV growth. (Why/how would they raise funds otherwise?)

What is perhaps not clear, although every bit as true, is that for valuation purposes it doesn't much matter whether or not the growth is funded internally or externally—the firm's externally funded growth contributes to firm value in precisely the same way as its internally funded growth. If, instead of retaining the earnings, the firm pays out dividends and then raises equity to fund the growth reinvestments, it is still the net present value of the reinvestment projects that must be added to the value of current operations.

We are valuing the firm by how it invests cash in assets and operations and how, in turn, those produce cash. Consequently, for valuation we do not have to worry a great deal about whether the expenditures are internally or externally funded. Our approach recognizes value creation (and depletion) through a venture's investment of funds, not through its raising of funds.

If the venture is expected to raise future funds at below-market prices, or with legal and other costs that are not included in the projected financial statements supporting the flows being discounted, valuing asset flows will not incorporate these negative hits on venture value. Good accountants won't let the venture book an opportunity loss expense for having to sell equity at $25 when it's worth $35. Consequently, we know the negative hit from selling equity for less than it is worth won't be included in the valuation. This will be a windfall to those who buy at $25. Valuing such a venture as though all equity is provided internally will overstate true value. The present value of opportunity losses in equity sales—and any external fundraising costs (like additional legal fees) that are not already in formal financial projections—causes the net present value of externally funded growth to fall below that of internally funded growth. Other than fundraising costs that are avoided for internally funded growth, there is no difference in the treatment of the value added by internally and externally funded growth.

Earlier we noted that a difference between the VCSC and the MDM and PDM is how one calculates terminal value. Given a terminal value, all of the given methods discount the value at the demanded (venture) return to get a present value that serves as the venture's valuation. We have shown that the differences in how terminal values are calculated are mostly cosmetic if the venture grows smoothly (is mature enough in the terminal value period to be approximated as constantly growing). If it does not, then the connection between the two approaches' terminal value calculations is not clean. One would be well advised to consider both approaches and compare and contrast the resulting valuations.

Learning Supplement 10B

PDC'S EQUITY VALUATION: SYNTHESIZING MDM, PDM, AND VCSC (ADVANCED)

To understand how the MDM and PDM of Chapter 9 relate to the VCSC, it is useful to produce a variation of financial statements closer in spirit to those implied by the VCSC. In this variation, as in the PDM, we project no dividends before Year 5, thereby forcing the venture to hold on to surplus cash. We make no adjustments to the discount rate, even though the venture gets riskier as it moves cash from marketable securities into venture operations and gets less risky as it begins to stockpile cash.

As we will demonstrate shortly, VCSCs are post-money versions of what we call a delayed dividend approximation. The *delayed dividend approximation (DDA)* treats all cash as an investment in the venture's working capital. It assesses the same required return on all cash irrespective of whether it is invested in venture operations or an interest-bearing checking account. Essentially, for valuation purposes, there is no distinction between required and surplus cash. The DDA net working capital calibration is all current assets (including required and surplus cash) less all current liabilities. Your intuition should lead you to conjecture that the DDA will produce a lower venture valuation.

Tables 10B.1 to 10B.3 present PDC's pre-money financial projections and the DDA. Any external offerings that PDC may be considering have not yet been incorporated into the balance sheet. Table 10B.4 presents the accompanying valuations.

As we discussed in Chapter 9, the MDM valuation agrees with the PDM valuation (both have initial PV = $399,170 and NPV = $405,657, including the $6,487 initial surplus). In contrast, when we value the venture assuming it must hold all surplus cash and make the required 25 percent return on that surplus cash even when invested in low-risk,

TABLE 10B.1
PDC's DDA Income Statements

		YEAR 1	YEAR 2	YEAR 3	YEAR 4	YEAR T = 5
	4/1/Y0– 7/31/Y0	8/1/Y0– 7/31/Y1	8/1/Y1– 7/31/Y2	8/1/Y2– 7/31/Y3	8/1/Y3– 7/31/Y4	8/1/Y4– 7/31/Y5
Sales	552,000	1,656,000	2,000,000	2,800,000	2,968,000	3,146,080
(growth rates)			20.8%	40.0%	6.0%	6.0%
Income Statements	Historical	Projected	Projected	Projected	Projected	Projected
Sales	552,000	1,656,000	2,000,000	2,800,000	2,968,000	3,146,080
– COGS	–386,400	–1,159,200	–1,400,000	–1,960,000	–2,077,600	–2,202,256
– Wages and commissions	–105,800	–317,400	–383,333	–536,667	–568,867	–602,999
– Rent, miscellaneous, and insurance	–47,840	–111,780	–135,000	–189,000	–200,340	–212,360
– Depreciation	–4,600	–5,796	–5,630	–6,800	–9,520	–10,091
Earnings before interest and taxes (EBIT)	7,360	61,824	76,036	107,533	111,673	118,374
– Interest expense	–988	0	0	0	0	–22,664
Earnings before taxes	6,372	61,824	76,036	107,533	111,673	95,709
– Taxes	0	–18,547	–22,811	–32,260	–33,502	–28,713
Net income	6,372	43,277	53,225	75,273	78,171	66,997
– Dividends	0	0	0	0	–378,959	–63,460
Retained earnings	6,372	43,277	53,225	75,273	–300,788	3,537

TABLE 10B.2
PDC's DDA Balance Sheets

PROJECTED BALANCE SHEETS	TODAY 7/31/Y0	EOY 1 7/31/Y1	EOY 2 7/31/Y2	EOY 3 7/31/Y3	EOY 4 7/31/Y4	EOY 5 = T 7/31/Y5
Current assets						
Required cash	23,000	24,840	30,000	42,000	44,520	47,191
Surplus cash	6,487	71,890	92,015	90,310	0	0
Accounts receivable	46,000	46,000	55,556	77,778	82,444	87,391
Merchandise inventory	97,520	82,800	100,000	140,000	148,400	157,304
Prepaid insurance	2,300	2,300	2,778	3,889	4,122	4,370
Total current assets	175,307	227,830	280,348	353,977	279,487	296,256
Net property, plant, and equipment	57,960	56,304	68,000	95,200	100,912	106,967
Total assets	**233,267**	**284,134**	**348,348**	**449,177**	**380,399**	**403,223**
Current liabilities						
Accounts payable	33,810	41,400	50,000	70,000	74,200	78,652
Accrued wages and commissions	11,500	11,500	13,889	19,444	20,611	21,848
Total current liabilities	45,310	52,900	63,889	89,444	94,811	100,500
Long-term debt	0	0	0	0	226,643	240,241
Owner's equity	187,957	231,234	284,459	359,733	58,945	62,482
Total liabilities and equity	**233,267**	**284,134**	**348,348**	**449,177**	**380,399**	**403,223**

TABLE 10B.3   PDC's DDA Statement of Cash Flows

ACCOUNTING STATEMENT OF CASH FLOWS	YEAR 1 8/1/Y0– 7/31/Y1	YEAR 2 8/1/Y1– 7/31/Y2	YEAR 3 8/1/Y2– 7/31/Y3	YEAR 4 8/1/Y3– 7/31/Y4	YEAR T = 5 8/1/Y4– 7/31/Y5
Cash flows from activities					
Net income	6,372	43,277	53,225	75,273	78,171	66,997
Adjustments to net income for cash flow					
+ Depreciation expense	4,600	5,796	5,630	6,800	9,520	10,091
− Change in prepaid insurance	1,840	0	−478	−1,111	−233	−247
+ Change in accrued liabilities	1,725	0	2,389	5,556	1,167	1,237
− Change in inventory	12,880	14,720	−17,200	−40,000	−8,400	−8,904
+ Change in accounts payable	−4,830	7,590	8,600	20,000	4,200	4,452
− Change in accounts receivable	−9,200	0	−9,556	−22,222	−4,667	−4,947
Total adjustments	7,015	28,106	−10,614	−30,978	1,587	1,682
Net cash flow from operations	13,387	71,383	42,611	44,296	79,758	68,678
Cash flows from investing					
Capital expenditures	−6,900	−4,140	−17,326	−34,000	−15,232	−16,146
Net cash from investing	−6,900	−4,140	−17,326	−34,000	−15,232	−16,146
Cash flows from financing					
+ Equity issues	0	0	0	0	0	0
− Dividends	0	0	0	0	−378,959	−63,460
(= −net dividend)	0	0	0	0	−378,959	−63,460
+ Debt issues	0	0	0	0	226,643	13,599
Net cash flows from financing	0	0	0	0	−152,316	−49,861
Net change in cash and equivalents	6,487	67,243	25,285	10,296	−87,790	2,671
Beginning cash balance	23,000	29,487	96,730	122,015	132,310	44,520
Ending cash balance	29,487	96,730	122,015	132,310	44,520	47,191

low-return marketable securities, we get the lower initial valuation of $371,831 in Table 10B.4. This value is both a PV and an NPV here, because this valuation retains the $6,487 surplus cash until the first dividend in Year 5. The only difference between the NPVs of Chapter 9 and those of the above DDA is the net present value of the timing difference between the dividend streams. The same is true for the differences in the PVs as long as we adjust for the initial $6,487. We verify this agreement in Table 10B.5.

The important point here is that the valuations differ only in the timing of *when* the surplus cash is paid out, not *whether* it is paid out. Most venture capital shortcuts delay all (credit for) dividends until an exit or terminal event. Like the delayed dividend method above, these shortcuts do not consider the increases in risk when a financing round's proceeds, initially parked in low-risk marketable securities or interest-bearing deposits, are subsequently invested in venture operations. The DDA, and its cousins the VCSCs, value the venture using the same required return whether or not funds are invested in venture operations. Perhaps even more troubling, they apply high venture period discount rates to the bloated cash balances in the projected later stages of a successful

TABLE 10B.4 PDC's DDA Valuations

EQUITY VALUATION	4/1/Y0– 7/31/Y0	YEAR 1 8/1/Y0– 7/31/Y1	YEAR 2 8/1/Y1– 7/31/Y2	YEAR 3 8/1/Y2– 7/31/Y3	YEAR 4 8/1/Y3– 7/31/Y4	YEAR T = 5 8/1/Y4– 7/31/Y5
Net income	6,372	43,277	53,225	75,273	78,171	66,997
− Depreciation and amortization	4,600	5,796	5,630	6,800	9,520	10,091
− Capital expenditures	−6,900	−4,140	−17,326	−34,000	−15,232	−16,146
− Change in net working capital	−4,072	−44,933	−41,529	−48,073	79,857	−11,081
+ Debt proceeds	0	0	0	0	226,643	13,599
Equity VCF (valuation cash flow)	0	0	0	0	378,959	63,460
(vs. dividends − equity issues)	0	0	0	0	378,959	63,460
VALUATION DATE	TODAY 7/31/Y0	EOY 1 7/31/Y1	EOY 2 7/31/Y2	EOY 3 7/31/Y3	EOY 4 7/31/Y4	EOY 5 = T 7/31/Y5
PV Equity (Excluding Current Equity VCF)	371,831	464,789	580,987	726,233	528,833	560,563
Capital gain on market equity		25.0%	25.0%	25.0%	−27.2%	6.0%
Dividend yield on market equity		0.0%	0.0%	0.0%	52.2%	12.0%
Total return on market equity		25.0%	25.0%	25.0%	25.0%	18.0%
NPV Equity (Including Current Equity VCF)	371,831	464,789	580,987	726,233	907,792	624,023

TABLE 10B.5 PDM Versus DDA Cash Flow Timing

VALUATION DIFFERENCE IS ONLY IN THE TIMING OF (CREDITING FOR) DIVIDENDS		YEAR 1	YEAR 2	YEAR 3	YEAR 4	YEAR T = 5
PDM pre-money equity valuation CF	6,487	65,403	20,125	−1,704	288,649	63,460
DDA pre-money dividends	0	0	0	0	378,959	63,460
Difference	6,487	65,403	20,125	−1,704	−90,310	0
Cumulative sum of differences		71,890	92,015	90,310	0	0
NPV of timing difference	33,825					
PV of timing difference (excluding $6,487)	27,338					
NPV equity: dividends in Year 5 forward	371,831					
+ NPV of timing difference	33,825					
Sum	405,657					
NPV equity: pseudo and maximum dividend methods	405,657					
PV equity: dividends in Year 5 forward	371,831					
+ PV of timing difference	27,338					
Sum	399,170					
PV equity: pseudo and dividend methods	399,170					

venture. The result can be dramatically lower valuations and the accompanying loss of a larger percent ownership for the same amount of fundraising.

We can see the difference in the price of a share if we know how many shares PDC currently has outstanding: 200,000. The MDM and PDM are both inherently pre-money valuations (because they are free cash flow methods and will pay out any idle cash, including proceeds). When the $6,487 is included, their share price is $2.0283 (= $405,657/ 200,000 = pre-money valuation/pre-money shares). This DDA valuation of $371,831 is also pre-money (before any proceeds) and includes the $6,487 since it is deferred until year 5. The pre-money DDA share price is $1.8592 = $371,831/200,000. The decrease in the calibrated value of founder shares is $33,825 = (2.0283 − 1.8592) × 200,000. Not surprisingly, the entire weight of the decrease in NPV is borne by PDC's founders. They lose when the DDA is used (other things being held equal). Note that we have produced this 8.3 percent difference while using 25 percent discount rates. If we were to use a more typical 40 to 70 percent VC rate, the penalty associated with the DDA would be even larger.

The common justification for not using a valuation approach that treats surplus cash as stripped out is that once the cash is given to the venture, the money usually cannot be recovered, if at all, other than in an exit event. While this may be descriptively true, we know from the accounting identity that the real risk in the venture is no more or less than the risk taken by the assets in the venture's operations. It is not the raising of funds that creates risk; it is the use. When a valuation fixes a discount rate for a period during which cash surpluses are forced to be retained, the valuation and equity dilution consequences can be significant.

In defense of the delayed dividend method (and its cousins the VCSCs), the surplus cash penalty in these methods can be reduced through the common industry practice of anticipating staging in the financing. Almost all ventures are financed in rounds, each involving a different rate of return and seeking to apply only enough cash to get to the next financing round or exit. Participants in the venture capital markets understand that financing all of the venture's present and future cash needs in an early round can lead to a massive loss in calibrated value because high discount rates are applied to the idle cash (even if they wouldn't say it this way). Injecting venture funding in stages simultaneously allows the founders to avoid the valuation hit on surplus cash and allows venture investors to wait and see if the venture is still on track and deserving of additional financing. To some extent, founders and venture investors both gain from staging the infusion of cash.

Summarizing to this point, we have covered three approaches:

1. *MDM*. Formally project all cash surpluses as being paid out as dividends. The balance sheet will have zeros for all surplus cash balances. The venture's equity can be valued directly using the dividends/issue line in the statement of cash flows (or by the equity VCF method, which gives the same amount). There is no excess cash in the end, and the balance sheet says so.

2. *PDM*. Formally retain all cash surpluses in a surplus cash account. Project all dividends at zero. Value the venture's equity using the equity VCF with working capital calculations that omit surplus cash. Remember that the projected balance sheets indicate surplus cash balances that have been treated by the valuation as already having been paid. These balances cannot be added to a terminal value or otherwise stripped out again.

3. *DDA*. Formally retain all cash surpluses on the balance sheet and in the valuation. Pay a catch-up dividend in the last year of the explicit forecasting period and pay all surplus cash thereafter as explicit dividends. Value the firm by its dividends (or its equity VCF, which is the same here) with working capital coming from all current assets less

all current liabilities. The resulting value will be lower than that found by the other approaches owing, solely, to the delay in crediting the venture for creating surplus cash (which eventually becomes a dividend or other flow to equity).

We have one additional step to take in getting from the above *pre-money* DDA to the inherently *post-money* VCSCs we have used earlier in this chapter. We need to include the proceeds of any equity financing that will result in new share issues. That is, just as in the examples used earlier (with a $10,000,000 exit value and two potential rounds of financing), the more formal VCSCs we consider involve *post-money* financial projections. PDC has been considering two equity financing rounds of $50,000 to take place immediately (at the beginning of Year 1) and at the end of Year 3. We need a new set of post-money financial projections that include the balance sheet impact of these financing rounds. Tables 10B.6 to 10B.8 provide those projections.

Since Table 10B.9 uses the equity VCF formula with no adjustments for proceeds, it may not be obvious but we are still getting a type of pre-money cash flow for valuation (and therefore should divide by the number of pre-money shares to get a share price). You can see this by comparing the equity VCFs from Tables 10B.4 and 10B.9. The equity VCFs in Table 10B.9 are lower by $50,000 initially and in Year 3. They are higher by the extra $100,000 dividend that can be paid in Year 4. This is just the Table 10B.4 pre-money DDA VCFs plus a project that pays out $50,000 immediately and in Year 3 to get the combined $100,000 back in Year 5 (when dividends are allowed to start) as though this project were paid for by pre-money shareholders. This extra project has NPV = −$34,640. If we take the valuation of $337,191 in Table 10B.9 and add back the NPV of this surplus cash penalty project, we would get the pre-money DDA value of $371,831 in

---

TABLE 10B.6   Post-Money DDA Income Statements

	4/1/Y0– 7/31/Y0	YEAR 1 8/1/Y0– 7/31/Y1	YEAR 2 8/1/Y1– 7/31/Y2	YEAR 3 8/1/Y2– 7/31/Y3	YEAR 4 8/1/Y3– 7/31/Y4	YEAR T = 5 8/1/Y4– 7/31/Y5
Sales	552,000	1,656,000	2,000,000	2,800,000	2,968,000	3,146,080
(growth rates)			20.8%	40.0%	6.0%	6.0%
Income Statements	Historical	Projected	Projected	Projected	Projected	Projected
Sales	552,000	1,656,000	2,000,000	2,800,000	2,968,000	3,146,080
− COGS	−386,400	−1,159,200	−1,400,000	−1,960,000	−2,077,600	−2,202,256
− Wages and commissions	−105,800	−317,400	−383,333	−536,667	−568,867	−602,999
− Rent, miscellaneous, and insurance	−47,840	−111,780	−135,000	−189,000	−200,340	−212,360
− Depreciation	−4,600	−5,796	−5,630	−6,800	−9,520	−10,091
Earnings before interest and taxes (EBIT)	7,360	61,824	76,036	107,533	111,673	118,374
− Interest expense	−988	0	0	0	0	−22,664
Earnings before taxes	6,372	61,824	76,036	107,533	111,673	95,709
− Taxes	0	−18,547	−22,811	−32,260	−33,502	−28,713
Net income	6,372	43,277	53,225	75,273	78,171	66,997
− Dividends	0	0	0	0	−478,959	−63,460
Retained earnings	6,372	43,277	53,225	75,273	−400,788	3,537

TABLE 10B.7 Post-Money DDA Balance Sheets

PROJECTED BALANCE SHEETS	TODAY 7/31/Y0	EOY 1 7/31/Y1	EOY 2 7/31/Y2	EOY 3 7/31/Y3	EOY 4 7/31/Y4	EOY 5 = T 7/31/Y5
Current assets						
Required cash	23,000	24,840	30,000	42,000	44,520	47,191
Surplus cash	56,487	121,890	142,015	190,310	0	0
Accounts receivable	46,000	46,000	55,556	77,778	82,444	87,391
Merchandise inventory	97,520	82,800	100,000	140,000	148,400	157,304
Prepaid insurance	2,300	2,300	2,778	3,889	4,122	4,370
Total current assets	225,307	277,830	330,348	453,977	279,487	296,256
Net property, plant, and equipment	57,960	56,304	68,000	95,200	100,912	106,967
Total assets	**283,267**	**334,134**	**398,348**	**549,177**	**380,399**	**403,223**
Current liabilities						
Accounts payable	33,810	41,400	50,000	70,000	74,200	78,652
Accrued wages and commissions	11,500	11,500	13,889	19,444	20,611	21,848
Total current liabilities	45,310	52,900	63,889	89,444	94,811	100,500
Long-term debt	0	0	0	0	226,643	240,241
Owner's equity	237,957	281,234	334,459	459,733	58,945	62,482
Total liabilities and equity	**283,267**	**334,134**	**398,348**	**549,177**	**380,399**	**403,223**

Table 10B.4. Since the equity VCF flows are a type of pre-money flow (with the newly incorporated surplus penalty project), we can find the share price by dividing by the pre-money number of shares. It is $1.6859574 (= $337,191/200,000) per share.

Attempting to conduct a pre-money valuation on post-money financial statements is a bit silly (and confusing) even when it gives the correct answer. We only provide it for the interested readers (if there are any) and for completeness. It's simpler and more logical to commit to post-money valuation when doing post-money financial projections. Table 10B.10 takes this approach.

Note that in the valuation in Table 10B.10 we have the new money ($50,000 immediately and in Year 3) to offset the pain of the surplus cash penalty project. This money is provided by new investors. Since the flows we are discounting include all payments to all post-money shareholders, we will find the share price by dividing by the total number of shares outstanding after the offerings. We are now in a position to proceed as we did in the simpler example we used (with a $10,000,000 exit value) earlier. To reproduce the "Share Distributions" section of Table 10B.10, we start with the Year 3 post-money value of $806,233. The Year 3 $50,000 investors get 6.2 percent (= 50,000/806,233) of the final total shares when they invest in Year 3. The initial $50,000 investors get 12.11 percent of what will be the final total shares when they invest in the first round (at 7/31/Y0). That will leave a total of 81.69 percent (= 1 − .1211 − .062) of the final total shares for the founders. If their 200,000 shares represent 81.69 percent of the total shares at the end, then there will be a grand total of 244,841 (= 200,000/.8169) shares outstanding at the end. Investors in the first round will be issued 29,657 shares (= .1211 × 244,841). Investors in the second round (Year 3) will be issued 15,184 shares (= .062 × 244,841). The first-round share price is $1.685974 (= $50,000/29,657), and the second-round price is $3.2928856 (= $50,000/15,184). Note that this first-round price is the same as that we

TABLE 10B.8 Post-Money DDA Statements of Cash Flow

ACCOUNTING STATEMENT OF CASH FLOWS	YEAR 1 8/1/Y0– 7/31/Y1	YEAR 2 8/1/Y1– 7/31/Y2	YEAR 3 8/1/Y2– 7/31/Y3	YEAR 4 8/1/Y3– 7/31/Y4	YEAR T = 5 8/1/Y4– 7/31/Y5
Cash flows from activities					
Net income	6,372	43,277	53,225	75,273	78,171	66,997
Adjustments to net income for cash flow					
+ Depreciation expense	4,600	5,796	5,630	6,800	9,520	10,091
− Change in prepaid insurance	1,840	0	−478	−1,111	−233	−247
+ Change in accrued liabilities	1,725	0	2,389	5,556	1,167	1,237
− Change in inventory	12,880	14,720	−17,200	−40,000	−8,400	−8,904
+ Change in accounts payable	−4,830	7,590	8,600	20,000	4,200	4,452
− Change in accounts receivable	−9,200	0	−9,556	−22,222	−4,667	−4,947
Total adjustments	7,015	28,106	−10,614	−30,978	1,587	1,682
Net cash flow from operations	13,387	71,383	42,611	44,296	79,758	68,678
Cash flows from investing					
Capital expenditures	−6,900	−4,140	−17,326	−34,000	−15,232	−16,146
Net cash from investing	−6,900	−4,140	−17,326	−34,000	−15,232	−16,146
Cash flows from financing					
+ Equity issues	50,000	0	0	50,000	0	0
− Dividends	0	0	0	0	−478,959	−63,460
(= −net dividend)	50,000	0	0	50,000	−478,959	−63,460
+ Debt issues	0	0	0	0	226,643	13,599
Net cash flows from financing	50,000	0	0	50,000	−252,316	−49,861
Net change in cash and equivalents	56,487	67,243	25,285	60,296	−187,790	2,671
Beginning cash balance	23,000	79,487	146,730	172,015	232,310	44,520
Ending cash balance	79,487	146,730	172,015	232,310	44,520	47,191

calculated using Table 10B.9's pre-money valuation (equity VCF) from the post-money financials. Pre-money and post-money valuations should give the same answers if done correctly using the same assumptions on surplus cash penalties. Table 10B.10 provides cross-checks for each round that validate these share prices.

Table 10B.10 also introduces the VCSC directly in order to compare it to these more detailed valuation approaches (the post-money DDA in particular). Since Year 4 is the first year the venture starts to return capital to the investors, the VCSC starts with a Year 4 terminal value guess of $1,007,792. This is a very good guess and magically coincides with the Year 4 NPV. Of this total exit pie, the round-one investors get $122,070 [= $50,000 × (1.25)^4] and the round-two investors get $62,500 (= $50,000 × 1.25), leaving $823,221 (= $1,007,792 − $122,070 − $62,500) for the founders. These lead directly to the percents of ownership, which lead directly (as in the last paragraph) to the distribution of shares and share prices. The VCSC we introduced in the extended example (with a $10,000,000 exit) is a post-money DDA method.

TABLE 10B.9 Pre-Money Valuation with Additional Penalty on Proceeds

EQUITY VALUATION	4/1/Y0– 7/31/Y0	YEAR 1 8/1/Y0– 7/31/Y1	YEAR 2 8/1/Y1– 7/31/Y2	YEAR 3 8/1/Y2– 7/31/Y3	YEAR 4 8/1/Y3– 7/31/Y4	YEAR T = 5 8/1/Y4– 7/31/Y5
Net Income	6,372	43,277	53,225	75,273	78,171	66,997
+ Depreciation and amortization	4,600	5,796	5,630	6,800	9,520	10,091
− Capital expenditures	−6,900	−4,140	−17,326	−34,000	−15,232	−16,146
− Change in net working capital	−54,072	−44,933	−41,529	−98,073	179,857	−11,081
+ Debt proceeds	0	0	0	0	226,643	13,599
Equity VCF (valuation cash flow)	−50,000	0	0	−50,000	478,959	63,460
(vs. dividends − equity issues)	−50,000	0	0	−50,000	478,959	63,460
VALUATION DATE	TODAY 7/31/Y0	EOY 1 7/31/Y1	EOY 2 7/31/Y2	EOY 3 7/31/Y3	EOY 4 7/31/Y4	EOY 5 = T 7/31/Y5
PV Equity (Excluding Current Equity VCF)	387,191	483,989	604,987	806,233	528,833	560,563
Capital gain on market equity		25.0%	25.0%	33.3%	−34.4%	6.0%
Dividend yield on market equity		0.0%	0.0%	−8.3%	59.4%	12.0%
Total return on market equity		25.0%	25.0%	25.0%	25.0%	18.0%
NPV Equity (Including Current Equity VCF)	337,191	483,989	604,987	756,233	1,007,792	624,023

For completeness, Table 10B.11 demonstrates again that the DDA/VCSC valuations differ from the PDM (or MDM valuation) only in the surplus cash penalty applied by the former.

The transition from traditional free cash flow valuation, which treats the venture as though it had a just-in-time equity line of credit, to the VCSC or post-money DDA method involves several hits on value. Table 10B.12 provides the details for how PDC's pre-money PDM share price of $2.02 falls to the VCSC/post-money DDA share price of $1.68. To see the share price impacts given in the table, we need to remember that share prices are found either by (i) using pre-money valuations divided by pre-money shares outstanding or by (ii) using post-money valuations divided by post-money shares outstanding. In practice, it also helps to remember that post-money financial statements do not necessarily lead to post-money valuations, particularly when we use formulas to get equity valuation cash flows.

Earlier in this chapter, we used VCSCs to emphasize how additional financing rounds compound each other, potentially causing massive dilution in the founders' ownership. Each of our examples is a "post-all-rounds" valuation, reflecting the rounds projected for that example. The dilution is a result of having to have *more* money to achieve the *same* final payoff ($10,000,000). If we think about this more carefully, what our VCSC examples assume is that additional proceeds are spent prior to the terminal (exit) value, without changing the terminal value. The financial shortfall necessitating the additional financing is due to expense overruns relative to the single-round example where we began. The invariance of the terminal value is an important assumption. The dilution will not be so dramatic if the proceeds lead to a higher terminal value (as in the above examples). Our VCSC examples are post-money analyses for a venture assumed to have a fixed terminal value.

TABLE 10B.10   Post-Money Valuation Using Post-Money DDA Projections

POST-MONEY VALUATIONS	4/1/Y0– 7/31/Y0	YEAR 1 8/1/Y0– 7/31/Y1	YEAR 2 8/1/Y1– 7/31/Y2	YEAR 3 8/1/Y2– 7/31/Y3	YEAR 4 8/1/Y3– 7/31/Y4	YEAR T = 5 8/1/Y4– 7/31/Y5
Equity VCF (including 6,487 paid in Year 5)	−50,000	0	0	−50,000	478,959	63,460
+ Equity issues	50,000	0	0	50,000	0	0
Post-money equity valuation cash flow (including 6,487)	0	0	0	0	478,959	63,460
PV Post-Money (incl. 6,487, excl. current flow)	412,791	515,989	644,987	806,233	528,833	560,563
NPV Post-Money (incl. 6,487, incl. current flow)	412,791	515,989	644,987	806,233	1,007,792	624,023

SHARE DISTRIBUTIONS	INVESTMENT	% POST-MONEY NPV	SHARES	SHARE PRICE
Existing shares		81.69%	200,000	N/A
Round 1 (Year 0)	50,000	12.11%	29,657	1.6859574
Round 2 (Year 3)	50,000	6.20%	15,184	3.2928856 (check growth of equity price = discount rate)
		100.00%	244,841	25.00% (consistent with accruing all VCF's)

CROSS-CHECK	PRE-MONEY SHARES	PRE-MONEY NPV/SHARE	PV PREVIOUS VCF'S	PRE-MONEY PRICE	POST-MONEY SHARE PRICE
Round 1 (Year 0)	200,000	1.6859574	0	1.6859574 per share	1.6859574
Round 2 (Year 3)	200,000	3.7811688	−0.48828125	3.2928856 per share	3.2928856

POST-MONEY VC SHORTCUT (VCSC)	EXIT PAYOFFS	% OWNERSHIP	SHARES	SHORTCUT PRICE
Founder	823,221	81.69%	200,000	
Round 1 investor requirements	122,070	12.11%	29,657	1.6859574
Round 2 investor requirements	62,500	6.20%	15,184	3.2928856
Totals	1,007,792	100.00%	244,841	

Alternative to get to first-round pre-money   1.6859574 (Post-Money Time 0 NPV − PV(Proceeds))/Founder Shares

Alternative to get to second-round pre-money   3.2928856 (Post-Money Time 3 NPV − PV(Remaining Proceeds))/ (Founder + Round 1 Shares)

TABLE 10B.11 Surplus Cash Penalty in the DDA/VCSC

VALUATION DIFFERENCE IS ONLY IN THE TIMING OF (CREDITING FOR) DIVIDENDS	4/1/Y0–7/31/Y0	YEAR 1 8/1/Y0–7/31/Y1	YEAR 2 8/1/Y1–7/31/Y2	YEAR 3 8/1/Y2–7/31/Y3	YEAR 4 8/1/Y3–7/31/Y4	YEAR 5 8/1/Y4–7/31/Y5
PDM post-money equity valuation cash flow	56,487	65,403	20,125	48,296	288,649	63,460
DDA post-money valuation cash flow	0	0	0	0	478,959	63,460
Difference	56,487	65,403	20,125	48,296	−190,310	0
Cumulative sum of differences		121,890	142,015	190,310	0	0
NPV of timing difference	68,465					
PV of timing difference	11,978					
Post-money NPV equity: dividends in Year 5 forward	412,791					
+ NPV of timing difference	68,465					
Sum	481,257					
Post-money PV equity: PDM and MDM	481,257					
Post-money PV equity dividends in Year 5 forward	412,791					
+ PV of timing difference	11,978					
Sum	424,770					
Post-money PV equity: PDM and DDM	424,770					
Difference (including 6,487)	MDM/PDM Shares	DDA/VCSC Shares	MDM/PDM Price	DDA/VSCS Price	Price Difference/Share	PV Loss Founder Shares
Viewed at Year 0 using round 1 pricing	24,651	29,657	2.028284549	1.6859574	−.3423271	−68,465 = 200,000 * Price Difference
Viewed at Year 0 using round 2 pricing	12,622	15,184	3.96149326	3.2928856	−.6686077	−68,465 = 200,000 * Price Difference/(1.25)^3
Conclude: More shares sold at lower prices!						
Proceeds and additional dividend flows	−50,000	0	0	−50,000	100,000	
Loss (NPV) from additional surplus penalty	−34,640					
Pre-money DDA with pre-money financials (Chapter 9)	371,831	371,831= 200,000 * 1.8591574				
Pre-money DDA with post-money financials (VCSC)	337,191	337,191= 200,000 * 1.6859574				

Conclude: Post-money DDA (and, therefore, VC shortcut) differs from pre-money DDA by the NPV of additional surplus cash penalty on proceeds.

TABLE 10B.12   Valuation Walk-Down from Pre-Money PDM to Post-Money DDA/VCSC

VIEW OF NPV DECREASE WITH POST-MONEY DDA (VCSC)	VALUATION	SHARES SPLITTING	SHARE PRICE
PDM/MDM on pre-money financials and equity VCF	405,657	200,000	2.028284549 (checks with pre-money PDM pricing)
− DDA penalty on pre-money surplus cash	−33,825		
= DDA on pre-money financials and equity VCF	371,831	200,000	1.859157402 (checks with DDA on pre-money financials)
+ PV of proceeds	75,600		
= DDA on post-money financials w/o proceeds penalty	447,431	240,664	1.859157402 (NPV = 0 issue since no additional penalty on proceeds)
− Additional DDA proceeds penalty	−34,640		
= VCSC or DDA on post-money financials and equity VCF	412,791	244,841	1.685957402 (given above)

Now we can return to Jim's FrothySlope microbrewery and ask if the analysis was pre-money or post-money. While we treated the valuation in Chapter 9 as pre-money, there was nothing in the setup that dictated that the analysis was pre-money. For that "quick-and-dirty" valuation, we employed a rather ad hoc set of cash flows and the following valuation:

	YEAR 1	YEAR 2	YEAR 3	YEAR 4	YEAR 5 (INCLUDING TERMINAL VALUE)
FrothySlope's DCF PV	$\dfrac{0}{1.4}$	$\dfrac{0}{(1.4)^2}$	$\dfrac{0}{(1.4)^3}$	$\dfrac{2,500,000}{(1.4)^4}$	$\dfrac{3,000,000 + 3,500,000/(.2 - .6)}{(1.4)^5}$

The important information that is missing is whether the cash flows that Jim inputs to this quick valuation include use of the investor's contribution. Does one or more of the cash flow projections ($2,500,000, $3,000,000, or $3,500,000) change when Jim accepts the investor's money? That is, will the investor's $100,000 contribution increase, for example, the initial $2,500,000? If the cash flows were those Jim could produce without the new financing, then the initial dividend can increase by $100,000. If the cash flow numbers were predicated on having already spent an additional $100,000 (relative to the current business plan), the cash flow predictions won't change. We need to know if the cash flow predictions are pre-money or post-money. In Chapter 9, we assumed the cash flow predictions were pre-money. Consequently, to get the percent of the venture that had to be sold for $100,000, we added the proceeds to the pre-money valuation to get a post-money valuation. We calculated the amount of the venture that Jim had to sell by noting that the proceeds were 1.68 percent of this post-money value. It could be that Jim's ad hoc cash flows already incorporated $100,000 of additional returns to investors. Then the cash flow would already be post-money and we would not need to add the proceeds. So, it's important to understand whether the cash flow predictions already have been bumped up to incorporate additional payouts due to additional financing. In the extreme, if Jim's investor put in $500,000,000, it would be pretty clear that the cash flow projections would need to be altered given the current business plan. In particular, the venture could immediately pay dividends. This is why we assumed that Jim's predictions were pre-money. To get an idea of the relevance of the assumption for FrothySlope, we provide a valuation for various assumptions about the nature of these cash flow predictions.

Scenario 1: We begin by assuming that the projected dividends are "post-money." That is, we assume the dividend projections include an estimate of a dividend of whatever remains of the 100,000, if anything:

	0	1	2	3	4	5
Dividends	0	0	0	0	2,500,000	3,000,000
Terminal value						25,000,000
Dividends paid	0	0	0	0	2,500,000	28,000,000

In this scenario, the time $4 + 5$ "pie" must be used to pay all investors, new and old. All claims must be funded out of the cash flows at times 4 and 5. Consequently, we solve for ownership of the final pie by simple division:

Time 5 "pie" (future value of time 4 dividend plus time 5 flows)		31,500,000
Time 5 value of investment		537,824
Ownership percent of "pie"		
100,000 investor	1.71%	
Founder	98.29%	

The same calibration can be done in present values as was done in Chapter 9, Section 9.2:

Time 0 "pie"	$5,856,935 (present value of time 4 and time 5 flows)	
Ownership percent of "pie"		
100,000 investor	1.71%	
Founder	98.29%	

Assuming the venture has 100 shares outstanding, it issues 1.737036 new shares in order to carve out the 1.71 percent ownership.

Scenario 2: Next, as in Chapter 9, we assume that the dividend projections are "pre-money." Consequently, there will be an additional 100,000 at time 0 or 537,824 at time 5 (the future value of the 100,000).

	0	1	2	3	4	5
Dividends	0	0	0	0	2,500,000	3,000,000
Terminal value, including FV 100,000						25,537,824
Dividends paid	0	0	0	0	2,500,000	28,537,824

As before, the time $4 + 5$ "pie" must be used to pay all investors, new and old. All claims must be funded out of the cash flows at times 4 and 5. Consequently we solve for ownership of the final pie by simple division:

Time 5 "pie" (future value of time 4 dividend plus time 5 flows)		32,037,824
Time 5 value of investment		537,824
Ownership percent of "pie"		
100,000 investor	1.68%	
Founder	98.32%	

The same calibration can be done in present values:

Time 0 "pie"	$5,956,935 (present value of time 4 and time 5 flows)	
Ownership percent of "pie"		
100,000 investor	1.68%	
Founder	98.32%	

Assuming the venture has 100 shares outstanding, it issues 1.707378 new shares in order to carve out the 1.68 percent ownership. It should not be surprising that this calibration results in fewer shares issued as the final pie is larger by the FV of the 100,000 investor.

Scenario 3: ("Add the proceeds variation"). When we don't assume that the projections include the payout of whatever is left of the proceeds from the offering, we can just add the proceeds to the "pre-money" time 0 value and then do the share issue calculations:

Scenario 1 PV	$5,856,935
Proceeds	$ 100,000
Total time 0 pie	$5,956,935
Ownership Percent of "pie"	
100,000 investor	1.68%
Founder	98.32%

The DDA is named for the restriction it imposes on dividends before the exit or terminal period (Year 4 in our example). This restriction applies whether or not projected cash surpluses could be used to pay dividends before the exit. It is a more rigorous version of a VCSC. The associated projected financial statements correctly track the cash account and record that no returns are expected to be paid to venture investors before the year of hypothesized exit. Valuation for the DDA can be calibrated by directly discounting the statement of cash flow's projected dividend (and terminal value) flows to investors. The approximation's main drawback, which appears largely to be ignored in practice, is that it cavalierly ignores potentially serious risk differences associated with (1) a new venture's periodic gluts of surplus cash in waiting and (2) a mature successful venture's potential cash account bloat. Of course, the VCSC shares these drawbacks. Applying a typical venture discount rate to these otherwise desirable surplus cash balances results in a depressed valuation (relative to the PDM and MDM) and could potentially distort the venture's incentives to create value through its business plan.

When the smoke clears, our academic side prefers the more equitable (and theoretically correct) PDM, while our practical side appreciates the simplicity and usefulness of the post-money DDA/VCSC. We admit that, when applying flat rates like 70 percent, we are already making gross approximations. For many ventures where cash is always scarce, little may be gained by a more equitable but complex treatment of surplus cash.

We could have provided an uncritical presentation of VCSCs (i.e., a post-money delayed dividend approximation). Such a presentation would have been blatantly pro–venture capitalist. While we are pro–venture capitalist, we are also pro-entrepreneur. We hope we have provided enough insight to let you see why stripping out surplus cash (and therefore treating its temporary use as a zero-NPV project separate from the venture) is the most precise approach to valuing the venture. Perhaps surprisingly, stripping out and reissuing through pseudo dividends and pseudo issues also grants entrepreneurs their wish for equity that acts like a just-in-time line of credit—at least for valuation purposes. The true justification for our preference for the PDM is that we want you to think about what creates value, and how and when that takes place.

Part 5

STRUCTURING FINANCING FOR THE GROWING VENTURE

Chapter 11

PROFESSIONAL VENTURE CAPITAL

PREVIOUSLY COVERED

In Chapter 10, we introduced the venture capital methods of valuation and related them to more formal equity valuation methods. We demonstrated that current and future valuations, ownership percent, and share counts are related. We provided a framework for combining multiple valuation scenarios into a single value for the venture.

LOOKING AHEAD

Chapter 12 discusses funding opportunities other than those provided by angels and venture capitalists. For certain ventures there may be opportunities to access capital through financial intermediaries, including commercial and investment banks. We discuss the advantages and disadvantages of these rarer forms of venture financing. We also cover, in some detail, borrowing opportunities associated with programs run by the Small Business Administration.

CHAPTER LEARNING OBJECTIVES

In this chapter, we consider the highest-profile segment of the venture investing markets: professional venture capital. We discuss the origins of venture capital and the periodic fluctuations accompanying major new technologies. We give special attention to the professional venture capital screening and investment processes. After completing this chapter, you will be able to:

1. Discuss the history and current status of venture investing in the United States

2. Explain the professional venture investing cycle and its relevance to entrepreneurs seeking professional venture capital

3. List major elements in the design and structure of a venture capital fund

4. Describe the venture capital screening process and list characteristics central to determining a venture capitalist's willingness to invest

5. Discuss the various roles a venture capitalist can take in providing financing and services to an emerging venture

6. Enumerate several terms or conditions to be negotiated when structuring venture capital financing

> *On average, venture capitalists pumped $160 million a day into entrepreneurial companies in the fourth quarter of 1999, a 50 percent increase over the prior record set in Q399 and a 290 percent increase over Q498. An average of 14 companies per day received an average of $11.6 million each.*
> —PricewaterhouseCoopers MoneyTree Survey, March 2000

The late 1990s and early twenty-first century experienced the hottest venture investing market in history. In 1999, more than 4,006 firms received professionally managed venture capital at an average funding level of $8.8 million per company.[1] This shattered the previous record total by 150 percent to end at $48.3 billion.[2] But the seeds of a spectacular decline had already been sown. Some appreciation for the historical boom-bust venture investing cycle may help investors and entrepreneurs understand the ups and downs of aggregate venture investing.

11.1   HISTORICAL CHARACTERIZATION OF PROFESSIONAL VENTURE CAPITAL

While there are many types of investors who put their money at risk in new and high-growth ventures, in this chapter we will concentrate on the professional intermediaries in the venture investing arena, venture capitalists (VCs). The distinguishing characteristic of professional VCs is that, in addition to having personal financial stakes in their portfolio of venture investments, they have raised funds from other investors to invest in the portfolio. That is, professional venture capitalists are intermediaries in the venture investment sector who raise capital from investors and invest that capital in a portfolio of risky ventures. This financial intermediation function distinguishes venture capitalists from their angel investor counterparts, who primarily invest their own capital or that of neighbors and friends.

Professional venture capital, as we know it today, did not exist before World War II. Most venturesome investing in the prewar era came from wealthy individuals and families. Like today's angels, many of these investors enjoyed stimulating new business formation. They wanted to contribute to the success of capitalism as an economic system and felt some obligation to plow a portion of their wealth back into the system. The genesis of professional venture capital intermediation is usually identified with the formation of American Research and Development (ARD) in 1946 by Harvard professor Georges Doriot and Boston

---

[1]   PricewaterhouseCoopers MoneyTree Survey 1999, http://www.pwcmoneytree.com.

[2]   News release, *Venture Economics,* February 8, 2000. (For data from the National Venture Capital Association and Venture Economics, see http://www.nvca.org.) The PWC MoneyTree amount for 1999 was $35.6 billion.

Federal Reserve president Ralph Flanders.[3] In 1945, Flanders suggested to attendees at a meeting of the National Association of Securities Dealers (NASD, the parent organization for the NASDAQ) that tapping into the capital controlled by institutional investors could facilitate new company formation. Doriot (a long-time advocate of entrepreneurial venturing) and Flanders believed that technologies developed at MIT during World War II could provide a solid foundation for commercial opportunities. Flanders and Doriot joined with several others to form ARD on June 6, 1946.

After some serious difficulties convincing investment bankers and investors, ARD's initial $3.5 million capitalization was held in a closed-end mutual fund structure (permitting no increase in the size of the fund). Almost $2 million of this came from institutional investors. ARD's first investment was in High Voltage Engineering Corporation, a venture organized by MIT physicists and engineers. The startup was one of the first venture-backed high-technology firms to have a New York Stock Exchange (NYSE) listing. By the end of 1947, ARD had invested in eight ventures, six of which were startups.

While ARD's prospectus emphasized the uncertainty and length of the investment horizon, investors still were not ready for the massive cash burn and the length of time before light appeared at the end of the tunnel. They were also unaccustomed to a complete lack of pacifying dividends along the way. Many other factors, including subjectivity in how to value ARD's portfolio companies, contributed to a decline in ARD's publicly traded share price. A second offering in 1949 was a failure, although some funds (about 43 percent of the target amount) were raised. By 1951, many of ARD's companies had achieved operating profits, and ARD's stock price stood at $19 (down from $25 for the 1946 offering). ARD's performance was at best lackluster during its early years. We will return to ARD's story after we discuss some characteristics of 1950s-era venture investing.

The first major government foray into venture investing came with the formation of the Small Business Administration (SBA) in 1953. Before the SBA, the government's involvement in fostering small businesses was restricted to agencies intended to assist small businesses in securing contracts from the Department of Defense. There were also some relatively minor small business lending activities. With the Small Business Administration came the legislative authority for the government to actively engage in assisting new business formation. In 1958, the SBA created Small Business Investment Companies (SBICs). SBICs, in addition to possessing some important tax advantages, were eventually eligible to borrow from the government up to four times their equity base, giving them a fourfold expansion in the size of their funds under management.[4] In return, the SBICs submitted to government regulation and caps on their investment strategies (such as never having a controlling stake or putting more than 20 percent of their funds in one

---

[3] See William Bygrave and Jeffry Timmons, *Venture Capital at the Crossroads* (Boston: Harvard Business School Press, 1992), which draws heavily on the 1969 Harvard dissertation research of Patrick Liles titled "Sustaining the Venture Capital Firm."

[4] The SBA's introduction to the current structure of SBICs is available on the Web at http://www.sba.gov/idc/ groups/public/documents/sba_program_office/inv_sbic_program_overview.ppt.

venture).[5] Because of the tax and leverage advantages, the SBIC quickly became the primary vehicle for professionally managed venture capital. By the mid-1960s, there were approximately 700 SBICs.

We return to ARD's pathbreaking experience. In 1957, ARD had invested $70,000 in the startup of the Massachusetts minicomputer company Digital Equipment Corporation (DEC). In 1960, DEC took off. By 1971, ARD's position in DEC was worth $355 million. When ARD was sold the following year at an equivalent of $813 per share, it provided a compound annual return of 14.7 percent, owing primarily to the performance of DEC. Without the DEC holdings, the annual return would have been only 7.4 percent.[6] Professional venture capital grew tremendously, partially in response to ARD's success with DEC.

At about the same time as DEC's success, it became apparent that the structure and incentives created by the government subsidy and regulation of SBICs distorted venture investing. By 1967, 232 SBICs were classified as problems,[7] more regulations were introduced, and the SBIC industry was headed for serious trouble. While the SBICs' access to leverage appeared attractive, as in many other contexts, debt service commitments introduced significant frictions to venture investing. During the mid- to late 1960s, the professional venture investing community widely abandoned the SBIC structure (although several still exist today and new SBICs are formed occasionally). The limited partnership structure for professional venture capital grew in influence during this period. By 1968, more funds were managed by VC partnerships than by SBICs. The venture capital partnership remains the dominant U.S. structure for professionally managed venture capital.

Between 1968 and 1969, new issues of public stock hit all-time highs with about a thousand small companies going public. By late 1969, however, the hot market was gone. The early 1970s shook the entire U.S. economy. The costs of the Vietnam War and the oil embargo of 1974 to 1975 finished off the equity markets. Entering 1970, the Dow Jones Industrial Average (DJIA) stood at about 800. It peaked at over 1,000 before losing 40 percent of its value by the end of 1974, dipping below 600. Needless to say, the first half of the 1970s was not a good time to be holding equity. The NASDAQ composite (which is made up of smaller firms than the DJIA) dropped by 60 percent during this period. Massive losses in smaller emerging companies basically killed both the new issues and the venture investing markets. Venture investing was flat during this time. While 1969 had seen about $171 million in professionally managed venture capital investments, only $10 million was invested in 1975. Many believe that the boom-bust cycle of the late 1960s and early 1970s demonstrates a pattern that will be repeated in the future.

During the turbulent early 1970s, venture capitalists began to seek partial protection from the ravages of the markets by changing their organizational structures (away from public company structures like ARD and toward private partnerships)

---

[5]   Section 107 of Title 13 in the U.S. Federal Regulations.

[6]   Bygrave and Timmons, *Venture Capital at the Crossroads*, p. 20.

[7]   Ibid., p. 21.

and by syndicating their deals with others so that their portfolios would retain significant diversification.

The 1978 founding and 1980 initial public offering of Apple are symbolic of the next major wave in venture investing. Rather than *mini*computer related (as with DEC), this wave was driven by the revolution in *micro*computers.[8] With first-round financing at $.09 per share and the public offering of $22, Apple's remarkable success was noted by many potential venture investors. Even though the prime rate of interest in 1981 was a remarkable 18.9 percent, the flow of funds to new ventures hit $1.8 billion in 1982, $4.5 billion in 1983, and $4 billion in 1984. By 1983, however, industry watchers were beginning to characterize the fever-pitched VC investing as "speculative excess." Evidence of the excess included unusually high price-earnings ratios (40 to 60) and dramatic changes in the venture capitalists' profit sharing (rising to 30 percent from the historical average of 20 percent). The Winchester disk drive manufacturing industry was one of the major victims of the overheated venture market and is frequently identified as the marker for the end of this venture boom-bust cycle.[9] With more than forty manufacturers funded by professional venture capital during 1978 to 1984, and more than one hundred manufacturers in total, there was little chance that venture capital investors would escape unharmed. Many disk drive companies went public between 1981 and 1983 and had stock prices fall by as much as 80 percent from their level in mid-1983. Most failed or were merged into better-financed competitors.

As can be seen in Figure 11.1, the recent expansion in venture investing was significant and continued until the late 1990s. The Internet fostered levels of investment never before experienced.

What does the future hold? Predicting financial markets is far harder than one might expect. William Bygrave and Jeffry Timmons recorded several comments made during the crunch of 1989 to 1991, including "Venture capital has changed forever, and when the shakeout is over, it won't return to the good old days." If the venture capital markets were at Bygrave and Timmons' "crossroads" in 1992, one wonders what, if anything, should be said about the future of venture investing as it appears looking forward from 2007.[10] We will stick to what we believe is evident. As Figure 11.1 indicates, all previous levels of venture investing are trivial relative to turn-of-the-century levels. Much of the most recent boom was Internet related. For example, in the fourth quarter of 1999, business-to-consumer venture capital investments reached $4.46 billion (in 98 ventures) and business-to-business levels reached $2.64 billion (in 128 companies).[11] These quarterly investment levels represent 1,092 and 908 percent increases, respectively,

---

[8] Federal legislation liberalizing institutional involvement in venture investing played an important part in pulling out of the venture investing recession in the early 1970s. Bygrave and Timmons provide a list of several major legislative actions that assisted in the return to vitality. Ibid., p. 24.

[9] Our short description of the crash of the Winchester disk drive venture investing is based on the Venture Economics–assisted discussion in "Note on the Venture Capital Industry—Update (1985)," a Harvard case note (#9-286-060).

[10] Bygrave and Timmons, *Venture Capital at the Crossroads.*

[11] These statistics are drawn from the quarterly surveys conducted by PricewaterhouseCoopers LLP in their MoneyTree Survey, available at http://www.pwcmoneytree.com.

FIGURE 11.1   Historical Levels of VC Investment

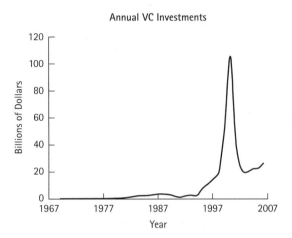

Source: Data compiled by authors from various financial sources.

over previous levels. Technology companies accounted for over 90 percent of investments in this quarter. The average technology funding round was at $9.63 million, up from $5.15 million in the previous period. Nontechnology raw dollars invested actually declined. Early-stage companies garnered 42 percent of these dollars. While the history of venture capital has proved that VCs are interested in a variety of different business models, the most recent boom-bust was heavily focused on Internet-related ventures.

As before, the venture investing market has cooled rapidly. Many popular Internet companies quickly ran out of cash because of incredibly high burn rates.[12] We believe that Internet-related companies have returned to being valued more on achievements and evidence than on speculative sentiment. While the Internet will continue to revolutionize global commerce, valuations are closer to normal. To many, this latest boom-bust was just another episode in a sequence of technology-driven venture capital cycles—although the swings in this cycle were larger than previously seen.

While the U.S. venture capital market is the largest and most mature in the world, there has been significant growth in venture investing in many other companies, particularly in Europe and the Pacific Rim. Venture investing has truly become a global reality. As the venture investing culture spreads, many regions organize venture capital associations that track the region's venture

---

[12] A *Wall Street Journal* article ("Burning Up; Warning: Internet Companies Are Running Out of Cash—Fast," March 20, 2000) stated that about 25 percent of the firms included in its study would burn through their cash within a year.

investments and provide summary statistics. More and more of these data are provided in Web-based formats. For example, if you are interested in the market for venture capital investments in Europe, the European Venture Capital Association provides hard copy and electronic versions of its reports. (See, for example, http://www.evca.com.) Academic studies of the international venture investing markets can be found in the journal *Venture Capital: An International Journal of Entrepreneurial Finance.*

In a quick Web search, we turned up references to country-specific venture capital associations for Australia, Belgium, Finland, France, Germany, Hong Kong, India, Indonesia, Italy, Japan, Korea, the Netherlands, Norway, Portugal, Singapore, Spain, Sweden, Switzerland, Taipei, Thailand, and the United Kingdom. Links to many international venture capital firms and service providers can be found at http://vcexperts.com/vce/community/directory.

CONCEPT CHECK

- What were the technologies that drove the first two venture capital booms in the twentieth century?
- What is the technology that drove the most recent venture capital boom?
- How are the venture capital and public offerings markets linked?
- What is the purpose of venture capital directories? Where can they be found?

11.2   PROFESSIONAL VENTURE INVESTING CYCLE: OVERVIEW

Now that we have an idea of the history and current conditions for professional venture capital, we can move on to a discussion most entrepreneurs find more interesting: What do VCs do and how do they do it? We begin by discussing what VCs do. It is important to remember that professional VCs are market intermediaries between suppliers and demanders of venture financing. Consequently, their time is split between maintaining relationships with investors and providing guidance and services to their portfolio ventures.

In a mature VC firm, these activities will cycle or occur simultaneously. Figure 11.2 graphically depicts a seven-stage view of the professional venture investing cycle that begins with determining fund objectives and policies and culminates with the distribution of cash and securities proceeds. At all times, the firm will maintain involvement in activities that lead to potential new deal flow (new ideas, technologies, and business plans). Each stage will now be addressed in a separate section.

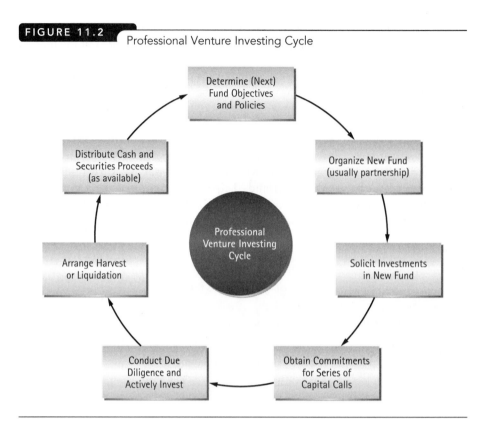

FIGURE 11.2   Professional Venture Investing Cycle

11.3   DETERMINING (NEXT) FUND OBJECTIVES AND POLICIES

Because of the potential and need for value-added investing by venture capitalists, VC firms tend to specialize in publicly identified niches. There are many different specializations in the venture capital industry. Three common identifying characteristics are industry, stage and size of investment, and geographic area. Firms and funds also come and go as the economy changes, new areas of expertise emerge, and new partnerships are forged. When considering contacting a VC firm for possible funding, it is worth your time to find out how the firm has described itself (perhaps on the firm's Web page). It is also worthwhile to check the firm's listing in the major venture capital directories, including *Pratt's Guide to Venture Capital* and the *National Venture Capital Association* (NVCA). You may be able to gather information on relevant VC firms' recent fundraising and investing activities from VC tracking services, like those provided by the National Venture Capital Association (http://www.nvca.org) or Pricewaterhouse-Coopers MoneyTree Survey (http://www.pwcmoneytree.com).

A typical directory entry for a venture capital firm will include addresses and contact information for the firm's offices. It is common for VC firms to have multiple offices in order to be geographically close to their portfolio firms as well as the talent pool they may need to develop and tap. The directory entry will also include a short description of the firm and a description of the types of investment opportunities the VC firm seeks. As an example, the firm may be described as a second-stage/mezzanine firm with a $500,000 minimum investment for ventures within two hours of the office, with no preferred industry and exclusions on real estate and oil and gas investing. The directory entry may also include some brief history on the origin of the firm and the amount of capital under management by the firm. The status of VC firms (seeking capital or seeking investments) changes quite rapidly, and static directories (even electronic ones) may provide stale information. The Internet Age has also reintroduced a debate among venture firms on whether they should be industry specific (e.g., Internet only) or diversified across industries (e.g., Internet, biomedical devices, and wireless).

As the global economy continues to expand and evolve, a given VC firm may change its concentration or its willingness to consider investing in different markets. In our venture investing cycle, we began with a firm defining a fund's objectives and policies. Based on past experience and the VC firm's reputation gained from previous investment, it may be advantageous to widen or narrow the objective for the next fund.

11.4   ORGANIZING THE NEW FUND

The venture firm must structure the governance of the new fund (determining the general partners), set the fee structure, and arrange profit sharing. The typical compensation and incentive structure provides a 2 to 2.5 percent annual fee on invested capital and a 20 percent share in any profits (**carried interest**) to the managing general partner(s). In the private equity money management markets, one hears such firms referred to as **two and twenty shops**, emphasizing the nature of the fee arrangement. For short periods of time during the more heated venture investing periods, one may even observe fee and carried interest structures of 3 percent and 30 percent. Some industry participants and observers, however, have interpreted such fees as a sign of an overheated irrational market poised for a downfall.

Having set the fund's objective, governance, and fee structure, the sponsoring venture capital firm can proceed with the requisite legal procedures and documents necessary to solicit and accept funds from investors. Typically, the details will be spelled out in a "private placement" or "confidential offering" memorandum. Figure 11.3 outlines the content of a recent software-oriented venture capital partnership offering memorandum.

As with the fund described in Figure 11.3, the typical new U.S. venture capital fund is organized as a limited partnership with a venture firm acting as the fund's general (managing) partner. The new fund will be formally organized, and money will be raised with the aid of a private placement memorandum similar to the one summarized in Figure 11.3. The promotional activities for the fund generally will be directed toward institutional investors, including pension funds, and wealthy individuals (all of whom will be accredited investors, providing virtually automatic exemption from SEC registration requirements). The placement

carried interest
portion of profits paid to the professional venture capitalist as incentive compensation

two and twenty shops
investment management firms having a contract that gives them a 2 percent of assets annual management fee and 20 percent carried interest

FIGURE 11.3 Elements of a Venture Capital Fund Placement Memorandum

FRONTMATTER DECLARATIONS	EXAMPLES
Description of Limited Manner of the Offering	to be delivered to a limited number of prospective investors
Imposition of Confidentiality	"each memorandum recipient agrees that it will not copy, reproduce or distribute to others this Memorandum, in whole or in part, at any time without the prior written consent of the Partnership, and that it will keep permanently confidential all information contained herein not already public"
Notice of Lack of SEC Registration	not registered with the Securities and Exchange Commission
Notice of Restriction on Resale	subject to restrictions on transferability and resale and may not be transferred or resold except as permitted under the Securities Act of 1933
Declaration of the Highly Risky Nature of Investment	"involves a high degree of risk . . . substantial risks involved"
State Securities Disclosures	
Generic Resale Restrictions	"investors should be aware that they will be required to bear the financial risks of this investment for an indefinite period of time"
California-Specific Remarks	sale is conditional on obtaining exemption under section 25100, 25102, or 25105 of the California Corporations Code
Offering Summary	
Objective of Formation	to invest in development-stage information technology companies
Geographic Concentration or Restriction	primarily, but not exclusively, in the Rocky Mountain region of the United States
Declaration of General Partner	a Delaware limited liability company
Targeted Fund Size	expects aggregate proceeds of $50 to $70 million
Minimum Fund Size	$35 million in aggregate proceeds
Minimum Capital Subscriptions	$1 million for institutions; $500,000 for individuals
Fund Overview	
Fund Size	$50 to $70 million
Investment Focus	information technology companies; very early stage; first institutional round; B2B
Geographic Focus	Rocky Mountain region
Fund Management	IT and VC professionals with distinguished advisory board
Fund Benefits and Advantages	unique in region; access to low valuation ventures, rapid exit opportunities
Portfolio Size	12 to 16 companies
Average First-Round Investment	$600,000
Amount Reserved for Follow-On Investments	66% to 75% of fund
Term	10 years
Management Fee	2.5% per annum of committed capital
General Partner's Carried Interest	20%
Executive Summary	
Summary of Terms	
Structure	Delaware limited partnership with a Delaware LLC as general partner
Objectives	"to provide a limited number of accredited investors the opportunity to realize significant long-term capital appreciation through investing in information technology companies"
Special Limited Partners	other venture capitalist participation and incentive structure

FIGURE 11.3   Elements of a Venture Capital Fund Placement Memorandum (*continued*)

FRONTMATTER DECLARATIONS	EXAMPLES
Size	$50 to $70 million expected with a minimum of $35; six-month window; and minimum capital commitments of $1 million (institutional) and $500,000 (individual)
Term	10 years
Location	determined by general partner
Fiscal Year	ends December 31
General Partners' Capital Contributions	1% of total capital with maximum of .25% as promissory note
Limited Partners' Capital Contribution	installments paid within thirty days of call notice; each call of no more than 20% of total committed capital; expect all calls in first four years
Limitation of Liability	limited partners' liability limited to their committed capital
Allocation of Gains and Losses	if net gain then 80% pro rata on committed capital and 20% to general partner; if net loss then 100% pro rata on committed capital
Tax Distribution	cash payment of 40% of allocated net income within ninety days of end of fiscal year
Distributions of Cash	pro rata in accordance with committed capital until committed capital returned; 80/20 split with general partner afterward
Management Fee	2.5% of committed capital, payable quarterly in advance
Expenses	allocated to general partner except for organizational and disposition expenses
Valuation	determined by general partner in accordance with methods set forth in the limited partnership agreement
Advisory Committee	duties include review of asset valuations and audit report, provision of investment advice and counsel
Powers and Duties of General Partner	manage and have sole control over the partnership's business and affairs
Restriction on Indebtedness	no debt on behalf of partnership; no SBIC or other venture partnership investments
Restrictions on the General Partner	cannot engage in transactions detrimental (at the time) to the partnership; two-thirds approval required for security sales from general partner to partnership; limitations on general partner investing alongside the partnership
Withdrawal of Capital	none allowed without consent of two-thirds of limited partners and general partner
Withdrawal of Limited Partner	none allowed
Early Dissolution of Partnership	upon 80% of limited partner approval or 180 days after bankruptcy or dissolution of general partner (unless voted otherwise)
Transfer of Limited Partnership Interests	requires approval of general partner other than in specific events like a merger
Transfer of General Partner's Interest	none allowed
Audit of Partnership	annually by accounting firm chosen by general partner
Reports to Limited Partners	annual audited financial statements; quarterly portfolio summary; unaudited quarterly financial statements; tax filing statements
Liquidation	supervised by general partner or, if requested by two-thirds of the limited partners, by a committee of designates of the general and limited partner
ERISA Partners	ERISA partners have special withdrawal privileges if the activities of the partnership involve material violations of ERISA
Future Amendments to Partnership Agreement	requires the consent of general partner and two-thirds of the limited partners
Indemnification	the partnership agrees to indemnify the general partner against claims and expenses arising from activities taken in good faith to promote the best interests of the partnership

materials will include the track record of the venture fund and other relevant marketing information.

CONCEPT CHECK

- What is carried interest?
- Why do venture capital firms use private placement memoranda in raising the money for their funds?
- What is the role of the general partner of a venture capital fund?
- What is the role of the limited partners?

11.5   SOLICITING INVESTMENTS IN THE NEW FUND

Thanks to the venture capital tracking activities of several firms, we know a lot about the sources of funds for professional venture capitalists. Using a fifteen-year average, Figure 11.4 displays the sources of professionally managed venture capital by the type of investor.

The most important trend obscured by the twenty-five-year (1980–2004) averages is an increased participation of pension funds. In 1979, the Department of Labor clarified [for the purposes of the Employee Retirement Income Security Act (ERISA)] that portfolio diversification was a legitimate consideration in determining the prudence of an individual investment. This clarification cleared the way for pension funds to invest a portion of their funds in venture capital. Since this

FIGURE 11.4   Suppliers of Venture Capital

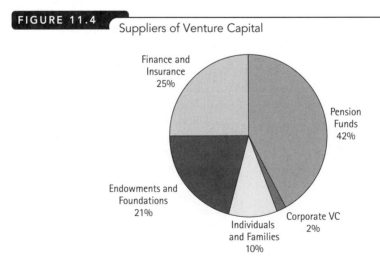

Source: National Venture Capital Association, 2004.

clarification, pension funds have remained the dominant source of funds for venture investing.[13]

The task of raising money from institutional and individual investors is not an easy one. Many potential venture capitalists have been frustrated by the difficulty of raising money. A track record of previous success is a requirement for credibility in dealing with institutional investors whose investment decisions are regulated and subject to great scrutiny. Perhaps one of the most misunderstood aspects of being a professional venture capitalist is the amount of time and energy devoted to raising money rather than investing it in new ventures. Of course, with a track record of previous success and with solid concept and structure for the new fund, the process will be easier. Nonetheless, there will always be market fluctuations that can bring failure to even the most careful and deliberate fundraising efforts.

As an entrepreneur dealing with a professional venture capitalist, it is important to remember the entire process in which the venture capitalist makes a living. The appeal of your venture, and the timing of your success and exit for the investors, are important in developing a successful venture portfolio that will become the basis for soliciting future funds. This is one reason that VCs tend to stick to investing in areas where they have expertise and previous success. It's all part of the job of establishing a solid reputation for successful venture investing and subsequent fundraising.

CONCEPT CHECK

- What is the largest source of funds for professional venture capitalists?
- List five different types of investors in venture capital funds.

11.6   OBTAINING COMMITMENTS FOR A SERIES OF CAPITAL CALLS

As we mentioned in earlier chapters, it is common to stage the investments in a new venture. Consequently, the total size of a fund is not necessarily achieved at its inception. For the fund described in Figure 11.3, the **capital call** policy was summarized as follows:

> *Installments paid within thirty days of call notice; each call of no more than 20 percent of total committed capital; expect all calls in first four years.*

It is common for a fund to stage its own capital infusion in this manner. Typically, the fund will allocate a certain amount of the total to initial investments in the venture and reserve some for the venture's future funding needs.

capital call
when the venture fund calls upon the investors to deliver their investment funds

---

[13] An interesting review of the history of venture fundraising is given in Paul Gompers and Josh Lerner, *What Drives Venture Capital Fundraising?* (Cambridge, MA: National Bureau of Economic Research, 1999).

When an investor has decided to invest in a venture capital fund, an agreement will be signed stipulating initial and subsequent investments consistent with the level of the investor's contribution. Once the fund has reached its minimum, the fund's (partnership) legal structure can be completed, initial capital calls can be made, and there is money to invest. The venture capitalist's focus can then change to placing the money in deserving new ventures.

CONCEPT CHECK

- What is a capital call?
- What is the purpose of staging in venture capital fundraising?

11.7 CONDUCTING DUE DILIGENCE AND ACTIVELY INVESTING

It always helps to understand the structure and motivations of a potential investor, particularly one who is a professional venture capitalist. Now that we have a basic understanding of the fundraising side of professional venture capital, we will consider the aspect of professional venture capital most relevant to the entrepreneur: determining the ventures in which to invest.

deal flow
flow of business plans and term sheets involved in the venture capital investing process

It is important to remember that venture capitalists are almost constantly on the lookout for new technologies and worthy ventures, even when they are in the process of raising funds. The **deal flow** is necessary to their existence; it is in their best interest to foster the environments and processes that give rise to new and rapidly growing ventures. Throughout the history of professional venture capital, it has been common for venture capital firms to develop and maintain relationships with research universities. For example, Doriot's ARD was closely affiliated with MIT and Harvard. Today, all of the major venture investing regions are in proximity to prominent research universities (e.g., Stanford University, University of California at Berkeley, Harvard University, Massachusetts Institute of Technology, University of Minnesota, University of North Carolina, Duke University, University of Colorado, University of Washington, and University of Texas). Research universities provide a fertile environment for the formulation, testing, and commercialization of new technologies.

Although new technology investment is not the only target for venture investing, it is the main driver. Many of these research universities have centers for entrepreneurship, incubators for new ventures, technology transfer offices for licensing university-owned technologies, and faculty and students eager to develop and commercially profit from new technologies. It is common for venture capitalists to take active roles in supporting the entrepreneurially inclined members of the university community. This is a classic example of a mutually beneficial arrangement. However, it would not be accurate to say that, historically, most venture capitalists have actively entered universities looking for new technologies to commercialize.[14] The relationship usually has been more indirect. Venture investing in the Internet Age appears to have greatly increased the number of ventures sprouting from formerly university-affiliated entrepreneurs. It is now common for venture capitalists to become involved with university business plan competitions (acting as sponsors and judges) and with mentoring and internship programs for entrepreneurially inclined students.[15]

CONCEPT CHECK

- Why is it reasonable to expect that research universities may attract venture capital firms to their geographic areas?

Even though contributing to, and fostering, the environments from which new business concepts and plans emerge is a central part of the venture capital process, it is not as widely studied or understood as the screening, gatekeeping, and monitoring processes for which VCs are known and frequently vilified. Once the business plan pump has been primed and plans are flowing, the VCs must select those plans worthy of further consideration, investigate the suitability of investing in the worthy candidates, and (politely) redirect or dispose of less worthy concepts and plans. The process of investigating a potentially worthy concept or plan is known as conducting **due diligence**.

The well-primed business plan pump can produce an overwhelming number of business proposals. Remembering that there are only twenty-four hours in a day and that occasional sleep is required makes one slightly more sympathetic to the incredible task we ask venture capitalists to conduct throughout the year. It is not uncommon for even small (three to four partners) venture firms to review more than a thousand business plans a year. The process is "noisy"; entrepreneurs are fortunate to have the freedom to discuss their business plans with several venture capital firms to get more than one shot at venture funding and, in the process, to get a more reliable signal of the venture's merits.

For those of us who are active observers of the venture investing industry, it is always interesting to watch VCs assess a given venture's prospects differently and, in rare cases, on opposite ends of the feasibility spectrum. As we examine some of the documented characteristics of venture capitalist screening processes, remember that no two VCs (even in the same firm) are identical. The diversity of

due diligence (in venture investing context)
process of ascertaining the viability of a business plan

---

[14] An interesting example of a venture firm that concentrates on commercializing "ivory tower technologies" is ARCH Venture Partners. A *Fortune* magazine article ("Extreme Venture Capital," October 26, 1998) discussed ARCH's strategy and provided several other examples of fruitful university entrepreneurial endeavors. In a contrary tone, however, the article stated, "Most venture capitalists regard such places as byzantine backwaters populated by fractious eggheads." To its credit, the article does point out that the propensity of venture capitalists to locate close to universities may not be due to any desire to redirect academics into business. After all, academics are not necessarily gifted in, or inclined to, running emerging commercial ventures. Nonetheless, universities do contribute significant new technologies that they are not particularly adept at commercializing.

[15] See, for example, Robert Strauss, "Class Action," in "Going Public 2000 Supplement," *Red Herring*, October 2000.

opinion in the venture investing community is part of the reason that this critical element of our capitalist economy works so well. With that said, it is still helpful to discuss some of the regularities you can expect to encounter in dealing with venture capitalists considering your business plan.

A venture capitalist may participate in funding and assisting a venture in a variety of different ways. The screening process must not only identify successful candidates for funding, but must also determine the extent of the venture firm's financial, managerial, and executive involvement in the governance and day-to-day venture activities. In boom times, when entrepreneurs hold some bargaining power in the venture funding negotiations, it is frequently the extent and quality of the nonfinancial contributions that determine which venture capital firm's money will be taken. Of course, in normal times, when entrepreneurs have less bargaining power, there may not be much freedom to negotiate the nonfinancial contributions. Nonetheless, the initial due diligence process significantly affects the venture capital firm's expectations regarding financial and nonfinancial contributions to the venture. These expectations will be an important component (probably the most important component) of the VC's position when negotiating any actual financing.

The initial VC screening focuses on the basic characteristics that make a venture attractive to venture investors. Many VCs specialize in industries where they have significant managerial and financial expertise. Consequently, it is not difficult for VCs to provide a quick initial "laugh test" on the basic market being addressed by the venture, the feasibility of the venture's business concept, and the potential financial rewards offered in the venture's general market and those specifically offered by the venture seeking funding. Owing to their current and former affiliations with the industries in which they invest, relevant external expertise is readily accessible when required. VCs can quickly render praise or condemnation for your new venture's business plan; they are in the business of making quick decisions, many of which will be justified, others that they will regret.

What do VCs look for in a venture seeking funding from them? This question has received considerable scrutiny in the academic literature on venture capital. Most of the insight we have into what venture capitalists look for is based on surveys where VCs are asked what they look for. Of course, such methods are subject to the criticism that what VCs say, and what they actually do, may be quite different (and VCs may not even realize it).

Early academic research on VC decision making emphasized the possible venture characteristics that are critical to the funding decision.[16] It has always been clear that the two primary venture characteristics that matter most are the entrepreneurial team and the market. Many VCs believe that a management team can be replaced and that a strong market is very forgiving. Such VCs claim their decisions are heavily influenced by their perceptions of the quality of the

---

[16] Summaries of the early literature are available in Hernan Riquelme and Tudor Rickards, "Hybrid Conjoint Analysis: An Estimation Probe in New Venture Decisions," and John Hall and Charles Hofer, "Venture Capitalists' Decision Criteria in New Venture Evaluation," *Journal of Business Venturing* 7 (1992) and 8 (1993), respectively. Silvia Sagari and Gabriela Guidotti also provide an overview of U.S. venture investing and relevant academic research, including VC criteria, in "Venture Capital: The Lessons from the Developed World for Developing Markets," *Financial Markets, Institutions and Instruments* 1, no. 2 (1992).

market the venture seeks to create or address. It probably would be fair, however, to say that more VCs would reason that a good entrepreneurial team will adapt and modify in order to penetrate or redefine a market and that without such a team the venture is a lost cause even if it addresses a strong market.

In a useful summary, John Hall and Charles Hofer compared the criteria considered in five different academic studies of VC decision making.[17] Figure 11.5 presents their classification scheme. More recent research has applied a variety of interesting methods to get a better picture of what goes on in a VC's mind when she evaluates the prospects of a new venture. It is a mysterious process but not completely veiled to the entrepreneur, thanks to some interesting research that considered actual comments made during recorded VC review sessions. In an examination of the relevance of the characteristics suggested in the survey literature, Hall and Hofer classified actual evaluative remarks made by VCs while screening business plans for possible investment.[18] Their findings suggest that the initial screening lasts, on average, about six minutes. Such a short review results in a large number of rejections for a variety of reasons, ranging from the shallow (not in the VC's investment area) to the relatively deep (consumer product, not proprietary, no management team, organization of company, unrealistic numbers). Interestingly, two proposals considered by Hall and Hofer's VCs were rejected due to the absence of financial information. They suggest that financial information in a business plan is an important signal of competence or effort but need not be an important basis for forming the VC's view of the venture's future. The rejection comments Hall and Hofer observed were typically based on inadequacies in the management team or the venture's target market, with several comments addressing inadequacies in the venture's approach to the market. Their summary remarks are:

> *Based on the observations made by the venture capitalists in the protocols, an idea for a product or service—no matter how brilliant—must be presented in a professional package. The plan also should be simple, including all relevant information while keeping extraneous information to a minimum. Despite the number of books and articles written as aids in preparing a business proposal, a well-written plan was no guarantor of success. However, a professionally presented proposal appeared to be a necessary but insufficient criterion for acceptance. The thrust of the protocol comments was that venture proposals should be short documents that provide the major pieces of information the venture capitalist needs to make a decision. This information includes an overview of the proposed business, the amount of funding requested, the use of these funds, a brief listing of the management of the proposed business, and a summary of both current financial information and financial projections.*

In the spirit of the old adage "The exception proves the rule," we note that during the last part of 1999 and the first quarter of 2000 there was at least one VC who stated that, if an Internet or e-commerce venture had taken the time to

---

[17] See Hall and Hofer, "Venture Capitalists' Decision Criteria in New Venture Evaluation."

[18] Ibid.

FIGURE 11.5   VC Screening Criteria

1. **Venture Capital Firm Requirements**
   a. Cash-out potential
   b. Equity share
   c. Familiarity with technology, product, market
   d. Financial provisions for investors
   e. Geographic location
   f. Investor control
   g. Investor group
   h. Rate of return
   i. Risk
   j. Size of investment
   k. Stage of development

2. **Characteristics of the Proposal**
   a. Requirement for additional material
   b. Stage of plan

3. **Characteristics of the Entrepreneur/Team**
   a. Ability to evaluate risk
   b. Articulate regarding the venture
   c. Background/experience
   d. Capable of sustained effort
   e. Managerial capabilities
   f. Management commitment
   g. References
   h. Stake in firm

4. **Nature of the Proposed Industry**
   a. Market attractiveness
   b. Potential size
   c. Technology
   d. Threat resistance

5. **Strategy of the Proposed Business**
   a. Product differentiation
   b. Proprietary product

write a business plan, then it was not the type of firm that would attract his funds. That was a heated time in the venture investing market, when a company could go from startup to publicly traded firm in less than a year. The longer run shows that a properly prepared business proposal or plan is a significant aid in attracting venture capital.

In a decidedly different approach to examining VC preferences in choosing ventures, we can look at a sample of firms that succeeded and failed to see if there are any systematic differences that appear correlated to success or failure in venture screening. Ronald Hustedde and Glen Pulver, in a study of 318 entrepreneurs who sought equity funding of at least $100,000 in 1987, provided evidence that entrepreneur characteristics correlated with success in receiving funding.[19] Of their responding sample, 59 percent received funding; perhaps more important, 41 percent of their sample did not. Although their study considered funding from angels and VCs alike, some of their conclusions are of interest to those seeking professional VC. Hustedde and Pulver argued that their data indicate that the most important elements of success in attracting financing were the willingness to give up a large share of the equity and the determination to look for funding in a variety of places. They also suggested, contrary to accepted wisdom, that in their sample of Wisconsin and Minnesota entrepreneurs, age and experience were not positive factors. Consistent with the diatribes of business school professors, they found that a written business plan increased the probability of receiving funding.

CONCEPT CHECK

- What is due diligence in venture investing?
- List the main aspects of a business plan in terms of how they appeal to venture capitalists.
- What is the role of financial statements in a written business plan?

Assuming your market and entrepreneurial team pass the initial six-minute screen, the venture capital firm will then move toward the more lengthy due diligence process. During this process, the VC firm will determine the roles it will play in the financing round and in the venture's governance and management. As an example of the decisions it must make, the VC firm might consider the following four outcomes of the screening process:

1. Seek the **lead investor** position: Organize the due diligence process; determine conditions of investment (financial, managerial, necessary changes); locate other interested VCs; conclude negotiations; disburse funds from initial and subsequent capital calls; help raise new financing when required; actively participate in governance and possibly management or operations; organize the financial harvest when the venture is ripe for an exit.

2. Seek a nonlead investor position: Refer low-fit desirable ventures to better-fit firms/funds—participate financially in syndicated deal organized by other firm; delegate monitoring and any governance or managerial participation to the lead investor.

lead investor
venture investor taking the lead for a group (syndicate) of other venture investors

---

[19] See "Factors Affecting Equity Capital Acquisition: The Demand Side," *Journal of Business Venturing* (1992).

3. Refer the venture to more appropriate financial market participants (e.g., angels or banks) or to other preparatory services (e.g., incubators or small business consultants).

SLOR
standard letter of rejection, or used as a verb to indicate the sending of such a letter

4. **SLOR** (standard letter of rejection) the venture; field questions from inquiring entrepreneurs.

In outcomes 1 and 2, the venture investing process will enter the negotiation phase where, if there are no fatal hitches along the way, the investment will be structured with a basic understanding of how the venture capitalist will be involved in the venture's governance and administration. Earlier in this text, we dealt with issues of valuation and financial structure. Here we concentrate on the VC's nonfinancial involvement.

While the professional venture capital investing cycle we have presented gives a good idea of the activities involved in being a venture capitalist, we have not discussed how a VC's time is allocated across the activities. Although VC attention and input vary widely by the stage and size of the funding, there is some evidence that a majority of a VC's time is spent monitoring and contributing to the ventures in the VC's portfolio. One industry observer has suggested that a venture capitalist's time is allocated as follows: about 20 percent to solicitation and selection of ventures, 5 percent to negotiations, 70 percent to monitoring and adding value to the venture portfolio, and 5 percent to implementing the exit strategy.[20]

One of the most common ways for the venture capitalist to contribute to the venture is by sitting on its board of directors. Some have described the typical arrangement as one that leaves day-to-day control with the entrepreneurial team while vesting overall governance with the board of directors. Depending on the size of the investment, the venture capital investors may actually control the majority of the voting stock and, therefore, exercise veto power over the entrepreneurial team. Nonetheless, it would be inaccurate and unfair to suggest that a venture capitalist's main goal is to control the venture. Day-to-day control is not necessarily a venture capitalist's comparative advantage, although his continuation in the venture investing cycle certainly depends on the financial returns produced by successful ventures. A VC's overriding concern will almost always be the creation of value and its ultimate realization in an exit event.

According to Joseph Rosenstein and his co-researchers, the typical venture board of directors grows by almost two members when venture capital investors fund a venture.[21] Interestingly, in their overall sample, the venture CEOs did not value the venture capitalists' advice any more highly than that of other board members.[22]

In addition to joining the venture's board, venture capitalists may take more invasive roles. VCs frequently become directly involved in attracting talent for the management team (e.g., by recruiting a CEO to take the venture to the

---

[20]   See Bob Zider, "How Venture Capital Works," *Harvard Business Review* (November–December 1998).

[21]   See Joseph Rosenstein, Albert Bruno, William Bygrave, and Natalie Taylor, "The CEO, Venture Capitalists, and the Board," *Journal of Business Venturing* 8 (1993).

[22]   There was, however, some indication that the advice of top-twenty venture capital firms was more valuable than that of other board members.

proverbial "next level"). VCs also have been known to work directly in the venture in roles where they have significant expertise. Although this direct rendering of services is not common, it can be critical to venture survival during transition periods when external expertise has not yet been retained.

Professional venture investors have a vested interest in fostering the growth and success of their portfolio companies; entrepreneurs should always keep this in mind. As an example, a VC guest speaker in one of our classes emphasized to students how the profit motive can create significant tension in dealing with a historically successful entrepreneur who, later in life, has become less profit oriented. For a venture in this VC's portfolio, the tension eventually resulted in a meeting between the entrepreneur and the venture investors to remind the entrepreneur that venture investors want returns for investors. Of course, the entrepreneur would eventually be free to donate all of his exit proceeds to charity if he pleased. Until then, the VCs informed him, the venture must seek increases in tangible financial value rather than intangible spiritual value. Ultimately, the venture investors sidelined the entrepreneur in a consulting arrangement and hired a new CEO. It is relatively uncommon for an entrepreneur to remain CEO all the way to venture maturity.[23]

The purpose of VC screening and due diligence is to determine a venture's viability and the potential gain from venture capital investment and venture capitalist involvement. With these findings, the VC and the venture team are ready to negotiate an investment and its structure and covenants. Chapters 9 and 10 discussed venture valuation methods and the structure of venture capital investments in detail. The venture capitalist will propose a set of terms in a **term sheet** upon which the investment will take place. Figure 11.6 lists typical issues addressed in a term sheet. The National Venture Capital Association provides examples of several legal documents related to venture financing. These "model" documents are available at http://www.nvca.org/model_documents/model_docs .html. The terms will specify the amount of the investment (across all investors in that round); the amount of shares (usually convertible preferred equity); and the voting, registration, and control rights of those shares. In some cases, the terms will include vesting clauses on the entrepreneurial team's equity holdings, incentive options, performance clauses, and indications of future financing availability. In any case, in order for the fund transfer to take place, the VCs and the venture must come to some set of mutually agreed-upon terms. Both should have competent legal counsel specializing in securities law.

Upon agreement on terms, the investment takes place. The venture gets its financing and goes to work on implementing its business plan. The VC firm begins its monitoring and assistance functions. Everyone starts looking at the calendar, wondering how long the money will really last and from where the next infusion will come.

term sheet
summary of the investment terms and conditions accompanying an investment

---

[23] Garry Burton, Vance Fried, and Robert Hisrich, in a study of CEO dismissals in VC-backed ventures, found that strategic rather than operational concerns were the more common cause of CEO dismissal. They also found that CEO dismissal had, on average, a positive effect on the venture's performance. See "Venture Capitalist and CEO Dismissal," *Entrepreneurship Theory and Practice* (Spring 1997).

FIGURE 11.6   Typical Issues Addressed in a Term Sheet

- Valuation
- Ongoing funding needs
- Size and staging of financing
- Preemptive rights on new issues
- Commitments for future financing rounds and performance conditions
- Form of security or investment
- Redemption rights and responsibilities
- Dividend structure
- Board structure (number of VCs and outsiders)
- Additional management
- Conversion value protection
- Registration rights
- Exit conditions and strategy
- IPO-dictated events (e.g., conversion)
- Cosale rights (with founders)
- Lockup provision
- Employment contracts
- Incentive options
- Founder employment conditions: compensation, benefits, duties, firing conditions, repurchase of stock on termination, term of agreement, postemployment activities, and competition
- Founder stock vesting
- Confidentiality agreements and protection of intellectual property

---

CONCEPT CHECK

- What are the different roles a venture capitalist can play in participating in a financing round for your venture?
- What is likely to happen to your board of directors when you accept venture capital financing?
- On average, approximately what percentage of a venture capitalist's time is allocated to monitoring and managing the firms in the VC's portfolio?
- What types of venture activities are more likely to involve VC participation?

11.8   ARRANGING HARVEST OR LIQUIDATION

For ventures that never make it, the venture investing process isn't over when the venture ceases operations. When there are patents or other intellectual property, some attempt to sell these assets will take place; any proceeds will be distributed to the investors and other claimants based on their priority. This is one of the reasons venture investors typically buy "preferred" equity. They will claim liquidation proceeds before the entrepreneur. A liquidation wind-down is not the expected outcome. The entrepreneur and venture investors tend to think about more lucrative exit possibilities: selling the venture's equity to the public in an initial public offering or selling the venture to another firm capable of capitalizing on the venture's success by taking it to the "next level." Such events (treated in detail in Chapter 14) mark the beginning of the end of the venture investment stage of the venture's life cycle. It is the beginning of the end (and not the end) due to restrictions on selling the privately placed stock, even when the venture goes public or sells itself. Such restrictions (imposed by securities laws, investment banks, or acquirers) are intended to keep the venture-stage investors engaged for a time and to keep their large equity holdings from flooding the market for the venture's or the acquirer's public equity.

The venture capital firm takes a great interest in making sure the exit event is timely (when possible) and lucrative. Even in a rapid acquisition, there is still much to do, and the VCs can help prepare the venture for assimilation. When the deal is done, the VCs will exercise any options they benefit from exercising and will convert their equity if required. While these details are not particularly burdensome, and are familiar to the VC from previous harvests, they are still an integral part of the winding down of the venture investment.

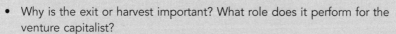

- Why is the exit or harvest important? What role does it perform for the venture capitalist?
- What are the most common exit strategies?

11.9 DISTRIBUTING CASH AND SECURITIES PROCEEDS

Once the venture capital firm has received exit proceeds from a venture in the form of cash or securities, some method of returning the proceeds (less the carried interest) must be determined. In many cases, the deciding factors will be the tax and liquidity implications. When the venture firm distributes its securities proceeds directly to its investors, they gain tax timing (deferred taxation) advantages. In addition, by distributing securities they also limit the impact that would occur if they sold the securities and then distributed the cash. Consequently, the distribution of securities is common.

When a venture fund's last investment reaches the exit event and the proceeds have all been distributed, the firm carefully calculates the return achieved for investors over the entire life of the fund. For high returns, there is little doubt that the performance will be a centerpiece in marketing the firm's next fund. For low returns, there is a liability going forward in construction and marketing of any new fund. Venture capitalists, however, are typically very fond of their particular role in funding, supporting, and profiting from emerging ventures; they will, in most cases, make any adjustments in strategy, organization, or marketing necessary to launch the next fund. Thus, the professional venture investing cycle continues.

SUMMARY

Venture capitalists are professional financial intermediaries. They raise money from investors in their funds, and they use the proceeds to fund a portfolio of ventures. Entrepreneurs' ventures are the ultimate recipients of these funds; they are expected to provide financial returns to the venture capital fund that are, in turn, distributed to the fund's investors. Venture capitalists must allocate their time between raising money, finding worthy ventures in which to invest, helping to create value in their invested ventures, and assisting in achieving eventual liquidity through an exit event such as an IPO or acquisition.

Because of the overwhelming volume of business plans reviewed each year, the venture screening process is quick and decisive. After an initial screening and a modest additional review, VCs typically engage in a due diligence process on surviving business plans to determine the terms they will offer for financing, and the role (if any) they will play in the venture's governance and management. Ultimately, some ventures in their portfolios will fail, some will succeed, and some will just get by. The venture capitalists will assist surviving ventures in achieving liquidity for the venture investors and founders in an exit event.

KEY TERMS

capital call
carried interest
deal flow

due diligence (in venture
    investing context)
lead investor

SLOR
term sheet
two and twenty shops

DISCUSSION QUESTIONS

1. What is a professional venture capitalist? How does this occupation differ from that of an angel investor?

2. Briefly describe how professional venture capital got started after World War II.

3. What was the early role of the Small Business Administration (SBA) in fostering venture investing?

4. Describe the development of professional venture investing in the 1960s, 1970s, and early 1980s.

5. What has happened to professional venture investing since the mid-1990s?

6. What are the components or stages in the professional venture investing cycle from inception to funding?

7. What are the components or stages in the professional venture investing cycle after funds have been raised until closure?

8. Who are the major suppliers of venture capital by type and size of commitment?

9. What is meant by the terms (a) "capital call," (b) "deal flow," and (c) "due diligence"?

10. What is meant by the terms (a) "lead investor," (b) "SLOR," and (c) "term sheet"?

11. Why should entrepreneurs care what pressures venture capitalists face in carrying out their professional money management (intermediation) function?

12. Why do venture capitalists make quick decisions on the infeasibility of some business plans? When a business plan is not quickly determined to be infeasible, what happens next and why?

13. What should be the goal of the financial projections in a business plan submitted to a venture capitalist?

14. Is the compensation paid to venture capitalists (e.g., 2 percent management fee and 20 percent carried interest) reasonable? What are a fund's investors buying with this compensation?

15. Why are venture capital funds typically organized as limited partnerships? In particular, why are they private firms instead of public firms?

16. What can be learned from the SBA's creation and the IRS's subsidy of venture investing through SBICs?

INTERNET ACTIVITIES

1. Summarize nationwide venture capital investing by industry for the last available quarter using a data source available on Web sites such as http://www.pwcmoneytree.com or http://www.nvca.org.

2. Visit a venture capital fund's Web site and summarize the fund's history and current activities.

EXERCISES/PROBLEMS

1. List three venture capital firms active in your region and describe their investing style and restrictions.

2. Locate a recent study covering venture capital fundraising (not investing) for the previous year. Determine what the current sources of funds tend to be.

3. Interview a local venture capitalist regarding what she looks for in a promising venture seeking funding. Summarize your discussion.

4. Determine the three largest venture capital firms in the United States. How much money do they have under management? In what areas, if any, do they specialize? Where are they located? Where are their branch offices?

5. Suppose you become an intern at a local VC firm and are asked to assist in due diligence on a proposed investment in a telecommunications company. Explain how you would approach such a task and where and how you would structure your investigation. What data sources would you use?

6. List ten terms you might find in a venture capital fund's term sheet (see Figure 11.3). Explain what they are and why it might make sense to structure them the way they are.

7. Find a recent *Wall Street Journal* article on venture investing and summarize it.

8. Update Figure 11.1 in terms of recent levels of VC investment.

9. List ten Web sites or hard-copy magazines that contain venture capital investing information that might be of use to entrepreneurs seeking venture capital.

10. Locate a venture capital–backed firm that recently completed an initial public offering (IPO). Provide a summary of the venture's history and success through the IPO and to date.

MINI CASE

Interact Systems, Inc.

Interact Systems, Inc., has developed software tools that help hotel chains solve application integration problems. Interact's application integration server (AIS) provides a two-way interface between central reservations systems (CRS) and property management systems (PMS). At least two important trends in the hotel industry are relevant. First, hotels are shifting away from the manual booking of room reservations; electronic bookings will continue to increase as more bookings are made over the Internet. Second, competitive pressures are forcing hotels to implement yield management programs and to increase customer service. By integrating the CRS and PMS through Interact's AIS, the company can better manage inventories, improve yields, and enhance customer service.

All reservation traffic is routed from the CRS to individual hotel properties. This allows Interact Systems to create a database that can be used to track customers and to facilitate marketing programs, such as frequent-stay or VIP programs, as a way of increasing customer satisfaction. Interact forecasts application integration expenditures in the hospitality industry to exceed $1 billion by 2009.

Greg Thomas founded Interact Systems in 2003 and developed the firm's middleware software and hospitality applications. He has twelve years of systems applications experience and currently is Interact's chief technology officer. Eric Westskow joined Interact in early 2006 as president and CEO. He had worked in sales and marketing in the software industry for more than twenty years.

Interact Systems' AIS software development, which began in 2003, went through several design changes in 2004. The first product was sold and installed in 2005. Sales were only $500,000 in 2006. However, now that the firm has dependable market-tested AIS products ready to be shipped, revenues are expected to reach $20.8 million in 2009.

Greg Thomas founded Interact Systems with $50,000 of his own savings plus $50,000 from friends. Two private investors provided an additional $200,000 in 2004. In addition, $1 million was obtained from a venture capital firm, Katile Capital Partners, in early 2006 in exchange for an equity position in Interact. The firm currently is seeking an additional $5 million to finance sales growth.

A. A VC is considering providing the additional $5 million. What type of fund (stage specialization, industry focus, etc.) would you approach? In what part of their investing cycle would you hope to approach them?

B. Discuss how Interact Systems would expect to fare in the VC screening process involving each element of Figure 11.5.

C. Discuss typical issues that might be addressed in a term sheet using Figure 11.6 as a reference.

Chapter 12

OTHER FINANCING ALTERNATIVES

PREVIOUSLY COVERED

Chapter 11 discussed professionally managed venture capital. We presented a brief history of the industry with its ups and downs and its sources and uses of funds. An important aspect of professional venture investing is the process of finding relevant venture capitalists and preparing for the screening processes they use in determining the basis upon which they will invest in a venture. We discussed the six-minute screening and the implications it has for the proper preparation and presentation of a business plan.

LOOKING AHEAD

Chapter 13 discusses important concepts in structuring a venture's securities. We provide an introduction to primitive securities (e.g., bonds and common stocks) and derivative securities (e.g., warrants and convertible preferred). We introduce the enterprise valuation method, an easier technique to apply when the venture uses complex financing. These materials will pave the way for discussing the methods available for harvesting a successful venture.

CHAPTER LEARNING OBJECTIVES

In this chapter, we consider a variety of government and private sources of new venture funding. We also consider financing traditionally available only to more mature ventures, including commercial banking loans. After completing this chapter, you will be able to:

1. Identify relevant sources of debt-oriented financing

2. Discuss government loan guarantee and microcredit programs

3. Identify several potential sources of funding for minority-owned enterprises

4. Explain what differentiates venture lending and leasing from traditional lending and leasing

5. Describe factor financing and compare it to receivables financing through a bank

As you may have discovered from our coverage of topics up to this point, we are serious advocates of the use of equity financing in emerging ventures. Professional venture capitalists and business angels almost always invest in equity. There are good reasons for this. High-growth ventures seldom wish to deal with the pressures and monitoring costs of debt instruments. Equity financing is a more natural fit. Fast-growing ventures don't really want to pay the regular interest costs of debt and are not particularly fond of the legal downsides should they miss a payment or default in some other way. For many entrepreneurs, debt imposes constraints that they would rather avoid.

On the other hand, most entrepreneurs don't like the ownership dilution that accompanies equity financing. They will have a natural tendency to seek out debt financing for its fixed upside, if at all possible. That is, (nonconvertible) debt gets only principal and interest when the venture lands in utopia. More of utopia belongs to the entrepreneurs. Convertible and equity financing grants a part (and sometimes most) of the upside to the investors, leaving substantially less for the entrepreneur. We know that debt usually has a lower expected return and is tax preferred in most cases. So, if you're willing to tolerate the rather noncooperative approach involved in debt financing, and you succeed in finding some, you can expect to retain greater control of the venture.

While we will begin our discussion with some general remarks on using financial intermediaries and consultants other than venture capitalists and angels to get to equity and debt financing, our focus in this chapter is on special financing opportunities more commonly associated with debt. Included among these opportunities are venture(some) lending, commercial bank loans, SBA program loans, minority loans, receivables factoring, mortgages, traditional leasing, and venture leasing.

12.1   FACILITATORS, CONSULTANTS, AND INTERMEDIARIES

While there are some intermediaries in the financial market who will help locate other people willing to invest money in your venture's equity (or debt), you should take great care in dealing with them. In particular, there are many operators who will, for an up-front fee, put your business plan before allegedly interested investors (at home and abroad). We implore you to consider the structure of such arrangements before paying any up-front fee. A small amount of simple reasoning will help.

Successful consulting or finance facilitation boutiques have ready investors and can absorb the risk of the time they spend placing your business plan in front of those investors. Accordingly, such boutiques will be more likely to take a contingency fee that pays them upon completion of the financing, and nothing otherwise. This is similar to the way almost all real estate agents and brokers, and many litigation attorneys, conduct business. They don't get paid until they produce.

For whatever reason, up-front fee solicitors for financing still survive. Many desperate entrepreneurs, disillusioned by the length of time it takes to raise new financing, have turned to these facilitators—only to find their up-front fees, sometimes in the $10,000 to $50,000 range, completely fruitless and responsible for an even earlier demise. The CBS television program *60 Minutes*, among others, has covered finance solicitation scams, perpetrated in some cases by relatively well known people. While there are ventures that shelled out up-front fees for such services and ended up with financing that would have been difficult or impossible to attract on their own, it is hard to determine in advance if the up-front fee is justified. Of course, it's safer just to negotiate a contingency that provides the intermediary with the appropriate amount (even more than the fixed fee) of incentive compensation upon completion of the financing. If you decide to engage an adviser or intermediary to assist in solicitation financing for your venture, make sure you understand the terms. Contact previous clients for references.

CONCEPT CHECK

- What is meant by up-front fee solicitors?

12.2 COMMERCIAL AND VENTURE BANK LENDING

One of the more common misunderstandings between new entrepreneurs and the financial services community is the role of commercial lending. Traditional bank commercial lending officers are trained to study the creditworthiness (see Figure 12.1) of businesses, using traditional conservative measures of the borrower's ability to pay and the value of any assets that may be recovered in the case of default. The recoverable assets are usually referred to as collateral. While commercial loan officers strongly prefer that a business pay off the interest and principal on a commercial loan, they also like the security of being able to attempt to recover some of their investment by seizing assets when the business defaults. Of course, the security that such assets offer will depend on the difficulty in seizing them and the ease and profit in reselling them. The bank has little or no use for the assets themselves. Needless to say, the collateral's value to the commercial lender is almost always less than its value to the business. Consequently, this type of secured lending will seldom be for 100 percent of the current value of the underlying collateral.

Although collateral value plays a significant role in determining the willingness to lend and the amount and terms of the loan, it is not the most important factor. A firm's ability to generate the cash flow necessary to pay the interest and principal due to the bank is the primary criterion. Commercial loan officers are very comfortable projecting your venture's performance into the future to see if

FIGURE 12.1   The Five Cs of Credit Analysis

Capacity to repay is the most critical of the five factors. The prospective lender will want to know exactly how you intend to repay the loan. The lender will consider the cash flow from the business, the timing of the repayment, and the probability of successful repayment of the loan. Payment history on existing credit relationships—personal or commercial—is considered an indicator of future payment performance. Prospective lenders also will want to know about your contingent sources of repayment.

Capital is the money you personally have invested in the business and is an indication of how much you have at risk should the business fail. Prospective lenders and investors will expect you to have contributed from your own assets, and to have undertaken personal financial risk to establish the business, before asking them to commit any funding.

Collateral, or guarantees, are additional forms of security you can provide the lender. Giving a lender collateral means that you pledge an asset you own, such as your home, to the lender with the agreement that it will be the repayment source in case you can't repay the loan. A guarantee, on the other hand, is just that—someone else signs a guarantee document promising to repay the loan if you can't. Some lenders may require such a guarantee in addition to collateral as security for a loan.

Conditions focus on the intended purpose of the loan. Will the money be used for working capital, additional equipment, or inventory? The lender also will consider the local economic climate and conditions both within your industry and in other industries that could affect your business.

Character is the general impression you make on the potential lender or investor. The lender will form a subjective opinion on whether or not you are sufficiently trustworthy to repay the loan or generate a return on funds invested in your company. Your educational background and experience in business and in your industry will be reviewed. The quality of your references and the background and experience levels of your employees also will be taken into consideration.

Source: Tracy L. Penwell, *The Credit Process: A Guide for Small Business Owners* (New York: Federal Reserve Bank of New York).

---

you can service their debt—on one condition. That condition is that you give them a couple of years of operating history on which to base their projections. With reasonable assumptions, they can move forward, size the loan and its terms, and provide a reasonable debt facility to accommodate the venture's future.

Unfortunately for entrepreneurs in new ventures, commercial loan officers are not particularly well adapted, nor inclined to produce the kind of wild conjectures necessary, to project a new venture into completely uncharted territory. Government regulatory bodies, including the Federal Reserve, the Comptroller of the Currency, and the Federal Depository Insurance Corporation (FDIC), also are not particularly fond of speculative lending and can impose harsh discipline on banks with large portfolios of nonperforming loans. In the preceding chapters, we emphasized the type of investors (professional venture capitalists and angels) that have the temperament, inclination, and skills to put a value on completely uncertain market innovations. Such investors are accustomed to enduring long periods of time when a venture's health is not clear and no return of principal or interest is achieved. Venture investors are compensated for their willingness and inclination with large exit returns. Commercial loan officers are compensated on how well their loan portfolios are currently performing and tend to place restrictive covenants in their debt agreements (see Figure 12.2). The two worlds could be no farther apart (in the finance universe). Don't go to a commercial lending officer expecting her to think, project, or act like a venture investor. It is an irrational expectation. The whole commercial lending system is set up to screen out risk takers. (This does not mean that there are not a few venturesome bankers who somehow slip through the screen.)

Frequently, within a region there will be a bank that has established a reputation for taking extraordinary risks. For example, there may be a commercial loan officer who extended a modest line of credit to an entrepreneur starting a new venture with only a résumé in hand. In all likelihood, that loan will be personally guaranteed, and the résumé will indicate prior success in the same industry. There won't be a new product without an existing prototype, and, chances are, there won't be a great deal of development work necessary to generate initial revenues. While banks that set up this type of reputation are generally highly regarded in the entrepreneurial community, they are still considered commercial banks and are not expected to bear significant responsibility in the funding of new ventures. It is not always pointless to talk to a banker, particularly when the banker is connected to the venture investing community. A commercial loan officer may not be willing to extend terms but may know how to contact local venture investors more suited to the job or may provide an introduction to a principal in an associated venture investing subsidiary.

In contrast to commercial banks, venture banks are hard to think of as banks at all. Banks like Silicon Valley Bank (http://www.svb.com) and Lighthouse Capital Partners (http://www.lcpartners.com) have developed reputations for lending to emerging ventures and are distinct in character and operation from traditional commercial banks. Venture banks typically provide debt facilities to ventures that have already received professional venture capital funding in the form of equity. While these debt facilities will carry interest and principal obligations (along with other covenants), these traditional debt obligations represent only a portion (sometimes small) of the venture lender's expected return. Warrants (the right to buy equity at a specific price) typically provide the remainder

---

FIGURE 12.2 Common Loan Restrictions

- Maintenance of accurate records and financial statements
- Limits on total debt
- Restrictions on dividends or other payments to owners and/or investors
- Restrictions on additional capital expenditures
- Restrictions on sale of fixed assets
- Performance standards on financial ratios
- Current tax and insurance payments

Source: Tracy L. Penwell, *The Credit Process: A Guide for Small Business Owners* (New York: Federal Reserve Bank of New York).

of the expected return. When a venture lending–backed venture is successful, the venture bank will receive interest, principal, and the proceeds from profitable exercise of the warrants.

While it is tempting for entrepreneurs to think of venture lending as "debt" rather than "equity," with the attractive feature that less ownership dilution will occur, keep in mind that the warrants are ownership dilutors. Traditional corporate finance, and our earlier treatment of convertible bonds and preferred equity, show that a loan with warrants is similar to a convertible bond or to convertible preferred equity. Of course, these are the preferred securities for professional venture capitalists. While it is true that the venture lender is getting a package similar to that given to professional venture capitalists, the mixture of warrants and bond-like payoffs is slanted more toward debt than is the typical venture capital investment. The warrants are sweeteners to the deal—not the main course. For traditional venture capitalists, the warrants (or the conversion feature on the convertible bond or preferred equity) is the main course. In this sense, venture lending is expected to have less ownership dilution and will also be available to fewer ventures. In particular, you will have a professional venture capitalist involved before receiving venture loans. To some extent, the venture lender is a bandwagon investor who leverages the due diligence and monitoring offered by professional venture capitalists.

CONCEPT CHECK

- Identify the five factors used in credit analysis.
- List some common restrictions in loan agreements.

12.3 UNDERSTANDING WHY YOU MAY NOT GET DEBT FINANCING

It is widely understood among startup businesses that bank debt, with the possible exception of a loan guaranteed by a government agency (e.g., the Small Business Administration), is not a very realistic source of financing for ventures with less than two years of (successful) operating performance. The following is a recapping of some of the reasons for this: (1) A large portion of startup assets are intangible (ideas, skills, etc.) and provide no collateral; (2) either receivables don't yet exist or collection history is inadequate; (3) it is not economically feasible for the bank to attempt to recover some of its outlay through managerial involvement in a defaulting new venture; and (4) the risk characteristics of a new venture, including its dependence on a very small number of irreplaceable people, is not a good match for demand deposits or other bank liabilities. One need only apply for a loan as a startup to add to this list of reasons.

In the theories of finance, one important idea (which is now accepted wisdom) is that when a business spirals down, the owners (shareholders), who get only the remainder after debts have been paid, have an incentive to take great risks. This can benefit the owner-manager in the following way. If the status quo is that the venture is going down to a value at or below the level of debt, then there will be no equity and the owner-manager will get nothing. If the manager has discretion over some assets (cash) and can run to the local convenience store and buy lottery tickets, then at least there is some chance that equity will have value (when one or more of the lottery tickets hits the jackpot). Of course, lottery tickets are not prudent investments; it is the endgame outlook that introduces this potentially destructive moral hazard problem.

A classic problem in the theory of gambling is the one faced by the gambler who is in a casino and has only $.50 left. A bus ride home costs $1.00, and failure to produce that dollar within the next hour will result in a night on the street with the homeless. While finance academics and practitioners alike normally extol the benefits of diversification, in this case, diversification is the enemy.

Suppose that the gambler had an opportunity that would provide an expected loss of only 6 percent (which is low for the casino's take). If the gambler could continuously invest infinitesimal amounts (summing to $.50) over the remaining hour, he would only guarantee that at the end of the hour he had $.47. Even if the casino ran at an expected loss, offering the gambler an expected 10 percent gain, the gambler could lock in only $.55. Betting a small amount a large number of times does provide diversification of risk. (There is no uncertainty in the outcome.) Unfortunately, the certain outcome is that the gambler will be sleeping on the streets.

If, instead, the gambler were to bet the whole $.50 on one spot on a wheel of fortune with at least one winning wedge paying at least $1, then he would have a positive probability of sleeping at home. To him, this is better than the certainty of sleeping on the street. Of course, there are many other possible strategies that give multiple chances at winnings of at least $1. The point is not to characterize the gambler's optimal strategy.[1] It is to recognize that the gambler is in a situation in which he will not try to maximize expected wealth. In a casino where the house expects to win, maximizing expected wealth would mean not gambling at all. This assures a night on the street. The alternative possibility of sleeping at home provides the irresistible temptation to gamble, and gamble boldly.

Now suppose the gambler had borrowed $1 at the beginning of the evening from the VISA® cash machine at the casino's entrance. Because the gambler is teetering on the edge of personal bankruptcy, after having committed to paying the cash advance fee, VISA® would be better off if he ceased gambling and sent it the remaining $.50. By continuing to gamble in an unfair casino, and particularly by doing so boldly, he diminishes the value of VISA®'s primary claim on his $.50 total assets.

The gambler who is not maximizing wealth acts at the expense of his creditors. Another basic tenet of finance is that bankers are not stupid. The interest costs of the $1 loan reflect the possibility that the $1 might be used for such

---

[1] The optimality of "bold" gambling strategies has been formally treated in Lester Dubins and Leonard Savage, *Inequalities for Stochastic Processes: How to Gamble If You Must* (New York: Dover Publications, 1965).

undesirable endgame gambling (after all, the bank put the machine in the casino). That is, bankers understand that gamblers do not look first to the bank's interest as they undertake last-ditch efforts to stay afloat. The profitability of casino cash machines is grounded in the notion that the average gambler is not close to gambler's ruin (personal bankruptcy) and, therefore, is not gambling only on the bank's money.

In a startup, continued existence and a shot at eventual success are undoubtedly central to the entrepreneur's self-perception and welfare. In addition to facing increased difficulties in starting future ventures if the current venture fails, the entrepreneur's ego is tied up in the venture's ability to communicate his vision and creativity to the marketplace. The ego aspect and the fulfillment of a desire to control the venture are personal benefits that accrue to the entrepreneur when the venture survives. These personal benefits are analogous to the gambler's desire to sleep in his own bed. Personal benefits compete with wealth-building motives and exacerbate the gambler's (entrepreneur's) temptation to seek risk even when, on average, it destroys value.

It is not rational to assume that an entrepreneur owner-manager will discontinue operations to preserve the value of creditors' investments. We should expect very high debt interest rates, or no debt at all, for venture firms having a significant probability of nearby failure. We would expect that, in a heroic attempt to keep the venture alive, the entrepreneur would take unwarranted risks and (on average) deplete the value that would otherwise be left for creditors. While similar conditions can arise in any firm with debt, early-stage firms almost always face the prospect of nearby failure. Traditional bank loans and other debt are not going to be a popular way to finance a new or growing venture—with one exception.

CONCEPT CHECK

- Why is it difficult for an entrepreneur to finance a startup with debt?
- How do an entrepreneur's personal nonfinancial motives complicate debt financing?

12.4   CREDIT CARDS

Although credit card financing is a type of bank loan, we have chosen to treat it separately because the associated credit lines and loans are not usually made to the venture. They are typically granted solely on the ability and demonstrated tendency of the individual cardholder to repay the unsecured loans. Bankruptcy is a risk when using credit card financing. However, it is also a risk for bank loans personally guaranteed by the entrepreneur.

When bank loans are offered to startups, the venture's principals, with few exceptions, will have to guarantee the loans. The guarantee gives the bank recourse to much more than the assets the venture is financing. Personal bankruptcy is a likely outcome in a failed small business that has undertaken a bank loan. It should not be surprising that many entrepreneurs use personal credit card debt to get through a cash crunch. The teaser rates that are offered on new cards and balance transfers are below prime lending rates. Given the multiplicity of competing credit card providers, it is not difficult to plug a cash gap or even produce a six-figure injection and roll it over at balance transfer rates. The debt produced is extraordinarily cheap for a while. Such an endeavor massively undercuts the rate the venture would have to pay on a traditional bank loan, if it could get one at all. Since personal bankruptcy is a risk in both credit cards and guaranteed bank loans, it is easy to see why unsecured credit card debt, combined with low introductory and balance transfer (teaser) rates, make credit cards an appealing, if not major, source of early-stage venture debt. Quick legal lending opportunities other than credit cards are difficult to find. However, a methodical rolling of credit card balances, to avoid high rates after the introductory period, takes serious planning. Early-stage ventures exploiting credit card debt have an even greater need to anticipate and prepare for cash cycles.

Given the ease of obtaining credit card debt, the potential low cost when rolling a balance across various cards, and the personal guarantees that will be required on regular bank loans, we should not be surprised to find that new and growing ventures use credit card financing. It is commonly accepted that around 50 percent of entrepreneurial ventures use credit card financing.[2] In the Arthur Andersen *Survey of Small and Mid-Sized Businesses (Trends for 2000)*, the top three types of debt financing are credit cards, commercial loans, and leasing, in that order, with 50 percent, 43 percent, and 20 percent of respondents reporting usage.[3] Among those reporting credit card financing, 24 percent carried a balance, 20 percent said they used two to three cards, and 7 percent said they used four or more cards. The usage of credit card financing has risen from 24 percent of respondents in 1996 to 34 percent in 1997, 47 percent in 1998, and 50 percent in 2000. Credit card financing, like it or not, is a significant factor in venture financing.

CONCEPT CHECK

- Why do entrepreneurs find credit cards an easy source of venture financing?
- What are teaser rates?
- What are the dangers of credit card financing?

2 See, for example, Knight-Ridder/Tribune Information Services, "Credit-Card Financing Is No Longer a Sin," December 10, 1998.

3 Six percent of respondents reported getting SBA-guaranteed loans; 2 percent reported receiving venture capital; angel financing and home equity/personal loans tied at 19 percent.

12.5   SMALL BUSINESS ADMINISTRATION PROGRAMS

By an act of Congress, the Small Business Administration (SBA) was created in 1953 for the purpose of fostering the initiation and growth of small businesses. The SBA is the division of the federal government primarily responsible for assisting small businesses.

OVERVIEW OF WHAT THE SBA DOES FOR SMALL BUSINESSES

The SBA provides access to financial capital through several different programs, as well as providing contract assistance and counselling.[4] Figure 12.3 identifies

FIGURE 12.3   Small Business Administration Sources of Financial Capital

CREDIT PROGRAM	LENDERS	LOAN CHARACTERISTICS	SBA ROLE
7(a) Loan	Commercial bank, credit union, or financial services firm	Up to $2,000,000; 7- to 10-year loan Can be used for most business purposes, including the financing of working capital needs	Approves loan and guarantees up to 85% of loan value
504 Loan	Commercial bank jointly with not-for-profit Certified Development Company	Up to $4,000,000 for fixed assets and up to $2,000,000 for other business needs	Approves and guarantees development company's portion of debt.
Microloan	Not-for-profit or government-affiliated Community Development Financial Institution (CDFI)	Up to $35,000 to very small firm for general business needs	Provides a direct loan to community organization, which reloans the funds in small amounts
Venture Capital	Small Business Investment Company (SBIC), a private for-profit organization	No limit, several-year loan provided by debenture SBIC SBICs also make loans in exchange for equity investments	Borrows money to be lent to SBICs and guarantees payment to investors

Source: Robb Mandelbaum, "Does the SBA Still Matter?" *Inc.* (May 2007), pp. 101–112.

---

[4]   This section benefits from an excellent summary of current Small Business Administration activities presented in Robb Mandelbaum, "Does the SBA Still Matter?" *Inc.* (May 2007), pp. 101–112.

four current credit programs whereby small businesses can access financial capital. These programs include 7(a) loans, 504 loans, microloans, and venture capital. The 7(a) loan traditionally has been the SBA's primary loan program and approached $14 billion in loans in 2006. Loans are made usually for 7 to 10 years in amounts up to $2,000,000, require collateral, and can be used for most business purposes, including the financing of the venture's working capital. Interest rates generally require a premium of 2.25 to 4.75 percent above the then-prevailing prime loan rate. The SBA approves the standard 7(a) loan and guarantees up to 85 percent of the loan value. The SBA also offers an "express" version of the 7(a) loan, which is easier for the borrower to apply for. Express loans are approved by the lending bank with a 50 percent guarantee by the SBA.

The 504 loan is the SBA's rapid-growth loan program. Maximum loans range from $2,000,000 for working capital and general business needs up to $4,000,000 for fixed assets such as equipment or real estate. Borrowers typically are required to make a 10 percent upfront deposit or payment as a form of collateral with interest rates on 504 loans being tied to prevailing interest rates in the bond markets. The SBA approves and guarantees the development company's portion of the debt.

As noted in Figure 12.3, microloans are intended for very small businesses with a maximum amount of $35,000 to be used for general purposes. These loans are made by not-for-profit or government-affiliated Community Development Financial Institutions (CDFIs), which make loans for up to six years. CDFIs also provide technical assistance to borrowers. The SBA provides a large loan to CDFIs, which re-lend a small portion of the funds to various very small businesses. In the event of small business borrower default, the SBA expects the CDFI to still repay the SBA loan amounts.

The SBA's venture capital credit program works through Small Business Investment Companies (SBICs), which are private for-profit investment firms. Small early-stage ventures can either borrow directly from SBICs or exchange a portion of their equity for early-stage financing. SBIC loanable funds come from the private investments of their investors supplemented by government-provided money. SBICs typically are classified as debenture SBICs if they specialize in making direct loans to early-stage ventures. Some SBICs are referred to as participating security SBICs in that they lend funds in exchange for equity in the early-stage ventures. Money to be lent to SBICs is first raised in the capital markets with the SBA guaranteeing repayment to the investors who purchase the debt obligations. However, due to a recent surge in defaults, the SBA has stopped providing licenses to new participating security SBICs.

In addition to the SBA's credit programs, the SBA's Office of Government Contracting helps small businesses obtain government contracts by explaining regulations and providing counsel on penetrating government bureaucracy. The SBA also provides counseling to small businesses through SCORE, Small Business Development Centers, and Women's Business Centers. SCORE stands for Service Corps of Retired Executives, which is a not-for-profit association of over 10,000 volunteers in nearly 300 chapters in the United States. SCORE offers counseling and seminars—particularly to startup-stage ventures. The SBA funds most of SCORE's operating funds. Small Business Development Centers (SBDCs) provide services similar to those provided by SCORE but focus instead on more established small businesses. There are approximately 100 Women's Business Centers in the United States, which support women who own and operate small businesses.

CONCEPT CHECK

- What are some characteristics of an SBA 7(a) loan?
- What are some characteristics of an SBA 504 loan?
- Briefly describe SBA credit programs involving microloans and venture capital.

SELECTED SBA LOAN AND OPERATING SPECIFICS

While the SBA is not the answer to the financing needs of the vast majority of the more than one million new business formations a year, it does have many programs that may be potential contributors to a growing venture. The following descriptions of the SBA's programs have been modified and updated from the SBA's 2002 report *Who We Are and What We Do*, Seventh Edition. SBA programs change from time to time. The latest information on specific programs should be available on the SBA's Web site: www.sba.gov.

FINANCING

Program: Basic 7(a) Loan Guaranty

Function: Serves as the SBA's primary business loan program to help qualified small businesses obtain financing when they might not be eligible for business loans through normal lending channels. It is also the agency's most flexible business loan program, since financing under this program can be guaranteed for a variety of general business purposes. Loan proceeds can be used for most sound business purposes, including working capital, machinery and equipment, furniture and fixtures, land and building (including purchase, renovation, and new construction), leasehold improvements, and debt refinancing (under special conditions). Loan maturity is up to 10 years for working capital and generally up to 25 years for fixed assets.

Customer:	Startup and existing small businesses, commercial lending institutions
Delivered Through:	Commercial lending institutions

Program: CAPLines

Function: Finances the short-term and cyclical working capital needs of small businesses. Under CAPLines there are five distinct, short-term, working capital loans: Seasonal, Contract, Builders, Standard Asset-Based, and Small Asset-

Based lines, which are designed to meet different short-term financing needs of small businesses. For the most part, the SBA regulations governing the basic 7(a) Loan Guaranty Program also apply to CAPLines. The SBA generally can guarantee a maximum of $1 million under the program.

Customer: Existing small businesses

Delivered Through: Commercial lending institutions

Program: Defense Loan and Technical Assistance (DELTA)
Function: Helps defense-dependent small businesses adversely affected by defense cuts diversify into the commercial market through financial and technical assistance. Must be used to retain jobs of defense workers, create new jobs in impacted communities, or modernize/expand to diversify operations and remain in the national technical and industrial base under 7(a). DELTA has a maximum total loan amount of $1.25 million. Under 504, the maximum guaranteed debenture is $1 million. Federal, state, and private-sector entities provide a full range of management and technical assistance.

Customer: Defense-dependent small companies adversely impacted
                       by defense cuts

Delivered Through: SBA district offices, resource partners

Program: Community Adjustment and Investment (CAIP)
Function: Creates new, sustainable jobs and/or preserves existing jobs in businesses at risk due to changed trade patterns related to the North American Free Trade Agreement. Business applicants must be located in CAIP-eligible communities. Applicants must demonstrate that within twenty-four months and as a result of the loan they will create or preserve at least one job per $70,000 of federally guaranteed funds they receive under the 7(a) program and $35,000 of each debenture under the 504 program. The only exception is when a job that otherwise would be lost to low-cost foreign competition will be saved by the CAIP 504 loan. CAIP is a partnership between the North American Development Bank and the federal government (primarily the SBA and the U.S. Department of Agriculture). NADBank pays the SBA the loan guaranty fee normally paid by the participating lender. See also Certified Development Company (CDC), a 504 Loan Program.

Customer: Businesses in communities with significant job losses
                       related to NAFTA

Delivered Through: NADBank, SBA, U.S. Department of Agriculture

Program: Export Working Capital Loan (EWCL)
Function: Enables the SBA to guarantee up to 90 percent of a secured loan, or $1 million, whichever is less. Loan maturity may be for up to three years with annual renewals. Loans can be for single or multiple export sales and can be extended for preshipment working capital, postshipment exposure coverage, or a combination of the two. Proceeds can be used only to finance export transactions.

See also Assistance for Exporters.

Customer:	Export-ready small businesses and suppliers of exporters
Delivered Through:	Commercial lending institutions

Program: International Trade Loan (ITL)

Function: Helps small businesses engaged in exporting, preparing to engage in exporting, or adversely affected by competition from imports. Under this program, the SBA can guarantee as much as $1.25 million in combined working capital and facilities and equipment loans. See also Assistance for Exporters.

Customer:	Export-ready small businesses
Delivered Through:	Commercial lending institutions

Program: Energy and Conservation Loan

Function: Provides financing for eligible small businesses engaged in engineering, manufacturing, distributing, marketing, and installing or servicing products or services designed to conserve the nation's energy resources. Up to 30 percent of the loan can be used for research and development.

Customer:	Small businesses
Delivered Through:	Commercial lending institutions

Program: Pollution Control Loan

Function: Assists small businesses that are planning, designing, or installing pollution control facilities. This includes most real or personal property that will reduce pollution. Unlike the Energy and Conservation Loan, this loan is for the end user of the pollution control facility.

Customer:	Businesses building, installing, or servicing pollution control facilities
Delivered Through:	Commercial lending institutions

Program: Qualified Employees Trust Loan

Function: The SBA can guarantee 7(a) loans to eligible employee trusts that meet the SBA's size and policy requirements, are part of a plan sponsored by their employer, and qualify under the Internal Revenue Code (as an Employee Stock Ownership Plan) or the Department of Labor (under the Employee Retirement Income Security Act). Loan proceeds may be used by an employee trust for a growth and development loan, whereby the trust relends the loan proceeds to the employer by purchasing qualifying securities (not necessarily voting stock) in the employer's business; or for change of ownership loans, whereby employees acquire controlling interest in the employer's business. Collateral for the loan includes the assets of the employer's business.

Customer:	Eligible employee trusts
Delivered Through:	SBA participating lenders

Program: Secondary Market

Function: Gives lenders making SBA-guaranteed loans an opportunity to improve their liquidity by selling both the guaranteed and the unguaranteed portions of the loans to investors. Frequent secondary-market buyers include banks, savings and loan companies, credit unions, pension funds, and insurance companies.

Customer:	Commercial lending institutions participating in SBA-guaranteed lending programs, securities dealers
Delivered Through:	Lenders, securities dealers, secondary market for guaranteed government obligations

FINANCING/STREAMLINED APPLICATIONS AND APPROVALS

Program: Certified and Preferred Lenders

Function: Provides expedited SBA approval for designated lenders. Certified lenders receive a partial SBA delegation of authority to approve loans. Preferred lenders receive full delegation of lending authority. Only the most active and expert SBA participating lenders are designated as certified or preferred. SBA district offices have listings of participating lenders.

Customer:	Small businesses and commercial lending institutions participating in SBA-guaranteed lending programs
Delivered Through:	Commercial lending institutions

Program: Low Documentation Loan (SBALowDoc)

Function: Reduces the paperwork a lender must complete to obtain a guaranty on loan requests of $150,000 or less. The agency uses a one-page application that allows the lender to rely on the strength of the applicant's character and credit history. Once an applicant satisfies all the lender's requirements, the lender may request a LowDoc guaranty from the SBA.

Customer:	Lenders providing loans to startup and existing small businesses
Delivered Through:	Self-certified commercial lending institutions

Program: SBAExpress

Funtion: Encourages lenders to make more small loans to small businesses. Participating banks use their own documentation and procedures to approve, service, and liquidate loans up to $250,000. In return, the SBA guarantees up to 50 percent of each loan.

Customer:	Lenders providing loans to startup and existing small businesses
Delivered Through:	Specially designated commercial lending institutions

Program: SBA ExportExpress

Function: Similar to the SBAExpress Program above, except that proceeds are oriented toward increasing exports and guarantee levels are 85 percent for loans up to $150,000 and 75 percent for loans between $150,000 and $250,000.

Customer:	Lenders providing loans to existing small businesses for export endeavors
Delivered Through:	Specially designated commercial lending institutions

Program: CommunityExpress

Function: Spurs economic development and job creation in untapped rural and inner-city communities by providing loans and technical assistance. This nationwide program is available in predesignated geographic areas. The maximum loan amount is $250,000. CommunityExpress lenders and the National Community Reinvestment Coalition (NCRC) provide hands-on technical training and support through community-based, not-for-profit NCRC member organizations.

Customer:	Lenders providing loans to businesses in low- and moderate-income urban and rural areas designated for participation
Delivered Through:	Specially designated commercial lending institutions, the National Community Reinvestment Coalition

Program: Loan Prequalification

Function: Allows business applicants to have their loan applications for $250,000 or less analyzed and potentially sanctioned by the SBA before they are taken to lenders for consideration. The program focuses on the applicant's character, credit, experience, and reliability rather than assets. An SBA-designated intermediary works with the business owner to review and strengthen the loan application. The review is based on key financial ratios, credit and business history, and the loan request terms. The program is administered by the SBA's Office of Field Operations and SBA district offices.

Customer:	Designated small businesses
Delivered Through:	Not-for-profit intermediaries such as Small Business Development Centers and certified development companies operating in specific geographic areas

FINANCING/OTHER SBA LOAN PROGRAMS

Program: Microloan, a 7(m) Loan Program

Function: Provides short-term loans of up to $35,000 to small businesses and not-for-profit child care centers for working capital or the purchase of inventory, supplies, furniture, fixtures, machinery, and/or equipment. Proceeds cannot be used to pay existing debts or to purchase real estate. The SBA makes or guarantees a loan to an intermediary, which, in turn, makes the microloan to the applicant. These organizations also provide management and technical assistance. The loans are not guaranteed by the SBA. The Microloan Program is available in selected locations in most states.

Customer: Small businesses and not-for-profit child care centers needing small-scale financing and technical assistance for startup or expansion

Delivered Through: Specially designated intermediary lenders (not-for-profit organizations with experience in lending and in technical assistance)

Program: Certified Development Company (CDC), a 504 Loan Program
Function: Provides long-term, fixed-rate financing to small businesses to acquire real estate or machinery or equipment for expansion or modernization. Typically, a 504 project includes a loan secured from a private-sector lender with a senior lien, a loan secured from a CDC (funded by a 100 percent SBA-guaranteed debenture) with a junior lien covering up to 40 percent of the total cost, and a contribution of at least 10 percent equity from the borrower. The maximum SBA debenture generally is $1 million (and up to $1.3 million in some cases). DELTA and CAIP funding are also available under this program.

Customer: Small businesses requiring "bricks and mortar" financing

Delivered Through: Certified development companies (private, not-for-profit corporations set up to contribute to the economic development of their communities or regions)

Program: Franchise Registry
Function: A national registry of franchises. The SBA reviews the franchise agreements of the franchisors listed on the registry. The benefit of being listed on the SBA Franchise Registry is that whenever a business operating under a franchise agreement of a listed franchise applies for a loan, the SBA's eligibility review process is expedited because the complex issues of control have already been satisfied. However, the business still must meet additional eligibility issues associated with an SBA loan such as size, use of proceeds, nondiscrimination, repayment ability, and so on. Franchises not listed on the registry are not necessarily ineligible for SBA financial assistance. The applications of such franchises take longer to process, however, because first a determination must be made that no affiliation between franchisee and franchisor exists. For further information, visit the Franchise Registry at www.franchiseregistry.com.

Customer: Lenders, franchisors, and franchisees

Delivered Through: The SBA's Office of General Counsel and a private contractor

Program: Small Business Investment Company (SBIC)
Function: Provides equity capital, long-term loans, debt-equity investments, and management assistance to small businesses, particularly during their growth

stages. The SBA licenses SBICs and supplements their capital with U.S. government–guaranteed debentures or participating securities. SBICs are privately owned and managed, profit-motivated companies, investing with the prospect of sharing in the success of the funded small businesses as they grow and prosper. Specialized SBICs provide the same services as SBICs. They invest in socially or economically disadvantaged small companies; typically, however, they invest in businesses during their growth stages and make smaller investments. The Small Business Improvement Act of 1996 repealed Section 301(d), and as a result no new SSBIC licenses are being issued. However, existing 301(d) licensees were "grandfathered" and are still in operation.

Customer: Small businesses seeking long-term capital

Delivered Through: Small Business Investment Companies (there are currently more than 415, including SSBICs)

Program: New Market Venture Capital (NMVC)

Function: Provides equity capital and intensive management assistance to businesses located in low-income areas. NMVC companies receive supplemental funding through the issuance of U.S. government–guaranteed debentures and matching technical assistance grants.

Customer: Businesses located in low-income areas

Delivered Through: New Market Venture Capital companies

Program: Surety Bond Guarantee

Function: Guarantees bid, performance, and payment bonds for contracts up to $2 million for eligible small businesses that cannot obtain surety bonds through regular commercial channels. By law, prime contractors to the federal government must post surety bonds on federal construction projects valued at $100,000 or more. In addition, many states, counties, municipalities, and private-sector projects and subcontracts also require surety bonds. Contractors must apply through a surety bonding agent, since the SBA's guaranty goes to the surety company.

Customer: Small construction and service contractors; surety and insurance companies and their agents; federal and state agencies; state insurance departments; federal, state, and other procurement officials

Delivered Through: Surety and insurance companies and their agents; four SBA area offices: Atlanta, Denver, Philadelphia, and Seattle

FEDERAL GOVERNMENT CONTRACTING ASSISTANCE

Program: Prime Contracting

Function: Increases small business opportunities in the federal acquisition process. This is accomplished through negotiating goals for small business set-asides, identifying new small business sources, counseling small businesses on doing business with the federal government, and investigating cases of contract bundling.

Customer:	Small businesses, other federal government agencies
Delivered Through:	SBA procurement center representatives

Program: Subcontracting
Function: Ensures that small businesses receive the maximum practical opportunity to participate in federal contracts as subcontractors and suppliers.

Customer:	Large and small contractors, other federal agencies
Delivered Through:	SBA commercial market representatives

Program: Certificate of Competency (CoC)
Function: Helps small businesses secure government contracts by providing an appeals process to businesses denied government contracts for a lack of "responsibility" or a perceived inability to perform satisfactorily.

Customer:	Small businesses denied government contracts for perceived lack of ability
Delivered Through:	SBA field office industrial and financial specialists

Program: Contract Assistance for Women Business Owners (CAWBO)
Function: Increases federal contracting opportunities for women-owned small businesses and works to increase the number that successfully compete in the federal marketplace.

Customer:	Women-owned businesses
Delivered Through:	SBA's Office of Federal Contract Assistance

Program: Procurement Marketing and Access Network (PRO-Net®)
Function: Serves as an Internet-based search engine for contracting officers, a marketing tool for small businesses, and a link to procurement opportunities and information. Contains business information on thousands of small firms. Provides online links to other sources of procurement opportunities. Administered by the SBA's Office of Government Contracting and Business Development, PRO-Net® registration is free.

Customer:	Contracting officers, small companies seeking federal procurement opportunities, federal and large prime contractors
Delivered Through:	SBA

Program: Sub-Net
Function: Primarily used by prime contractors to post subcontracting opportunities, which may or may not be reserved for small businesses.

| Customer: | Contracting officers; small businesses seeking procurement opportunities; federal, state, and local governments; large prime contractors; not-for-profit organizations; and colleges and universities |
| Delivered Through: | PRO-Net® home page at pronet.sba.gov under "Subcontracting Opportunities" |

Program: Small Business Size Standards

Function: Serves to determine which businesses meet the federal criteria for designation as a small business. The SBA Office of Size Standards develops and prepares regulations on size standards as needed following agency and federal government rule-making procedures. The regulations determine which businesses are eligible for the SBA's financial and procurement assistance programs.

| Customer: | Small businesses, large and small federal contractors, federal agencies, and financial institutions |
| Delivered Through: | SBA's Office of Size Standards |

Program: HUBZone Empowerment Contracting

Function: Encourages economic development in historically underutilized business zones—HUBZones—through the establishment of federal contract award preferences for small businesses located in such areas. After determining eligibility, the SBA lists qualified businesses in its PRO-Net® database. See also Procurement Marketing and Access Network (PRO-Net®).

| Customer: | Small businesses located in historically underutilized business zones |
| Delivered Through: | SBA's Office of HUBZone Empowerment Contracting Program |

Program: Natural Resources Sales Assistance

Function: Aids and assists small businesses in obtaining their fair share of federal property offered for sale or disposal by other means. The focus of the program is concentrated on the sales of federal timber, royalty oil, coal leases, other mineral leases, and federal surplus property.

| Customer: | Small businesses |
| Delivered Through: | SBA Industrial Specialists (Forestry) |

Program: Small Business Innovation Research (SBIR)

Function: Provides a vehicle for small businesses to propose innovative ideas in competition for Phase I and Phase II awards, which represent specific research and R&D needs of the participating federal agencies. These awards may result in commercialization of the effort at the Phase III level. Administered by the SBA's Office of Technology.

Customer: Innovative small businesses interested in competing for federal R&D awards

Delivered Through: Ten participating federal agencies with $100 million in extramural R&D budgets

Program: Small Business Technology Transfer (STTR)
Function: Requires each small business competing for a federal R&D project to collaborate with a not-for-profit research institution. This program is a joint venture from the initial proposal to project completion. Administered by the SBA's Office of Technology.

Customer: Small, innovative R&D businesses

Delivered Through: Five federal agencies with extramural research and R&D budgets of $1 billion: NASA; the National Science Foundation; and the Departments of Defense, Energy, and Health and Human Services

Program: Small Business Research, R&D Goaling
Function: Measures and reports the amount of federal funding for research and R&D (excluding the amounts for SBIR and STTR) awarded to small businesses each year by the major research and R&D federal agencies. Administered by the SBA's Office of Technology.

Customer: Small businesses that compete for federal R&D awards

Delivered Through: Eighteen federal agencies with annual research or R&D budgets in excess of $20 million

Program: Federal and State Technology Partnership
Function: Enhances or develops within the states the technological competitiveness of small businesses. Grants or cooperative agreements are awarded on a competitive basis to eligible entities, organizations, or individuals who, among other things, receive an endorsement from the governor of the state.

Customer: Technology-based small businesses

Delivered Through: Network of service providers, including, but not limited to, colleges and universities, state economic development agencies, not-for-profit organizations, collaboratives, etc.

Program: Rural Outreach
Function: Provides grants and cooperative agreements to approximately twenty-five states to increase participation of businesses located in underserved states and territories in the SBIR and STTR programs. Projects funded under this program are used to provide outreach and other types of assistance to the technology-based small business community.

Customer: Technology-based small businesses

Delivered Through: Network of service providers, including, but not limited to, colleges and universities, state economic development agencies, not-for-profit organizations, collaboratives, etc.

Program: Technology Access Network (TechNet)
Function: Serves as a chief resource for federal acquisition agencies, venture capitalists, and others seeking to do business with small high-technology businesses under all the Research and Development Assistance programs.

Customer: Small high-tech businesses, researchers, scientists, state, federal, and local government officials, investors, and other sources of capital

Delivered Through: SBA

BUSINESS COUNSELING AND TRAINING

Program: Small Business Development Center (SBDC)
Function: Provides management and technical assistance, counseling, and training to current and prospective small business owners through SBDCs. Administered by the SBA, the SBDC program is a cooperative effort of the private sector, the educational community, and federal, state, and local governments. See also Business Information Services.

Customer: Prebusiness, startup, and existing small businesses

Delivered Through: More than 1,000 locations, including universities, colleges, state governments, and private-sector organizations

Program: Paul D. Coverdell Drug-Free Workplace (DFWP)
Function: Provides grants to intermediaries and contracts to SBDCs to assist small businesses in setting up drug-free workplace programs. A DFWP program consists of a written policy, drug and alcohol abuse prevention training, drug testing, an employee assistance program, and continuing education.

Customer: Small businesses wanting to set up a DFWP program

Delivered Through: Intermediaries, SBA's Office of Small Business Development Centers

Program: Business Information Center (BIC)
Function: Provides the latest in high-tech hardware, software, and telecommunications at multiple locations to help small businesses start and grow. BIC counseling and training are provided by the Service Corps of Retired Executives, other SBA resource partners, and community organizations. See also Business Information Services.

Customer: Prebusiness, startup, and existing small businesses

Delivered Through: Approximately eighty locations throughout the country

Program: Service Corps of Retired Executives (SCORE)
Function: Offers counseling and training for small business owners who are starting, building, or growing their businesses. Funded by a grant from the

SBA, SCORE's services are free of charge. See also Business Information Services.

Customer: Prebusiness, startup, and existing small businesses
Delivered Through: 11,500 volunteers in 389 chapters nationwide

For specialized business counseling and training, see Assistance for Exporters, Assistance for Native Americans, Assistance for Small and Disadvantaged Businesses, Assistance for Veterans, and Assistance for Women.

BUSINESS INFORMATION SERVICES

Program: Answer Desk
Function: Helps callers with questions and problems about starting and running businesses. The computerized telephone message system is available nationwide twenty-four hours a day, seven days a week. Counselors are available Monday through Friday, 9 A.M. to 5 P.M. Eastern time.

Customer: General public
Delivered Through: Toll-free telephone number: 1-800 U ASK SBA

Program: Publications
Function: SBA field offices and the Answer Desk (see above) offer free publications that describe the SBA's programs and services.

Customer: General public
Delivered Through: SBA field offices, Answer Desk and SBA resource partners, the federal Consumer Information Center

Program: Home Page
Function: Offers detailed information on all SBA programs and services, including SBA publications and local resources; other business services; and access to the SBA classroom, an online vehicle for reading articles, taking courses, and researching small business development issues, PRO-Net®, the U.S. Business Advisor, and other Web sites.

Customer: General public
Delivered Through: www.sba.gov

Program: Small Business Classroom
Function: Brings easy-to-use, electronic business courses twenty-four hours a day to anyone with a standard Internet connection. Classes include such titles as How to Start a Small Business, The Business Plan (English and Spanish), Building Your Business, and Small Business Opportunities in Federal Procurement. Classes are added on a regular basis. Also contains a calendar of SBA-sponsored training events around the country.

Customer: General public

Delivered Through: www.sba.gov/services/training/index.html

Program: U.S. Business Advisor

Function: Provides a one-stop link to the government's business information and services. Now small businesses no longer have to contact dozens of agencies and departments to access applicable laws and regulations or figure out on their own how to comply. They can download business forms and conduct a myriad other business transactions through this Web site.

Customer: General public

Delivered Through: www.business.gov

Program: www.business.gov/guides/business_law

Function: Provides information on legal and regulatory issues for small businesses. Provides access to critical information in plain English on topics from advertising to zoning. Links to state and local laws, including hiring and managing employees. Links for personalized assistance in local area or for e-filing of tax returns. Keeps potential owners and small business owners current on changes in laws and regulations. Provides opportunity to confer with other business owners.

Customer: General public

Delivered Through: www.business.gov/guides/business_law

ADVOCACY

Program: Office of Interagency Affairs

Function: Monitors regulatory and other policy proposals of more than twenty federal agencies to assess their impact on small business to suggest alternatives for consideration. The office provides information to Congress on legislative issues and drafts testimony on public policy issues of concern to small businesses. Monitors regulatory agencies' compliance with the Regulatory Flexibility Act, as amended by the Small Business Regulatory Enforcement Fairness Act, and reports annually to Congress on the agencies' activities.

Customer: Small businesses, regulatory agencies, Congress

Delivered Through: Regulatory agencies, Congress, trade associations

Program: Office of Economic Research

Function: Serves as the principal source for small business statistics and helps fund and analyze major databases to monitor/identify small business trends. Produces the annual report to Congress, The State of Small Business: A Report to the President; oversees research on small business issues, banking, and the economy; and compiles and interprets statistics on small businesses according to size, industry, and geographic distribution.

Customer:	Small businesses, Congress, the media, academic institutions, government agencies, foreign governments
Delivered Through:	The White House, federal agencies, Congress, state and local governments, the media, and independent researchers

Program: Office of Public Information
Function: Publicizes and disseminates information on small business issues, statistics, research, and advocacy; prepares reports for Office of Advocacy–sponsored economic research, policy, and conferences; and provides outreach to small businesses, trade associations, the legal community, and others interested in small business policy.

Customer:	Small businesses, Congress, state legislatures, the media, government agencies, economic-research organizations
Delivered Through:	SBA's Office of Advocacy; www.sba.gov/advo

Program: Regional Advocate
Function: Serves as the SBA chief counsel's direct link to local communities. Regional advocates monitor the impact of federal and state regulations and policies on communities within their regions. They also work with state officials to develop policy and legislation that shape an environment in which small companies can prosper and grow.

Customer:	Local business owners, state and local government agencies, and legislatures
Delivered Through:	SBA's ten regional offices

Program: Small Business and Agriculture Regulatory Enforcement Ombudsman
Function: Receives comments from small businesses about the regulatory enforcement and compliance activities of federal agencies and refers comments to the appropriate agency's inspector general on a confidential basis. Coordinates the efforts of the ten small business regulatory fairness boards and reports annually to the SBA Administrator and to the heads of the affected agencies on the boards' activities, findings, and recommendations.

Customer:	Small businesses, federal agencies
Delivered Through:	The SBA ombudsman, SBA's ten regional fairness boards, SBA's Office of Field Operations; toll-free number 1-888-REG-FAIR or www.sba.gov/aboutsba/sbaprograms/ombudsman/nationalombudsman/index.html

Disaster Assistance
The SBA Disaster Assistance Program, administered by the Office of Disaster Assistance, is the primary federally funded disaster-assistance loan program for funding long-range recovery for private-sector, nonagricultural disaster victims. Eligibility is based on financial criteria. Interest rates fluctuate according to statutory formulas. A maximum interest rate of 4 percent is provided to applicants

without credit available elsewhere; the maximum is 8 percent for those with credit available elsewhere. In addition to presidential declarations, the program handles disaster loans when the SBA Administrator makes a disaster declaration. There are five disaster loan programs: loans for homes and personal property, physical disaster loans to businesses of any size, predisaster mitigation loans to businesses, economic injury loans to small businesses without credit available elsewhere, and economic injury loans to eligible businesses affected by the call-up of an essential employee to active duty in the role of military reservist.

LOANS FOR HOMES AND PERSONAL PROPERTY

Program: Real Property Loan

Function: Provides qualified homeowners with uninsured losses up to $200,000 with funds to repair or restore a primary residence to predisaster condition. This is the major long-term recovery program for individual disaster losses. Loans may be increased by as much as 20 percent to protect the damaged real property from possible future disasters of the same kind.

Customer:	Individuals
Delivered Through:	SBA's four disaster area offices, disaster-specific hotline number

Program: Personal Property Loan

Function: Provides qualified homeowners and renters who have sustained uninsured losses up to $40,000 with funds to repair or replace personal property such as clothing, furniture, cars, etc. This loan is not intended to replace extraordinarily expensive or irreplaceable items such as antiques, pleasure craft, recreational vehicles, fur coats, etc.

Customer:	Individuals
Delivered Through:	SBA's four disaster area offices, disaster-specific hotline number

LOANS FOR BUSINESSES

Program: Physical Disaster Business Loan

Function: Provides qualified businesses of any size that have sustained uninsured losses up to $1.5 million with funds to repair or replace business property to predisaster conditions. Loans may be used to replace or repair equipment, fixtures, and inventory and to make leasehold improvements.

Customer:	Large and small businesses, not-for-profit organizations
Delivered Through:	SBA's four disaster area offices, disaster-specific hotline number

Program: Predisaster Mitigation Loan

Function: Provides loans of up to $50,000 for eligible small businesses without credit elsewhere to fund specific projects to prevent disaster damage. The businesses must be located in participating predisaster mitigation community locations designated by the Federal Emergency Management Agency.

Customer:	Eligible small businesses without credit available elsewhere
Delivered Through:	SBA's four disaster area offices, disaster-specific hotline numbers

Program: Economic Injury Disaster Loan (EIDL)

Function: Provides up to $1.5 million in working capital loans for businesses that suffer economic injury as a direct result of a disaster, regardless of whether the property was damaged. The loans are made to help small businesses pay ordinary and necessary operating expenses that they would have been able to pay if the disaster had not occurred.

NOTE: The maximum loan amount is $1.5 million for EIDL and physical-disaster business loans combined, unless the business meets the criteria for a major source of employment.

Customer:	Small businesses without credit available elsewhere
Delivered Through:	SBA's four disaster area offices, disaster-specific hotline number

Program: Military Reservist Economic Injury Disaster Loan

Function: Provides working capital loans of up to $1.5 million for businesses that suffer economic injury because an essential employee has been called to active duty as a military reservist. The loans are for small businesses without credit elsewhere. Loan proceeds are to provide working capital needed by a small business until operations return to normal following the release of the essential employee from active military duty.

Customer:	Small businesses without credit available elsewhere
Delivered Through:	SBA's four disaster area offices, disaster-specific hotline number

Program: Loan for Major Source of Employment (MSE)

Function: Serves to waive the $1.5 million loan limit for businesses that are major sources of employment, as defined in the SBA regulations. Generally, businesses employing 250 or more persons in the disaster area are considered MSEs.

Customer:	Large and small businesses, not-for-profit organizations
Delivered Through:	SBA's four disaster area offices, disaster-specific hotline number

ASSISTANCE FOR EXPORTERS

Program: U.S. Export Assistance Center (USEAC)

Function: Delivers international programs and services. U.S. Export Assistance Centers offer a full range of federal export programs and services from the SBA, the U.S. Department of Commerce, the Export-Import Bank of the United States, and other public and private organizations. Located in nineteen cities nationwide, USEACs use the latest technology to provide export marketing and trade finance assistance, customized counseling for companies committed to exporting, and customer service. The SBA's Office of International Trade delivers its export loan and technical assistance programs at the USEACs.

Customer:	Export-willing, export-ready, and exporting small businesses
Delivered Through:	Nineteen centers around the country; www.sba.gov/aboutsba/sbaprograms/internationaltrade/index.html

Program: Export Legal Assistance Network (ELAN)

Function: Offers a complimentary initial legal consultation with an international trade attorney. Under an agreement among the SBA, the U.S. Department of Commerce, and the Federal Bar Association, experienced trade attorneys volunteer their time to answer exporters' legal questions.

Customer:	Export-willing, export-ready, and exporting small businesses
Delivered Through:	SBA, U.S. Department of Commerce, Federal Bar Association; www.fita.org/elan/index.html. See also Export Working Capital Loan (EWCL), International Trade Loan (ITL), and Loan Prequalification.

Program: Export Trade Assistance Partnership (E-TAP)

Function: Assists small business owners in becoming export-ready and competing in global markets. The program consists of four distinct segments: partnership, training, counseling, and international trade shows or missions. The ultimate goal is for U.S. small businesses to participate in trade events in the country or countries with the greatest market potential for the businesses' exports. See also U.S. Export Assistance Center (USEAC).

Customer:	Export-willing, export-ready, and exporting small businesses
Delivered Through:	Nineteen USEACs around the country; www.sba.gov/aboutsba/sbaprograms/internationaltrade/index.html

Program: Trade Mission Online (TM Online)

Function: Online database of U.S. small businesses that seek to export their products. Also a search engine for foreign companies that seek U.S. business alliances through direct product purchases, licensing, or franchising agreements.

Customer:	Export-willing, export-ready, and exporting small businesses
Delivered Through:	www.sba.gov/aboutsba/sbaprograms/internationaltrade/tmonline/index.html

ASSISTANCE FOR NATIVE AMERICANS

Program: Native American Affairs
Function: Develops initiatives that ensure Native Americans have access to business development resources, training, and services in their communities. The primary focus of the Office of Native American Affairs is economic development and job creation through small business ownership and education. Works with individual and tribally owned organizations; other federal, state, and local agencies; not-for-profit organizations; and national Native American organizations.

Customer:	American Indians, Alaskan Natives, and Native Hawaiians
Delivered Through:	SBA field offices, Small Business Development Centers; www.sba.gov/naa

ASSISTANCE FOR SMALL AND DISADVANTAGED BUSINESSES

Program: Small Disadvantaged Business (SDB) Certification
Function: Ensures that small businesses owned and controlled by individuals claiming to be socially and economically disadvantaged meet the eligibility criteria. Once certified, the businesses are eligible to receive price evaluation credits when bidding on federal contracts.

Customer:	Small socially and economically disadvantaged businesses
Delivered Through:	SBA's Office of Business Development; www.sba.gov/sdb

Program: 8(a) Business Development
Function: Uses the SBA's statutory authority to provide business development and federal contract support to small disadvantaged businesses.

Customer:	Small socially and economically disadvantaged businesses
Delivered Through:	SBA and other federal contracting officers, small business specialists at federal procurement activities; www.sba.gov/services/contractingopportunities/contracting/8a/index.html

Program: 7(j) Management and Technical Assistance
Function: Authorizes the SBA to provide grants and enter into cooperative agreements with service providers for specialized assistance to 7(j) eligible small businesses in areas such as accounting, marketing, and proposal/bid preparation. Industry-specific technical assistance and entrepreneurial training are also available. This program does not provide grants to individuals or small businesses to start or expand the business.

Customer:	Small disadvantaged businesses, low-income individuals, businesses in either labor-surplus areas or areas with a high proportion of low-income individuals

Delivered Through: Service providers (including SBA contractors and educational institutions), SBA's Office of Business Development

ASSISTANCE FOR VETERANS

Program: Veterans Business Outreach Center (VBOC)
Function: Provides entrepreneurial training, business development assistance, counseling, directed referrals, mentoring, and management assistance through four VBOCs to service-connected disabled veterans who own or want to start a small business. The program is currently in effect in Florida, New York, Texas, and Virginia.

Customer: Service-connected disabled veterans
Delivered Through: Four VBOC grant recipients

ASSISTANCE FOR WOMEN

Program: Women's Business Center (WBC)
Function: Through cooperative agreements with the SBA, WBCs provide long-term training and counseling in all aspects of owning or managing a business, including financial, management, marketing, and technical assistance, and procurement.

Customer: Women-owned small businesses, startups, prebusiness startups
Delivered Through: Nationwide network of more than eighty WBCs

Program: Online Women's Business Center

Function: Serves as an interactive, state-of-the-art Web site that offers the information an entrepreneur needs to start and build a successful business. The numerous features of the center include training, mentoring, individual counseling, and message boards and calendar of events. Information is available in several languages.

Customer: Women-owned small businesses, startups, prebusiness startups
Delivered Through: SBA home page; www.sba.gov/aboutsba/sbaprograms/onlinewbc/index.html

Program: Women's Network for Entrepreneurial Training (WNET)
Function: Provides a vehicle for established women business owners to serve as mentors, passing on knowledge, skills, and support to protégées who are ready to expand their businesses. WNET roundtables offer support and guidance in group settings. WNET sponsors include Small Business Development Centers, local business leaders, government representatives, and SCORE.

Customer:	Women-owned small businesses
Delivered Through:	SBA field offices, women's business and professional organizations, SBDCs, Women's Business Centers, SCORE, more than 160 WNET roundtables around the country. See also Loan Prequalification and Contract Assistance for Women Business Owners (CAWBO).

CONCEPT CHECK

- Describe some of the SBA advisory and counseling programs.
- What specific SBA programs might apply to your venture idea?

12.6 OTHER GOVERNMENT FINANCING PROGRAMS

In addition to the many programs available through the federal government, numerous state and municipal agencies have been charged with supporting the formation and growth of small businesses. In 1994, Congress created the Treasury Department's Community Development Financial Institutions (CDFI) Fund. About 1,000 CDFIs are in operation today. Most CDFIs currently still focus on promoting affordable housing and homeownership. However, CDFIs are increasing their financing of small businesses through the making of microloans as well as larger loans.[5] Recall from our discussion of SBA credit programs that the SBA makes direct loans to CDFIs, which, in turn, make microloans to small businesses.

Some CDFIs specialize in lending to small firms in specific industries while others specialize in specific geographic locations such as inner-city-based or rural-area-based small businesses. Figure 12.4 provides a checklist of questions that the owner of a small business should ask to determine whether a CDFI loan is a good fit. One should begin by asking "How much financing is needed?" While many CDFIs make microloans, some will provide financing in the $150,000 to $500,000 level, and a few might lend up to $1,000,000 or more. It is also important to remember that CDFIs often prefer, or are restricted, to lend to small businesses located in rural or economically depressed areas. CDFIs typically offer technical and managerial assistance and seek small business owners who are receptive to coaching and counseling help. Some CDFIs also impose other requirements relating to accounting systems and social missions as conditions for making loans to small businesses.[6]

---

[5] For individual examples of CDFI loans and other information, see "High-Risk Loans from a NonProfit," *Inc.* (June 2007), pp. 42–44.

[6] The U.S. Treasury Department provides a partial list of CDFIs at www.cdfifund.gov. Also, see the Web site for the Coalition of Community Development Financial Institutions at www.cdfi.org for additional information on CDFIs.

FIGURE 12.4   Does a CDFI Loan Fit Your Venture's Financing Need?

Questions to Ask When Considering a Community Development Financial Institutions (CDFI) Loan:

1. How much money is needed?

   Most CDFIs make microloans up to $35,000. Some CDFIs will lend between $150,000 and $500,000 to small businesses, and a few CDFIs may make loans for $1,000,000 or more.

2. Is the venture located in a low-income geographical area?

   CDFIs usually concentrate lending to small businesses in rural or economically depressed areas to support increased job opportunities.

3. Am I receptive to technical advice and coaching?

   CDFIs provide technical advice and business skills and are looking to lend to ventures whose managers are receptive to such advice and education.

4. Do I meet business operation requirements and social commitments?

   CDFIs require small businesses to have accounting record keeping and control systems in place and often expect successful borrowers to have stated social objectives or missions.

Source: "High-Risk Loans from a NonProfit," *Inc.* (June 2007), pp. 42–44.

As an example, financing programs available in 2004 for small businesses in Colorado are detailed in the Appendix. The list indicates that there are many potential government-related sources of funding, particularly if your venture has an ownership structure or objectives consistent with those of the relevant government programs. Although this historical list is only for Colorado, we encourage you to contact your state's equivalent office to find the relevant list for your venture.

CONCEPT CHECK

- Describe some characteristics of a Community Development Financial Institutions (CDFI) loan.

12.7   RECEIVABLES LENDING AND FACTORING

As we have emphasized in earlier chapters, one of the more imposing cash crunchers that can threaten a new venture's survival is the extension of trade credit to customers. In cash planning and valuation, it is critical that we treat receipts and not sales. One important gap between these two is the changes in accounts receivable. A potential narrowing of the time gap between the booking of a sale and the receipt of the related cash is the use of factoring or receivables financing. **Factoring** is the sale of receivables to a third party at a discount from their face value. Factoring can be *with recourse* to the venture, when the receivable is uncollectible, or it can be *without recourse* to the venture.

When a venture factors its receivables, it collects the cash related to a sale much earlier than it would otherwise. However, as with any debtlike claim, there will be charges for the time value of money and the credit risk associated with the receivables. Factoring discounts can run anywhere from 2 to 5 percent on low-risk receivables to more than 10 percent. A local factor in our area quoted 4 to 5 percent plus an additional 1 percent for each expected ten-day period over thirty days. In addition to the fee, the factor may advance only a portion of the factored amount, keeping the remainder in a factor's rebate account to be cleared when the receivables are actually collected. Factoring accounts can be set up in about ten days. The delay is caused by the due diligence the factor will conduct on those holding venture accounts. Typically, factors look for business rather than consumer accounts.

Local factor brokers may offer to facilitate your connection with a factor (in return for a fee or a cut). Such brokers can provide some value through their familiarity and relationship with factoring companies working in your geographic area. There is no professional certification or training required of factor brokers, although an education program is offered through the American Cash Flow Association (www.americancashflow.com), which also provides a directory of affiliated factors (and, more generally, "cash flow brokers").

Many factors have industry preferences. Factoring is common in the manufacturing, service, telecommunications, transportation, health care, high-tech, and government contracting industries. There are also industries where factoring financing is difficult to obtain—for example, consumer, retail, and construction industries.[7] When seeking factor financing, make sure to check out the factor's reputation. Speak to some of the factor's customers and check with the local Better Business Bureau.

Receivables lending is traditional debt that is secured by a venture's receivables. The venture retains the obligation to pay the debt irrespective of whether the receivables are collected. The receivables are merely a source of collateral for the bank or lending institution. The major difference between factoring and receivables lending is that a venture sells its receivables (transfers ownership) to a factor and only pledges them as collateral in receivables lending. If, however, the factoring is with recourse to the venture, meaning that the venture is still on the hook for uncollectible receivables, then the two become substantially more similar.

factoring
selling receivables to a third party at a discount from their face value

receivables lending
use of receivables as collateral for a loan

CONCEPT CHECK

- What is the difference between factoring and receivables lending?

---

[7] For a good introductory description of the factoring process, see Barbara Drazga, "Factors Offer Alternative Financing: Last-Resort Option Helps Cash-Hungry Companies," *Denver Business Journal*, April 6, 1998.

12.8   DEBT, DEBT SUBSTITUTES, AND DIRECT OFFERINGS

VENDOR FINANCING: ACCOUNTS PAYABLE AND TRADE NOTES

In our financial projections and cash-planning exercises, we emphasized the importance of projecting the working capital accounts. Accounts receivable were a particularly important use of funds. Similarly, accounts payable are an important source of funding. There are some basic concepts to grasp in the cost of using this type of spontaneous financing. A typical accounts payable policy is "2 in 10, net 30," which means a 2 percent discount can be taken if the bill is paid in ten days and, if not, the amount is due in thirty days. Of course, if such an arrangement is enforced, this amounts to keeping your funds an additional twenty days for 2 percent. It doesn't take a genius to figure out that this is one of the most expensive loans you'll ever see. In fact, you should know enough finance by now to see that this is a compound annual rate of over 43 percent. It makes credit card rates of 21 percent look appealing. Think long and hard before you forego an offered discount for paying early. On the other hand, if the terms are simply "net 30," why not take the free thirty-day loan?

MORTGAGE LENDING

Mortgage lending can be an important source of venture financing, particularly when real estate assets are required by the venture. As with leasing, which we discuss next, it is almost always worth taking the time to ask, "Should we buy and mortgage (borrow) or should we lease?" In many cases, assets that support mortgage debt can also be leased.

When a venture requires significant real estate, it should consider approaching potential real estate partners. Such partners may consider building or modifying existing structures to accommodate the venture's real estate needs. It has become increasingly common for real estate partners to have an ongoing equity interest in the venture, usually through the use of warrants. This provides the real estate developer with important incentives to accommodate the venture's real estate needs. It also makes the developer's involvement very similar to venture leasing, a type of equity-sweetened leasing arrangement that applies to more than just real estate assets.

TRADITIONAL AND VENTURE LEASING

Some venture requirements for equipment and real estate can be funded through leasing arrangements. In an operating lease, the venture never takes ownership of the assets. The lease frequently includes maintenance payments. The venture makes monthly payments, and the asset is available and operational. Operating leases can be month to month or have fixed terms with cancellation penalties. Typically, leases conserve a venture's cash because they include the financing for the asset. Capital leases also include the financing but often do not include maintenance and may be considered as installment purchases for tax purposes. While taxes are not usually an item of primary concern in an early venture, operating lease payments are entirely deductible whereas capital lease payments are not. When a capital lease is treated as an installment purchase for tax purposes, the monthly expense comes as depreciation. There are many subtle clauses and conditions in leases; you would be well advised to read one carefully before signing it, particularly when the item being leased is subject to immediate obsolescence. Do you really want a desktop computer on a five-year lease when it will be obsolete in two years? Perhaps, but remember that years from now you will be making payments on a machine no one wants to use.

Venture leasing refers to leases of equipment and other assets where the lessor takes an equity interest (usually through warrants) in the venture. In most cases, this is a logical extension of the notion of venture lending, when the lender takes a similar equity position. In fact, capital venture leasing is essentially equivalent to buying the asset and then borrowing through a venture bank.

venture leasing
leasing contracts where one component of the return to the lessor is a type of ownership in the venture, usually through warrants

One area where venture leasing has branched out beyond venture banking is in the sale and leaseback of intellectual property. In relatively rare cases where a venture has created an important piece of protected (patented) intellectual property, the venture may have the opportunity to sell the property to a lessor who agrees to lease the property back to the venture. Such a structure may have accounting and financing advantages in some cases and is a modern variation on research-and-development partnerships where the intellectual property was spun off to an R&D partnership (funded externally) that leased the intellectual property back to the venture. Typically, such exotic arrangements are created to exploit an explicit funding opportunity, to exploit tax advantages of a certain structure, or to tailor a venture's apparent financial condition.

Traditional and venture leasing of tangible operating assets and real estate are important potential sources of venture funding and should almost always be considered.

DIRECT PUBLIC OFFERS

Under U.S. federal and state securities laws, for certain small offerings (less than $1 million) a venture can, in some situations, sell directly to the public without a complete registration. This exemption for small offerings ("504" at the federal level and "SCOR" at the state level) is one of the bases for direct public offerings. Most often, **direct public offerings** attempt to raise money over the Web or from an existing customer base. Such offerings are still considered an inferior way to raise venture funding; while some have succeeded, others have been significant failures. A Web search for "direct public offerings" will introduce you to

direct public offerings
security offering made directly to a large number of investors

the current firms seeking capital in this manner. We encourage you to investigate this potential source of funds and to do your own research regarding its efficacy. We believe that, while this may become a more effective way to raise venture financing, currently it appears quite risky and may actually stigmatize a firm seeking financing in this manner. Direct public offerings, owing to limitations on their size (up to $5 million if Regulation A is used), have not succeeded in mounting a significant challenge to traditional venture capital funding. Needless to say, they have not succeeded in replacing public offerings underwritten by investment banks.

CONCEPT
CHECK
 • What is a direct public offering?

SUMMARY

Almost all emerging ventures are best served by obtaining equity financing through selling shares of common and preferred stock. The major sources of equity financing for such ventures are business angels and professional venture capitalists. Equity financing has the advantage of not requiring periodic payments; there is no default clause that allows the venture to be forced into bankruptcy proceedings. Nonetheless, equity financing, by design, dilutes the founders' ownership of the venture. Many entrepreneurs wishing to preserve ownership will seek out debt financing wherever feasible.

We have discussed traditional and government-guaranteed loan programs, state- and municipal-backed initiatives for revolving loans to small business, factoring and receivables financing, venture lending and leasing, mortgage financing, and direct public offerings as alternative sources of debt, equity, and hybrid financing. While we believe that most ventures will be served best by seeking equity financing, some of these alternative sources can bridge a current or ongoing financial gap. Perhaps more important, the mere presence of alternatives can provide important competition to those seeking to provide equity financing. Thus, they can affect the bargain that the venture strikes with its equity investors.

KEY TERMS

direct public offerings	receivables lending
factoring	venture leasing

DISCUSSION QUESTIONS

1. What are the five Cs of credit analysis?

2. Name three of the common loan restrictions and explain how they relate to new venturing financing. What are some additional common loan restrictions?

3. What is meant by venture banks? How do they differ from traditional commercial banks?

4. Why are new ventures at a disadvantage in receiving debt financing?

5. Why is credit card financing attractive to entrepreneurs? What are the risks?

6. What is the Small Business Administration (SBA), when was it organized, and what was its purpose?

7. Identify and briefly describe four basic SBA credit programs.

8. Compare the characteristics in terms of loan amounts, lenders, and SBA role in 7(a) loans versus 504 loans.

9. What is a Small Business Investment Company (SBIC)?

10. What types of advisory services are available from the SBA?

11. What is a debt guarantee and how does the SBA back a small business loan?

12. In which research areas does the SBA provide supplemental programs?

13. What are some characteristics of a Community Development Financial Institutions (CDFI) loan?

14. What is factoring? What is receivables lending?

15. What is venture leasing? How does it differ from traditional leasing?

16. What is a direct public offering?

INTERNET ACTIVITIES

1. Locate your state's small business credit facilitation Web page. Describe the resources your state makes available in broad categories.

2. Find the Web solicitation for a direct public offering. (You might start at http://www.vipo.com or other similar facilitation sites.) Describe the venture and its prospects.

EXERCISES/PROBLEMS

1. Assume you started a new business last year with $50,000 of your own money, which was used to purchase equipment. Now you are seeking a $25,000 loan to finance the inventory needed to reach this year's sales target. You have agreed to pledge your venture's delivery truck and your personal automobile as support for the loan. Your sister has agreed to cosign the loan. During your initial year of operation, you paid your suppliers in a timely fashion.

A. Analyze the loan request from the viewpoint of a lender who uses the five Cs of credit analysis as an aid in deciding whether to make loans.

B. Assume that you are currently carrying an accounts receivable balance of $10,000. How might you use accounts receivables to obtain an additional bank loan?

C. Assume that at the end of next year you will have an accounts receivable balance of $15,000 and an inventories balance of $30,000. If a bank normally lends an amount equal to 80 percent of accounts receivable and 50 percent of inventories pledged as collateral, what would be the amount of a bank loan a year from now?

2. Assume that the operation of your business resulted in sales of $730,000 last year. Year-end receivables are $100,000. You are considering factoring the receivables to raise cash to help finance your venture's growth. The factor imposes a 7 percent discount and charges an additional 1 percent for each expected ten-day average collection period over thirty days.

A. Estimate the dollar amount you would receive from the factor for your receivables if the collection period was thirty days or less.

B. Estimate the dollar amount you would receive from the factor for your receivables if the average collection period was sixty days.

C. Show how your answer in Part B would change if the factor charges an 8 percent discount and charges an additional .5 percent for each expected fifteen-day average collection period over thirty days.

D. If the $730,000 in sales last year were evenly distributed throughout the year, an average $100,000 in receivables outstanding would imply what average collection period? Given the original terms stated in the problem, what dollar amount would you expect to receive for your receivables?

M I N I   C A S E

Jen and Larry's Frozen Yogurt Company (Revisited)

In 2008, Jennifer (Jen) Liu and Larry Mestas founded Jen and Larry's Frozen Yogurt Company, which was based on the idea of applying the microbrew or microbatch strategy to the production and sale of frozen yogurt. Jen and Larry began producing small quantities of unique flavors and blends in limited editions. Revenues were $600,000 in 2008 and were estimated at $1.2 million in 2009.

Since Jen and Larry were selling premium frozen yogurt containing premium ingredients, each small cup of yogurt sold for $3, and the cost of producing the frozen yogurt averaged $1.50 per cup. Administrative expenses, including Jen and Larry's salaries and expenses for an accountant and two other administrative staff, were estimated at $180,000 in 2009. Marketing expenses, largely in the form of behind-the-counter workers, in-store posters, and advertising in local newspapers, were projected to be $200,000 in 2009.

An investment in bricks and mortar was necessary to make and sell the yogurt. Initial specialty equipment and the renovation of an old warehouse building in lower downtown (known as LoDo) of $450,000 occurred at the beginning of 2008 along with $50,000 being invested in inventories. An additional equipment investment of $100,000 was estimated to be needed at the beginning of 2009 to make the amount of yogurt forecasted to be sold in 2009. Depreciation expenses were expected to be $50,000 in 2009 and interest expenses were estimated at $15,000. The tax rate was expected to be 25 percent of taxable income.

A. How much net profit, before any financing costs, is the venture expected to earn in 2009? What would be the net profit if sales reach $1.5 million? What would be the net profit if next year's sales are only $800,000?

B. If inventories are expected to turn over ten times a year (based on cost of goods sold), what will be the venture's average inventories balance next year if sales are $1.2 million? How much might the venture be able to borrow if a lender typically lends an amount equal to 50 percent of the average inventories balance? If the borrowing rate is 12 percent, how much dollar amount of interest would have to be paid on the loan?

C. How might the venture acquire and finance the new equipment that is needed?

D. Identify potential government credit resources for the venture.

E. Prepare a summary of the benefits and risks of Jen and Larry's continued use of credit card financing.

Jen and Larry's Frozen Yogurt Company (Revisited) (continued)

F. Prepare a summary of how the venture might benefit from receivables financing if commercial customers are extended credit for thirty days on their purchases.
G. Discuss the impact of potential loan restrictions should the venture seek commercial loan financing.
H. Comment on how the venture might be evaluated in terms of the five Cs of credit analysis.

Appendix

FUNDING SOURCES FOR COLORADO (AS OF 5/7/2004)

| | $25,000 OR LESS | | |
PROGRAM/CONTACT	TYPE OF PROGRAM/ SERVICE AREA	TYPES AND LIMITS OF FINANCING	TARGET MARKET
Business Capital of Colorado, Inc. *(303) 832-8647*	A for-profit multibank community development corporation created to make loans to existing small businesses that cannot qualify for conventional bank financing. Service area: Denver Metro Area.	The maximum loan amount under the program is $50,000.	Borrowers must have been turned down by at least two banks and have been in business for at least one year.
Clear Creek Economic Development Corp. *(303) 569-2133*	The RLF offers loans, in conjunction with conventional loan sources, to new and expanding businesses to create new employment and expand the economic base of the region. Service area: Clear Creek and Gilpin Counties.	Up to $100,000. On a case-by-case basis may offer loans greater than $100,000; however, additional state approval is required.	The RLF may also offer loans specifically for microenterprises.

continued on next page

$25,000 OR LESS			
PROGRAM/CONTACT	**TYPE OF PROGRAM/ SERVICE AREA**	**TYPES AND LIMITS OF FINANCING**	**TARGET MARKET**
Colorado Enterprise Fund, Inc. *(303) 860-0242*	Business counseling and direct loans. Service area: Adams, Arapahoe, Boulder, Denver, Douglas, Elbert, El Paso, Jefferson, Larimer, and Weld Counties.	Startups and existing businesses; loans up to $25,000.	Ten-county region. Sales less than $1 million. Owners net worth less than $250,000.
Community Enterprise Lending Initiative *(303) 585-4150*	U.S. Bank provides financing for startups and emerging businesses; administered by selected Small Business Development Centers. Service area: statewide.	Loan amounts range from $500 to $25,000.	Small businesses referred by training sponsors.
Community Entrepreneurial Microloan Program *(303) 894-9495*	Microloan, business training, and technical assistance program. Service area: NE Denver: Five Points, Curtis Park, and Cole neighborhoods.		Clients needing job-readiness training; microenterprise technical assistance and loans.
Credit for All, Inc. *(303) 320-1955*	Peer-lending groups; microloans. Service area: East Denver and Aurora.	$500–$5,000.	
Denver Community Development Credit Union *(303) 292-3910*	Cooperative and low-income credit union consumer loans. Money management programs. Service area: Metro Denver area.		Focus on low-income.
El Pueblo Interdevelopment Corp. (EPIC) *Pueblo SBDC (719) 549-3224*	Emerging loan program. Service area: Custer, Fremont, Huerfano, Otero, and Pueblo Counties.	Loan minimum of $3,000, with no maximum.	Startup and existing businesses that can't meet conventional underwriting criteria.
Guadalupe Small Business Empowerment, Inc. *(303) 477-8113*	Business loans to members of worker cooperatives, support services. Business training in Spanish. Service area: West Denver.	$500–$2,000.	Low income.
Larimer-Weld Revolving Loan Fund *Greeley/Weld Economic Development Partnership (970) 356-4565*	Gap financing designed to assist with the financing of companies expanding or locating to the rural areas of Weld and Larimer Counties. Service area: Larimer and Weld Counties (outside Greeley and Ft. Collins city limits).	Up to $100,000. On a case-by-case basis may offer loans greater than $100,000; however, additional state approval is required.	
Loveland Microloan Guarantee Program *Loveland Center for Business Development (970) 667-4106*	Business counseling and credit enhancement. Service area: Loveland area.	Loans of $1,000 to $10,000; program deposits up to 75 percent guarantee in participating bank.	Sales less than $500,000; low- to moderate-income and minority targets; enterprise zone location.

| | TYPE OF PROGRAM/ | $25,000 OR LESS | |
| | | TYPES AND LIMITS | |
PROGRAM/CONTACT	SERVICE AREA	OF FINANCING	TARGET MARKET
Mi Casa Individual Microlending Program *Mi Casa Business Center for Women* *(303) 573-1302*	Business counseling and direct loans. Service area: Denver/ Metro.	Stepped loans: first: $500 to $2,000; second: up to $5,000.	Women ownership, low-income household.
MicrocreditWorks! *MicroBusiness Development Corp.* *(303) 308-8121*	Provides unsecured credit, training, and technical assistance for self-employment through microcredit lending circles. Service area: Adams, Arapahoe, Boulder, Denver, and Douglas Counties.	Stepped loans, starting at $500, up to $5,000, for members who have completed lower steps successfully.	Low-income people, especially women without access to traditional lending resources.
Northeastern Colorado Revolving Loan Fund Program *(970) 332-4335*	The RLF offers loans, in conjunction with conventional loan sources, to new and expanding businesses to create new employment and expand the economic base of the region. Service area: Logan, Morgan, Phillips, Sedgwick, Washington, and Yuma Counties.	Up to $100,000. On a case-by-case basis may offer loans greater than $100,000; however, additional state approval is required.	The RLF may also offer loans specifically to microenterprises.
Northwest Loan Fund (Region 12 Revolving Loan Fund Corporation) *(970) 468-0295 Ext. 119*	Startup and/or expansion financing for small businesses that are unable to secure conventional financing in the region. Service area: Eagle, Garfield, Grand, Jackson, Moffat, Pitkin, Rio Blanco, Routt, and Summit Counties.	Up to $100,000. On a case-by-case basis may offer loans greater than $100,000; however, additional state approval is required.	The goals of the fund are to create and retain jobs for individuals of low to moderate income and diversify the economy throughout the service area.
Otero–Las Animas Counties Revolving Loan Fund *(719) 383-3006*	The RLF offers loans, in conjunction with conventional loan sources, to new and expanding businesses to create new employment and expand the economic base of the region. Service area: Otero and Las Animas Counties.	The RLF provides low-interest gap-financing loans for business expansion, startups, and retentions. Businesses applying for RLF funding must provide permanent jobs for low- or moderate-income persons.	
PACEWorks! *MicroBusiness Development Corp.* *(303) 308-8121*	Microenterprise support program, offering technical assistance and loan guarantees. Service area: Self-selected communities throughout the state.	Initial loan guarantees of $500–$5,000; follow-on loan guarantees of $6,000–$30,000.	

continued on next page

		$25,000 OR LESS	
PROGRAM/CONTACT	**TYPE OF PROGRAM/ SERVICE AREA**	**TYPES AND LIMITS OF FINANCING**	**TARGET MARKET**
Pikes Peak Regional Development Corp. *(719) 471-2044*	Gap financing designed to assist with the financing of emerging companies. Service area: El Paso County except City of Colorado Springs.	Up to $100,000. On a case-by-case basis may offer loans greater than $100,000; however, additional state approval is required.	
Prairie Development Corp. (PDC) *(719) 348-5562*	Gap financing designed to assist with the financing of companies expanding or locating in the region. Service area: Cheyenne, Elbert, Lincoln, and Kit Carson Counties.	Direct loans up to $150,000. Microenterprise loans up to $25,000 targeted toward small businesses with five or fewer employees. PDC also has four other loan programs.	Job creation or retention of full-time employment located in PDC's service area is a primary objective with all six of the PDC loan programs.
Pueblo County Development Corp. *(719) 583-6382*	Gap financing designed to assist with the financing of companies expanding or locating to the rural areas of Pueblo County. Service area: Pueblo County except City of Pueblo.	Up to $100,000. On a case-by-case basis may offer loans greater than $100,000; however, additional state approval is required.	The RLF may also offer loans specifically for microenterprises.
Region 9 Economic Development District of Southwest Colorado *(970) 247-9621*	The RLF offers loans, in conjunction with conventional loan sources, to new and expanding businesses to create new employment and expand the economic base of the region. Service area: Archuleta, Dolores, La Plata, Montezuma, and San Juan Counties.	Up to $100,000. On a case-by-case basis may offer loans greater than $100,000; however, additional state approval is required. MicroEnterprise Lending Program provides loans up to $25,000.	Target industries are basic manufacturing and exporting, high-tech software and telecommunications companies, and agricultural processing.
Region 10 Revolving Loan Fund and Microloan Program *(970) 249-2436*	The RLF offers loans, in conjunction with conventional loan sources, to new and expanding businesses to create new employment and expand the economic base of the region. Region 10 serves as an intermediary lender for an SBA-funded microloan program for small businesses. Service area: Delta, Gunnison, Hinsdale, Montrose, Ouray, and San Miguel Counties.	Loans from the microloan program may range from $1,000 to $25,000.	Small businesses that cannot obtain financing on reasonable terms through other channels.
San Luis Valley Development Resources Group *(719) 589-6099*	The RLF provides low-interest gap-financing loans for business expansion, startups, and retentions. Businesses applying for RLF funding must provide permanent jobs for low- or moderate-income persons. Service area: Alamosa, Conejos, Costilla, Mineral, Rio Grande, and Saguache Counties.	Up to $100,000. On a case-by-case basis may offer loans greater than $100,000; however, additional state approval is required.	The RLF may also offer loans specifically to microenterprises.

		$25,000 OR LESS	
PROGRAM/CONTACT	**TYPE OF PROGRAM/ SERVICE AREA**	**TYPES AND LIMITS OF FINANCING**	**TARGET MARKET**
Southeast Colorado Enterprise Development (SECED) *(719) 336-3850*	Gap financing designed to assist with the financing of companies expanding or locating in the region. Service area: Baca, Bent, Crowley, Kiowa, and Prowers Counties.	Up to $100,000. On a case-by-case basis may offer loans greater than $100,000; however, additional state approval is required.	The RLF may also offer loans specifically to microenterprises.
Upper Arkansas Area Development Corp. *(719) 395-2602*	Gap and direct financing designed to assist with the financing of companies expanding or locating in the region. Service area: Chafee, Custer, Fremont, Lake, and Park Counties.	Gap-financing loans from $5,000 to $125,000. Direct loans from $5,000 to $30,000.	The RLF may also offer loans specifically to microenterprises.
Western Colorado Business Development Corp. *(970) 243-5242*	Gap financing designed to assist with the financing of companies expanding or locating in the county. The Peterson Fund microloan program combines business education with small loans for eligible low-income entrepreneurs. Service area: Mesa County.	$8,000 to $300,000. Microloans from $1,500 to $5,000 are available for low-income persons interested in business startup.	Preference is given to businesses that will create new jobs or retain existing jobs.

		$100,000 OR LESS	
PROGRAM/CONTACT	**TYPE OF PROGRAM/ SERVICE AREA**	**TYPES AND LIMITS OF FINANCING**	**TARGET MARKET**
Colorado Housing and Finance Authority (CHFA) *Business Finance Division* *(303) 297-7329* or *(800) 877-2432*	CHFA's Business Finance Division provides a variety of business financing programs, primarily for small- to medium-sized firms. Service area: Colorado.	Type and loan size depend on the loan programs.	For-profit and not-for-profit enterprises located in Colorado.
Denver Revolving Loan Fund *Mayor's Office of Economic Development* *(720) 913-1640*	Gap financing for new or expanding businesses in targeted Denver neighborhoods. Service area: targeted neighborhoods in City and County of Denver.	Maximum $350,000; maximum 25 percent of project costs (30 percent for minority- and women-owned businesses).	Majority of new or retained jobs must be made available to low- and moderate-income Denver residents.
La Junta Capital, Inc. Revolving Loan Fund *(719) 384-7638* or *(800) 634-2130*	Revolving loan fund to increase the pool of funds available to new and expanding businesses in the area. Service area: City of La Junta, the La Junta Industrial Park, and nearby unincorporated areas.	$5,000–$500,000.	Businesses that diversify the local economy or provide a product or service not currently available in the City of La Junta. Highest priority is given to manufacturing concerns.

continued on next page

$100,000 OR LESS			
PROGRAM/CONTACT	TYPE OF PROGRAM/ SERVICE AREA	TYPES AND LIMITS OF FINANCING	TARGET MARKET
SBA Express *SBA District Office* *(303) 844-2607*	This program makes it easier and faster for lenders to provide small business loans in smaller amounts and helps lenders provide smaller revolving credit loans. Service area: statewide.	Loans up to $150,000 (SBA guaranties 50 percent).	Small businesses under SBA size standards.
SBA LowDoc *SBA District Office* *(303) 844-2607*	This program streamlines the application process and simplifies the credit analysis. Service area: statewide.	Up to $150,000 (SBA guaranty up to 85 percent); no revolving credit loans.	Small business under SBA size standards.
SBA 7(a) Guaranteed Loans *SBA District Office* *(303) 844-2607*	One of SBA's primary lending programs. The program operates through private-sector lenders that provide loans that are, in turn, guaranteed by the SBA. Service area: statewide.	Maximum guaranty amount is generally $1,000,000; 85 percent on loans of $150,000 or less and 75 percent on loans of more than $150,000.	Small business under SBA size standards. Unable to obtain financing on reasonable terms through other channels.

$100,000 OR MORE			
PROGRAM/CONTACT	TYPE OF PROGRAM/ SERVICE AREA	TYPES AND LIMITS OF FINANCING	TARGET MARKET
CHFA Rural Development Loan Program *CHFA Commercial Division* *(303) 297-7329 or (800)* *877-2432 Ext. 329*	For-profit and not-for-profit enterprises located in rural communities. Service area: Colorado communities with fewer than 25,000 people.	The maximum loan amount is $150,000 or 75 percent of the project cost, whichever is less. Loans may have terms for up to twenty years.	Businesses that are unable to receive money from sources such as CHFA's QIC and Access programs or SBA loans.
Rural Community Infrastructure Assistance Program *Office of Economic Development* *(303) 892-3840*	Funds for the construction and/ or improvement of publicly or quasi-publicly owned water, sewer, road, and other infrastructure in support of specific business projects that will create or retain jobs. Service area: Nonntitlement (rural) areas of Colorado.		Businesses creating permanent jobs and/or retaining existing jobs for low- to moderate-income persons.
SBA 504 Certified Development Companies *SBA District Office* *(303) 844-2607*	Provides long-term, fixed-asset financing through five Certified Development Companies (CDC). These CDCs are not-for-profit organizations. Service area: statewide.	SBA can guarantee debentures covering as much as 40 percent of a 504 project up to $1 million ($1.3 million if the business meets a public policy goal, such as business district revitalization, rural development, or expansion of exports).	Small businesses as defined by SBA.

$100,000 OR MORE			
PROGRAM/CONTACT	**TYPE OF PROGRAM/ SERVICE AREA**	**TYPES AND LIMITS OF FINANCING**	**TARGET MARKET**
USDA Community and Business Program *(720) 544-2931*	Direct loans and guarantee business loans. Service area: rural areas with a population of 50,000 or fewer.	Larger loan amounts not to exceed $25 million.	Businesses located in rural areas.

SPECIALTY FUNDING			
PROGRAM/CONTACT	**TYPE OF PROGRAM/ SERVICE AREA**	**TYPES AND LIMITS OF FINANCING**	**TARGET MARKET**
Colorado Brownfields Revolving Loan Fund *Colorado Department of Public Health and Environment* *(303) 820-5660*	Revolving loan fund to assist in approved cleanup of environmental contamination, including necessary site monitoring. Service Area: Denver Metro Area.	Up to $425,000, depending on balance in loan fund.	All cleanups financed through the fund must have previous approval under the Colorado Department of Public Health and Environment's Voluntary Cleanup Program.
Englewood Brownfields Revolving Loan Fund *(303) 762-2599*	The BRLF offers a line of credit to fund potential environmental assessments and environmental engineering studies necessary to overcome environmental concerns. Service area: City of Englewood.		Properties that are impacted by real or perceived environmental contamination, where concerns over environmental liability have hindered reuse.
Export-Import Bank *(562) 980-4583*	Guarantee direct loans, credit enhancement, information service, export business counseling, and export credit insurance program.	Loan amounts and guarantees vary according to the export financing programs.	Small business exporters.
SBA CAPLines (General Contractor) Loans *SBA District Office* *(303) 844-2607*	CAPLines is the umbrella program under which the SBA helps small businesses meet their short-term and cyclical working capital needs. Service area: statewide.	The maximum amount the SBA can guarantee is generally $750,000.	There are five short-term working capital loan programs for small businesses, including seasonal, contract, builders, standard asset-based credit line, and small asset-based line.
SBA Export Working Capital Program (EWCP) *SBA District Office* *(303) 844-5652*	Guarantee loans that provide short-term working capital to exporters. The EWCP is a combined effort of the SBA and the Export-Import Bank. Service area: statewide.	SBA guarantees up to 90 percent of EWCP loan requests of $1,111,111 or less. Requests over that amount may be processed through the Export-Import Bank.	Small businesses engaging in exporting.

continued on next page

	SPECIALTY FUNDING		
PROGRAM/CONTACT	**TYPE OF PROGRAM/ SERVICE AREA**	**TYPES AND LIMITS OF FINANCING**	**TARGET MARKET**
SBA International Trade Loan Program *SBA District Office* *(303) 844-9461*	Service area: statewide.	SBA guarantees up to $1.25 million. Loan amounts up to $1 million for facilities and equipment and $750,000 for working capital.	Small businesses planning to export or increase existing exports. Small businesses adversely affected by competition from imports.
U.S. Department of Transportation Short-Term Lending Program *(800) 532-1169*	The STLP provides revolving lines of credit to finance accounts receivable arising from transportation-related contracts.	Maximum line of credit is $500,000.	Certified disadvantaged business enterprises.

Chapter 13

SECURITY STRUCTURES AND DETERMINING ENTERPRISE VALUES

PREVIOUSLY COVERED

In Chapter 11, we discussed the characteristics and operations of professionally managed venture capital organizations. This was followed by Chapter 12, which focused on other financing alternatives available to entrepreneurs. Topics included commercial and venture bank lending, the use of credit cards, Small Business Administration (SBA) credit programs, and other types of government financing programs. Most ventures that successfully move through their life cycle stages while growing rapidly will find it necessary to obtain financial capital by issuing bonds and common stocks. They may also issue warrants and convertible securities. As ventures take on more complex capital structures, discounted cash flow valuation methods should shift from the previously discussed direct equity methods to enterprise methods that consider all of the firm's financing.

LOOKING AHEAD

Part 6 covers exit strategies and turnaround opportunities. Chapter 14 focuses on how investors and founders exit an ultimately successful venture. An entrepreneur who has committed her time, effort, and personal financial assets to convert an idea into a successful business venture and has weathered one or more bouts of financial distress is, in all likelihood, looking forward to a fruitful harvest. We will cover the various ways one harvests a successful venture. In Chapter 15, we focus on financially troubled ventures and discuss opportunities for turning them back into successful ventures.

CHAPTER LEARNING OBJECTIVES

In this chapter, we discuss important concepts in structuring the securities a venture uses to raise funding. We introduce the notion of primitive securities (such as bonds and common stocks) and consider more complex securities (such as warrants and convertible preferred securities) that derive their values from the primitive securities.

517

We introduce the enterprise valuation method, a straightforward technique for valuing a venture that has issued complex financial securities. After completing this chapter, you will be able to:

1. Describe the types of securities often involved in venture financing

2. Discuss the structural considerations involved in designing venture securities

3. Draw simple diagrams describing the payoffs to calls, puts, and warrants

4. Value a venture as a complete enterprise and relate that value to the value of the securities involved in supporting the enterprise

Up to this point, we have concentrated our treatment of valuation techniques on the class of securities affiliated with a venture's residual or basic ownership. For a corporation, the holders of its common equity are the basic owners. In a partnership, basic ownership is vested in partnership interests. For a limited liability company, basic ownership resides with the holders of the LLC's memberships. Many businesses acquire funding by selling off portions of this basic ownership. The valuation techniques in Chapters 9 and 10 that we labeled "equity methods" directly apply to the sale of basic (residual) ownership. Our methods make sure all senior claims against the venture are paid (or projected to be paid) before treating the amount remaining as the equity valuation cash flow, forming the basis of the value of venture ownership.

It is common for high-growth ventures to engage in financing by selling combinations of basic securities (e.g., debt and equity in combination) and by selling more complicated securities (e.g., preferred equity and warrants). Some important concepts and techniques can help entrepreneurs navigate the minefield of security design and valuation. We begin with some definitions and a list of potential ingredients that a venture's (or an investor's) legal counsel may suggest as part of the venture's financial structure. We will couch our discussion using terminology applicable to corporate organizational structures.

CONCEPT CHECK

• What is the basic form of ownership in the common organizational forms?

13.1   COMMON STOCK (COMMON EQUITY)

common stock
the least senior claim on a venture's assets (residual ownership)

We start with basic, or residual, ownership. The least senior claim on a venture's assets is the claim held by the holders of the venture's **common stock** (or common equity). Generally, a venture's other security holders receive their promised payments before common stockholders receive any payment. For example, in bankruptcy liquidation, common stockholders generally get only what remains after all the creditors (debtholders) and other investors have taken their share. Common shareholders' claims are subordinated to those other claims. Unless it is specifically organized otherwise, a venture's common stockholders have the voting rights, including those needed to appoint a board of directors.[1] The venture's common stockholders have the right to legal dividends so long as they are not due to others (e.g., as we discuss later, they may be due to the holders of the venture's preferred equity). By law in some states, and by choice in others, the holders of a venture's common stock may have the right to maintain their percent ownership through subsequent financings. Such **preemptive rights** allow existing owners to buy sufficient shares in each round of financing so that their ownership is not automatically diluted. Of course, if existing shareholders do not have the financial resources to participate adequately in a new round, or if for other reasons they do not choose to exercise their preemptive rights, their ownership percentage will decline. Common shares can be held, sold to others (subject to the resale restrictions we covered in Chapter 8), or sold back to the venture (where they usually become "treasury shares").[2]

preemptive rights
the right for existing owners to buy sufficient shares to preserve their ownership share

CONCEPT CHECK

- What is common equity?
- What is a preemptive right?

13.2   PREFERRED STOCK (PREFERRED EQUITY)

Preferred stock grants its holders preferential (senior) treatment relative to the holders of a venture's common equity. In particular, preferred stockholders generally receive dividends and liquidation proceeds (in case of bankruptcy) before they are distributed to common stockholders. The specific preferential treatment accorded must be set forth in the venture's organizational documents (e.g., a corporation's articles of incorporation). While in some jurisdictions it may be possible for the board of directors to amend the articles directly, in many other cases a postorganizational addition of preferred equity requires shareholder approval in a process that can be time consuming and expensive. If your venture ever plans to have preferred equity, it is probably worth the time and energy to organize the venture so that such shares are authorized. This will keep any necessary changes (subsequently mandated by the buyers of the venture's preferred equity) to a minimum.

preferred stock
equity claim senior to common stock and providing preference on dividends and liquidation proceeds

Preferred dividends, unlike common dividends, are usually stated as a percent of the par value of the preferred stock. That is, if the preferred stock was originally issued at $1, then the dividend covenant might specify a 4 percent

---

[1] While the voting rights for different classes of common shares may differ (with regular and "super voting" classes of common stock), there are some significant issues for ventures that opt to avoid the more common "one share, one vote" structure. In particular, the venture may have serious difficulties if, and when, it later decides to sell regular voting shares to the public and have them traded on an exchange.

[2] Although it is not typical, if the venture has the right to repurchase a class of common shares (obviously not all of them), the shares in that class are called "redeemable common stock."

annual preferred dividend. This dividend, having preferential status to common dividends, must be paid prior to any common dividend. If the preferred dividend is *noncumulative*, missing it imposes no restriction on the payment of future dividends. If it is *cumulative*, all previously unpaid preferred dividends must be paid (in arrears) before any common dividend. If the preferred dividend is "cumulative if earned," it is cumulative when there are (and noncumulative when there are not) sufficient earnings to pay the preferred dividend.[3] The penalties imposed for repeated failure to pay preferred dividends may include (but are certainly not limited to) the right of preferred stockholders to elect members to the board or a mandatory, and possibly irreversible, increase in the dividend rate.

As you may imagine, there are some serious incentive problems in structuring preferred equity investments. For example, suppose one year that the 4 percent dividend is paid. If the venture, by paying the 4 percent dividend, becomes free to declare a common dividend sufficiently large to assure that no preferred dividends will be paid in the foreseeable future, there can be serious investor versus owner conflicts. Purchasers of the venture's preferred equity can, and will, seek protection against this treatment in a variety of ways. **Participating preferred stock** can be structured to assure preferred shareholders that they will participate (dollar for dollar, or otherwise) in the payment of any dividends to common shareholders. Such a provision significantly raises the cost of declaring any common stock dividend. For instance, if the venture wanted to pay a $1 dividend and the preferred shareholders had equal participation in the dividend, the cost to the venture would be $2. The possibilities for structuring the terms of participation and preference are unlimited. Some common structures are predividend return of par, predividend twofold return of par (2X preferred), equal participation, partial participation (at less than equal), threshold participation (granting participation above a certain level of common dividend), and capped participation (limiting the amount of the participation to some maximum amount).

An interesting recent design feature for corporations wishing to conserve cash is **paid in kind (PIK) preferred stock**, where the dividend obligation can be satisfied in cash or by issuing additional par amounts of the preferred security. Although not common in new venture funding, it is easy to see why PIK preferred stock acts like cumulative preferred with an additional bite. That additional bite comes from the fact that the issue of new par value equity formally confers additional senior claim to a venture's underlying assets if and when it liquidates. Depending on the context, such a formal claim may be treated differently from unpaid preferred dividends on cumulative preferred. In any case, the venture may want the flexibility of paying either in cash or in more of the same security. If this is the case, PIK preferred equity might be worth investigating.

In almost all new venture funding cases, preferred stock contains important features that allow a venture to redeem (buy back) the preferred security and allow an investor facing possible redemption to convert the preferred stock to common stock. These covenants are typically structured to balance the investors' demands

participating preferred stock

preferred stock with rights to participate in any dividends paid to common stockholders; stock with an investment repayment provision that must be met before distribution of returns to common stockholders

paid in kind (PIK) preferred stock

preferred stock that has the option of paying preferred dividends by issuing more preferred stock

---

[3] The accumulation covenants may be more complex than those falling neatly into the three categories we present. As always, the legal structure and interpretation of the securities covenants are best discussed with legal counsel (in this case, counsel specializing in corporate finance and securities law).

(to be like common stock but senior to it) with the venture's demands (to avoid an eternal overhang of a senior security having the unexercised right to convert to common stock).

Redemption clauses can involve elements of venture obligation and discretion. Regarding venture obligation, for example, sinking fund clauses may compel a venture to set aside funds (and use them) to repurchase specific amounts of the preferred stock. The redemption price would typically be the issue price plus any accrued dividends. Redemption dates can be contractually specified and create creditor-like liabilities to replace the existing preferred equity claim. To maintain an element of fairness, the preferred shares to be redeemed at a given date can be prorated on all outstanding shares or chosen by lot.

Regarding redemption that is at the venture's discretion, many preferred stocks have call features that dictate dates at which the venture can repurchase the preferred equity by paying a contractually specified amount. For example, if the preferred equity was originally issued for $1, it might contain a one-year call protection period, at the end of which the venture has the right to repurchase the preferred share during the second year for $2.75. The option might also include the right to repurchase the preferred share in the third year for $3.25. You can easily construct scenarios where the venture would not repurchase the share until it had to pay the full $3.25. In many new venture contexts, the preferred stocks have a declining redemption price schedule. For example, the venture might have to pay only $2 in the second year. With an issue price of $1, an adequate return may have already been assured at $2. The declining price may make the preferred holder more willing to surrender preferred status.

CONCEPT CHECK

- What is preferred stock?
- What are the cash flow advantages of PIK preferred stock?

Typically, the surrender of preferred status occurs when the preferred holder exercises a conversion option to convert the preferred share into common stock. Generally, holders of a venture's **convertible preferred stock** have the right to convert a preferred share into a specified number (usually one) of common shares at any time before the expiration date, if any, of the preferred security.[4] Of course, the venture needs to ensure that it has set aside enough authorized but unissued shares to fulfill the common share issue obligations dictated by conversion. Conversion can also be forced upon preferred shareholders (if the appropriate covenants exist) at specific events in the venture's life. The most common example is that of convertible preferreds' being automatically converted to common stock

convertible preferred stock
preferred stock with option to exchange it into common stock

---

4   Although it can be, preferred equity is not necessarily perpetual. It can have a fixed life span and dictate a final payment analogous to the return of principal on debt. Also, the number of common shares received in exchange for a preferred share (the conversion ratio) need not be one.

upon the registration of the venture's common stock with the SEC for the venture's initial public offering (IPO).

As should be clear after a little thought, the conversion feature of convertible preferred stock can confer a great deal of value to the investor. While the venture is struggling, the preferred status places the preferred shareholder above the common shareholders (including the entrepreneur and founders) in dividends and any liquidation proceeds (if the venture folds). When the venture takes off, the conversion feature ensures the preferred shareholder equal status to participate in the venture's meteoric rise in value. Two points here are important: (1) the propensity of convertible preferred stock to remain unconverted and (2) the impact new issues can have on the value of the conversion feature.

One should not expect the conversion option to be exercised unless some serious loss can result from not exercising it. Because convertible preferred stock can be converted into common stock, it must be worth at least as much as common stock. Because it is senior to, and therefore worth more than, common stock in bad outcomes (liquidation), preferred stock can be more valuable than common stock. Faced with this value proposition, convertible preferred stockholders have a rational aversion to converting. This aversion creates what is known as overhanging convertibles. Overhang tendencies are a natural part of the incentives structured into convertible securities (including convertible preferreds).

The response to "I won't convert if I don't have to" is "If you don't convert, you'll miss out." What will the unconverted miss? Importantly, having a dividend set at 4 percent (and less than full participation in common dividends) means the unconverted miss out on some, if not all, of the common dividends. Lack of compensation for erosion of venture value (and correspondingly for erosion in the value of preferred equity) owing to the payment of common dividends is a major reason for participation clauses for convertible preferred equity. If no participation clauses are present, one could expect the threat of a large common dividend to cause massive conversion. If we assume that this dividend "threat" is recognized and participation clauses are embedded in the preferreds, we see that the incentive for convertible preferred stockholders to convert lies outside the threat of paying large dividends. We must look elsewhere for a solution to overhanging convertibles.

The most effective incentive to convert comes from the redemption right (or call feature) granted to the venture. As we have mentioned, it is common for the venture to be able to repurchase the convertible preferreds at a specific price for a specific period of time. Suppose that a $1 par value preferred stock can be converted into one share of common stock currently worth $10. With full participation in common dividends, there is little (if any) reason to convert the preferred into common. If, however, there is a $2 call feature, the venture can repurchase the convertible preferred stock for $2. You can be assured that between the time when the call is announced and the time it is effective (usually a period of a few days to a few weeks), the conversion will take place. It is usually better to get $10 of value rather than $2. Now we can see how the call feature imposes the necessary "If you don't convert, you'll miss out" to force conversion. A properly designed call feature mitigates the overhang problem created by making preferred stock convertible into common stock. You will probably not observe a conversion feature without an accompanying call feature designed to force conversion and control overhang.

Our second point addresses the relationship of new issues to the value of the conversion feature. Conversion value can be severely limited when a venture continues to issue new securities in such a way that conversion is never desirable. For example, suppose a preferred stock is perpetually worth $5 for its stream of dividends and can be converted into one share of common stock. If the venture adopts a policy of splitting the stock two for one every time its value reaches $3, resulting in a share value of $1.50, the conversion option will never be worth exercising. Clearly, convertible preferred shareholders will demand some protection against stock splits and stock dividends that can rob the value of their conversion option. In addition to straightforward stock split and stock dividend protection, convertible preferred shareholders will bargain for antidilution clauses that further protect the value of their conversion option. While there may be specific clauses related to distributions of securities and assets, of particular interest are clauses related to what is known as price protection.

Price protection clauses seek to compensate current investors for subsequent decreases in the offering price of common stock. As we have already argued, subsequent decreases in the issue price for common stock (even without splits) limit, or even destroy, the value of the conversion feature. Such dilutive offerings are an observable sign that previous investors' conversion options have relatively low value. Investors wanting to preserve the conversion value will seek some form of compensation for this unexpected failing. Whether they deserve such compensation is questionable. Whether they get it depends on the venture's bargaining strength. Before we discuss important aspects of the bargaining over price protection clauses, we should look at a few examples.

In order to make sense of price protection clauses and formulas, we first need to move from the notion of a *conversion ratio* to the notion of a *conversion price*. For example, if the par value of a preferred stock is $5 and the stock can be converted into one share of common stock, we say the conversion ratio is one and the conversion price is $5. If the preferred stock could be converted into two shares, we would say that the conversion ratio is 2:1 and that the conversion price is $2.50. The par value can be used to pay for the stock at $2.50 per share. In this second case, it is reasonable to ask how the conversion price should change if and when the venture subsequently sells new shares for $1.25. Clearly, it will be hard to derive any value from conversion at $2.50 per share (assuming the preferred is worth its par) when the company is selling shares at $1.25.

CONCEPT CHECK

- How are the conversion price and the conversion ratio related?
- What is the purpose of an antidilution clause?

The easiest and harshest adjustment is known as a *full ratchet* clause. For the full ratchet in our example, a new issue at $1.25 would change the conversion price for the existing preferred to $1.25 (from $2.50). That is, an existing share of convertible preferred would convert to four shares of common (twice as many as before the dilutive round). While a full ratchet involves simple calculations, the shadow such a clause casts on future investment rounds can be considerable. How this shadow affects investors may not be clear. Subsequent investors can bargain knowing that the convertibles are being made more attractive in the process. As a consequence, they will demand more shares than they otherwise would. Full ratchet–protected investors will receive enough postconversion shares to protect their preissue conversion value. They certainly are not paying the cost of their own price protection. That leaves the entrepreneur, founders, and other non-price-protected investors to pick up the tab. In short, if we assume that the ratchet price protection shadow does not kill a subsequent dilutive round, the entire cost is borne by existing investors who do not have price protection. Price protection covenants other than the full ratchet are more common and usually involve some cost sharing between non-price-protected and partially price-protected investors.

As an example of these partial price protection formulas, we examine the conversion price formula and the market price formula.[5]

Conversion Price Formula (CPF)

$$\text{New Conversion Price} = \frac{\text{Shares Before Issue} \times \text{Old Conversion Price} + \text{New Issue Price} \times \text{New Shares}}{\text{Total Shares After Issue}}$$

Market Price Formula (MPF)

$$\text{New Conversion Price} = \text{Old Conversion Price} \times \frac{\text{Shares Before Issue} + \dfrac{\text{New Issue Price} \times \text{New Shares}}{\text{Share Value Without New Shares}}}{\text{Total Shares After Issue}}$$

Assuming 100,000 shares outstanding before the current issue, 25,000 shares to be issued in the current round priced at $1.25, and prefinancing market value per share of $1.50, we get new conversion prices of $2.25 and $2.42 for the conversion price and market price formulas, respectively. Note that the CPF is invariant to a hypothesized prefinancing valuation, whereas the MPF requires one (in "Share Value Without New Shares"). To compare these formulas, consider what happens when shares are sold at the previous conversion price and at market. If we change the new issue price to $2.50, we get new conversion prices of $2.50 and $2.83. When shares are issued at the current conversion price, the CPF suggests no change in the conversion price, as the new issue is thought to be supporting the existing conversion value. For this case, the MPF is problematic. In recognition that $2.50 is above the specified "Share Value Without New" of $1.50, it suggests increasing the conversion price to $2.83. The market price formula is intended to address new issue prices no greater than the "Share Value Without New Shares." More importantly, these two formulas reflect different

---

[5] These terms are taken from the price protection treatment given in Richard Harroch, "Negotiating Venture Capital Financing," *Start-Up Companies: Planning, Financing, and Operating the Successful Business* (New York: Law Journal Seminars-Press, 1993).

approaches to defining what is meant by dilution. The CPF compensates for any issue below the current conversion price. The MPF compensates only for issues below current fair market value, whatever that is. To see this, note that changing the new issue price to the current market value of $1.50 gives conversion prices of $2.30 and $2.50. The CPF, recognizing that $1.50 is below the current conversion price of $2.50, compensates the convertible preferred owner. Nonprotected investors pay the penalty for issuing below the protected investors' conversion price. The MPF suggests no damage for which nonprotected investors should pay when the venture must sell to the market at a price below protected investors' conversion prices. Consequently, it recommends no adjustment to the $2.50 conversion price. When the venture issue is below the current market price, the MPF begins to adjust the protected investors' conversion prices. As you can see, the differences in these formulas suggest different distributions of the responsibility when the current issue price falls below the existing conversion and market prices.

Having different conversion price formulas allows negotiation and variation in how dilution costs are allocated to existing investors when the venture must undertake a **down (reset) round**. There is little doubt that everyone in the venture will be upset when the reset round is priced below previous rounds. After all, other things being equal, the entrepreneur, founders, and all existing investors would certainly prefer to sell the shares for a higher price. Persuasive current investors, seeking as much protection as possible, may bargain to be granted conversion price concessions if a subsequent round takes place at a lower price. While this at first appears unambiguously to new investors' benefits, it need not be.

When the venture requires external financing beyond that targeted in the current round, subsequent investors may be unwilling to pay current issue prices. These potential subsequent investors will have to be told that previous investors have antidilution clauses granting them free shares in this subsequent round. What subsequent investors are going to like granting conversion price concessions to previous investors? Sometimes the antidilution clauses are sufficient to kill the deal. If not, then, at a minimum, subsequent investors will demand sweetened terms (more shares for the same dollars), price-protected current investors will get their free shares, and all non-dilution-protected investors (like the entrepreneur and founders) will be left "holding the bag."[6] Seen in this light, granting price protection is a gutsy signal from the non-dilution-protected founders. The venture could be betting its future on making its projections and not having to reset the issue price. If you become involved in price protection negotiations, it is important to remember that, by granting price protection, you increase your "carry" of the costs of a future dilutive round. While the amount and type of price protection you offer can be an important signal, it can also materially affect the probability that your venture will survive.

down (reset) round
venture round priced below most recent previous price

---

[6] To get an idea of the subsequent investor's problem, return to the CPF and MPF and ask how we got the notion that 25,000 new shares would be sold at $1.25. Clearly, a potential new investor would want to see how the terms and their effect on existing securities would affect postinvestment percent share ownership. As the 25,000 shares' percent of ownership declines through changes in the conversion price on existing securities, the potential investor might demand, say, 27,000 shares for the same proposed investment of $31,250 (= 25,000 × $1.25) or might demand a price of, say, $1.10. Clearly, the terms of 25,000 shares at $1.25 must include the feedback effect those same terms have on existing securities.

Generally, it is difficult (and undesirable) to provide complete price protection against every possible move the venture could make to diminish existing conversion value. One situation where one would expect price protection concerns is a venture issuing new convertibles at nondilutive par prices while having dilutive conversion options. When a venture sells a share of stock bundled with an option to buy another share (frequently called stock units), where the option confers the right to buy at advantageous (below market or conversion price) prices, concerns about dilution are warranted and protection will be sought.

While we have discussed price protection at length in order to uncover some of the natural concerns investors and entrepreneurs have about the structure of a venture's securities, we do not want to imply that these issues are necessarily central to an investor's willingness to purchase securities. For example, the willingness and right to participate pro rata in subsequent investing rounds (preemptive rights) grants some protection against unwelcome dilution by outsiders. That is, if the outside price is so attractive that it is a problem, then one should expect existing investors to participate in the dilutive round, if they can. If the new round is completely funded by existing investors, the dilution is really only a rearrangement of existing percent ownerships.

One side note of this discussion is that, if you are considering investing in someone else's venture, you should make sure you have the resources to participate in subsequent rounds (possibly at lower prices) or anticipate having your ownership diluted.

CONCEPT CHECK

- What is a reset round?
- How do price protection clauses hedge against reset rounds?

13.3   CONVERTIBLE DEBT

Some new ventures fund themselves with convertible debt. While this debt is usually structured like the more common convertible preferred equity financing, there are some notable distinct differences.[7] Convertible debt holders have bankruptcy rights that can kick in when coupon payments are missed. These rights are much stronger than those of preferred shareholders, who don't receive a scheduled dividend. Convertible debt holders also have a security interest in the venture's assets that is senior to preferred shareholders' interests. Unlike preferred equity, debt can

---

[7] When a venture issues securities, it is almost always issuing some type of equity-related instrument. New ventures are, almost by definition, too young to attract sizable financing structured as straight debt. Consequently, most new venture debt issues involve debt that converts into common equity, which is the subject of this section. The exceptions to the no-straight-debt new venture characterization are ventures funded by Small Business Administration–guaranteed loans, traditional bank debt, and credit cards, all of which are treated elsewhere in this text.

be structured to provide senior interest in specific assets such as inventory or property, plant, and equipment (collateral).

It is frequently claimed that a major advantage in a mature corporation's use of debt over preferred equity is the tax deductibility of interest. Preferred dividends are not tax deductible on the venture's tax returns. Two important characteristics make this traditional advantage less important in structuring a new venture's securities. First, tax shields are widely available in startups. These come from depreciated new equipment and the accumulation of net operating loss carryforwards. It may be several years before the tax deductibility of interest confers any marginal tax benefit, and delay erodes the value of the tax benefits. Second, some of the potential purchasers of a venture's securities are themselves corporations that can exclude most of the preferred dividends from income but would have to pay taxes on interest received on bonds. When a new venture compares the diminished relative tax benefits from issuing debt to the increased downside from missing a periodic payment, the balance may tip in favor of convertible preferred rather than convertible debt.

What may not be obvious is that forfeiting the bankruptcy rights bundled with the use of debt may benefit the venture and its investors. By issuing preferred equity instead of debt, investors may commit to an internal reorganization rather than court reorganization in bankruptcy when the venture hits hard times. Without such a commitment, as the venture gets into trouble and faces loss of control in a bankruptcy proceeding, it has strong incentives to undertake risky projects to avoid losing control. The incentive to undertake these projects can easily exceed the venture's incentive to undertake only those projects that are expected to increase value. To put it bluntly, if we are off to the bankruptcy court tomorrow, tonight you have a great incentive to buy today's lottery tickets (with the money on which I will have a senior claim tomorrow in court). I should expect this because, with lottery tickets today, you will have some chance of staying out of bankruptcy court tomorrow. The problem is that lottery tickets, on average, destroy value. If investors were threatening an internal reorganization (or cooperative workout) tomorrow rather than bankruptcy, your incentive to buy lottery tickets would be greatly reduced. It might be in our mutual best interest to use financing that implicitly incorporates the promise of a less destructive internal reorganization.[8] While we recognize that convertible debt is used in funding some ventures, its use in professional venture capital is relatively rare (about 2 percent), and its structural issues are similar to those of convertible preferred.[9]

CONCEPT CHECK

- What is convertible preferred stock?
- What advantage does convertible preferred stock offer venture investors?

---

[8] For formal treatment of this potential advantage of preferred stock in a venture investing context and an empirical investigation of the frequency of debt and preferred usage, see Jeffrey Trester, "Venture Capital Contracting Under Asymmetric Information," *Journal of Banking and Finance* 22 (1998).

[9] Ibid.

13.4   WARRANTS AND OPTIONS

Options to buy additional shares at specified prices are common "sweeteners" or "equity kickers" used to increase the attractiveness of a securities offering. These options offer their holders an increased participation in the venture's upside, with no obligation on the venture's downside. Options are also a common (and usually highly desirable) component of venture employee incentive compensation. Granting employees some participation in the venture's upside can increase their motivation to work as a team and provide strong incentives to seek opportunities to increase the value of the founders' and investors' investments. When current investors have preemptive rights on newly issued securities (in order to maintain their percent ownership), those rights are options on the venture's new stock. A different sort of option, the right to sell, is structured into the design of some ventures' securities. In such arrangements the venture can be forced to repurchase an investor's shares, usually at some multiple of earnings at some future date. We begin with some formal definitions:

Call Option: the right, not the obligation, to purchase a specified asset at a specified price

Put Option: the right, not the obligation, to sell a specified asset at a specified price

American-Style Option: an option that can be exercised at any time until expiration

European-Style Option: an option that can be exercised only at the expiration date

Bermudan-Style Option: an option that can be exercised only at a specific set of dates

The call and put options embedded in securities issued by a venture can have American, European, or Bermudan characteristics. In addition, for American and Bermudan embedded options, the exercise price can change over time in a way that is specified in the security agreement.

When thinking about options, it helps to diagram the option to see how the option holder benefits. An example is a call option's payoff diagram. Figure 13.1 displays the payoff diagrams for call options that are "out of the money" (not currently worth exercising), "at the money" (breakeven current exercise), and "in the money" (profitable current exercise).

As these diagrams illustrate, if the venture's stock price is $2 at the exercise date for the option, a call option to buy the stock at $1 ($2) is worth $1 ($0). A call option to buy at $3 will not be exercised.

Our understanding of put options also can be enhanced by examining their payoff diagrams as in Figure 13.2.

In summary, call option holders benefit dollar for dollar in stock price increases above the exercise price (note the 45-degree line heading northeast from the exercise price). Put option holders benefit dollar for dollar in stock price decreases below the exercise price (note the 45-degree line heading northwest from the exercise price). As you might guess, the call option holder wants the stock

FIGURE 13.1 Call Option Payoff Diagrams

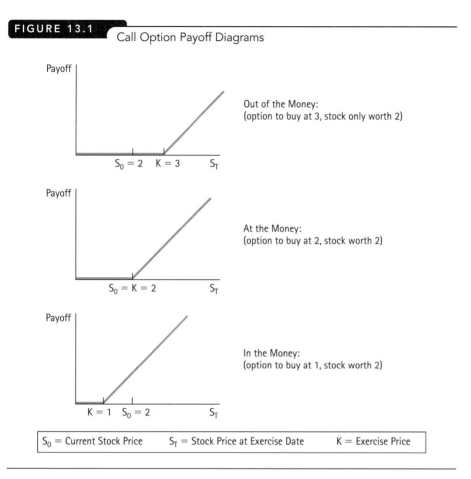

Out of the Money:
(option to buy at 3, stock only worth 2)

At the Money:
(option to buy at 2, stock worth 2)

In the Money:
(option to buy at 1, stock worth 2)

S_0 = Current Stock Price	S_T = Stock Price at Exercise Date	K = Exercise Price

price to rise, and the put option holder has an incentive to want the stock price to fall. Of course, call options are used for employee and founder incentive compensation. Put options are a type of assurance given to investors worried about not being able to sell their stock for a reasonable price otherwise. Usually, put options are a fallback bundled in the purchase of a stock. When we look at a combination of stock and put, the gains on the put are canceled by losses on the stock and, as one would hope, there is no net gain from a decline in the value of the venture.

Warrants are call options issued by the company and typically involve the issue of new shares rather than the purchase of existing ones. Warrants involving the creation of new (dilutive) shares are worth less than options on existing shares; how much less depends on how many new shares will be issued upon the exercise of the warrants. The simplest way to see this is to think about a venture having only one share outstanding. An option on that one existing share is an option on 100 percent ownership. A warrant on a new share is an option on 50 percent ownership (with two shares outstanding after warrant exercise). Clearly, although this is an extreme example, the value received under exercise of the warrant is strictly less

warrants
call options issued by a company granting the holder the right to buy common stock at a specific price for a specific period of time

FIGURE 13.2   Put Option Payoff Diagrams

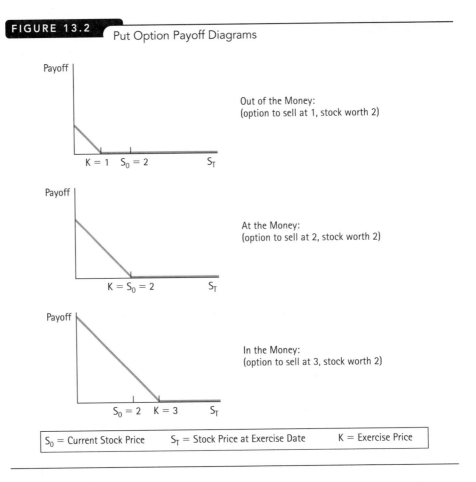

S_0 = Current Stock Price	S_T = Stock Price at Exercise Date	K = Exercise Price

than that received under exercise of the option.[10] It is common for a venture financing round to include the purchase of a share bundled with a warrant on an additional share. We have seen warrants issued to resolve disputes between founders. We have also seen them given out virtually free as a type of pacifier for disgruntled investors. When the current stock value is \$1, you may be tempted to throw off options to buy at \$5 as though they cost you nothing. This is foolishness. When we look back at the payoff diagrams, it is easy to see that put and call holders never lose when exercising in the future. When they do exercise, you will be the one explaining why you're selling a \$50 stock for \$5 because of options you granted when the stock value was \$1 and you thought an option to buy at \$5 was next to worthless. Since options are options on behalf of the holder, they will be exercised to the holder's advantage (venture's disadvantage), other things being equal.

---

[10] While we use "warrant" to denote an option that creates a new share, in practice, there is much overlap in the use of the words "warrant" and "option." In some cases, corporations may have discretion over whether the exercise of a call "option" or "warrant" is satisfied by the issue of a new share or the repurchase and delivery of an existing share.

With stock options that are "deep in the money" (say, a call with a $1 exercise price and a $20 current stock price), it is easy to approximate an option value. In almost all cases, the value will be close to, but higher than, the exercise value ($20 − $1 = $19). In fact, it is relatively easy to see that a call option, in the money or not, should always be worth at least its exercise value. What takes a little more work to see is that the value of a call option will never exceed the value of the stock upon which it is an option. While we could formally show this in a variety of ways, the easiest approach, for our current purposes, is to ask what the option is worth when the exercise price is zero. Having an option to buy the stock at zero price is the same as holding the stock. You can't find a more valuable stock option, since the least the exerciser can pay is zero.[11] A call option is worth more than its exercise value but less than the stock.

While an in-depth treatment of the mechanics of option valuation would take us too far afield, it is important to have some intuition about how the value of an option varies with venture aspects and option design. Figure 13.3 summarizes the characteristics of American-style option value that can be deduced by relatively straightforward reasoning. As the underlying stock price increases in value, a call (put) option to buy (sell) it becomes more (less) valuable. We can see this by tracking how the exercise profits change. As the amount a call (put) option holder pays (receives) increases, the value of the option decreases (increases). This is just common sense. The value of American-style puts and calls increases with the time remaining. Because the holder has discretion over the time of exercise, the longer the period of time over which the holder has exercise discretion the better.[12] For option holders, riskiness in the venture's stock price is a good thing. This can be seen from a quick example. Suppose I have two ventures. One has equally likely possible exercise date stock prices of $1 and $9; the other has equally likely exercise date stock prices of $4 and $6. Both stocks have an expected exercise date price of $5. Having the same expected stock price, but a wider spread of possible stock prices, the first venture is riskier. Suppose the call option has an exercise price of $5.25. The payoff diagram would look like that in Figure 13.4.

The payoffs to the holders of both options are the same (zero) when the two ventures fall below expectations. The option holder doesn't care how bad the downside is. Dispersion in prices below the exercise price is irrelevant. In contrast, dispersion in prices above the exercise price is great. It's better to buy a stock worth $9 than one worth $6, given that I have to pay $5.25 to exercise. This gain from dispersion (risk) is due to what is known as the "convexity" of the option (its shape). Because the call and put payoff diagrams are convex

---

[11] In the United States and most of the rest of the world, stock is limited liability and therefore is guaranteed to have a nonnegative value. By convention, call options require payment of some nonnegative amount in exchange for receiving the stock.

[12] That option values are increasing in the time left on the option is clear with American-style options that can be exercised at any time. For European-style options, the result need not hold, owing to the inability of the European option holder to exercise at any time. For example, if the venture is to pay a liquidating dividend one month from now, a two-week in-the-money European call is worth more than a similar in-the-money European call with two months to expiration.

FIGURE 13.3 Value Relationships for American-Style Options

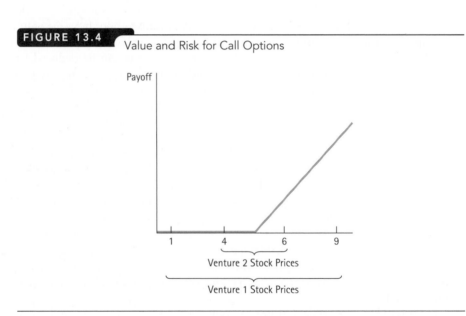

FIGURE 13.4 Value and Risk for Call Options

(similar to a U shape), they benefit from increased dispersion in possible stock prices. Risky stock prices are a benefit to option holders.

The prevailing interest rates and the opportunity for depleting firm value through dividends (more generally, payouts) remain important factors in a qualitative treatment of option value. Generally, a rise in interest rates is good for a call option (where the exercise price *paid* decreases in present value as interest rates rise) and bad for a put option (where the exercise price *received* decreases in present value as interest rates rise). The option value effect of payouts is clear. If firm value declines with payouts, then call exercise brings forth a lower-valued stock and put exercise surrenders the same lower-valued stock in return for a fixed exercise price. When the venture distributes its value, puts benefit and calls suffer.

Reflecting on our previous discussions of convertible preferred equity and convertible debt, you can see that these instruments are combinations of debt or debtlike securities with a warrant to purchase new shares. The only difference is that the bond or preferred equity must be surrendered as the exercise price paid in exchange for venture shares. We highlighted the issues with overhanging convertibles, which are really securities with embedded American-style options. The overhang is the result of having an in-the-money option that is worth at least as much unexercised (unconverted) as it is exercised (converted). Since options are worth at least as much as their exercise value, we would expect overhanging convertibles in the absence of any incentive for exercise. Of course, as we mention in our discussion, the typical solution to overhanging convertibles with their embedded American-style options is to make the convertible callable by the venture (the redemption call option). Redeemable (callable) convertible securities only overhang until they are called (redeemed) by the venture. Although it might be confusing, the value conveyed by the conversion call option is capped by the venture's call option on the convertible security. We have a type of callable call option, as it were. For a simplified view of the interactions of the options held by the investor and the venture, consider the payoff diagram of Figure 13.5.

Callable convertible securities have this same characteristic. The conversion feature allows the investor to participate dollar for dollar in venture stock price increases, to a point. The redemption provision of the same callable convertible security limits the range of stock prices over which dollar-for-dollar participation is granted. When all of this makes sense, you may consider yourself as having passed your first lesson in the mysterious but lucrative art of "financial engineering," where one customizes an exposure to specific financial risks.

We have taken a rather extensive detour from our main treatise on structuring securities in order to drive home an important point. While the options embedded in the venture's securities or sold outright may appear to have little current effect on venture ownership, control, or progress, many entrepreneurs awaken in venture utopia to find that some of the golden apples have mysteriously disappeared from the trees in their quadrant of that utopia. A little awareness and understanding regarding options could make their portion more fruitful.

FIGURE 13.5   The Payoff of a "Callable Call Option"

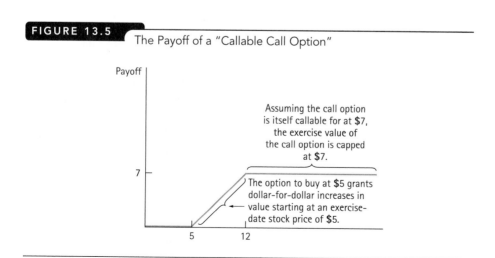

- What is a European-style call option?
- What is an American-style put option?
- Why is the value of an option increasing in the dispersion of future stock prices?

13.5   OTHER CONCERNS ABOUT SECURITY DESIGN

Wrapping up our discussion of elements you can expect to see in the design of securities your venture will consider, we should say something about voting and registration rights and negative covenants.

In many cases, a venture's securities may be structured to grant current majority ownership to the entrepreneur and founders. We say "current majority," because all of those options to buy additional shares, if exercised, could change the balance of power. As the venture increases the investor sophistication level from friends and family to angels and then to venture capitalists, it will be increasingly difficult for founders to retain voting control. Many of the securities will have clauses dictating that the holders "vote as if converted," meaning they are effectively already converted for voting purposes. Others will have embedded escalation clauses that increase the voting strength of investors when things don't go according to plan. Perhaps the best description of the typical venture capital–backed firm is that daily control resides with the entrepreneurial team, and board control resides with outside investors. While this is not always the case, it is common and is usually the target for which venture capitalists aim. As we previously mentioned, the willingness to give up a large share of ownership (and the board control that goes with it) is a significant factor in an entrepreneur's ability to raise funds.

Registration rights embedded in a venture's securities grant certain classes of shareholders the right, under certain circumstances, to have their securities registered with the SEC. Since the securities are restricted, under SEC rules they cannot be sold to the public and are difficult to resell to other private investors of any kind. (See Appendix B of Chapter 8 for an introduction of SEC Rule 144.) Registration with the SEC is a first step in the process of allowing venture investors to achieve liquidity through a sale of existing shares to the public. Registration rights generally fall into two types: demand and piggyback. Demand registration rights typically grant investors the right to demand (under specific conditions) that the venture undertake the process of registering the investors' securities. As registration can be an expensive procedure, the burden of such costs is typically spelled out in the demand registration clauses. Piggyback registration rights allow investors to have their securities registered when a venture's other securities are being registered. As most of the registration costs will be fixed and undertaken by the venture in order to sell other securities, piggyback registration rights usually impose less direct costs (if any) on existing venture investors.

The negotiations over venture securities can result in restrictions on what the venture can and cannot do. These so-called negative covenants typically deal with venture actions relating to classes of securities and, possibly, to the use of venture assets. Of course, such covenants will not be so important if the current securities offering will result in outsiders' control of the board. There are many other types of clauses and terms that you will find in venture financing arrangements. As we have previously mentioned, there is no substitute for competent legal advice. One word of nonlegal advice we would give you is that it could be very informative to ask your securities attorney whether she has various drafts of security agreements. In particular, you might want to ask for versions falling into such classifications as "favorable to issuer" and "favorable to investors." Comparing and contrasting such documents can be enlightening, may help you be a more astute purchaser of legal services, and can certainly make you a more competent venture funding negotiator.

CONCEPT CHECK

- What are demand registration rights?
- What are piggyback registration rights?

13.6 VALUING VENTURES WITH COMPLEX CAPITAL STRUCTURES: THE ENTERPRISE METHOD

Our discussion thus far has highlighted the abundance of structures one may use in designing venture financing. In many cases, a venture will fund itself by packaging multiple securities together (e.g., preferred equity and a warrant) in order to close the deal. Our equity valuation methods are a bit simplistic for ventures in which ownership of the venture's equity implies ownership of nonequity securities. While there is no magic valuation bullet to solve this problem, there are many contexts where it is better to value simultaneously the portfolio of equity and nonequity securities held by venture investors. Valuing the debt piece, then the equity piece, and, finally, the warrant piece is unnecessarily tedious since the securities do not trade separately. We may not even care what the value of the equity is when it cannot be purchased separately from the other securities.[13] To take a first step toward valuing ventures with complex, but linked, securities in their financial structure, we introduce the **enterprise (entity) method** of valuation.[14]

In the enterprise valuation method, rather than distilling all cash flows down to a residual flow to equity (as we did in Chapters 9 and 10), we distill all cash

enterprise (entity) method
valuation method for the entire financial capital structure

---

[13] As in many other contexts, the residual ownership held by the venture's equity holders is what is usually coveted. One can hear other securities, in particular debt, referred to as "cram down," when investors take them only because they want a piece of the equity.

[14] The older term for the enterprise method is "entity method." We will use the terms interchangeably.

flows down to an amount that belongs to, and must eventually flow to, the firm's investors *as a whole*, be they debtholders, common stockholders, preferred stockholders, or warrant holders. There is nothing more, and nothing less, from the asset/operations side of the balance sheet to be paid to security holders on the liability and equity side of the balance sheet. The value of the enterprise cash flows is, therefore, the combined value of all the firm's securities—that is, the value of its entire capital structure. It is the value of the venture's entire portfolio of issued securities, irrespective of what specific securities make up that portfolio. Figure 13.6 provides a graphical depiction of the enterprise method analogous to those in Chapter 9 for the equity method and the accounting statement of cash flows.

What this boils down to in terms of formula is that the cash flow available to pay investors a return starts with a measure of operating income, earnings before interest and taxes, or EBIT (so that debtholders' flows and tax effects will still be in the enterprise flow). We then deduct taxes that would be applied to EBIT and make the same types of adjustments as in the statement of cash flows and the direct calculation of the equity VCF.[15] In a departure from the equity VCF, we do not make any adjustments for retirement or issue of debt (principal payments) because we want the enterprise flow to include all payments to debtholders. The result is:

$$\begin{aligned}
\text{Enterprise Valuation Cash Flow} = \ &\text{EBIT} \times (1 - \text{Enterprise Tax Rate}) \\
&+ \text{Depreciation and Amortization Expense} \\
&- \text{Change in Net Operating Working Capital} \\
&\ (\text{Without Surplus Cash}) \\
&- \text{Capital Expenditures}
\end{aligned}$$

As you may have guessed, we will have to use a different type of discount rate to value these flows. Because we have included the flows that make up the payments to all security holders, we should use a rate that will apply to the portfolio of all the venture's securities. Such a rate is called a weighted average cost of capital (WACC). For this example, we will incorporate the tax benefit of debt (omitted when we calculated taxes on EBIT rather than on net income) in the debt rate to get an after-tax weighted average cost of capital.[16]

Before using the enterprise method to check the equity value we derived in Chapter 9, we need to discuss how one gets from an enterprise value (for all securities) to an equity value (for the least senior security in the venture's entire capital structure). First, in rare cases, we may not care about the individual values of the various securities that a venture issues. When a venture finances itself so that all investors (and incentive-compensated employees) own proportional pieces of each of the venture's securities, the enterprise value is "home." We need go no further. We don't need to know the value of the various securities since they always appear as a portfolio. Owners of 1 percent of the venture's securities are entitled to 1 percent of this enterprise flow and, therefore, 1 percent of

---

[15] After-tax EBIT is also known as NOPAT (net operating profit after taxes) or EBIAT (earnings before interest after taxes).

[16] See Chapter 7 for an explanation of WACC.

Valuation Cash Flow for the Enterprise Method

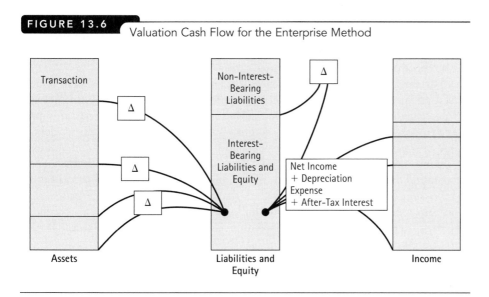

enterprise value. Of course, such a financial structure, while simplifying valuation, would certainly be an oddity. More typically, we will use the enterprise value to get to some other security's value: for example, the value of a share of the venture's common stock.

To use the enterprise method to get values for some subsets of securities, we start with enterprise value and subtract the value of all securities senior to the subset. The value derived will be the value of the subset and all other securities with equal or lower seniority. For example, suppose there are three securities in a venture's capital structure: debt, preferred equity, and common equity. If our objective is to value the portfolio of preferred and common equity, we start with enterprise value and subtract the value of all debt securities. The result is the value of the venture's entire equity base, preferred and common. If we then subtract the value of the preferred, what is left is the value of the common equity.[17]

Returning to the example of Chapter 9, we can see that, when executed properly and consistently (including using the same assumption on the treatment of surplus cash), the common equity value derived from the enterprise value is the same as that directly calculated by the equity method of valuation. The

---

[17] When starting with enterprise value and backing into the value of individual securities in a hierarchy, we are tempted to call it the "tranche" method rather than the "enterprise" method. In the mortgage-backed securities market, pools of mortgages are frequently "securitized" into hierarchical layers, called tranches, having different seniority in their claims to principal and interest payments from the pool. As flows to the mortgage tranches can only originate from flows from the mortgage pool (the asset side of the balance sheet), the sum of the value of the tranches equals the value of the mortgage pool the tranches repackage. To get the value of the lowest-seniority tranche, one could start with the value of the mortgage pool and subtract the values of all senior tranches. To get the value of the combined lower three tranches, one can start with mortgage pool value and subtract the value of all tranches senior to those lowest three, and so on. This approach to mortgage tranche valuation is entirely analogous to our enterprise method approach to equity valuation.

income statements, balance sheets, and statements of cash flow for the PDC venture in Chapter 9 (under the pre-money pseudo dividend method) are presented in Tables 13.1, 13.2, and 13.3 (pages 538–540). For reference, Table 13.4 (page 540) reproduces the equity method valuation.

For this example, the after-tax WACC is calculated period by period. It is based on (i) a 25 percent cost of equity during the first four years, dropping to 18 percent during the terminal value period; (ii) a 10 percent interest rate applicable to debt assumed just before the terminal value period; (iii) a target debt to value of 0 percent for the first four years and 30 percent in the terminal value period; and (iv) a tax rate of 30 percent. In summary, the first four years have an after-tax WACC of 25 percent and Year 5 and beyond have a 14.7 percent after-tax WACC. Table 13.5 (page 541) gives the spreadsheet for the enterprise valuation. After subtracting the market value of the payments promised to debtholders, the difference is the same equity values as we found in the PDM and MDM equity methods of Chapter 9: PV = $399,170 to start with (Year 0) and PV = $560,563 in Year 5.

While the indirect calculation of equity PV involves only a subtraction of the market value of debt [titled "Market value of debt (end of period)"], the indirect calculation of the equity NPV is a bit more complex. Since NPV includes current flows, it may include a tax-deductible payment of interest to debtholders. While the tax benefit of interest in future periods is handled by using an after-tax WACC rate for discounting, there is no discounting for the current flow. The tax deductibility of interest must be handled as a flow since it cannot be handled with a rate. Accordingly, to get the equity NPVs from the enterprise NPVs, we

---

TABLE 13.1   PDC's Projected Income Statements

	4/1/Y0– 7/31/Y0	YEAR 1 8/1/Y0– 7/31/Y1	YEAR 2 8/1/Y1– 7/31/Y2	YEAR 3 8/1/Y2– 7/31/Y3	YEAR 4 8/1/Y3– 7/31/Y4	YEAR T = 5 8/1/Y4– 7/31/Y5
Sales	552,000	1,656,000	2,000,000	2,800,000	2,968,000	3,146,080
(growth rates)			20.8%	40.0%	6.0%	6.0%
Income Statements	Historical	Projected	Projected	Projected	Projected	Projected
Sales	552,000	1,656,000	2,000,000	2,800,000	2,968,000	3,146,080
– COGS	–386,400	–1,159,200	–1,400,000	–1,960,000	–2,077,600	–2,202,256
– Wages and commissions	–105,800	–317,400	–383,333	–536,667	–568,867	–602,999
– Rent, miscellaneous, and insurance	–47,840	–111,780	–135,000	–189,000	–200,340	–212,360
– Depreciation	–4,600	–5,796	–5,630	–6,800	–9,520	–10,091
Earnings before interest and taxes (EBIT)	7,360	61,824	76,036	107,533	111,673	118,374
– Interest expense	–988	0	0	0	0	–22,664
Earnings before taxes	6,372	61,824	76,036	107,533	111,673	95,709
– Taxes	0	–18,547	–22,811	–32,260	–33,502	–28,713
Net income	6,372	43,277	53,225	75,273	78,171	66,997
– Dividends	0	0	0	0	0	0
Retained earnings	6,372	43,277	53,225	75,273	78,171	66,997

TABLE 13.2 PDC's Projected Balance Sheets

PROJECTED BALANCE SHEETS	TODAY 7/31/Y0	EOY 1 7/31/Y1	EOY 2 7/31/Y2	EOY 3 7/31/Y3	EOY 4 7/31/Y4	EOY 5 = T 7/31/Y5
Current assets						
Required cash	23,000	24,840	30,000	42,000	44,520	47,191
Surplus cash	6,487	71,890	92,015	90,310	378,959	442,419
Accounts receivable	46,000	46,000	55,556	77,778	82,444	87,391
Merchandise inventory	97,520	82,800	100,000	140,000	148,400	157,304
Prepaid insurance	2,300	2,300	2,778	3,889	4,122	4,370
Total current assets	175,307	227,830	280,348	353,977	658,446	738,675
Net property, plant, and equipment	57,960	56,304	68,000	95,200	100,912	106,967
Total assets	**233,267**	**284,134**	**348,348**	**449,177**	**759,358**	**845,641**
Current liabilities						
Accounts payable	33,810	41,400	50,000	70,000	74,200	78,652
Accrued wages and commissions	11,500	11,500	13,889	19,444	20,611	21,848
Total current liabilities	45,310	52,900	63,889	89,444	94,811	100,500
Long-term debt	0	0	0	0	226,643	240,241
Owner's equity	187,957	231,234	284,459	359,733	437,904	504,900
Total liabilities and equity	**233,267**	**284,134**	**348,348**	**449,177**	**759,358**	**845,641**

must subtract the debt NPVs. The NPV of debt is the beginning period market value of debt minus the current payment plus the tax benefit, the three lines between "NPV enterprise" and "NPV equity" at the bottom of Table 13.5.

An alternative approach to enterprise method valuation adds the tax shield from paying interest back into the flows and discounts at a before-tax weighted average cost of capital.[18] If we start with EBIT after taxes and add the tax shield of interest (tax rate times interest payment), we get the same result as when starting with net income plus interest. The rest of the calculation follows our procedures as usual. Table 13.6 (page 542) provides the details.

Clearly, there are several paths to this particular enlightenment. One advantage of enterprise methods is that you do not need to project complete balance sheets and income statements. In particular, knowing that the targeted debt to value is 30 percent, and knowing the investment items on the balance sheet and pre-EBIT income statement items, allows you to complete an enterprise valuation. Nonetheless, there is great value in projecting complete financial statements, even if not necessary for valuation. Once you have done the projected financial statements, the valuation method you choose is irrelevant as long as you use consistent assumptions.

---

[18] Note the give and take here. If we get the benefit as a flow, we do not take it in the rate. If we get it in the rate, we do not take it in the flow. This is another variation of the principle "Pay me with a rate or pay me with a flow, but not both."

TABLE 13.3 PDC's Projected Statement of Cash Flows

ACCOUNTING STATEMENT OF CASH FLOWS	YEAR 1 8/1/Y0– 7/31/Y1	YEAR 2 8/1/Y1– 7/31/Y2	YEAR 3 8/1/Y2– 7/31/Y3	YEAR 4 8/1/Y3– 7/31/Y4	YEAR T = 5 8/1/Y4– 7/31/Y5
Cash flows from activities					
Net income	6,372	43,277	53,225	75,273	78,171	66,997
Adjustments to net income for cash flow					
+ Depreciation expense	4,600	5,796	5,630	6,800	9,520	10,091
+ Change in accrued liabilities	1,725	0	2,389	5,556	1,167	1,237
− Change in inventory	12,880	14,720	−17,200	−40,000	−8,400	−8,904
+ Change in accounts payable	−4,830	7,590	8,600	20,000	4,200	4,452
− Change in accounts receivable	−9,200	0	−9,556	−22,222	−4,667	−4,947
Total adjustments	7,015	28,106	−10,614	−30,978	1,587	1,682
Net cash flow from operations	13,387	71,383	42,611	44,296	79,758	68,678
Cash flows from investing					
Capital expenditures	−6,900	−4,140	−17,326	−34,000	−15,232	−16,146
Net cash from investing	−6,900	−4,140	−17,326	−34,000	−15,232	−16,146
Cash flows from financing					
+ Equity issues	0	0	0	0	0	0
− Dividends	0	0	0	0	0	0
(= net dividend)	0	0	0	0	0	0
+ Debt issues	0	0	0	0	226,643	13,599
Net cash flows from financing	0	0	0	0	226,643	13,599
Net change in cash and equivalents	6,487	67,243	25,285	10,296	291,169	66,131
Beginning cash balance	23,000	29,487	96,730	122,015	132,310	423,479
Ending cash balance	29,487	96,730	122,015	132,310	423,479	489,610

TABLE 13.4 PDC's Valuation by Equity Cash Flow

EQUITY VALUATION	YEAR 1 4/1/Y0– 7/31/Y0	YEAR 1 8/1/Y0– 7/31/Y1	YEAR 2 8/1/Y1– 7/31/Y2	YEAR 3 8/1/Y2– 7/31/Y3	YEAR 4 8/1/Y3– 7/31/Y4	YEAR T = 5 8/1/Y4– 7/31/Y5
Net income	6,372	43,277	53,225	75,273	78,171	66,997
+ Depreciation and amortization	4,600	5,796	5,630	6,800	9,520	10,091
− Capital expenditures	−6,900	−4,140	−17,326	−34,000	−15,232	−16,146
− Change in net working capital	2,415	20,470	−21,404	−49,778	−10,453	−11,081
+ Debt proceeds	0	0	0	0	226,643	13,599
Equity VCF (valuation cash flow)	6,487	65,403	20,125	−1,704	288,649	63,460
(vs. dividends − equity issues)	0	0	0	0	0	0

VALUATION DATE	TODAY 7/31/Y0	EOY 1 7/31/Y1	EOY 2 7/31/Y2	EOY 3 7/31/Y3	EOY 4 7/31/Y4	EOY 5 = T 7/31/Y5
PV Equity (Excluding Current Equity VCF)	399,170	433,560	521,825	653,985	528,833	560,563
NPV Equity (Including Current Equity VCF)	405,657	498,962	541,949	652,281	817,481	624,023

| TABLE 13.5 | The Enterprise Method of Valuation: After-Tax WACC Variation |

ENTERPRISE VALUATION

EBIT (earnings bef. int. and taxes)	7,360	61,824	76,036	107,533	111,673	118,374
− Tax rate*EBIT (except year 0)	0	−18,547	−22,811	−32,260	−33,502	−35,512
EBIAT (earnings bef. int. after taxes)	7,360	43,277	53,225	75,273	78,171	82,862
+ Depreciation and amortization	4,600	5,796	5,630	6,800	9,520	10,091
− Capital expenditures	−6,900	−4,140	−17,326	−34,000	−15,232	−16,146
− Change in net working capital	2,415	20,470	−21,404	−49,778	−10,453	−11,081
Enterprise VCF (valuation cash flow)	7,475	65,403	20,125	−1,704	62,006	65,726

VALUATION DATE	7/31/Y0	7/31/Y1	7/31/Y2	7/31/Y3	7/31/Y4	7/31/Y5
Long-term debt/market value of equity		0.0%	0.0%	0.0%	0.0%	30.0%
After-tax WACC (wtd. avg. cost of cap.)		25.0%	25.0%	25.0%	25.0%	14.7%
PV Enterprise (Excluding Current Ent. VCF)	399,170	433,560	482,141	653,985	755,475	800,804
Capital gain on market value of enterprise		8.6%	11.2%	35.6%	15.5%	6.0%
Yield on market value of enterprise		16.4%	4.6%	−0.4%	9.5%	8.7%
Total return on market value of enterprise		25.0%	15.8%	35.3%	25.0%	14.7%
− Market value of debt (end of period)	0	0	0	0	−226,643	−240,241
PV Equity (Excluding Current Equity VCF)	399,170	433,560	482,141	653,985	528,833	560,563
PV Enterprise (Excluding Current Ent. VCF)	399,170	433,560	482,141	653,985	755,475	800,804
+ Current enterprise VCF	7,475	65,403	20,125	−1,704	62,006	65,726
NPV Enterprise (Including Current Ent. VCF)	406,645	498,962	502,266	652,281	817,481	866,530
− Interest (paid during period)	−988	0	0	0	0	−22,664
+ Tax shield on current interest	0	0	0	0	0	6,799
− MV debt (outstanding at beginning)	0	0	0	0	0	−226,643
NPV Equity (Including Current Flows)	405,657	498,962	502,266	652,281	817,481	624,023

Regarding more complex capital structures, the approach is very much the same. Starting with an enterprise value, we subtract the market value of senior securities; what is left belongs to the juniors (subordinated securities). While this approach is straightforward when you want to value the venture's common equity, you will have to take additional care when dealing with warrants, options, and convertibles. Warrants and options, when issued, are not yet common equity but typically can become common equity at any time. Ventures considering a harvest must remember that many, if not all, outstanding options and warrants may be automatically converted to common equity during the harvest.

Frequently, valuation procedures will assume that all warrants and options have been exercised. Consequently, the share count will be as though the warrants and options were already exercised. When we treat the options and warrants as exercised, it is best to add the exercise proceeds to the venture's calibrated value before dividing by the fully diluted (postexercise) number of shares.

If one is tempted to try a more precise valuation by pricing the options directly and then subtracting the calculated option value (along with the values of senior

TABLE 13.6   Enterprise Method of Valuation: Before-Tax WACC Variation

COMPRESSED APV/CAPITAL CASH FLOWS/BEFORE-TAX WACC

Net Income	6,372	43,277	53,225	75,273	78,171	66,997
+ Before-tax interest	988	0	0	0	0	22,664
+ Depreciation and amortization	4,600	5,796	5,630	6,800	9,520	10,091
− Change in net working capital	2,415	20,470	−21,404	−49,778	−10,453	−11,081
− Capital expenditures	−6,900	−4,140	−17,326	−34,000	−15,232	−16,146
Capital cash flow	7,475	65,403	20,125	−1,704	62,006	72,526

	TODAY	EOY 1	EOY 2	EOY 3	EOY 4	EOY 5 = T
VALUATION DATE	7/31/Y0	7/31/Y1	7/31/Y2	7/31/Y3	7/31/Y4	7/31/Y5
Long-term debt/market value of equity		0.0%	0.0%	0.0%	0.0%	30.0%
Before-tax WACC (wtd. avg. cost of cap.)		25.00%	25.00%	25.00%	25.00%	15.60%
PV Enterprise (Excluding Current Ent. VCF)	399,170	433,560	482,141	653,985	755,475	800,804
Market value of debt (end of period)	0	0	0	0	−226,643	−240,241
PV Equity (Excluding Current Equity VCF)	399,170	433,560	482,141	653,985	528,833	560,563
PV Enterprise (Excluding Current Ent. VCF)	399,170	433,560	482,141	653,985	755,475	800,804
+ Current capital cash flow (CCF)	7,475	65,403	20,125	−1,704	62,006	72,526
− Tax shield on current interest*	0	0	0	0	0	−6,799
NPV Enterprise (Including Current Ent. VCF)	406,645	498,962	502,266	652,281	817,481	866,530
− Interest (paid during period)	−988	0	0	0	0	−22,664
+ Tax shield on current interest	0	0	0	0	0	6,799
− MV debt (outstanding at beginning)	0	0	0	0	0	−226,643
NPV Equity (Including Current Equity VCF)	405,657	498,962	502,266	652,281	817,481	624,023*

* We subtract the tax shield on current interest because we have defined the enterprise flows to exclude the tax shield of interest. While the discount rate has been adjusted to handle the presence of the tax shield in future flows, the current tax shield must be removed to be comparable to our enterprise net present valuation.

securities) from the value of the enterprise, then some serious work needs to be completed. The Learning Supplement to this chapter provides an example where the venture's warrants are priced by a variation of the famous Black-Scholes option-pricing model.

CONCEPT CHECK

- What is an enterprise value?
- What discount rate is used to determine enterprise value?
- How is the equity value derived from the enterprise value?
- How are options and warrants incorporated into an enterprise valuation?

SUMMARY

The structuring of a venture's securities is an important aspect of fundraising. Many ventures have unwittingly hamstrung future financing efforts by granting apparently innocuous terms protecting current investors from future dilution or price decreases. Others have carefully considered such terms during their venture financing negotiations.

Venture financing regularly includes options features that allow investors increased participation in gains with no symmetric exposure to losses. While these securities can be priced fairly, it is important for an entrepreneur to understand how, and to whom, the future pie is being sold off. When dealing with complex capital structures, it is frequently easier to value the entire venture's ability to pay all investors (the enterprise value) and subtract senior security, warrant, and convertible values to arrive at the value of existing common equity.

KEY TERMS

common stock
convertible preferred stock
down (reset) round

enterprise (entity) method
paid in kind (PIK) preferred stock
participating preferred stock

preemptive rights
preferred stock
warrants

DISCUSSION QUESTIONS

1. What is common stock or common equity? What is the purpose of preemptive rights?

2. What is preferred stock? What is participating preferred stock, and what is meant by paid in kind (PIK) preferred stock?

3. What are the basic design features for financial securities used in venture investing?

4. Why is the conversion feature in convertible preferred important for venture investors?

5. What is meant by (a) a full ratchet clause and (b) a down (reset) round?

6. Which is more favorable to the founders, the market price formula (MPF) or the conversion price formula (CPF)?

7. How does convertible debt differ from convertible preferred stock?

8. Why are options to buy additional shares of stock used in venture financing? What are warrants?

9. How do (a) American-style options, (b) European-style options, and (c) Bermudan-style options differ?

10. How are put and call options similar? How are they different?

11. What are the "factors" that influence the values of American-style options?

12. Why is price protection an issue when convertibles or warrants are used?

13. Why is it important that convertible securities also be callable (redeemable)?

14. Is the sale of an out-of-the-money warrant a future sale of equity at a favorable price?

15. What is the enterprise (entity) method of valuation and how does it differ from the equity methods of Chapters 9 and 10?

16. Describe how the enterprise valuation cash flow is determined. That is, identify the components included in determining the enterprise valuation cash flow.

17. What is meant by (a) NOPAT and (b) EBIAT? How do they compare with each other?

18. Why is the weighted average cost of capital (WACC) used as the discount rate in the enterprise method?

19. How do debt investors get paid in the enterprise method?

INTERNET ACTIVITIES

1. Web-surfing exercise: Search the Web for a direct offering of a convertible preferred security. Possible search words include "direct public offering" or "small corporate offering registration" ("SCOR"). Analyze the conversion and dilution clauses offered in the security.

2. Get a current price for a traded call option on a publicly traded security having publicly traded options (e.g., http://www.cboe.com). Compare the option price to the value of exercise (stock price − exercise price) and comment on the difference.

EXERCISES/PROBLEMS

1. A share of a venture's preferred stock is convertible into 1.5 shares of its common stock. The dividend on the preferred stock is $.50 per share.
   A. If the firm's common stock is currently trading at $9.75, what is the conversion value of a share of the preferred stock?
   B. What would be the dividend yield on the preferred stock based on its conversion value?
   C. What explanation would you give if the venture's preferred stock currently trades at $15? What would be the dividend yield?
   D. If the venture doubles the number of shares of its common stock that are outstanding (and cuts its stock price in half) but increases the conversion terms on its preferred stock to 2.5 shares of common stock, what would be the conversion value of a share of preferred stock after the new common stock issue? What would be the dividend yield on the preferred stock based on this new conversion value?
   E. If the venture increased its common stock offering by 50 percent (instead of 100 percent), what common stock conversion ratio would be needed on a share of preferred stock to keep its conversion value the same as it was before the new common stock issue?

2. The CCC (triple C) Venture has issued convertible preferred stock to its venture investors. Each share of preferred stock is convertible into .80 shares of common stock and pays an annual cash dividend of $.25.
   A. If each share of preferred stock has a market value of $4, what is the minimum price that a share of the CCC Venture's common stock should be selling for (ignore the dividend yield on the preferred stock)?
   B. If a share of the CCC Venture's common stock is actually trading at $3 per share, what are the implied conversion terms? Given the above actual conversion terms, explain how the common stock could be trading at $3 per share while the preferred stock is trading at $4 per share.

3. Calculate the conversion price formula (CPF) and market price formula (MPF) prices for an offering involving an existing conversion price of $1, a hypothesized market price of $2, and a new offering price of $.95 for 1,000 shares with 2,000 shares outstanding before the new issue. Relate the new conversion price to the implied new conversion ratio.

4. Show how your answers for Problem 3 would change if the new offering price was $.80 for 1,500 shares. Assume other things remain the same.

5. Draw the payoff diagram for the following options:
   A. Call option to buy a venture's stock at $3.
   B. Put option to sell a venture's stock back to the venture at $15.

6. Draw the payoff for a portfolio of a share of venture equity and a short (sold) call option to buy that share at $5.

7. Sometimes the combination of a share and a warrant is called a stock unit. What does the payoff diagram look like for such an investment?

8. Find the enterprise valuation cash flow expected for the current year given the following information:

   Capital expenditures (CAPEX) = $150,000

   Depreciation and amortization expenses = $40,000

   Earnings before interest and taxes = $400,000

   Effective income tax rate = 30%

	LAST YEAR	CURRENT YEAR
Required cash	$ 50,000	$ 75,000
Surplus cash	20,000	40,000
Accounts receivable	200,000	250,000
Inventories	300,000	360,000
Accounts payable	100,000	120,000
Accrued liabilities	40,000	50,000
Bank loan (short-term)	90,000	110,000

9. Rework Problem 8 assuming that the earnings before interest and taxes are only $320,000 while CAPEX is $110,000. Assume the other information remains the same.

10. Calculate the after-tax WACC for a firm with a 25 percent tax rate, a 10 percent cost of debt, a 30 percent cost of equity, and a target debt to value of .30. Explain how investing to provide the WACC returns keeps the debt and equity investors happy. (Review Chapter 7.)

11. Why is the (1 − tax rate) in the WACC? How do we model the government's payment of the tax rebate on interest—through a flow or in the rate? (Review Chapter 7.)

12. Given a WACC of 15 percent, a target debt to value of .50, a tax rate of 28 percent, and a cost of debt of 10 percent, what is the implied cost of equity?

13. Assume a venture has a perpetuity enterprise value cash flow of $800,000. Cash flows are expected to continue to grow at 8 percent annually and the venture's WACC is 15 percent.
   A. Calculate the venture's enterprise value.
   B. If the venture has $2 million in interest-bearing debt obligations, what would be the venture's equity value?
   C. Show how your answers to Parts A and B would change if the perpetuity cash flow growth rate was only 6 percent and the WACC was 16 percent.

14. A venture has a $500,000 bank loan outstanding, a long-term debt obligation of $900,000, accounts payable of $200,000, and accounts receivable of $350,000.
    A. If the venture's equity value is $2.45 million, what would be the associated enterprise value?
    B. Assume the venture's enterprise value has been estimated to be $5.3 million (ignore any information from Part A). What would be the venture's equity value?
    C. Now assume that the venture has surplus cash of $700,000. Show how your answers would change (if at all) for Parts A and B.

15. Why is the market value of currently issued debt subtracted from the enterprise value (in a debt-and-equity-only firm) to arrive at the value of equity? Why are future debt issues ignored in this subtraction?

16. The Datametrix Corporation has been in operation for one full year (2007). Financial statements are shown below. Sales are expected to grow at a 30 percent annual rate for each of the next three years (2008, 2009, and 2010) before settling down to a long-run growth rate of 7 percent annually. The cost of goods sold is expected to vary with sales. Operating expenses are expected to grow at 75 percent of the sales growth rate (i.e., be semifixed) for the next three years before again growing at the same rate as sales beginning in 2011. Interest expense is expected to grow with sales. Depreciation can be forecasted either as a percentage of sales or as a percentage of net fixed assets (since net fixed assets are expected to grow at the same rate as sales growth). Individual asset accounts are expected to grow at the same rate as sales. Accounts payable and accrued liabilities are also expected to grow with sales.

    Because Datametrix is in its startup stage, management and venture investors believe that 35 percent is an appropriate weighted average cost of capital (WACC) discount rate until the firm reaches its long-run or perpetuity growth rate. At that time, it will have survived, recapitalized its capital structure, and become a more typical firm in the industry with an estimated WACC of 18 percent. Calculate Datametrix's enterprise value as of the end of 2007. Also indicate what the equity would be worth.

Datametrix Corporation

INCOME STATEMENT FOR DECEMBER 31, 2007
(THOUSANDS OF DOLLARS)

Sales	$20,000
Cost of goods sold	−10,000
Gross profit	10,000
Operating expenses	−7,500
Depreciation	−400
EBIT	2,100
Interest	−100
EBT	2,000
Taxes (40%)	−800
Net income	$ 1,200

Datametrix Corporation

BALANCE SHEET AS OF DECEMBER 31, 2007
(THOUSANDS OF DOLLARS)

Cash	$ 1,000	Accounts payable	$ 1,500
Accounts receivable	2,000	Accrued liabilities	1,000
Inventories	2,000	Total current liabilities	2,500
Total current assets	5,000	Long-term debt	1,000
Gross fixed assets	5,400	Common stock	5,300
Accumulated depreciation	400	Retained earnings	1,200
Net fixed assets	5,000	Total equity	6,500
Total assets	$10,000	Total liabilities and equity	$10,000

M I N I   C A S E

Wok Yow Imports, Inc.

Wok Yow Imports, Inc., is a rapidly growing, closely held corporation that imports and sells Asian-style furniture and accessories at several retail outlets. The equity owners are considering selling the venture and want to estimate the enterprise or entity value and then determine the value of the venture's equity. Following is last year's income statement (2007) and projected income statements for the next four years (2008–2011). Sales are expected to grow at an annual 6 percent rate beginning in 2012 and thereafter.

	ACTUAL	PROJECTED			
[$ THOUSANDS]	2007	2008	2009	2010	2011
Net sales	$150.0	$200.0	250.0	$300.0	$350.0
Cost of goods sold	−75.0	−100.0	−125.0	−150.0	−175.0
Gross profit	75.0	100.0	125.0	150.0	175.0
SG&A expenses	−30.0	−40.0	−50.0	−60.0	−70.0
Depreciation	−7.5	−10.0	−12.5	−15.0	−17.5
EBIT	37.5	50.0	62.5	75.0	87.5
Interest	−3.5	−3.5	−3.5	−3.5	−3.5
EBT	34.0	46.5	59.0	71.5	84.0
Taxes (40% rate)	−13.6	−18.6	−23.6	−28.6	−33.6
Net income	20.4	27.9	35.4	42.9	50.4

Selected balance sheet accounts at the end of 2007 are as follows: Required cash, accounts receivable, and inventory accounts totaled $50,000; net fixed assets were $50,000; and accounts payable and accruals totaled $25,000. Each of these accounts was expected to grow with sales over time. Long-term debt was $30,000, and there were 10,000 shares of common stock outstanding at the end of 2007.

Data have been gathered for Fine Furniture Products, a comparable publicly traded firm in Wok Yow's industry. Fine Furniture's risk index is judged to be 2.00, compared to a risk index of 1.00 for firms of average riskiness. Management believes that a 2.00 adjustment factor should be multiplied times the expected market risk premium for average firms to reflect Wok Yow's (and Fine Furniture's) relatively greater riskiness. Wok Yow's long-term debt to long-term capital (long-term debt plus equity) ratio was 40 percent at the end of 2007. The interest rate on long-term U.S. government

continued on next page

Wok Yow Imports, Inc. (continued)

bonds is 7 percent, Wok Yow could issue new long-term debt at a 12 percent rate, and the average expected market risk premium (common stocks over government bonds) is 7.5 percent for average firms.

A. Project Wok Yow's net operating profit after-tax (NOPAT) statements for 2008 to 2012.
B. Determine the annual increases in required net working capital and capital expenditures (CAPEX) for Wok Yow for the years 2008 to 2012.
C. Project annual operating free cash flows to the entity for the years 2008 to 2012.
D. Management initially thought that an 18 percent discount rate was reasonable.
E. Use the information from Part D to estimate Wok Yow's terminal value cash flow at the end of 2011.
F. Estimate the firm's enterprise or entity value at the end of 2007.
G. Adjust the enterprise value to determine Wok Yow's equity value in dollars and on a per-share basis at the end of 2007.
H. Now estimate Wok Yow's after-tax cost of long-term debt. Use the risk-free rate, the expected market risk premium, and the risk index for Fine Furniture Company to estimate Wok Yow's cost of equity capital. Determine Wok Yow's weighted average cost of capital (WACC).
I. Reestimate Wok Yow's enterprise value using the WACC calculated in Part H. Then adjust the enterprise value to determine Wok Yow's equity value in dollars and on a per-share basis at the end of 2007.

M I N I   C A S E

RxDelivery Systems, Inc. (Revisited)

RxDelivery Systems is an R&D venture specializing in the development and testing of new drug delivery technologies. The market for alternative drug delivery systems grew rapidly during the 1990s. Driving factors behind this growth include efforts to reduce drug side effects through site-specific delivery, the need to maintain the activity of new biopharmaceutical compounds, and the extension of drug patent life. Improved drug delivery methods are expected to reduce the number of surgical interventions and the length of hospital stays and promote patient compliance in taking prescribed drugs.

The world market for biopharmaceuticals (including peptide, protein, RNA, and DNA drugs) was more than $50 billion in 2004. Sales of polymer-based drug delivery systems are forecasted to exceed $2.0 billion in 2011. Pulmonary delivery systems currently account for about one-third of the drug delivery market, and sales are projected to exceed $25 billion by 2011.

RxDelivery Systems believes it can compete effectively in both the polymer-based and pulmonary drug delivery areas. The venture's delivery technology is expected to utilize hydrophobic ion pairing and supercritical carbon dioxide precipitation to incorporate water-soluble drug molecules into biodegradable controlled-release microspheres. The resulting microspheres will take the form of dry powders and will contain drug molecules small enough to allow for intravenous, intranasal, or pulmonary delivery. It is anticipated that this technology will be incorporated into products for controlled-release applications, including treatment of cancer, infectious diseases, and gene therapy.

RxDelivery Systems, through an agreement with its pharmaceutical parent, a major drug company, will initially operate as an independent corporation but will be merged into the parent at

---

RxDelivery Systems, Inc. (Revisited) (continued)

the end of its second year. At that time, RxDelivery Systems' entrepreneurial team will be paid a lump sum of $2.5 million as the terminal value for the venture. Following are limited financial statement projections for the next two years for the RxDelivery Systems Corporation:

First-year revenues	$12,500
Second-year revenues	$16,000
Expenses (including depreciation)	$125,000 per year
Initial time-zero (net) fixed assets	$50,000
Depreciation	10% of beginning-of-year net fixed assets
Accounts payable (Years 1 and 2)	$750
Inventories (Years 1 and 2)	$0
Corporate marginal tax rate	30%
Accounts receivable (Years 1 and 2)	$0
Accrued expenses (Years 1 and 2)	$300
Required cash	$3,000
Debt (all years)	$0

A. Construct the venture's balance sheet at startup. Then construct financial statements for Years 1 and 2. (Put initial fixed-asset investments in Year 0 and initial working capital investments in Year 1. Assume the initial $50,000 is equity financed.)
B. Construct the enterprise valuation cash flows, including the $2.5 million terminal payment. Treat existing liabilities at the terminal time as though the pharmaceutical firm assumes them. (The $2.5 million is "free and clear.") Strip all nonrequired cash out of net working capital (effectively declaring a pseudo dividend).
C. What is the value of the enterprise at time zero?
D. What is the value of the equity at time zero?
E. Why does this value differ from the value for the equity method in the RxDelivery Systems mini case at the end of Chapter 9?

Learning Supplement 13

To begin such an approach, we need an option-pricing formula (like the famous Black-Scholes formula). Such a formula typically requires, as input, the current value of common equity. Of course, this is the value we will get after we deduct the value of the options from the enterprise value. Put differently, the option value and the equity value will have to be determined simultaneously.

Since this is a somewhat complicated point, we digress to give an example. Suppose we have determined that the enterprise value, exclusive of the warrant proceeds, is $1,000. There are no senior securities, nine shares of common stock, and one warrant to create a tenth share upon the payment of an exercise price of $80. We need to determine both the value of the warrant and the value of the underlying nine common shares at the same time. Black and Scholes' famous call option-pricing formula for the value of a call option at time t is:

$$C_t = N(h) \times S_t - N(h - \sigma\sqrt{\tau}) \times PV(K)$$

where:

$N(\tau)$ = normal distribution function (probability)

σ = annual standard deviation (volatility) for the stock

K = exercise price

t = today's date

τ = time to expiration

$PV(K)$ = present value of the exercise price K

h = $\{\log(S_t/K) + r\tau + \sigma^2\tau/2\}/\sigma\sqrt{\tau}$

The value of a warrant can be directly derived from the value of a call. In particular, the value of a warrant (W) as a function of the value of a call option (C) having the same parameters is $W = 1/(1 + \lambda)C$, where $1/(1 + \lambda)$ is a dilution factor and λ is the ratio of new shares to preexercise shares outstanding. For our current example, $\lambda = 1/9$ and the dilution factor is .9. In our first approach, we consider the value of the single warrant to buy a newly minted tenth share at $80. We apply the Black-Scholes formula for an option to buy at $80 on an underlying security worth $111.11 ($1,000/9). We shrink this value by 10 percent (applying the dilution factor) to get the warrant value. We then subtract the warrant value from the enterprise value, and what is left is the value of the original nine shares of equity. This is an application of the enterprise method; we start with total asset–oriented enterprise value and subtract other securities to get to the value of equity.

	A	B	C	D	E	F
1	K	TIME TO EXPIRATION	ANNUAL INTEREST RATE	ENTITY VALUE PER SHARE	ANNUAL STOCK VOLATILITY	PRESENT VALUE OF K
2	80	1	.1	111.11	.3	72.73
3						
4	h	N(h)	N(h − σ × t^{1/2})	Dilution	BS Option	BS Warrant
5	1.5783	.9428	.8994	.9000	39.34	35.40
6						
7	Single Warrant Value		35.40			
8	Equity Value		107.18 = (9 × 111.11 − 35.40)/9			
9	Preexercise Enterprise Value		1,000 = (9 × 107.18) + 35.40			
10						

Example with One Warrant (Enterprise Per-Share Variation)

1. Preexercise enterprise value is $1,000.
2. Note that $1,000 is what is divided among nine shares and one warrant.
3. The option to buy an existing share is worth $39.34.

4. Think of warrant as optioning 1/10 of nine calls on enterprise value per existing share ($111.11).

5. Warrant value is therefore only 90 percent of call value (dilution factor = .9).

6. The warrant has value $35.40 = .9 × $39.34.

7. Value per share of existing nine shares is $107.18 = (9 × $111.11 − $35.40)/9.

8. Note that this value is the same as $111.11 − $35.40/9 = $107.18.

9. Each existing shareholder bears 1/9 of the warrant "burden."

For an intuition check, when there is no time value in the option, we can compare the pre-exercise and postexercise valuations directly. If the warrant were certain to be exercised immediately, the option value would be 31.11 = 111.11 − 80. For a dilution factor of .9, the warrant value would be 28. This gives a preexercise equity valuation of 108 [= (1,000 − 28)/9]. To see that this is consistent with the postexercise valuation, note the postexercise enterprise value is 1,080 (= 1,000 + 80) and there are ten shares outstanding for a postexercise share price of 108.

To see how this method also works for multiple warrants, we consider a second example, identical to the first except that there are five warrants outstanding.

	A	B	C	D	E	F
		TIME TO	ANNUAL INTEREST	ENTITY VALUE	ANNUAL STOCK	PRESENT VALUE
1	K	EXPIRATION	RATE	PER SHARE	VOLATILITY	OF K
2	80	1	.1	111.11	.3	72.73
3						
4	h	N(h)	N(h − σ × t$^{1/2}$)	Dilution	BS Option	BS Warrant
5	1.5783	.9428	.8994	.6429	39.34	25.29
6						
7	Single Warrant Value		25.29			
8	Equity Value		97.06 = (9 × 111.11 − 5 × 25.29)/9			
9	Preexercise Enterprise Value		1,000 = (9 × 97.06) + (5 × 25.29)			
10						

Example with Five Warrants (Enterprise Per-Share Variation)

1. Preexercise enterprise value is $1,000.

2. Note that $1,000 is what is divided among nine shares and five warrants.

3. The option to buy an existing share is worth $39.34.

4. Think of warrant as optioning 1/14 of nine calls on enterprise value per existing share ($111.11).

5. Warrant value is therefore only 64.29 percent of call value (dilution factor = .6429).

6. The warrant has value $25.29 = .6429 × $39.34.

7. Value per share of existing nine shares is $97.06 = (9 × $111.11 − 5 × $25.29)/9.

8. Note that this value is the same as $111.11 − (5/9) × $25.29 = $97.06.

9. Each existing shareholder bears 1/9 of each warrant's "burden."

An equivalent alternative approach is to consider an enterprise warrant on all nine existing shares and proceed from there:

	A	B	C	D	E	F
		TIME TO	ANNUAL INTEREST	ENTITY	ANNUAL STOCK	PRESENT VALUE
1	K	EXPIRATION	RATE	VALUE	VOLATILITY	OF K
2	720	1	.1	1,000.00	.3	654.55
3						
4	h	N(h)	$N(h - \sigma \times t^{1/2})$	Dilution	BS Option	BS Warrant
5	1.5783	.9428	.8994	.6429	354.04	227.59
6						
7	Total Warrant Value		227.59 (Value of 9-Warrant Block)			
8	Single Warrant Value		25.29 = 227.59/9			
9	Equity Value Per Share		97.06 = (1,000 − 5 × 25.29)/9			
10	Preexercise Enterprise Value		1,000 = (9 × 97.06) + (5 × 25.29)			

Example with Five Warrants (Enterprise Warrant Variation)

1. The enterprise warrant exercise price would be 720 = 9 × 80.
2. The dilution factor is still .6429.
3. The value of the enterprise option is 354.04.
4. The value of the enterprise warrant is 227.59 (= 354.04 × .6429).
5. Each warrant in enterprise warrant is worth 1/9 of the value of the block.
6. Single warrant value = 25.29 (= 227.59/9).
7. Total equity value is enterprise value less five single warrants, 873.56 (= 1,000 − 5 × 25.29).
8. Equity value per share is total equity value divided by 9, 97.06 (= 873.56/9).

For our intuition check, if the warrants were certain to be exercised immediately, the option value would be 31.11 = 111.11 − 80. For a dilution factor of .6429, the warrant value would be 20. This gives a preexercise equity valuation of 100 [= (1,000 − 100)/9]. To see that this is consistent with the postexercise valuation, note the postexercise enterprise value is 1,400 (= 1,000 + 400) and there are fourteen shares outstanding for a postexercise share price of 100.

As a final example, we can examine what would happen if the exercise price on the warrants were effectively zero. Note that a pure option (as opposed to a warrant) would have the same value as a share of the underlying. The warrant still dilutes and is worth less than the share.

	A	B	C	D	E	F
		TIME TO	ANNUAL INTEREST	ENTITY VALUE PER	ANNUAL STOCK	PRESENT VALUE
1	K	EXPIRATION	RATE	SHARE	VOLATILITY	OF K
2	.00001	1	.1	111.11	.3	.00
3						
4	h	N(h)	$N(h - \sigma \times t^{1/2})$	Dilution	BS Option	BS Warrant
5	54.5615	1.0000	1.0000	.6429	111.11	71.43
6						
7	Single Warrant Value		71.43			
8	Equity Value		71.43 = (9 × 111.11 − 5 × 71.43)/9			
9	Preexercise Enterprise Value		1,000 = (9 × 65.63) + (5 × 71.43)			
10						

Zero Exercise Warrants (Enterprise Per-Share Variation)

1. Preexercise enterprise value is $1,000.
2. Note that $1,000 is what is divided among nine shares and five warrants.
3. The option to buy an existing share is worth $111.11 (call = underlying when K = 0).
4. Think of warrant as optioning 1/14 of nine calls on enterprise value per existing share ($111.11).
5. Warrant value is therefore only 64.29% of call value (dilution factor = .6429).
6. The warrant has value $71.43 = .6429 × $111.11.
7. Value per share of existing nine shares is $71.43 = (9 × $111.11 − 5 × $71.43)/9.
8. Note that this value is the same as $111.11 − (5/9) × $71.43 = $71.43.
9. Each existing shareholder bears 1/9 of each warrant's "burden."

For a last intuition check, if the warrants were certain to be exercised immediately, the option value would be 111.11 = 111.11 − 0. For a dilution factor of .6429, the warrant value would be 71.43. This gives a preexercise equity valuation of 71.43 [= (1,000 − 357.16)/9]. It should not be surprising that the warrant (with exercise price 0) has the same value as the stock. Postexercise enterprise value is still 1,000. Postexercise share price is 71.43 (= 1,000/14).

As far as plugging and chugging with a given option-pricing formula, we are set to go; the enterprise method brings us to the equity bottom line after the required deductions from enterprise value. In order to apply the Black-Scholes formula, we have assumed that the underlying enterprise value has a particular statistical behavior (geometric Brownian motion). The biggest difficulty this creates is that normally the equity (rather than the enterprise) value is assumed to have this statistical behavior. One does not imply the other when a venture's capital structure includes warrants. While our treatment is typical, the serious reader would benefit by considering more detailed treatments of option (and warrant) pricing; for example, see Mark Rubinstein, *Options Markets* (Englewood Cliffs, NJ: Prentice-Hall, 1985).

For options and warrants on entrepreneurial ventures, we have made an invisible giant leap to apply an option-pricing formula. Option-savvy readers may note that, while option-pricing formulas can be manipulated this way, something is not quite right in cavalierly using this approach. We agree. The principle behind most option-pricing formulas is that an option derives its value from the stock. In particular, the stock price is assumed to be known, observable, tradable, and functionally independent of the option price. Here we have a simultaneously determined (codependent) warrant price and stock price, the latter of which is not traded in observable transactions at predetermined prices from which we can assume an option would derive its value. We see some usefulness in (mis)using an option-pricing formula, as we have in this example; however, such exercises would more rightly be deemed "abusefulness." While some evaluators will settle for a valuation that treats options, warrants, and convertibles as though they are already converted, our use of the Black-Scholes formula has highlighted that the single warrant granting one-tenth of the pie (in the first example) has a value of about $35.40. A possible simplification that avoids options formulas is to value the warrant as if currently exercised ($1,080/10 − $80) = $28. An unacceptable alternative is to value the warrant as if it were already a share (exercise price = 0), which gives $1,000/10 = $100.

The moral of the story is that one must take care when calculating the value of warrants (or convertibles) to be subtracted from enterprise value to arrive at equity value. First best is to use an option-pricing approach. Second best is to add the proceeds to enterprise value, calculate a share price, and then subtract the exercise price. Last, and not really acceptable, is treating the warrant as a share (the zero exercise price approximation).

CONCEPT CHECK

- What are the parameters for the Black-Scholes option-pricing formula?
- What are the issues and difficulties in using option-pricing formulas to determine the value of venture warrants when the process is simultaneously pricing the optioned equity?

Part 6

EXIT AND TURNAROUND STRATEGIES

Chapter 14

HARVESTING THE BUSINESS VENTURE INVESTMENT

PREVIOUSLY COVERED

So far, we have ventured fearlessly through the early, survival, and rapid-growth stages. Our emphasis has been on organizational, financial, legal, and strategic preparation for new venture success. An entrepreneur who has committed her time, effort, and personal financial assets to convert an idea into a successful business venture and has probably weathered financial distress also is, in all likelihood, looking forward to a fruitful harvest. We are now ready to discuss the various ways investors and founders exit or harvest a successful venture.

LOOKING AHEAD

The last chapter in this text focuses on how an entrepreneur deals with financial trouble. We will discuss ways an entrepreneur can turn a problematic financial situation into a turnaround success story. Most ventures face financial trouble or distress at least once during their life cycle. The successful venture is one that can overcome financial distress by restructuring operations, assets, or the venture's financing.

CHAPTER LEARNING OBJECTIVES

This chapter focuses on ways that a successful entrepreneur can harvest or exit the venture. After completing this chapter, you will be able to:

1. Plan an exit strategy

2. Understand the meaning of systematic liquidation

3. Describe outright sales of the venture to various potential buyers

4. Discuss the terms "leveraged buyouts" and "management buyouts"

5. Describe the process of going public

6. Identify what investment banking involves

harvesting

process of exiting the privately held business venture to unlock the owners' investment value

Harvesting is the process of selling ownership in a privately held business venture to realize the appreciated value of the founders' and venture investors' contributions. By harvest time, the set of owners often includes friends and family, angels, venture capitalists, and other later-stage equity investors. A venture is typically harvested in one of three ways: (1) through a systematic distribution of assets directly to the owners, (2) through an outright sale of the going concern to others (e.g., family members, managers, employees, or external buyers), or (3) through a two-step public equity registration and sale—an IPO (initial public offering) of new shares followed by a secondary offer of existing owners' shares. In the discussion that follows, we will refer to these methods as (1) systematic liquidation, (2) outright sale, and (3) going public.

14.1   VENTURE OPERATING AND FINANCIAL DECISIONS REVISITED

As we begin the last part of this text, it is time to revisit the major operating and financial decisions faced by business ventures as they progress through their life cycles. Figure 14.1 graphically depicts these decision areas. In the earliest chapters, we focused on turning an idea into a viable business opportunity and getting started. Initially, we were concerned with early-stage financing sources and how organizational form impacts the ability to raise funds and the liability assumed by investors.

Next, we turned to the preparation and use of historical financial statements, with specific attention to their role in monitoring and recording venture progress. We emphasized projecting the venture's cash flow throughout the various life cycle stages. Cash flow is central to survival and to providing a return for venture investors. Projected cash flows are also the basis of rigorous financial valuation.

Along the way to venture success, the entrepreneurial team makes many financial decisions. Perhaps the most trying are those involving the possibility of venture restructuring, sale, or liquidation. For ultimately successful ventures that have endured rapid growth and are perhaps entering maturity, it is important to understand how to harvest the venture's financial rewards.

Major operating and financial decisions must be made throughout a venture's life cycle. The development stage begins at the top of Figure 14.1. The entrepreneur begins with an idea for a new product or service. The road from the idea to a viable business opportunity, however, is often a rocky one. Ideas are modified or discarded, and the capabilities and composition of the management team changes. Even during the development stage, the entrepreneur must consider regrouping and reorganizing. Coincident with a decision about whether to regroup is a decision about whether to abandon or liquidate. We will discuss ways by which an entrepreneur may regroup or restructure a venture in Chapter 15.

In this chapter, we focus on harvesting the successful venture. The lower portion of Figure 14.1 shows that a successful venture that is still growing rapidly can be harvested by going public, selling the venture, or merging the venture with

FIGURE 14.1

Life Cycle Approach: Venture Operating and Financial Decisions

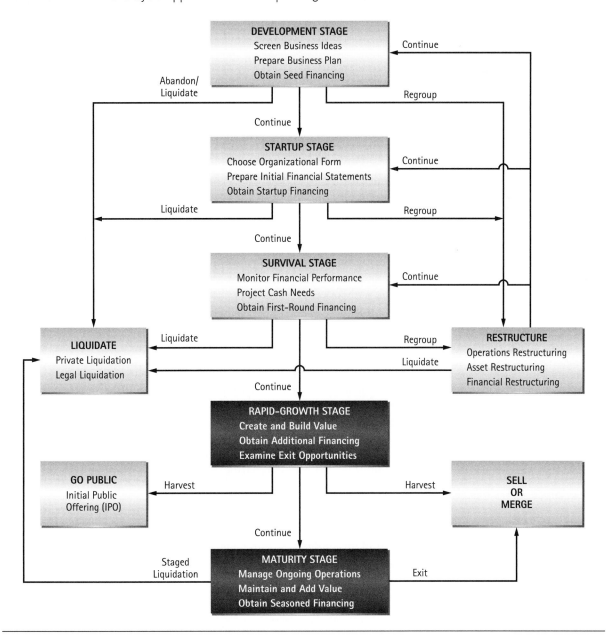

another firm. Mature ventures that are no longer rapidly growing (and not already publicly traded) typically provide investor liquidity through a sale, a merger, or a staged liquidation.

CONCEPT CHECK

- What are the major stages in a successful venture's life cycle?

14.2 PLANNING AN EXIT STRATEGY

It is important that the entrepreneur be keenly aware of investors' and founders' desires for eventual liquidity. When an initial business plan is prepared, serious consideration should be given to how and when the entrepreneur plans to provide a harvest for venture investors.

In many contexts, it is best to plan an exit strategy from the beginning. Waiting until there is significant pressure for an exit is likely to be much more traumatic than planning and anticipating when a harvest would be appropriate. An awareness of, and concern for, exit possibilities and timing is an important signal to potential investors. Some venture capitalists may insist on having an exit strategy in place before they will commit financial capital to early-stage ventures.[1] There is value to having a consensus among investors and founders regarding the type of exit that eventually will be sought.

Evidence suggests that over one-half of entrepreneurs either develop formal exit strategies or have thought about harvest strategies at the outset of the venture.[2] J. William Petty, John Martin, and John Kensinger interviewed twelve entrepreneurs who each harvested at least one business, ten venture investors who had harvesting experience, and two investment advisers who specialized in helping ventures go through the harvesting process. The interviewees emphasized how important it was to begin preparing for the harvest from the very beginning. Comments included:

- You plan for an acquisition and hope for an IPO.
- Exit strategy begins before the money goes in.
- The worst of all worlds is to suddenly realize that for health or other reasons you have to sell the company right now and you haven't planned for it.

---

[1] We are not promoting an obsession with, or commitment to, a particular exit strategy. Our point is that visible awareness of a concern about venture investor exit is usually a good thing. Obsession with an exit plan could annoy the subset of venture investors who prefer that entrepreneurs concentrate on building a sustainable business rather than on how they plan to "get out."

[2] See S. Holmburg, "Value Creation and Capture: Entrepreneurship Harvest and IPO Strategies," in *Frontiers of Entrepreneurship Research*, ed. N. C. Churchill et al. (Wellesley, MA: Babson College, 1991), pp. 191–204. Holmburg conducted a survey of CEOs at computer software ventures that went public during the 1980s. He found that 20 percent of the respondents had developed a formal harvest strategy that was either contained in the original business plan or developed shortly thereafter. An additional 40 percent of the CEOs indicated that they had at least thought about a future harvest.

Petty, Martin, and Kensinger suggested that having a harvest plan in place makes it easier to take advantage of windows of opportunity to exit. Willing and able buyers may come and go quickly, and the markets for initial public offerings often move quickly between being "hot" or "cold."[3] Venture investors and founders should recognize, and give advance consideration to, available exits for venture investors. Common alternative exits include:

- Systematic liquidation
- Outright sale to:
  - Family members
  - Managers
  - Employees
  - Outside buyers
- Going public

We will return to these alternative harvesting methods after we review the process of valuing ventures at the exit date. Of course, the chosen path for exit may depend on prevailing market conditions at the time.

CONCEPT CHECK

- Do entrepreneurs consider a formal exit strategy in the earliest stages of a venture?

14.3 VALUING THE EQUITY OR VALUING THE ENTERPRISE

As we have discussed in earlier chapters, we can value a firm's equity or value the whole enterprise (debt and equity). We can do so using either present or future values, depending on the focal point of the decision at hand. Ultimately for harvesting purposes, we need to decide on the venture's value at exit and how that exit value pie will be divided up among investors.

Exit values for many mature ventures are usually determined by (1) discounted cash flow (DCF) methods (equity or enterprise) or (2) relative valuation models based on some form of multiples analysis. Chapter 9 described the DCF equity approach (MDM and PDM alternatives). Chapter 10 employed a version of relative valuation by multiplying a forecasted net income at exit by a price-earnings multiple taken from a comparable firm or transaction. While our concern in Chapter 10

---

[3] J. William Petty, John D. Martin, and John W. Kensinger, *Harvesting Investments in Private Companies* (Morristown, NJ: Financial Executives Research Foundation, 1999), pp. 54–55. For a further discussion of the importance of timing when planning an exit or harvest strategy, see Jeffry A. Timmons and Stephen Spinelli, *New Venture Creation*, 7th ed. (New York: McGraw-Hill/Irwin, 2007), pp. 620–621.

was early-stage firms with very uncertain futures, a similar valuation analysis can be conducted for more mature firms.

For ventures with more complex financial structures, we often begin by estimating the enterprise value at exit. Chapter 13 described a formal DCF approach to estimating a venture's enterprise value. Analysts also estimate a firm's enterprise value by calculating multiples of earnings before interest, taxes, depreciation, and amortization (EBITDA). This works because EBITDA gives a "crude" estimate of cash flow available to both debtholders and equity holders.

As an example, let's assume that a group of managers have the opportunity to buy the equity in their employer's firm for $3,000,000. The managers have $500,000 to invest and have identified venture investors who are willing to invest $2,500,000 in return for an expected 25 percent annual rate of return. In addition, to complete the buyout, the managers must assume an additional $5,000,000 of a five-year-term bank debt venture mandating 12 percent annual interest.

The left side of Figure 14.2 depicts an initial enterprise value of $8,000,000 consisting of a $5,000,000 long-term bank loan and $3,000,000 in equity capital. The question is whether the managers can get the deal done. That is, how much of the equity ownership will the management team have to give up to provide the venture investors with an expected 25 percent compound annual rate of return? To answer this question, we need to estimate the venture's exit value five years from now. Let's assume that both a DCF enterprise valuation method and an EBITDA multiples-based relative valuation model suggest an enterprise exit value of $15,000,000. The right side of Figure 14.2 illustrates a $15,000,000 value based on an EBITDA of $1,500,000 times a multiple of 10 (determined by examining other similar exit transactions).

Panel A of Figure 14.3 shows how the $15,000,000 enterprise value will be divided up at exit in five years. First, the $5,000,000 bank loan will be paid off, resulting in an equity value of $10,000,000. Since the venture investors expect a 25 percent compound annual rate of return, their portion of the equity value at

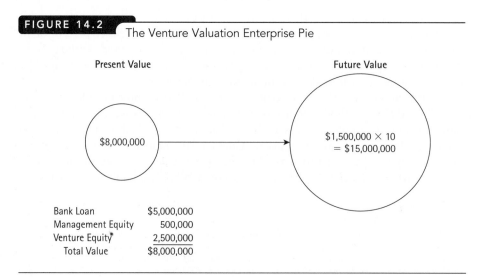

FIGURE 14.2   The Venture Valuation Enterprise Pie

Present Value

Future Value

$8,000,000

$1,500,000 × 10
= $15,000,000

Bank Loan	$5,000,000
Management Equity	500,000
Venture Equity	2,500,000
Total Value	$8,000,000

FIGURE 14.3 Determining the Future Value Venture Enterprise Valuation Pie and Dividing the Future Value Equity Pie

Panel A: Future Value Enterprise Valuation Pie

FV = $15,000,000

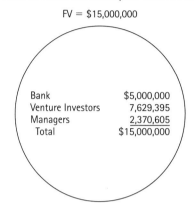

Bank	$5,000,000
Venture Investors	7,629,395
Managers	2,370,605
Total	$15,000,000

Panel B: Equity Ownership Percentages

FV = $15,000,000 − $5,000,000 = $10,000,000

Managers 23.71%

Venture Investors 76.29%

exit would be $7,629,395 [i.e., $2,500,000 times $(1.25)^5$]. The managers would receive the residual or remaining equity value of $2,370,605 (i.e., $10,000,000 − $7,629,395). Panel B of Figure 14.3 illustrates the percentage ownership (using future values) of the equity that the venture investors would need up front (now) to get the deal done. For the $2,500,000 initial equity investment, the venture investors would expect ownership of 76.29 percent ($7,629,395/$10,000,000 using future value relationships) of the equity to enable the expected 25 percent compound annual rate of return.

Of course, if the deal develops as projected, the management team will earn a very handsome rate of return on their initial $500,000 investment. Since the managers are expected to receive $2,370,395 at the end of five years, their anticipated rate of return is 36.5 percent compounded annually.

CONCEPT CHECK

- What are the methods available for estimating equity and enterprise values at exit?

14.4   SYSTEMATIC LIQUIDATION

We begin our discussion of available methods for exiting a privately held venture with systematic liquidation. A **systematic liquidation** occurs when a venture is liquidated by systematically distributing the venture's assets to the owners. By the time a venture reaches the maturity stage of its life cycle, it may be generating substantial amounts of free cash flow. That is, internally generated funds may

systematic liquidation venture liquidated by distributing the venture's assets to the owners

greatly exceed the amount needed to maintain the venture's sustainable growth. An entrepreneur may consciously slow or cease growth by not reinvesting in working capital and plant and equipment. As this use of cash ceases, the cash account bulges. The venture can distribute the cash through dividends (or the equivalent in partnerships and LLCs) and repurchases of outstanding equity. As a nongrowing venture frequently dies, eventually the remaining assets can be sold and the business can cease operations.

Why might an entrepreneur choose to plan an exit through a systematic liquidation? The venture's industry may be in decline, offering immediate (but not long-term) profit opportunities. As we know, industries come and go over time; the market for buggy whips evaporated with the introduction of the automobile. The demand for typewriters virtually ceased with the introduction of the personal computer. While some firms move into the production and sales of replacement products, other firms make the most of the decline and then cease to exist (at least in that market).[4] There are advantages to a systematic liquidation: (1) The entrepreneur and other owners maintain control throughout the harvest period; (2) the harvesting of the investment value can be spread out over a number of years; and (3) the time, effort, and costs of finding a buyer for the venture can be avoided.

Other than when the venture is operating in a declining industry, it is difficult to think of cases when the advantages of liquidation outweigh the disadvantages. Potential disadvantages include (1) the treatment and taxation of liquidation proceeds as ordinary income (rather than capital gains); (2) the commitment of the entrepreneur's wealth, abilities, and focus to a dying venture, rather than other venture pursuits that might be more lucrative; and (3) the acceleration of the rate of decline in the going concern's value as other industry participants respond to the reduction in investment.

With respect to the tax disadvantages: If the venture is organized as a corporation, distributing cash flow in the form of dividends to owners can result in double taxation of income. Taxes are paid first at the corporate level; then dividends are taxable income to the owners. As for focus issues, many entrepreneurs start, operate, and exit multiple ventures over their lifetimes. An exit strategy that pays out the investment value of a venture over several years may inhibit an entrepreneur from starting a new venture because adequate financial capital has not been released from the existing venture. The entrepreneur is still tied emotionally and financially to the dying venture. Finally, and possibly most important, a venture is typically most valuable as a going concern. Large systematic withdrawals of venture cash flow are likely to inhibit growth opportunities because of inadequate reinvestment. Customers and competitors will respond to the venture's declining posture. Except when an industry is in decline, systematic liquidation is typically the least attractive harvest strategy.

---

[4] Although it has a wide variety of products and is still operating in various market segments, Radio Shack pursued an interesting and lucrative strategy during the demise of the nine-channel citizens' band radio market.

CONCEPT
CHECK

• What is a systematic liquidation?

14.5 OUTRIGHT SALE

An **outright sale** occurs when an entrepreneur sells the venture to family members, managers, employees, or outside buyers. We will consider each of these potential purchasers.

FAMILY MEMBERS

Business ventures started by one or more family members often are sold to other family members when the initial founder (or founders) decides to exit. The two basic ways by which an entrepreneur can transfer a business, or interest in a business, to heirs (e.g., children or grandchildren) are (1) giving or "gifting" the venture or (2) selling the venture to them. Sometimes a combination of these methods can be used if the exit strategy is planned well in advance.

The Internal Revenue Code levies a tax on the transfer of property by gift. While the tax law provides for an annual gift exclusion of $10,000 by a donor per recipient, the tax on transferring a venture via gifting can be quite onerous. This is because federal gift tax rates are progressive and have a 55 percent maximum rate. Why, then, might a venture be gifted to heirs? The most likely reason is that the heirs are unable to generate the necessary financial capital to purchase the venture outright.

When businesses are sold or transferred between family members, it is important that the sales price reflect the venture's fair value. The Internal Revenue Service (IRS) states that the value of property is:

> the price at which the property would change hands between a willing buyer and a willing seller when the former is not under any compulsion to buy and the latter is not under any compulsion to sell, both parties having reasonable knowledge of relevant facts. (Revenue Ruling 59-60, 159-1 [13237])

When property is transferred for an amount that is less than what the property is worth, the federal gift tax may be imposed on the difference between the sales price and the fair value of the venture. Consequently, a strategy of selling a venture to a family member below its fair value, to make it easier for the new purchaser to finance the purchase, could be very costly. In most instances, it is better to pay the fair value and incur the financing costs associated with the purchase.

The seller of a family business can help heirs purchase the business in a number of ways. For example, the seller can provide financing by taking back a promissory note that will cover part of the venture's purchase price. The seller may enter into a net gift of stock that is actually a combination sale and gift transaction, whereby the seller sells stock at a price below its fair value. Of course, the difference between the fair value and the selling price would be taxed at the gift tax rate. However, if

outright sale
venture sold to others, including family members, managers, employees, or external buyers

the seller pays the tax out of the sale proceeds, the seller is providing another form of seller financing. Finally, the seller might enter into a private annuity whereby the buyer pays the venture's fair market value to the seller in annual installments over the seller's lifetime.[5]

MANAGERS

The entrepreneur might choose to sell the firm to some of its management team. Managers usually have limited personal resources insufficient for an outright purchase. Consequently, external investors would be brought in to finance the purchase. In a **leveraged buyout (LBO)**, the purchase is financed largely with debt financial capital provided by private equity investors,[6] banks, or purchasers of high-risk junk bonds collectively referred to as LBO financiers. In an LBO, much of the existing investors' equity is retired using the proceeds from an aggressive debt issue. The organizers of the LBO hold the greatly reduced equity portion of the venture's financial (debt and equity) structure. If the organizers and subsequent owners include members of the venture's existing management structure, we also may refer to the LBO as an **MBO**, or **management buyout**.[7]

When initially planning a harvesting strategy, the entrepreneur might help attract key management talent by suggesting that the mature venture be sold to management. An MBO may be the only way for the entrepreneur and top management to get such a deal done. In an MBO, the management team may use personal financial resources to put up as little as 5 or 10 percent of the purchase price and borrow the remainder from LBO private equity specialists, venture capitalists, banks, or other junk-bond investors.[8]

Of primary concern in an LBO/MBO is whether the firm can survive the short run of heavy debt service. An LBO/MBO exit strategy requires a tight plan for streamlining operations and cutting costs—even for previously well-managed firms. Evidence suggests that MBOs do achieve almost immediate operating efficiencies that are maintained over time.[9] Candidates for LBOs/MBOs usually are firms with relatively stable operating income and an ability to protect market share. Stable and adequate operating cash flows are essential to meeting current

leveraged buyout (LBO)
purchase price of a firm is financed largely with debt financial capital

management buyout (MBO)
special type of LBO where the firm's top management continues to run the firm and has a substantial equity position in the reorganized firm

---

[5] For a discussion of intrafamily business purchases and sales, as well as the importance of estate planning in terms of family businesses, see Michael Friedman and Scott Friedman, *How to Run a Family Business* (Cincinnati, OH: Betterway Books, 1994), chaps. 7 and 8.

[6] Venture capitalists who provide high-risk debt capital usually require that an equity "kicker" in the form of warrants be issued along with the debt. An alternative is to make the debt convertible into an equity position in the future.

[7] Non-MBO LBOs are one type of acquisition by "outside buyers," discussed later, although the financial mechanics are basically the same as those we present for an MBO.

[8] We have used the term "venture capitalist" to refer to private equity investors concentrating on the earlier stages in a venture's life. It is true that some venture capitalists also use their funds to invest in LBO and turnaround private equity. "Private equity investor" is a more general term for this broader type of investor.

[9] For example, see Steven Kaplan, "The Effects of Management Buy-Outs on Operating Performance and Value," *Journal of Financial Economics* 24 (1989): pp. 217–254, and "The Staying Power of Leveraged Buyouts," *Journal of Financial Economics* 29 (1991): pp. 287–313. Evidence on small-firm MBOs is provided in M. S. Wright, K. Robbie Thompson, and P. Wong, "Management Buy-Outs in the Short and Long Term," in *Frontiers of Entrepreneurship Research*, pp. 302–316.

interest commitments, as well as being able to pay off debt principal in a timely manner.

An Example

E-Calendar Company is a closely held corporation founded by Ryan McFee, who—along with some other members of the McFee family—owns all of the shares of stock in the firm. As the name suggests, the firm manufactures and sells electronic calendars and graphical enhancements to standard computer and personal decision assistant (PDA) time management software programs.

McFee plans to retire at the end of this year. He and his family want to sell the firm for $40 million. Three members of E-Calendar's top management team would like to purchase the firm, but they have only $2 million of personal equity capital to invest. The old equity will be retired upon the purchase of the firm, and two million shares at a par value of $1 each will be issued to the three new owners.

Since these three individuals have been long-term loyal employees with excellent operating expertise, McFee is interested in making the deal work. LBO financiers will put up $20 million in 9 percent, five-year subordinated debt funds with attached two million warrants that can be converted into two million shares of common stock. By exercising their warrants, the LBO financiers will own 50 percent of the venture's equity in the future. A bank specializing in making risky loans to firms undergoing LBOs will lend $10 million at a rate of 12 percent. Furthermore, the bank will require that the loan be fully amortized over a four-year period. Finally, to get the deal done, McFee will be asked to provide some seller financing in the form of a 10 percent, five-year, $8 million seller's note. The note will be subordinated to the bank loan but will have a claim on income and assets superior to the LBO financiers' debt claims.

To summarize, the proposed LBO/MBO will be financed with $2 million in equity and $38 million in debt, resulting in a 5 percent weight for equity and 95 percent for debt. McFee (and the other current owners) will receive $32 million in cash ($2 million in equity from management, $20 million from the LBO financiers, and $10 million from the bank) and will receive an additional $8 million when his $8 million loan is repaid at the end of five years. This proposed financing package will be a real test of how committed McFee is to selling E-Calendar Company to his top three managers. First, the effective selling price is less than $40 million because McFee will earn a below-market interest rate on the loan, and he will have to wait five years for the return of his principal. Even the bank is getting a 12 percent interest rate; the LBO financiers, while receiving only a 9 percent interest rate, have warrants that can handsomely raise their returns.

Using material presented earlier in this text, we should, with some additional information, be able to answer several questions.

1. In present value terms, how much are McFee and his family receiving for the sale of E-Calendar Company under the proposed LBO/MBO financing plan?

    We know that $32 million will be received in the form of cash proceeds. In addition, we need to calculate the present value of the 10 percent, five-year, $8 million seller's loan. Recall that we find the present value (PV) of a stream of periodic cash flows plus a terminal or ending value as follows:

$$\text{Present Value (PV)} = \text{Discounted Stream of Cash Flows}$$
$$+ \text{Discounted Terminal Value}$$

$$\text{PV} = \frac{\text{VCF}_1}{1+r} + \frac{\text{VCF}_2}{(1+r)^2} + \frac{\text{VCF}_3}{(1+r)^3} + \cdots + \frac{\text{VCF}_T}{(1+r)^T} + \frac{\text{TV}_T}{(1+r)^T}$$

$$= \sum_{t=1}^{T} \frac{\text{VCF}_T}{(1+r)^T} + \frac{\text{TV}_T}{(1+r)^T} \qquad \textbf{(14.1)}$$

In the case of a debt security, the stream of cash flows is the interest payments, and the terminal or ending value is the principal repayment.

Since the bank loan will carry a 12 percent interest rate and the seller's loan has subordinate claims, a 14 percent interest rate is probably a reasonable approximation of the market interest rate at that time for such a loan. The dollar interest on the 10 percent rate loan would be $800,000 (i.e., .10 × $8 million). We can find the present value (PV) of the loan by discounting the interest and principal payments at 14 percent as follows:

$$\text{PV at 14\%} = \$800,000/(1.14)^1 + \$800,000/(1.14)^2 + \$800,000/(1.14)^3$$
$$+ \$800,000/(1.14)^4 + \$800,000/(1.14)^5 + \$8,000,000/(1.14)^5$$
$$= \$6,901,410, \text{ or } \$6.9 \text{ million rounded}$$

Assuming no default on his seller's note, McFee would receive an effective price of $38.9 million ($32 million plus $6.9 million) for E-Calendar Company. Will a selling price that is effectively a little less than $39 million be adequate for the deal to be consummated? Only McFee and his family can decide.

2. Will LBO financiers invest in the proposed LBO/MBO?

The answer depends on the rate of return expected by the LBO financiers on their $20 million investment. LBO financiers often are willing to take a delayed equity investment position in an LBO/MBO. By accepting debt with an equity kicker, the private equity investors will receive some periodic cash flow, in the form of interest, in addition to their future cash-out value. Furthermore, the LBO debt, while subordinated to the bank loan and to McFee's seller's note, will have a priority claim (before management's claims) on the firm's income and assets.

The 9 percent interest rate on the LBO loan will provide $1.8 million in cash flow per year (i.e., .09 × $20 million). However, the major portion of the LBO financiers' expected return comes from the value of the equity (kicker) portion of their investment. Because E-Calendar Company has been operating for several years, and demand for calendars is relatively stable from year to year, operating risk is relatively low. The risk associated with the LBO/MBO is primarily associated with the ability to service the large debt burden. Given the proven operating track record for E-Calendar, a target rate of return of 20 to 25 percent per year might be acceptable to the LBO financiers.

Let's assume that the management team and the LBO financiers agree on an exit plan to sell the firm to another buyer at the end of five years at a target price of $50 million. The LBO financiers will exercise their warrants (their form of equity kicker) by exchanging the two million warrants for two million shares of stock. Since the management team also owns two million shares, the $50 million selling price will be split equally between the LBO financiers and the management team. Just before selling the firm, the LBO loan will be retired or replaced with a new $20 million privately placed debt issue. Because the bank loan and McFee's seller's loan will have been repaid earlier, a new $20 debt issue should carry a favorable interest rate at that time.

We can use an internal rate of return (IRR) calculation to estimate what the LBO financiers' expected rate of return would be if their debt is paid off and they receive $25 million as their portion of the selling price at the end of five years. In general terms, we have:

$$\text{Debt Investment} = \text{Discounted Stream of Cash Flows} \\ + \text{Discounted Terminal Value} \qquad \textbf{(14.2)}$$

The LBO financiers' investment was $20 million. Interest of $1.8 million will be paid at the end of each year to the LBO financiers. In addition, they will receive a return of their $20 million debt principal plus $25 million in proceeds from the sale of the firm at the end of five years. Thus, in this example, we actually have two terminal values. We now are ready to solve for the discount rate that will equate the initial LBO financiers' investment with the stream of expected cash inflows as follows:

$$\begin{aligned} \$20 \text{ million} = \ & \$1,800,000/(1+r)^1 + \$1,800,000/(1+r)^2 \\ & + \$1,800,000/(1+r)^3 + \$1,800,000/(1+r)^4 \\ & + \$1,800,000/(1+r)^5 + \$20,000,000/(1+r)^5 \\ & + \$25,000,000/(1+r)^5 \\ r = \ & 24.4\% \end{aligned}$$

A 24.4 percent rate of return falls into the LBO financiers' target range of 20 to 25 percent. Of course, they might also want to know what would happen to their return if the total selling price were only $40 million (rather than $50 million) at the end of five years. By substituting $20 million in the place of $25 million in the above equation and again solving for r, we would have a 21.94 percent internal rate of return. Thus, even at a lower than expected selling price ($40 million), the internal rate of return still falls within the LBO financiers' target range. These results suggest that the LBO financiers are likely to take part in the LBO/MBO.

3. Can the debt interest and principal be serviced or paid according to the contractual terms?

The answer to this question is found in precisely the same manner as that introduced in Chapter 6. With a proper set of projected financial statements, this question can be answered easily. Rather than duplicate the rather tedious material already covered, we refer you to that chapter. The new financial information that the LBO adds to the existing financials relates to the projected debt payments (principal and interest).

CONCEPT CHECK

- What are LBOs and MBOs?

EMPLOYEES

Rather than simply selling the venture to management in an LBO, some entrepreneurs harvest the fruits of their labor by establishing a leveraged employee stock ownership plan (ESOP). The idea (and financial analysis) is similar to that in an LBO/MBO, except that the debt used to purchase the venture's equity is issued by the venture's ESOP and guaranteed by the venture (rather than issued directly by the venture). The ESOP uses the proceeds of the debt to purchase venture equity that belongs to the employees. The venture promises to pay retirement contributions to the ESOP. In turn, the ESOP uses the contributions to retire the debt and purchase any retiring or departing employees' shares. As in an LBO, the founders achieve liquidity by having their shares purchased by a leveraged entity (in this case, an ESOP). The employees gain an ownership stake in the private company. The more traumatic harvest strategies, such as going public or being acquired, are avoided.

The ESOP harvest strategy was made possible by an act of Congress and is available in leveraged and unleveraged varieties. Of course, if the initial leveraging doesn't take place, the founders have a much longer road to liquidity because they sell shares to the ESOP only as the ESOP needs them. Recent studies indicate that about 9,000 private companies and 1,000 public companies have ESOPs in place.[10]

OUTSIDE BUYERS

For many ventures, the stated or unstated exit strategy involves the sale of the going concern, or its tangible and intangible assets, to a user of the venture's products or intellectual property or to a competitor attempting to consolidate the industry or incorporate the innovation into an existing product or service line. Discussions about possible acquisition may arise more than once in the normal course of business for an early-stage venture. As the venture creates relationships with customers and suppliers, and as competitors recognize the threat or contribution

---

[10] There was a flurry of press coverage in the spring of 1999 as Hewitt Associates, in conjunction with faculty at Northwestern University, released a study indicating superior performance by companies with ESOPs. The 10,000 number we provide comes from the discussion in "Your Money," *Time*, May 10, 1999, p. 95.

of the venture's products and services, a successful venture will generate informal (and possibly even formal) discussions about being acquired.

In a well-capitalized venture, early discussions of a possible acquisition may be taken lightly, as they distract from the venture's core mission of building a sustainable enterprise. In a less well capitalized venture, however, where the financial condition is tenuous, it may pay to consider more seriously occasional inquiries about the possibility of being acquired. As an example, one of the authors was involved in a dot-com investment that was on its third round of financing. The previous rounds exhibited reasonable price increases, raising several million dollars, and the venture had on several occasions discussed the possibility of being acquired. Its burn rate was relatively high, and it had a serious need for cash during the dot-com crunch of 2000. After notifying the existing investors that a down round (priced below the previous round) was under way, the venture abruptly changed course, began serious acquisition discussions, and sold itself to a publicly traded company desiring the venture's intellectual property. The cash-strapped venture had waited to begin serious acquisition discussions until it was facing a down round that looked like it might not be fully subscribed. Needless to say, it was not in the best position to negotiate favorable acquisition terms. Although the venture violated a main principle of venture financing—"Think about raising money before you need it"—it was successfully acquired with an absorption of the main assets, management, and employees into the publicly traded entity.[11] The return to most of the venture investors was a check for a portion of their initial investment and an IRS Section 1244 write-off for the remainder. In tough times with tight capital markets, it can be especially important to have a good idea of what, if any, are the possible acquisition opportunities.

There is some evidence that a venture's value to an acquirer may exceed the value of the same venture sold to the public markets.[12] Variations in public market conditions, and in the types of firms perceived to be "hot," make it difficult to offer generic remarks about the valuation (dis)advantage of being acquired (versus going public). We can, however, discuss some of the elements of valuation analysis for an acquisition.

The basic valuation approach is similar to what we have covered earlier in this text. Firms typically will have investment bankers (and insiders, if they have the staff) attempt to calibrate the venture's acquisition value, looking at both discounted cash flow and multiples approaches. Perhaps the most interesting practice (although a bit controversial) is what is done to these calibrations after they are determined. Typically, there are premiums and discounts applied to these numbers that dramatically increase or decrease the valuation from its base.

---

[11] At times like these, the original venture investors are keenly aware of the potential conflicts of interest. The entrepreneur-managers negotiate how they will fare when absorbed, and the external investors begin to see that they will get left behind as they are absolved (of their interest in the venture). The landing can be softer for the entrepreneur than for the external investors.

[12] For example, see the somewhat persuasive promotional piece by Daniel Donoghue and Michael Murphy (both of Piper Jaffrey), "Small Public Companies: Hidden M&A Value," Minneapolis, MN: Piper Jaffrey Corporate Finance, Spring 1998. Their statistical analysis addresses the valuation costs and benefits of going public or being acquired. Many firms that go public subsequently experience large downward revisions in their valuations.

- *Control Premium.* Typically applied to the base valuation to reflect the value of controlling the venture rather than being a minority shareholder. Although some suggest this premium may average as high as 40 percent during some periods, it does fluctuate. It is generally agreed, however, that some premium to control the venture is necessary to get the deal done. Of course, if you have done the discounted cash flow (DCF) valuation and there doesn't appear to be any way to justify a 40 percent premium for control, it may be a sign that the acquisition is not feasible with current market conditions and expectations for the venture. The rationale for a control premium is the common observation that publicly traded companies cannot typically be acquired for their trading price, which should (in efficient markets) be related to their true value.[13]
- *Illiquidity Discount.* Typically applied to the base valuation to compensate for the resale disadvantages of private equity. Public investors in equity are usually (as individuals) minority owners who cannot significantly influence the aspects of the public firm. As such, they pay a price that does not include a control premium. This is why an acquirer of a public firm typically pays (a control premium) more than what minority shareholders have been paying. If the firm is not publicly traded, the acquirer may calibrate the value to include a liquidity discount because of the lack of a liquid market for the acquired equity. In some cases, the discount may be based on empirical studies of the discount on restricted (letter) stock issued by publicly traded companies.[14] If the investor wishes to control a nonpublic venture, the value calibration may need to include a control premium and an illiquidity discount.

Full-service investment banks offer mergers and acquisitions services, in addition to those required to sell part of the venture's equity to the public. In many industries, mergers and acquisitions boutiques specialize in arranging for the purchase and sale of entities operating in those industries. Both full-service and boutique banks will provide estimates of anticipated acquisition prices and will address the issues of the types of acquirers and conditions of acquisition that lead to a control premium or an illiquidity discount.

If an investment bank, or mergers and acquisitions boutique, has been retained, typically the solicitation process (for acquisition offers) will involve confidential meetings with the venture, the preparation of promotional materials involving limited disclosure about the venture (possibly not even including the name), and the preparation of a targeted acquirer list. Once potential acquirers have been contacted, bids usually are solicited with some understanding of a feasible bid range. Once the finalist pool has been determined, the venture may provide supplemental disclosure and establish a bid cutoff date.

---

[13]   A starting point of classic academic studies discussing takeover premiums is Michael Bradley, Anand Desai, and E. Han Kim, "The Rationale Behind Interfirm Tender Offers: Information or Synergy?" *Journal of Financial Economics* 11 (1983): pp. 183–206, and "Synergistic Gains from Corporate Acquisitions and Their Division Between the Stockholders of Target and Acquiring Firms," *Journal of Financial Economics* 21 (1988): pp. 3–40. For a commercial support site offering useful current data on control premiums (and other valuation factors), see http://www.bvmarketdata.com

[14]   For an example of an empirical study on liquidity discount, see Michael Hertzel and Richard Smith, "Market Discounts and Shareholder Gains for Placing Equity Privately," *Journal of Finance* 48 (1993): pp. 459–485.

Although it is tempting to characterize this process as an auction, frequently the venture's consideration of nonmonetary terms (such as culture, managerial succession, and employee retention) may heavily influence the selection of a successful bidder. In some cases, even if the venture is not heavily influenced by the nonfinancial terms, the financial portions of the bids are hard to compare because of the mixture of debt, equity, options, and cash in the offer. One does not have to look very far (perhaps not even outside one's family) to find a venture that has been sold other than to the highest bidder—even using an objective determination of the value of the bids (e.g., all cash). The entrepreneur's objectives seldom boil down to maximizing a financial return. There are almost always legacy issues and ego involvement in the venture's future.

CONCEPT CHECK

- Identify the buyers who should be considered when the equity owners wish to harvest the venture.

14.6 GOING PUBLIC

There is no doubt that many venture investors and entrepreneurs consider an initial public offering of venture stock as the symbol of venture success. In the typical **initial public offering (IPO)**, a firm registers new (and sometimes "used") shares with the Securities and Exchange Commission (SEC) and state securities regulators and proceeds to sell those shares to the public. The sale of new shares is a **primary offering**, and the sale of used shares is a **secondary offering**. While there usually are restrictions on how many secondary shares can be sold, an initial public offering can involve primary and secondary shares.

During the IPO process, the firm presents itself to the public and prepares for its new life under the "microscope" that the public applies to publicly traded companies. Typically, firms retain the services of an investment bank to facilitate the IPO process. We begin with a discussion of investment banking.

initial public offering (IPO)
a venture's first offering of SEC-registered securities to the public

primary offering
the sale of new shares (or securities)

secondary offering
the sale of used shares (or securities)

INVESTMENT BANKING

When a firm employs an intermediary to assist in the creation, sale, and distribution of its financial assets, the intermediary's activities are referred to as **investment banking**. Institutions involved in the investment banking process are known as investment banks. Employees of investment banks are loosely referred to as investment bankers.

In the investment banking process, investment banks act neither like investors nor like banks. That is, investment banks are not the targeted investors for a firm's securities, and investment banking is not about offering banking services such as checking accounts. Investment bankers specialize in the critical process of finding buyers for a firm's securities. They initiate markets for a venture's newly issued public securities.

investment banking
an intermediary assisting in the creation, sale, and distribution of financial assets

Owing to their extensive network of possible buyers for the securities (through their affiliated brokerage and client services activities), investment bankers are considered experts in predicting the value of the newly issued securities. It seems reasonable, therefore, to assume they have some comparative advantage in taking mispricing risk. Investment banks assume mispricing risk by buying newly issued shares from the corporation at a price that is typically set just (the night) before the shares are available for public purchase (from the investment banks). If the investment bankers have done their homework, the public offering of the securities at a slightly higher price will be successful.

The underwriting process is designed to lock in the corporation's proceeds before the securities are legally offered to individual or institutional investors. The difference between what the investment banks get from public investors and what they pay to the issuing firm is called the investment banker's **underwriting spread** and is typically 7 to 10 percent. This spread is the largest component of compensation for the investment banks' provision of marketing services and for bearing their portion of overnight pricing risk.

underwriting spread
difference between what the investment bank gets from selling securities to public investors and what it pays to the issuing firm

Of course, it is not always the case that investment banks make a profit when reselling the securities to the public. If the investment bankers misjudge the demand for the new securities, they can end up unable to sell the securities at an average price above what they must pay the corporation. Such instances are rare. In a case in 1974, the investment banks lost $8 million on a bond issue by New Jersey Sporting Arena. There were major losses on a British Petroleum offering in 1987 when the overall market crashed during the offering. Given that the public offering price is set just before the actual offering, and given that many underwriting contracts now include clauses protecting the underwriters from major marketwide declines, the mispricing risks do not appear to be as large as they may have been in the past or as large as the underwriting community might suggest.

While securities laws prohibit formal agreements with the public to buy the soon-to-be-offered securities, investment bankers contact many potential buyers and construct reasonable demand curves for the new securities. While all such conversations must be informal and nonbinding, investors who back away from their stated nonbinding intent to buy may find future opportunities to buy other issues somewhat altered. We are not suggesting anything improper here; we are merely noting that the verbal indications are not merely "cheap talk."

Figure 14.4 presents an example of the prominent advertising technique (which is simultaneously an SEC-required disclosure) used to generate interest in upcoming issues. Such ads are known as *tombstone ads*.[15] They list the security, the offering price, and the investment banks participating in the offering (called the syndicate of underwriters) in descending order of importance and risk taking. The tombstone ad also carries the obligatory **red herring disclaimer** (at the top) that disavows any intent for the ad to act as an offer to sell or solicitation of an offer to buy the securities. Such an offer is illegal before the actual offering date. These ads, however, may appear after the securities have been allocated. That is, once you've seen the ad, it may not be possible to get a member of the

red herring disclaimer
obligatory disclaimer disavowing any intent to act as an offer to sell, or solicit an offer to buy, securities

---

[15]   Investment banks keep records of their securities transactions, and some make them available on the Web.

This advertisement is neither an offer to sell nor a solicitation of an offer to buy any of these securities. The offering is made only by the Prospectus.

December 6, 1995

2,600,000 Shares

 PHARMACOPEIA

Common Stock

Price $16 Per Share

Copies of the Prospectus may be obtained from such of the Underwriters as may legally offer these securities in compliance with the securities laws of the respective states.

ALEX. BROWN & SONS
INCORPORATED

COWEN & COMPANY

UBS SECURITIES INC.

DILLON, READ & CO. INC.	HAMBRECHT & QUIST LLC	LEHMAN BROTHERS
MERRILL LYNCH & CO.	MORGAN STANLEY & CO. INCORPORATED	OPPENHEIMER & CO., INC.
ROBERTSON, STEPHENS & COMPANY		SMITH BARNEY INC.
ROBERT W. BAIRD & CO. INCORPORATED	DOMINICK & DOMINICK INCORPORATED	FIRST OF MICHIGAN CORPORATION
FURMAN SELZ INCORPORATED	GRUNTAL & CO., INCORPORATED	JOSEPHTHAL LYON & ROSS INCORPORATED
PENNSYLVANIA MERCHANT GROUP LTD	RAGEN MACKENZIE INCORPORATED	VECTOR SECURITIES INTERNATIONAL, INC.

investment banking syndicate to indicate informally that you will be able to buy some of the securities when they are legally offered.

Investment bankers have an extensive set of security holders who may act as purchasers of newly distributed securities. There are two major issues with this. The first is the quality of the distribution. Public companies usually do not wish to have an entire offering land in the hands of a small group of investors. If the company is selling off a significant portion of ownership, a concentrated distribution could effectively overthrow the control of the existing shareholders (and result in the displacement of management). Investment bankers argue that part of their function is providing a widely dispersed security-holding base, which is particularly valuable when the security being sold is the common stock of the firm. The second aspect of distribution is simply physical. Firms need the distribution channel for new securities only when they are issuing new stocks. It is not efficient for firms to maintain an in-house investment banking department to carry out securities issuing functions on the rare occasions when they are required. It is much cheaper to contract for these services when needed. Investment banking firms, specializing in such services and maintaining continuous contact with potential investors, have a comparative advantage.

In addition to the underwriting and marketing services, investment banks provide advice and consulting. They also can help locate potential acquirers or possible acquisition targets. Since they are accustomed to taking mispricing risk, investment banks take reasonable care in reviewing the company's investment plans and may be in a position to provide valuable insights into the company. Investment banks also expend relatively large amounts of human and financial capital discovering and introducing new financial products.

The investment banking function relies heavily on reputations gained through repeated interactions with buyers and issuers in the market for new securities. Retaining an investment bank involves leaning on that bank's reputation, a carefully guarded asset. It is not hard to find investment banks that have walked away from deals that they thought would damage their long-term reputations. Woe to the firm that spends hundreds of thousands of dollars before finding out that the credible investment banks are no longer interested in assisting the firm in placing new securities.

CONCEPT CHECK

- What is a red herring disclaimer?
- What is the purpose of a tombstone ad?

SOME ADDITIONAL DEFINITIONS

due diligence
the process of ascertaining, to the extent possible, an issuing firm's financial condition and investment intent

In a manner similar to the term's use in venture capital screening, investment banks are responsible for conducting **due diligence** when assisting in the placement of securities with public investors. The assisting investment bank has a legal obligation to consider the firm's financial situation and investment intent. Assuming that everything checks out (to the extent possible), the investment bank's legal team will work with the issuer's legal team to prepare the necessary SEC and state registration documents. This process can be time consuming. It helps to have competent legal advisers and insiders who have had previous experience with public securities offerings. In a traditional registration, the issuer registers a specific security to be sold at a specific time, at a price in a specific range, and in accordance with a specific investment banking arrangement to be executed by a specific set of investment banks. Such an offering is, by far, the most common arrangement for equity offerings.

Issuing firms may complete an umbrella registration arrangement that allows security sales presently, and in the future, under the SEC's shelf registration process (Rule 415). Shelf registration, introduced only recently, permits the firm to register securities to be issued within the next two years. This method is more common for debt issues. Some of the advantages include timing the market (if possible), low transaction costs, short-notice delivery to arriving demand, and the ability to easily auction the firm's securities.

Most issuers prefer to have an investment bank underwrite their securities offerings. The underwriting agreement is frequently referred to as a **firm commitment** to purchase and distribute the new securities. There are, however, other less common arrangements available. If the issuer prefers to purchase only the marketing and distribution efforts and does not wish the issue to be guaranteed, then a **best efforts** agreement would be more appropriate. Best efforts services do not involve the actual transfer of ownership from the issuer to the investment banking syndicate. While such an arrangement may seem appealing, the total cost of issuing new securities is the sum of direct *and* opportunity costs. Perhaps the largest component of costs in best efforts arrangements is selling new securities for less than they could be sold in an underwritten offering. There is some evidence that the total costs (viewed this way) are higher for best efforts offerings.[16]

In addition to the compensation inherent in the spread between the share price the issuer receives and that at which the underwriters sell, the underwriters typically will have an option to buy additional shares. Such *greenshoe* options allow underwriters to sell more shares when an issuer is heavily oversubscribed. A greenshoe option on 10 percent additional shares is not uncommon. Of course, such options are exercised for the benefit of the option holder (the syndicate), not the option writer (the issuer). Consequently, they will be exercised when the issue price is below the realized market price. This is typically when the issuer would prefer not to sell any more shares than initially anticipated.

We previously mentioned primary offerings (for new securities) and secondary offerings (for previously issued securities). When the new securities are for a firm that already has publicly traded shares, the offering is called a *seasoned offering*. When the issuer has not previously issued that type of security, the offering is called an *unseasoned offering*. An IPO is an unseasoned offering of a firm's equity. When an issuer is first attempting to sell shares to the public, the investment bankers (and some securities regulators) usually try to restrict the current owners from selling their shares for a period of time following the offering. Large amounts of insider sales could make it difficult to stabilize the share price during the offering and would send a bad signal to new investors. A *lockup provision* is the negotiated period around an offering during which insiders are prohibited from selling their existing shares. Sometimes the insiders' shares are registered along with the new shares being sold to the public. This is the essence of the piggyback registration rights we discussed in earlier chapters. A lockup provision is useful in preventing such shares from coming to market at the same

firm commitment
type of agreement with investment bank involving the investment bank's underwritten purchase and resale of securities

best efforts
type of agreement with investment bank involving only marketing and distribution efforts

---

[16] For one of the earliest studies on the direct and indirect costs of a securities offering, see Jay Ritter, "The Costs of Going Public," *Journal of Financial Economics* 19 (December 1987): 269–281. Some useful descriptive statistics are also provided by Reena Aggarwal and Pietra Rivoli, "Evaluating the Costs of Raising Capital Through an Initial Public Offering," *Journal of Business Venturing* 6 (September 1991): pp. 351–361.

time as the public offering. In other cases, investment bankers will be able to avoid registering existing owners' shares. Of course, if they are not registered, they cannot be (immediately) sold to the public and there is little danger of flooding the market with existing shares. Eventually, insiders will want their shares registered, the lockup period (typically about 180 days) will expire, and the existing owners will push for a secondary offering of their shares to the public. The secondary offering becomes the exit or liquidity event for venture investors (and the entrepreneurial team). While many entrepreneurs and students think of the IPO as the major liquidity event, if the IPO falters it could be a long time before the liquidity event they seek actually takes place.

CONCEPT CHECK

- What is due diligence?
- What is a firm commitment underwriting?

OTHER COSTS IN ISSUING SECURITIES

In our discussion of best efforts and underwritten securities offerings, we have mentioned three important aspects of the cost of a public offering: spread, mispricing, and greenshoe. While these costs represent a large majority of the costs of a public offering, they are contingent costs. That is, these costs are borne when the offering takes place and securities are sold. By the time the firm bears these costs, the process is completed. Before incurring these costs, however, there are other costs that the firm must bear irrespective of the outcome of the actual offering. Such costs include the legal, printing, registration, and travel expenses accrued before the offer date. We know of a small firm that, during the process leading to its public offering, committed to pay noncontingent costs exceeding several hundred thousand dollars. Given these looming bills and a rather desperate need for cash by the time of the offering, the firm was in no position to bargain on issue price at the time. Entrepreneurial ventures seeking to go public should realize that incurring extensive costs in preparation for an initial public offering could, in some cases, be a precommitment to go public.

Mispricing risk is the somewhat loose notion that an issuing firm might be selling a security for less than it is worth. To make this notion more precise, academics and practitioners frequently make reference to **IPO underpricing**. Underpricing results when the syndicate's offering price is less than the market price immediately following an offering. For instance, if the syndicate is selling shares at $7 to the investors it contacted before the formal sale, and shares are trading through an exchange at $27, there is $20 of underpricing. While this is not a direct cost to the issuer, it can easily be the largest opportunity cost borne by existing owners. To sell a share for less than it is worth certainly "costs" existing shareholders.

As might be expected, many of the direct costs involved in issuing securities are not sensitive to volume. Therefore, it's no real surprise that there are economies

IPO underpricing
a reference to a syndicate's offering price when it is less than the market price immediately following the offering

of scale in offerings. The average total cost for IPO common stock offerings is around 14 percent but can be below 10 percent for large offerings.[17]

- What is underpricing and how is it a cost of selling new securities?

POST-IPO TRADING

In the preceding discussion, we considered how a firm places new securities in the market. When the securities are registered, they can be traded. Trading in the securities provides less timing risk for the security holders. That is, purchasers will be hesitant to hold securities that they cannot trade when needed. Trading in the secondary markets, such as the New York Stock Exchange (NYSE), greatly increases the attractiveness of a security and the efficiency of a decentralized capitalistic economy. Consequently, a venture's choice of location for post-IPO trading can be important.

Stock exchanges are clubs that exist primarily to further the interests of their members. While one may not frequently hear this said about the NYSE or the American Stock Exchange, it is best not to forget it. We will talk primarily about the NYSE, but many of the points carry over to other exchanges.

The NYSE has existed in some form since the early eighteenth century, when people gathered to trade everything from food to slaves. In 1792, several men agreed to meet and exclusively trade stocks. The exchange finally incorporated in 1971.

The exchange neither buys nor sells securities; it only coordinates the exchange of securities among its members. An example of the NYSE listing requirements is:

- $\geq$ 2,000 holders of $\geq$ 100 shares[18]
- $\geq$ 1,100,000 shares outstanding, held by the public
- $\geq$ $60 million in market value[19]
- $\geq$ $2.5 million before-tax profits in the latest year
- $2 million in each of the previous two years

There are other issues that the exchange mandates for the firms that trade, like those involving the distribution of voting rights. The NYSE is on record as being a strong supporter of one share, one vote.

---

[17] For a discussion of the breakdown of IPO costs and an introduction to the academic literature on the IPO process, see Ritter, "The Costs of Going Public."

[18] There are three alternative holdings standards for firms. We have used the most commonly cited one. For full information on the current NYSE listing standards, consult http://www.nyse.com

[19] The market value requirement for IPOs, spinoffs, and carve-outs is only $60 million, although it is $100 million for other issues.

From the trading side, one joins the NYSE club by purchasing a *seat*, which is a misnomer since few, if any, members of the exchange sit at any time during the trading day. Suppose you wished to buy 100 shares of IBM at the prevailing market price. You would contact your local broker, who would forward the order to the home office, which would, in turn, forward the order to its booth on the floor of the exchange. There, a broker would walk to the position where IBM is traded and inquire about the current prices at which traders are willing to buy and sell.[20] These prices are known as the bid and ask, respectively. If there is no one there actively trading IBM, the specialist quotes a bid and ask. A specialist is a member of the exchange appointed to trade a particular stock. The specialist acts as a buyer and seller of last resort and is charged with providing smooth transitions in price (continuity).

When the transaction is agreed upon, each party records its understanding of the transaction, and the accounts are reported to a central processor, which then sends out confirmation reports. Discrepancies are worked out as they arise. When the transaction is reported, it is broadcast across the ticker tape. If a trade of IBM occurred at $85 5/8 for 100 shares, the ticker tape would have $IBM_{85\ 5/8}$. If the trade were for more than 100 shares, the price in the subscript would be preceded by the count in 100s and S: 2S 85 5/8. Sometimes, in periods of high volume, the quotes are abbreviated. You should be aware of such abbreviations if you plan to trade based on ticker tape quotes.

In the aftermarket trading for the venture's securities, there are many different types of orders. We will consider only the most common types:

- *Market Order.* An order that is to be executed as soon as possible at the prevailing market price.
- *Limit Order.* An order that can be executed only at a specified price or better. A limit buy at 80 can be executed only at prices below 80. A limit sell at 90 can be executed only at prices above 90.
- *Stop Order.* An order that converts to a market order once a certain price is achieved. A stop buy at 80 will convert to a market order to buy once the price hits 80. The reason the order is called a stop order is that it frequently is used to stop losses. For example, if I have sold IBM short at 75, I might wish to place a stop buy at 80 to keep from losing more than $5 per share. However, the stop is no guarantee, since the stop may be activated at 80 even though 80 is not available to the stop, and the market order that is created by the stop need not execute at any particular price.

The market makers (e.g., specialists on the NYSE) usually book limit and stop orders. Some feel that this gives the market makers an advantage in discerning how the market will move over the near term. They argue that such an advantage may help offset the costs of providing liquidity when others are unwilling to do so.

---

[20]   If the order reached your broker's booth on the floor and he was too busy to trade at that instant, he might delegate the order to a $2 broker whose sole task is to execute the order.

Note that the specialist trades on his own account as well as for others. There are strict rules of precedence for trading that the specialist must obey.

Other stock exchanges in the United States are the American, Midwest, Philadelphia, Pacific, and the smaller exchanges in Boston, Cincinnati, Salt Lake City, and Spokane. Outside the United States, there are, among many others, the Canadian, London, Tokyo (Nikkei), and Paris (Bourse) exchanges.

Smaller companies, and those not wishing to undergo the hassles of an exchange listing, frequently can be traded through the National Association of Securities Dealers (NASD) Automated Quotation (NASDAQ) system. This is a popular option for firms that undertake an IPO. On the NASDAQ, dealers offer to buy and sell securities from their own accounts, via computer connections. If you wish to buy a security in a local small firm or the typical IPO, the NASDAQ is probably the best place to look for the market.

There are two markets administered by the NASD, the National Market System (NMS), and the SmallCap Market. Table 14.1 presents the initial listing standards for the NMS. Table 14.2 presents the listing requirements for the Small-Cap Market.

TABLE 14.1
NASDAQ NMS Listing Requirements

REQUIREMENTS	INITIAL LISTING 1	INITIAL LISTING 2	INITIAL LISTING 3	CONTINUED LISTING A	CONTINUED LISTING B
Net tangible assets[1]	$6 million	$18 million	N/A	$4 million	N/A
Market capitalization[2]	N/A	N/A	$75 million	N/A	$50 million
			or		or
Total assets			$75 million		$50 million
			and		and
Total revenue			$75 million		$50 million
Pretax income (in latest fiscal year or two of last three years)	$1 million	N/A	N/A	N/A	N/A
Public float (shares)[3]	1.1 million	1.1 million	1.1 million	750,000	1.1 million
Operating history	N/A	2 years	N/A	N/A	N/A
Market value of public float	$8 million	$18 million	$20 million	$5 million	$15 million
Minimum bid price	$5	$5	$5	$1	$5
Shareholders (round lot holders)[4]	400	400	400	400	400
Market makers	3	3	4	2	4
Corporate governance	Yes	Yes	Yes	Yes	Yes

[1] Net tangible assets means total assets (excluding goodwill) minus total liabilities.

[2] For initial or continued listing under option 3, a company must satisfy one of the following to be in compliance: the market capitalization requirement or the total assets and the total revenue requirement.

[3] Public float is defined as shares that are not held directly or indirectly by any officer or director of the issuer and by any other person who is the beneficial owner of more than 10 percent of the total shares outstanding.

[4] Round lot holders are considered holders of 100 shares or more.

TABLE 14.2   NASDAQ SmallCap Listing Requirements

REQUIREMENTS	INITIAL LISTING	CONTINUED LISTING
Net tangible assets[1]	$4 million	$2 million
	or	or
Market capitalization	$50 million	$35 million
	or	or
Net income (in latest fiscal year or two of last three fiscal years)	$750,000	$500,000
Public float (shares)[2]	1 million	500,000
Market value of public float	$5 million	$1 million
Minimum bid price	$4	$1
Market makers	3	2
Shareholders (round lot holders)[3]	300	300
Operating history[4]	1 year	N/A
	or	
Market capitalization	$50 million	N/A
Corporate governance	Yes	Yes

[1]   For initial or continued listing, a company must satisfy one of the following to be in compliance: the net tangible assets requirement (net tangible assets means total assets, excluding goodwill, minus total liabilities), the market capitalization requirement, or the net income requirement.

[2]   Public float is defined as shares that are not held directly or indirectly by any officer or director of the issuer and by any other person who is the beneficial owner of more than 10 percent of the total shares outstanding.

[3]   Round lot holders are considered holders of 100 shares or more.

[4]   If operating history is less than one year, initial listing requires market capitalization of at least $50 million.

CONTEMPLATING AND PREPARING FOR THE IPO PROCESS

When thinking about the IPO as a venture exit strategy, it is important to remember that the changes to the culture can be just as dramatic, if not more so, as when the venture is acquired. In particular, certain changes may prove much more difficult.

For the officers of a publicly traded corporation, there is minimal personal privacy. They are public figures, and their lives are subject to scrutiny in a way that most entrepreneurs have never imagined or desired. In addition to the lack of personal privacy, many entrepreneurs who stay on to help direct the public company must learn about quiet periods, and what they can or cannot say about the company. This can be a difficult adjustment for an entrepreneur whose entire self-image and sense of well-being are related to the current vitality of the publicly traded version of the venture.

In an odd counterbalance to the notion of taking extreme care in what one says about the venture, the required public disclosure in the proxy statement (and on a regular basis after the IPO) can be shocking to the managers of a formerly private corporation. In order to provide accountability to shareholders, shield the public entity from shareholder lawsuits, and keep the SEC happy, the venture's publicly traded version will have to disclose (to the public and, therefore, its competitors) a much greater portion of its strategically sensitive information. Regular financial statements by business segment will reveal where margins and investment are high (or low). When the public (specifically, analysts who follow the stock) somehow get it in their minds that the future is better than the insiders see it, the disparity in beliefs may have to be publicly addressed through warnings. The public company also will be under some obligation to answer questions put to it by the public. Consequently, public ventures frequently have to staff a shareholder relations office. All of these changes can be incredibly invasive, time consuming, and, overall, burdensome to the previously private venture.

As a partial offset to the downside of public scrutiny, an IPO may bring a huge benefit to the marketing of the venture's products and services. An IPO buzz can be contagious and may generate extensive national and international interest. For those who lived in the southeastern part of the United States, there was little doubt that Krispy Kreme (doughnut chain) was special in product, technology, and approach to its market. There is also little doubt that Krispy Kreme's franchising and IPO propelled the company to a national presence previously never imagined by the founders and owners of the private company. In the Denver area, for instance, not only did campers await the opening of the initial store, it was months before one could avoid a sizable line to purchase the hot commodities produced by the patented automated doughnut machinery. Krispy Kreme's spectacular IPO and subsequent performance clearly contributed to the national market for their product.

Crafting a successful IPO is important for venture investors. Although they are unlikely to participate in the proceeds from that initial offering, they stand to benefit from future secondary offerings, the success of which depends on the IPO and subsequent performance. An important element in planning for a successful IPO is being in an industry where investors expect fast growth. Typically, the investment banking firm leading the offering opens the trading for the venture's public securities and commits to provide ongoing research so that trading interest will be reasonable if not exuberant. It is important to stimulate initial trading interest so that new and existing investors will know that if they have to sell the stock, they will not be hammered by a lack of interest.[21]

There are crucial preparations that the venture can undertake to increase the possibility of IPO success and streamline the occasionally rough road to an IPO. There is no substitute for officers and board members who have IPO experience. Of particular interest is the CFO. In many early-stage ventures, the lead financial person is more an accountant and less a treasurer than the publicly traded venture will require. It is not uncommon for a venture to hire a CFO to assist during the going-public process. Such individuals are not to be confused with controllers,

---

[21] For example, in some collectors' investments (not securities), it is not difficult to find 30 percent brokerage fees to facilitate locating a buyer. If you are expecting a 14 percent annual return, a 30 percent selling fee certainly dampens buyer enthusiasm. Consequently, it is always important for a public corporation to consider how analyst following, public disclosure, and other interactions contribute to, or detract from, the liquidity of the company's securities. For reference, liquid public companies can easily have selling costs of less than 1 percent.

whose chief purpose is to coordinate financial protocol and reporting. The CFO needs to be an articulate individual capable of presenting the financial and nonfinancial venture aspects to a potentially hostile, finance-oriented audience. If a new CFO is to be brought in for the IPO, it is good practice to do so sufficiently in advance of the event to allow the CFO to get to know the venture on a personal basis. The CFO should be able to speak with conviction about the venture's condition and prospects.

Typically, the CFO becomes the main coordinator for the collection and preparation of the material contained in the offering prospectus. Preparation for audits, development of the unaudited projections for the immediate post-IPO firm, and initial drafting of the prospectus document are also the CFO's responsibility. Typically, a candidate for the CFO possesses strong financial analysis skills; has been an auditor or has extensive experience with auditors; and is comfortable with accounting systems, controls, and reporting.

In preparation for a public offering, certain internal compensation arrangements should be solidified. Compensation that is too low will suggest potential instability in management or, at least, degradation in future earnings as compensation rises to market levels. Compensation that is too high will suggest self-dealing and may cause future difficulties with management's concern for external shareholders. Consequently, it is usually a good idea to have salaries that are reasonable relative to other, similar publicly traded ventures. As we emphasized in the venture capital chapters, incentive compensation plans should be in place. Long-term employment guarantees usually are not a good idea, although it is not uncommon to see a public company holding the option to retain key employees and restraining those who leave from disclosing trade secrets or competing with the firm.

As anyone who has been involved in the senior management of a small business knows, private enterprises have a great deal of discretion in how they can provide legal perks and benefits to help attract and retain key employees. When a creative and efficient venture has taken advantage of some of these flexibilities, the underlying arrangements may fall under the SEC's designation of "Certain Transactions" under Regulation S-K that must be disclosed in the prospectus. Although there is no list of all arrangements that must be disclosed, in general the regulation deals with transactions with management, or to the benefit of management. Examples include:

- Subsidized housing, including indefinite rent arrangements
- Lease or purchase of corporate jet, yachts, and lodges
- Business relations with affiliated supplier or contractor
- Sales to, and then leaseback from, founder/CEO, even if advantageous
- Miscellaneous loans for no apparent purpose

Even if not a concern for Regulation S-K, certain pre-IPO structures may be confusing to investors. Owing to buyers' potential decreased willingness to pay when the structures make the financial conditions unclear, investment bankers may recommend simplifying and clarifying such relationships before going public. Examples of these potentially confusing structures include:

- Complex relationships and partnerships
- Holding structure organization
- More than two classes of equity
- Royalty (limited) partnerships
- "Off-the-balance-sheet" financing
- Equity (limited) partnerships not dissolved in the IPO process

As we mentioned before, in preparing for an IPO it is always important to have sufficient financing so that the IPO can be delayed. (Figure 14.5 presents a hypothetical time line.) To enter the market as a desperate cash-starved venture signals weak management, a lack of interest or ability for insiders to secure non-IPO financing, and a weak bargaining position. Mezzanine and bridge financing alternatives should be available as insurance against having to do an IPO in down markets or during a negative market attitude toward the venture or its industry. If the venture is given some discretion on an oversubscribed IPO, then it may want to think about the institutional and private investors it would like to see participating. Certain investors can lend credibility in the IPO and the after-market. By way of final comments on preparing for an IPO, it is usually advantageous to court early contact with the financial community (a built-in advantage of professional venture capital financing). The earlier that you have serious (major accounting firm) auditing and competent securities law representation, the better. Never promise more to those considering the IPO than the venture can deliver. Don't use (or allow the investment banks to suggest to potential investors) financial projections that are unrealistic. Although they are not typical characteristics of startup ventures, consistency and reliability are important financial characteristics for a publicly traded firm.

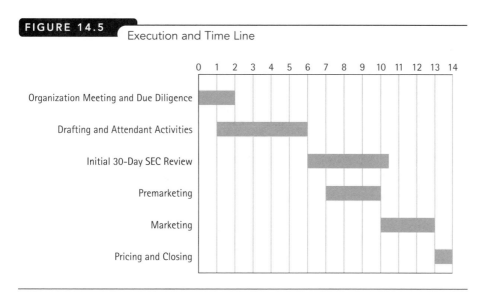

FIGURE 14.5 Execution and Time Line

CONCEPT CHECK

- What is the difference between a CFO and a controller?
- What are the main processes involved in taking a venture public?

SUMMARY

This chapter focused on ways an entrepreneur can harvest or exit a venture nurtured from initial idea into a valuable business enterprise. One typically harvests a venture (1) by a systematic liquidation of assets, (2) by an outright sale of the venture, or (3) by going public. Liquidation is the selling of remaining assets and the distribution of any proceeds (and remaining assets) to the venture's owners. An outright sale can be to family members, managers, employees, or outside buyers. Going public is a two-step registration and sale when an initial public offering (IPO) is followed by a secondary offering of the venture investors' shares.

KEY TERMS

best efforts	investment banking	primary offering
due diligence	IPO underpricing	red herring disclaimer
firm commitment	leveraged buyout (LBO)	secondary offering
harvesting	management buyout (MBO)	systematic liquidation
initial public offering (IPO)	outright sale	underwriting spread

DISCUSSION QUESTIONS

1. What is the meaning of harvesting a venture?

2. What evidence exists on whether entrepreneurs think about and/or develop exit strategies?

3. What is a systematic liquidation of a venture? What are some of the advantages and disadvantages of a systematic liquidation?

4. Describe an outright sale of a venture. What are the four categories of possible buyers?

5. Describe what is meant by (a) a leveraged buyout (LBO) and (b) a management buyout (MBO).

6. What is an employee stock option plan (ESOP)? How is an ESOP used to buy out a venture?

7. Describe the terms (a) "control premium" and (b) "illiquidity discount" when discussing possible external or outside buyers of a venture.

8. Describe an initial public offering (IPO). What are the differences between a primary offering and a secondary offering?

9. What is investment banking? What is an underwriting spread?

10. Describe the terms "tombstone ad" and "red herring disclaimer."

11. What is meant by due diligence? How does a traditional registration differ from a shelf registration?

12. When an investment banking firm decides whether to underwrite or market a securities issue, what is meant by a firm commitment and best efforts?

13. Describe the two following terms that may be involved in underwriting a new securities issue: (a) green shoe and (b) lockup provision.

14. What is meant by initial public offering (IPO) underpricing?

15. Briefly describe how securities are traded on an organized stock exchange such as the New York Stock Exchange.

16. Indicate some of the differences between the NASDAQ's National Market System and SmallCap listing requirements.

17. Describe some of the preparations that a venture can undertake that may increase the possibility of IPO success.

18. What are the steps or stages in a "typical" execution and time line schedule used in planning and executing an IPO?

EXERCISES/PROBLEMS

1. The venture investors and founders of ACE Products, a closely held corporation, are contemplating merging the successful venture into a much larger diversified firm that operates in the same industry. ACE estimates its free cash flows that will be available to the enterprise next year at $5,200,000. Since the venture is now in its maturity stage, ACE's free cash flows are expected to continue to grow at a 6 percent annual compound growth rate in the future. A weighted average cost of capital (WACC) for the venture is estimated at 15 percent. Interest-bearing debt owed by ACE is $17.5 million. In addition, the venture has surplus cash of $4 million. ACE currently has five million shares outstanding, with three million held by venture investors and two million held by founders. The venture investors have an average investment of $2.50 per share while the founders' average investment is $.50 per share.
   A. Based on the above information, estimate the enterprise value of ACE Products. What would be the value of the venture's equity?
   B. How much of the value of ACE would belong to the venture investors versus the founders? How much would the venture be worth on a per-share basis?
   C. What would be the percentage appreciation on the stock bought by the venture investors versus the investment appreciation for the founders?
   D. If the founders have held their investments for five years, calculate the compound annual or internal rate of return on their investments. The venture investors made a first-round investment of 1.5 million shares at $2 per share four years ago. What was the compound annual rate of return on the first-round investment? Venture investors made a second-round investment of 1.5 million shares at $3 per share two years ago. Calculate their compound rate of return on this investment.

2. The BETA firm is proposing to acquire ACE Products, described in Problem 1. BETA estimates that ACE's free cash flow for next year could be improved to $5.5 million because of synergistic benefits in the form of operating or distribution economies. The potential acquirer also believes that ACE's perpetuity growth rate could be increased to 7 percent annually. However, the riskiness of the cash flows would be increased, causing the appropriate WACC to increase to 16 percent. Interest-bearing debt owed by ACE is $17.5 million. The venture also has surplus cash of $4 million. ACE Products has five million shares of common stock outstanding.
   A. Determine ACE's enterprise value from the perspective of BETA. What is ACE's equity worth to BETA in dollar amount and on a per-share basis?
   B. Use the per-share value of ACE from Problem 1 and the per-share value from this problem and establish a range of values (i.e., without and with expected synergistic benefits). If one-half of the synergy-derived benefits were allocated to ACE's venture investors and founders, at what price per share would the merger take place?

C. BETA has thirty million shares of stock outstanding with a market capitalization value of $600 million. What is BETA's stock price? Determine the exchange ratio between ACE's stock value and BETA's stock price at each of ACE's values established in Part B. That is, what would ACE's venture investors and founders receive in BETA's shares for each share of common stock they currently hold in ACE Products?

3. The WestTek privately held venture is considering the sale of the venture to an outside buyer. WestTek's net sales are $21.2 million, its EBITDA is $11.1 million, and its net income is $2.9 million. Three publicly traded comparable firms or competitors in the industry have the following net sales, EBITDA, net income, and market capitalization (stock price times number of shares of common stock outstanding) information:

	EASTTEK	SOUTHTEK	NORTHTEK
Net sales	$25,000,000	$37,500,000	$ 80,000,000
EBITDA	12,500,000	20,000,000	37,500,000
Net income	2,500,000	3,000,000	10,000,000
Market "cap"	60,000,000	80,000,000	200,000,000

A. Calculate the market capitalization or "cap" to net sales ratios for each of the three competitors (EastTek, SouthTek, and NorthTek), as well as the average ratio for the competitors.

B. Calculate the market "cap" to EBITDA ratios for each of the three competitors, as well as the average ratio for the competitors.

C. Calculate the market "cap" to net income ratios for each of the three competitors, as well as the average ratio for the competitors.

D. Estimate the market value or market "cap" for WestTek using the net sales ratios or multiples from EastTek, SouthTek, and NorthTek, as well as for the average of the three competitors or comparable firms. Show the valuation ranges from high to low.

E. Estimate the market value for WestTek using the EBITDA multiples from each comparable firm, as well as the average multiple for the three "comps." Show the valuation ranges from high to low.

F. Estimate the market value for WestTek using the net income multiples from each comparable firm, as well as the average multiple for the three "comps."

G. Establish a range of market value estimates for WestTek based on the highest and lowest overall values generated from the multiples analyses in Parts D, E, and F. Also establish a range of market value estimates for WestTek based on the highest and lowest average values from the multiples analyses in Parts D, E, and F.

H. From the perspective of the selling venture investors and founders, would you recommend that they negotiate for the final selling price based on the use of top-side valuation multiples (i.e., using net sales) or bottom-side valuation multiples (i.e., using net income)?

4. Benito Gonzalez founded and grew the BioSystems Manufacturing Corporation over a several-year period. However, Benito has decided to exit BioSystems as of the end of 2007 with the intention of starting a new entrepreneurial venture. The Fuji Electronics Company is considering acquiring BioSystems, which is 60 percent owned by Benito Gonzalez; the other 40 percent of the equity is held by venture investors who also

desire to exit the venture. BioSystems' sales are expected to grow from the 2007 level at a 20 percent annual compound rate over each of the next three years. Cost of goods sold, marketing, depreciation, and interest expenses are expected to move or vary with sales (i.e., they are variable expenses). General and administrative (G&A) expenses are expected to remain at their 2007 level (i.e., they are fixed expenses). Beginning in Year 4 (2011), sales are expected to grow at a 6 percent annual compound rate over the then-foreseeable future. No cash dividend distributions are planned before exiting the venture.

A. Prepare BioSystems' income statements for the next four years.

B. Fuji Electronics has examined other recent acquisitions in BioSystems' industry and believes that a seventeen times price-earnings multiple would be appropriate for determining BioSystems' value in the future. Calculate the value of BioSystems as of the end of 2010.

C. How much should Fuji Electronics be willing to pay for BioSystems Manufacturing at the end of 2007 if Fuji's management believes the appropriate discount rate is 25 percent?

D. What is Gonzalez's portion of the exit proceeds? What is the venture investors' portion of the exit proceeds?

E. Benito Gonzalez invested $50,000 of his own funds in BioSystems at the end of 2002. What would be the compound rate of return on his investment when the exit (sale to Fuji Electronics) from BioSystems occurs at the end of 2007?

F. The venture investors contributed $500,000 at the end of 2003. What would be their compound rate of return on their investment if BioSystems is sold at the end of 2007?

Biosystems Manufacturing Corporation

INCOME STATEMENT FOR 2007 ($ THOUSANDS)

Net sales	$10,000
Cost of goods sold	6,000
Gross profit	4,000
Marketing expenses	1,000
G&A expenses	2,000
Depreciation	200
Interest	100
Income before taxes	700
Taxes (35%)	245
Net income	$ 455

5. Gamma Systems Manufacturing Corporation has reached its maturity stage, and its net sales are expected to grow at a 6 percent compound rate for the foreseeable future. Management believes that, as a mature venture, the appropriate equity discount rate for Gamma Systems is 18 percent.

A. Forecast the free cash flows to the equity investors for 2008.

B. Estimate the value of Gamma Systems equity at the end of 2007 by applying the terminal value perpetuity equation that was presented in Chapter 9.

C. By applying the terminal value equation at the end of 2007, what are we assuming about the future?

Gamma Systems Manufacturing Corporation

	2006	2007
Cash	$ 50,000	$ 40,000
Accounts receivable	200,000	260,000
Inventories	450,000	500,000
Total current assets	700,000	800,000
Fixed assets, net	400,000	500,000
Total assets	$1,100,000	$1,300,000
Accounts payable	$ 130,000	$ 170,000
Accruals	50,000	70,000
Bank loan	90,000	90,000
Total current liabilities	270,000	330,000
Long-term debt	300,000	400,000
Common stock ($10 par)	300,000	300,000
Capital surplus	50,000	50,000
Retained earnings	180,000	220,000
Total liabilities and equity	$1,100,000	$1,300,000

	2006	2007
Net sales	$1,400,000	$1,600,000
Cost of goods sold	780,000	900,000
Gross profit	620,000	700,000
Marketing	130,000	150,000
General and administrative	150,000	150,000
Depreciation	40,000	53,000
EBIT	300,000	347,000
Interest	45,000	57,000
Earnings before taxes	255,000	290,000
Income taxes (40%)	102,000	116,000
Net income	$ 153,000	$ 174,000

6. Assume that some of the information relating to Gamma Systems Manufacturing Corporation has changed. Answer the following questions using the financial statement data in Problem 5.
   A. How would your valuation estimate change if the sales growth rate had been 6 percent but the discount rate had been 20 percent?
   B. How would your valuation estimate change if the sales growth rate had been 5 percent and the discount rate 18 percent?
   C. How would your valuation estimate change if the perpetuity growth rate had been 7 percent and the discount rate 20 percent?

7. New information for Gamma Systems Manufacturing Corporation has been brought to management's attention. Use the financial statement information in Problem 5 and take into consideration that sales will grow at a 15 percent rate in 2008 and a 10 percent rate in 2009 before settling down to a 6 percent perpetuity growth rate.
   A. Estimate the free cash flows for 2008 and 2009.
   B. Estimate the terminal value of all future cash flows at the end of 2009.
   C. Estimate the value of Gamma Systems at the end of 2007 under these assumptions.

M I N I   C A S E

MiniDiscs Corporation

Brian Motley founded MiniDiscs Corporation at the end of 2002. After nearly one year of development, the venture produced an optical storage disk (about the size of a silver dollar) that could store more than 500 megabytes of data, along with a mechanism allowing the device to be integrated into a variety of portable consumer electronic devices, including e-books, music discs, and video games.

In addition to Brian Motley's role as the venture's CEO, Susan Sharpe, with six years of prior financial management experience at two high-technology ventures, was hired as the CFO. The vice president of marketing was Steven Davis, and the vice president of operations was Sanjay Chavarti. Before being hired by MiniDiscs, Davis had twelve years of marketing experience in the technology area. Chavarti worked in high-tech operations for eight years before pursuing the opportunity with MiniDiscs.

Leading electronic manufacturers were eager to incorporate the minidisc in their products. Brian Motley obtained $7 million in financing at the end of 2003 from venture investors in exchange for 43 percent of the stock in the venture. After this round of venture financing, Brian retained 50 percent ownership in MiniDiscs, and the other three members of the management team (Sharpe, Davis, and Chavarti) owned 7 percent of the venture.

Over a four-year period, MiniDiscs moved quickly through its startup and survival stages and is now in the midst of its rapid-growth stage. Brian Motley has recently decided to harvest his investment by selling the firm. However, the other three members of the management team want to continue and proposed a leveraged buyout to Brian Motley. An external valuation firm estimated that $45 million represented a fair price for all of the equity in the MiniDiscs Corporation.

An abbreviated balance sheet in thousands of dollars for year-end 2007 follows:

Current assets	$15,000	Payables and accruals	$ 5,000
Fixed assets, net	15,000	Long-term debt	10,000
		Common equity	15,000
Total	$30,000	Total	$30,000

It is the beginning of 2008, and the management team has $5 million of its own capital, including its share of the sales price, available to purchase all of the venture's existing equity capital. The intent is to retire all of the old stock and issue two million shares of common stock in the new venture to the management team. LBO financiers will put up $20 million in 8 percent, five-year subordinated debt funds plus 1.9 million warrants that can be converted into 1.9 million shares of common stock. A bank will also offer a $10 million, 14 percent interest rate, four-year fully amortized loan. To make the deal work, Brian Motley was asked to provide seller financing in the form of a below-market 10 percent, five-year seller's note. The amount of the note was to be for the difference between the $45 million selling price and the amount of funds raised from management, the LBO financiers, and the bank.

In exchange for the seller financing by Motley, the existing venture capitalists agreed to reduce their ownership rights from 43 to 40 percent. The management team also lowered its claim on the existing venture from 7 to 5 percent. Thus, as the result of agreeing to provide seller financing, Motley's percentage ownership of the $45 selling price was 55 percent. Motley estimated that the interest rate being paid on similar risk-subordinated seller loans was currently at 16 percent.

A. What will be the dollar amount of seller financing that Motley will need to provide to complete the financing of the $45 million selling price?

B. How much cash will be available to distribute to the existing owners of the MiniDiscs Corporation? What will be the dollar breakdown for Brian Motley, the management team, and the venture capitalists?

continued on next page

MiniDiscs Corporation (continued)

C. In present value terms, how much is Motley receiving for his share of the sale proceeds from the MiniDiscs Corporation?

D. What compound rate of return did the venture capitalists earn on their $7 million investment?

E. After five years of operating as a private venture owing to the LBO, assume that the common equity in the MiniDiscs Corporation could be sold for $60 million. What compound rate of return would the management team earn on its $5 million investment?

F. Assume that when MiniDiscs is sold at the end of 2012 for $60 million, the LBO financiers will have their debt retired and will sell their share of interest in the venture. What compound rate of return will the LBO financiers receive?

Chapter 15

FINANCIALLY TROUBLED VENTURES: TURNAROUND OPPORTUNITIES?

PREVIOUSLY COVERED

In the first thirteen chapters of this text, we focused on moving a venture through its successful life cycle—from its early stages through rapid-growth success. Chapter 14 focused on how investors and founders can exit or harvest a successful venture (1) through systematic liquidation, (2) through outright sale, or (3) by going public. Most entrepreneurs, of course, will experience one or more financial distress situations while operating their ventures. In this chapter, we focus on how the entrepreneur might change a financially troubled venture into a turnaround success story.

THE END

Our entrepreneurial finance text ends with the current chapter. We have presented many concepts and techniques to help entrepreneurs deal with venture origination, growth, reorganization, and realization. Of course, the end of this process offers the prospect of great personal and financial rewards for those left standing at the ultimate harvest. Now it is up to each of you to formulate your entrepreneurial idea, craft it into a viable business opportunity, and begin your own venture life cycle. Get going and good luck!

CHAPTER LEARNING OBJECTIVES

We direct attention in this chapter toward recognizing and managing a troubled venture that is in financial distress. The inability to pay creditor obligations as they come due poses a major financial threat and distracts the venture from its primary mission. A successful entrepreneur copes with such financial distress and finds a way to turn the troubled venture around. The alternative to a successful turnaround is venture liquidation. After completing this chapter, you will be able to:

1. Explain financial distress faced by troubled ventures

2. Define and describe insolvency

3. Describe how troubled ventures emerge from financial distress

4. Describe how private reorganizations and liquidations take place

5. Describe reorganization under Chapter 11 of the U.S. bankruptcy laws

6. Describe liquidation under Chapter 7 of the U.S. bankruptcy laws

How can we even suggest that an entrepreneurship textbook of any kind (including one on entrepreneurial finance) include a chapter on financially troubled ventures with specific treatment of reorganization and bankruptcy? Won't an examination of this topic dampen the entrepreneurial enthusiasm we are supposed to be fostering? Perhaps. On the other hand, wouldn't a responsible treatment of entrepreneurship introduce techniques for recognizing, managing, and recovering from financial distress? Don't entrepreneurs who accept external financing have an obligation to cope with financial distress and, at times, even plan for the softest possible landing in the failed venture? We believe so.

Other than under outright fraud, no entrepreneur initially plans to fail. Nonetheless, we know that many ventures become financially troubled and some even fail. Deciding if and when a financially troubled venture should reorganize, and how to proceed when reorganizing, may not be pleasant. Nevertheless, practically all ventures involve some period of financial distress. Fortunately, many financially troubled ventures can be saved, reenergized, and crafted into profitable businesses. Some troubled ventures, however, will be beyond repair; the entrepreneur may exit with only a valuable learning experience and the hope that the next venture will get the benefit.

15.1   VENTURE OPERATING AND FINANCING OVERVIEW

Throughout this text, we have taken a life cycle approach to entrepreneurial finance. We started in Chapter 1 with Figure 1.3, "Life Cycle Approach: Venture Operating and Financial Decisions," and in Chapter 14 we revisited the major operating and financial decisions faced by business ventures as they progress through this cycle and discussed how successful ventures are ultimately harvested or exited. However, most ventures must successfully navigate through one or more periods of financial troubles on their way to harvest. Our topic in this chapter focuses on the recognition and management of financial troubles and distress.

Reorganizing or even discarding a venture idea can be relatively straightforward when the financial resources involved are small and are primarily those of the entrepreneur, family, and friends. The process is quick and involves little interaction with investors. Nevertheless, because the financial capital comes from individuals the entrepreneur is likely to see again (perhaps often), there will be pain and suffering in the anticipation and experience of uncomfortable conversations about the venture's drawbacks and failures.

As ventures start operations and sales, they invest in assets and a qualified management team. This often requires the external financial capital of venture investors and others. As the venture begins full-scale operations, it needs even more assets and financial capital. The corresponding organizational and financial complexity makes it increasingly more difficult to reorganize informally. At these later stages, even failed ventures have salvageable assets. It no longer becomes possible, or at least ethical, merely to walk away from the venture. Planning the remainder of the demise becomes a part of the entrepreneur's job description (assuming the entrepreneur is still running the venture). Liquidation may take the form of private liquidation or legal liquidation.

Many struggling or troubled ventures attempt to restructure rather than liquidate. Restructuring takes place in one or more of the following areas: operations, assets, and financing. These restructuring areas were depicted in our Figure 14.1 review of venture operating and financial decisions. Operations restructuring often involves cost-cutting efforts, including layoffs for some employees and expanded job descriptions for others. It can also include efforts to achieve production and distribution economies of scale. Asset restructuring involves selling noncore assets to help refocus the venture and alleviate financial distress.

Financial restructuring, the primary focus of this chapter, involves informal or formal efforts to help a venture emerge from financial distress. An unsuccessful restructuring may lead to liquidation. Of course, as a venture progresses, the amount and complexity of scheduled contractual payments increase. The likelihood of a formal liquidation or reorganization grows as contractual complexity increases.

CONCEPT CHECK

- What are three methods used for restructuring a financially troubled venture?

15.2 THE TROUBLED VENTURE AND FINANCIAL DISTRESS

Jeffry Timmons and Stephen Spinelli use the term "troubled company" when referring to ventures suffering economic or financial difficulties that may lead to a turnaround plan or, eventually, liquidation.[1] While trouble can originate from changes in the venture's external markets, many difficulties are the result of poor internal management. Ventures get into trouble by mishandling strategic issues, failing to unite management on key initiatives, and having poor finance and accounting

---

[1] See Jeffry A. Timmons and Stephen Spinelli, *New Venture Creation*, 7th ed. (New York: McGraw-Hill/Irwin, 2007), chap. 18.

practices and controls. Since we are primarily examining entrepreneurial *finance*, we concentrate on the finance and accounting origins of venture troubles, including overextension of credit, excessive use of financial leverage (borrowed funds), and lack of adequate cash planning and financial forecasting.

Not surprisingly, the factors that cause ventures to get into financial trouble are very similar to those that bring about venture failure. For example, in Chapter 1 we cited data from the U.S. Small Business Administration that over two-thirds of business failures are due to either economic factors (inadequate sales, insufficient profits, etc.) or financial factors (excessive debt, insufficient financial capital, etc.). Whether entrepreneurs are successful in turning around their troubled ventures, they will surely suffer both emotional and financial distress in the process.

"Distress" is typically defined as anxiety, acute suffering, or a state of extreme necessity. **Financial distress** exists when a venture's cash on hand is insufficient to pay currently due liabilities.[2] Financial distress related to making payroll or to an overdue account payable, debt obligation, or tax deprives many entrepreneurs (and venture investors) of sleep. Others get ulcers and high blood pressure.[3] Such shortages and their physiological implications should be anticipated and avoided where possible.

Loan default occurs when an interest or principal payment is not paid by its due date. Most loans have provisions or clauses to protect lenders or creditors in the case of default. An **acceleration provision** provides that all future interest and principal obligations on a loan become immediately due when default occurs. A **cross-default provision** found in many loan agreements provides that defaulting on one loan places all loans in default. **Foreclosure** is a legal process used by creditors to try to collect amounts owed on loans in default. In most instances, if there is reason to believe that the financial distress situation is temporary, it is in the best interests of owners and creditors to move quickly to initiate negotiations with the creditors to try to restructure the venture and avoid foreclosure. As we will cover in detail later in this chapter, these negotiations can be handled informally (privately) or formally (legally) under the U.S. Bankruptcy Code.

The word "insolvent" often is used interchangeably with financial distress but is somewhat different. Insolvency can be viewed from both balance sheet and cash flow viewpoints. A venture is said to be **insolvent** if it has a negative book equity or net worth (balance sheet viewpoint) or when its cash flow is insufficient to meet current debt obligations (cash flow viewpoint).[4]

financial distress
when cash flow is insufficient to meet current debt obligations

loan default
occurs when there is a failure to meet interest or principal payments when due on a loan

acceleration provision
provides that all future interest and principal obligations on a loan become immediately due when default occurs

cross-default provision
provides that defaulting on one loan places all loans in default

foreclosure
legal process used by creditors to try to collect amounts owed on loans in default

insolvent
when a venture has a negative book equity or net worth position and/or when its cash flow is insufficient to meet current debt payment obligations

---

2   For further discussion of the meaning of financial distress, see Karen H. Wruck, "Financial Distress, Reorganization, and Organizational Efficiency," *Journal of Financial Economics* 27 (October 1990): p. 421.

3   Bonds issued by business firms have similar provisions or clauses relating to default on interest or principal payments. Failure to pay taxes when due to the government will result in actions taken under the Internal Revenue Service (IRS) Code. Failure to pay employees on time or suppliers of trade credit when payments are due may result in lawsuits by employees and/or creditors in the courts. A venture, of course, suffers from being in financial distress under any and all of these debt defaults.

4   A detailed discussion of these two types of insolvency is provided in Edward Altman, *Corporate Financial Distress: A Complete Guide to Predicting, Avoiding and Dealing with Bankruptcy* (New York: John Wiley & Sons, 1983).

- What are the causes of financial difficulty or trouble?
- What is meant by financial distress?
- When is a venture considered to be insolvent?

BALANCE SHEET INSOLVENCY

Balance sheet insolvency exists when a venture has negative book equity or net worth; that is, the book value of total debt exceeds the book value of total assets.[5]

Balance sheet insolvency is not uncommon during the early stages of a venture's life cycle. For example, a venture may have several years of operating losses during its startup and survival stages.[6] These losses are accumulated as negative retained earnings (or accumulated losses) on the venture's balance sheet. At some point, the cumulative amount of losses can more than offset the infusion of equity capital, and the venture's total equity account can become negative. Typically, this will only occur if the venture has engaged in debt financing or extensive trade credit at some point in time.

Consider Northland Industries, which started with an initial equity (common stock) investment of $200,000 with $100,000 spent for current assets (working capital) and $100,000 spent for fixed assets. Northland had a net loss of $100,000 during the first year of operations and $150,000 during the second year. The entrepreneur "borrowed" funds from suppliers and others to cover the operating losses. Year-end balance sheets were as follows:

balance sheet insolvency
exists when a venture has negative book equity or net worth because total debt exceeds total assets

Northland Industries

	YEAR 0	YEAR 1	YEAR 2
Current assets	$100,000	$100,000	$100,000
Fixed assets	100,000	100,000	100,000
Total assets	$200,000	$200,000	$200,000
Total debt	$ 0	$100,000	$250,000
Equity			
Common stock	200,000	200,000	200,000
Retained earnings	0	−100,000	−250,000
Total equity	200,000	100,000	−50,000
Total debt and equity	$200,000	$200,000	$200,000

5 Using the market, rather than the book, value of equity provides an alternative version of balance sheet insolvency.

6 The generation of operating losses usually implies that the venture is burning cash faster than it is building cash from operations. Of course, if additional equity financing sources can be found, a venture's equity position could remain positive even though the venture is in a net cash burn situation.

We can see that, by the end of Year 2, total debt ($250,000) exceeds the venture's total assets ($200,000), resulting in a negative equity position (−$50,000). Northland is balance sheet insolvent. What should the entrepreneur do? The answer depends on whether the balance sheet insolvency is expected to be temporary (a turnaround opportunity) or permanent. Is the venture worth more alive than dead? The answer, of course, depends on the entrepreneur's (or a replacement's) ability to correct the underlying causes of the balance sheet insolvency.

CONCEPT CHECK

• What is balance sheet insolvency?

CASH FLOW INSOLVENCY

cash flow insolvency
exists when a venture's cash flow is insufficient to meet its current contractual debt obligations

Cash flow insolvency, or financial distress, exists when a venture's cash flow is insufficient to meet its currently due liability obligations. We illustrate this concept with an example for the Westland Industries venture. Westland started its business in Year 0 with a $100,000 equity investment used to purchase assets. Westland had no sales in Year 0 but incurred $50,000 in startup costs and administrative expenses. Sales were $100,000 in both Year 1 and Year 2 with operating expenses, before depreciation, of 75 percent of sales. Interest on borrowed funds in Year 1 was $20,000. Interest payments due in Year 2 increased to $40,000 because more debt funds were needed to support the venture's operations. Westland's cash flow insolvency is evident through simple calculations:

Westland Industries

	YEAR 0	YEAR 1	PROJECTED YEAR 2
Sales	$50,000	$100,000	$100,000
Operating expenses	−50,000	−75,000	−75,000
EBITDA	0	$ 25,000	$ 25,000
Interest	0	−20,000	−40,000
EBIT	0	$ 5,000	−$ 15,000

In Year 2, the $40,000 due in interest obligations exceeds the EBITDA cash flow of $25,000, and the venture is cash flow insolvent to the tune of $15,000. What should the entrepreneur do? Again, this becomes an issue of whether the venture is worth more alive than dead. Stated differently, is this an opportunity for a successful turnaround or is the venture doomed to failure?

As an example of principal-induced cash flow insolvency, consider Eastland Industries, which, at the end of Year 0, made a $100,000 investment in current assets (working capital) and a $100,000 investment in gross fixed assets (GFA). No debt was used to finance these purchases. Depreciation on the purchased fixed assets was $20,000 in Years 1 and 2. Eastland had a net loss after all expenses of $70,000 in Year 1 and net income of $20,000 in Year 2. Net working capital

(NWC) increased by $50,000 in Year 1 and by $70,000 in Year 2 to support the venture's sales growth. Therefore, additional investments made in accounts receivable and inventories were only partially offset by increases in accounts payable and accruals. No additional increases in gross fixed assets were necessary. Eastland was obligated to make a $50,000 repayment of debt principal at the end of Year 2. Following is an illustration of cash flow insolvency as viewed in terms of cash build or cash burn:

Eastland Industries

	YEAR 0	YEAR 1	YEAR 2
Net income (loss)	0	−70,000	20,000
+ Depreciation	0	20,000	20,000
− Increase in NWC	−100,000	−50,000	−70,000
− Increase in GFA	−100,000	0	0
+ Equity/debt issues	200,000	100,000	0
− Debt repayment	0	0	−50,000
Net cash build (burn)	0	0	−80,000

The cash burn of $200,000 in Year 0 was financed by the initial $200,000 equity investment. The additional $100,000 cash burn for Year 1 was financed with debt borrowings. Year 2 projects a cash burn of $30,000. While this is substantially less than the cash burn for Year 1, not only is there a cash shortfall for Year 2, the $50,000 in debt principal payment that is due can't be repaid. Thus, Eastland is currently cash flow insolvent. (It is at the end of Year 2.) What should Eastland do? Again, this depends on whether the entrepreneur (or others) can turn the venture around.

While we have demonstrated the two cases of insolvency—balance sheet and cash flow insolvency—it is important to understand that both types generally go hand in hand. A venture producing net losses from operations and therefore having negative changes in retained earnings is in a net cash burn situation. If it continues to net burn cash, in the absence of adequate new capital infusion, its balance sheet will eventually indicate negative book equity. Continued cash flow insolvency leads to balance sheet insolvency.

CONCEPT CHECK

- What is meant by cash flow insolvency?
- How does cash flow insolvency lead to balance sheet insolvency?

TEMPORARY VERSUS PERMANENT CASH FLOW PROBLEMS

Figure 15.1 shows a graphical view of cash flow insolvency. Financial distress occurs when cash flows are inadequate to meet current debt obligations. Panels

FIGURE 15.1   Financial Distress as a Cash Flow Concept

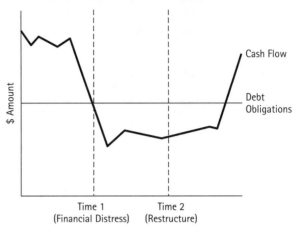

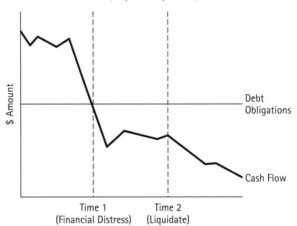

A and B illustrate two ventures, WebTek and JiffySoft, that become insolvent at time 1. Both are in the business of providing core networks that transmit data rapidly and safely over long distances via the Internet. Both ventures have identical cash flow patterns up to time 1. For illustration purposes, the current debt obligations are shown as being level over time. Of course, the amount of debt obligations could, and likely would, change over time if more debt is needed (issued) to support the venture's operations.

The period between time 1 and time 2 in Figure 15.1 is the same for WebTek and JiffySoft. The cash flow after time 2, however, differs dramatically for the two ventures. WebTek, in panel A, is clearly a turnaround opportunity. The venture is able to restructure so that cash flow returns to a level above the debt obligations amount and long-term financial distress is avoidable. In contrast, JiffySoft in panel B suffers from a permanent problem of deteriorating cash flow. As a consequence, JiffySoft should be liquidated at time 2—or as soon as it is determined to be worth more dead than alive.

CONCEPT CHECK

- For a venture suffering financial distress, illustrate what a successful turnaround would look like in terms of cash flows and debt service obligations over time.

15.3 RESOLVING FINANCIAL DISTRESS SITUATIONS

Most entrepreneurs believe that, even though their ventures are suffering financial distress, a turnaround is possible and desirable. Once serious financial troubles are recognized, the entrepreneur should move quickly to prepare a turnaround plan involving immediate remedial actions and detailing their financial ramifications. Such a plan must result in creditor and investor buy-in. Often, the immediate goal of a turnaround plan is raising survival cash quickly and beginning to restore creditor confidence in order to buy time to turn the financially troubled venture around. Components of the plan may involve employee unpaid leaves or layoffs, the sale of receivables at deep discounts, and the liquidation of finished goods inventories. The turnaround plan needs to explain credibly how both short-term survival and long-term financial health will result from such actions.[7]

Figure 15.2 depicts the two basic options—restructure or liquidate—when trying to resolve a venture's financial distress. A turnaround opportunity suggests that a distressed venture can be restructured to escape. Financial restructuring can take the form of either a private workout or a court-supervised reorganization using Chapter 11. Ventures having permanent financial distress can fold through a private liquidation or through a court-supervised Chapter 7 liquidation.

Ventures operating in the startup or survival stages of their life cycles continually review and revise their business models. They also periodically regroup and restructure their operations, assets, and financings. In some instances, they do so when teetering on the edge of financial distress. In other cases, they are firmly in

---

[7] For further discussion of turnaround plans, see Timmons and Spinelli, *New Venture Creation*, chap. 18. Of course, all ventures can't be saved or turned around. For example, Friendster, which was the first online social network venture, "flamed out." See Max Chafkin, "How to Kill a Great Idea," *Inc.*, June 2007, pp. 84–91.

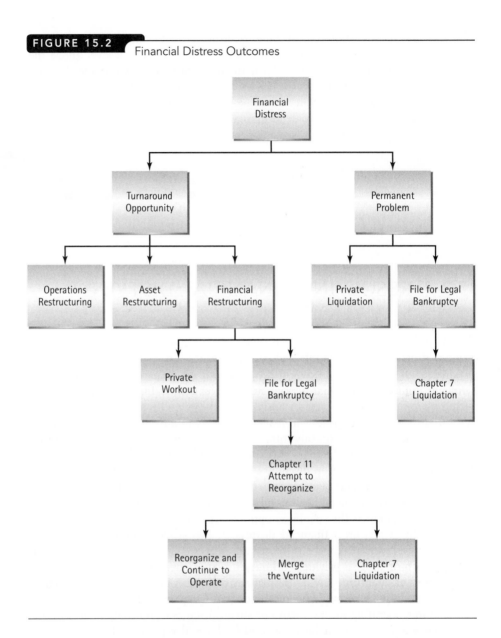

FIGURE 15.2   Financial Distress Outcomes

its grasp. An entrepreneur who remains at the helm through venture maturity is likely to have to try to turn the venture around several times. Of course, in some instances specialists may be brought in to execute the turnaround. It is not surprising that few entrepreneurs stay at the helm throughout the entire venture life cycle.

At each turnaround opportunity, failure to successfully restructure may result in abandonment or liquidation. Recall that nearly one-fourth of all businesses dissolve within two years of beginning their operations. Over one-half of new ventures cease operations within four years.[8] While some of these ventures are just dissolved, sold, or merged with other firms, the venture (in any case) ceases to exist as an independent entity. Private liquidations are more common for early life cycle ventures because of their simple capital structures and small number of debtors. As capital structure complexity and the number of investors increases, a court-supervised Chapter 7 liquidation is more likely.

As depicted in Figure 15.2, and previously presented in Figure 14.1, the process of turning around a venture in financial distress involves employing one or more of the three methods of restructuring. These methods are:

- Operations restructuring
- Asset restructuring
- Financial restructuring

A successful restructuring of operations, assets, and/or financial structure can avoid the need for a private workout or the need to file for legal bankruptcy under Chapter 11, which allows the venture to continue to operate during its efforts to reorganize.

CONCEPT CHECK

- What are the three types of restructuring available to try to turn around a financially distressed venture?

OPERATIONS RESTRUCTURING

Operations restructuring involves growing revenues or cutting costs. A financially distressed venture needs to improve its operating cash flow to allow it to meet its debt obligations. An increase in sales without an equal increase in costs will help. Likewise, a reduction in costs with a less-than-proportionate decrease in revenues will also help increase cash flow.[9]

Increasing revenues or cutting costs typically requires that the venture undergo changes in structure and strategy. Creditor intervention can force the entrepreneur to refocus or alter the venture's business model. Financial distress forces the entrepreneur to reevaluate how the venture generates revenues and controls costs.

operations restructuring
involves growing revenues relative to costs and/or cutting costs relative to the venture's revenues

---

[8] The Facts About Small Business, 1999," Small Business Administration, Office of Advocacy, Washington, DC, September 2000. Of course, it is important to point out that business failure may have a bright side if the entrepreneur can learn from prior mistakes. For one example of an entrepreneur who started several unsuccessful businesses before he succeeded, see Mark Lacter, "How I Did It: William Wang," *Inc.*, June 2007, pp. 106–108.

[9] Some ventures in financial distress may even find it necessary to reduce capital spending (CAPEX) and research and development (R&D) expenses. However, if CAPEX and/or R&D expenditures are not temporary, such cutbacks will reduce future growth opportunities and the viability of the venture.

Poor decision making on the part of the entrepreneur and/or other members of the management team may have contributed to the financial distress situation. Operations restructuring may require replacing a part of the management team or hiring professional managers to handle the day-to-day operations. Managers with new or different skills may be needed to improve the venture's performance. Incumbent directors, through weak governance, also may have been contributors to the financial distress situation. Thus, operations restructuring may also involve restructuring a venture's board of directors.[10]

Let's look at a possible operations restructuring for the WebTek Corporation that was depicted in panel A of Figure 15.1. WebTek entered into financial distress in time 1 and is now at time 2. WebTek can continue operating "business as usual" (BAU) next year or attempt an operations restructuring that focuses on revenue growth while controlling costs. These scenarios are depicted below in terms of an EBITDA cash flow perspective:

WebTek Corporation

1. REVENUE EXPANSION SCENARIO		
	BUSINESS AS USUAL FORECAST	RESTRUCTURED OPERATIONS FORECAST
Revenues	$5,000,000	$6,000,000
Variable expenses		
Cost of goods sold (60% of sales)	−3,000,000	−3,600,000
Fixed expenses		
General and administrative costs	−1,000,000	−1,000,000
Marketing costs	−1,000,000	−1,000,000
EBITDA	0	400,000

The BAU scenario forecasts a zero EBITDA for next year. WebTek will remain in financial distress because it will be unable to pay interest on its debt obligations. Creditors will continue to be unhappy. If they believe the problem is a permanent one, they may move to foreclose on the venture in hopes of retrieving a portion of their loan amounts. A negative EBITDA would indicate a progressively worsening financial distress situation much like that faced by JiffySoft in panel B of Figure 15.1. In the case of a permanent financial distress problem, it is usually in the best interests of both owners and creditors to liquidate the venture relatively quickly.

On the other hand, the "shock" of being unable to meet current debt obligations again next year may result in an immediate effort to restructure the venture's current operations. The restructured operations scenario projects an increase in revenues from $5 million to $6 million, a 20 percent increase, relative to the BAU scenario. Although variable costs increase with sales, by holding fixed costs

---

[10]   Stuart Gilson documents turnover of management and directors for firms involved in financial distress. See Stuart Gilson, "Management Turnover and Financial Distress," *Journal of Financial Economics* 25 (1989): pp. 241–262; and "Bankruptcy, Boards, Banks, and Blockholders," *Journal of Financial Economics* 27 (October 1990): pp. 355–387.

constant, the EBITDA is forecasted to be $400,000. This amount will allow WebTek to move out of financial distress and back into a situation where cash flow exceeds current debt obligations. This scenario would be consistent with viewing WebTek's financial distress as only a temporary problem, as depicted in panel A of Figure 15.1.

Of course, the entrepreneur may have to take several actions to achieve the benefit from restructuring operations. First, a management retreat might be held to refocus on the venture's core business and strategies developed to grow the core business. Second, a new marketing manager might be hired from the outside to stimulate sales growth. Third, an outside director with marketing experience might be added to the venture's board of directors to help the venture grow its sales. Of course, for WebTek to benefit from sales growth and alleviate its financial distress situation, the management team must control and constrain operating costs while growing sales—a task that undoubtedly will cause pain to management and the other employees. It is important for the entrepreneur to face up to the fact that restructuring the venture will be painful. For entrepreneurs who are unable to stomach laying off, firing, and replacing existing employees (including members of the management team), outside professional restructuring experts may have to be hired to turn around the venture.

Alternatively, a restructuring of operations could focus on cost-cutting efforts while trying to maintain revenues at existing levels.[11] The following scenario focuses on cutting general and administrative (G&A) expenses while trying to maintain sales:

WebTek Corporation

2. COST-CUTTING SCENARIO	BUSINESS AS USUAL FORECAST	RESTRUCTURED OPERATIONS FORECAST
Revenues	$5,000,000	$5,000,000
Variable expenses		
Cost of goods sold (60% of sales)	−3,000,000	−3,000,000
Fixed expenses		
General and administrative costs	−1,000,000	−600,000
Marketing costs	−1,000,000	−1,000,000
EBITDA	0	400,000

The BAU scenario will not solve WebTek's current financial distress situation. However, a concerted effort to reduce general and administrative overhead expenses by $400,000 will produce a positive EBITDA of $400,000, so that the venture's cash flow will again exceed its current debt obligations. This is another way to produce the cash flows necessary to relieve the temporary financial distress problem as was depicted graphically in panel A of Figure 15.1.

---

[11] Of course, many restructuring efforts will jointly attempt to grow sales while simultaneously cutting costs. Here we are illustrating these activities as separate events.

Of course, it is important not to underestimate the pain that will be associated with the restructuring of operations through cost-cutting efforts. Employees in staff positions will have to be let go, and the remaining G&A employees will have to be asked to work harder. The remaining management team also may be required to take over some of the G&A responsibilities, which will effectively increase their own workloads. Some entrepreneurs will find the cost-cutting task distasteful, particularly if it involves management and other employees. Creditors, however, will move quickly to foreclose if they believe that the entrepreneur is unable or unwilling to quickly turn the venture around. A convincing plan to restructure operations must be quickly developed. Otherwise, WebTek will mimic the cash flow pattern of JiffySoft as depicted in panel B of Figure 15.1.

CONCEPT CHECK

- What is meant by the phrase "restructuring a venture's operations"?

ASSET RESTRUCTURING

asset restructuring
involves improving the working-capital-to-sales relationship and/or selling off fixed assets

Asset restructuring involves improving the working-capital-to-sales relationship and/or selling off fixed assets.[12] Many ventures get into financial distress because their working capital is too large relative to revenues. Sales growth often is emphasized, with less effort devoted to the management and control of accounts receivable and inventories. In order to support sales growth, management may begin to sell to lower-quality credit customers who, at best, will be slower in paying their bills (and, at worst, may become bad debts). The result will be that the days sales outstanding (DSO) will increase, and the average accounts receivable balance will become larger. Similarly, management may increase the rate of production to meet anticipated future sales growth and to avoid possible merchandise stockouts. If inventory levels are built up in anticipation of future sales and safety stocks of inventories are also increased, the venture will turn its inventory more slowly (i.e., have a higher inventory conversion period) and have larger average inventory balances that must be financed. Furthermore, larger inventory balances will increase the likelihood of a portion of inventory becoming obsolete. Investments in accounts receivable and inventories must be financed. To the extent that this working capital is financed with debt funds, there will be an increased probability that the venture will suffer financial distress. Too much money tied up in accounts receivable and inventories, relative to sales, is often an underlying cause of financial distress.

---

[12] Asset restructuring also may take the form of merging with another firm. Synergies in production may result in a reduction in the combined premerger fixed assets of the merging firms. Merger-related synergies also may accrue in terms of required working capital investments. Although we are viewing merging with another firm as primarily a form of asset restructuring, mergers may also result in a form of operations restructuring associated with economies of scale in terms of production and distribution.

We can view the working capital problem in terms of a venture's operating cycle. Let's assume that WebTek, currently in financial distress, forecasts the following partial income statement and balance sheet information under both business as usual and restructured working capital scenarios:

WebTek Corporation

3. RESTRUCTURED WORKING CAPITAL SCENARIO		
	BUSINESS AS USUAL FORECAST	RESTRUCTURED WORKING CAPITAL FORECAST
Partial Income Statement		
Revenues	$5,000,000	$5,000,000
Cost of goods sold	3,000,000	3,000,000
Partial Balance Sheet		
Cash	0	0
Accounts receivable	$ 500,000	$ 410,970
Inventories	600,000	493,140
Total working capital	$1,100,000	$ 904,110
Accounts payable	$ 200,000	$ 200,000
Accruals	100,000	100,000
Loans	800,000	604,110
Total liabilities	$1,100,000	$ 904,110

We are setting cash at a level of zero. In actual practice, some safety stock of cash is needed to cover fluctuations in cash flows over time. Also, since total working capital and total liabilities are equal, the venture's fixed assets are equal to the equity. Thus, given that there are fixed assets, WebTek is not insolvent in a balance sheet context because the equity account is positive. However, WebTek is insolvent in a cash flow context since this is depicted in panel A of Figure 15.1.

Under the BAU scenario, we calculate the days sales outstanding (DSO) as:

$$\text{DSO} = \text{Receivables}/(\text{Revenues}/365)$$
$$= \$500,000/(\$5,000,000/365)$$
$$= \$500,000/\$13,699$$
$$= 36.5 \text{ days}$$

Likewise, the inventory conversion period (ICP) under the BAU scenario is calculated as:

$$\text{ICP} = \text{Inventories}/(\text{Cost of Goods Sold}/365)$$
$$= \$600,000/(\$3,000,000/365)$$
$$= \$600,000/\$8,219$$
$$= 73.0 \text{ days}$$

Then, by adding together the DSO and ICP under the BAU scenario, we get an operating cycle of 109.5 days (36.5 + 73.0). The result of having a nearly 110-day operating cycle is that $1,100,000 in working capital in the form of receivables ($500,000) and inventories ($600,000) must be financed. For illustration, let's assume that the $800,000 in loans carries an average 10 percent interest rate. Thus, WebTek must pay $80,000 in interest annually to finance its working capital. An asset restructuring that would lead to lower amounts of investments in working capital might allow the venture to move out of financial distress, because some of the loans could be paid off and interest obligations reduced.

To understand the basis for forecasting receivables and inventories under the working capital restructuring plan, we need to establish targets for days sales outstanding and the inventory collection period. To do so, we might turn to the industry averages for these time-to-conversion measures. The BAU and industry averages follow:

	WEBTEK BAU	INDUSTRY AVERAGES
Days sales outstanding	36.5 days	30.0 days
Inventory conversion period	73.0 days	60.0 days
Total operating cycle	109.5 days	90.0 days

If WebTek could reach the industry averages for DSO of thirty days and ICP of sixty days, working capital could be reduced and the proceeds used to pay off some of the loans. Under the restructured working capital forecast, the average investment in accounts receivable would be determined as follows:

$$
\begin{aligned}
\text{Receivables} &= (\text{Revenues}/365) \times \text{Target DSO} \\
&= (\$5{,}000{,}000/365) \times 30.0 \\
&= \$13{,}699 \times 30.0 \\
&= \$410{,}970
\end{aligned}
$$

Likewise, the average investment in inventories based on the industry norm would be:

$$
\begin{aligned}
\text{Inventories} &= (\text{Costs of Goods Sold}/365) \times \text{Target ICP} \\
&= (\$3{,}000{,}000/365) \times 60.0 \\
&= \$8{,}219 \times 60.0 \\
&= \$493{,}140
\end{aligned}
$$

The result would be an average working capital investment in receivables and inventories of $904,110 ($410,970 + $493,140) versus $1,100,000 under the BAU scenarios. This reduction in average balances, if achieved, would allow WebTek to reduce its outstanding loans by $195,890. Assuming this amount would be adequate to produce cash flows higher than current debt obligations, the financial distress problem would be a temporary one similar to that illustrated in panel A of Figure 15.1.

A second form of asset restructuring involves the selling off of fixed assets. Ideally, property, plant, and equipment not needed for the venture's core business could be sold to free up cash that would enable the venture to pay its debt obligations when due. Of course, a venture in financial distress may also need to sell off fixed assets employed in the core business area. Remaining assets will have to be used more efficiently if a negative impact on the ability to grow sales is to be avoided. In essence, while shrinking the physical size of the venture may provide some immediate cash flow, such action could be costly in the long term if it hinders the venture's ability to grow its sales.

CONCEPT CHECK

- What do we mean when we refer to asset restructuring?

FINANCIAL RESTRUCTURING

Financial restructuring involves changing the contractual terms of the existing debt obligations and/or the composition of the existing debt claims against the venture.[13] For example, the due dates for interest and principal on existing loans may be lengthened to make it easier for the venture to service its debt. Also, the size of the interest payments and/or loan principal may be reduced through a change in the composition of the claims of existing creditors. For example, in exchange for a reduction in interest rates and loan principal, creditors may be offered an equity position in the venture. This is a process of swapping equity for a reduction in the amount of existing debt.

A **debt payments extension** involves postponing the due dates for interest and principal payments on loans and cash payments on credit purchases. In the case of loans, interest payments can be lowered (or suspended) and/or loan due dates lengthened until the venture's cash flow is expected to be adequate to service the debt. For example, let's assume that a venture has a two-year $50,000 loan that requires annual interest payments at 10 percent. At the end of one year, an interest payment of $5,000 would be due. At the end of two years, another interest payment of $5,000 would be required, along with the repayment of the $50,000 loan principal amount. For a venture that is in temporary distress, a lender who otherwise might lose the interest payments, or not recover the full loan principal if liquidation occurs, might be willing to extend the loan maturity to three years and, possibly, delay the first interest payment by one year.

A **debt composition change** occurs when creditors reduce their contractual claims against the venture. These reductions can take the form of a lower interest rate, a lower debt claim (principal amount), and/or an equity position that is accepted in lieu of a portion of the debt claim. For example, a lender might lower the interest rate on a loan from 10 to 7 percent. Alternatively, a loan principal amount of $50,000 might be reduced to $40,000. Finally, the loan balance of $50,000 might be cut in half to $25,000 in exchange for 10 percent equity ownership in the business venture. In a similar fashion, a supplier might accept a

financial restructuring
involves changing the contractual terms of the existing debt obligations and/or the composition of the existing debt claims against the venture

debt payments extension
involves postponing due dates for interest and principal payments on loans and cash payments on credit purchases

debt composition change
occurs when creditors reduce their contractual claims against the venture

---

[13] Financial restructuring may also involve the issuing of new securities to help the venture get through its immediate liquidity problem. To do so, however, typically requires that the newly issued debt have a claim that is senior to existing unsecured debt. Equity, at a high dilution cost, also may be sold to "vulture" investors who are willing to wager that the venture can be turned around through restructuring.

partial equity ownership position in exchange for reducing the credit balance owed by the venture. Of course, these creditor concessions would be offered only if the venture's financial distress were perceived to be temporary and liquidation perceived to be a less profitable alternative for the creditors.

CONCEPT CHECK

• What is financial restructuring?

15.4   PRIVATE WORKOUTS AND LIQUIDATIONS

When a venture suffers from financial distress, the entrepreneur and other owners must meet with the venture's creditors to attempt to reach an agreement as to whether the current situation represents a viable turnaround situation or is projected to be permanent. Figure 15.2 shows that if owners and creditors agree to pursue a financial restructuring, they may do so in a private restructuring or more formally by filing for legal bankruptcy.

PRIVATE WORKOUTS

private workout
voluntary agreement between a venture's owners and its creditors that provides for a financial restructuring of the venture's outstanding debt

A **private workout**, or restructuring, is a voluntary agreement between a venture's owners and its creditors that provides for a financial restructuring of the venture's outstanding debt. A study by Stuart Gilson, Kose John, and Larry Lang found that approximately one-half of public firms suffering from financial distress engaged in private workouts, while the other half filed for bankruptcy reorganization under Chapter 11 of the U.S. Bankruptcy Code.[14] Firms that privately reorganized primarily owed their debts to a few banks and had relatively fewer creditors compared to firms using the formal bankruptcy alternative. Bank debt often can be restructured through negotiation. Rather than entering into very costly legal actions, banks frequently find it less costly to negotiate debt repayment extensions with their customers who are believed to be suffering from temporary financial distress.

Ventures that are experiencing financial distress in the early stages of their life cycles usually have to negotiate with fewer creditors. Thus, younger entrepreneurial ventures are much more likely to engage in private workout plans with their creditors. However, as ventures move into their rapid-growth and maturity life cycle stages, they probably have one or more bond issues outstanding. If bonds have been sold previously to the public, there are potentially hundreds of

---

[14] Stuart C. Gilson, Kose John, and Larry H. P. Lang, "Troubled Debt Restructurings: An Empirical Study of Private Reorganization of Firms in Defaults," *Journal of Financial Economics* 27 (October 1990): pp. 315–353. Actual percentages were 47 percent for private workouts and 53 percent for Chapter 11 filings.

individual bondholders who could make a private reorganization difficult to achieve.

Evidence suggests that private workouts or reorganizations generally take less time to complete, and are less costly than formal reorganizations. Some evidence also indicates that senior creditors make relatively more concessions to shareholders and junior creditors in private workouts.[15] This leads one to ask: "Why, then, aren't almost all financial reorganizations in the form of private workouts?" Many firms do start by seeking a negotiated financial restructuring of existing debt. We have already seen that firm size can make a difference. Larger firms usually have more complex financial structures. The more complex the financial structure, the less likely that the venture will get complete agreement on a reorganization plan. To complicate matters, individual creditors may find it in their best interests to foreclose even when the venture is worth more alive than dead, while other creditors may believe it is in their best interests to hold out and not agree to a negotiated restructuring. As we will discuss later, these two problems, known as the "common pool" and "holdout" problems, can keep a venture from achieving a cooperative workout. The alternative is for a venture to file for protection against its creditors so that it can reorganize under the U.S. Bankruptcy Code.

CONCEPT CHECK

- What are private workouts?

PRIVATE LIQUIDATIONS

In instances when the venture's financial distress problem is viewed as permanent, the venture should be worth more dead than alive. That is, continual operation of the venture would result in the entrepreneur's and creditors' losing more of their funds than if the venture were liquidated immediately. For early-stage ventures, an informal liquidation procedure referred to as **assignment** is often used. The process of assignment involves the transfer of title to the venture's assets to a third-party assignee or trustee. The assignee is responsible for liquidating the venture's assets and distributing the proceeds to the creditors.

assignment
transfer of title to the venture's assets to a third-party assignee or trustee

Generally, the amount of the liquidation proceeds generated via a public auction or private sale is not sufficient to cover the full amount of creditor claims. Thus, in most instances, the proceeds will be distributed on a pro rata basis. For example, let's assume that creditor claims total $400,000 and that liquidation proceeds total $300,000. If the level of all creditor claims is the same, the pro rata distribution would be 75 percent ($300,000/$400,000), or $.75 per dollar of claim. If a private liquidation cannot be agreed upon, the remaining alternative is to file for legal bankruptcy and have the bankruptcy court administer the liquidation of the venture's assets.

---

[15] J. R. Franks and W. N. Torous, "How Shareholders and Creditors Fare in Workouts and Chapter 11 Reorganizations," *Journal of Financial Economics* 35 (May 1994): pp. 349–370.

Venture Example: Jeremy's MicroBatch Ice Creams, Inc.

In Chapter 3, we mentioned Jeremy Kraus's idea of making premium ice cream in small quantities in limited editions.[16] Kraus initially raised $70,000 in 1997 by selling stock to others in the venture and then was able to secure $1 million in venture capital from Bluestem Capital Partners. Sales in 1998 were $416,000 and increased to $854,000 for the first half of 1999. Jeremy's MicroBatch ice cream was sold primarily through supermarkets in the Northeast. In an effort to expand and possibly have a national rollout, the venture completed a $5.9 million initial public offering in 1999. An aggressive $2.4 million advertising campaign was undertaken. However, sales were lower during the first half of 2000 than in the first half of 1999. Competition in the premium ice cream category was fierce; "slotting fees," payments for shelf space, amounted to nearly one-half of revenues.

The cash burn continued at high levels, and Jeremy's MicroBatch was running out of cash by mid-2000. Bluestem Capital Partners, which had controlling interest in the venture, replaced Kraus as CEO in July 2000. Efforts were made to cut back on marketing expenditures and to lower slotting fees by switching distribution channels from supermarket chains to convenience stores. However, sales continued to decline, and the venture's operations ceased in early October 2000. Thus, Jeremy Kraus's idea for a premium quality microbatch ice cream went from startup in 1997 to private liquidation by the end of 2000.

CONCEPT CHECK

• What is a private liquidation?

15.5   FEDERAL BANKRUPTCY LAW

Modern U.S. bankruptcy law is set forth in the Federal Bankruptcy Reform Act of 1978, which became effective in late 1979.[17] Currently, there are nine parts, or "chapters," to the law.[18] Chapters 1, 3, and 5 set out general bankruptcy provisions, while Chapter 15 provides for a system of trustees to help administer the bankruptcy proceedings. Several chapters are very specific: Chapter 9 focuses on municipalities, Chapter 12 on family-owned farms, and Chapter 13 on individuals with incomes.

The two chapters that are most applicable to entrepreneurial ventures are Chapter 11, relating to business reorganizations, and Chapter 7, specifying the

---

[16] Sources for this example were "Hot Start-Ups," *Inc.*, July 1999, pp. 35–50, and "Despite Student 'Army,' Ice-Cream Venture Is Frozen Out," *Inc.*, February 2001, p. 33.

[17] The origin of U.S. bankruptcy law began with legislation in 1898 and was followed by major modifications in 1938. Minor revisions of the 1978 Reform Act were made in 1986 and 1995.

[18] The current chapters are not consecutively numbered because most of the old even-numbered chapters were eliminated under the 1978 Reform Act revision.

procedures to be followed when liquidating a venture. Chapter 7 usually is implemented as a last recourse when reorganization under Chapter 11 is not considered feasible.[19] Some ventures that decide to shut down operations and sell their assets choose to file under Chapter 11 so that management has time to sell off the assets rather than have the sales done through the bankruptcy courts.[20] U.S. bankruptcy laws are designed to protect ventures that are worth more as operating businesses than if liquidated. The protections encourage a collective discussion of the venture's future and financial structure in an attempt to counterbalance specific creditors' incentives to act in ways that increase the total damage done to the venture's claimants as a group.

The change from a situation of financial distress to actual bankruptcy has both formal and legal consequences. A venture is **bankrupt** when a petition for bankruptcy is filed with one of nearly 300 federal bankruptcy courts. A petition filed by the venture's management is said to be a **voluntary bankruptcy petition**; a petition filed by the venture's creditors is deemed an **involuntary bankruptcy petition**. Once a petition has been filed, the bankruptcy court appoints a committee of the venture's unsecured creditors to negotiate a reorganization acceptable to both management and creditors. In instances when feasible and equitable agreements can't be reached, the court will order the venture liquidated.

bankrupt
a venture is "bankrupt" when a petition for bankruptcy is filed with a federal bankruptcy court

voluntary bankruptcy petition
petition for bankruptcy filed by the venture's management

involuntary bankruptcy petition
petition for bankruptcy filed by the venture's creditors

CONCEPT CHECK

- What two chapters of the U.S. Bankruptcy Code are most important for ventures considering legal bankruptcy?

BANKRUPTCY REORGANIZATIONS

Figure 15.2 shows that attempts to reorganize under Chapter 11 may result in (1) a successful reorganization and continuing of operations, (2) merging the venture with another firm, or (3) liquidating the venture under Chapter 7 of the bankruptcy law. Dale Morse and Wayne Shaw examined what happened to firms that filed for Chapter 11 bankruptcy. They found that about two-thirds (65 percent) of the examined firms reorganized, 28 percent liquidated, and 7 percent merged with other firms.[21]

---

[19] In a study of thirty-seven bankruptcies, Weiss found that only two firms filed directly under Chapter 7 while thirty-five filed under Chapter 11. See Lawrence A. Weiss, "Bankruptcy Resolution: Direct Costs and Violation of Priority of Claims," *Journal of Financial Economics* 27 (October 1990): pp. 285–314.

[20] Webvan Group, Inc., an online grocer that had burned up $830 million since 1999, decided to shut down its operations and sought protection under Chapter 11 instead of filing under Chapter 7. This choice was made even though there were no plans for resuming operations and the intent was to sell the venture's assets. See "Webvan Shuts Down," *CNN America*, July 9, 2001, and "Webvan Joins List of Dot-Com Failures," *Wall Street Journal*, July 10, 2001, p. A3.

[21] See Dale Morse and Wayne Shaw, "Investing in Bankrupt Firms," *Journal of Finance* 45 (December 1988): pp. 1193–1206. In another study of thirty-five firms that filed under Chapter 11, Weiss found thirty were reorganized and five were liquidated. See Weiss, "Bankruptcy Resolution: Direct Costs and Violation of Priority of Claims."

REASONS FOR LEGAL REORGANIZATIONS

Although an informal reorganization generally can be accomplished in less time, and at a lower cost, than a formal court-supervised reorganization, potential problems often cause ventures to seek court supervision under Chapter 11. The common pool and holdout problems often make it necessary to reorganize formally.

The **common pool problem** exists when individual creditors have the incentive to foreclose on the venture even though it is worth more as a going concern relative to being liquidated. MeTwo.com is an Internet retailer that specializes in high-end "fad" clothing for preteens. Unfortunately, MeTwo.com has recently defaulted on a $1 million loan from TelCom Products. There are three additional creditors with loans of $1 million each to MeTwo.com. All four creditors are unsecured creditors and thus have equal priority claims against the venture's assets. The entrepreneur and a team of outside consultants used cash flow projections to estimate the venture's going concern value at $3 million. However, if the firm is liquidated now, the proceeds are projected to be only $2 million. Thus, while the going concern value is less than the book value of the $4 million owed to creditors, continuing to operate the venture has a higher value relative to immediate liquidation. As a going concern, the creditors can expect to get back $.75 per $1 of loan amount. In contrast, if MeTwo.com is liquidated, creditors will receive only $.50 per $1 of the amount loaned.

TelCom Products has an incentive to try to foreclose quickly on its loan to MeTwo.com; it hopes to recover the full amount of the loan. MeTwo.com's management team may find it difficult to negotiate a loan extension with TelCom Products. Furthermore, each of the other three creditors may perceive an incentive to foreclose, hoping to be paid in full. Thus, the common pool problem makes it difficult for MeTwo.com to get private workout financial restructuring. Rather, MeTwo.com may be forced to seek "protection from creditors" under Chapter 11 of the Federal Bankruptcy Code so that it may restructure and continue as a going concern. An **automatic stay provision** in Chapter 11 restricts the ability of individual creditors to foreclose to try to recover their individual claims. This clause, however, does not prohibit creditors from collectively foreclosing.

The intent of Chapter 11 is to allow management an opportunity to restructure the venture and recover from financial distress while being protected from creditor foreclosure. At the same time, management is restricted from operating the firm to the disadvantage of the creditors. Creditor preapproval of major management decisions may be required, and management cannot freely transfer the venture's assets to the detriment of the creditors.[22]

The second problem is the **holdout problem**, which exists when one (or more) of the creditors refuses to agree to the reorganization terms because of the potential for a larger individual recovery. Let's return to the MeTwo.com example. Under the guidance of the bankruptcy courts, each of the four creditors is

common pool problem
when individual creditors have the incentive to foreclose on the venture even though it is worth more as a going concern

automatic stay provision
a restriction on the ability of individual creditors to foreclose to try to recover their individual claims

holdout problem
when one or more of the creditors refuse to agree to the reorganization terms because of the potential for a larger individual recovery

---

[22] When in bankruptcy, creditors are protected by fraudulent conveyance statutes that prohibit managers from making unjustified transfers of the venture's assets.

offered $.65 per each $1 of their outstanding loans. Thus, each creditor is offered $650,000 in new restructured debt for a total of $2.6 million. Recall that the going concern value was estimated to be $3 million. Equity in the restructured venture is thus $400,000 ($3 million − $2.6 million). Of course, TelCom Products or some of the other creditors may not agree to exchange their old debt claims for the new claims. For example, assume that the other three creditors accepted the reorganization plan. They would each have $650,000 in claims for a total of $1.95 million. By holding out, TelCom would still have a $1 million claim, making the total debt claims $2.95 million—which is slightly less than the estimated $3 million going concern value. This suggests a likelihood that TelCom Products might be paid in full. Of course, if the other creditors think like TelCom, no one will agree to the reorganization plan.

The federal bankruptcy courts can alleviate the holdout problem in a Chapter 11 reorganization by not requiring unanimous acceptance by all creditors in a particular class. Creditors are grouped on the basis of the priority of their claims on the firm's assets.[23] The plan is approved by a creditor class if (1) one-half of the number of creditors and (2) creditors holding two-thirds of the value of the debt vote for the reorganization plan. In our MeTwo.com example, recall that the four unsecured creditors have the same priority claim against MeTwo.com's assets. Let's assume that while TelCom votes against the proposed reorganization plan, the other three creditors vote for it. This would result in three-fourths of the number of creditors, and three-fourths of the pre-reorganization value of the debt, voting for acceptance of the plan.

Now let's assume that the four creditors are grouped into two classes instead of one. Creditors 1 and 2 are together and creditor 3 and TelCom are together. Creditors 1 and 2 will vote for the reorganization plan. However, while creditor 3 supports the plan, TelCom will vote against it. The result is that while the first creditor class supports the plan, the second creditor class does not because only 50 percent of the value of the pre-reorganization debt supports the plan—TelCom's dissenting vote constitutes one-half of the $2 million total debt for this class. Since at least one creditor class approves the plan, the bankruptcy court may evoke a "cram down" procedure to render the plan operational. In a **cram-down procedure**, the bankruptcy court accepts the plan for all creditors, including dissenting classes, and judges the plan to be both fair and equitable.

The filing of formal bankruptcy under Chapter 11 has other advantages. To help meet its short-term liquidity needs during the reorganization process, the venture can issue **debtor-in-possession financing**, which is made senior to all existing unsecured debt. Also, equity investors seem to be able to bargain more effectively in legal reorganizations than in private workouts. Studies show that pre-reorganization equity investors often retain an interest in the venture when it is successfully reorganized under Chapter 11. One study found that, in about four-fifths of the bankruptcies studied, equity investors received some compensation,

cram-down procedure
bankruptcy court accepts a reorganization plan for all creditors, including dissenting creditor classes

debtor-in-possession financing
short-term financing, made senior to all existing unsecured debt, to help meet liquidity needs during the reorganization process

---

[23]   Shareholders also may be grouped into more than one class. For example, preferred stockholders would be a different class than common stockholders since the preferred holders have a prior or higher claim against the firm's assets.

usually securities, in the reorganized venture.[24] Two other studies found that about two-thirds of the equity investors received some form of compensation in conjunction with the reorganizations.[25]

There is also the possibility of using a combination of a private workout and a Chapter 11 filing. This hybrid reorganization is called a **prepackaged bankruptcy**; it involves an initial private attempt to convince a majority of the creditors to go along with a reorganization plan that will be proposed after the venture files for legal bankruptcy under Chapter 11. The reorganization time should be relatively short because the holdout problem can be avoided through the use of the cram-down provision in the case of dissenting creditors.

One caveat is in order at this time. The fact that a venture is able to reorganize, restructure, and successfully emerge from Chapter 11 does not guarantee that the venture will be successful in the future. In one study of firms that emerged from Chapter 11, about one-third eventually refiled or privately restructured.[26]

prepackaged bankruptcy

an initial private attempt to convince a majority of the creditors to go along with a reorganization plan that will be proposed after the venture files under Chapter 11

CONCEPT CHECK

- What two problems often lead to a venture's choosing a legal reorganization instead of a private reorganization?

LEGAL REORGANIZATION PROCESS

Several common steps are followed in a Chapter 11 filing:

1. A bankruptcy petition is filed with one of the bankruptcy courts for "protection under Chapter 11" while the firm attempts to reorganize. Since formal bankruptcy proceedings are designed to protect both creditors and the firm, the petition may be filed by management (voluntary) or by creditors (involuntary).

2. A bankruptcy judge may accept or reject the petition. If the petition is accepted, a time schedule is established for the filing of claims by creditors and shareholders.

3. The firm's management usually is allowed to continue operating the firm. However, if there has been fraud or mismanagement, the court can appoint a trustee. Usually, management is given 120 days to submit a reorganization plan. An additional sixty days are allotted management to get creditor and investor approval of the plan. A court often extends these dates if progress is being made in the reorganization. If management does not submit a plan within the allotted time, other involved parties can submit their own reorganization plans.

---

[24]   Weiss, "Bankruptcy Resolution: Direct Costs and Violation of Priority of Claims."

[25]   J. R. Franks and W. N. Torous, "An Empirical Investigation of U.S. Firms in Reorganization," *Journal of Finance* 44 (July 1989): pp. 747–770; and W. Beranek, R. Boehmer, and B. Smith, "Much Ado About Nothing: Absolute Priority Deviations in Chapter 11," *Financial Management* (Autumn 1996): pp. 102–109.

[26]   E. S. Hotchkiss, "Postbankruptcy Reform and Management Turnover, *Journal of Finance* 50 (March 1995): pp. 3–21.

4. Creditors and stockholders are grouped into classes for voting purposes. A claimant class accepts a plan if one-half of the claimants and two-thirds of the dollar amount of the claims vote in favor of the plan. However, as was previously noted, if all classes don't vote for the plan, the bankruptcy judge has the option of employing the cram-down procedure as a means of accepting the plan for all claimants.

5. The accepted plan is implemented by the exchange of old creditor claims and securities for new ones. The plan also may involve payments of cash property and even the issuance of new securities. Interest rates and debt maturities usually are lengthened (debt payments extensions), and a portion of the old debt becomes equity (debt composition changes) in the reorganized venture.

An acceptable reorganization plan must be feasible in an operating sense and be fair and equitable to the claimants. Feasibility involves determining the extent to which the debt (interest and principal) can be serviced after the venture is reorganized. To assure adequate cash flow for debt-servicing purposes, the reorganization plan may involve operations and asset restructurings, as well as financial restructuring. The process of determining how the venture's financial structure will need to change begins with an estimation of the going concern value of the venture.[27] An appropriate post-reorganization financial structure is established, and the new securities are allocated to the existing claimants.

Bankruptcy reorganization and liquidation are intended to provide fair and equitable treatment of all claimants. At least in theory, fair and equitable treatment is achieved by applying the **absolute priority rule**, which establishes a hierarchical order for the payment of claims for firms in bankruptcy, starting with senior creditors and ending with the existing common stockholders. Senior claims are to be paid in full, followed by the full payment of junior claims with equity holder claims considered last. In actual practice, many deviations from the absolute priority rule take place. For example, Lawrence Weiss found that secured creditors received full payout in a little over 90 percent of the reorganizations studied. Unsecured creditors did not receive full payout after secured creditors in nearly four-fifths of the reorganizations. And, as previously noted, while equity investors were last in the hierarchy of claims and generally did not expect to receive anything, they received some payout in four-fifths of the reorganizations studied.[28]

Let's illustrate a basic bankruptcy reorganization. Table 15.1 contains selected balance sheet data for WebTek Corporation. Recall from our earlier discussion that WebTek is suffering from financial distress. However, both creditors and equity investors believe that the situation is temporary and that the venture can be reorganized and its operations continued into the future.

After filing a petition for bankruptcy, WebTek's management team, along with outside professional consultants, estimates the venture's entity value to be $1 million. This value turns out to be the same as the book value of the venture's

absolute priority rule the hierarchical order for the payment of claims for firms in bankruptcy starting with senior creditors and ending with the existing common stockholders

[27] Recall that going concern values are determined by discounting future free cash flows and/or by applying a market-based multiples approach that utilizes data from comparable firms. It is also important to recognize that we are referring to the value of the overall entity when trying to develop a fair reorganization.

[28] Weiss, "Bankruptcy Resolutions: Direct Costs and Violation of Priority of Claims."

TABLE 15.1   WebTek Corporation: Balance Sheets: Actual and Pro Forma Reorganization Plan Under Chapter 11

ASSETS	PRIOR TO REORGANIZATION	ASSETS	PROPOSED REORGANIZATION
Cash	$ 10,000	Cash	$ 10,000
Accounts receivable	200,000	Accounts receivable	200,000
Inventories	290,000	Inventories	290,000
Fixed assets, net	500,000	Fixed assets, net	500,000
Total assets	$1,000,000	Total assets	$1,000,000
LIABILITIES AND EQUITY		**LIABILITIES AND EQUITY**	
Accounts payable	$ 200,000	Accounts payable	$ 160,000
Notes payable (10% bank loan)	400,000	Notes payable (10% bank loan)	320,000
Accrued liabilities (wages and taxes)	100,000	Accrued liabilities (wages and taxes)	100,000
Long-term mortgage loans		Long-term mortgage loans	
(12%; 8 years)	300,000	(10%; 10 years)	300,000
Long-term subordinated loans		Long-term subordinated loans	
(14%; 10 years)	300,000	(10%; 12 years)	60,000
Common stock	100,000	Common stock	60,000
Retained earnings	(400,000)	Retained earnings	0
Total liabilities and equity	$1,000,000	Total liabilities and equity	$1,000,000

assets before reorganization. Of course, the going concern entity value easily could be estimated to be below or possibly even above the total asset value carried on the balance sheet. When the entity value is lower than the book value of assets, the asset values can be "written down" to the entity value level. For example, accounts receivable might be reduced because of expected bad debts, inventories might be written down to reflect obsolescence, and even fixed assets might be lowered to reflect more accurately their ability to generate future revenues. In a similar sense, if the estimated entity value is higher than the book value of the assets, some assets might be "written up," or intangible assets such as goodwill might be added to the balance sheets.

Our focus here, of course, is on the financial restructuring needed to produce a feasible reorganization, as well as one that will be fair and equitable to all claimants. Table 15.1 shows that the current net equity value is −$300,000, based on a common stock value of $100,000 and cumulative retained earnings of −$400,000. A financial restructuring should include a reduction in interest rates, a lengthening of some loan maturities, and an exchange of some of the debt for an equity position in the reorganization. First, the accrued liabilities in the form of wages and taxes will remain at $100,000. Actually, these amounts are continually turning over, with old amounts being paid out of operations as new wages and taxes payable replace the old ones. Second, the absolute priority rule calls for senior creditors to be paid in full prior to consideration being given to junior creditors. Holders of the mortgage loans will have a senior claimant position. However, while the reorganization may honor the dollar value of the mortgage debt ($300,000) to these senior creditors, the interest rate might be reduced from 12 to 10 percent, and the maturity of the debt lengthened from eight to ten years.

The bank loan (notes payable) and the suppliers of trade credit (accounts payable) will hold unsecured creditor positions and, thus, will be next in line since the holders of the subordinated loans are considered to have a claim position subordinate to (lower than) the claims of unsecured creditors. The absolute priority rule will maintain the obligations at their existing levels for accounts payable ($200,000) and notes payable ($400,000). Thus, the commitments made before considering the holders of the subordinate loans would be:

Accrued liabilities	$ 100,000
Mortgage loans	300,000
Accounts payable	200,000
Notes payable	400,000
Total claims	$1,000,000

This means that the $1 million entity value will be totally allocated after the unsecured creditors are accommodated. As a result, there will be nothing left for either the subordinated loan holders or the existing shareholders. Such a plan's fairness will mostly likely be questioned.

Some form of compromise will be necessary to get this reorganization done. A possible successful reorganization plan is presented on the right side of Table 15.1. The amount of accrued liabilities is honored in full, as is the case for the mortgage loan holders. However, the mortgage debtholders are offered a lower interest rate and a longer maturity on their debt. The unsecured creditors (accounts payable and notes payable) are offered $.80 on the dollar of their prior claims, and the 10 percent interest rate on the bank loan is maintained. The holders of the subordinated loans are offered $.20 of the dollar amount of their existing claims. The new loan maturity will increase to twelve years, and a new interest rate will be set at 10 percent. The holders of the subordinated loans will also be given a 75 percent interest in the venture's equity, leaving the existing shareholders a 25 percent equity position.

To summarize, the proposed reorganization plan calls for some debt payment extensions in the form of lower interest rates and longer maturities. Some debt amounts also are reduced, and some debt conversion occurs with the holders of the subordinated loans receiving a controlling equity position in the reorganized venture. These actions are necessary so that WebTek's cash flows are adequate to service the debt and, thus, allow the venture to escape its financial distress situation. The plan is consistent with the venture's estimated going concern value. Thus, the plan seems feasible and tries to be fair and equitable to all claimants. The hope is that the plan will be accepted and the venture can continue to operate and be successful. Of course, if a reorganization plan agreement cannot be reached, the alternative is to liquidate.

CONCEPT CHECK

- What is meant by the absolute priority rule?

BANKRUPTCY LIQUIDATIONS

Chapter 7 of the U.S. Bankruptcy Code covers the formal liquidation of businesses. The process begins with a filing of a petition of bankruptcy in a federal bankruptcy court in a fashion similar to that described in terms of Chapter 11 filings. However, instead of seeking protection from creditors in order to reorganize, the Chapter 7 bankruptcy petition involves shutting down the business and liquidating the venture's assets. As previously noted, some ventures that initially file under Chapter 11 are unable to produce an acceptable reorganization plan and end up filing for a Chapter 7 bankruptcy.

A Chapter 7 bankruptcy is costly and usually very time consuming. Why, then, don't firms engage in a private liquidation? First, if the venture previously chose to file for a legal bankruptcy under Chapter 11, it is likely that claimants in an unsuccessful reorganization attempt will demand a legal liquidation. A Chapter 7 liquidation also (1) restricts management from fraudulently transferring the venture's assets, (2) provides a court-decided "fair and equitable" basis for allocating the asset proceeds to all claimants, and (3) allows the entrepreneur and other shareholders to "walk away" from the venture with no further obligations. A formal liquidation of an unsuccessful venture wipes the slate clean and makes it easier for the entrepreneur to start a new venture.

After a court accepts the Chapter 7 petition for bankruptcy, a trustee is elected by the creditors to take over and liquidate the venture's assets. The proceeds from the sale of the assets are then distributed according to a set priority of claims, which is summarized as follows:

1. Administrative costs associated with the venture's liquidation
2. Wages and other unpaid employee benefits (limited to amounts earned within the past three months with a maximum of $2,000 per employee)
3. Specific consumer claims ($900 maximum per claim)
4. Tax claims (property and income taxes)
5. Secured creditors (entitled to the proceeds from sale of plant and equipment pledged as security for mortgage loans or bonds)[29]
6. Unfunded pension plan liabilities (a portion may have a prior claim over general creditors while the remainder has a claim equal to the general creditors)[30]

---

[29]   In the event that the proceeds from the sale of the pledged fixed assets do not cover the amount of the debt claim, secured creditors are grouped with general creditors for purposes of recovering the remaining amounts of their debt claims.

[30]   Pension plans may be funded or unfunded. For plans that are fully funded, cash needed to pay retiree pensions was previously placed with a bank or insurance company. For unfunded plans, although the firm is obligated to pay retiree pensions, all the necessary funds have not been put aside. The Employee Retirement Income Security Act of 1974 (ERISA) provides some protection for employees with unfunded plans. A portion of the pension claims (an amount up to 30 percent of a firm's equity) has a priority over general creditors while the remaining portion has claims equal to those of general creditors. The allocation process is further complicated because many ventures declaring legal bankruptcy have negative equity positions on their balance sheets.

7. General (unsecured) creditor claims (includes holders of trade credit, unsecured loans including debenture loans, and unpaid portions of secured loans)[31]

8. Preferred stockholder claims

9. Common stockholder claims (differential priorities might exist if different classes of common stock had been previously issued)

The trustee claims any cash account amounts (currency on hand and checking balances) and considers them part of the distributable funds. The venture's accounts receivable are sold at a discount from their face value to firms that will attempt to collect the receivables. Likewise, inventories will be sold to competitors or to other firms called inventory liquidators. The selling firm usually receives pennies on the dollar for its inventories. Purchasers try to turn the inventory as quickly as possible by selling the merchandise at low markups. Fixed assets in the form of property, plant, and equipment are sold or liquidated. Prices fetched are often well below accounting book values because they are liquidated on a "distressed sale" basis and because many fixed assets are special-purpose assets for which there are likely to be few potential buyers.

Before the asset proceeds are available for distribution, two possible adjustments may be necessary to determine the amount available for distribution to claimants. The first possible adjustment is referred to as the right of offset. Short-term bank loans, or lines of credit, usually specify that bank lenders have a first-priority claim against deposits held at the bank by the bankrupt firm. These deposits are taken by the lending bank as an offset against the amount of the bank loan. In essence, the amount of the bank loan is reduced by the amount of the deposits. Let's assume that Westland Industries had borrowed $500,000 on its line of credit with Banc First at the time of its bankruptcy declaration. The loan agreement stated that the lender had a first-priority claim against deposits. At the time that Westland Industries filed a petition for Chapter 7 bankruptcy, deposit balances at Banc First were $50,000. Banc First would immediately seize or attach the $50,000 in deposit balances, which would, in turn, reduce the amount of its loan claim to $450,000 (i.e., $500,000 − $50,000). Moving quickly to attach bank balances is in the bank's best interest, since Banc First would be classified as a general or unsecured creditor.

The second possible initial adjustment to proceeds made available from the liquidation of assets relates to secured creditor claims. A secured creditor is one who has a claim or lien on specific assets or property. In an effort to keep borrowing costs low, a venture's management will first issue or sell **mortgage debt or bonds**, which is debt secured by a pledge of plant (buildings) and equipment. In the event of liquidation, the holders of this mortgage debt have first claim on the proceeds from the sale of the specified plant and equipment. Let's assume that Westland Industries' mortgage debt amounts to $3 million and that the

mortgage debt or bonds
debt secured by a pledge of plant (buildings) and equipment

---

[31] Holders of subordinated debt also are included in this category. However, the act of making unsecured debt junior to other general creditor claims means that their share of any proceeds would first be used to repay all senior creditor claims. Only if any asset proceeds remain after senior creditors have been paid in full would funds be paid to the holders of subordinated debt.

assets that secure the debt are liquidated for $3 million. In this case, all the proceeds from the sale of the pledged assets are paid to the secured creditors, and they have no further claim on the venture's assets. If the proceeds had been less than the face amount of the debt (say, $2 million), the secured creditors would receive all of the sale proceeds and still have a remaining claim of $1 million, which then would be made equal in priority with the unsecured creditors.

Bank loans with maturities greater than one year are sometimes secured by pledging the venture's receivables and/or inventories as collateral to guarantee the loans. The proceeds from the sale of pledged working capital would first be applied to pay off the secured bank loans. Let's assume that Banc Two lent Westland $1 million last year for three years and that the loan was secured by the pledge of Westland's accounts receivable. The receivables were subsequently liquidated for $1.5 million. In this case, Banc Two would receive a $1 million payment; the remaining $500,000 would be distributed to help cover remaining claims.

Let's illustrate a legal liquidation for the JiffySoft Corporation. Shareholders and creditors have decided that JiffySoft's financial distress situation is permanent and that the venture should be liquidated under Chapter 7. Table 15.2 shows the venture's balance sheet before liquidation. The reader may recognize the similarity between the balance sheets for JiffySoft and WebTek. However,

TABLE 15.2   JiffySoft Corporation: Actual Balance Sheet and Cash Receipts and Disbursements Liquidation Plan Under Chapter 7

PRELIQUIDATION BALANCE SHEET		LIQUIDATION OF JIFFYSOFT	
ASSETS	PRIOR TO LIQUIDATION	ASSETS	LIQUIDATION RECEIPTS
Cash	$ 10,000	Cash	$ 10,000
Accounts receivable	200,000	Accounts receivable	160,000
Inventories	290,000	Inventories	145,000
Fixed assets, net	500,000	Fixed assets, net	300,000
Total assets	$1,000,000	Total receipts	$615,000
LIABILITIES AND EQUITY		**DISBURSEMENT OF FUNDS**	
		Administrative fees	$ 18,700
Accounts payable	$ 200,000	Accounts payable	54,000
Notes payable (10% bank loan)	400,000	Notes payable (10% bank loan)	115,300
Accrued liabilities (wages and taxes)	100,000	Accrued liabilities (wages and taxes)	100,000
Long-term mortgage loans		Long-term mortgage loans	
(12%; 8 years)	300,000	(12%; 8 years)	327,000
Long-term subordinated loans		Long-term subordinated loans	
(14%; 10 years)	300,000	(14%; 10 years)	0
Common stock	100,000	Common stockholders	0
Retained earnings	(400,000)		
Total liabilities and equity	$1,000,000	Total disbursements	$615,000

WebTek was able to reorganize and continue to operate. In contrast, JiffySoft is shutting down its operations and liquidating the venture.

JiffySoft's bank has exercised its right of offset and has attached the $10,000 in the cash account held in the form of deposits in the bank. This reduces the bank's claim to $390,000 ($400,000 − $10,000). The trustee responsible for liquidating JiffySoft sells or factors the accounts receivable to a firm that specializes in collecting accounts receivable at $.80 per dollar of receivable and receives $160,000. The inventories are sold to an inventory liquidator at $.50 on the dollar, which nets $145,000. Fixed assets are sold to a prior competitor for $300,000. The bank loan was not secured by either receivables or inventories; thus, the bank has no first claim against these proceeds. Total liquidation proceeds available for distribution are:

PROCEEDS FROM	AMOUNT
Accounts receivable	$160,000
Inventories	145,000
Fixed assets	300,000
Total proceeds	$605,000

These amounts are also given in the last column of Table 15.2, showing the proceeds from the proposed liquidation of assets.

Now let's look at how these proceeds are likely to be dispersed. First, administrative fees are $18,700. Second, funds are used to pay the $100,000 owed for back wages and taxes. Third, the holders of the mortgage loans have first claim against the proceeds from the sale of the fixed assets that had been pledged as security for the loan. However, the $300,000 received repays the mortgage loan holders only three-fourths of the amount of their claim, so that the remaining $100,000 claim ($400,000 − $300,000) is reclassified into the general creditor priority class.[32] JiffySoft does not have any outstanding consumer claims, and it does not have an unfunded pension plan. The disbursements of funds at this point are:

CLAIMANT	AMOUNT
Administrative fees	$ 18,700
Accrued liabilities	100,000
Mortgage loans	300,000
Subtotal	$418,700

Since the total liquidation proceeds were $605,000, and $418,700 has been allocated, there is $186,300 remaining for disbursement. The general creditor claims would be:

---

[32] Technically speaking, in the rare instance that the only liquidation proceeds received were from the sale of assets used to secure the mortgage loans, the holders of these loans would have the first claim to the proceeds. Of course, it is hard to believe that a Chapter 7 liquidation would go forward if there were reason to believe that the liquidation proceeds might not cover legal fees and other administrative expenses.

GENERAL CREDITOR CLAIMS	AMOUNT
Accounts payable	$200,000
Notes payable (bank loan)	390,000
Mortgage loans (remaining amount)	100,000
Subordinated loans	300,000
Total remaining creditor claims	$990,000

Recall that the bank loan claim had been reduced from $400,000 because the bank attached the $10,000 that JiffySoft held in deposits at the time of the Chapter 7 filing. Since the holders of the subordinated loans originally agreed that their loans would be subordinated to all other general creditors, they will not receive any of the liquidation funds unless all senior creditors have been paid in full.

If we divide the remaining funds for disbursement of $186,300 by the general creditor claims of $690,000 ($990,000 − $300,000), a ratio of .27, or 27 percent, is established for disbursal of the $186,300. Following are the amounts to be received by each claimant group:

GENERAL CREDITOR CLAIMS	ORIGINAL AMOUNT	PERCENT PAID	AMOUNT PAID
Accounts payable	$200,000	.27	$ 54,000
Notes payable (bank loan)	390,000	.27	105,300
Mortgage loans (remaining amount)	100,000	.27	27,000
Total claims and disbursements	$690,000		$186,300

Thus, the general creditors receive $.27 per dollar of preliquidation claim. Unfortunately, since all of the liquidation funds have been allocated, neither the holders of the subordinated loans nor the common stockholders receive anything from the liquidation of JiffySoft under Chapter 7. Table 15.2 shows the disbursement of these proceeds by claimant category on JiffySoft's balance sheet. Of course, these are shown only for the purpose of comparison with the preliquidation amounts since, in reality, there are no financial statements after liquidation.

CONCEPT CHECK

- Why do ventures choose legal liquidation when it is generally less costly and consumes less time to complete a private liquidation?

SUMMARY

No entrepreneur likes to fail. However, business failure is a fact of life. On the positive side, analyzing and understanding why the venture failed provides the entrepreneur with an opportunity to avoid the same pitfalls in his next venture.

Many of the factors that cause ventures to become financially troubled are related to accounting and financial practice. They include the overextension of credit, excessive use of borrowed funds, and inadequate use of cash budgeting and financial projections. In this chapter, we defined financial distress and discussed cash flow insolvency. Financial distress either will disappear in a successful turnaround or will become a permanent problem resulting in venture liquidation. Financial distress can be resolved if a venture can be turned around by restructuring operations, assets, or financing. Operations restructuring involves growing revenues faster than costs or cutting costs while revenues fall (if at all) at a lower rate than costs. Asset restructuring focuses on improving existing working-capital-to-sales relationships or selling some of the venture's fixed assets. The aim is to generate additional cash flow to service its debt obligations.

Financial restructuring usually involves extending or changing the composition of debt. Restructuring can also involve reducing the debt amount by exchanging equity for the troublesome debt. Financial restructuring can occur through a private workout between the venture's shareholders and creditors. It may also take the form of a court-supervised reorganization under Chapter 11 of the U.S. Bankruptcy Code. Early-stage ventures, with fewer creditors and less complicated financial structures, frequently find it easier to engage in private workouts. Chapter 11 provides protection from creditors when more complex ventures attempt to reorganize and alleviate their financial distress.

The alternative to restructuring a financially troubled venture is liquidation. Liquidation, like reorganization, can occur privately or under court supervision (Chapter 7 of the U.S. Bankruptcy Code). Private liquidation requires the agreement of the creditors and shareholders. This is typically easier for early-stage ventures. As ventures grow in size and their financial structures become more complex, Chapter 7 liquidation is more likely than private reorganization.

KEY TERMS

absolute priority rule	cram-down procedure	insolvent
acceleration provision	cross-default provision	involuntary bankruptcy petition
asset restructuring	debt composition change	loan default
assignment	debt payments extension	mortgage debt or bonds
automatic stay provision	debtor-in-possession financing	operations restructuring
balance sheet insolvency	financial distress	prepackaged bankruptcy
bankrupt	financial restructuring	private workout
cash flow insolvency	foreclosure	voluntary bankruptcy petition
common pool problem	holdout problem	

DISCUSSION QUESTIONS

1. What are the three types or methods of restructuring available when trying to turn around financially troubled ventures?

2. Identify major factors that cause ventures to get into financial trouble.

3. What is meant by financial distress?

4. What is meant by loan default? Also, describe (a) an acceleration provision and (b) a cross-default provision.

5. What do we mean when we say a venture is insolvent?

6. Compare and contrast (a) balance sheet insolvency and (b) cash flow insolvency.

7. Use the concept of cash flow insolvency over time and describe what could happen if the problem is temporary rather than permanent.

8. What are some of the basic requirements of a successful turnaround plan?

9. Define operations restructuring and describe how it can be implemented to escape financial distress.

10. Define asset restructuring and describe how it can be implemented to escape financial distress.

11. Define financial restructuring and describe what is meant by (a) debt payments extension and (b) debt composition change.

12. What is a private workout? Also, describe some of the characteristics of ventures that are likely to engage in private workouts.

13. What is a private liquidation? What does the process of assignment mean?

14. What is Chapter 11 bankruptcy and how is it used by ventures?

15. Describe a venture bankruptcy. Also, indicate the difference between (a) a voluntary bankruptcy petition and (b) an involuntary bankruptcy petition.

16. Briefly describe the common pool and holdout problems that often make it necessary for a venture to enter into a court-supervised reorganization.

17. Briefly define the following terms: (a) "cram-down procedure," (b) "debtor-in-possession financing," and (c) "prepackaged bankruptcy."

18. Describe the absolute priority rule.

19. What is the purpose of Chapter 7 of the U.S. Bankruptcy Code? What are some of the characteristics of ventures that use Chapter 7 instead of private liquidation?

INTERNET ACTIVITIES

1. Go to the *Wall Street Journal* or some other financial publication such as *Inc.* magazine and identify a venture that has recently filed for reorganization or liquidation with the U.S. bankruptcy courts. Then access the Securities and Exchange Commission's Web site at http://www.sec.gov/edgar/searchedgar/webusers.htm and find recent financial statements for the venture you identified as being in financial distress. By way of a hint, you will probably want to access the most recent Form 10Q, which provides quarterly information. Determine whether the venture was suffering from balance sheet insolvency, cash flow insolvency, or both. Explain the bases for your insolvency assessments.

EXERCISES/PROBLEMS

1. It was shown earlier in this chapter that Northland Industries was suffering from balance sheet insolvency. Two scenarios are possible for Northland in Year 3. In scenario 1, Year 3 for Northland is expected to result in an additional $150,000 operating loss. On the other hand, scenario 2 is expected to be a "breakout" year for Northland when higher sales and lower costs owing to economies of scale are forecasted to produce operating profits of $250,000 in Year 3. Total assets are expected to remain at $200,000 under either scenario. Total debt will be increased to finance additional operating losses. On the other hand, operating profits will be used to reduce total debt.
   A. Show Northland's basic balance sheets under both scenarios.
   B. Based on your analysis, will Northland Industries still be balance sheet insolvent in Year 3 under scenario 1? If this trend continues, would you describe Northland's financial distress as a temporary or a permanent problem?
   C. Based on your analysis, will Northland Industries still be balance sheet insolvent in Year 3 under scenario 2? If this trend continues, would you describe Northland's financial distress as a temporary or a permanent problem?

2. It was shown earlier in the chapter that Westland Industries was suffering from cash flow insolvency in terms of its earnings before interest, taxes, and depreciation (EBITDA). Two scenarios are possible for Westland in Year 3. Scenario 1 suggests that the results from operations for Year 2 are expected to be repeated in Year 3 and thereafter. In scenario 2, Westland is expected to have a breakout year in terms of sales of $400,000 and operating expenses before depreciation of 60 percent of sales. Interest is expected to remain at $40,000 because of the need to finance the venture's growth. Prepare basic income statements (from sales to EBIT) under both scenarios. Comment on your findings.

3. It was shown earlier in the chapter that Eastland Industries was suffering from cash flow insolvency. Assume that scenario 1 projects that Year 3 and following years will be like the results incurred for Year 2, where profitability is low and continued large investments in net working capital are required. In contrast, an optimistic scenario for Eastland Industries for Year 3 suggests that a sales breakout year will lead to operating efficiencies resulting in net income projections of $100,000. Improved management of working capital also will result in a net working capital increase of only $30,000. Estimate the net cash build or burn after a $50,000 debt repayment under both scenarios. Comment on your findings.

4. Following are the financial statements for the Chenhai Manufacturing Corporation for 2006 and 2007. The venture is in financial distress and hopes to turn around its financial performance in the near future.

Chenhai Manufacturing Corporation

	2006	2007
Cash	$ 50,000	$ 10,000
Accounts receivable	200,000	250,000
Inventories	450,000	490,000
Total current assets	700,000	750,000
Fixed assets, net	400,000	400,000
Total assets	$1,100,000	$1,150,000
Accounts payable	$ 130,000	$ 170,000
Accruals	50,000	70,000
Bank loan	90,000	90,000
Total current liabilities	270,000	330,000
Long-term debt	300,000	400,000
Common stock ($10 par)	300,000	300,000
Capital surplus	50,000	50,000
Retained earnings	180,000	70,000
Total liabilities and equity	$1,100,000	$1,150,000

	2006	2007
Net sales	$1,400,000	$1,000,000
Cost of goods sold	−780,000	−700,000
Gross profit	620,000	300,000
Marketing	−130,000	−150,000
General and administrative	−150,000	−150,000
Depreciation	−40,000	−53,000
EBIT	300,000	−53,000
Interest	−45,000	−57,000
Earnings before taxes	255,000	−110,000
Income taxes (40%)	102,000	0*
Net income	$ 153,000	$−110,000

* Note that a tax credit would be generated and could be used if the firm returns to profitability in the future.

A. Calculate the days sales outstanding (DSO) for Chenhai in both 2006 and 2007.
B. Calculate the inventory conversion period (ICP) for Chenhai in both 2006 and 2007.
C. Determine the total operating cycle for Chenhai in both 2006 and 2007.
D. What type of working capital restructuring might Chenhai undertake to turn around its financial performance? What other type of asset restructuring might Chenhai consider undertaking?
E. What type(s) of operations restructuring might Chenhai attempt during 2008?
F. What type(s) of financial restructuring might Chenhai attempt during 2008?
G. What prevailing conditions (economic, competitive, etc.) might cause you to believe that Chenhai's situation may be a turnaround opportunity versus a permanent problem?

5. EnCal is a small California-based power company specializing in power generation methods that use clean-burning fuels and renewable natural resources. However, due to California's complex and confusing power-pricing structure, EnCal is reeling from the aftereffects of the state's attempt at power deregulation. EnCal has been unable to pass its operating costs on to its consumers. To make matters worse, EnCal has recently completed construction of several power production centers in efforts to double its capacity and to help diminish the frequency of power outages that are wreaking havoc on local commerce. As a result, it has accumulated a massive debt load to help finance these facilities and is on the verge of default. However, raising the prices of the power it supplies to its consumers involves a slow and laborious bureaucratic process and regulatory approval. EnCal is forced to reorganize its financing.

EnCal's partial income statements and balance sheets for the 2006 and 2007 fiscal years follow. An incomplete income statement for 2008 is also provided.

INCOME STATEMENT ($ MILLIONS)	2006	2007	2008
Revenue	$240	$ 360	?
COGS (70% in 2006, 80% in 2007/2008)	−168	−288	?
Gross profit	72	72	?
SG&A	−30	−35	−35
EBITDA	42	37	?
Depreciation	−20	−30	−40
EBIT	22	7	?
Interest	−22	−92	?
Earnings before taxes	0	−85	?
Taxes (40%)	0	0	?
Net income	$ 0	−$ 85	?

BALANCE SHEET ($ MILLIONS)		
Assets		
Cash	$ 10	$ 10
Accounts receivable	20	30
Inventories	10	15
Fixed assets, net	510	1,080
Total assets	$550	$1,135

Liabilities and Equity

Accounts payable	$ 14	$ 24
Notes payable (8% bank loan)	50	140
Accrued liabilities (wages and taxes)	4	4
Long-term mortgage loans (10%)	180	460
Long-term subordinated loans (12%)	0	290
Common stock	300	300
Retained earnings	2	−83
Total liabilities and equity	$550	$1,135

A financial restructuring that would reduce EnCal's debt burden has been proposed. The proposal is to reduce the interest rate on its bank loan to 6 percent and loan principal to $100 million, to reduce the interest rate on its mortgage loans to 8 percent, and to replace all of its subordinated loan balance with a 50 percent equity stake in the company.

A. Assuming a 25 percent increase in revenue with no additional capital investment, what will EnCal's new income statement and balance sheet look like in the business as usual and financial restructuring scenarios?

B. Will EnCal be able to service its debt under either scenario?

C. Would EnCal be a likely candidate for Chapter 7 bankruptcy?

D. Suppose the governor has called an emergency legislative session on the utility's behalf to prevent its eventual bankruptcy. If the governor is able to get a bill passed supporting a rate hike on electrical power, how much must EnCal charge per kilowatt if it is going to be able to cover its interest payments under the new financial restructuring plan? Assume EnCal's power generation facilities have a maximum capacity of 800 megawatts with an average capacity utilization of 50 percent.

M I N I   C A S E

ENDCO, INC.

Endco is a wireless solutions provider that facilitates wireless Internet access through small remote devices that connect to portable computers. During the aggressive venture financing era of the 1990s, Endco was lavished with an abundance of equity financial capital from a variety of venture investors. Although initial adoption rates for this new service were far below expectations, most were confident that expanding the service area, and thus increasing the service's availability to new and existing users, would result in rapid increases in the volume of new subscribers. Helping to fund this massive expansion, Endco arranged tremendous amounts of debt financing, much of which was secured by the expansion assets themselves (i.e., wireless towers and transmission facilities). However, toward the end of 2000, the technology bubble began to burst and optimism in telecommunications waned. It became clear that Endco would never become profitable and would only continue to burn large amounts of cash if it proceeded to operate. Using the financial data provided, answer the following questions regarding Endco's Chapter 7 bankruptcy liquidation.

Administrative and legal fees are $370,000, and the bank underwriting the notes payable has the right of offset on cash deposits, the amount indicated in the cash account on the balance sheet.

continued on next page

ENDCO, INC. (continued)

A. Who are considered to be the priority claimants in this liquidation?
B. Who are considered to be general creditors?
C. Create a table indicating the cash distribution to each creditor and the percentage of the original liability that is satisfied.

Balance Sheet ($ Millions)

ASSETS		LIQUIDATION RECEIPTS
Cash	$ 2.4	$ 2.4
Inventory	16.0	5.0
Accounts receivable	5.6	3.0
Net plant	200.0	165.0
Net equipment	100.0	57.0
Total assets	$324.0	$232.4

LIABILITIES AND EQUITY	
Accounts payable	$ 3.5
Notes payable (12% bank loan)	29.0
Accrued liabilities (wages and taxes)	1.5
Long-term mortgage loans (12%, 10 years)	140.0
Long-term subordinated loans (14%, 15 years)	80.0
Debentures (subordinated to notes payable)	20.0
Preferred stock	300.0
Common stock	100.0
Retained earnings	−350.0
Total liabilities	$324.0

Part 7

CAPSTONE CASES

CORAL SYSTEMS, INC.

On a sunny Colorado afternoon in late August 1997, Eric Johnson was pondering the future of the company he had started in 1991. "In my role now as CEO, I'm responsible for the strategic vision, and the M&A activity of the company. Coral's future is really going to come from being merged into another company." Over the past six years, Johnson had founded Coral Systems, took it through four major rounds of financing, and built a company that achieved over $6.8 million in revenues through the first nine months of 1996. However, the company had planned to float an initial public stock offering in late 1996, but withdrew the offering by the beginning of 1997.

In May 1997, John Fraser was appointed president of Coral Systems. He hit the ground running, as he was immediately plunged into the end of Coral's second quarter of 1997. Tim Hayes had also been named senior vice president of engineering and development at the same time. They took over the day-to-day operations of the company from the founder, Eric Johnson. As Fraser sat in his office, contemplating the future of Coral Systems, he had this to say: "In the short term, the two core markets we are focusing on are fraud detection and customer retention. Wireless is one of the fastest-growing markets in the world, so we are thinking if we could just do everything right and be there for a while, we will be doing great."

The company was the first graduate of the Boulder Technology Incubator (BTI). A recent study by the International Association of Business Incubation indicates that businesses connected with incubators are two to three times more likely to thrive than those started without such assistance. Coral Systems was just such a success story. Coral provides software solutions to wireless carriers, their primary product being a fraud protection device. Through creative financing means, a vision of the marketplace that was ahead of its time, and the creation of key strategic partner relationships, Coral Systems was playing with some heavy hitters in the big leagues of the exploding wireless communications boom. With competition like IBM and GTE, how did this Colorado startup company manage to grow out of nothing into a force to be reckoned with by the industry?

This entrepreneurship case study was prepared by David A. Stenman, under the supervision of Professor G. Dale Meyer, as the basis for class discussion and not to illustrate the effective or ineffective handling of an administrative situation.
Copyright © 1998 by the Deming Center for Entrepreneurship, University of Colorado at Boulder. Case preparation was funded through a grant from the Coleman Foundation. Used by permission.

THE DEVELOPMENT OF CORAL SYSTEMS

For a brief discussion of the wireless industry, and the technology underlying Coral Systems products, please refer to Appendix A.

THE FOUNDATION

Before founding Coral Systems in 1991, Eric Johnson spent many years in San Diego as director of business development with PacTel Cellular, which is now AirTouch Cellular. ACI Telecom, a software division of US West, then hired Johnson. US West was doing some software work that was considered "providing information services," and this caused the company to run afoul of the Modified Final Judgment (MFJ). The MFJ is the federal court ruling that broke up the AT&T and Bell Systems monopoly. ACI Telecom was also performing services that could have been problematic in the future for US West and the MFJ, so US West ended up selling ACI Telecom to Tandem Computers. Johnson was concerned with Tandem's strategic vision and felt it would not devote the resources to grow the telecommunications division. Therefore, he left Tandem Computers shortly after the sale. Through his prior experience with PacTel, he saw that there was a niche with carriers for highly targeted intelligent computing solutions to solve problems of analyzing data at carriers.

Coral Systems was not the first company Johnson founded. Johnson taught himself to program computers and has a degree in biology and psychology. He began his career as a genetic technician for the Salk Institute. During the 1980s the research scientists Johnson was working with had to solicit funding for their projects from corporate sponsors, largely because of funding cuts by the Reagan administration. Johnson felt that he was not conducting the valuable research he had been doing before the budget cuts, so he left the genetic research field. With no money and working out of his car, he started a company called NCAS. While this was Johnson's first entrepreneurial venture, his father was a successful entrepreneur in the boating business. NCAS conducted legal investigations, courier services, process serving, and computer work for lawyers. Over seven years he grew the company to three offices, with around thirty employees and independent contractors before selling the business.

Upon leaving ACI Telecom, Eric Johnson brought two people he had met at ACI to start Coral. He decided to divide the original ownership shares equally among the three original founders. Throughout the development stage of the company, Johnson grew with the company and the other two shareholders left to pursue other opportunities, while retaining their vested stock.

At the time of the company's inception, the wireless carriers were very receptive to the idea of a quiet solution to cell phone fraud. The carriers did not want the problem of fraud to be drawn to the public eye, primarily because it would contribute to the public perception that the network was not secure. In addition, if the shareholders of a carrier knew the company was losing 2 to 4 percent of their revenue to fraud, it could create undue hardships for the board. If the problem could be solved quickly and quietly, there would be great reception from the carriers. Coral Systems was the first to address the problem. However, nobody wanted a fraud solution from a small company in Colorado. Coral Systems was in the bind of being a first mover. The company had to wait until competition formed in order to establish the validity of the profiling product among carriers.

STRATEGIC RELATIONSHIP DEVELOPMENT

Major wireless phone switch manufacturers (Ericsson, Nortel, and Motorola) wanted to move the telecommunications industry forward by allowing everyone to work with their equipment, and not have any proprietary interface. As a result of this, the switch manufacturers provided a gateway to the information their switches produced. These gateways would package the data that the switches produced, which was used primarily for billing information, and provide that information to the rest of the world, including Coral. The information package is of no value unless there is some way of using that information. Coral provided a way to use this information, and Johnson approached these large companies to strike up a mutually beneficial strategic relationship.

Johnson states that the key reason he struck up the strategic relationships with the switch manufacturers was to receive their endorsement, their distribution channels, and their knowledge. The switch makers either resold or comarketed the application with Coral. The large switch manufacturers would market Coral's fraud software utilizing their already existing infrastructure equipment relationships with the carriers. Coral therefore was able to implement a market penetration strategy through its alliances with the large switch manufacturers. The customers (carriers) would in turn benefit because now there would be a "one-stop" shop for the infrastructure equipment purchased from a switch manufacturer, and the carrier could also pick up a fraud solution.

MANAGEMENT TEAM AND EMPLOYEE DEVELOPMENT

The company initially used outside contractors to develop the software. Coral found that this was much easier, because it allowed the company to better manage its cash burn. "It was a bad decision to hire independent contractors," stated Eric Johnson. Johnson saw that as he hired these contractors, they did the work, but once they were done there was no experience gained by the company. "It's the knowledge transfer that you lose with independent contractors. We had no employees who retained that knowledge early on." The product was very detailed and customized, so when Coral had to go back and make changes or upgrades, the company had to hire new engineers all over again. "We were essentially paying for the service twice," stated Johnson on the reuse of contractors. If Coral were writing specific, off-the-shelf software packages, the contractors would have been the best solution. However, Johnson felt that with specific, customized applications like FraudBuster, Coral needed to hire people who would have stayed with the company in order for Coral to retain that knowledge. As the product became more developed, management eventually hired some of the contractors for the long term.

After two years, Coral had grown to ten employees. Then as the likelihood of a return on its investment seemed possible, the employee base grew to twenty-five. By September 1996, the company had eighty employees in various functions (see Figure 1).

FIGURE 1	Historical Growth in Revenues and Employees	
YEAR	**NUMBER OF EMPLOYEES**	**REVENUES**
1991	5	$0
1992	12	699,000
1993	25–30	504,100
1994	35–45	1,416,900
1995	50–60	3,889,800
1996		
Research and development	29	*(9 months of 1996)*
Customer support	7	$6,852,400
Field operations	13	
International sales	2	
Consulting services	6	
Marketing	8	
Finance and administration	15	
Total at the end of 1996	80	

Howard Kaushansky, legal counsel and one of the first members of Johnson's management team, had this to say on the attitudes of the employees as Coral traveled from a startup to a professionally managed company:

There's people who like [the startup] environment. They thrive in that, and they don't thrive in where, all of a sudden, you start to look at more sophisticated, deliverable, end-use products and the responsibilities associated with it. You start moving out of that "development, think tank, coke cans piling up in the cubes' environment" into "people are relying on this software. People are paying money for this software's environment." You have an obligation to deliver the best-quality software possible. Not that it wasn't high quality to begin with; it's just a different mind-set.

We definitely would take steps along the way where people would reach their comfort level in what was being asked of them and restrictions that were being placed on them. Because rather than saying "You're responsible for whatever you get done," it became "You are now responsible for this piece of code. It needs to do this, it needs to be tested. It needs to be done by this date and this is your responsibility, this is your world. You make sure it's going to plug in with this person's piece." [Early growth] is a different environment. A different way of doing business.

Eric Johnson looked for creative intelligence, high energy levels, and adaptability in the employees he hired in the early stages. Johnson created a whole new industry within the wireless space, so it was difficult to rely on a potential employee's previous experience, since nobody would have any direct experience in Coral Systems' product. Johnson would rely on advertising, employee head hunters, and extensive interviews when looking at potential employees. Johnson found that it was extremely difficult to let employees go when they did not perform well at certain levels of growth. If an employee had an outstanding skill set in building and creating the company at a smaller revenue level, but did not exhibit the same skill proficiency at a higher revenue level, it led to some strenuous times with the officers, especially when that person had to be let go. Johnson felt that hiring and firing people was one of the biggest hurdles he has ever faced in the growth of the company.

MARKETING

CORAL SYSTEMS' SOLUTION TO FRAUD

Coral Systems' main product, FraudBuster, is a fraud profiling system, and it was first offered in June 1993. Eric Johnson had this to say on the fraud profiling concept: "The value behind FraudBuster is that Coral built it from the very beginning to be a pan-specific fraud solution. It was independent of the analog or digital technology, and it was independent of the type of fraud being committed. It was an approach that would work against all types of fraud, on any standard."

A fraud profiler tracks the customer's calling patterns through nearly real-time call detail records by interfacing with the cellular switch. If a customer's account suddenly shows characteristics of potential fraudulent uses, the phone can be red flagged and possibly disconnected. FraudBuster looks at many possible characteristics (see Figure 2) such as the following:

- Changes in call patterns inside or outside the subscriber's calling area
- Call patterns that typically indicate some form of fraudulent activity
- Simultaneous calls on one account.

FIGURE 2 Illustration of How FraudBuster Works

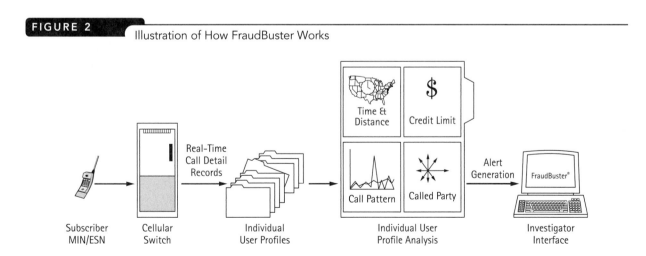

How FraudBuster Works

Source: Coral Systems.

Using sophisticated patterning software, the profiler would recognize these unusual patterns, and it could notify the carrier to contact the subscriber, or even disconnect service immediately. There is even the possibility that the potentially fraudulent charges could be eliminated on the subscriber's bill, even before the subscriber receives the monthly invoice. If the charges were eliminated early, the subscriber would never know he had been a victim of fraud and therefore would not experience the customer dissatisfaction of knowing about vulnerability to fraud.

The newer digital standards, as well as the advent of placing authentication chips in the phone, have made cloning fraud less of a problem. The equipment needed to effectively clone a digital phone is much more advanced and expensive than the equipment needed to clone an analog phone. The Federal Communications Commission (FCC) has also required modifications on scanners sold to the public, making it more difficult to find a scanner that is capable of picking up a cell phone's signal. However, the criminals are still out there, with a tendency to attack the weakest link. As preventative technology has taken over most of the fight against cloning fraud, subscription fraud is emerging as the predominate problem. FraudBuster is able to deal with this type of fraud in exactly the same way it deals with cloning. The user profiling system is very versatile because it uses nearly real-time data and is able to act quickly in identifying these acts.

PRICING MODEL

One of the principal goals of the company was to establish a recurring revenue stream. Coral feels that is one of the keys to building value. If Coral sells a product, such as a software license, then each period the company's sales start at zero and the hope is that the sales staff can beat the prior period's sales. In a good quarter, Coral's sales team may sell three or four licenses to a carrier, while a bad quarter may be zero new sales. With a fixed product, such as a software license, the company's sales performance is only as good as the last quarter.

A recurring revenue stream is much steadier. For example, US West can sign up a customer and then bill the customer on a monthly basis for telephone services. With this revenue stream, a company is assured of a large percentage of revenue each period. US West still has to focus on retailing its current customers, as well as adding new ones, but for the most part it can concentrate its efforts on reducing costs associated with this revenue stream. US West starts each quarter not from zero, as is the case with a fixed product company, but from the ending point of the last period's subscriber base. This recurring revenue model allows for more predictability in forecasting the financing needs of the company, as well as establishing the company's value.

Unfortunately for Coral Systems, the customers wanted to buy the application and then control their own destiny. Therefore, the pricing model Coral developed to solve this potential problem was a hybrid of the recurring revenue model and the per-product licensing fee. Coral would sell a one-time license per subscriber, based on the number of subscribers at the time of license. For example, if a carrier purchased the FraudBuster solution directly from Coral

Systems, the current number of subscribers the carrier served would determine the price of the license. If this hypothetical carrier had 500,000 subscribers when the solution was purchased, the carrier would pay a license fee based on that number. Each quarter the carrier would tabulate the current number of subscribers. If in the following quarter the carrier had increased to 650,000 subscribers, the carrier would have to pay a license fee to Coral for the additional 150,000 subscribers. That way as long as the customer base grows, Coral gets some recurring revenue.

EARLY MARKETING STRATEGY

The early marketing strategy was primarily to sell the product. Coral had a product that was a very good idea, and the company brought that to the market. The primary thrust was simply to get the products out to the market, and the engineers really did not listen to the customers. The marketing and engineering were completely disconnected. There was no specific marketing department at the time. Johnson had this to say on the subject: "The marketing function was supposed to be the bridge between sales and engineering, but it never did that. Somewhere around the third stage of the product, there was a connection, and the engineers finally began listening to the customers."

One of the major value-added resources of Coral Systems is the fact that FraudBuster supports all standards of the wireless telecommunications industry. Johnson designed the product to be usable with any standard and now that vision is very beneficial. The GSM standard is widely used in Europe but hardly used in North America. Some competitors have geared their fraud solutions to a specific technology, and if the telecommunications industry shifts away from that technology, the company could lose its product. Coral Systems' fraud solution is the only product that can support any digital standard, as well as analog. This has given Coral a competitive value-add in the emerging digital PCS market, as well as internationally.

MARKET PENETRATION

For a small, emerging company like Coral Systems to compete with its large competitors like GTE-TSI, IBM, and DEC is a difficult problem. Howard Kaushansky had this to say about the early market distribution with the major switch manufacturers:

> We had the product, [the switch manufacturers] have a distribution channel. But, we also provided some unique development to maximize some of the unique aspects of one switch versus another. We also have built, simultaneously, a direct marketing and distribution channel. The reason why that is necessary is that a small company in Longmont cannot hand an application over to a company like Motorola and say, "Here, sell this for us and send us huge checks." They have got hundreds . . . thousands of applications that people want to sell to [the switch manufacturers]. It is incumbent upon you as a company to basically sell the product to the company that's going to buy it from Motorola.

Howard Kaushansky also commented on the first sales of Coral Systems:

One thing that we didn't lack was being audacious enough to think that if we just could call up Lucent and Ericsson and work our way into those organizations and convince them that they needed to distribute FraudBuster, that they had customers crying out for it. It's based on personal relationships. We happened to strike up personal relationships either at a trade show, or you know somebody, who knows somebody, and you call and you pursue and you work your way up the chain. Especially with a company like us. You really need to secure internal sponsorship as quickly as you can.

CURRENT MARKETING STRATEGY

Tom Prosia, vice president of marketing, was brought on board in February 1996, with ten years of software and hardware industry management, marketing, and sales experience. Before joining Coral Systems, Tom was with Covia Technologies, a provider of middleware software and services. While at Covia he held two key positions as vice president of sales and vice president of marketing and communications. Before his tenure at Covia, Prosia worked as manager of new product planning for UNISYS Corp.

With the addition of Prosia, the company shifted its marketing focus from an "engineering-driven, get the product out the door focus," to a customer-oriented focus. The key is business development, including focusing on existing product evolution and new product analysis. This includes looking at other potential partners or strategic relationships and talking to a number of systems integrators. A systems integrator is a large consulting company (e.g., Andersen Consulting or Cap Gemini) that typically bids on very large projects and assists in establishing networks and building infrastructures for a company. These systems integrators are looking for a one-stop shop to bring in all the clients' needs. Coral is trying to establish a relationship in which the integrator will subcontract to Coral Systems, thus leading to another key strategic relationship.

Another key function of the current market strategy is to pave the way in the marketplace for Coral's salespeople. This is primarily achieved through news reports on the wireless space. If Coral can establish its engineers as experts on fraud or other telecommunications customer retention products, the press will not only write articles on those subjects, but also refer to Coral Systems as subject experts. Once the salespeople actually come in, they can simply refer to a trade journal or article listing Coral Systems as leaders in the field. Coral prefers to send its people to speak at conferences or talk with the trade press as a means to teach others about products such as FraudBuster or ChurnAlert, as well as raise awareness of the company's presence.

Finally, the marketing team can obtain information about the marketplace, even before the sales team approaches a customer. Owing to the high cost of sending someone to Europe or elsewhere overseas, Coral needs to have its intelligence done prior to the sale. Through the strategic relationships, the market team can "mine" the partner, such as the switch manufacturer, for potential helpful information on the customer. Tom Prosia had this to say on making an international sale, after the market team has gone through:

> [Coral] still has to do some selling. The sale won't be done, but we'll know [the potential customer] has dollars in their budget this year. [The potential customer] won't have to create a budget, or wait to the next budget cycle. That's pretty straightforward, if you don't have dollars in your budget, you're going to have trouble making a purchase. Particularly with software, where internationally it's going to be a million, million and a half, two million dollars. So the budget has to exist. Our partners have relationships where they can get answers to those types of questions. "Who are the decision makers?" These are big companies, they have people all over the place. "Whose office do we need to be sitting in, making our presentation, and who do we actually have to sell? What's their buying process? Do they tend to go through a very lengthy process? Should we expect an eighteen-month sales cycle, or will they decide if we establish that they've got budget and need, will they buy it in three and four months?"
>
> All of those things and many others, as kind of an environmental profile of a customer, are really important for us to have. Then we can make a prioritization of where we want to spend our resources, and where we think we can get a return on the investment. That's exactly what it is for us—a return on investment.

COMPETITION

"The day GTE announced they were going to do the same product was one of the biggest red letter days for Coral," said Eric Johnson. Johnson had created a whole new field, and one of his biggest concerns early on was competition. He was not sure that if one of the larger companies in the wireless space rolled out a similar product, whether that could significantly damage the company. Then GTE issued a press release, introducing a product similar to Coral's. GTE had contracted with DEC to create its own fraud product. Other competitors quickly followed suit. Once again, Coral had to overcome an obstacle faced by a small startup. Johnson felt that a small startup company could have missed out on some of the early deals in fraud prevention products. This was due to the fact that the larger carriers and competitors traveled in a type of social circle that was difficult and expensive for a small company like his to penetrate. A competitor could easily get the ear of a potential customer through its big-name recognition, such as GTE or IBM. A company like Coral Systems had to work much harder to get a potential customer to listen to it.

The market for Coral Systems' FraudBuster product, in addition to being fairly new, is intensely competitive. The carriers who supply service to North America include AT&T Wireless Services, BellSouth Cellular Corp., GTE Mobilenet, AirTouch Cellular, and Ameritech Cellular Services, just to name a few. The top-twenty carriers accounted for over 89 percent of the wireless subscribers at the beginning of 1996. Coral Systems not only has to compete with other fraud profiling systems for the carriers' business, but with the numerous other fraud prevention device makers as well. These include authentication chips, PIN numbers, voice recognition, and other methods used to combat fraud. The following is a summary of Coral Systems' primary competition:

GTE-TSI FraudForce^{SM} service line—GTE-TSI has a product line that includes several services that allow a carrier to block, restrict, and reinstate roamers in selected high-fraud markets. It could also route restricted roamers to an automated challenge and response system, in order to ensure the validity of the subscriber. GTE-TSI also uses artificial intelligence software on an individual switch basis to detect possible cloning activity. The company has products in the authentication, PIN, and profiling market. This is the closest profiler to FraudBuster in terms of functionality. One major weakness of GTE-TSI's product is that it does not support the GSM or digital standard, thus significantly limiting its growth potential in the foreign markets. GTE-TSI has not readily adapted to the new PCS market.

IBM FMS—IBM purchased the profiler from a small company called I-NET. The product was initially developed for AT&T by I-NET. IBM's primary customer for its FMS product is AT&T Wireless. AT&T has purchased FMS and modified it substantially, in essence making it AT&T's own product. This development has left IBM's product fairly stagnant and deficient in the emerging PCS markets. Besides supplying the number-one carrier in terms of subscribers (AT&T Wireless), IBM FMS also supplies Southwestern Bell Mobile Systems, which was the number-two North American carrier. These top-two carriers made up 30.5 percent of the subscriber base at the beginning of 1996.

Digital Equipment Corporation Fraud Management System—DEC is the largest competitor to Coral Systems' FraudBuster in international markets. It is also a profiling system that detects and analyzes fraud and recommends fraud counter-actions. It runs on a UNIX operating system and requires Informix database software. The pricing structure is similar to Coral's, where as the carrier increases its subscriber base, it must purchase additional licenses.

SystemsLink FraudTec—This major competitor is closest in company size to Coral Systems. SystemsLink is a small operation and has limited product support, but its product is also less expensive. FraudTec only supports analog networks and does not support international or digital standards. SystemsLink only had one of the top-twenty carriers at the beginning of 1996, but that carrier (Bell Atlantic Nynex Mobile) accounted for 11.3 percent of the total cell phone subscribers.

FINANCING

ROUND ONE

Early in 1991, Eric Johnson applied for support and occupancy in the Boulder Technology Incubator (BTI). One member of BTI's board, Pete Bloomer, was the president of Colorado Venture Management (CVM), a small venture capital/management firm. CVM offered $300,000 of seed money (in two stages, $120,000 and $180,000). Johnson immediately received the first stage of $120,000, with the second stage coming at a later date. These dollars were invested without a written business plan. Bloomer became a member of Coral's board of directors. Coral Systems had several distinctions with BTI, including being the first graduate, the company to be admitted the fastest (the decision to admit Coral was made in a day), and the company to receive the quickest funding (this was also made in one day with a handshake).

Eric Johnson had this to say on Pete Bloomer, the first investor of Coral Systems:

> *Pete looked me in the eye and said, "This guy has the drive, he's going to do it and it's a solid idea." To this day, of the investors in Coral, he is the largest because he took a risk at a very early stage. How many venture capitalists would do it with no business plan and a guy with no venture capital history? They wouldn't do it. But Pete did it. I respect the fact that he did do it, and I never begrudged him his stock. He should get something for his risk.*

The unusual mix of residents in the BTI at the time occasionally made for an interesting working environment, one that is often characteristic of an entrepreneurial startup. When Howard Kaushansky described working out of the incubator, he said, "You hope you don't get hit by the guy next to you. He may have a laser and might drill through the wall every now and then, if he missed his end target or something." Johnson stated that he enjoyed the excitement of being around these emerging businesses. He was able to help other participants with his own advice, as well as share in the pleasure of seeing a fellow BTI member reach a major milestone, such as receiving financing.

In order to continue developing the company after the first round of venture capital money, Johnson came up with a creative method of financing. Early on Coral Systems struck up strategic relationships with Computer Sciences Corporation (CSC), Stratus Computer, and Sun Microsystems (Sun). CSC funded the development stage software in exchange for distribution rights. Sun was looking for applications that could sell servers and equipment. Sun donated roughly $2 million in equipment and some cash, in exchange for Coral Systems to develop the FraudBuster software solution on the Sun platform. This not only gave Sun a customer that would exclusively use their platform, but it also allowed Sun to gain an avenue into the growing wireless telecommunications industry. The same applied for Stratus, except for on a smaller scale.

Owing to the creative structure of some of their early funding relationships, Coral was able to keep much of the equity control by obtaining nonequity-based forms of funding. This also increased the value to the seed round investors. It did not dilute their stake to the degree a normal development company would have. Through the development stage of the company, Coral had received roughly $6 million in cash and equipment and only gave away approximately 20 percent of the equity.

Eric Johnson offered the following thought regarding the first deal with Sun:

> *A short definition of an entrepreneur is "insanity." Everyone always tells you "you can't do something, that can't be done, that shouldn't be done." You get so used to it as an entrepreneur that you probably are a little insane. Everybody told me that there is no way Sun Microsystems would do the first deal. It was $300,000 with no equity, no payback, the whole thing was just one page. We called it a marketing agreement. I committed that the first release of the product would be on a Sun Microsystems box, and that was it.*

ROUND TWO

In February 1993, when Coral was still an early stage development company, the first financial officer, Kyle Hubbart, was hired. Hubbart worked in public accounting for three years and then moved into the restaurant industry. He was CFO for Round the Corner and Good Times restaurants and helped take them public. After eleven years in the restaurant industry, Hubbart felt he wanted to move to the high-tech arena where the risks were high, but the rewards were also high if the company was successful. He commented that taking the risk of going from a well-established role in a stable company to an entrepreneurial venture was "a step back, with hopefully a big step forward in the future." As the new CFO of Coral, Kyle Hubbart's main tasks were to establish financial connections, to provide additional funding for the growth of the company, and to come in and set up the accounting systems and finance department. When he came in, Coral had yet to make its first sale of a product.

As the money and equipment from the strategic relationships in the beginning ran to the end of their course, Coral looked for its second round of major financing. Once again, Coral Systems did not have to look far for its second round. Although sales had been nominal to that point, Coral was able to sell the value of the concept to potential investors. Kyle Hubbart estimated the valuation of the company, primarily through market potential, before the second round to be in the neighborhood of $10 to $12 million. A group of investors that had spun off of Alex Brown was very interested in the business concept. These investors had heard about Coral through an analyst who was tracking Coral in the wireless market. This group of investors put together a $2 million private placement of forty to fifty private individuals as Coral's second major round of financing.

Coral Systems was able to get $600,000 from the investors at the beginning of the deal. The money would be taken out of the final proceeds, but either way Coral got this money up front to continue operations. While the private placement group found the rest of the investors to complete the placement, Johnson was able to start using some of the proceeds right away. This solved the problem often faced by a startup of having to wait a long time for the cash from an investor.

ROUND THREE

The next year, Coral Systems embarked on its third round of financing. The company had placed a product on the shelf and was actively making sales. Software license revenue in 1993 was $1,036,400. Coral was fully out of the development stage and into a functioning business. Through attendance at trade shows, venture fund conferences, and word of mouth, the venture capitalists were very interested in meeting them. The VC firms did not necessarily bust down the door at Coral, but it wasn't difficult to get an audience to listen to the Coral management team. Coral's staff discussed a deal with approximately twenty venture capital firms and investment banks, and they found some who were willing to invest in Coral Systems at this particular stage of growth. When asked why it was much easier for Coral Systems to raise money than other firms, Kyle Hubbart, CFO, had this to say:

> *Definitely, I think a big part was the business concept itself. They saw what a dynamic growth industry wireless telecommunications was and they could easily understand the applications of the FraudBuster [product] we were developing, and what a need there was for that. They just wanted . . . to invest in that space.*

In addition to having a sound business concept, Johnson stressed the need to make the business plan easy for anyone to understand. Venture capitalists spend a significant portion of time analyzing business plans and may have trouble looking past the numbers. If the concept is put in a form that is simple for anyone to understand, there is a much better chance that someone will listen to it. For Coral the main question was, "Would you pay money for someone to stop stealing from you?" When put this way, it is very difficult to say no to the business.

Coral put together a $4.5 million deal with four VC firms: Bessemer Venture Partners of Boston, Vertex Management Inc. of San Francisco, the P/A Fund L.P., and the investment banking firm Unterberg Harris of New York. After the deal was announced, Eric Johnson was quoted as saying:

> *I wanted to send a message to the marketplace. With these investors, we're a substantial force to execute on any opportunity we have. I wanted to make sure I have a lot of dry powder stored.*

ROUND FOUR

Finally, the fourth round of financing brought a real endorsement from within the telecommunications industry. Cincinnati Bell Information Systems (CBIS), working through a mergers and acquisition firm, Broadview Associates, approached Coral Systems about the possibility of buying 100 percent of Coral and integrating it into CBIS. CBIS is the global leader in the provision and management of customer care and billing solutions for the communications industry. It produces over 225 million bills for cable TV, wireless, and wireline telephone systems. It is also a subsidiary of Cincinnati Bell, Inc. CBIS felt Coral's fraud and customer retention solutions could be used to help drive its business in terms of billing systems.

The management at Coral did not feel they had grown the company to the point they wanted and still felt there was much more value that could be built through the company before they gave up control. They did, however, realize Coral needed an additional round of venture capital and worked out a deal with CBIS. This round netted Coral an additional $4.2 million in equity financing. The fact that it came from a leader in the wireless industry, as opposed to another venture capital firm, helped validate Coral's current valuations.

Figure 3 (page 646) shows the history of Coral's equity and major rounds of financing position since its inception, as well as the amount of cash invested in the company to date.

FIGURE 3

Schedule of Financing and Equity

	Series A Preferred Stock Shares	Amount	Series B Preferred Stock Shares	Amount	Series C Preferred Stock Shares	Amount	Common Stock Shares	Amount	Additional Paid-in Capital	Accumulated Deficit	Treasury Stock Shares	Amount	Total S/HS Equity (Deficit)
December 31, 1990	—	—	—	(0)	—	—	—	(0)	(0)	—	—	—	(1)
1st Round Original Capital							3,731,729	3,733	123,268				$ 127,001
Net Loss										(125,000)			$ (125,000)
December 31, 1991	—	—	—	(0)	—	—	3,731,729	3,733	123,268	(125,000)	—	—	2,000
Miscellaneous Equity Transactions									50,500				$ 50,500
Net Loss										(502,500)			$ (502,500)
December 31, 1992	—	—	—	(0)	—	—	3,731,729	3,733	173,768	(627,500)	—	—	(450,000)
Buy Treasury Stock											676,887	(18,000)	$ (18,000)
Net Loss										(1,049,800)			$(1,049,800)
December 31, 1993	—	—	—	(0)	—	—	3,731,729	3,733	173,768	(1,677,300)	676,887	(18,000)	(1,517,800)
Miscellaneous Equity Transactions							392,630	392	131,108				$ 131,500
2nd Round Sell													
Series A Stock	2,000,000	2,000							1,858,300				$ 1,860,300
Net Loss										(1,227,800)			$(1,227,800)
December 31, 1994	2,000,000	2,000	—	(0)	—	—	4,124,359	4,125	2,163,176	(2,905,100)	676,887	(18,000)	(753,800)
3rd Round Sell													
Series B Stock			2,083,333	2,083					4,269,317				$ 4,271,400
Miscellaneous Equity Transactions							141,150	141	16,759				$ 16,900
Buy Treasury Stock											290,078	(6,000)	$ (6,000)
Net Loss										(3,390,900)			$(3,390,900)
December 31, 1995	2,000,000	2,000	2,083,333	2,083		—	4,265,509	4,266	6,449,251	(6,296,000)	966,965	(24,000)	137,600
Buy Treasury Stock											108,185	(164,600)	$ (164,600)
Retire Treasury Stock							(1,074,400)	(1,074)	(187,326)		(1,074,400)	188,400	$ (0)
4th Round Sell													
Series C Stock					1,824,920	1,825			4,191,275				$ 4,193,100
Miscellaneous Equity Transactions							44,075	44	13,956				$ 14,000
Net Loss										(741,700)			$ (741,700)
September 30, 1996	2,000,000	2,000	2,083,333	2,083	1,824,920	1,825	3,235,184	3,235	10,467,156	(7,037,700)	750	(200)	$ 3,438,400

HISTORICAL FINANCIAL PERFORMANCE

Exhibit 1 (page 648) shows the historical income statements for Coral Systems for the years 1991 through 1995 and for the first nine months of 1996. While the firm has never shown a net profit, the net loss was reduced substantially in 1996. Exhibit 2 (page 648) provides a history of selected balance sheet items and Exhibit 3 (page 649) provides a historical graphic description of selected income statement items. Exhibit 4 (page 650) provides balance sheet information at the end of 1994 and 1995, as well as for the end of September 1996. Total assets increased from about $1 million at the end of 1994 to nearly $7.5 million by the end of September 1996. This asset growth was financed primarily through equity financings in 1995 and 1996. Exhibit 5 (page 651) contains cash flow statements for the years 1993 through 1995 and for the first nine months of 1996. Cash at the end of September 1996 was in excess of $3 million.

THE WITHDRAWN IPO

At the end of 1996 Coral Systems had planned on issuing 2.7 million additional shares to the public, with an estimated price at $11 per share, equating to $26,800,000 (after deducting underwriting expenses). The 2.7 million shares issued to the public would have constituted approximately 21 percent of the company's common stock. In October 1996, Coral filed with the SEC for the initial public offering. The need for additional funding and a way to bring the company to the next level of growth were cited as the main reasons why Coral wanted to go public. In addition, the IPO would allow the original investors a way to exit their investment. The company would benefit by having directors on the board who represented more than just each round of financing. By December, the offering was listed as scheduled for immediate sale, but the company postponed it indefinitely. There were several factors cited for the decision to withdraw the public offering.

1996 FOURTH QUARTER

With the advent of the PCS technology, many new carriers were emerging in the market. They were trying to get their telecommunications networks up and running, and fraud solutions were secondary on their list of priorities. Coral was one of the few fraud management solutions that would support digital, so it was poised to grab a huge market share of this new U.S. market, and it anticipated closing these deals prior to going public. Unfortunately, some of the PCS carriers held off on closing the deals with Coral, resulting in a down fourth quarter. This was the final quarter before putting the stock on the market.

COMPARABLE COMPANIES

In addition to the problem of not having the attractive recurring revenues in place, several comparable technology stocks were having a downturn as well.

Coral Systems, Inc.

EXHIBIT 1 Income Statements

STATEMENT OF OPERATIONS DATA	YEAR ENDED DECEMBER 31,					NINE MONTHS ENDED 9/30/96
	1991	1992	1993	1994	1995	
Revenue						
Software licenses	$ —	$ —	$ 215,200	$ 1,036,400	$ 2,484,600	$5,828,700
Services and other	—	699,000	178,700	239,700	624,700	408,400
Hardware	—	—	110,200	140,800	780,500	615,300
Total revenue	—	699,000	504,100	1,416,900	3,889,800	6,852,400
Cost of revenue						
Software licenses	—	—	57,600	122,000	526,000	419,100
Services and other	—	140,000	74,500	258,000	644,700	584,800
Hardware	—	—	111,800	128,300	738,300	469,600
Total cost of revenue	—	140,000	243,900	508,300	1,909,000	1,473,500
Gross profit	—	559,000	260,200	908,600	1,980,800	5,378,900
Operating expenses						
Research and development	37,000	514,000	414,000	572,700	2,159,700	1,953,100
Sales and marketing	2,000	133,000	158,300	645,300	1,869,700	2,614,000
General and administrative	86,000	417,000	677,100	885,600	1,351,000	1,765,400
Total operating expenses	125,000	1,064,000	1,249,400	2,103,600	5,380,400	6,332,500
Loss from operations	(125,000)	(505,000)	(989,200)	(1,195,000)	(3,399,600)	(953,600)
Other income (expense), net	—	3,000	(60,600)	(32,800)	8,700	(31,400)
Loss before extraordinary item	(125,000)	(502,000)	(1,049,800)	(1,227,800)	(3,390,900)	(985,000)
Extraordinary item						
Gain on extinguishment of debt	—	—	—	—	—	243,300
Net loss	$(125,000)	$(502,000)	$(1,049,800)	$(1,227,800)	$(3,390,900)	$ (741,700)

EXHIBIT 2 History of Selected Balance Sheet Information

BALANCE SHEET DATA (IN THOUSANDS)	DECEMBER 31,					SEPTEMBER 30, 1996
	1991	1992	1993	1994	1995	
Cash and cash equivalents	$25	$ 215	$ 62	$ 83	$1,023	$3,374
Total assets	35	312	355	1,092	2,958	7,454
Long-term debt, noncurrent portion	—	167	500	22	146	313
Stockholders' equity (deficit)	2	(450)	(1,518)	(754)	138	3,438

The comparable companies of Coral Systems, selected by the underwriters, were not doing as well as anticipated in the public market. Figure 4 indicates the performance of several comparable companies over the last several months. These comparable companies were categorized as being similar to Coral Systems in two separate groups: telecommunications service companies and client/server applications companies.

EXHIBIT 3 History of Revenues, Gross Margin, and Net Income

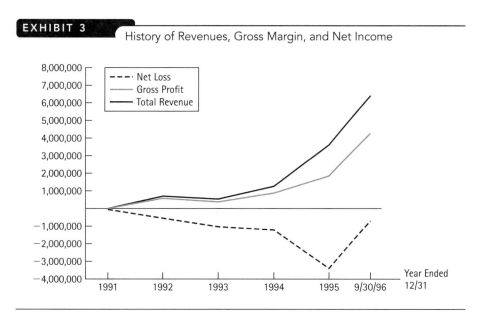

REVENUE RECOGNITION ISSUES

The CFO, Kyle Hubbart, stated that one of the more interesting problems he has had to deal with in terms of accounting issues is revenue recognition on a sale of software. One of the smaller problems Coral had to deal with in going public was to align its revenue recognition standards with that of the SEC. The question was, "When do you recognize the revenue on a sale of a license, particularly when that sale may be related to further obligations down the road?" For example, let's say Coral made a sale to a carrier, but as part of the agreement Coral is required to give the carrier an upgrade one year from now. Would Coral credit the sales account in this period, or would it have to wait until the final portion of the sales agreement—the upgrade—is completed a full year from now, even if Coral received the cash today? This revenue recognition issue on one of its sales held up the final SEC approval until the entry was resolved.

With all three of these factors pushing Coral to the point where it would likely miss the underwriter's deadline, the company withdrew the offering. The pricing model was another concern of the management team. The pricing structure did not directly impact the decision to withdraw the public offer. However, the fact that the predictability in the revenue stream was not to the point the management had envisioned it would be at the time of the offering may have indirectly influenced the decision. John Fraser, president, had this to say about the IPO:

> We believe that it was probably a good thing that it didn't go through, because all of the fundamentals were not in place and Q1 was not strong. So having come from a company that was one of the darling stocks for five years, which Sybase was, went from a 100 million to a billion, made sixteen quarters in a row of exceeding expectations, and in the seventeenth quarter missed by four cents, and the stock lost 50 percent of its value in one day.

Coral Systems, Inc.

EXHIBIT 4	Balance Sheet Information		
BALANCE SHEET ASSETS	**DECEMBER 31, 1994**	**DECEMBER 31, 1995**	**SEPTEMBER 30, 1996**
Current assets			
Cash and cash equivalents	$ 82,900	$1,022,500	$3,373,500
Accounts receivable	740,800	1,119,300	2,449,200
Other current assets	2,800	149,300	328,000
Total current assets	826,500	2,291,100	6,150,700
Property and equipment	398,500	914,000	1,827,000
Accumulated depreciation	(143,100)	(288,200)	(562,700)
Property and equipment, net	255,400	625,800	1,264,300
Other assets (plug)	10,000	41,100	39,100
Total assets	$1,091,900	$2,958,000	$7,454,100
Liabilities and Stockholders' Equity (Deficit)			
Current liabilities			
Accounts payable	$ 291,500	$ 412,900	$ 446,800
Accrued liabilities	90,000	526,100	1,010,800
Current portion of long-term debt	666,700	796,700	380,100
Deferred revenue	300,300	463,700	1,479,600
Total current liabilities	1,348,500	2,199,400	3,317,300
Deferred revenue and other (plug)	475,200	475,200	385,000
Long-term debt	22,000	145,800	313,400
Total liabilities	1,845,700	2,820,400	4,015,700
Stockholders' equity (deficit)			
Series A preferred stock	2,000	2,000	2,000
Series B preferred stock	—	2,083	2,083
Series C preferred stock	—	—	1,825
Preferred stock	—	—	—
Common stock	4,124	4,265	3,235
Additional paid-in capital	2,163,176	6,449,252	10,467,157
Accumulated deficit	(2,905,100)	(6,296,000)	(7,037,700)
Less: Treasury stock	(18,000)	(24,000)	(200)
Total stockholders' equity (deficit)	(735,800)	137,600	3,438,400
Total liabilities and stockholders' equity (deficit)	$1,091,900	$2,958,000	$7,454,100

I'm a pretty firm believer that you better have your fundamentals and your predictability in place before you go public.

AFTER THE WITHDRAWN IPO

In early 1997, the company had a major management shakeup as well. Eric Johnson retained his position as chairman of the board and CEO but was no

EXHIBIT 5 Cash Flow Information

STATEMENT OF CASH FLOWS	YEAR ENDED DECEMBER 31,			FOR THE NINE MONTHS ENDED SEPTEMBER 30,
	1993	1994	1995	1996
Cash Flows from Operations				
Net loss	(1,049,800)	(1,227,800)	(3,390,900)	(741,700)
Depreciation	38,100	90,100	198,700	296,100
Provision for doubtful accounts	—	—	—	75,000
Write-offs of uncollectible receivables	—	—	—	26,900
Gain on disposal of equipment	—	—	(2,600)	(5,300)
Extraordinary gain	—	—	—	(243,300)
Change in				
Accounts receivable	(136,800)	(604,000)	(378,500)	(1,553,200)
Other assets	(2,000)	(7,000)	(177,600)	(310,800)
Accounts payable and accruals	198,400	158,600	576,900	719,000
Deferred revenue	—	291,200	163,400	1,010,000
Net cash used in operations	(952,100)	(1,298,900)	(3,010,600)	(727,300)
Cash Flows from Investing				
Proceeds from the sale of property	—	—	198,300	206,400
Property and equipment additions	(95,200)	(195,400)	(514,000)	(542,900)
Net cash used in investing	(95,200)	(195,400)	(315,700)	(336,500)
Cash Flows from Financing				
Proceeds from sale of preferred stock, net	—	1,580,300	3,874,500	4,193,100
Proceeds from sale of common stock	—	1,500	13,900	14,000
Purchase of treasury stock	—	—	(6,000)	(164,600)
Proceeds from the issuance of loans	921,500	205,200	760,000	250,000
Payments on borrowings	(27,000)	(271,900)	(376,500)	(877,700)
Net cash used in financing	894,500	1,515,100	4,265,900	3,414,800
Net increase (decrease) in cash	(152,800)	20,800	939,600	2,351,000
Beginning cash	214,900	62,100	82,900	1,022,500
Ending cash	62,100	82,900	1,022,500	3,373,500

longer responsible for the day-to-day operations of the company. John Fraser was brought in as EVP of sales and operations in the middle of April and Tim Hayes was named VP of engineering at approximately the same time. At the end of May, John Fraser was appointed president, and Tim Hayes became senior VP of engineering and development. Fraser and Hayes were also responsible for all of the day-to-day operations of the company.

FIGURE 4

FIGURE 4   Recent Stock Price Performance of Comparable Firms

COMPANY	PRICE ON 7/15/96	PRICE ON 5/22/97	NET CHANGE	% CHANGE FROM 7/15/96
Telecommunications Services				
Boston Communications Group	$ 14.13	$ 7.31	$ (6.82)	−48.3%
CSG Systems International	$ 22.50	$17.63	$ (4.87)	−21.6%
Cellular Tec	$ 13.88	$12.75	$ (1.13)	−8.1%
Premiere Technologies Services	$ 21.00	$27.50	$ 6.50	31.0%
Lightbridge	$ 11.00	$ 8.75	$ (2.25)	−20.5%
Saville Systems	$ 23.88	$41.25	$ 17.37	72.7%
TCSI	$ 23.25	$ 5.88	$(17.37)	−74.7%
Client/Server Applications				
Documentum	$ 22.25	$19.25	$ (3.00)	−13.5%
HNC Software	$ 30.81	$30.63	$ (0.18)	−0.6%
Objective Systems Integrators	$ 27.50	$ 6.69	$(20.81)	−75.7%
PeopleSoft*	$ 58.75	$51.00	$ (7.75)	−13.2%
Remedy Corporation*	$ 51.13	$37.63	$(13.50)	−26.4%
Scopus Technology	$ 9.50	$34.25	$ 24.75	260.5%
Workgroup Technology	$ 14.50	$ 4.25	$(10.25)	−70.7%
	$344.08		$(39.31)	

Average Change   −11.4247%

* two-for-one split

THE BOARD OF DIRECTORS

Coral Systems has had a board of directors since its incorporation. The board consisted primarily of people who had put money into the company at each of its various rounds of financing. Johnson brought in the outside board of directors to create accountability to the company for his actions. However, the majority of the directors are financial contributors who are also concerned with making a return on their investment. Eric Johnson did bring in an outside director from the wireless industry, with the intention of rounding out the board. Johnson feels that if he had to create the board all over again, he would look for a more well-rounded board, with skill sets in a variety of areas.

Much of the literature discussing startup companies emphasizes the creation of an independent board of directors early on. Usually giving a director's seat comes with taking money from an investor. A new director can also be a rich source of consulting to the management of the company, at very little cost to the startup. In Coral Systems' case, the board was built primarily through each round of investment, with a representative being placed on the board at each new stage.

THE EXECUTIVE LIMIT

It is not unusual for the founder of a high-technology startup company to be removed from the day-to-day operations of the company he started. Yet other founders grow with and create very large companies. Usually, it is the board of directors that will make the decision to have the founder removed. Oftentimes it takes a different skill set of managerial tools to start a company from scratch (usually, the founder is extremely technically competent) than that needed to grow a young company into the next level of commercial success (when the manager or team of managers needs sound, fundamental business skills). The founder may not want, or be able to learn, the skill sets required in the commercialization stage of the company for reasons as simple as the founder's lack of interest in the management aspects. These skills may be necessary in order to fill the gap between startup and growth. This difference is often compounded by the fact that venture capital firms were used to fund the early growth of the company. This may create a difference in the goals of the shareholders versus the goals of the founder. The founder may want to continue to work and grow in the choppy waters of the entrepreneurial environment, but the investors in the company will most likely want to see a return on their investment at some point.

For the most part, the way the investors achieve this return is through the growth of the company into a commercially successful vehicle. In order to bring on this commercial success, the company may have to learn to manage it at a different level than the startup. Often professional management is brought in to replace the founder, primarily because this new management team may have the proper skills to grow the company. The new management team also will likely have the same goal of commercial success that is desired by the equity providers. The point where this change occurs is termed the "Executive Limit" by Meyer and Dean.[1] Coral's board of directors made a decision after the IPO process that founder Eric Johnson should perform new roles with the company he founded. In an interview with the board, Johnson questioned the conclusion of some of the board members. He remains convinced that he has the skill set needed at this stage and that he could successfully manage the company to its next stage of development.

THE FUTURE: CHURN

Coral Systems, to date, has been a primarily one-product company—FraudBuster. It has two customers using its second major product, ChurnAlert, and is working on not only making a market, but also dominating the market space for customer retention products.

Churn is described by the telecommunications industry as a user who drops his service or switches to another carrier. In the United States, through very competitive tactics, wireless carriers have compelled their subscribers to churn. Carriers can give new subscribers free phones, batteries, and better price plans; claim higher

---

[1] G. Dale Meyer and Thomas J. Dean, "An Upper Echelons Perspective on Transformational Leadership Problems in High Technology Firms." *Journal of High Technology Management Research*, 2(1) (1990), pp. 223–242.

voice quality; offer better coverage area; provide better service; have more accurate billing; and make other offers to effectively attract new customers.

Figure 5 shows the various reasons why a customer may drop or switch carriers. There is one commonly accepted, unpreventable reason for canceling service, and that is the death of a subscriber. According to one wireless industry publication, "The only good deactivated user is a dead one."

Carriers are very concerned if customers start leaving. Leading industry analysts estimate that it's five to six times more expensive to acquire a new customer than it is to retain an existing one. In addition, it takes six to thirteen months to break even on acquisition costs of a new customer. Sixty to 70 percent of the churn takes place in the first three months of the customer's service, so with the high churn rates, a carrier could turn over its customer base once every two to four years. The alarming customer turnover rate has in large part gone unnoticed owing primarily to the fact that the new customer base has steadily outpaced it. For one customer lost, two to three are signing up.

ChurnAlert was introduced September 1995 and had met with limited success through the end of 1996. It had been installed quickly at one of Coral's customers but was still being tested and refined to meet the customer's current expectations. To date, Coral has focused its most recent efforts primarily on capturing market share for FraudBuster in the international markets.

ChurnAlert works using the same software interface into the call detail records as the FraudBuster product. It tracks customer calling habits in near real-time, analyzing factors such as price, plans, air time, feature usage, and dropped and blocked calls. A red flag is raised when customer profiles match known churn

---

FIGURE 5   Reasons for Customer Switching

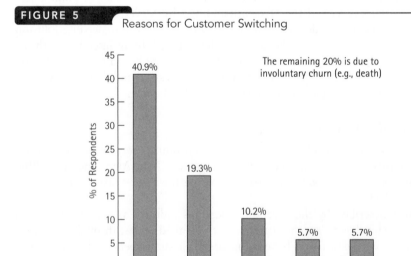

Source: RCR Reports, Link Resources, Yankee Group.

drivers. Once the at-risk subscribers are identified, a strategy can be developed to retain the customer. These strategies could be implemented by the carrier, and they could be as simple as a personalized letter or phone call, to a more complex handling of the issue, such as replacement phones or assistance with phone reprogramming. Not only does ChurnAlert provide the customer retention suggestions, but it also allows the vendor to sort customers by specific segments and create customized customer data reports for targeting preferred subscribers.

For example, the carrier may segment the top 10 percent of its customers, and this 10 percent represents 80 to 90 percent of the carrier's revenue. This segment is the "golden customer," and for the most part, these customers are fairly price insensitive. Their company pays for their phones, and quality may be a much higher priority than price. This segment may be willing to make the trade-off of higher price for higher quality. Therefore, the carrier had better make sure it is watching blocked and dropped calls more closely with the "golden customer" than the price plan. Conversely, with the growth in the market over the last two years, the new subscriber additions have primarily been described as "safety users," or basic consumers. These are people who buy the phone for convenience factors. They are not going to be as quality sensitive as someone who uses her cell phone constantly for business purposes. These safety users are on a very inexpensive plan, with limited minutes. They may also use their phone to order a pizza on the way home, or call the day care center to say they are going to be late picking up their kids, but they are going to be very price sensitive. If they can take their plan from $19.95 to $16.95 a month, they may switch. ChurnAlert might want to have the analysis of price plan much higher for this particular segment. ChurnAlert allows the carrier to segment its customers on a matrix-type relationship.

COMPETITION IN THE CHURN SPACE

The churn product industry is not entirely without competition against Coral's ChurnAlert, despite the recent emergence of the market. ChurnAlert's primary feature is that it is a near real-time profiler, with information taken directly from the switch. This is beneficial to Coral because it's the same interface that FraudBuster uses. It allows Coral to leverage its experience and technological knowledge into a brand-new arena. The benefit to having the data in near real-time is that it monitors information continuously over time as factors change. The carrier can factor a dropped call today, or a price plan introduced by the competitor today. The carrier can then pull the at-risk subscriber profile, based on the segments mentioned previously, so the carrier can take some action to secure the at-risk user before the user drops the service. ChurnAlert puts the information on a proactive basis, even before the customer calls the service desk.

The following is a summary of the two major competitors in the churn space. All the competition is in churn management, but the other two companies' approaches are unique, and the market has not really discerned the benefits or detriments to any method.

Lightbridge Churn Prophet—Lightbridge uses predictive modeling. The company has a very sophisticated tool set of data mining tools, and it draws correlations and trends based on analysis of massive amounts of data. When the confluence of around three to five factors come together, which Lightbridge has patterned over time, it will pinpoint a subscriber or group of subscribers who are likely to churn. Then Lightbridge gives its prediction to its carrier, so that the carrier can take action. Information is taken from a data warehouse, not off the switch.

GTE-TSI ChurnManager[SM]—GTE-TSI uses a customer care approach. If a customer calls in, the operator may get an indicator on his screen warning that this person is liable to churn. When the indicator appears in front of the customer service rep, it will warn the rep and suggest possible action steps. It's a reactive churn system. It only addresses churn if and when a customer does in fact call in, which is a very low percentage. There is not a lot of competitive information on the product, because it has not been installed at a customer site as of the writing of this case.

One of the hopes for Coral is that ChurnAlert will become a product that is accepted in the wireless market space. The marketing team feels strongly that ChurnAlert will be poised to take over as the primary product for the company, as FraudBuster's sales taper off. The goal is to have the churn product sales increase in the new product market, just as FraudBuster is reaching the peak of its success in the product life cycle. Once Coral has placed two strong products in the wireless industry, it may shift its focus in using its innovative fraud and churn solutions in an altogether different industry.

ASSIGNMENTS

A. Describe Coral Systems' "business model" in terms of revenues, profits, and cash flows.

B. What intellectual property, if any, does Coral Systems possess?

C. Describe the experience and expertise characteristics of the management team.

D. Describe Coral Systems' pricing model and its current marketing strategy.

E. Discuss the competition faced by Coral Systems in conjunction with its current product, FraudBuster, and expected competition for its second major product, ChurnAlert.

F. Describe the four successful rounds of financing achieved by Coral Systems in terms of sources and amounts.

G. Conduct a ratio analysis of Coral Systems' past income statements and balance sheets. Note any performance strengths and weaknesses and discuss any ratio trends.

H. Use the cash flow statements for Coral Systems to determine whether the venture has been building or burning cash, as well as possible trends in building or burning cash.

I. Discuss possible reasons why Coral Systems' plan for an initial public offering (IPO) of common stock at the end of 1996 was withdrawn.

J. Describe how you might prepare a discounted cash flow (DCF) model to determine whether the proposed IPO price of $11 per share was reasonable.

K. Discuss how you would evaluate the proposed $11 IPO price using comparable firms and a multiples analysis. What multiples would you propose using?

L. Optional: Attempt to value Coral Systems by first identifying several comparable firms. Find various price to income statement or balance sheet item multiples for these firms.

Then use these multiples to value Coral Systems. (Note: This exercise requires the use of information external to the case.)

M. What strategic and financial options are available to Coral Systems at this time that would help ensure a viable future for the venture? What should Coral Systems do?

Appendix A

BACKGROUND

INDUSTRY CONTEXT

Cell Phone Usage and Fraud Costs. The telecommunications industry was rapidly expanding as the popularity of car phones and portable phones increased dramatically during the early 1990s. The following shows the increase in the number of subscribers of cell phones over time:

1983	1st Subscriber
1987	1 million
1992	10 million
1996	30 million
1997	50 million
Projected 1999[2]	200 million

*   Subscribers estimated by the Cellular Telecommunications Industry Association.

The cell phone has grown from a modification of a mobile radio telephone, or "walkie-talkie," in 1946. The cell phone is now a personal communications network that can provide a wide range of services, as well as integrating taxes, modems, and many other telecommunications devices into the palm of your hand.

TECHNOLOGY STANDARDS

In order to understand how cell phones are cloned, a brief explanation of cell phone technology is necessary. There are currently two types of wireless telecommunications networks: analog and digital.

ANALOG

The first wireless network in the cell phone industry was analog, and it uses AMPS (Advanced Mobil Phone Services) as its transmission standard. Analog works by establishing a radio link from the handheld cell phone to the wired telephone system.

When the customer picks up the cell phone and dials a number, the phone immediately assigns two channels to the call, a voice channel and a control channel. This control channel allows the phone to communicate with the switch. It will communicate all the time with the switch, even if the caller is not talking. This is how the carrier will know where to send a call transmitted to a particular cell phone.

A city or county is divided into several cells, and each cell has a low-powered radio transmitter/receiver on a tower. Once combined, these transmitter/receiver towers make up a service area for the phone. The phone searches available channels for the cell tower with the strongest signal and then locks onto it, thus connecting the call to the cell system. The call's strength is then monitored by a Mobile Telephone Switching Office (MTSO, or "switch") that is linked to this multiple cell system through a central computer. The MTSO is also linked to the local telephone system and long-distance carriers, which in turn connect the subscriber to the number called.

The MTSO monitors a subscriber's signal as she travels through the cell network, using the control channel. Once the switch detects that the signal is fading in that cell, owing to the subscriber traveling out of the cell range, it automatically switches it to a stronger cell and radio frequency. This switch is done so quickly that it is not noticeable to the caller. If the subscriber travels out of a service area into another area, the phone will still connect, but additional "roaming" charges are assessed. Since all analog carriers use the AMPS standard, a caller is able to connect in any area serviced by a carrier. Once a caller reaches an area that is out of range of their own service area, the phone will display an "out of service" indicator or a "roam" indicator, depending on whether or not the call is picked up by a different cell network. In addition to switching calls, the MTSO creates a call detail record (CDR), which is passed on to a carrier database. The CDRs are used to compile billing statistics, process diagnostic information, and verify the validity of the phone.

DIGITAL

An improvement over the analog network in recent years is the digital network. The analog networks were reaching capacity, and during the early 1990s many companies began implementing a new type of telecommunications network using digital technology. Digital cellular transforms the human voice into computer language. It transmits the voice in a series of 0s and 1s, which requires less radio spectrum and allows greater system capacity. In addition to greater capacity, the digital signal is much clearer. In analog, the actual voice waveform is transmitted. The transmission loses its strength and progressively picks up distortions, static, and interference. As the analog signal is amplified, so is this additional "noise." With digital, as the signal is regenerated, it is put through a series of yes-no questions, "Is what is being transmitted a 'one' or a 'zero'?" The signal is then reconstructed and demodulated, or "squared off," to its original form, thus producing a cleaner signal. Another major benefit is that a digital signal can be interweaved with other digital signals, such as those from computers or fax machines.

Unlike analog using one transmission standard (AMPS), carriers have elected to implement different digital transmission standards, including Time Division

Multiple Access (TDMA), Code Division Multiple Access (CDMA), and Global System for Mobile Communications (GSM). These transmission standards are not compatible with each other or with analog standards. The lack of a single digital standard across the world has led many digital network carriers to use existing analog networks to allow customer roaming services when compatible digital networks are not available. The result is a multimode digital/analog phone that defaults to analog mode in the absence of a compatible digital transmission standard.

PCS ARCHITECTURE

Recently, many carriers have begun offering PCS, which stands for Personal Communications Services. The FCC auctioned off six blocks of spectrum, which covered the United States, to a variety of carriers. These blocks of spectrum were made available as a result of the Telecommunications Act of 1995 and brought in billions of dollars in license revenue to the government. The deregulation also resulted in the creation of the PCS market. These PCS systems use many interlocking micro cell sites, unlike the analog cellular architecture that uses large tower cell sites with great radius. A PCS transmitter/receiver is very small and could be placed on buildings rather inconspicuously. The micro cell covers a very small service area. A cellular transmitter/receiver requires a large tower and covers miles and miles of radius. PCS architecture is very common in densely populated areas, since an analog cell tower would not be able to handle all the subscribers in its service area. With the advent of digital technology, many of the new PCS carriers use the multimode digital/analog phone. PCS has advantages over the old cellular, since it creates more system capacity, experiences fewer dropped calls, and offers a variety of other advanced features.

Digital transmissions are much more difficult to clone, owing to the fact that there are many more combinations of possible frequencies at a higher bandwidth. In Europe and other foreign markets, PCS architecture is employed using the European digital standard GSM. If a subscriber wanted seamless roaming capabilities in Europe or Asia, it would require a handset that is compatible with the GSM standard. This handset would work in a North American PCS network that is based on the GSM standard, but not in any North American network based on TDMA or CDMA. There are a few carriers setting up GSM networks in the United States, but currently these service areas are not nearly as numerous as the analog and PCS networks. U.S. PCS carriers have not agreed on a uniform digital standard.

PROBLEMS OF FRAUD

CLONING

Cloning fraud involves the scanning and capturing of a cell phone's electronic serial numbers from the airwaves. These serial numbers are called the ESN/MIN (electronic serial number/mobile identification number). The ESN uniquely identifies each cellular phone. It is fixed in the phone and cannot readily be changed. The MIN corresponds to the subscriber's uniquely assigned telephone number, which is used for both billing and receiving calls. When a subscriber switches services, the MIN in the phone handset can be changed for a new user, thus reusing the phone. When the ESN is paired with the MIN, the MTSO checks the ESN/MIN combination in order to ensure that it is a valid combination. The control channel transmits this ESN/MIN number to the switch. The MTSO also checks that the phone has not been reported stolen, and that the user's monthly bills have been paid, before putting a call through.

Since these codes are broadcast over the airwaves, a techno criminal can get these codes using a simple scanner purchased at an electronics store. It's so easy to do there are even cell phone hacker Web sites that give equipment-ordering information and detailed instructions on how to clone phones. The criminals first cloned phones using a laptop and some other peripheral equipment. These criminals duplicate the scanned and stolen code on a chip, and install this chip in another phone. The cell phone with the copied chip in it is called a cloned phone. Today, a criminal can obtain a "vampire" phone that actually scans the airwaves for the ESN/MIN itself and automatically programs the number into its own chip. The cloner can then make calls to nearly anywhere, and all the calls will be billed to the current subscriber's account. Only when the valid subscriber receives the enormous bill showing the calls that were not made by that person is the fraud detected. By then, the calls have been placed and the damage is done.

Usually the criminal will steal the numbers from one location and then use the cloned phone outside the victim's service area, thus incurring expensive roaming charges as well. A cloned call in the valid user's service area is simply lost revenue to the carrier, but when the carrier has to pay the roaming charges to other carriers, it becomes a hard, direct cost. In addition to the actual cash expense, fraud has a significant detrimental effect on a subscriber. If the subscriber is a business person who has to change phone numbers due to fraud, the carrier may face the risk of having this steady customer switch carriers, because of dissatisfaction.

OTHER METHODS OF FRAUD

One other method of fraud is "subscription fraud," where a subscriber could walk into a dealer with falsified or stolen information and sign up for wireless service. When the fraudulent subscriber receives his cell phone, he could make, or even sell, as many calls as he wants without paying the bill. The carrier would eventually disconnect the fraudulent subscriber for nonpayment, and it may take two to three months to detect the fraud without clone protection software. However, there is little recourse against the subscriber, since the phone was obtained using a false identity.

There are many other methods of committing fraud in the cell phone industry. Thieves used to be able to take the ESN number off the airwaves and then have a phone that would rotate a series of MIN numbers each time the criminal places a new call. This "tumbling" type of fraud has been all but eliminated due to switches that are more intelligent and wireless protocols that verify that the ESN number being transmitted is the valid match with the MIN number also being reported. In addition, a subscriber's phone could be stolen, and the thief could use the phone at will until the victim reports the crime. A dealer can put through fraudulent sales orders, to build up sales for the quarter, and receive extra incentives from the carrier. Also, technical criminals can hack directly into the carrier network and set up an invalid account for their own illegal use.

COMBATING FRAUD

There are a number of different methods the industry has developed to combat the various types of fraud. The radio frequency signature of the phone being transmitted can be verified by the cell site in the customer's service area, in order to ensure that the phone transmitting the information is the valid subscriber's phone. Phone manufacturers have been adding an authentication chip in each new phone that sends a scrambled code to the switch. The switch descrambles the code and verifies it's a valid number, as well as authenticates the ESN/MIN number. The authentication chip prevents a criminal from scanning the signal and cloning the phone. However, approximately 80 percent of all phones currently do not have the chip, and all carriers would have to recognize the authentication protocol. If a criminal clones a phone in a service area with no authentication standard, the chip is ineffective. The dealers can prevent fraud by implementing a more sophisticated check of a potential subscriber's credit and identification, to verify the person's identity. There are also PIN numbers and voice recognition software that is being tested in limited capacities.

All of the aforementioned fraud prevention techniques are effective in preventing one form of fraud or another. For example, a PIN number is extremely useful against phone theft, but it is completely ineffective against subscription fraud. None of the aforementioned techniques effectively combats all types of fraud. One method that does address all types of cell phone fraud is a "profiler." Coral Systems has built the company through the development of its main product, Fraud-Buster, which is a fraud profiling system.

SPATIAL TECHNOLOGY, INC.

It was late afternoon on Thursday, October 10, 1996, when Richard "Dick" Sowar leaned back in his office chair and tried to organize his thoughts. Only minutes earlier the CEO and founder of Spatial Technology had concluded a phone conference with his vice president of finance, his New York venture capitalist, and his Minneapolis-based investment bank. The phone conference had marked the end of what seemed to be the longest thirty-six hours of Sowar's life. During this time Spatial's investment bankers had tried to solicit a sufficient number of buy orders for the company's initial public offering, which had been scheduled for the following day. Having twice failed to fill the order book, however, the lead investment bank had canceled the IPO. As Spatial's CEO assessed his situation, he recalled the company's founding ten years earlier.

THE ORIGIN OF SPATIAL TECHNOLOGY

After receiving a BS in mathematics from Marietta College and an MS in operations research, Sowar worked at the Air Force Graduate School in Ohio for several years. He then began doctoral studies in computer science at the University of Colorado while working as a research associate at Bell Laboratories and later joined a startup company. Sowar recalled:

> My partner Dave Lehman and I were part of starting up a CAD/CAM company called Graftek in 1980 in Boulder. We were using solid modeling technology from Shape Data Co. in England. I was VP of research and development; Dave Lehman was VP of engineering. Graftek was venture funded and ended up having more than thirty investors. When the Venture people wanted to cash out, Cyrus (Cy) Lynch was brought in to sell the company. Graftek was eventually acquired by Burroughs for $23 million in 1984. Subsequently, the

This entrepreneurship case study was prepared by Professor J. Chris Leach and Research Assistant Thomas Bleyer, as the basis for class discussion and not to illustrate the effective or ineffective handling of an administrative situation.

entrepreneurial nature of Graftek changed and it became a very slow moving company.

With Graftek's culture change, Sowar started to think about how he could pursue his own, somewhat different vision for 3D technology:

I was interested in the applied use of solid modeling, and I had very good contacts with the people at Shape Data Co., among them Dr. Ian Braid, the "father" of solid modeling. The idea when we started Spatial was to make use of Shape Data's modeling technology as a foundation for building a system for machine tool manufacturers: CAM machining software that could automatically drive a machine to cut parts.

I wrote up a little eleven-page white paper to explain the concept. It was far from being a business plan. It basically said: "Hey, this is how we're going to put the technology together and we should make a lot of money off this thing." I think I was fairly convincing in some of the things I talked about in this paper. So I took this little white paper to Cy (who had already left Graftek) in 1985 and asked him, "How do I get money?"

During the search for capital to cold-start the high-tech venture, Sowar and Lehman drew on the connections they had built at Graftek. According to Sowar:

Cy had sold Graftek and he knew the venture capital community, so he introduced me to Fred Nazem, a New York venture capitalist. Fred Nazem got very excited about the idea; he's a technologist at heart, having studied physics and chemistry. He loves technology, but he invests more in people than in the technology. Our advantage was that Fred already knew Cy, Dave, and me, because he had been one of the investors in Graftek. So we managed to work out a deal where he would invest $1 million in the company. At the same time I had set up an arrangement with Ian Braid (who in 1986 had founded his own company, Three Space Ltd.). Three Space Ltd. would become our technology partner to build the 3D modeler on which we would base our applications. We had a handshake in July '86, so Dave and I turned our resignations into Graftek.

With a mission to design, develop, and market 3D modeling software with targeted applications in the machine tool industry, Sowar, Lehman, and Lynch incorporated Spatial later that month in the state of Delaware. Although Spatial was principally located in Boulder, Colorado, the founding president, Lynch, lived in Dallas and commuted to Boulder once or twice a month to take care of the administrative work. Spatial had no difficulties attracting additional talented developers. "We lured five really good technologists away from Graftek. We hadn't approached them before, but I knew that they would be in love with our idea," Sowar said.

The company closed financing in September 1986 with an initial capitalization of $1 million from Nazem & Company (see Exhibit 1). With capital, seven talented developers, strategic development partners at Three Space Ltd. in England, and a plan providing a two-year development process, the startup was set to go.

EXHIBIT 1

Financing History of Spatial Technology

	STARTUP JULY 1986 SHARE PRICE: $0.01			VENTURE ROUND A SEPT. 86 SHARE PRICE: $1.00			VENTURE ROUND B JUNE 89 SHARE PRICE: $3.75			ROUND B WARRANTED SHARES $3.75 EXERCISE PRICE	VENTURE ROUND C APRIL 91 SHARE PRICE: $3.84		
	%	SHARES	$ NEW CAPITAL	%	SHARES (CUMULATIVE)	$ NEW CAPITAL	%	SHARES (CUMULATIVE)	$ NEW CAPITAL	SHARES (F)	%	SHARES (CUMULATIVE)	$ NEW CAPITAL
Total	100.0	440,000	4,400	100.0	1,440,000	1,000,000	100.0	3,408,665	7,300,000		100.0	4,165,956	3,100,000
R. Sowar (Founder)	45.5	200,000	2,000	13.9	200,000		5.9	200,000			4.8	200,000	
D. Lehman (Founder)	45.5	200,000	2,000	13.9	200,000		5.9	200,000			3.6	150,000 (E)	
C. Lynch (Founder)	9.1	40,000	400	2.8	40,000		1.8	62,000 (A)			1.5	62,000	
Nazem & Company				69.4	1,000,000	1,000,000	46.5	1,586,666	2,200,000 (B)		44.3	1,847,083	1,000,000
Benefit Capital							15.6	533,333	2,000,000 (B)		20.0	832,812	1,150,000 (B)
New York Life							5.9	200,000	750,000	30,000 (L)	9.5	395,312	750,000 (B)
Allied Signal							5.9	200,000	750,000		6.1	252,083	750,000 (B)
Hewlett-Packard							12.5	426,666	1,600,000 (B)		10.2	426,666	200,000
Management & Directors													
Total	100.0	440,000	4,400	100.0	1,440,000	1,000,000	100.0	3,408,665	7,300,000	30,000	100.0	4,165,956	3,100,000

All numbers based on common stock

(A) Cyrus Lynch received 10,000 and 12,000 shares as payment for consulting.
(B) Minimal rounding differences (adjustment for stock-splits).
(C) These warrants were never exercised.
(D) Fully exercised.
(E) Dave Lehman had sold 50,000 shares back to the company when he left (at the original price).
(F) No net revenue was collected for the issue of these warrants/options.
(G) Fully exercised in April 1996.
(H) Not exercised as of October 1996.
(I) 15,000 shares (at $3.84 per share) issued to Cy Lynch on 10/08/96 as settlement.
(J) Additional granted warrants exercised by Nazem & Company: 100,000 shares at $0.99 per share, 16,666 at $0.99 per share. 16,667 shares bought directly from John Rowley at $5.25 in August 1993.

(K) 66,666 warranted shares (exercise price $8.22 per share) from series D outstanding and options for 15,000 shares (exercise price $5.00 per share) for Fred Nazem.
(L) Fully exercised in the beginning of October 1996.
(M) Two granted warrants for a total of 43,333 shares (exercise price $8.22 per share).
(N) Options that are exercisable within 60 days of an IPO, granted to the directors and executives of the company through a stock-option plan (various exercise prices) e.g., Dick Sowar: 130,000 shares exercisable at $5.00 and 19,995 shares exercisable at $1.50.

EXHIBIT 1

Financing History of Spatial Technology (continued)

	ROUND C WARRANTED SHARES $3.84 EXERCISE PRICE	VENTURE ROUND D FEB. 93 SHARE PRICE: $8.22			ROUND D WARRANTED SHARES $0.03 EXERCISE PRICE	ADDITIONAL STOCK ISSUES (BETWEEN 03/93 AND 10/96)	ADDITIONAL WARRANT ISSUES (F) (BETWEEN 03/93 AND 10/96)	STATUS OCTOBER 10, 1996 (ACCORDING TO PLANNED IPO PROSPECTUS) FULLY DILUTED SHARE NUMBERS — ASSUMING ALL WARRANTS/OPTIONS HAVE BEEN EXERCISED	
	SHARES (F)	%	SHARES (CUMULATIVE)	$ NEW CAPITAL	SHARES (F)	SHARES	SHARES	SHARES (CUMULATIVE)	%
Total	141,245	100.0	4,499,599	2,742,557	42,915		149,995 (N)	5,502,404	100.0
R. Sowar (Founder)		4.4	200,000					349,995	6.4
D. Lehman (Founder)		3.3	150,000					150,000	2.7
C. Lynch (Founder)		1.4	62,000			15,000 (I)		77,000	1.4
Nazem & Company	83,645 (G)	41.8	1,878,891	261,462	4,091 (D)	133,333 (J)	81,666 (K)	2,181,624	39.6
Benefit Capital	28,103 (C)	21.9	986,285	1,261,551	19,741 (D)			1,006,026	18.3
New York Life	18,345 (G)	11.5	516,966	1,000,001	15,648 (H)		43,333 (M)	624,291	11.3
Allied Signal	11,152 (C)	5.6	252,083					252,083	4.6
Hewlett-Packard		10.1	453,374	219,543	3,435 (D)			456,809	8.3
Management & Directors							404,576 (N)	404,576	7.4
Total	141,245	100.0	4,499,599	2,742,557	42,915	148,333	679,570	5,502,404	100.0

Total per principal & selling stockholder table (fully diluted)   5,502,404 (fully diluted)

Less: Options and warrants included   5,502,404

    −749,054

    consisting of:

Add: Other stockholders (employees—not listed)   434,819

Outstanding stock before planned IPO   5,188,169

Sowar (N)	149,999 (B)
Nazem (K)	81,666
Nazem (D)	4,091
Benefit (D)	19,741
N.Y.L. (M)	58,981
N.Y.L. (L)	30,000
Others (N)	404,576
	749,054

EARLY COMPANY HISTORY

The basis of Spatial's product strategy was to be sophisticated 3D modeling technology. Sowar wanted his partners at Three Space to further develop and enhance the modeling software Spatial planned to license from Shape Data:

> We planned to license the base modeling technology from Shape Data, but by the time we had our financing and everything in place, Shape Data had decided not to license its product anymore. From September '86 to March '87, we had been using almost half of our financing at Spatial to work on our application software. In parallel, we had Three Space evaluating alternative modeling technology, but in March it became clear to us that there wasn't a viable alternative to the Shape Data license. We were almost in a panic.

Finding himself six months behind schedule, Sowar quickly had to change his plans:

> We were able to convince Three Space to develop a modeler for us from scratch. We would fund the development, but we told them that they had to do it in two years. They said they could build the modeler in two years, but they couldn't develop the surface modeling inside in that time frame. So we found surface modeling in Seattle: there were two mathematicians who had broken away from Boeing and started their own company [Applied Geometry], and they licensed their surface modeling to us.
>
> It was May of '87, we had all the partners we needed and all the contracts signed, but had only six months of cash left. And we had already shifted our delivery date back. Fred Nazem had us look for new sources of funding—VCs in Boston mostly, which we met over the summer. But then there was the stock market crash in October 1987; we didn't have any money and the whole VC community stopped investing in new technology companies and shifted their focus on LBOs instead. So, Fred Nazem kept funding us for nearly two more years, until mid-1989 [see Exhibit 2]. By that time, the modeling technology was coming together, the machining software was presentable . . . it was fairly impressive. We had applied for a patent, and we started getting a little press.

EXHIBIT 2   Loan Financing of Spatial Technology

DATE THAT LOAN WAS GIVEN	LOAN PROVIDER	$ AMOUNT	DATE THAT LOAN WAS PAID BACK
End of 1987	Nazem & Company	1,200,000	June 1989, paid back with proceeds of series B financing
1990	Nazem & Company	1,800,000	April 1991, paid back with proceeds of series C financing
1992	Nazem & Company	1,500,000	February 1993, paid back with proceeds of series D financing
November 1993	Autodesk	500,000	February 1996
	Silicon Valley Bank	500,000	January to June 1996

Unfortunately, during the first two development years, the machine tool industry for which Spatial had targeted application software underwent a major crisis. "During 1988 it became clear that our original strategy wasn't going to work because the machine tool industry was in a decline and wasn't investing in anything. They were just trying to keep their companies alive," Sowar said.

Abandoning the original target end-user market, Spatial decided to focus on licensing the 3D modeling technology as its core business. The modeling kernel emerging from two years of internal and partnered development was unrivaled in its technological standards; it held the promise of becoming an industry standard. The change in direction was reflected in the new business model developed by John Rowley, who had joined Spatial as CEO in the summer of 1988. Spatial would license its 3D modeling engine, known as ACIS, to other CAD/CAM software developers who would fold it into end-user applications software, thereby generating revenues in three ways: (1) an initial license fee paid by the software companies, (2) royalty fees on units of end-user software incorporating ACIS, and (3) revenues from customer support for ACIS users.

As Sowar recalled, this shift in the technological focus precipitated Lehman's departure:

> *Dave was a great hardware engineer. That was the primary reason why he was involved at the start of the company. We needed Dave to pursue our original idea of putting our software into the machine tool controls, because he was really good at that sort of stuff. But with our new concept, it turned out that we became totally software focused and Dave didn't have a major role in the company anymore, so he left Spatial in 1990.*

By mid-1989, the first version of the ACIS product was brought to market and gained immediate recognition with initial customers like Hewlett-Packard. Enthusiasm for the company was high and Spatial easily obtained additional funding to bring its product to market and begin building an infrastructure. Nazem & Company, some of the limited partners of the Nazem Funds (Benefit Capital, New York Life, Allied Signal), and Hewlett-Packard invested in the next round (series B) of venture financing (see Exhibit 1).

With its open design, ACIS had the potential to provide core 3D modeling capability for numerous commercial CAD software applications on a variety of platforms. Although ACIS was quickly embraced by universities and the research community, convincing its potential key customers to rely fully on ACIS was more difficult. Companies like Shape Data (a subsidiary of Electronic Data Systems), Ricoh, and, in many cases, the customers' own in-house modeling platforms competed with the adoption of ACIS. In order to convince important customers (including Bentley Systems, CDC, Intergraph, and Hitachi-Zosen) to commit to ACIS, and to improve the quarterly cash flows, Spatial offered a somewhat unusual licensing agreement. The company began to sell an ACIS license to targeted customers for a one-time lump sum that included a specific level of prepaid but heavily discounted royalty fees. These prepaid royalty deals (see Exhibit 3) were a key element in the company's revenue streams from 1990 to 1993.

Despite the accelerated revenues provided by prepaid royalties, overall cash flow was not yet positive. An additional round of venture financing (round C)

EXHIBIT 3   Prepaid Royalties Collected by Spatial Technology

YEAR	PREPAID ROYALTIES $ AMOUNT COLLECTED	FACE VALUE OF REVENUES (AT LIST PRICES)
1991	300,000	
1992	2,600,000	
1993	1,500,000	
1994	400,000	
Total	4,800,000	7,200,000

was needed and executed in April of 1991 (see Exhibit 1). With its investors reluctant to supply more capital, and an increasing industry presence, Spatial considered an IPO in 1992. Sowar said:

> We had some pretty impressive licensees, and in terms of technology, we were the darlings of the industry. The CAD/CAM world used to be very conservative and slow moving and closed . . . a bunch of closed systems. And here was Spatial, professing open modeling, and sharing, and passing models from one system to the other . . . we were sort of a breath of fresh air. So we generated a lot of interest in the company, we were getting a lot of press. We were also building up a potential royalty stream that was very attractive. And that's why the investment bankers got interested in us. They saw that we did have a good customer base, we had the technology, and we had the leading developers. Also, at that time object-oriented programming was coming into vogue, and we'd been doing it for years. We were in all the leading universities and research institutions like Stanford, MIT, the Fraunhofer-Institute in Germany, the University of Tokyo, and so on. . . . ACIS was the up and coming thing.

The IPO, planned for the end of 1992, was called off, however, when the investment bankers found several reasons to back out. Apparently, investors believed that Spatial's management team was not broad enough. Rowley, then CEO, was perceived to control the entire business side of the company. Although he had remarkable success in selling ACIS's promise, his aggressive style was an issue for some customers and investors. In addition, customers complained that the core ACIS product was still not stable enough for them to ship their ACIS-based applications. Consequently, revenue projections were not met. Spatial's customer relations became even more strained when the company announced a new product called Personal ACIS, aimed at the lower-end PC market. According to Sowar:

> People in the industry loved the product [Personal ACIS] when we demonstrated it in November 1992, but our customers were furious. They essentially said, "We paid you all this money to develop a product [core ACIS] that still isn't stable enough for us to use and you turn around and start chasing the low-end PC market for which your technology is sufficient. . . . You screwed us!" Our customers hated us for this initiative. They thought we would make

all this money on the PC market and stop developing the sophisticated model-
ing product they needed from us. They thought we totally screwed them, be-
cause they couldn't shift their focus and develop the modeler on their own.
We did a terrible job of communicating with our customers.

The controversy peaked at the end of 1992 with a public announcement that
Autodesk, Spatial's largest customer, was dropping ACIS. Sowar continued:

Not surprisingly, upon completion of their due diligence, our investment
bankers ended up saying that it was too early for an IPO. They thought our
company was poisoned: the product was not stable enough, our customers
hated us, and they were beginning to question John as the CEO. I don't
think anybody doubted that we had the right technology, but you invest
more in people than in technology and we were told that we didn't have the
right management team. So the investment bankers just withdrew and said,
"Let's wait."

A subsequent attempt by the company to arrange a private placement with
the help of Donaldson, Lufkin & Jenrette failed because of the high valuation
Spatial was seeking. Despite the critical situation, Spatial's management was able
to convince its existing investors to put up another round of capital. In the beginning of 1993, John Rowley (CEO) and Kevin Walsh, who was Spatial's CFO at
the time, negotiated a fourth round of venture financing. The preferred stock series D (see Exhibit 1) was priced at $8.22 per share, indicating a $45 million valuation of the company.

As a consequence of the feedback from the investment bankers, the board of
Spatial Technology began looking for industry people to fill out Spatial's management team. During the second quarter of 1993, eight new managers were
hired (see Exhibit 4). Dick Sowar recalled that John Rowley took issue with the
new management structure:

We rounded out the team and had individual executives running each of the
different functions and John became lost. He was a real entrepreneur-type
CEO who liked to have his hands in everything. It got really hard for him to
handle the fact that he had other people underneath him running things he
liked to do day to day.

The new management team, in opposition to the CEO, also wanted to drop
Personal ACIS in order to rekindle the relationships with larger customers. As
the opinions and management styles continued to diverge, Spatial and Rowley
parted ways in July 1993. Dick Sowar and Chuck Bay (then CFO) were in
charge.

AFTER THE RESTRUCTURING

Rebuilding customer relationships in the reorganized Spatial became a priority.
A major step in the process was the decision to drop Personal ACIS and convince
customers that all development efforts would focus on stabilizing the core ACIS
product. The sincere refocusing and numerous hours with industry contacts and

EXHIBIT 4   Management and Personnel Development

Name	1986	1987	1988	1989	1990	1991	1992	1993	1994	1995	1996
Richard Sowar (Founder)	VP & Treasurer		VP					Senior VP Technology	Chief Executive Officer		
Dave Lehman (Founder)	VP of Technology										
Cy Lynch (Founder)	Pres. & CEO										
Mike Schuhmacher		Pres. & CEO									
Kathy Cunningham			CFO								
Jim Feenstra			VP Mktg								
John Rowley			CEO								
Doug Hakala				ACIS Development							
Kevin Walsh						COO | CFO					
Denny Chrismer							Worldwide Sales				
Ricardo Fuchs								Japan Sales			
Chuck Bay							CFO | President				
Ron Belcher									VP of Development		
Jerry Sisson								VP US Sales	President and COO		
Mark Vellequette								Controller	Dir. of Fnce. | CFO		
Ronald Davidson								VP Pacific Rim Sales			
Karlheinz Peters								VP European Sales			
Bruce Morgan					Consultant to Spatial				VP US Sales		
John Einberger											VP Bus. Dvlp.
David Sefton											VP US Sales

media helped rebuild ACIS's ailing reputation. Autodesk, the highest-volume CAD software producer, returned as a customer in the middle of 1993. In 1994, the development efforts started to pay off, as ACIS became stable enough for Spatial's customers to ship their ACIS-enabled applications. Financially, however, times were rough. Dropping the Personal ACIS product had resulted in significant overstaffing in sales. Management decided to lay off 25 percent of the entire work force in September 1993. In addition, by the end of 1993, Chuck Bay and Mark Vellequette (then corporate controller) had written down accounts receivables by $1 million to eliminate the inflated (recognized) revenue related to marginal deals that never materialized. The overall result of the restructuring was a loss of $3 million (see Exhibits 5a, 5b, and 5c).

Mark Vellequette, who became vice president of finance at the end of 1994 after Chuck Bay had left the company, described the situation:

Nineteen ninety-three was a rough year and we had to work our way back from there. It's been hard. In November '93, we got Autodesk, one of our largest customers, to loan us half a million dollars as part of a larger deal, and at the same time we pulled half a million from an existing credit line at Silicon Valley Bank (see Exhibit 2). But cash was still extremely tight; the loan was barely enough to keep us going.

As the new management worked on stabilizing the product and the revenue streams, the restructuring and settlement of outstanding bills stressed Spatial's cash reserves. Vellequette said:

When I got here in July 1993 we had an outstanding legal bill over $200,000 for the failed 1992 IPO, the private placement efforts by DLJ, and the series D arrangement. Our company had effectively only collected $1.2 million from the series D and they hadn't even paid the lawyers. So then we had to deal with them and stretched their payment out into '94. . . . It was just a nightmare. In addition, we had an employment lawsuit with a former Spatial vice president who had left in August 1993. He had sued us for everything under the sun, which seems to be the American way . . . and we lost. As a result, the company got slapped with a $419,000 judgment in the beginning of 1995. That means we had huge legal bills we were paying throughout 1994 and in 1995. But the management pretty much turned it around in a year and got things stabilized. Operationally, we were doing OK. We started turning a profit in Q3 1994, but we still had to pay off all that old crap and we wanted to keep investing in new technology, so we were dying for cash all the way to 1996 (see Exhibit 6 on page 676). I remember that at the end of Q4/95 we had one week of cash left. So basically on New Year's Day 1996 I woke up with a hangover and cash to get me 'til Friday.

According to Vellequette, the remarkable valuation of the series D offering in February 1993 had some unintended consequences:

After this round D in 1993 we had to lay off people, we were out of cash, it was hell. And we couldn't go out and easily raise capital because all these venture financing rounds have a so-called antidilution trigger. So if you

EXHIBIT 5a Income Statements

| | YEAR ENDED DECEMBER 31, | | | | | SIX MONTHS ENDED JUNE 30, | |
	1991	1992	1993	1994	1995	1995	1996
	(IN THOUSANDS, EXCEPT PER SHARE DATA)						
Statements of Operations Data							
Revenue							
License fees	$ 4,731	$ 3,528	$ 3,687	$ 3,087	$4,850	$2,386	$2,348
Royalties	—	85	562	876	1,207	627	1,228
Prepaid royalties	250	2,571	1,475	448	—	—	—
Maintenance and training	748	1,341	1,657	2,137	2,572	1,273	1,461
Total revenue	5,729	7,525	7,381	6,548	8,629	4,286	5,037
Cost of sales	873	1,364	1,150	705	677	299	403
Gross profit	4,856	6,161	6,231	5,843	7,952	3,987	4,634
Operating expenses							
Sales and marketing	2,411	2,907	3,220	2,710	2,942	1,506	1,674
Research and development	2,499	2,770	3,843	3,166	3,123	1,495	1,913
General and administrative	1,016	1,851	1,776	950	1,210	660	767
Severance costs	—	—	300	—	—	—	—
Total operating expenses	5,926	7,528	9,139	6,826	7,275	3,661	4,354
Earnings (loss) from operations	(1,070)	(1,367)	(2,908)	(983)	677	326	280
Other expense, net	(52)	(19)	(61)	(42)	(115)	(30)	(51)
Earnings (loss) before income taxes and extraordinary items	(1,122)	(1,386)	(2,969)	(1,025)	562	296	229
Income tax expense (1)	—	25	42	137	174	97	45
Earnings (loss) before extraordinary item	(1,122)	(1,411)	(3,011)	(1,162)	388	199	184
Extraordinary item (2)	—	—	—	298	—	—	—
Net earnings (loss)	$(1,122)	$(1,411)	$(3,011)	$ (864)	$ 388	$ 199	$ 184

Source: Spatial Technology Prospectus

EXHIBIT 5a Income Statements (continued)

| | | | | | THREE MONTHS ENDED | | | | | |
| | MAR. 31, 1994 | JUN. 30, 1994 | SEP. 30, 1994 | DEC. 31, 1994 | MAR. 31, 1995 | JUN. 30, 1995 | SEP. 30, 1995 | DEC. 31, 1995 | MAR. 31, 1996 | JUN. 30, 1996 |
					(IN THOUSANDS)					
Revenue										
License fees	$ 390	$ 835	$ 909	$ 953	$1,212	$1,174	$1,173	$1,291	$ 951	$1,397
Royalties	127	302	228	219	338	289	234	346	718	510
Prepaid royalties	100	98	—	250	—	—	—	—	—	—
Maintenance and training	288	539	669	641	649	624	652	647	716	745
Total revenue	905	1,774	1,806	2,063	2,199	2,087	2,059	2,284	2,385	2,652
Cost of sales	158	177	143	227	155	144	222	156	232	171
Gross profit	747	1,597	1,663	1,836	2,044	1,943	1,837	2,128	2,153	2,481
Operating expenses										
Sales and marketing	552	650	647	861	776	730	684	752	735	939
Research and development	852	790	635	889	745	750	796	832	935	978
General and administrative	288	217	238	207	409	251	256	294	330	437
Total operating expenses	1,692	1,657	1,520	1,957	1,930	1,731	1,736	1,878	2,000	2,354
Earnings (loss) from operations	(945)	(60)	143	(121)	114	212	101	250	153	127
Other expense, net	(20)	(8)	(13)	(1)	(11)	(19)	(12)	(73)	(30)	(21)
Earnings (loss) before income taxes and extraordinary item	(965)	(68)	130	(122)	103	193	89	177	123	106
Income tax expense	0	36	8	93	51	46	18	59	64	(19)
Earnings (loss) before extraordinary item	(965)	(104)	122	(215)	52	147	71	118	59	125
Extraordinary item—gain on early extinguishment of debt	—	—	—	298	—	—	—	—	—	—
Net earnings (loss)	$ (965)	$ (104)	$ 122	$ 83	$ 52	$ 147	$ 71	$ 118	$ 59	$ 125

Source: Spatial Technology Prospectus

EXHIBIT 5b   Balance Sheets

SPATIAL TECHNOLOGY INC. AND SUBSIDIARIES
CONSOLIDATED BALANCE SHEETS
(AMOUNTS IN THOUSANDS, EXCEPT SHARES)

ASSETS

	DECEMBER 31,		JUNE 30,	PRO FORMA (1) JUNE 30,
	1994	1995	1996 (UNAUDITED)	1996 (UNAUDITED)
Current assets				
Cash and cash equivalents	$ 288	$ 153	$ 390	
Accounts receivable, net of allowance of $102, $34, and $94 in 1994, 1995, and 1996, respectively	1,742	1,893	2,293	
Prepaid expenses and other	185	179	171	
Total current assets	2,215	2,225	2,854	
Equipment, net	256	377	373	
Purchased computer software, net	292	246	410	
	$ 2,763	$ 2,848	$ 3,637	

LIABILITIES AND STOCKHOLDERS' DEFICIT

	DECEMBER 31,		JUNE 30,	PRO FORMA (1) JUNE 30,
	1994	1995	1996 (UNAUDITED)	1996 (UNAUDITED)
Current liabilities				
Notes payable	$ —	$ 500	$ —	
Accounts payable	279	585	410	
Accrued royalties payable	286	455	398	
Other accrued expenses	1,130	848	1,231	
Deferred revenue	1,726	1,220	1,779	
Total current liabilities	3,421	3,608	3,818	
Notes payable	500	—	—	
Total liabilities	3,921	3,608	3,818	
Mandatory redeemable convertible preferred stock, $.01 par value; 7,566,324 shares authorized; 6,381,473 shares issued and outstanding; liquidation preference of $14,154,550	14,155	14,155	14,155	—
Stockholders' deficit				
Common stock, $.01 par value; 20,000,000 shares authorized; 1,023,208, 1,060,791, and 1,088,571 shares issued in 1994, 1995, and 1996, respectively (5,188,169 shares pro forma)	10	11	11	52
Additional paid-in capital	143	183	419	14,533
Accumulated deficit	(15,260)	(14,872)	(14,688)	(14,688)
Treasury stock at cost; 250,000 shares of common stock	(176)	(176)	—	—
Foreign currency translation adjustment	(30)	(61)	(78)	(78)
Total stockholders' deficit	(15,313)	(14,915)	(14,336)	(181)
Commitments and contingency	$ 2,763	$ 2,848	$ 3,637	

EXHIBIT 5c   Cash Flow Statements

SPATIAL TECHNOLOGY INC. AND SUBSIDIARIES
CONSOLIDATED STATEMENTS OF CASH FLOWS
(AMOUNTS IN THOUSANDS)

	YEARS ENDED DECEMBER 31,			SIX MONTHS ENDED JUNE 30,	
	1993	1994	1995	1995	1996
				(UNAUDITED)	
Cash flows from operating activities					
Net earnings (loss)	$(3,011)	$ (864)	$ 388	$ 199	$ 184
Adjustments to reconcile net earnings (loss) to net cash provided (used) by operating activities					
Extraordinary item—gain on early extinguishment of debt	—	(298)	—	—	—
Depreciation and amortization	317	267	174	87	115
Common stock issued for services	4	4	—	—	20
Interest accrued on conversion of stockholder notes	7	—	—	—	—
Changes in operating assets and liabilities					
Accounts receivable	—	142	(151)	212	(400)
Prepaid expenses and other	81	(43)	6	47	8
Accounts payable	(51)	(117)	306	63	(175)
Accrued expenses	410	32	(113)	(141)	326
Deferred revenue	997	(8)	(506)	(119)	559
Net cash provided (used) by operating activities	(1,246)	(885)	104	348	637
Cash flows from investing activities					
Additions to equipment	(238)	(2)	(249)	(64)	(75)
Additions to purchased computer software	—	(210)	—	—	(200)
Net cash used by investing activities	(238)	(212)	(249)	(64)	(275)
Cash flows from financing activities					
Principal payments on notes payable and capital leases	(166)	(501)	(100)	—	(725)
Proceeds from exercise of common stock options and warrants	60	4	41	3	392
Proceeds from notes payable	2,200	100	100	—	225
Proceeds from issuance of preferred stock, net	1,202	—	—	—	—
Purchase of treasury stock	(175)	—	—	—	—
Net cash provided (used) by financing activities	3,121	(397)	41	3	(108)
Foreign currency translation adjustment affecting cash	—	(30)	(31)	4	(17)
Net increase (decrease) in cash and cash equivalents	1,637	(1,524)	(135)	291	237
Cash and cash equivalents at beginning of period	175	1,812	288	288	153
Cash and cash equivalents at end of period	$ 1,812	$ 288	$ 153	$ 579	$ 390
Supplemental disclosures					
Cash paid for interest	$ 34	$ 71	$ 76	$ 20	$ 29
Cash paid for income taxes	$ 42	$ 83	$ 127	$ 101	$ 91

Source: Spatial Technology Prospectus

EXHIBIT 6   Cash Reserves at Quarter's End

QUARTER	1/93	2/93	3/93	4/93	1/94	2/94	3/94	4/94
Weeks of cash left at end	12	10	1	9	5	4	5	2

QUARTER	1/95	2/95	3/95	4/95	1/96	2/96
Weeks of cash left at end	2	4	1	1	2	2

Calculation = Cash/(Cost of Sales + Expenses)

Source: Spatial Technology

---

closed a subsequent round of financing at below $8.22 per share, you would have to make an equity adjustment to the series D because it was priced above that. And since there was strong reluctance to get into the whole anti-dilution issue, you always had this floor on the valuation of the company. Yet on the investors' side we were told that there was no way in hell that they would invest any more for $8.22 per share. They would invest, but only at a much lower price. So it seemed good in the beginning of 1993 to have this high valuation . . . it would be fine if it were the last round of financing you'd ever need. But if you ever needed to go back for more money, then it was going to be a real problem. And for us it was, indeed, a real problem.

TIME TO GO PUBLIC

To support the strategic goal of having ACIS adopted as an industry standard for 3D modeling, Spatial made the radical move of publishing the ACIS file format (called SAT) in mid-1996. As prepaid revenues were depleted and development problems continued, Spatial sought new revenue sources. Spatial's president (from April 1994) Jerry Sisson explained:

You have to keep in mind that the license fee for ACIS is a one-time payment. All of our big customers had paid us the license fee years ago. Today we are looking at annualizing that license fee, but so far all of them are initial one-time payments. That's why the license fee revenue doesn't really grow rapidly over the years. The theory is that we wouldn't have to collect a lot of license fees because once our customers start shipping their ACIS based products, the increasing royalty revenues come in. But guess what happened: it took our customers a lot longer to bring their products to market than what they told us. People said they were going to build a product in a year. It took Autodesk two and a half years. It took Bentley Systems almost two years to get their product to the marketplace. So we were not receiving as much royalty revenue as forecast.

Since the dropping of Personal ACIS in 1993, the company had continued to seek a product that could be sold to customers other than those in the market for mechanical CAD. Sisson said:

Dick Sowar always writes a column in our company newspaper, and in one 1996 issue he came out with this comment about how we were going to expand into other markets. Immediately, we had one of our major customers on the phone, saying, "What the hell are you doing?" That's because our traditional marketplace always wanted to put us in a box; they wanted us to stick with our traditional CAD/CAM stuff that we built for them. The only time an established customer like that one would listen to me is when I said, "Yes, sir, but when was the last time you sent me a check? We have $600,000 worth of prepaid royalties from you, so I'm not going to see a check there. You haven't bought a product from me since the initial license acquisition. How am I supposed to run the company if I don't find other people to buy my products? I'm not going to get any more money from you."

To leverage its ACIS 3D modeling technology, make it easier to use, expand to new markets, and broaden the use of ACIS-based applications, the company developed a new product called 3D Building Blox. 3D Building Blox was targeted at visual programming developers in the rapidly growing 3D markets such as virtual reality, animation, architecture, entertainment, filmmaking, and Internet applications. The commercial rollout of the product was scheduled for the first quarter of 1997, and it was to be packaged and delivered to developers as an ActiveX control. The company believed 3D Building Blox would not compete with the ACIS 3D Toolkit (the core product) since it would not allow direct access to the modeling engine and would have a reduced set of procedural interfaces, limiting the functionality to those procedures appropriate for the visual programming market. (See Exhibits 7a and 7b.)

An excerpt from the product description said:

3D Building Blox enables developers to create 3D models using basic geometry construction and will provide the ability to import and export models generated by other applications built using the company's 3D modeling software ACIS. The product also supports real-time rendering, texture mapping, and model manipulation and will include capabilities such as virtual walkthroughs and animation. The product is delivered with several sample applications that serve as templates for basic modeling, rendering and object manipulation functions, and easing application development.

Throughout 1995 and 1996 the software market greatly increased the attention given to 3D products. Market leaders like Microsoft and Intel started to target the 3D market (graphics applications) and press coverage became more and more enthusiastic. Spatial's management was convinced that, just as sound cards had become a standard in almost any PC in the beginning of the 1990s, the next three to five years would see the standard PC become 3D enabled with a graphics accelerator (see Exhibit 8 on page 681).

As management anticipated these market developments in 1995, Spatial seemed to be, once again, in a critical situation. Cash reserves were either extremely tight or nonexistent. To establish ACIS as the industry standard and introduce Building Blox to the emerging 3D markets, the company had to expand

---

EXHIBIT 7a   Technology and Product

3D modeling refers to the ability to create and modify 3D objects on a computer and manipulate those objects by moving, sizing, rotating, stretching, intersecting, and performing other operations on them. 3D solid modeling uses mathematical definitions of edges, surfaces, and volumes and, in addition, may integrate other physical attributes such as density, hardness, dimensions, and light reflectance to model an object. As a result, 3D applications employing solid models incorporate more accurate, lifelike, and intuitive modeling capabilities than other modeling technologies.

Spatial's 3D modeling software incorporates a solid modeling engine and component extensions. The company's core product, the ACIS 3D modeling engine, is used for the creation, definition, and manipulation of 3D shapes, while the component extensions enhance the modeling engine and provide optional functionalities. In 1994, Spatial introduced the ACIS 3D Toolkit, which includes a suite of component extensions packaged with the modeling engine. This packaging allows developers to quickly produce prototype applications, greatly reducing their development costs and time to market.

Spatial's 3D modeling software is designed as an open, component-based software technology that is compatible with a variety of platforms. Open architecture allows applications developers to integrate the ACIS 3D modeling engine and component extensions to mix and match "best of breed" applications and tools in order to better address the requirements of specific markets, products, and applications. Open architecture also allows end users to share 3D models generated with different ACIS-based applications.

ACIS COMPONENT-BASED APPLICATIONS

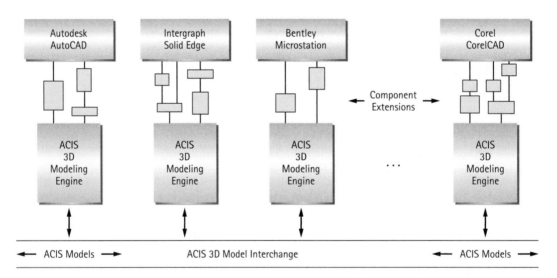

ACIS 3D Modeling Engine

The ACIS 3D modeling engine enables solid, surface, and wire-frame modeling in a single modeling environment. The ACIS 3D modeling engine uses a solid modeling technique known as analytic and spline-based modeling, which is a means of precisely representing the characteristics of a 3D model using mathematical definitions of edges, surfaces, and volumes and, in addition, may integrate other physical attributes such as density, hardness, dimensions, and light reflectance. This technique offers greater precision than competing 3D modeling techniques, such as wire-frame and surface modeling techniques, and is better at producing complex objects with smooth flowing lines, resulting in richer, more robust models. The completeness of ACIS 3D solid models allows software applications to calculate other attributes such as strength, center of gravity, mass, flexibility, and momentum. As a result, 3D applications employing ACIS 3D models can incorporate lifelike and intuitive operations for building and manipulating 3D shapes. In addition, because the ACIS 3D modeling engine defines 3D shapes using mathematical formulas, the resulting 3D models have relatively compact data requirements for transmission of rich 3D content, which, Spatial believes, provides it with significant competitive advantages for low bandwidth environments such as intranets and the Internet.

EXHIBIT 7a Technology and Product (continued)

ACIS 3D Toolkit

The ACIS 3D Toolkit has been designed for rapid, low-cost development of 3D applications and is currently the primary packaging for delivery of the ACIS 3D modeling engine. The ACIS 3D Toolkit consists of the ACIS 3D modeling engine and a suite of component extensions that make it easy to create, manipulate, visualize, and interact with 3D models and develop prototype applications. Component extensions include geometry construction, which facilitates the creation of geometric shapes; graphical interaction, a graphical user interface for modeling; and basic rendering, which applies shading, coloring, and other visual features to the model. The componentry of the ACIS 3D Toolkit provides a powerful LISP-based scripting language allowing Spatial's customers to quickly create and prototype ACIS-based 3D applications. Applications developers may also utilize an Applications Procedural Interface and direct C++ access to integrate the functionality of the ACIS 3D modeling software directly into their 3D applications. The ACIS 3D Toolkit has also been designed to enable developers to integrate common graphical user interface (GUI) tools into their ACIS-based 3D applications. The company offers its customers development licenses for the ACIS 3D Toolkit that range in price depending on the range of functionality and distribution rights. Optional maintenance services, including product updates, are available for an annual fee. In addition, most licensees are required by their license agreements to pay royalties typically based on a percentage of the net revenue generated by their sales of applications incorporating ACIS-based products.

Optional Component Extensions

In addition to the component extensions packaged with the ACIS 3D Toolkit, Spatial offers a series of optional component extensions that increase the functionality of the ACIS 3D Toolkit. Spatial's introduction of new component extensions allows it to market new products to new and existing customers. The open architecture of the ACIS 3D modeling technology also enables licensees to integrate additional functionality through independently developed ACIS-compatible component extensions. Optional component extensions are priced separately from the ACIS 3D Toolkit. Examples of component extensions recently released by the company include advanced blending, deformable surfaces, local operations, mesh surfaces, and shelling.

---

its development, support, and sales operations. Therefore, Spatial desperately needed to raise new capital.

In addition, the pressure from Spatial's investors to find an exit strategy increased. Venture capitalist Fred Nazem had been in this investment for nine years. One of his funds owning Spatial shares was already being extended on a yearly basis. Faced with the valuation of series D in 1993 and the resulting antidilution clause issues, the board of directors seriously considered selling the firm in May 1995. They employed Broadview Associates to find suitable buyers. Although the company met with representatives of Silicon Graphics, Microsoft, Intel, and a number of other firms, none were interested in buying at the price Spatial's investors demanded, about $50 million.

In October 1995, the board decided to renew its attempts at an initial public offering. Spatial's IPO plans immediately generated significant interest in the investment banking community, and the early 1996 IPO market was hot. Spatial's management began to look at a number of investment banks and many of them traveled to Boulder for interviews. Numerous banks showed enthusiasm for the company's technology, its position in the CAD/CAM market, and the expansion plans for the 3D markets. In addition, by the end of 1995, Spatial had six profitable quarters in a row. Vellequette recalled:

We went through and interviewed a number of investment banks, had them come out and explain what their strengths are. You try to make sure that they can understand what you do, so that they could adequately represent

EXHIBIT 7b Technology and Product Development

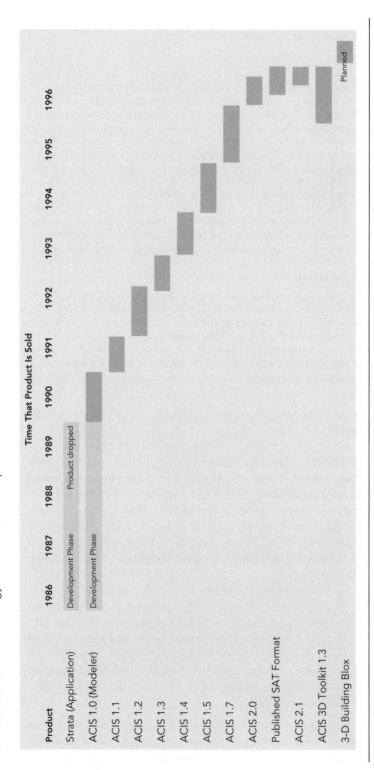

EXHIBIT 8	Sales Projections for 3D-Enabled PCs					
YEAR	1995	1996	1997	1998	1999	2000
Units sold (in millions)	0.4	6	30	76	89	102

Source: Spatial Technology (Road Show Presentation)

Spatial to their customers and explain why our company would be a good investment. You also want to look at what their customer bases are. Some banks are stronger in retail, others are stronger with institutional investors, some have a regional strength, and so on. So you're looking for some diversity there. But I think the really big thing is that they have to understand what you do. We had some investment bankers come in here where it was clear at the end of the day that they didn't understand our technology. We make a very technical product; it can be very difficult to grasp, but that's what these investment bankers do for a living; they're supposed to come in and understand what you do. These analysts supposedly had some familiarity with the sector we are in . . . but we've had people think we're a graphics company, we've had people think we make hardware, we had others thinking we make software applications . . . and so on. With one of them, even after two or three times here, it was clear they wouldn't get it. Some of the times it was just a particular analyst . . . but if the analyst that you were going to sign to didn't get it, how was this person supposed to explain to the investment bank's sales force, let alone their customers, what we did? It would never happen . . . if this person was going to write the research we'd be dead. So we went through that whole process. Most of the investment bankers came back and, especially because they were all so busy, a number of them said, "We think it's too early" . . . which was a very legitimate concern for Spatial in 1996. Some of the investment banks we eliminated, because we didn't think they'd ever get it and we didn't want to be their guinea pig. Others I think were simply too busy. And then there were others that were really aggressive, saying, "Spatial, you are in our sweet spot: you're a small cap company, you're a high-tech company, that's what we do!"

Even though a number of investment banks said they thought it was too early (and, in the case of J.P. Morgan, even offered bridge financing to postpone the IPO), Spatial's board and management decided that the market still offered a good opportunity to take the company public in mid-1996. In May 1996, the board made the decision to accept the offers of the investment bank's Dain Bosworth as lead underwriter and Cruttenden Roth as comanager (see Exhibit 9).

However, as Spatial and Dain Bosworth were preparing the IPO, "the market absolutely tanked," Vellequette said, in July 1996. The subsequent uncertainty in a nervous market led the underwriters to believe an IPO in August or September would be too risky. They decided to postpone the offering until the beginning of October. Finally, Sowar and Vellequette began their long and exhausting road show in mid-September. According to Vellequette:

We went out and Dick and I traveled for what seemed to be forever. We did a couple of weeks of dry runs with Nazem in New York, Dain Bosworth in Minneapolis, and Cruttenden Roth in Irvine. One round of dry runs was three days of travel. So we did that a couple of times and then started marketing the deal around the 20th of September. We went out and did the East Coast for a week (September 23–27) and then went over to the West Coast (September 30–October 4) and got caught up at the Montgomery Technology Conference, which is one of the key technology conferences. We couldn't get time to present at Montgomery, yet all the institutional investors we wanted to talk to were there. So we did some presentations (up to eight on a single day) in L.A., in Houston, and some in the Bay Area. We went back out to the West Coast the next week (October 7–9) to catch some more of those people we couldn't get the first time. After that we went to Minneapolis to get a couple of people we hadn't talked to there. Those were crazy weeks.

The final pricing was to take place on Wednesday, October 9, 1996, at Dain Bosworth's office in Minneapolis. Sowar's reflection was:

Mark and I were at Dain Bosworth in Minneapolis, with Fred Nazem on the phone, and the Dain guys were calling their investors, soliciting the orders. We wanted to sell 2.1 million shares and they wanted an overallotment of 2.4 million. We were sitting at about 2 million shares at $9–$11 . . . and then, all of a sudden, they said, "We're not going to be able to close this book." It just went silent in the room. You could have heard a pin drop. I said: "You have got to be kidding me! We went through all this stuff and you're telling me this thing is off?" And they didn't know what to say. I'll never forget this. I mean for five weeks I couldn't go anywhere without someone with white gloves holding open the door to a limousine and all of a sudden no one in there even wanted to talk with me. I'll never forget the irony of this: the deal went soft, and they just forgot about everything we had talked about. I think they were just embarrassed. I ended up walking two blocks to a hotel so I could get a cab to the airport.

Mark Vellequette tried to explain what had happened from his point of view:

When the investment bank sales force gets on the phones and tries to put the book together that means they're soliciting the orders from their customers. We were originally selling 2.1 million shares and they generally want a book that is "3x," so they want orders for around 6 million. That's because of simple investor psychology: if you ask for 100,000 shares of Spatial and you get 100,000 shares, then it's a bad deal. But if you can't get everything you wanted, it must be a hot deal. It seems totally perverse, but that's just the way the psychology works. They also want a strong aftermarket. As soon as it goes public they want buy orders in there; they want it to seem desirable and precious and rare.

One of the comments I've heard was that, when the sales force was still soliciting orders at $9–$11, all the potential investors wanted to know who else is going to the party. They all wanted to know who the other buyers are and who's in for 10 percent (of the shares). Observing which other investors

EXHIBIT 9   Dain Bosworth Offer Letter

April 22, 1996

Mr. Fred F. Nazem
Managing General Partner
Nazem & Company
645 Madison 12th Floor
New York, NY 10022

RECEIVED
APR 23 1996
FRED F. NAZEM

Dear Mr. Nazem:

Dain Bosworth is pleased to present you with our proposal regarding the initial public offering of Spatial Technology. Our due diligence meetings with Dick Sowar, Jerry Sisson, and Mark Vellequette have convinced us that Spatial is in the midst of terrific growth and is well positioned for continued financial and strategic progress in 1996, 1997, and beyond. The purpose of this letter is to confirm our interest in serving as the lead manager in Spatial's initial public offering and to set forth our preliminary recommendation on structure, valuation, and timing.

First, however, we want to emphasize our software analyst's enthusiasm for Spatial and the industry in which it operates. Barry Randall, who joined us in 1995, has selected 3D graphics and CAD as a specific focus of research. Spatial Technology would be an excellent addition to his research coverage. Specifically, Barry highlights Spatial's combination of leading-edge 3D technology, the "free" leverage provided by enormous Visual Basic marketplace and an existing core modeling business that is growing and already profitable. Barry has met with some of Spatial's key developers and is comfortable with the company's aggressive technology strategy. Barry's prior experience as a software developer for NASA and his investment research experience with software tools companies enhance both his technical and financial strengths. These experiences also give him the ability to effectively communicate Spatial's strategy to investors.

We consider Barry to be one of our best analysts at Dain Bosworth. We hope that you have had a chance to speak with Dick to confirm Barry's understanding of Spatial and his knowledge of 3D and software in general. Furthermore, Barry would welcome an opportunity to speak with you personally about his prior background as a software developer and also how he intends to position Spatial with investors.

As we have stressed to Dick, Jerry, and Mark, Dain Bosworth views the initial public offering as the first step in building a long-term relationship. We have focused the firm's institutional and retail sales, trading, and research efforts to provide the finest possible underwriting service and strength in the aftermarket. Furthermore, Barry is not asked to cover as many companies as is numerically possible; rather, he is highly selective in his coverage in order to provide investors high quality, in-depth research in the aftermarket.

From a timing perspective, there is some merit to marketing the offering to investors in either the fourth quarter of 1996 or the first quarter of 1997 as a result of the anticipated financial performance of Spatial's Web strategy. However, we believe that the equity markets would be very receptive to a Spatial Technology offering at the present time. We unreservedly like the Spatial growth strategy and wish to manage the offering whenever you choose to access the market. Outlined below is our recommendation for an offering assuming a third quarter 1996 pricing off of Spatial's June 30, 1996, financial results.

Preliminary Structure and Valuation

In determining valuation and structure, we have analyzed a variety of financial and market related information. We believe that the public marketplace will value the Spatial investment opportunity using multiple parameters, including revenue, price-to-earnings, and P/E-to-growth rate multiples. Our assumptions for the IPO are as follows:

1. We assumed that a $20 million offering is completed in the third calendar quarter of 1996 and that the offering will include at least 25 percent secondary shares. In addition, we reverse split the outstanding shares in order to achieve an offering price in the range of $10 to $12 per share.

2. Owing to the assumed timing of the offering, we valued Spatial based on projected pro forma forward four quarters and calendar 1997 revenue and earnings and P/E-to-growth rate multiples. Furthermore, we very conservatively assumed that the net proceeds of the offering to Spatial are invested to generate a 5 percent return. This investment income was applied as additional income to the projections that were provided to us.

continued on next page

EXHIBIT 9   Dain Bosworth Offer Letter (continued)

3. Given that Spatial's growth will be derived from both the base ACIS business and new Web capabilities, our comparable companies consist of those in the CAD, tools, and 3D markets.

4. As a result of our discussions and after analyzing the growth opportunities of the Web strategy, we assumed a 35 to 40 percent projected five year earnings growth rate.

Based on an estimated fully taxed forward four quarters net income of $3.4 million and pro forma calendar 1996 and 1997 earnings of $1.7 million and $5.4 million, respectively, we believe it is reasonable to target a post offering valuation range of approximately $75 million to $87 million. Assuming a $20 million initial public offering and $15 million of gross company proceeds, this would imply a preoffering valuation range of $60 million to $72 million and the sale of approximately 25 percent of the company's stock to investors. The price-to-earnings multiple of this range is within 21.7 to 25.2 times the company's forward four quarters pro forma earnings estimates; 44.0 to 51.0 times pro forma 1996 earnings estimates; and 14.0 to 16.2 times pro forma 1997 earnings estimates. Our expectation is that this valuation range appropriately rewards the existing shareholders for the value created to date as well as provides an attractive opportunity for prospective public investors based on the offering analysis as outlined in the attached material.

In closing, Dain Bosworth believes that we can add significant value to Spatial Technology's initial public offering and, more important, in the aftermarket. Barry Randall's knowledge of 3D tools and the software industry will allow us to effectively communicate Spatial's growth strategy and offering highlights to investors. For these reasons and others, we believe there exists an outstanding "fit" between Spatial and Dain Bosworth.

I have included in the attached material our summary positioning of Spatial, detail of our valuation analysis, a time line of the IPO process, and next steps. On behalf of Dain Bosworth, Dick Stebbins, John Siegler, and Barry Randall, we appreciate the opportunity to discuss your initial public offering and we would very much look forward to joining the Spatial team. Please do not hesitate to contact any of us with questions or comments.

Best regards,

Hugh Hoffman

---

go in for 10 percent is apparently a major indicator. If an investor who is known for his competence in the software industry goes in for 10 percent, then others start to think: "If he's in for 10 percent, then it must be a good deal; therefore, I'll go in for 10 percent as well."

But from what I heard, the sales force at Dain Bosworth couldn't get a couple of the key players in at 10 percent, a move that many other investors were waiting for. Once you get three or four of those key players in, your book fills pretty quickly. But the first domino never fell and the book didn't get oversubscribed.

In a phone conference that evening, the representatives of Dain Bosworth and Spatial's board members and management assessed the situation. A quick decision had to be made. Spatial's investors still had a strong intention to complete the IPO; all parties had already put a lot of time and effort into the project. Consequently, it was decided that the investment bankers should try the next day at $7–$9 per share. Vellequette said:

After we couldn't close the deal the first night, we lowered the pricing to $7–$9 and they tried to put the book together on Thursday. But then you quickly had the investor psychology setting in that says, "Hold it, I put an order in at $9–$11 . . . it didn't come together, what did I miss?" So as an *investor you ask yourself, "Is there something wrong with this deal that I didn't notice? Is it any better at $7–$9?" You don't know, and you don't have time to go look, but you have thirty other deals on your desk, so you just invest your money in something else that looks good and you're not going to bother with Spatial anymore.*

The deal started to get cold very quickly in a hot market because the investors were off to other IPOs and the investment bankers couldn't force it together. So, at the end of that second day we had another phone conference with Dick, the board members, and the guys from Dain and they basically said, "We don't think there's a deal here, we can't get the book together."

Since the book was not full at the end of that Thursday, the deal was not effective. As is customary for initial public offerings, no legally binding contracts had been signed between Spatial and the underwriters. (The underwriting agreement is usually signed the evening after an offer has been fully subscribed and the book has been closed.) Neither Spatial's board nor its management had any legal, financial, or personal means to change the decision of the lead underwriter. Vellequette said:

You have to put yourself in my shoes as the finance guy. I knew we had spent about $600,000 at that point to prepare the IPO and we didn't have a lot of cash lying around. I had no idea of how we were going to pay for those bills. In addition, there was now a stigma that was going to stick with us when it would ever come to doing anything else (in terms of financing) in the future. . . . "Hey, you guys were going to go public, what happened?" Future potential investors would consider us as the "unclean," asking themselves "What is it that's wrong with this company that we aren't seeing?" before they would ever do a private investment in us or whatever the other financing options were. On top of it all, the crushing part was the time and the energy we put into doing this versus doing other things. The emotional blow to the company would be huge, let alone to Dick and me for doing all this work on the road. . . . That Thursday night I flew home: a very, very long and unhappy flight.

THE MORNING AFTER: A LAST CHANCE?

On Friday morning, things suddenly took a new direction. Vellequette continued:

I arrived at Spatial Friday morning at 8:30 and walked into Dick's office. He immediately dragged me into a phone conference where we had several guys from Cruttenden Roth as well as Fred Nazem on the phone. Apparently what had happened was that, an hour after the end of the phone conference the night before, Cruttenden had called back Dick Sowar and said that regardless of Dain Bosworth's walkout, they still thought they had a deal. They had indications from their institutional investor base that they could put the deal together.

Sowar recalled the situation:

We got another phone call from Cruttenden Roth that Friday morning. They had five guys on the phone: a couple from L.A. and a couple from Seattle. They basically said: "Dick, you guys got screwed. The guys in Minneapolis dropped the ball. Look, if you're flexible on the price we know we can get you out next week. If you go on the road with us Monday, Tuesday, and Wednesday, we'll get this thing closed for you on Thursday."

Cruttenden Roth said that it had a strong institutional investor base behind it that would support the deal and made an aggressive and simple offer (see Exhibit 10):

EXHIBIT 10   Cruttenden Roth Offer Fax

October 11, 1996

The Board of Directors
Spatial Technology, Inc.
2425 55th Street, Bldg. A
Boulder, CO 80301

Gentlemen:

This letter will confirm that Cruttenden Roth Incorporated ("CRI") will act as manager of the initial public offering of Common Stock ("Shares") of Spatial Technology, Inc. As we discussed, CRI intends to underwrite as soon as is practicable, on a firm commitment basis, an offering consisting of 2,100,000 newly issued Shares and 900,000 existing Shares to be sold by existing shareholders. The company's capitalization shall otherwise be as described in the preliminary prospectus dated September 12, 1996. In addition, CRI shall be granted an overallotment option consisting of a number Shares equal to 15% of those sold in the offering. The overallotment option shall be exercisable for a period of 45 days from the date of the offering. The price range for the offering and the overallotment option shall be $5.00 to $6.00 per Share.

As compensation for such underwriting, CRI will be paid in cash a gross underwriting spread equal to 8% of the gross proceeds of the offering and a non-accountable expense allowance equal to 2% of the gross proceeds of the offering, with such percentages to be calculated based on the total gross proceeds of the offering and the overallotment option (if exercised). In addition, CRI shall receive warrants to purchase a number of shares equal to 7% of the total sold by the Company and shareholders through the offering and the overallotment option with such warrants to be exercisable for a five year period beginning one year from the date of the offering. The exercise price of such warrants shall be 120% of the per Share price achieved in the offering. While this letter constitutes an expression of our mutual intent, all legal obligations of the parties shall be contained in a duly executed underwriting agreement.

Please indicate your agreement with the above by proving an authorized signature below and sending a copy of this letter to us at your earliest convenience. We appreciate your decision and look forward to completing the offering in the very near future.

Sincerely,

James Stearns   Fred Nazem
Managing Director   Chairman

                                            Richard Sowar
                                            Chief Executive Officer, Director

cc: Byron Roth, Dave Walters, Jay Beaghan
     Debra Fagan

- They alone would de facto be in charge of the IPO the next week.
- The price per share would be 5 to 6 dollars.
- Spatial would have to sell 3 million shares (2.1 million new issued and 900,000 from existing shareholders) instead of 2.1 million and face an even stronger dilution.
- The effective commission costs for the underwriters would be about 10 percent of the share price.
- Spatial would have to come up with a revised prospectus in twenty-four hours.

Sowar paused for a moment to reflect on the offer. Nazem and the other Spatial investors seemed to be willing to accept it. Sowar looked at Mark Velle-quette; they both knew that, under the circumstances, Cruttenden Roth did not have to entertain any negotiations. It was a take-it-or-leave-it deal. "We looked at the reasonable options we had. We still didn't have the cash to go fund the new product development and marketing, and we now had $600,000 in unpaid bills," Sowar said.

ASSIGNMENTS

A. Describe Spatial Technology's "business model" in terms of revenues, profits, and cash flows.

B. What intellectual property, if any, does Spatial Technology possess?

C. Describe the experience and expertise characteristics of the management team.

D. Describe Spatial Technology's pricing and marketing strategy.

E. Discuss the competition faced by Spatial Technology in conjunction with 3D modeling technology in general and specifically with its ACIS product.

F. Describe the four successful rounds of venture financing (A through D) achieved by Spatial Technology in terms of sources and amounts. What additional financing sources have been used?

G. Conduct a ratio analysis of Spatial Technology's past income statements and balance sheets. Note any performance strengths and weaknesses and discuss any ratio trends.

H. Use the cash flow statements for Spatial Technology, Inc. to determine whether the venture has been building or burning cash, as well as possible trends in building or burning cash.

I. Discuss possible reasons why the plan by Spatial Technology for an initial public offering (IPO) of common stock at the end of 1992 was withdrawn.

J. Describe the IPO market conditions in 1996 and discuss possible reasons why the proposed IPO at a price of about $10 per share planned for October 1996 and involving Dain Bosworth as lead underwriter failed.

K. Evaluate the compound return on investments made at startup, Round A, Round B, Round C, and Round D if the acquired shares eventually sell at $10 and $5. Evaluate the compound return on all investments of each existing investor. Analyze the incentives of each investor and founder for taking the Cruttenden Roth offer to execute a $5 IPO.

L.   Using the provided financial statements as a starting point:

1. Prepare and present a DCF valuation and pro forma financials with five years of explicit forecasts using license fees and royalties growth rates consistent with recent history (e.g., two to three years) at Spatial.

2. Modify your analysis to consider a more successful scenario where Spatial's main revenue sources (combined) grow at 50 percent for five years and then flatten to a more sustainable growth rate.

3. Prepare and present DCF valuations and pro forma financial statements (five-year explicit period) that justify a $10 and a $5 share price at the IPO. Make sure the ratios embedded in your projections conform to reasonable operating ratio assumptions.

4. In all cases be sure to explain your modeling assumptions on revenue and costs and provide a summary comparison of the four scenarios.

M.   Discuss the $5 and $10 IPO prices for Spatial within the context of comparable firms and their multiples. (There are some glimpses of multiples in the case materials, but you may wish to use some outside historical reference material. Please state your sources.)

N.   Prepare an executive summary discussing the events and decisions (technological and financial) leading to its situation, the options it had, and your recommendations for Spatial's future. Would (could) you have done anything differently?

O.   Take a position on whether you would recommend the $5 IPO. Take a position on whether, as an investor, you would have purchased shares in the $5 IPO.

P.   Discuss what you believe would have been the strategic (product lines, licensing, competitors, etc.) outlook for Spatial at the time and what you believe would have been the financial market's view of a publicly traded Spatial Technology.

Glossary

A

absolute priority rule Establishes a hierarchical order for the payment of claims for firms in bankruptcy, starting with senior creditors and ending with the existing common stockholders.

acceleration provision Provides that all future interest and principal obligations on a loan become immediately due when default occurs.

accrual accounting The practice of recording economic activity when it is recognized rather than waiting until it is realized.

accrued wages Liabilities owed to employees for previously completed work.

accumulated depreciation Sum of all previous depreciation amounts charged to fixed assets.

additional funds needed (AFN) Gap remaining between the financial capital needed and that funded by spontaneously generated funds and retained earnings.

articles of incorporation Basic legal declarations contained in the corporate charter.

asset intensity Total assets divided by revenues; the reciprocal of asset turnover.

asset restructuring Involves improving the working-capital-to-sales relationship and/or selling off fixed assets.

assets Financial, physical, and intangible items owned by the business.

assignment Transfer of title to the venture's assets to a third-party assignee or trustee.

automatic stay provision A restriction on the ability of individual creditors to foreclose to try to recover their individual claims.

B

balance sheet Financial statement that provides a "snapshot" of a business's financial position as of a specific date.

balance sheet insolvency Exists when a venture has negative book equity or net worth because total debt exceeds total assets.

bank loan Interest-bearing loan from a commercial bank.

bankrupt A venture is "bankrupt" when a petition for bankruptcy is filed with a federal bankruptcy court.

best efforts Type of agreement with investment bank involving only marketing and distribution efforts.

blue-sky laws State laws designed to protect individuals from investing in fraudulent security offerings.

bond rating An assessment that reflects the default risk of a firm's bonds as judged by a bond-rating agency.

bridge financing Temporary financing needed to keep the venture afloat until the next offering.

business angels Wealthy individuals who invest in early-stage ventures in exchange for the excitement of launching a business and a share in any financial rewards.

business plan Written document that describes the proposed product or service opportunity, current resources, and financial projections.

C

capital call When the venture fund calls upon the investors to deliver their investment funds.

capital leases Long-term, noncancelable leases whereby the owner receives payments that cover the cost of equipment plus a return on investment in the equipment.

capitalization (cap) rate Spread between the discount rate and the growth rate of cash flow in terminal value period.

carried interest Portion of profits paid to the professional venture capitalist as incentive compensation.

cash Amount of coin, currency, and checking account balances.

cash budget A venture's projected cash receipts and disbursements over a forecast period.

cash build Net sales less the increase in receivables.

cash build rate Cash build for a fixed period of time, typically a month.

cash burn Cash a venture expends on its operating and financing expenses and its investments in assets.

cash burn rate Cash burn for a fixed period of time, typically a month.

cash conversion cycle Sum of the inventory-to-sale conversion period and the sale-to-cash conversion period less the purchase-to-payment conversion period.

cash flow breakeven Cash flow at zero for a specific period (EBDAT = 0).

cash flow insolvency Exists when a venture's cash flow is insufficient to meet its current contractual debt obligations.

closely held corporations Corporations whose stock is not publicly traded.

coefficient of variation Measure of the dispersion risk per unit of expected rate of return.

commercial banks Financial intermediaries that take deposits and make business and personal loans.

common pool problem When individual creditors have the incentive to foreclose on the venture even though it is worth more as a going concern.

common stock The least senior claim on a venture's assets (residual ownership).

confidential disclosure agreements Documents used to protect an idea or other forms of intellectual property when disclosure must be made to another individual or organization.

constant-ratio forecasting method Variant of the percent-of-sales forecasting method that projects selected cost and balance items at the same growth rate as sales.

contribution profit margin Portion of the sale of a product that contributes to covering the cash fixed costs.

conversion period ratios Ratios that indicate the average time it takes in days to convert certain current asset and current liability accounts into cash.

convertible preferred stock Preferred stock with option to exchange into common stock.

copyrights Intellectual property rights to writings in printed and electronically stored forms.

corporate bylaws Rules and procedures established to govern the corporation.

corporate charter Legal document that establishes the corporation.

corporation A legal entity that separates personal assets of the owners, called shareholders, from the assets of the business.

cost of goods sold Cost of materials and labor incurred to produce the products that were sold.

cram-down procedure Bankruptcy court accepts a reorganization plan for all creditors, including dissenting creditor classes.

cross-default provision Provides that defaulting on one loan places all loans in default.

cross-sectional analysis Comparison of a venture's performance against another firm at the same point in time.

current assets Cash and other assets that are expected to be converted into cash in less than one year.

D

deal flow Flow of business plans and term sheets involved in the venture capital investing process.

debt composition change Occurs when creditors reduce their contractual claims against the venture.

debt payments extension Involves postponing due dates for interest and principal payments on loans and cash payments on credit purchases.

debtor-in-possession financing Short-term financing, made senior to all existing unsecured debt, to help meet liquidity needs during the reorganization process.

default risk Risk that a borrower will not pay the interest and/or principal on a loan.

default risk premium (DRP)   Additional interest rate premium required to compensate the lender for the probability that a borrower will default on a loan.

depreciation   Reduction in value of a fixed asset over its expected life, intended to reflect the usage or wearing out of the asset.

development stage   Period involving the progression from an idea to a promising business opportunity.

direct capitalization   Valuation by capitalizing earnings using a cap rate implied by a comparable ratio.

direct comparison   Valuation by applying a direct comparison ratio to the related venture quantity.

direct public offering   Security offering made directly to a large number of investors.

discounted cash flow (DCF)   Valuation approach involving discounting future cash flows for risk and delay.

down (reset) round   Venture round priced below most recent previous price.

due diligence   The process of ascertaining, to the extent possible, an issuing firm's financial condition and investment intent.

due diligence (in venture investing context)   Process of ascertaining the viability of a business plan.

E

early-stage ventures   Firms in their development stage, startup stage, survival stage, or just entering their rapid-growth stage.

EBDAT   Earnings before depreciation, amortization, and taxes.

EBDAT breakeven   Amount of revenues (i.e., survival revenues) needed to cover a venture's cash operating expenses.

EBIT   Earnings before interest and taxes; also called operating income.

EBITDA   Earnings before interest, taxes, depreciation, and amortization.

e-commerce   The use of electronic means to conduct business online.

economic value added (EVA)   Measure of a firm's economic profit over a specified time period.

employment contracts   Employer employs the employee in exchange for the employee agreeing to keep confidential information secret and to assign ideas and inventions to the employer.

enterprise (entity) method   Valuation method for the entire financial capital structure.

entrepreneur   Individual who thinks, reasons, and acts to convert ideas into commercial opportunities and to create value.

entrepreneurial finance   Application and adaptation of financial tools and techniques to the planning, funding, operations, and valuation of an entrepreneurial venture.

entrepreneurial opportunities   Ideas with potential to create value through different or new, repackaged, or repositioned products, markets, processes, or services.

entrepreneurial ventures   Entrepreneurial firms that are flows and performance oriented as reflected in rapid value creation over time.

entrepreneurship   Process of changing ideas into commercial opportunities and creating value.

equity valuation cash flow   Cash flow used for valuing equity.

expected PV   Valuation method calculating PVs for each scenario, applying probabilities, and summing.

expected rate of return   Probability-weighted average of all possible rates of return.

expected value   Weighted average of a set of scenarios or possible outcomes.

explicit forecast period   Two- to ten-year period in which the venture's financial statements are explicitly forecasted.

F

factoring   Selling receivables to a third party at a discount from their face value.

financial bootstrapping   Minimizing the need for financial capital and finding unique ways of financing a new venture.

financial capital needed (FCN)   Funds needed to acquire assets necessary to support a firm's sales growth.

financial distress When cash flow is insufficient to meet current debt obligations.

financial ratios Relationships between two or more financial variables or between financial variables and time.

financial restructuring Involves changing the contractual terms of the existing debt obligations and/or the composition of the existing debt claims against the venture.

firm commitment Type of agreement with investment bank involving the investment bank's underwritten purchase and resale of securities.

first-round financing Equity funds provided during the survival stage to cover the cash shortfall when expenses and investments exceed revenues.

fixed assets Assets with expected lives of greater than one year.

fixed expenses Costs that are expected to remain constant over a range of revenues for a specific time period.

foreclosure Legal process used by creditors to try to collect amounts owed on loans in default.

free cash Cash exceeding that which is needed to operate, pay creditors, and invest in assets.

free cash flow Change in free cash over time.

free cash flow to equity Cash remaining after operating cash outflows, financing and tax cash flows, investment in assets needed to sustain the venture's growth, and net increases in debt capital.

G

generally accepted accounting principles (GAAP) Guidelines that set out the manner and form for presenting accounting information.

government assistance programs Financial support, such as low-interest-rate loans and tax incentives, provided by state and local governments to help small businesses.

gross earnings Net sales minus the cost of production.

gross profit Revenues less the cost of goods sold.

gross profit margin Gross profit divided by revenues.

H

harvesting Process of exiting the privately held business venture to unlock the owners' investment value.

holdout problem When one or more of the creditors refuse to agree to the reorganization terms because of the potential for a larger individual recovery.

I

income statement Financial statement that reports the revenues generated and expenses incurred over an accounting period.

industry comparables analysis Comparison of a venture's performance against the average performance of other firms in the same industry.

inflation Rising prices not offset by increasing quality of the goods or services being purchased.

inflation premium (IP) Average expected inflation rate over the life of a risk-free loan.

initial public offering (IPO) A corporation's first sale of common stock to the investing public.

insolvent When a venture has a negative book equity or net worth position and/or when its cash flow is insufficient to meet current debt payment obligations.

intellectual property A venture's intangible assets and human capital, including inventions that can be protected from being freely used or copied by others.

interest Dollar amount paid on the loan to a lender as compensation for making the loan.

interest rate Price paid to borrow funds.

interest tax shield Proportion of a venture's interest payment that is paid by the government because interest is deductible before taxes are paid.

internal rate of return (IRR) Compound rate of return that equates the present value of the cash inflows received with the initial investment.

internally generated funds Net income or profits (after taxes) earned over an accounting period.

inventories Raw materials, work-in-process, and finished products that the venture hopes to sell.

Investment Advisers Act of 1940 Federal law that focuses on people and organizations that seek to provide financial advice to investors and defines "investment adviser."

investment banker Individual working for an investment banking firm who advises and assists corporations in their security financing decisions and regarding mergers and acquisitions.

investment banking An intermediary assisting in the creation, sale, and distribution of financial assets.

investment banking firms Firms that advise and assist corporations regarding the type, timing, and costs of issuing new securities.

Investment Company Act of 1940 Federal law that defines an "investment company."

investment risk of loss Chance or probability of financial loss from a venture investment.

investment risk premium (IRP) Additional return that investors can expect to earn when investing in a risky publicly traded common stock.

involuntary bankruptcy petition Petition for bankruptcy filed by the venture's creditors.

IPO underpricing A reference to a syndicate's offering price when it is less than the market price immediately following the offering.

J

joint and several liability Subsets of partners can be the object of legal action related to the partnership.

joint liability Legal action treats all partners equally as a group.

L

lead investor Venture investor taking the lead for a group (syndicate) of other venture investors.

leverage ratios Ratios that indicate the extent to which the venture has used debt and its ability to repay its debt obligations.

leveraged buyout (LBO) Purchase price of a firm is financed largely with debt financial capital.

lifestyle firms Firms that allow owners to pursue specific lifestyles while being paid for doing what they like to do.

limited liability Creditors can seize the corporation's assets but have no recourse against the shareholders' personal assets.

limited liability company (LLC) A company owned by shareholders with limited liability; its earnings are taxed at the personal income tax rates of the shareholders.

limited partnership Certain partners' liabilities are limited to the amount of their equity capital contribution.

liquid assets Sum of a venture's cash and marketable securities plus its receivables.

liquidity How quickly an asset can be converted into cash.

liquidity premium (LP) Premium charged when a debt instrument cannot be converted to cash quickly at its existing value.

liquidity ratios Ratios that indicate the ability to pay short-term liabilities when they come due.

loan default Occurs when there is a failure to meet interest or principal payments when due on a loan.

loan principal amount Dollar amount borrowed from a lender.

long-term debts Loans that have maturities of longer than one year.

M

management buyout (MBO) Special type of LBO where the firm's top management continues to run the firm and has a substantial equity position in the reorganized firm.

market capitalization (or "market cap") A firm's current stock price multiplied by the number of shares that are outstanding.

market risk premium (MRP) Excess average annual return of common stocks over long-term government bonds.

marketable securities Short-term, high-quality, and highly liquid investments that typically pay interest.

maturity premium (MP) Premium that reflects increased uncertainty associated with long-term debt.

maturity stage Period when the growth of revenue and cash flow continues but at a much slower rate than in the rapid-growth stage.

maximum dividend method (MDM) Valuation method involving explicitly forecasted dividends to provide surplus cash of zero.

mezzanine financing Funds for plant expansion, marketing expenditures, working capital, and product or service improvements.

mortgage debt or bonds Debt secured by a pledge of plant (buildings) and equipment.

N

net cash burn When cash burn exceeds cash build in a specified time period; also cash burn less cash build.

net cash burn rate Net cash burn for a fixed period of time, typically a month.

net income (or profit) Bottom-line measure of what's left from the firm's net sales after operating expenses, financing costs, and taxes have been deducted.

net operating working capital Current assets less surplus cash less non-interest-bearing current liabilities.

net present value (NPV) Present value of a set of future flows plus the current undiscounted flow.

net profit Dollar profit left after all expenses, including financing costs and taxes, have been deducted from the revenues.

net profit margin Net profit divided by revenues.

net working capital (NWC) Current assets minus current liabilities.

nominal interest rate Observed or stated interest rate.

NOPAT Net operating profit after taxes or EBIT times one minus the firm's tax rate.

NOPAT breakeven revenues (NR) Amount of revenues needed to cover a venture's total operating costs.

O

operating cash flow Cash flow from producing and selling a product or providing a service.

operating cycle Time it takes to purchase required materials, assemble, and sell the product plus the time needed to collect receivables if the sales are on credit.

operating income Also called earnings before interest and taxes (EBIT), the firm's profit after all operating expenses, excluding financing costs, have been deducted from net sales.

operating leases Leases that provide maintenance in addition to financing and are also usually cancelable.

operations restructuring Involves growing revenues relative to costs and/or cutting costs relative to the venture's revenues.

organized securities exchange A formally organized exchange typically having a physical location with a trading floor where trades take place under rules set by the exchange.

other current liabilities Catchall account that includes borrowing in the form of cash advances on credit cards.

other long-term assets Intellectual property rights or intangible assets that can be patented or owned.

outright sale Venture sold to others, including family members, managers, employees, or external buyers.

over-the-counter (OTC) market Network of brokers and dealers that interact electronically without having a formal location.

owner-debtholder conflict Divergence of the owners' and lenders' self-interests as the firm gets close to bankruptcy.

owner-manager (agency) conflicts Differences between manager's self-interest and that of the owners who hired him.

owners' equity Equity capital contributed by the owners of the business.

P

paid in kind (PIK) preferred stock Preferred stock that has the option of paying preferred dividends by issuing more preferred stock.

participating preferred stock Preferred stock with rights to participate in any dividends paid to common stockholders; stock with an investment repayment provision that must be met before distribution of returns to common stockholders.

partnership Business venture owned by two or more individuals who are jointly and personally liable for the venture's liabilities.

partnership agreement An agreement that spells out how business decisions are to be made and how profits and losses will be shared.

patents Intellectual property rights granted for inventions that are useful, novel, and nonobvious.

payables Short-term liabilities owed to suppliers for purchases made on credit.

percent-of-sales forecasting method Forecasting method that makes projections based on the assumption that most expenses and balance sheet items can be expressed as a percentage of sales.

post-money valuation Pre-money valuation of a venture plus money injected by new investors.

preemptive rights The right for existing owners to buy sufficient shares to preserve their ownership share.

preferred stock Equity claim senior to common stock and providing preference on dividends and liquidation proceeds.

pre-money valuation Present value of a venture prior to a new money investment.

prepackaged bankruptcy An initial private attempt to convince a majority of the creditors to go along with a reorganization plan that will be proposed after the venture files under Chapter 11.

present value (PV) Value today of all future cash flows discounted to the present at the investor's required rate of return.

primary offering The sale of new shares (or securities).

prime rate Interest rate charged by banks to their highest-quality (lowest default risk) business customers.

private equity investors Owners of proprietorships, partners in partnerships, and owners in closely held corporations.

private financial markets Markets for the creation, sale, and trade of illiquid securities having less standardized negotiated features.

private workout Voluntary agreement between a venture's owners and its creditors that provides for a financial restructuring of the venture's outstanding debt.

profitability and efficiency ratios Ratios that indicate how efficiently a venture controls its expenses and uses its assets.

proprietorship Business venture owned by an individual who is personally liable for the venture's liabilities.

pseudo dividend method (PDM) Valuation method involving zero explicitly forecasted dividends and an adjustment to working capital to strip surplus cash.

public financial markets Markets for the creation, sale, and trade of liquid securities having standardized features.

publicly traded stock investors Equity investors of firms whose stocks trade in public markets such as the over-the-counter market or an organized securities exchange.

R

rapid-growth stage Period of very rapid revenue and cash flow.

real interest rate (RR) Interest one would face in the absence of inflation, risk, illiquidity, and any other factors determining the appropriate interest rate.

real options Real or nonfinancial options available to managers as the venture progresses through its life cycle.

receivables Credit sales made to customers.

receivables lending Use of receivables as collateral for a loan.

red herring disclaimer Obligatory disclaimer disavowing any intent to act as an offer to sell, or solicit an offer to buy, securities.

Regulation D Regulation that offers a safe harbor from registration of securities with the SEC.

required cash   Amount of cash needed to cover a venture's day-to-day operations.

return on assets   Net after-tax profit divided by total assets.

return on assets (ROA) model   Return on assets as the product of the net profit margin and the asset turnover ratio.

reversion value   Present value of the terminal value.

risk-free interest rate   Interest rate on debt that is virtually free of default risk.

ROA model   The decomposition of ROA into the product of the net profit margin and the sales-to-total-assets ratio.

ROE model   The decomposition of ROE into the product of the net profit margin, the sales-to-total-assets ratio, and the equity multiplier.

S

S corporation   Corporate form of organization that provides limited liability for shareholders; plus, corporate income is taxed as personal income to the shareholders.

salary-replacement firms   Firms that provide their owners with income levels comparable to what they could have earned working for much larger firms.

seasoned firms   Firms with successful operating histories and operating in their rapid-growth or maturity life cycle stage.

seasoned securities offering   The offering of securities by a firm that has previously offered the same or substantially similar securities.

secondary offering   The sale of used shares (or securities).

secondary stock offering   Founder and venture investor shares sold to the public.

second-round financing   Financing for ventures in their rapid-growth stage to support investments in working capital.

Securities Act of 1933   Main body of federal law governing the creation and sale of securities.

Securities Exchange Act of 1934   Federal law that deals with the mechanisms and standards for public security trading.

seed and startup financing   Sources of financing available during the development and startup stages of a venture's life cycle.

seed financing   Funds needed to determine whether an idea can be converted into a viable business opportunity.

senior debt   Debt secured by a venture's assets.

sinking-fund payments   Periodic repayments of a portion of debt principal.

SLOR   Standard letter of rejection, or used as a verb to indicate the sending of such a letter.

Small Business Administration (SBA)   Established by the federal government to provide financial assistance to small businesses.

sound business model   A plan to generate revenues, make profits, and produce free cash flows.

spontaneously generated funds   Increases in accounts payables and accruals (wages and taxes) that accompany sales increases.

staged financing   Financing provided in sequences of rounds rather than all at one time.

standard deviation   Measure of the dispersion of possible outcomes around the expected return of an investment.

startup financing   Funds needed to take a venture from having established a viable business opportunity to initial production and sales.

startup stage   Period when the venture is organized and developed and an initial revenue model is put in place.

statement of cash flows   Financial statement that shows how cash, as reflected in accrual accounting, flowed into and out of a company during a specific period of operation.

stepping-stone year   First year after the explicit forecast period.

subordinated debt   Debt with an inferior claim (relative to senior debt) to venture assets.

surplus cash   Cash remaining after required cash, all operating expenses, and reinvestments are made.

survival revenues (SR)   Amount of revenues just offsetting variable and cash fixed costs (EBDAT breakeven).

survival stage   Period when revenues start to grow and help pay some, but typically not all, of the expenses.

sustainable sales growth rate   Rate at which a firm can grow sales based on the retention of profits in the business.

SWOT analysis   An examination of strengths, weaknesses, opportunities, and threats to determine the business opportunity viability of an idea.

systematic liquidation   Venture liquidated by distributing the venture's assets to the owners.

T

term sheet   Summary of the investment terms and conditions accompanying an investment.

term structure of interest rates   Relationship between nominal interest rates and time to maturity when default risk is held constant.

terminal (or horizon) value   The value of the venture at the end of the explicit forecast period.

trade credit   Financing provided by suppliers in the form of delayed payments due on purchases made by the venture.

trade secrets   Intellectual property rights in the form of inventions and information, not generally known to others, that convey economic advantages to the holders.

trademarks   Intellectual property rights that allow firms to differentiate their products and services through the use of unique marks.

trend analysis   Examination of a venture's performance over time.

two and twenty shops   Investment management firms having a contract that gives them a 2 percent of assets annual management fee and 20 percent carried interest.

U

underwriting spread   Difference between what the investment bank gets from selling securities to public investors and what it pays to the issuing firm.

unlimited liability   Personal obligation to pay a venture's liabilities not covered by the venture's assets.

utopia discount process   Valuation by discounting utopian projections at utopian required returns.

V

variable expenses   Costs or expenses that vary directly with revenues.

venture capital   Early-stage financial capital often involving substantial risk of total loss.

venture capital firms   Firms formed to raise and distribute venture capital to new and fast-growing ventures.

venture capital (VC) method   A valuation method that estimates a venture's value by projecting only a terminal flow to investors at the exit event.

venture capitalists (VCs)   Individuals who join in formal, organized firms to raise and distribute venture capital to new and fast-growing ventures.

venture hubris   Optimism expressed in business plan projections that ignore the possibility of failure or underperformance.

venture law firms   Law firms specializing in providing legal services to young, fast-growing entrepreneurial firms.

venture leasing   Leasing contracts where one component of the return to the lessor is a type of ownership in the venture, usually through warrants.

venture leverage   Measure of how changes in top-line revenues relate to changes in EBDAT.

venture life cycle   Stages of a successful venture's life from development through various stages of revenue growth.

venture opportunity screening   Assessment of an idea's commercial potential to produce revenue growth, financial performance, and value.

viable venture opportunity   An opportunity that creates or meets a customer need, provides an initial competitive advantage, is timely in terms of time to market, and offers the expectation of added value to investors.

voluntary bankruptcy petition   Petition for bankruptcy filed by the venture's management.

VOS Indicator™   Checklist of selected criteria and metrics used to screen venture opportunities for potential attractiveness as business opportunities.

W

warrants   Call options issued by a company granting the holder the right to buy common stock at a specific price for a specific period of time.

weighted average cost of capital (WACC)   Weighted average of the cost of the individual components of interest-bearing debt and common equity capital.

Y

yield curve   Graph of the term structure of interest rates.

Index

Italic page numbers indicate material in tables or figures.